THE
AMERICAN
ENCOUNTER

THE
AMERICAN
ENCOUNTER

THE UNITED STATES
AND THE MAKING
OF THE MODERN WORLD

Essays from 75 Years of *Foreign Affairs*

Edited by
James F. Hoge, Jr., and Fareed Zakaria

BASIC
BOOKS

A Member of the Perseus Books Group

Grateful acknowledgment is made for permission to reprint the following essays:

"Can the Soviet Union Reform?" copyright © 1984 by Richard Pipes.

"A Monetary System for the Future," copyright © 1984 by Richard N. Cooper.

"Misconceptions About Russia Are a Threat to America," copyright © 1980 by Aleksandr Solzhenitsyn.

"Technology and Sovereignty," copyright © 1988 by Walter B. Wriston.

Library of Congress Cataloging-in- Publication Data

The American encounter : the United States and the making of the modern
    world : essays from 75 years of Foreign Affairs / edited by James F. Hoge,
    Jr. and Fareed Zakaria.
        p.   cm.
    Includes index.
    ISBN 0-465-00170-X (cloth)
    ISBN 0-465-00171-8 (paper)
        1. United States—Foreign relations—20th century.   2. World politics—
    20th century.   I. Hoge, James F.   II. Zakaria, Fareed.   III. Foreign affairs
    (New York)
    E744.A5324   1997
    327.73—dc21   97-20120

---

10 9 8 7 6 5 4 3

Contents

After Versailles, the 1920s

The Gathering Storm, the 1930s

Contents

War and Victory, the 1940s

A Cold War, the 1950s

The Quagmire of Vietnam, the 1960s

An Age of Limits, the 1970s

Contents

The Collapse of Communism, the 1980s

An Uncertain New Order, the 1990s

Contents

Editors' Note

AS READERS will note, *The American Encounter* has been crafted less as a traditional anthology than as a record of the United States' journey through the twentieth century: in some senses it is an intellectual history of the American century. Our 75 years of publication offered us a bounty of articles. We finally selected those that were seminal, elegantly written, and relevant. Naturally there were many fitting these qualifications that we still had to omit; what appears here should be regarded as a selection of our best essays, not a ranked list. An author's fame was not in itself a criterion. We passed up pieces, not without regret, by Leon Trotsky, J. Robert Oppenheimer, both Franklin and Eleanor Roosevelt, Golda Meir, Jawaharlal Nehru, Richard Nixon, and others. Over the course of several painstaking cuts, we pared down our selections to the 40-odd articles that best illuminated America's encounter with the world.

In order to streamline the articles, we trimmed away some digressions or tangents, rarely amounting to more than five percent of the original essay; these are always noted with ellipses. The trims are designed to remove only material that is now dated or obscure and do not alter the thrust of the author's argument. We have also done away with most footnotes.

Because the book is constructed as a narrative, the articles are grouped by decade. We have occasionally placed an article from one decade into another section for thematic reasons. For instance, Isaiah Berlin's famous musings on nationalism in "The Bent Twig" were prescient in 1972; they seemed an appropriate way to describe the widely remarked-on "return of nationalism" of the 1990s. Within each chapter, the articles are ordered thematically, not strictly chronologically. All the articles conform to current *Foreign Affairs* style, with a few exceptions. For example, most of the essays from the Vietnam era spelled "Vietnam" as "Viet Nam." In these cases, we have retained these evocative period spellings.

Some of the quirks of this collection reflect both the magazine's editorial history and the changing focus of U.S. foreign policy. The earlier decades are notably Eurocentric, as was the diplomacy of the day, although *Foreign Affairs* did publish many articles on what we would today call the Third World, including five passionate essays by W. E. B. Du Bois on race, colonialism, and Africa.

This book literally could not exist without the vision of the magazine's previous editors, Archibald Cary Coolidge, William P. Bundy, William G. Hyland, and above all Hamilton Fish Armstrong, who was the first managing editor of *Foreign Affairs* and then was editor from 1928 to 1972. If institutions are, as Emerson said, lengthened shadows of men, *Foreign Affairs* is a very long shadow of Hamilton Fish Armstrong. We are indebted to the Council on Foreign Relations and its directors for providing unstinting support and thank its chairman, Peter G. Peterson, and its president, Leslie H. Gelb, for their confidence. David Kellogg, our gifted publisher, has helped steer the magazine in new and innovative directions. It has been our pleasure to work with a talented staff of associate editors during our tenure at *Foreign Affairs'* helm: Patricia Lee Dorff, Kirk Krauetler, Warren Getler, Joseph Saxon O'Keefe, and our current team of Alice H. G. Phillips, Jacob Kramer, and William J. Dobson. James Chace and Peter Grose, both former managing editors, offered valuable insights. Amy Rowe, our copy editor, has kept careful watch, and Anna Papatheodorou, our editorial assistant, provided much-needed support work. We cannot imagine how the office would run without our incomparable assistants, Rosemary Hartman and Deborah Millan. Paul Golob of Basic Books was everything an editor should be: creative, clear-eyed, and erudite.

The American Encounter would not have been possible without the assistance of Warren Bass, our project editor, who helped select the articles, draft the section introductions, and edit the essays. Warren's talent and enthusiasm kept this project moving when other tasks could have overwhelmed it. Finally, *Foreign Affairs*—and therefore this book—would not be what it is without our loyal readers. Our thanks.

James F. Hoge, Jr., Editor
Fareed Zakaria, Managing Editor
New York City
September 1997

THE
AMERICAN
ENCOUNTER

America's Past,
America's Future

An Introduction

James F. Hoge, Jr., and Fareed Zakaria

"IN EVERY CENTURY," Henry Kissinger observes, "there seems to emerge a country with the power, the will and the intellectual and moral impetus to shape the entire international system in accordance with its own values." If the sixteenth century was Spain's, the seventeenth century France's, and the nineteenth century Britain's, the twentieth century is surely America's. The American encounter with the world, however, has been one marked by profound ambivalence. More than any great nation in modern history, the United States has been uninterested in foreign affairs. Its parochialism and isolationism are matters of fact and historical record. Yet through the twentieth century, this same nation has undertaken international projects of an unprecedented size, reach, and scope. Indeed, at its most ambitious the United States has sought to achieve nothing less than the transformation of international relations, obliterating the familiar pattern of power political struggles to bring forth an ever-expanding realm of stability, commerce, and law. All the great twentieth-century agreements, from the League of Nations to the United Nations Charter to the Bretton Woods accords to the Helsinki Final Act, are, as Kissinger says, "embodiments of American values." The great events of the century are marked by Washington's involvement, for better or worse. The United States provided the might and the political and moral leadership for victory in two world wars and the Cold War. It is also in some part responsible, however, for tragedies like interwar isolationism and the war in Vietnam.

The theme of this volume is America's fitful encounter with the world. It spans the century in an intellectual sense, because chronology aside, the twentieth century really began as World War I ended, and the century is closing now amidst the confusion of the present. The historian E. J. Hobsbawm has characterized it as a short century marked by extremes: World Wars I and II; the rise of fascism and communism; the collapse of European imperialism; and through it all, the rise of America and its distinctive ideology, liberal democratic capitalism. These events are presented through an unusual prism, the pages of one journal that was itself the expression of America's desire to better understand the world. In its pages you will see the American encounter take shape. Not all the essays were written by Americans, nor are they all about American foreign policy, narrowly conceived, but they are about concerns, interests, and values that were uppermost in the minds of Americans who thought about the world and their country's relationship to it. It is, in a sense, the American window on the American century.

World War I was supposed to have been "the war to end all wars." Only months after the armistice, however, it became clear that hopes for a stable and just peace were steadily diminishing. "Nothing but blackness in the future," wrote the British diplomat Harold Nicholson in his diary at the climax of the Versailles Conference of 1919. The Versailles treaty turned into a document more concerned with retribution for the past than peace for the future. Its child, the League of Nations, assumed extravagant responsibilities for world peace, without any power to enforce it. America, having refused to join the League, quickly became uninterested in the problems of the world and danced into the Roaring Twenties to its own tune. In this climate of general indifference, a group of Americans set up a private organization composed of public-minded citizens who hoped to educate and involve their country in the affairs of the world to make less likely the horrors and mistakes from which it had just emerged. The Council on Foreign Relations was officially founded in 1921 and within a year began publishing a quarterly journal, *Foreign Affairs*. Its purpose was magnificently summed up in these words from the lead essay of the first issue, written by Elihu Root, a former secretary of state, secretary of war, and United States senator:

> When foreign affairs were ruled by autocracies and oligarchies, the danger of war was sinister purpose. When foreign affairs are ruled by democracies, the danger of war will be in mistaken beliefs. The world will be the gainer by the change, for while there is no human way to prevent a king from having a bad heart, there is a human way to prevent a people from having an erroneous opinion. That way is to furnish the whole people, as part of their

ordinary education, with correct information about their relations to other peoples.

Which was a polite way of saying that now that foreign policy was the people's business, they had better learn something about it.

It was a novel idea at the time, a serious forum for essays on world affairs and with no political or party line. From the beginning, *Foreign Affairs* would not, in the words of its founding editor, Archibald Cary Coolidge, "devote itself to the support of any one cause," but rather would "tolerate wide differences of opinion." Thus over the years it published, with equal interest, Leon Trotsky, Franklin D. Roosevelt, John Foster Dulles, Nikita Khrushchev, Aleksandr Solzhenitsyn, Anwar al-Sadat, William F. Buckley, Jr., and Margaret Mead. Over the years it has been seen in various countries as the mouthpiece of the State Department. In fact, even a cursory reading would highlight the many occasions on which essays in *Foreign Affairs* have been deeply critical of the administration at the time. Its audience has never been a mass one, but it has achieved some influence at home and abroad because of the quality of its readership, reaching leaders, activist citizens, and, through amplification in popular media, the general public. Through these readers the journal has also influenced American foreign policy. This is in large part a product of America's unusual political structure. In the United States, business leaders, lawyers, journalists, and academics are solicited by, influence, and actually move in and out of the government. By serving as a forum in which these groups discuss international issues, *Foreign Affairs* has an effect on government policy. *Foreign Affairs'* reputation, in this sense, is the result of the porous structure of the American state, which is open to ideas and influence from the outside. In a country dominated by state elites rather than societal elites, a private journal like this one would have little impact on government policy.

The first two decades of *Foreign Affairs'* existence proved to be rich in opportunities to inform and educate the public, if not influence governments that seemed engaged in wishful nonthinking. Having published many essays on the breakdown of the peace agreements of 1919, the young editor of *Foreign Affairs*, Hamilton Fish Armstrong, was the first American journalist to meet with Adolf Hitler; he did so in April 1933, less than three months after the latter's accession to power. Armstrong, editor of the journal since 1928, returned convinced that the Nazis were a new and sinister force to be reckoned with. *Foreign Affairs* began publishing articles about this extraordinary new phenomenon: among others, the liberal columnist Dorothy Thompson attacked its ideology, the American socialist leader Norman Thomas denounced its labor policies, and the historian Charles Beard wrote an essay on its distortions of education. While continuing to publish mainstream and quasi-official pronouncements on the virtues of appeasement throughout the 1930s, *Foreign Affairs* became an important outlet for those who believed that the democracies of the West had to stand up against fascist aggression.

Pearl Harbor ended America's debate, and World War II became its paramount national cause. As America prepared for war, *Foreign Affairs* and the Council on Foreign Relations gave a great deal of thought to the peace that would follow, especially with the collapse of Versailles and the League still in the minds of many of the organization's elders. The council undertook a secret project, innocuously called the "War and Peace Studies," which prepared 682 memoranda on American interests and policies during and after the war for the State Department, which marked them confidential and circulated them throughout the government. *Foreign Affairs*, for its part, published a number of articles preparing the groundwork for an activist, engaged America when this war was over. The man who could be said to have inherited Elihu Root's mantle as the elder statesman of the Eastern establishment, Secretary of War Henry L. Stimson, who was also a former secretary of state, put forth "A Challenge to Americans," asking them to step up to their responsibilities as the world's greatest power.

In 1945, with Europe in ruins, theoretical questions about the postwar world became practical ones as America began putting into place institutions and programs to secure a new peace. Soon it became clear that all plans for the future hinged on whether the other remaining great power at the end of World War II, the Soviet Union, would be a partner or foe of the United States. A young diplomat named George F. Kennan helped make up Washington's mind. In 1946 in a telegram and then one year later in an article in *Foreign Affairs*, "The Sources of Soviet Conduct," Kennan explained that cooperation between the two superpowers was impossible. The "X" article, as it was popularly called (for the pseudonym under which it was originally published), is certainly the most important essay that *Foreign Affairs* has published. It has been translated and reprinted across the world for half a century. In it Kennan proposed a strategy to counter Soviet influence that, he predicted, would eventually result in the collapse of the Soviet regime. That policy, "containment," became the grand strategy of the United States for 45 years, adopted in some form or other by nine presidents.

By the 1950s the United States had taken on the material responsibilities of a world power: alliances, bases, intelligence services, foreign aid, the whole gamut. What it lacked, however, was an intellectual tradition of great power statesmanship. *Foreign Affairs* filled this gap with essays by new strategic thinkers. One of the most impressive was a young professor at Harvard University who applied the lessons of his area of expertise, the nineteenth-century Concert of Europe, to the choices facing America in the Cold War. Henry

Kissinger's "Reflections on American Diplomacy" can still be read with reward and not simply because its author went on to become one of the chief architects of the subject of his essay. *Foreign Affairs* published the work of other rising intellectual figures like Zbigniew Brzezinski, Albert Wohlstetter, and Arthur Schlesinger, Jr., not to mention elder statesmen like Dean Acheson and John Foster Dulles.

If the Cold War was the dominating strategic event of the 1950s, the other colossal force that was transforming the world was nationalism. In the two decades following World War II, Europe's great powers decolonized their far-flung empires, resulting in the creation of dozens of new nations in Africa and Asia. These two tectonic plates of geopolitics—the Cold War and decolonization—were to intersect repeatedly and noisily throughout the 1950s and 1960s, nowhere more discordantly than in Vietnam. Vietnam was as far away from the United States as almost any point on the globe could be, yet it dominated the discourse of American foreign policy, and for a while of all American politics, for nearly a decade. The pages of *Foreign Affairs* from those years were filled with analyses of Vietnam (or Viet Nam, as it was often written then) and America's involvement in it. *Insurgency warfare, escalation dominance,* and *strategic hamlets* all became commonplace terms for foreign policy experts.

By the 1970s Vietnam had become a symbol of the limits of American power and purpose. It was an era when all order seemed to break down: Bretton Woods, the oil cartels, Middle East stability, Western economic productivity. It took a decade for the United States to regain some measure of its confidence and position in the world. For the Soviet Union, the decades after the Vietnam War proved even more complex. The empire expanded while the economy contracted, a combination that resulted, by the late 1980s, in total crisis. Facing a hard-line administration, a spiraling arms race, and insurgency movements around the world, Mikhail Gorbachev began a process of reform that snowballed out of control into the collapse of the Soviet Union and its communist regime and, by the early 1990s, the breakdown of the centuries-old Russian empire. George Kennan's prophecy had finally come true.

The collapse of the Soviet Union has ended an era in international history, one marked by uneasy but peaceful relations among the great powers. But what will this post–Cold War world look like? Will Europe come together or split apart? Will East Asia rise to challenge the West? Will technology make war obsolete—or more dangerous still? This flux, its nature and its dizzying pace, causes great uncertainty for the political leader who must make policy and for the businessman who must bet on the future. But for the observer, it is endlessly interesting. For the editors of *Foreign Affairs*, the Chinese curse "May you live in interesting times" is something of a blessing.

We can make a few observations about the present, uncertain world order. The current scene bears marked similarities to the opening years of *Foreign Affairs*. Once again we are in a postwar era in which relief at the end of a protracted struggle and the immediate absence of security threats has bred public complacency. The public's disinterest is mirrored in the behavior of politicians and government officials, who make little effort to persuade the American people of the importance of foreign policy and the need to handle early on the conditions that breed threats. There are also issues from those early years that remain unresolved. Security arrangements in Europe, much on the minds of statesmen in the 1920s, are still the subject of heated debate. The incorporation of Russia into the family of nations remains unfinished business. Then, as now, the rise of new great powers was a critical challenge. Then, it was Japan and Germany; now it is China and the smaller but growing nations of Asia. The rise of non-Western regions may create for the first time in history a truly global system, one comprising Western and non-Western powers and cultures that will have to live together as equals.

The Cold War era added other issues, and they, too, are still with us in one form or another. The potential horror of nuclear conflict is no longer essentially one of rival superpowers, for the proliferation of the means and the weapons of mass destruction in aggrieved nations and groups is very much a contemporary concern. Passionate nationalism, venerable yet unpredictable, is still a dynamic force taking new shapes and forms across the globe.

We enter the new century more aware of the need to protect the planet's environment, but awareness has yet to translate into sufficiently effective international cooperation. That awkward word *globalization* may well turn out to represent the most powerful force we face today. Globalization has already transformed business practices in every industrialized land and is beginning to affect most aspects of how we live and are governed. These changes will not come without turmoil because all will not benefit equally from them. In a world where much is new, the inequality of nations will persist.

One feature of this inequality that was clear in 1922 is still clear today. The United States is the most powerful country in the world, and no stable world order can exist without its active participation. Obviously it must do its part in concert with other great nations and international institutions, but ultimately they have neither the capability nor the will to supplant America. For America to play its natural role in the world, the American public must be led, and by the president. Others can help—an articulate secretary of state, congressional leaders, and a conscientious media—but without conspicuous and sustained presidential involvement, America's dealings with the world will remain reactive, tentative, and frustrated. Many Americans have the suspicion that foreign policy is the realm of ambition and fancy, that it is unnecessary, even wasteful, to spend time, energy, and money on it while problems persist at home. It is odd that such sentiments are widespread today, because America as an economy and a society is more tightly intertwined in the world than it has ever been. As a country, however, we remain ambivalent, and, remarkably, this ambivalence exists as we look upon a world utterly transformed by American power and purpose. Life at the end of the twentieth century is dominated by the idea and the reality of America's distinctive creed, liberal democratic capitalism. Nations and people of every culture are adapting their old world to these new ideas, and their countries are being revolutionized, slowly but surely, by it. Some of this transformation is the result of broad structural shifts like industrialization and modernization, but much of it is the result of one nation's efforts to stand for and fight for certain political and economic ideals. The American encounter has changed the world. What remains to be seen is whether it has changed America. Having defeated the doubters and challengers abroad, we have not yet banished the doubts at home.

A Requisite for the Success of Popular Diplomacy

Elihu Root

SEPTEMBER 1922

THE CONTROL OF foreign relations by modern democracies creates a new and pressing demand for popular education in international affairs. When the difficult art of regulating the conduct of nations toward each other, in such a way as to preserve rights and avoid offense and promote peaceful intercourse, was left to the foreign offices of the world, the public in each country could judge policies by results, and, in the various ways by which public opinion expresses itself, could reward or punish the success or failure of government. To perform that particular function, it was not very important that the public should be familiar with the affairs out of which success or failure came. That condition, however, is passing away. In the democratic countries generally, the great body of citizens are refusing to wait until negotiations are over or policies are acted upon or even determined. They demand to know what is going on and to have an opportunity to express their opinions at all stages of diplomatic proceedings. This tendency is due partly to a desire to escape from certain well recognized evils in diplomacy as it has been practiced. It is due in part doubtless to the natural disposition of democracies to revert to the conditions which existed before the invention of representative government and thus to avoid the temporary inequalities involved in delegations of power to official representatives however selected.

The new condition has undoubtedly been accelerated by the great war and its lessons. We have learned that war is essentially a popular business. All the people in the countries concerned are enlisted in carrying it on. It cannot be carried on without their general participation. And whoever wins the war, all the people of all the countries involved suffer grievous consequences. There is a general conviction that there has been something wrong about the conduct of diplomacy under which peoples have so often found themselves embarked in war without intending it and without wishing for it, and there is a strong desire to stop that sort of thing. Democracies determined to control their own destinies object to being led, without their knowledge, into situations where they have no choice.

The demand for open diplomacy and contemporaneous public information, although in its application there is frequently an element of mere curiosity or news gathering business, nevertheless rests upon the substantial basis of democratic instinct for unhampered self-government. It is incident to the awakening sense of opportunity which, among the unskilled majority, has followed the exercise of universal suffrage, the spread of elementary education, and the revelation of the power of organization. The change is therefore not to be considered as temporary but as a step in the direct line of development of democratic government, which, according to the nature of democracies, will not be retraced. The new conditions and such developments as may grow from them are the conditions under which diplomacy will be carried on hereafter. Of course, as in all practical human affairs, limitations and safeguards will be found necessary, but the substance will continue, and public opinion will be increasingly not merely the ultimate judge but an immediate and active force in negotiation.

The usefulness of this new departure is subject to one inevitable condition. That is, that the democracy which is undertaking to direct the business of diplomacy shall learn the business. The controlling democracy must acquire a knowledge of the fundamental and essential facts and principles upon which the relations of nations depend. Without such a knowledge there can be no intelligent discussion and consideration of foreign policy and diplomatic conduct. Misrepresentation will have a clear field, and ignorance and error will make wild work with foreign relations. This is a point to which the sincere people who are holding meetings and issuing publications in opposition to war in general may well direct their attention if they wish to treat the cause of disease rather than the effects. Given the nature of man, war results from the spiritual condition that follows real or fancied injury or insult. It is a familiar observation that in most wars each side believes itself to be right and both pray with equal sincerity for the blessing of heaven upon their arms. Back of this there must lie a mistake. However much ambition, trade competition, or sinister personal motives of whatever kind may have led towards the warlike situation, two great bodies of human beings, without whose consent war cannot be carried on, can never have come to two diametrically opposed genuine beliefs as to the justice of the quarrel without one side or the other, and probably both, being mistaken about their country's rights and their country's duties. Here is the real advantage of the change from the old diplomacy to the new. Irresponsible governments may fight without being in the least degree mistaken about their rights and duties. They may be quite willing to make cannon fodder of their own people in order to get more territory or more power; but two democracies will not fight unless they believe themselves to be right. They may have been brought to their belief by misrepresentation as to facts, by a misunderstanding of rules of right conduct, or through having the blank of ignorance filled by racial or national prejudice and passion to the exclusion of inquiry and thought; but they will fight not because they mean to do wrong but because they think they are doing right. When foreign affairs were ruled by autocracies or oligarchies, the danger of war was in sinister purpose. When foreign affairs are ruled by democracies, the danger of war will be in mistaken beliefs. The world will be the gainer by the change, for while there is no human way to prevent a king from having a bad heart, there is a human way to prevent a people from having an erroneous opinion. That way is to furnish the whole people, as a part of their ordinary education, with correct information about their relations to other peoples, about the limitations upon their own rights, about their duties to respect the rights of others, about what has happened and is happening in international affairs, and about the effects upon national life of the things that are done or refused as between nations; so that the people themselves will have the means to test misinformation and appeals to prejudice and passion based upon error.

This is a laborious and difficult undertaking. It must be begun early and continued long, with patience and persistence, but it is the very same process as that by which all the people of the great democracies have learned within their own countries to respect law and to follow wise and salutary customs in their communities, and to consider the rights of others while they assert their own rights, and to maintain orderly self-government.

It so happens that our own people in the United States have been peculiarly without that kind of education in foreign affairs. Not only have we been very busy over the development of our own country and our own institutions, but our comparatively isolated position has prevented the foreign relations of the old world from becoming matters of immediate vital interest to the American people, and they have not been interested in the subject. Naturally enough, a great part of our public men have neglected to study the subject. The great body of Americans in office would study questions of transportation and tariff and internal improvements and currency because their constituents were interested in these subjects; but there was no incentive for them to study foreign affairs because their constituents were indifferent to them. The conditions are now widely different. Our people have been taught by events to realize that with the increased intercommunication and interdependence of civilized states, all our production is a part of the world's production, and all our trade is a part of the world's trade, and a large part of the influences which make for prosperity or disaster within our own country consist of forces and movements which may arise anywhere in the world beyond our direct and immediate control. I suppose that the people of the United States have learned more about international relations within the past 8 years than they had learned in the preceding 80 years. They are, however, only at the beginning of the task.

The subject is extensive and difficult, and a fair working knowledge of it, even of the most general kind, requires long and attentive study. Underlying it are the great differences in the modes of thought and feeling of different races of men. Thousands of years of differing usages under different conditions forming different customs and special traditions have given to each separate race its own body of preconceived ideas, its own ways of looking at life and human conduct, its own views of what is natural and proper and desirable. These prepossessions play the chief part in determining thought and action in life. Given two groups of men, each having a different inheritance of custom and tradition, each will have a different understanding of written and spoken words, of the reasons for conduct and the meaning of conduct, and each will to a very considerable degree fail to understand the other. Neither can judge the other by itself. If the instinctive occidental reformer and the instinctive oriental fatalist are to work together, they must make biological studies of each other. Add to these differences the selfish passions which have not yet been bred out of mankind and there inevitably follow in the contacts of international intercourse a multitude of situations which cannot be solved by the men of any one nation assuming that the rest of the world is going to think and feel as they themselves do and to act accordingly.

The organization of independent nations which has followed the disappearance of the Holy Roman Empire is in the main the outgrowth of that progress in civilization which leads peoples to seek the liberty of local self-government according to their own ideas. Whatever may be the form of local governments, there can be no tyranny so galling as the intimate control of the local affairs of life by foreign rulers who are entirely indifferent to the local conceptions of how life ought to be conducted. National independence is an organized defense against that kind of tyranny. Probably the organization of nations is but a stage of development, but it is the nearest that mankind has yet come towards securing for itself a reasonable degree of liberty with a reasonable degree of order.

It is manifest that the differences of thought and feeling and selfish desire which separate nations in general have to be dealt with in particular in the multitude of controversies which are sure to arise between them and between their respective citizens in a world of universal trade and travel and intercommunication. The process of such adjustment without war is the proper subject of diplomacy. During some centuries of that process, many usages have grown up which have been found necessary or convenient for carrying on friendly intercourse, and many of these have hardened into generally accepted customs in manners or in morals which no longer require to be discussed but which every nation has a right to assume that other nations will observe. Many rules of right conduct have been accepted and universally agreed upon as law to govern the conduct of nations. In England and America these rules of international law are authoritatively declared to be a part of the municipal law of the country enforceable by the courts. In this way the nations founded upon differences have been gradually rescuing from the field of difference and controversy, and transferring to the field of common understanding and agreement, one subject after another of practical importance in the affairs of the world. The process is in the direction of that unity of thought and feeling, the absence of which hitherto has caused the failure of all schemes and efforts for the unity of mankind. The study of international relations means not only study of some particular controversy but study of this long history of the process of adjustment between differing ideas and of the prejudices and passions and hitherto irreconcilable differences which have baffled adjustment and which affect the relations and probable conduct of the nations concerned. All these are in the background of every international question and are often of vital importance to its right understanding.

The process I have described has created a community of nations. That community has grown just as communities of natural persons grow. Men cannot live in neighborhood with each other without having reciprocal rights and obligations towards each other arising from their being neighbors. The practical recognition of these rights and obligations creates the community. It is not a matter of contract. It is a matter of usage arising from the necessities of self-protection. It is not a voluntary matter. It is compelled by the situation. The neighbors generally must govern their conduct by the accepted standards or the community will break up. It is the same with nations. No nation whose citizens trade and travel; that is to say, no nation which lives in neighborhood with other nations need consider whether or not it will be a member of the community of nations. It cannot help itself. It may be a good member or a bad member, but it is a member by reason of the simple fact of neighborhood life and intercourse. The Bolshevik rulers of Russia are illustrating this. They have been trying to repudiate all the obligations resulting from their country's membership in the community of nations, and one result is that intercourse is impossible.

This great fact of the community of nations is not involved at all in any question about the "League of Nations" or any other association of nations founded upon contract. The "League of Nations" is merely a contract between the signers of the instrument by which they agree to super-add to the existing usages, customs, laws, rights, and obligations of the existing community of nations certain other rights and obligations which shall bind the signers as matter of contract. Whether a country enters into that contract or not, its membership of the community of nations continues with all the rights and obligations incident to that membership.

A self-respecting democracy which undertakes to control the action of its government as a member of this community of nations, and wishes to respond fairly and fully, not only to the demands of its own interests, but to the moral obligations of a member of the community, is bound to try to understand this great and complicated subject so that it may act not upon prejudice and error but upon knowledge and understanding.

There is one specially important result which should follow from such a popular understanding of foreign affairs. That is, a sense of public responsibility in speech and writing, or perhaps it would be better stated as a public sense of private responsibility for words used in discussing international affairs. More fights between natural persons come from insult than from injury. Under our common law, libel was treated as a crime, not because of the injury which it did to the person libeled but because it tended to provoke a breach of the peace. Nations are even more sensitive to insult than individuals. One of the most useful and imperative lessons learned by all civilized governments in the practice of international intercourse has been the necessity of politeness and restraint in expression. Without these, the peaceful settlement of controversy is impossible. This lesson should be learned by every free democracy which seeks to control foreign relations.

It cannot, however, be expected that every individual in a great democracy will naturally practice restraint. Political demagogues will seek popularity by public speeches full of insult to foreign countries, and yellow journals will seek to increase their circulation by appeals to prejudice against foreigners. Hitherto these have been passed over because the speakers and writers were regarded as irresponsible, but if the democracy of which the speakers and publishers are a part is to control international intercourse, that irresponsibility ends, and it is the business of the democracy to see to it that practices by its members which lead directly towards war are discouraged and condemned. Offenses of this character are frequently committed in this country by political speakers and sensational newspapers, and because we are a great nation the expressions used become known in the other countries concerned and cause resentment and bitter feeling. What especially concerns us is that these are very injurious offenses against our own country. Such public expressions by our own citizens bring discredit upon our country and injure its business and imperil its peace. They answer to the description of crime in the old indictments as an act "against the peace and dignity" of the state. They will practically cease whenever the American public really condemns and resents them so that neither public office nor newspaper advertising or circulation can be obtained by them. That will come when the American public more fully understands the business of international intercourse and feels a sense of the obligations which it incurs by asserting the right to control the conduct of foreign relations.

After Versailles

THE NINETEEN TWENTIES

IN 1918 A shattered Europe looked for the first time to America for guidance. Seizing this newfound role, Woodrow Wilson, a man fired with idealism, tried to turn the wreckage of the First World War into a new international order. Wilson's ideals—national self-determination, the thwarting of aggression, and collective security as embodied in the League of Nations—were written into the postwar peace settlement signed in the glittering halls of Versailles.

Two years later, it was all over. Wilson had been incapacitated by a stroke, the U.S. Senate rejected the Versailles treaty, and hopes for a new era in international relations after "the war to end all wars" were dashed. The pleas of thinkers like Alfred E. Zimmern, whose "Nationalism and Internationalism" argued that there need be no contradiction between a vigorous nationalism and support for international organizations, fell on ears that were not so much deaf as distracted. Americans were content with the postwar prosperity of the Roaring Twenties and determined not to be dragged into another catastrophic European conflict.

European affairs were, indeed, dominated by what the historian Arnold J. Toynbee called "things not foreseen at Paris." In the spirit of Versailles, the world's major powers—especially France and Britain—began drives for disarmament that remain unparalleled in modern history. But by 1920, Europe had entered a nervous interlude when the League demanded $33 billion in reparations from Weimar Germany for the kaiser's sins in the Great War. Berlin refused to pay up and instead began printing huge amounts of money to devalue the mark, prompting the French to occupy the Ruhr valley in 1923. Karl Kautsky, a leading German socialist, offered a prescient critique of the instability at the heart of the post-Versailles European order in his essay, "Germany Since the War."

Further east, Russia's new Bolshevik government managed to hold on to the power it gained in the October Revolution of 1917. The founding of the Communist International in 1919 created a source of inspiration for socialists in the West and anticolonialists in the Third World. At the center of it all was Vladimir Lenin. Despite its theoretical emphasis on broad structural forces, in practice Marxism was brought into the world by one dominant personality. By introducing communism to Russia, Lenin changed the course of the twentieth century. When he died in 1924, Victor Chernov, a Russian democrat and revolutionary, penned a classic retrospective of his erstwhile colleague that put Soviet communism's early growing pains on fascinating display.

Postwar optimism reached its high-water mark in 1928 with the signing of the Kellogg-Briand Pact, which famously outlawed war itself. (There were some voices of skepticism. Walter Lippmann, Washington's most influential columnist and the forefather of today's punditocracy, crafted in "Concerning Senator Borah" an elegantly scathing profile of Senator William E. Borah— the powerful head of the Senate Foreign Relations Committee—that was both a literary tour de force and an anti-isolationist broadside.) While Washington stayed politically detached, America deployed what Herbert Feis famously called "the diplomacy of the dollar" to encourage foreign trade. Politicians everywhere wanted to push aside any thoughts of instability and war. Even the Soviet Union signed the Kellogg-Briand Pact. The 1920s were a time of economic growth, creeping political instability, and wishful thinking. But perhaps we feel that way only because we know today what happened next.

Germany Since the War

Karl Kautsky

DECEMBER 1922

I

WHEN THE ARMISTICE between the Allied Powers and Germany went into effect in November 1918, the whole world drew a breath of relief. The slaughter, the suspension of intercourse between nations, was at an end; peace was bound to come, and with it a resuscitation of the afflicted peoples. To imagine that the peace treaties would without further ado prove guarantees of everlasting peace would have been a utopian dream. But it was reasonable to expect that the conclusion of peace in 1919 would bring about a pacific state of affairs which would last at least as long as that effected by the Congress of Vienna in 1814 and 1815, to which, until 1853, no European war succeeded. Instead, however, we find an uninterrupted, nay, in many cases a constantly increasing unrest—war in the east, a series of political and economic crises in the west. Europe is unable to free herself from the fear of new disruptions which threaten to involve in ruin the entire civilized world.

Why did this latest world war come to a close so different from that which terminated the Napoleonic wars? We are able to look back upon the century since the Napoleonic wars as one of most brilliant economic growth, of fabulous progress in science and technology, of uninterrupted advance in democracy. Were not the conquerors of 1815 narrow-minded and reactionary? Were not those of 1918, on the contrary, progressive and enlightened? Certainly. But for the very reason that narrow, absolutist governments were made possible by the political and economic conditions of a hundred years ago, the problems of such governments, whenever they came to make peace, were of an extremely simple nature. The peoples had no recourse save passively to accept the dictates of their governments. And, except in rare instances, they were still economically dependent one on another. Nowadays all the people of Europe are inspired with an intense passion for self-determination, and even the peoples of the Orient are today harder to hold in leash than were those of the continent of Europe a century ago. At the same time international intercourse has so increased that, collectively, nations are living in close economic community. They are not always aware of this solidarity, and it is often interrupted by the antagonisms of competition or of monopolization. Yet every major violation of this solidarity not only injures those against whom it is directed, but in the end avenges itself even on its authors, no matter how powerful they may be.

The problems attending the laying of a foundation for world peace were in 1919, therefore, far more complicated than had been those facing the Congress of Vienna. They were such as could be solved only by the widest application of democratic principles and by the calmest consideration of economic questions, scrutinized in the light of all their consequences. But, as a matter of fact, the peace terms were evolved by methods and on principles suggestive of the era of absolutism and commercialism rather than those of an era of democracy and international intercourse.

In many respects the authors of the Versailles peace terms proved even less advanced than had been the statesmen at the Congress of Vienna. The latter had made a clear distinction between Napoleon and the French people. It was against Napoleon alone that they had waged war, not against his nation. Napoleon they deposed and banished, but to France they left the same frontiers she had had in 1792, and they imposed no war indemnity upon her. Even after Napoleon had returned from Elba and, to the great exultation of part of the French people, had recommenced the war, the peace conditions offered to France after he had succumbed a second time were only slightly more harsh. France had to cede a few communities and to pay a small war indemnity of 700 million francs—far less than the sum which the new France tossed to her nobles on their return from banishment by way of indemnity for the confiscation of their estates by the revolution. French patriotism was so little aggrieved by the readjustment of the French frontiers in 1815 that even the Treaty of Versailles failed to extend them in 1919. Nor was this peace one-sidedly dictated to the French by the victors. At the Congress of Vienna, where the peace was negotiated and where its conditions were determined, France herself had a seat and a voice, on a footing of national equality; and she was, as an equal, abundantly able to defend her interests, thanks to the superior diplomacy of her representative, Talleyrand.

There were good reasons for this concession. The reactionary monarchs of 1814 were well able to distinguish between the government and the people. They had not waged war against the French nation, but against Napoleon. It was he whom they had wished to render powerless. But they realized very plainly that to attain their ends it was not only necessary to conquer him by the power of their armies, but also to see that the new government erected in France in opposition to him should win the favor of the country generally. It was possible to accomplish this only if the new government were successful in efficiently defending the interests of France against her conquerors.

But the Allies of 1918 were far from giving weight to these considerations of the Allies of 1814. It is true that Par. 227 of the Treaty of Versailles indicts "William II of Hohenzollern, formerly German Emperor, for a supreme offence against international morality and the sanctity of treaties." But in Par. 231 William II is no longer named as responsible for the war; it is Germany.

Now one may estimate as highly as one likes William's responsibility for the war; I myself do not consider it to have been small. But it was not he who signed the treaty of peace—it was the government of the German Republic. And the latter certainly bore not the least responsibility for the war. Moreover, in 1918 Germany had repudiated her war-guilty emperor far more decisively than France did her Napoleon in 1814. The German people had risen in irresistible revolt against William. France, on the other hand, left it to the Allies to remove Napoleon from his throne.

The great bulk of the German population had turned from the emperor as from the author of the war who was therefore the author of all its misery. When, however, the republic came to be charged with as full a responsibility for the war as was that attributed to the emperor, when it was deprived of power to guard the people's interests against the conqueror, then the idea of the empire again began gradually to gain ground. If today Germany is confronted with the possibility of a monarchist *coup d'etat,* if she faces the threat of civil war, it is the fault of the Peace of Versailles, which is compelling the republic to do penance for the sins of the emperor. The monarchs of the Holy Alliance of 1814 understood better how to protect the interests of the Bourbons against Napoleon in France than did the democracies which took the field against the military monarchy of Germany in 1918 know how to guard those of the democratic republic against kaiserism. Despite their intentions, they have, by the Treaty of Versailles, worked "pour le roi de Prusse."

Furthermore, by their refusal to discuss the terms of peace with the conquered, they have injured themselves in yet another way. The economic and political conditions of a modern state are so complicated that no contemporary statesman, no matter how great his genius, is capable of foreseeing the consequences of every legislative proposal, even in his own country. Victors as well as vanquished have suffered severely as a result of numerous requirements of the peace treaties which were either incapable of fulfillment or which brought about economic confusion for them as well as for us. It is not by chance that simultaneously a cry is being sounded in Russia for the revi sion of the communist system of administration and in the countries of the victors for the revision of the peace treaties. Both were evolved simultaneously and by the same methods, methods which are incompatible with the conditions and the necessities of modern existence. Nevertheless, let it not be denied that, just as in the Soviet administrative system, so in the peace treaties there are a number of excellent requirements. But these treaties were unable to do justice to their task of creating a permanent state of peace because their authors did not take counsel with the representatives of the peoples affected and because they did not consistently follow the course of modern social development.

II

IT WAS A good thing that Germany was compelled to disarm by land and by sea. Unfortunately, the act was not followed by consequences correspondingly good. It was said before the war that German armament was forcing all the nations to increase their fleets and armies. But this incitement to the extension of armaments has now disappeared. France might reduce her army, thereby remedying her finances. What she is doing in this respect, however, is altogether insufficient. Poland, also, feels obliged to maintain in service a great and extravagant army at the expense of her economic welfare. This is not exactly the way to strengthen the pacifist idea in Germany and to make German disarmament lasting. The whole business is nothing but imitation of the disarming of Prussia after Jena by a Bonapartism bristling with weapons—an act by which the peace of the world was in no way assured. Disarmament can only become a lasting institution, a source of economic prosperity and an instrument of peace, when it is general, not one-sided. When it is only an individual affair it does nothing but excite the predatory and belligerent passions of the strong.

While disarming the vanquished, the peace treaties also brought about numerous alterations of frontiers, among them several of an excellent character which represent a permanent advance. Such are the breaking-up of moribund Austria, the restoration of Poland, the return of Northern Schleswig to Denmark, and the return of Alsace-Lorraine to France.

The violent severance of the inhabitants of Alsace-Lorraine from France, to which they remained devotedly attached, was the original sin with which the new German Empire entered upon its existence in 1871. Therewith commenced the dislike of the democracies of the world for the German Empire; and thereby was the French Republic driven into the arms of the Russian czar. Thus was evolved the concatenation of circumstances which led to the world war of 1914 and to the collapse of the Hohenzollern dynasty, and for which the German Republic is now doing such sore penance.

But the Peace of Versailles set about cutting Germany to pieces. The Saar Basin, with 600,000 inhabitants, was separated from Germany for 15 years, its purely German population being robbed of their civic rights for this period and subjected to an alien rule which owes them not the least responsibility. Nominally the government of the Saar Basin is appointed by the League of Nations. Actually it governs in the interest of France. Matters were not improved by the decision that the population should, after the lapse of 15 years, be polled on the question of whether or not they would prefer union with France. This decision merely constitutes an incitement to the French-controlled administration to torment as much as possible inhabitants of pro-German proclivities, in order either to intimidate them or to drive them out, thus establishing a population in agreement with the views of France.

Furthermore, as a guarantee for the performance of the terms of the peace treaty, there is the occupation by the victors' troops of the German territory west of the Rhine, with its six and a half million inhabitants. This comes near to being government of those regions by a military dictatorship. This condition of affairs is to last for 15 years. But it may be extended by the conquerors even beyond that period, if they should be of the opinion that Germany had not given them sufficient guarantees against unprovoked attack. This authorizes an interminable stay of foreign troops in the occupied territory. But besides this, the treaty of peace gives the victors the right, if they believe themselves able to establish a "deliberate non-fulfillment" of the treaty by Germany, to take all such measures "as the respective governments may determine to be necessary in the circumstances." This clause is being construed, by France at least, in a manner which delivers Germany wholly over to the option of the conquerors. Indeed, French troops have already occupied districts eastward of the Rhine, near Düsseldorf and Frankfurt.

No less provocative are the frontiers laid down in the east. The authors of the peace treaty attempted to replace the Austrian state with a series of nationalistic states. That was a great step in advance. The object was not easy to achieve, for in the east the various nationalist groups were not definitely separated territorially, but were much intermingled. It was inevitable that each of the succession states carved from the body of the old Austria-Hungary should contain not only its dominating race but also fragmentary groups of other nationalities. But, except in the cases of German-Austria and of Hungary, the establishment of the frontiers of these new states was carried far beyond the limits indicated by the circumstances. Each of the new states sought to embrace not only the entire body of the nationality which gave it its name, but also, for reasons of strategy or from a desire for important traffic routes c rich districts, to expand its borders as much further as was possible. Hence, with the aforementioned exceptions of German-Austria and Hungary, every one of the succession states has become a new little Austria.

The oppression of the Germanic people by the peace treaties reached its climax in the determination to forbid Austria from attaching herself to Germany. Until 1866 Austria had belonged to the German confederation. The Germans of Austria had never ceased to look upon themselves as Germans. Only the antagonism between the Hohenzollern and Hapsburg dynasties had excluded them from the German Empire. These dynasties were overthrown by the victory of the Entente, which had taken the field for the liberation of subjugated peoples; and now it celebrated its victory by enslaving and dismembering the German nation, already given over to ruin by the Hohenzollerns and Hapsburgers, to an even greater degree than had been done by those guilt-burdened dynasties. . . .

III

I HAVE ALREADY referred to the fact that in 1814 the allies refrained from imposing any war indemnity upon vanquished France. But even though the principal intention of the victorious monarchs may have been to give the new French government a good standing in the opinion of its people, their moderation also proved economically advantageous to the whole world. If that policy had not been followed, Europe would never have calmed down and recovered so quickly after the downfall of Napoleon, nor, without it, would peace have endured four decades. It is true that the return of Napoleon from Elba led to the imposition upon France, after his overthrow, of a charge for war costs, but it was inconsiderable—700 million francs.

It was a long time before large war indemnities again made their appearance. The terms of the Peace of Paris, which terminated the Crimean War in 1856, imposed upon Russia no payment of indemnity. Nor did the vanquished Austria have to pay any war compensation in 1859; and in 1866 she had to pay only 30 million gulden to Prussia while she received 35 millions from Italy in part payment for the cession of Venice.

Hence the astonishment was all the greater when that same Bismarck who in 1866 had shown himself in such a moderate light broke 4 years later with all the traditions of the past few decades in his dealings with vanquished France and demanded 5 billion francs as a war indemnity. To be sure, France caused even greater astonishment by producing this sum through loans so quickly that within two years she was able to pay her conquerors and rid French territory of foreign troops. From that time until the world war, Russia alone of all the European powers was engaged in great conflicts. In 1877–1878, she defeated Turkey and at the Congress of Berlin imposed upon her a war indemnity of 300 million rubles. An even greater war, that between Russia and Japan, came to an end in 1905, the quarrel being settled through the mediation of America, who saved Russia from the payment of any indemnity. A few years before, in 1898, the United States had conducted a victorious war against Spain. By the treaty of peace the victors not only dispensed with the payment of any damages or war indemnity, but even paid the vanquished 20 million dollars as compensation for the cession of the Philippines.

In the face of such precedents, the procedure of the conquerors at the conclusion of peace in 1919 could not but seem astonishing. During the whole century following the Napoleonic wars there had been concluded only *one* peace by the terms of which a huge war indemnity had been imposed. The victor—Germany—had not only suffered therefor the stern condemnation of the vanquished—France—but also that of the greater part of the civilized world. And yet, what were the 4 billion marks demanded by Bismarck in 1871 compared to the reparation claims of the Entente half a century later?

IV

ON THE PRESENT occasion the demand for an indemnity was nevertheless quite comprehensible. For four long years France and Belgium had been forced to submit to a horrible invasion which, especially in the north of France, resulted in widespread devastation. England had suffered severely from the new weapons, the airplane and the submarine. Were they finally to be victorious in the bloody conflict, only to bear alone the damages which had been sustained? Germany not only expected but was also willing, after her military collapse, to pay an enormous war indemnity out of which the victors would be able to make good a large portion of their damage. Had negotiations with the German government been opened, and on the basis of these negotiations had there been fixed a sum of such size that Germany would have been able to pay it without overstepping the limits of her capacity—Germany herself figured this sum in 1921 at 50 billions of gold marks—this amount might long ago have been raised through international loans. Northern France would have been restored, Germany would have been freed from foreign troops and foreign control, world commerce would have been again in full swing and general prosperity restored. Unfortunately, the victors were unable to adopt this simple, farsighted procedure.

They wanted no payments made on the basis of military law, but an indemnification on that of higher morality; the Germans were to pay not because they had been conquered, but because they were wicked rascals, criminals who had brought on the war.

I have already pointed out the injustice of holding a people responsible for the deeds of a government which it has driven out. . . .

However, if the republic was supposed to be responsible for the misery brought about by the empire, it should have sufficed for the victors to have announced this as their conviction. They could, furthermore, have called to witness the fact that the decisive declarations of war were made by Germany and have coupled with this the invasion of Belgium. But that was not enough for the authors of the Treaty of Versailles. They demanded that the representatives of Germany should themselves recognize her responsibility—even her sole responsibility—for the war. Without this confession there was not to be any peace; the war was to continue—no longer against the armies of the Central Powers, for these had been dissolved, but against starving children, women, old men, whose every avenue of sustenance had been cut off by the victors.

Nevertheless, the German signature to a confession of guilt was exacted. And today many statesmen even dare to proclaim this signature as the evidence of German guilt and as a legal title to complete indemnification by Germany for all damages.

The reparation charges which were imposed upon Germany were divided into two groups. On one side they were definite and exact. They consisted of the delivery of the most widely diverse materials, including the transfer of the entire German fleet to the victors. The handing over of the war fleet was not a bad thing. It relieved Germany of a heavy load and rescued her from the false position into which she had been brought by her naval armaments, which, without purpose and without the possibility of success, had called forth the enmity of England and the mistrust of America. But the surrender of the merchant fleet was another matter. Germany had to deliver nearly 5 million tons of shipping, gross register. That was a hard blow to German commerce. Like blows to German industry were the loss of the Saar coal district, together with a great portion of the Upper Silesian coal district, and the annual loss of the great quantities of coal—in round figures about 40 million tons a year—which Germany had to deliver to Belgium, France, and Italy. Along with all this, countless deliveries of chemical products, live-stock, etc., were required.

In addition there must be figured the expenses, annually renewed, of maintaining the conquerors' troops in the occupied territory. Up to the present they have already cost 4 billions of gold marks, nearly as much as the entire war indemnity which France had to pay in 1871. The occupation is to last another quarter of a century. How many billions are in this way going to be needlessly wasted in the name of reparations, to which not even a penny of them is applied?

All these requirements serve the purpose of restoring the devastated regions and repairing the damages of the war far less than they serve that of creating, year in, year out, ever-renewed sources of friction with Germany.

V

WORST OF ALL, however, are those reparation charges which have to be paid straight-out in cash, for by the treaty of peace their amount is in no way definitely stipulated. To determine them there was appointed a commission on which Germany is not represented, which is not even required to negotiate with the German government, which consults *in camera*, and which "shall not be bound by any particular code or rules of law or by any particular rule of evidence or of procedure, but shall be guided by justice, equity and good faith." This is unrestricted dictatorship, after the kind of the Bolsheviks, and it is extended over a very wide territory. "The Commission shall in general have wide latitude as to the control of the present treaty and the handling of the whole reparation problem." Unbelievable sums were spoken of as to be raised in the shape of reparations by the commission. Mention was made of more than 300 billions—about as much as the national wealth of Germany before the war. This wealth, too, has been considerably reduced since by the demands of the war, by the loss of territory, and by the deliveries of raw materials. Very conservative estimates put this diminution at one-third of the whole.

At the Paris conference in January 1921, the total amount of reparations to be paid in money to the allied governments was fixed at 226 billion gold marks. This was to be paid in full within 42 years, in annual installments which, commencing with 1 of 2 billions in 1921, were to be made at the rate of 6 billions a year from 1932 to 1963. In addition to this there was to be paid 12 percent of the value of German exports over a period of 42 years, which might amount in all to between 40 and 60 billions. Altogether, nearly 300 billions. Messrs. Briand, Lloyd George, and the others who formulated this marvelous demand seemed to believe it possible that Germany could keep on paying, one year after another, about twice the sum which France, in 1871, had to pay but once and which she was then enabled to get together merely in the form of a loan on which she had only to pay the annual interest.

And this mad state of affairs was to last for over 40 years! For that length of time Germany and the world were not to be allowed to quiet down!

Even the Reparations Commission itself was startled at such madness. A few months later it set the sum of Germany's reparation obligations at 132 billions, less than half of what the leaders of the Entente had shortly before demanded. Nothing can more clearly indicate the frivolity with which suc' demands were conceived—a frivolity fully equal to that with which the German government set going a world war in 1914. It is also a very plain indication of the rationality and precision of a treaty which left such enormous sums hanging absolutely in the air.

The authors of the Treaty of Versailles cannot say that they wandered on to the wrong road unwarned. Keynes early pointed out its perils with admirable clearness, advising that there be fixed a definite total for the war indemnities which would not overtax the power of Germany. Today this demand is being reechoed everywhere. In the meanwhile, however, Germany's affairs have become so thoroughly entangled that their reclamation is much more difficult. They could nevertheless be improved in time to prevent catastrophe in Europe if the reparations demands were to be so modified that German credit could be reestablished in the money markets of the world. That Germany has no such credit at the present moment is the most striking proof of the fact that in the opinion of the world's bankers the reparations demands as at present conceived surpass Germany's capacity to pay.

A moratorium, whatever relief it might have afforded earlier, would no longer suffice today. . . .

Yet even disregarding the reparations, the German payments balance is for the moment on the wrong side of the book. Germany is an industrial nation, producing an insufficient amount of food supplies and raw materials. Such nations, as a rule, have a balance of trade against them; England has, Germany had even before the war. The war wiped out Germany's reserve stocks of food and raw materials, and peace deprived Germany of a number of districts producing such supplies and materials. The result is that today Germany's need for foreign raw materials and foodstuffs is greater than ever, far greater than her industrial exports. Germany's special trade in 1920 consisted of imports to the total value of 99 billions of paper marks and exports to the value of 69 billions. The imports of raw materials and foodstuffs amounted to 72 billion marks, the exports of industrial products only to 52 billions. The balance of trade deficit, which in the last years before the war amounted annually to a round 2 billions (in gold marks), was in those days covered by the receipts of the mercantile marine on the one hand and on the other by the interest payments on German capital investments abroad, the proceeds from which flowed back to Germany. The war, with its consequences, destroyed both these means of compensating for the deficit of the balance of trade, at the same time forcing German capitalists to seek credit abroad or to sell their holdings to foreigners. Thus the flow of interest is headed away from Germany. All this has combined to make the deficit of Germany's payments balance even larger than that of her balance of trade. The only way of compensating for this deficit remains, for the moment, that easy but universally destructive process, note inflation.

The foes of Germany are fond of asserting that she is less heavily loaded with taxation than are the victorious countries. This assertion is contested by the German government. In January 1922, Dr. Wirth, chancellor of the German Republic, presented to the Reparations Commission a memorial in which, among other matters, it was reckoned that in Germany roughly 30 percent of the popular income was being paid in taxes, while in France the ratio was but 15 percent. According to the proposal of the German national budget, appearing in the recently published "Statistical Year-Book of the German Reich," out of an estimate of expenditures totaling 352 billion marks, not less than 226 billions—64 percent—were designated as expenditures in connection with the execution of the peace treaty. Only 36 percent were to be used for German purposes.

That a budget of this sort should constantly be broken down by the force of circumstances is evident, nor is it any less plain that the falling rate of exchange should make it impossible to calculate with certainty in advance either in the commercial or the political field. A tax levy may appear enormously high at the moment of its establishment, and by the time of its collection its money value may have shrunk materially. When its proceeds are applied to the compensation of expenditures, the value of the tax may be at a minimum.

It is quite hopeless to expect to rehabilitate Germany's finances and to put an end to money inflation until Germany is granted credits that will permit her for a time to meet her obligations without issuing further notes. Then such issuance can be forbidden; then it will be possible to construct a stable and provident system of taxation; then the taxes can be so ordered that they will suffice to cover expenditures—unless reparations make further senseless demands. And then we should be given time to draw our breath and an opportunity of attaining a surplus of exports which, together with the income from a growing mercantile marine and from capitalistic accumulations, might serve to pay interest and amortization charges on the reparations debt.

As to getting a loan that would save us, there are various means of accomplishing that end. This is not the place for me to discuss them. I can only emphasize here once more that such a loan is an urgent necessity, and that very soon.

One should not be led astray by misleading tales of comfort and swollen luxury discovered by foreign observers in Germany. Moscow, also, has similar pictures to offer. But no one would venture to assert for that reason that the Russian people were living in comfort.

German conditions so far are naturally not as bad as those of Soviet Russia. But each approximation to the latter must here in Germany have a far more disintegrating effect than in Russia, because there the agricultural element is preponderant and many industrial laborers can become simple peasants. That way out is closed to the mass of German workmen. Even emigration is today open to but few of them. If their industrial labor fails them, if their products become incapable of purchasing food from abroad, there will be a terrible mortality.

There are, of course, capitalists in Germany who have been interested in the fall of the rate of exchange because they believed that it would make German industry capable of more effective competition. Such a belief is based on the fact that wages rise more slowly than the value of money declines, and that in this way the German working classes are constantly becoming more miserable. But now even these shortsighted capitalists are beginning to groan over the decline of exchange value, for it constantly is increasing their difficulty in obtaining foreign raw materials and foreign credits.

The only ones who still have a personal interest in the decline of the exchange and in inflation are the speculators, those vultures who always foregather wherever a people is dying. They make their profits from the uncertainty of circumstances, they become rich not by any productive activity but through dealings that are the counterpart of gambling. And, gamblerlike, they never think of accumulating their winnings, but squander them in the most frivolous and prodigal fashion.

Such are the elements that give rise to the appearance of well-being and of luxury in Germany. That the consumption of champagne within the customs jurisdiction of Germany has not decreased is to be laid at their door. In 1913 this consumption reached a total of twelve and a half million bottles; in 1920 (I have at hand no later figures) ten and one-tenth million. The per capita consumption, therefore, of the population since the war is practically the same as in the days that preceded it. It might be fair to investigate to what degree exchange-favored foreigners and officers of the armies of occupation are concerned in this consumption. But in any case, the figures relating to the consumption of champagne testify to a notable looseness of conduct among certain higher elements of the population. The statistics tell quite a different story, however, when we look into the use of luxuries by the lower classes. The consumption of beer within the German excise jurisdiction declined from 69 million hectoliters in the year 1913 to 23 million in the year 1920.

The intellectual workers are hit even harder than are the manual laborers by the results of the fall in exchange. Everywhere, whenever there is a rise in prices, it becomes plain that many of the actual laborers, whose activities cannot for a moment be dispensed with, are much better able to protect themselves against the consequences of the rise than are the intellectual workers, without whose labor the world can, in case of need, get along for a while. But nowhere, except perhaps still in Austria, is the privation of scholars and artists so distressingly manifest as in Germany. Many of them are literally starving. And they are starving not only physically; they are finding it more and more impossible to satisfy their intellectual hunger, to purchase books, instruments, and other scientific means of support.

In this wise Germany is steadily becoming more and more impoverished by the fall in the exchange value of her currency. She is losing not only in material values, but also in her physical ability to work and in the field of scientific qualifications.

Nearly a hundred years ago Charles Dickens showed, with masterly delineation, how imprisonment for debt deprives the debtor of every capacity for and enjoyment in labor and demoralizes him to the utmost, without the slightest advantage to the creditor and to the disadvantage of society as a whole.

The German nation is now undergoing imprisonment for debt. It is wasting away and is more and more losing in the process the capacity to make its labors pay its debts.

VI

WHEN THE conditions of the Treaty of Versailles became known in Germany, we were all horrified. The German people had been far from unanimous in their attitude toward the war. Those of us who judged the war to have been brought about by the German government, either by design or through incompetence, were not, even from the beginning, merely an isolated portion of the population, and the longer the war continued the larger became the number of those who opposed its continuation and who demanded of the German government that it express its readiness to enter into a peace of understanding. But all of us, even the most determined denouncers of Germany's military policy, were fully agreed that the Versailles treaty was terrific and impracticable, and that, if mention were to be made of moral guilt, the criminal war-responsibility of Germany was more or less matched by the criminal peace-responsibility of the authors of the treaty provisions. We held it to be our duty to criticize this peace-guilt as sharply as we had criticized that war-guilt.

When the German people learned the conditions of peace in May 1919, they were completely united for the first time since the outbreak of the war.

They condemned them with a single voice. But a new disagreement arose as to whether or not, despite all condemnation, the treaty should be signed.

We who demanded that it be signed were at first very few in number. But as the decisive moment approached, the majority came over to us. No one, however, demanded that it be signed because he deemed it tolerable or practicable; the reason of everyone who made the demand was merely that there was nothing else to do. After the evidence we had received from the victors, it seemed to us that there was no possibility that a refusal would influence them to reconsideration and to negotiation. Refusal would have been taken as a defiant denial of any sort of reparation; it would have roused the victors to unmeasured fury, to deeds of violence which would have imparted to Germany's desperate situation an even more dreadful aspect and which would not have saved us in the end from having to sign under even more unfavorable circumstances.

But although nobody in Germany who advocated the signing of the treaty regarded its complete execution as possible, that must not be taken to mean that the treaty was signed with a *reservatio mentalis*, with the intention of not carrying it out. It was signed with the firm determination to fulfill all of its obligations as far as should prove possible. A revision was considered inevitable, but this was not expected as the result of passive resistance. By that our opponents would only be irritated and made still more implacable. The revision was hoped for as the result of a change of mind on the part of the conquerors. But this change of mind was to be expected only in the event that the most loyal fulfillment of the terms of the treaty was contemplated. . . .

The governments committed to the policy of fulfillment have been not only weak, they have also been responsible for many blunders, and have thus interfered with their own objectives: the cooling of the war hatred against Germany and the growth of a realization that under present conditions of international intercourse the economic collapse of any great civilized nation, even of Germany, would create uncertainties all over the world.

This policy of fulfillment has not yet accomplished its aim of stabilizing conditions in Germany. But during the past year there has been unmistakably a softening of the previous attitude of Germany's late opponents. They have begun to abandon the Bolshevistic method of dictation and to adopt the democratic one of negotiation between parties equally entitled to justice. For all that, the process of modification is going on all too slowly and too inadequately, while the ruin which the peace terms brought in their train advances swiftly. It is not always enough to do the right thing; it must be done at the right time. The words "too late" have played a fateful role in every great historical catastrophe.

VII

FOR ALL THIS holding off and hanging back and postponing of the inevitable, the French government is principally to blame.

It is a well known fact, and one that needs no further elaboration, that it is the French government which most bitterly opposes every suggestion of discussion or of alleviation of the reparation terms and which is first in the field to threaten fresh violence, such as for instance the occupation of the Ruhr district.

Since the German population is growing while that of France scarcely increases at all, the German nation will soon be twice as numerous as the French. For France that is a very alarming outlook. And it goes far toward explaining her present policy.

There is no doubt that a rehabilitated Germany could become terrible to France as an enemy. But one would think that a realization of this fact would lead her to consider the necessity of pursuing a policy which would not isolate her from the world and which would render it possible for her to live on friendly terms with Germany. Otherwise she is left with no alternative but to strive from now until eternity to prevent Germany's recuperation, to tear open afresh, day by day, the wounds inflicted on her by both war and peace, thus permanently depriving all Europe of tranquillity, security, and welfare— a policy which would finally rally all Europe in support of Germany and lead to a catastrophe for herself.

There could be an excuse for this suicidal policy only if Germans and Frenchmen were fashioned by nature to be as hostile toward each other as cats and dogs, a state of affairs which could never be altered. This conception is as senseless as was the one which counted for so much throughout the eighteenth century and into the beginning of the nineteenth, namely that a natural enmity existed between Englishmen and Frenchmen. Enmity between two nations always is only the result of historical circumstance, and it passes with the historic causes which occasioned it. The historic causes which brought France as well as many other nations into opposition with Germany are practically passed.

This opposition was fundamentally an opposition to Prussian militarism. Prussia as the youngest, smallest, and poorest of the great powers in the eighteenth century was only able to assert herself by making sure that her army was equal to that of any other important state, an achievement requiring of her that more than any other state she should devote all her energies to her army. . . .

The policy of Prussia increased the aversion toward Germany in the most influential European nations. We have already designated the violent annexation of Alsace-Lorraine as the original sin of the new German Empire. With this mistake of Bismarck's, William II associated the second and far greater one of a competition in naval armament, whereby England felt herself threatened. Finally German policy committed still a third error, the most fateful of all. Being able to find only a single ally whom she trusted under all circumstances, Germany allowed herself to be influenced in her decisions by that ally. And the ally was the empire of Austria, which had become wholly moribund. For Austria's sake Germany came into opposition with Russia, with the growing Balkan states and even with her old associate Italy. It was not in defense of a German but of an Austrian claim that the world war broke out. Thus the German Empire made all the world its enemy and consequently it had in the end to fight against almost all the world.

Along with the German Empire, all these stumbling blocks have been removed. The old Austria has vanished, the German war fleet has been surrendered, Alsace-Lorraine has been given back to France. At the same time the root of all the evil, Prusso-German militarism, has ceased to exist. Nor was it overcome only from outside by the act of compulsory disarmament; it was vanquished also from within. It has lost the commanding influence that it used to exert on the mind of the German people.

No great army in Europe ever had such an almost unbroken series of victories to point to as did the Prussian army. True, this army which believed itself almost invincible was disastrously smitten in 1806 at Jena; but in 1913 it had ironed out this dent in its shield. From 1870 on, the confidence of the entire German people in its army reached almost unbelievable heights.

And now, at the conclusion of the world war, came crushing defeat, all the more paralyzing because it was not due to any lack of stoutness in the troops but to the incompetent policy of the military command, which had taken upon itself to lead the German nation into the field against an overwhelmingly superior force. From the heights of wealth and glory, Germany was cast down by the war into the depths of bitter poverty and indignity. Hereafter only absolute despair could make it try once more a passage at arms, which, under the circumstances, would but lead to renewed, to absolutely crushing disaster.

The German people are therefore becoming more and more convinced that Germany's salvation no longer depends on competitive armaments, but on a general disarmament; not on the increase of her own army, but on the decrease of the armies of others. The role that she would play in the society of nations is the exact opposite of what it has hitherto been. From a menace she is becoming a promise; from a martial peril she is turning into a pledge of world peace.

In many quarters the sincerity of this intention is not trusted. People seem to think that it would vanish again upon the economic rehabilitation of Germany.

It must be admitted that this new intention is not yet universal, although it already inspires a majority of the nation. The old generation cannot easily rid itself of inherited trains of thought. But the new idea is being developed by the new conditions themselves and will root itself ever more deeply in the minds of the young generation which is growing up under its influence and is no longer being dazzled by militaristic stage-shows.

The strengthening of Germany's economic life will not impede but will further a pacifistic development. The stronger the peaceably inclined body of workmen becomes, the less numerous will be those déclassés who are bent on desperate schemes.

It is not Germany's economic resuscitation but her economic collapse which means danger to her neighbors. If the victors pursue a policy tending to plunge the German people ever deeper into misery, they will be adopting the best means of bringing again to life ideas of armed opposition and revenge.

What the German nation wants and needs is peace—lasting, actual peace, with complete self-determination for all its parts and with no slave labor to perform for the benefit of its conquerors. It demands nothing but that these shall at last proceed to make good what they promised in Wilson's Fourteen Points. The principal obstruction in the matter up to the present has been offered by France. But it is not from outside that this obstruction can be overcome. It is wholly mistaken to expect Germany's rescue to result from a conflict between England and France. Such a conflict would only put the climax to Europe's hapless situation and would not improve French relations with Germany. The world needs peace and friendship between France and England just as urgently as it needs peace and friendship between these two and Germany. Should these three become united and join in a hearty understanding with the great transatlantic republic, the peace of the world would be assured; then would be possible a League of Nations which would not be a gendarme of the conquerors, but one to which all nations would belong, which all nations would trust, and which would be in a position to solve peacefully all the problems which have grown out of the peace pacts concluded in 1919.

Nationalism and Internationalism

Alfred E. Zimmern

JUNE 1923

IT IS A COMMON theme among the pessimists that the world has relapsed since the armistice into a temper of nationalism which renders illusory the hopes and dreams of internationalism so widely entertained during the war. These two movements or moods, nationalism and internationalism, are regarded as opposing and mutually exclusive, and the very evident ascendancy of the former is too often unquestioningly accepted as involving, if not the final defeat, at least the indefinite postponement of the latter. If this were really so, the outlook for mankind would be black indeed, for nationalism, not only in Europe and America but throughout the world, is clearly a rising power. But the belief that nationalism and internationalism are incompatibles, although superficially plausible, is based upon ignorance of men and nations and a complete misunderstanding of the two movements themselves. As this belief is widespread and is acting as a serious hindrance to the advance of a real understanding between nations, it may be worthwhile to subject it to the test of a brief analysis.

Let us look first at the complaint brought by the disillusioned idealists and antinationalists against the postwar world. What is the general indictment that lurks behind the manifold grumbling about the Balkanization of Europe, the unreasonableness of France, the commercialism of Britain, the impenitence of Germany, the self-assertion of the Little Entente states and of the British Dominions, and the recrudescence of isolationism and Monroeism in the United States? We are often told, when these topics are mentioned, that the world has relapsed from the principles and standards of internationalism into a state of blind and unreflecting nationalism. But when we look at the facts, this explanation is obviously insufficient. If nationalism were really rampant in East-Central Europe, how could the Little Entente between Czechoslovakia, Rumania, and Jugoslavia ever have come into existence or been maintained for three years? How indeed could these three states and their Polish neighbor, all of them inhabited by a variety of peoples, have succeeded in preserving their identity at all? Or how, if nationalism were the world's ruling passion, could the British Commonwealth, with its manifold variety of peoples, have been held together? How could France have maintained the unity of her empire, or even of her newly integrated home country? How could bilingual Belgium and trilingual Switzerland have survived? How, finally, could the United States have avoided serious conflicts with the unassimilated nationalisms of millions of her recent arrivals? Clearly, even if we grant that nationalism has been one of the forces at work, it has not been the most powerful and determining factor. What we really find, when we examine the counts of the indictment against the postwar world more closely, is that the policies complained of are quite as marked in the case of states consisting of several nations acting in cooperation as in those consisting of but a single nation. The real trouble in fact is not nationalism, in any of the many forms which that movement is capable of assuming, but something which may be described by the less romantic and more comprehensive designation of selfishness. In other words, the indictment should be drawn not against nations but against states; not against statesmen acting as the spokesmen of nationalities and the interpreters of nationalism but against statesmen acting as the instruments of sovereign states, great or small, uninational or multinational; not against Mr. Lloyd George as a Welshman, M. Briand as a Breton, President Masaryk as a Slovak, M. Venizelos as a Cretan, but against the policies of the British Empire, the French and Czechoslovak Republics, and the Kingdom of Greece.

Some such relapse into selfish policies was almost inevitable after the strain of war and of wartime cooperation. We are not concerned here with its details or degrees—with the question whether it would have been possible, by wiser and more farsighted statesmanship, to have prevented the pendulum from swinging back so far. What is important for our present purpose is to note that the existing political troubles of the world arise not from the passions of nations but from the policies of states, and that it is with the adjustment of these policies, not with the sublimation of national passions, that constructive political work in the field of foreign affairs is concerned. "Internationalism," in the political sense in which the word is customarily used, is in fact concerned with promoting the cooperation of states, not with controlling or even canalizing the undue self-expression of nations. It is unfortunate that this vital truth should be concealed by the vagaries of our political terminology. The League of Nations is, of course, a misnomer. It is a League of States, and it will be subject to perpetual misunderstanding if it is thought of as anything else. If its membership is extended to Ireland and not to Scotland, to Haiti and not to the Afro-American nation, it is because Ireland and Haiti have a distinct political status which Scotland and the Negroes of the American continent cannot claim.

The work of internationalism, then—or, as it would be more properly called, the work of interstate organization—is concerned with the mutual relations of sovereign bodies, however composed, and has nothing directly to do with the relations of nations.

From this it would appear that internationalism and nationalism, so far from being conflicting forces, do not impinge upon one another at all, and that the current impression to the contrary is completely unfounded. Nevertheless, there is no smoke without fire, and it will probably be felt that the above summary analysis does less than justice to the common view. Theoretically and in principle, it will be said, the two movements dwell on separate planes and ought not to conflict. But in point of fact they frequently do. Both in Europe and America there is a large admixture of what cannot be described otherwise than as nationalist sentiment in the conduct of affairs of state. To explain why this is so and to understand its significance we must subject the whole movement of nationalism to closer scrutiny.

It is difficult for a European to discuss this subject with Americans, not merely because of the differences in current nomenclature which have already been mentioned but because the whole course and direction of national sentiment has been different on the two sides of the Atlantic. The nations of the American continent, north and south, are not only far younger than the nations of Europe, but they have also come into existence by a wholly different historical process. Nevertheless, the resultant sentiment of nationalism is of much the same character in America as in Europe, and the likeness will undoubtedly become more marked as the accidents of origin are smoothed out by the normal processes of development and the life of the two continents tends more and more to beat with a similar pulse and rhythm. The nationalism of America, or at any rate of the United States of America, to use a phrase of Mr. Van Wyck Brooks, is coming of age. The difference between 15 and 25 in the life of an individual is akin to the difference between one century and three or four in the life of a nation. When the youth of 15 has come to 40 and the man of 25 has touched 50, the common element in their experience becomes much more apparent. The same will be true of the inner experience of the nations of Europe and America as the generations go on.

What is nationalism? It is a movement or manifestation of the sentiment of nationality. It is often employed in a derogatory sense to denote a violent, intolerant, and even aggressive manifestation; but it may equally well be employed of manifestations of a more equable temper. It will, however, conduce to clearness in the discussion to set aside the term nationalism and to deal rather with "nationality" and "nation" than with their manifestations in "nationalist" movements of various types. "Nationality," then, is the group-consciousness of which nationalism is one of the outward expressions; and a nation is a body of people bound together by the particular form of group-consciousness described as "nationality" or "the sense of nationality."

What is this particular form of group-consciousness which constitutes nationality? What is it that distinguishes a nation or body of people held together by a sentiment of nationality from other human groups and corporate bodies? It is easier to say what a nation is not than to define satisfactorily what it is. As we have seen, it is not a state or political body. The English nation is something different from the British Commonwealth and (though this is not so commonly recognized) the American nation is something different from the American Commonwealth. English nationality does not necessarily imply British citizenship, nor did Henry James cease to be an American when he surrendered his American citizenship during the war. Again, a nation is not a church or religious body. Turkish nationality is something different from Mohammedanism and Jewish nationality is something different from Judaism. It is true that practically all Turks are Moslems and that many, if not most, of those who share the sentiment of Jewish group-consciousness share also in the Jewish religious belief and observances; but the distinction between church and nation, though frequently denied by Jews, as the distinction between commonwealth and nation is denied by Americans, is nevertheless undeniable.

Again, a nation is not a territorial unit. There are probably more Irishmen outside Ireland, more Norwegians outside Norway, more Jews outside Palestine, perhaps also more Scotsmen, Slovaks, and Letts outside Scotland, Slovakia, and Latvia than in the compact area of territory with which their national sentiments are related.

Again, a nation is not a race. None of the existing nations, not even those who, like the Jews, have laid most stress on purity of stock, correspond to the racial divisions and subdivisions of the anthropologists. The attempts made at repeated intervals by anti-Semitic writers such as Houston Stewart Chamberlain in Germany and less doctrinaire and more frankly abusive writers in America to enlist racial prejudice in the cause of nationalist intolerance spring from pure obscurantism.

Finally, a nation is not a linguistic unit. The English-speaking peoples, whether under the Union Jack or not, are, with one exception, not English; neither are the German-speaking Swiss and Austrians German, nor the French-speaking Swiss and Belgians and Canadians French. Conversely, cases occur in which national sentiment exists not only, as in English-speaking North America and Australasia, without a national medium of expression, but without any common medium of expression at all. Among Welshmen, for instance, there is a large mass who know no Welsh and a very considerable body who know no English, and the same phenomenon can be found on a smaller scale in Ireland. Thus these two bodies of Welshmen and Irishmen, each of them participating consciously and deliberately in the deep-lying sentiment of their nationality, have no means of communicating with one another in speech—an example which is striking not so much for the light it throws on the vicissitudes of Welsh and Irish history as for the revelation it affords of the inadequacy of words as a means for the expression of thought. Another example of the same kind is the survival of the Jewish national consciousness in spite of the varieties of Jewish speech. A heroic effort is now indeed being made to revivify Hebrew and make it the current speech of the Jewish homeland in Palestine. This experiment, like the parallel experiment in Ireland, may possibly succeed; but it is possible that such success may be accompanied by a narrowing and stiffening of the national soul. On the other hand it may fail; but its failure, whilst in some ways regrettable, would certainly not entail the disintegration of the Jewish national personality, which has survived far deeper disappointments during its long and chequered career. The fact is that we are only at the beginning of the study of the interrelations between language and personality, whether individual or national. Students of phonetics, of music, and of psychology have yet to join hands in investigating the subconscious region whence proceed the infinite variations of pitch and intonation, of idiom, metaphor, and symbolism, of gesture and phonation which, to the student of modes of human expression, are like a warm covering of flesh and blood over the bare skeleton of a mere vocabulary.

If a nation is neither a state nor a church nor a race nor a geographical or linguistic unit, what is it? No definition is satisfactory in a matter which goes so deep or has such widespread ramifications, but the following, put forward by the present writer some years ago, may at least serve as a working basis: *a nation is a body of people united by a corporate sentiment of peculiar intensity, intimacy, and dignity, related to a definite home-country.*

National sentiment is intense: men feel towards their nation as towards something which plays a large part in their life and inner experience. How intense this feeling is can be tested by the joy which every normally constituted man feels when, after sojourning in a strange atmosphere, he is once more brought into contact with his nationality, whether it be in a gathering in a strange country or on his return to his territorial base. The Englishman who feels a catch in his throat when he sees the white cliffs of Dover after an absence in distant lands (whether under the Union Jack or not) and the

American who raises his hat to salute the Statue of Liberty as he steams into New York harbor are both giving expression, not to their sense of patriotism or state obligation, but to their sense of nationality.

National sentiment is intimate: whether it be mainly compounded of influences of heredity (as in Europe) or of environment, as in the older Americans, or whether it be something newly acquired and deliberately cherished, as among the new arrivals, it is something that goes deep down into the very recesses of the being. Europeans are accustomed to believe that nationality is something so intimate that it cannot be acquired; nationality to them is akin to the family; it is the element of heredity which is paramount. Americans, on the other hand, are accustomed to the idea of an acquired nationality but perhaps do not always sufficiently realize how intimate such an acquirement may be. The nationality of a European and the nationality of a recent American may perhaps be compared to a man's relation to his parents and his relation to his wife. Both sentiments are intimate; both can legitimately be compared, in the sphere of personal relations, to the sense of nationality in the wider sphere of corporate relations. But the one is hereditary, the other is elective. The European and the older American are born into their nation; the recent American has chosen his nationality and attached himself to it as to a wife. And, as parentage and marriage both go to make up a complete personality, so nationality, even among members of the older nations, will not be complete without an element of election and deliberation, or, to use a more appropriate term which the war brought home to so many, rededication.

National sentiment is dignified: it is on a larger and grander scale than a man's feeling towards a country or a parish, a club or a group of professional or other intimates, however warm such a feeling may be. No outsider can judge at what point a group attachment related to a definite territory reaches the degree of dignity entitling it to be described as national. Is Malta the home of a nation or is it a mere municipal port of call? Is Newfoundland the home of a nation or a mere elderly colony? Was Virginia ever a nation? Was the Old South ever a nation? Every student of these problems of sentiment must make these nice valuations for himself. In general we can only say that a nation is a nation, however small its territory, when its members feel it to be one and bear themselves accordingly. "It is not walls but men that make a city," said the Greek orator long ago; and it is not space and population but a sense of great things experienced in the past and greater lying before in the future, if we may thus deepen the implication of a phrase of Renan's, which constitutes the soul and consciousness of a nation.

Every nation has a home. The sentiment of nationality cannot gather simply round an idea or a memory or a programme or about some function or status, such as a priesthood or an aristocracy or a Legion of Janissaries. That does not mean that membership in a nation, participation in its common life and consciousness, necessarily involves residence within a fixed area or contact with it by visits or economic ties. Consciousness can overleap the barriers and ignore the qualifications fixed by political authority for the world of statehood. No period of residence for naturalization is required to relate an Emmet born in New York to Ireland, or Theodor Herzl the Viennese journalist to Palestine, or to defer the acceptance by America of the wholehearted offering of mind and spirit made by so many of those lately landed on her shores. But without the element of environment, the actual physical territory and what man has made of it, to form the framework and receptacle, as it were, of the national ideal, the sentiment of nationality would lose the warmth and concreteness which constitute so large a part of its appeal and would disappear into the clouds which have swallowed up so many unattached idealisms in the past.

We have defined nationality. Let us now observe it in operation in various parts of the world.

It is often said that the nineteenth century witnessed the dawn of nationality in Europe. Of some parts of Europe this may be true, but of Western and Central Europe, to which this judgment is usually applied, it is certainly untrue. Englishmen were already Englishmen in the days of Chaucer and Langland, and the France of Froissart and Villon was already France. So too Dante's Italy, though still only lisping Italian, was Italy, and, in spite of the unhappy vicissitudes and backwardness of German political history, the men for whom Luther translated the Bible were already Germans. The history of the rise of the different European nationalities, from Ireland in the west to the various Slav and Baltic peoples in the east, would form a fascinating study. . . . But, until the French Revolution, this history is, broadly speaking, nonpolitical. Government being still almost everywhere regarded, according to the feudal tradition, as the concern of a special class, the people, in whom the national consciousness was alive or in process of formation, did not concern itself with what are nowadays loosely described as "national" problems and policies. The territorial lords of Europe, kings and electors and grand dukes and bishops and petty barons, fought and plotted and intrigued, extended their frontiers hither and thither by conquest, marriage, and barter, and turned the balance of power this way and that without enlisting in their causes (which would hardly bear too close a scrutiny) the deep-lying passions and sentiments which were growing up in the hearts of the populations from whom they drew tribute. It was in England and Holland that nationality was first enlisted in the political field, but it was the great outburst of the French Revolution which mingled and muddied the two streams and brought about a confusion of thought and a perplexity in action from which the world, on both sides of the Atlantic and of the Pacific, has not yet recovered.

When President Wilson, picking up a phrase from the great mischief-maker Lenin, flung the slogan of "self-determination" into the world's arena, he was using a word capable of many interpretations. But the majority of mankind, under the influence of vague nineteenth-century shibboleths, understood him to be associating himself with the doctrine that every nation has a right to be a sovereign state. "It is in general a necessary condition of free institutions," said John Stuart Mill, "that the boundaries of governments should coincide in the main with those of nationalities." What Mill thus cautiously stated as a maxim of convenience (how in all sincerity could an inhabitant of the United Kingdom of England, Scotland, Wales, and Ireland put it any higher?) had long since been elevated by more ardent liberals into a gospel of indefeasible right. The necessary result of such a doctrine, as Lenin foresaw and desired, was disintegration—the breakup of that bourgeois nationalist society which he so detested.

A survey of the workings of political nationalism and of the theory of self-determination is instructive. A gospel that claims to be of universal validity and application can only show results in a limited region of Europe and western Asia. It has helped to break up the Austro-Hungarian Empire, but it has left trinational Switzerland untouched; it has disintegrated Russia—if indeed, for most Russians, there ever was, in the deepest sense, a Russia—but it has not brought independence either to Armenia or to the Ukraine. It has torn Southern Ireland from Westminster but has left Scotland, Wales, and Ulster where they were. It has taken German-speaking Alsace from the German Empire and restored it to France; it has rescued the Germanic peasants of Flanders from their invading kinsmen and reunited them with their French-speaking fellow-citizens. It has destroyed the dream of an Illyrian Republic and brought a joint Serbo-Croatian-Slovenian Kingdom into existence. Finally, having demolished three autocratic empires, it has left the indescribably heterogeneous and multinational dominion of Britain standing upright amid the débris of imperialisms. In other words, national sentiment, whilst proving an invaluable ally for a movement of resistance against the abuses of misgovernment, as in Austria-Hungary, or against the pinpricks of misunderstanding, as in Ireland, is unable by its own unaided efforts to make the political map conform more nearly to its pattern design.

Turn now to America. What application can be found, either in North or South America, for Mill's doctrine? Here it is not a question of redrawing a political map so as to carve new frontiers to fit old and existing nations. It is a case of fitting nations into existing frontiers, or rather of helping nations to find themselves and be themselves within the fixed framework of an established political society. The malady of Europe has not arisen, as is so often said, from its nationalisms. It has arisen from a simpler cause, from bad government. Europeans have had to wage a long fight, of which the recent war, we may hope and believe, is the last phase, against autocracy and its consequent injustice, not against the denial of "rights" to "nations," but against the denial of justice and liberty to men and women. The malady of America, on the other hand, the growing restlessness and perplexity of which every student of the United States must be conscious, arises not from bad government (Europe has had to suffer more, in these last years, than America from the defects of the American constitutional machine) but from its nationality problem or problems. It sounds paradoxical yet it is substantially true to say that each continent has wrongly diagnosed its malady. The Europeans who have given their lives, from Ireland to Poland and the Ukraine, for the cause of self-determination and an independent national republic have been waging a hopeless battle for an unrealizable ideal. In all three countries, diverse as is their present status, Mill's coincidence of government with nationality is a practical impossibility. What their champions have really been fighting for, if they only knew it, has been conditions of government which would enable them to be themselves—in other words, for the supreme political goods, for Justice and Liberty—Justice and Liberty for all dwellers in Ireland, for all dwellers in Poland and the Ukraine, irrespective of race, religion, or nationality.

Americans, on the other hand, who have been much concerned in recent years over the external problems of their community life, are beginning to look back on their muckraking campaigns with an uneasy sense that they have not probed the real roots of the national dissatisfaction. It is true that American government and American society leave much to be desired; but surely the real problems of America are national, belong, that is, to the intimate region of mind and spirit which has been spoken of above. Let Europe, from Galway to Lemberg, from Algeciras to Helsingfors, consolidate its newly established democracies, establish firm guarantees of mutual protection among its states, reduce its infantile mortality, introduce labor-saving science into its homes and factories, and ameliorate its plumbing. These are the tasks, practical and positive, whether high or humble, for a continent, such as Europe now is, of self-conscious and satisfied nationalism. America's domestic problems are of a different order. They are not so much political and social (the tasks in this region are clearly indicated and not difficult of accomplishment by an energetic and organizing people) as national in the deepest sense—to work inwards from the influences of environment to the unalterable values of heredity, to discover the quality and substance of the diverse populations that have married themselves to this great continent, and to make the men and women and, still more, the children, who have entered into the new national consciousness, at home and at ease, in the deepest region of their manifold natures, in the home of their choice.

Once the problems of nationality and the problems of statehood and citizenship have been disentangled, they will easily yield to treatment. It is from their century-old confusion that so much mischief and bloodshed have arisen, whether in the insane German design to base the dominion of the world on the "culture," that is, the intimate expression of a single people, or in the futile and suicidal efforts, now happily discredited, of the straitest sect of "Americanizers." The way is becoming clear, then, both in Europe and America, for a real internationalism, in the truest and purest sense of the word.

For internationalism, properly understood, is not contact between states; nor is it contact between supernationalists and cosmopolitans who have torn themselves loose from affiliation with their nation. It is at home neither round the green table of the diplomatists nor "above the melee" with the minority minds. True internationalism is contact between nations in their highest and best and most distinctive representatives and manifestations. The true contact between the West European national triangle which is so disquieting the world must be a contact, not between trust-magnates or labor-leaders or even statesmen from the three countries, but, so to speak, between Shakespeare, Molière, and Goethe. It is the most characteristic figures of a national literature who are also the most international, and it is through them that understanding must come. Our efforts at internationalism have failed hitherto because they have followed the line of least effort. Any fool can book a ticket for a foreign country, just as any fool can learn Esperanto. But contacts so established effect nothing. They tell us no more than that the German or the Frenchman is a human being, a father, a workman, and a lover of beer or coffee, which we knew before. It is through a deeper exploration and enjoyment of the infinite treasures of the world's nationalities, by men and women whose vision has been trained and sensibilities refined because they themselves are intimately bound up with a nation of their own, that an enduring network of internationalism will some day be knit and a harmony of understanding established in a world of unassailable diversity.

Lenin

Victor Chernov

MARCH 1924

LENIN IS DEAD—this time dead physically, for spiritually and politically he has been dead a year at least. We have got in the habit of speaking of him as a thing of the past; and for that very reason it will not be difficult now to write of him dispassionately.

Lenin was a great man. He was not merely the greatest man in his party; he was its uncrowned king, and deservedly. He was its head, its will, I should even say he was its heart were it not that both the man and the party implied in themselves heartlessness as a duty. Lenin's intellect was energetic but cold. It was above all an ironic, sarcastic, and cynical intellect. Nothing to him was worse than sentimentality, a name he was ready to apply to all moral and ethical considerations in politics. Such things were to him trifles, hypocrisy, "parson's talk." Politics to him meant strategy, pure and simple. Victory was the only commandment to observe; the will to rule and to carry through a political program without compromise, that was the only virtue; hesitation, that was the only crime.

It has been said that war is a continuation of politics, though employing different means. Lenin would undoubtedly have reversed this dictum and said that politics is the continuation of war under another guise. The essential effect of war on a citizen's conscience is nothing but a legalization and glorification of things that in times of peace constitute crime. In war the turning of a flourishing country into a desert is a mere tactical move; robbery is a "requisition," deceit a stratagem, readiness to shed the blood of one's brother military zeal; heartlessness towards one's victims is laudable self-command; pitilessness and inhumanity are one's duty. In war all means are good, and the best ones are precisely the things most condemned in normal human intercourse. And as politics is disguised war, the rules of war constitute its principles.

Lenin was often accused of not being and of not wanting to be an "honest adversary." But then the very idea of an "honest adversary" was to him an absurdity, a smug citizen's prejudice, something that might be made use of now and then jesuitically in one's own interest; but to take it seriously was silly. A defender of the proletariat is under an obligation to put aside all scruples in dealings with the foe. To deceive him intentionally, to calumniate him, to blacken his name, all this Lenin considered as normal. In fact, it would be hard to exceed the cynical brutality with which he proclaimed all this. Lenin's conscience consisted in putting himself outside the boundaries of human conscience in all dealings with his foes; and in thus rejecting all principles of honesty he remained honest with himself.

Being a Marxist, he was a believer in "class struggle." As an individual contribution to this theory, he used to confess his belief that civil war was the unavoidable climax of class struggle. We may even say that to him class struggle was but the embryo of civil war. Dissent in the party, whether serious or merely trifling, he often tried to explain as an echo of class antagonisms. He would then proceed to eliminate the undesirable by cutting them off from the party, and in doing this he "honestly" resorted to the lowest means. After all, is not a nonhomogeneous party an illegitimate conglomeration of antagonistic class-elements? And all antagonistic class-elements should be treated according to the precept "war is war."

His whole life was passed in schisms and factional fights within the party. From this resulted his incomparable perfection as a gladiator, as a professional fighter, in training every day of his life and constantly devising new tricks to trip up or knock out his adversary. It was this lifelong training that gave him his amazing cool-headedness, his presence of mind in any conceivable situation, his unflinching hope "to get out of it" somehow or other. By nature a man of single purpose and possessed of a powerful instinct of self-preservation, he had no difficulty in proclaiming *credo quia absurdum* and was much like that favorite Russian toy, the Van'ka-Vstan'ka boy, who has a piece of lead in his rounded bottom and bobs up again as fast as you knock him down. After every failure, no matter how shameful or humiliating, Lenin would instantly bob up and begin again from the beginning. His will was like a good steel spring which recoils the more powerfully the harder it is pressed. He was a hardy party leader of just the kind necessary to inspire and keep up the courage of his fellow fighters and to forestall panic by his personal example of unlimited self-confidence, as well as to bring them to their senses in periods of high exaltation when it would be extremely easy for them to become "a conceited party," as he used to say, resting on their laurels and overlooking the perils of the future.

This singleness of purpose was the thing that most imposed respect among his followers. Many a time when Lenin managed to survive, thanks only to some blunder of his foes, the credit for his survival was attributed to his unflinching optimism. Often it used to be mere blind luck—but then blind luck mostly comes to those who know how to hold out through a period of desperate ill-luck. Most persons soon give up. They do not care to sacrifice their strength in evidently futile attempts; they are sensible—and it is this good sense that precludes good luck. There is some supreme common sense, on the other hand, in a man who will spend his last ounce of energy in spite of all odds—in spite of logic, destiny, and circumstance. And with such "unreasonable common sense," nature endowed Lenin to excess. Thanks to this tenacity, he more than once salvaged his party from apparently inextricable straits, but to the masses at large such occurrences were miracles and were ascribed to his genius of foresight. Foresight on a large scale, however, was the very thing he lacked. He was a fencing master first of all, and a fencer needs only a little foresight and no complicated ideas. In fact, he must not think too much; he must concentrate on every movement of his adversary and master his own reflexes with the quickness of inborn instinct, so as to counter every hostile move without a trace of delay.

Lenin's intellect was penetrating but not broad, resourceful but not creative. A past master in estimating any political situation, he would become instantly at home with it, quickly perceive all that was new in it, and exhibit great political and practical sagacity in forestalling its immediate political consequences. This perfect and immediate tactical sense formed a complete contrast to the absolutely unfounded and fantastic character of any more extensive historical prognosis he ever attempted—of any program that comprised more than today and tomorrow. . . . His concrete plans of attack were superbly practical; but his grandiose program of action after victory, which was to cover a whole historical period, went to pieces at the first touch of reality. His "nearer political outlook" was unexcelled; his "further political outlook" went permanently bankrupt.

As a man who already had the truth in his pocket, he attached no value to the creative efforts of other seekers after truth. He had no respect for the convictions of anyone else, he had none of the enthusiastic love of liberty which marks the independent creative spirit. On the contrary, he was dominated by the purely Asiatic conception of a monopoly of press, speech, justice, and thought by a single ruling caste, agreeing therein with the alleged Moslem saying that if the library of Alexandria contained the same things as the Koran it was useless, and if it contained things contrary it was harmful.

Granting that Lenin was absolutely lacking in creative genius, that he was merely a skilful, forcible, and indefatigable expounder of other thinkers' theories, that he was a man of such narrowness of mind that it could almost be called limited intelligence, nevertheless he was capable of greatness and originality within those limitations. His power lay in the extraordinary, absolute lucidity—one might almost say the transparency—of his propositions. He followed his logic unflinchingly even to an absurd conclusion and left nothing diffuse and unexplained unless it were necessary to do so for tactical considerations. Ideas were made as concrete and simple as possible. This was most evident in Lenin's rhetoric. He never was a brilliant orator, an artist of beautiful speech. He would often be coarse and clumsy, especially in polemics, and he repeated himself continually. But these repetitions were his very system and his strength. Through the endless redigesting, uncouth pounding, and clumsy jokes there throbbed a live, indomitable will that would not be deviated by an inch from the appointed path; it was a steady, elemental pressure whose monotony hypnotized the audience. One and the same thought was expressed many times in many different shapes till finally in one way or another it penetrated each individual brain; then, as a drop of water perforates the rock, constant repetition was applied to implant the idea into the very essence of the hearer's intelligence. Few orators have known how to achieve such admirable results by dint of repetition. Besides, Lenin always *felt* his audience. He never rose too high above its level, nor did he ever omit to descend to it at just the necessary moment, in order not to break the continuity of the hypnosis which dominated the will of his flock; and more than anyone he realized that a mob is like a horse that wants to be firmly bestrode and spurred, that wants to feel the hand of a master. When needed he spoke as a ruler; he denounced and whipped his audience. "He's not an orator—he's more than an orator," someone remarked about him, and the remark was a shrewd one.

The will of Lenin was stronger than his intellect, and the latter was everlastingly the servant of the former. Thus when victory was finally won after years of clandestine toil, he did not embark upon the task of embodying his ideas as would a constructive socialist who had pondered over his creative work in advance; he merely applied to the new, creative phase of his life's program the same methods which had been used in his destructive struggle for power, "On s'engage et puis on voit"—he was very fond of these words of Napoleon's.

Lenin has often been painted as a blind dogmatist, but he never was such by nature. He was not the kind to become attached for better or worse to a symmetrically finished system; he merely set his mind on succeeding in his political and revolutionary gamble, where to catch the proper moment meant everything. This is how he often became a quack, an experimenter, a gambler; this is why he was an opportunist, which is something diametrically opposed to a dogmatist.

Many critics have thought Lenin greedy for power and honors. The fact is he was organically made to rule and simply could not help imposing his will on others, not because he longed for this but because it was as natural for him to do so as it is for a large astral body to influence the planets. As for honors, he disliked them. His heart never rejoiced in pomp. Plebeian in his tastes and by his inmost nature, he remained just as simple in his habits after the October Revolution as he had been before. He has often been represented, too, as a heartless, dry fanatic. This heartlessness of his was purely intellectual and therefore directed against his enemies, that is, against the enemies of his party. To his friends he was amiable, good-natured, cheerful, and polite, as a good comrade should be; so it was that the affectionate, familiar "Iliich" became his universally accepted name among his followers.

Yes, Lenin was good-natured. But good-natured does not mean good-hearted. It has been observed that physically strong people are usually good-natured, and the good nature of Lenin was of exactly the same description as the amiability of a huge Saint Bernard dog toward surrounding pups and mongrels. So far as we can guess, real good-heartedness most probably was considered by him one of the pettiest of human weaknesses. At least it is a fact that whenever he wanted to annihilate some socialist adversary, he never omitted to bestow upon him the epithet of "a good fellow." He devoted his whole life to the interests of the working class. Did he love those working people? Apparently he did, although his love of the real, living workman was undoubtedly less intense than his hatred of the workman's oppressor. His love of the proletariat was the same despotic, exacting, and merciless love with which, centuries ago, Torquemada burned people for their salvation.

To note another trait: Lenin, after his own manner, loved those whom he valued as useful assistants. He readily forgave them mistakes, even disloyalty, though once in a while calling them sternly to task. Rancor or vengefulness were alien to him. Even his foes were not live, personal enemies but certain abstract factors to be eliminated. They could not possibly excite his human interest, being simply mathematically determined points where destructive force was to be applied. Mere passive opposition to his party at a critical moment was a sufficient reason for him to have scores and hundreds of persons shot without a moment's consideration; and with all this he was fond of playing and laughing heartily with children, kittens, and dogs.

It has been said that what the style is the man is. It would be even truer to say that what the thought is the man is. If it has been given to Lenin to leave any imprint of himself upon the doctrine of class struggle, it is to be found in his interpretation of the dictatorship of the proletariat, an interpretation permeated with the conception of that will which was the essence of his own personality. Socialism means the enfranchisement of labor; and the proletariat is the warp and woof of the working mass. In the proletariat itself, however, there are purer and less pure strains of proletarians. Now if a dictatorship of the proletariat over the working masses is required, there must be, on the same principles, within the proletariat itself a vanguard-dictatorship over the proletarian rank and file. This must be a kind of quintessence, a true proletarian party. Within this proletarian party there must likewise be an inner dictatorship of the sterner elements over the more yielding ones. We have thus an ascending system of dictatorships, which culminates and could not help culminating in a personal dictator. Such Lenin came to be.

His theory of concentric dictatorships—which reminds one of the concentric circles of Dante's Inferno—thus developed into a universally applicable theory of socialist dictatorial guardianship over the people, that is, into the very antithesis of true socialism as a system of economic democracy. This favorite and most intimate conception of Lenin—and the only one really his own—was a *contradictio in adjecto.* Such an inner contradiction could not help but become, ultimately, a source of disintegration inside the party he had created.

He is dead. His party is now headed by men whom for a long period of years he moulded after his own image, who found it easy to imitate him but who are finding it extremely difficult to continue his policy. That party as a whole is now beginning to experience the fate of its supreme leader: gradually it is becoming a living corpse. Lenin is no longer there to galvanize it with his surplus energy; he spent himself to the dregs—spent himself on a party which is now, in its turn, exhausted. Over his freshly made grave it may for a moment draw closer together and pronounce vows of fidelity to the revered teacher who has told it so much in the past, but who today is telling it no more, and who will tell it no more in the future. Then it will fall back into everyday life and again be subject to the law of disintegration and dissolution.

Concerning Senator Borah

Walter Lippmann

JANUARY 1926

I

IN DUE COURSE Senator Borah has been made chairman of the Committee on Foreign Relations. He has come into this high estate not by election of the people or by choice of his own party but under the rule of seniority. He has outlasted his predecessors. I mention this fact because it establishes his independence at the outset. A man who has attained an office because he is alive and because he continues to be elected by the people of Idaho is under no great compulsion to regard himself as the mere mouthpiece of a president or of a secretary of state. *Deo volente,* he will survive them both. If only he continues to eat moderately, to exercise regularly, to sleep well, and to keep about half the voters in the state of Idaho on his side, he can look with cool detachment on any suggestion that issues from the White House.

The ordinary inducements to conformity count for little in Mr. Borah's case. There are many more voters on the island of Manhattan alone than in the whole state of Idaho; with such a small constituency to nurse, Senator Borah does not have to worry about the favors and threats of the national administration. His constituency is manageable. He can really talk to it and make a direct personal contact with the local leaders who dispose of votes. No wonder his faith in an appeal to the people is unshaken, for there are so few people to whom he has to make his appeal. A loyal following of less than 75,000 voters in Idaho is enough to make his reelection certain. Mr. Borah does not need to worry. A national administration cannot help or hurt him much.

But he can help or hurt the administration. He is the greatest figure in the Northwest, and the Northwest is about as warmly attached to the Republican Party as the Irish Free State is to the United Kingdom. The Northwest votes Republican in presidential years and then forms a coalition with the

Democrats against almost all major Republican policies. President Coolidge and the Republicans of the East know that there are good reasons for being very kind to Senator Borah. For although he has never actually run away as Roosevelt did in 1912, there is something about him which suggests that he might. He is allowed to go his own way, therefore, in the reasonable hope that if he is given enough space to roam about within the party, he will find it convenient to stay inside the party.

Thus it has come to pass that wholly domestic considerations have given Mr. Borah a peculiar independence in international affairs.

II

HE EXERCISES the power of protest and of veto. It is a power exactly suited to his temperament. For Senator Borah has little interest in what is usually called constructive statesmanship. He is not possessed by a desire to make two institutions grow where one grew before. He does not like and he does not trust officials and committees and administrative hierarchies and executive orders and large payrolls and pensions. When someone comes to him with a proposal for elaborating the machinery of society, be it to maintain peace, to protect children, or to pension and instruct mothers, it is no lack of interest in the object but a congenital dislike of the machinery which brings him finally into opposition. Borah was born and bred on the frontier far from the complexity of modern civilization; it is in his bones to distrust formality and collective red tape, and to rely upon direct speech, common knowledge, individual salvation, and his own conception of the sovereign power of the moral law. The strain of Jefferson, and of Rousseau, of the Reformers before them, runs strongly in Borah. He believes in the natural goodness of man and, when that goodness is deficient, in the natural right of man to be damned in his own way. Thus recently he wrote to me, quoting Buckle, that "the most valuable additions made to legislation have been enactments destructive of preceding legislation." The real business of the statesman, in his philosophy, is not to construct institutions for the regimentation of men but to tear down those vested follies of the ages which thwart the natural goodness of mankind. Therefore, when Borah considers a new proposal he does not ask himself: What does this add to the machinery of living? Borah asks himself: Does it subtract from a machinery which is already top-heavy? Thus, the word constructive casts no spell upon him; he has read history with a deeply protestant mind and has concluded that what statesmen have usually constructed is a prison house for the soul.

It follows inevitably that the career of Borah is built upon opposition. He has been against the League, and against the Court, and against the Pacific

Pact, and against the British funding arrangements, and against the Wilson-Hughes Russian policy, and against the Caribbean policy, and against the Isle of Pines Treaty, and against the exclusion of Count Karolyi and Mr. Saklatvala, and against the alien property administration, and against the bonus, and against the Child Labor Amendment, and against Coolidge Republicanism, and against LaFollette insurgency. He is an instinctive conscientious objector, and his mind seizes swiftly upon the reasons why anything that is about to be done should not be done. His passion is to expose, to ventilate, to protest, to prevent, and to destroy. Since he does not have a hankering to create institutions, pass laws, or facilitate agreements, he has no use for the reticences and frustrations that are required in public affairs. Thus, for example, he was once arguing with Senator Brandegee that treaties should be discussed publicly in the Senate, and Mr. Brandegee had made the point that too much plain speech might give offense to foreign countries. "What are these delicate questions," retorted Senator Borah, "which may offend foreign powers? These delicate questions are too often questions of dubious righteousness." Only a man who has risen by appealing to audiences rather than by making executive decisions would, I think, have said that.

III

NOW ORDINARILY such a man would find himself extremely unpopular in a country where the passion for doing something, or even anything, is so highly regarded. He would be labelled a chronic kicker and dismissed from the society of the righteous and the efficient.

That has not been Senator Borah's fate. It may be that he has lost a little in prestige since he became the chairman of the Committee on Foreign Relations. Many people say he has, but I am not so sure they are right. For they are the same people who think that the whole term of Mr. Coolidge will be like the present honeymoon when nobody is seriously dissatisfied with anything. It is in the nature of things that a great protestant like Borah should lose lustre in a time of fabulous complacency and contentment. But as surely as there will be new causes for discontent, so there will be a revival of Borah's influence. For in the existing confusion and paralysis of the Democratic Party, he is the natural rallying point of the opposition.

In America today anyone who is out of sorts with anything thinks first of Mr. Borah. That is why he has grown great on opposition rather than weak by his chronic objecting. Within the last few years most of the large blocs of voters have been more deeply opposed to something than they have been eager for anything. The internationally minded wanted the League and the Court but Borah touched their hearts by his outspoken opposition to the

Ruhr, by his Russian attitude, his Haitian attitude, and his Chinese. The strong nationalists deplored Borah's affection for the underdog nations, but where could they find a champion comparable to him in their fight against cooperation with Europe? He delighted the upper classes in the East with his attack on the bonus, and he delighted the people of the West by his attack on the international bankers who desire an easy settlement of the debts. He opposed the Child Labor Amendment and pleased the conservatives, and he opposed the suppression of free speech and pleased the liberals. Mr. Borah has not become an outcast like most objectors because he has made common cause at one time or another with every influential group.

On whichever side he fights he is a host in himself, and those who have had him as their champion in one cause readily forgive him for all the pet projects of theirs which he has brought to nothing. Borah is a very inspiring man to have on one's own side of the argument. He knows what is theatrically effective, he has an air of common sense, a resourcefulness, and an eloquence, which have made him the most successful debater in the Senate. He has a still greater quality than these. Borah's opposition has no poison in it. For some subtle reason, Borah does not make enemies of his opponents. One would expect that a man who had fought everybody's dearest project at one time or another would be hated throughout the land. Borah is not hated anywhere. On the contrary there is not a gathering from a bankers' convention to a communist meeting where Borah is not respected. He was the one irreconcilable enemy of the League with whom the friends of the League were on friendly terms. He has opposed almost everybody and has embittered almost nobody.

This is due in part to the liking which everyone feels for a man who is known to be brave, in part also to his vitality and his poise, and to the sense that he is not bitten and driven by jealousies and animosities. There is a natural well-ventilated health in Borah which distinguishes him from the run of overfed, tobacco-laden, anecdotal indoor politicians. But there is also a deeper ground of confidence. Borah's opposition has nothing exotic about it. He is not against this or that because he believes in strange doctrines. When a man denies he also affirms, and Borah always affirms the oldest American traditions and the simplest popular prejudices. He believes in helping the underdog, in distrusting powerful foreigners, in distrusting politicians, in preserving the Constitution, and in holding onto the taxpayer's money. When Borah is in opposition to the Child Labor Amendment nobody thinks he wishes to exploit children; when he opposes the League nobody thinks he is a militarist and a jingo; when he opposes the Haitian occupation nobody supposes he has fallen in love with the Haitians; and when he pleads for Russia, *mirabile dictu,* nobody, not even the most furious patrioteer, thinks he is in the pay of Moscow. He has fought the battle of the jingo and the pacifist, the reactionary and the radical, and yet he has not merged his identity with any of them.

IV

IT WOULD NOT occur to Senator Borah, I think, that he must sacrifice any of his liberty of action because he had become chairman of the Committee on Foreign Relations. He has always spoken his mind on all subjects, and he continues to speak it. If he does not like French policy in Morocco, or British policy in China, he says so just as plainly as if he were still a mere senator. If he does not like what he hears about the intentions of the president in respect to the French debt, he says so loudly and publicly. He feels perfectly free to indulge in running comment on the acts of foreign powers, on the domestic affairs of other nations, on their statesmen and their national habits, on their ambitions and supposed purposes, and on any and all negotiations however delicate at any time while they are in progress. He is not concerned apparently about the difficulty which foreigners experience because they do not know whether they are being lectured by William E. Borah of Idaho or by the Senate of the United States as a coordinate part of the treaty-making power.

He feels himself privileged to use the prestige of his office to promote the influence of his opinions. The ensuing troubles of the executive do not break his heart, and the demands of all institutions that men suppress themselves and conform mean very little to him. Mr. Borah is a confirmed bachelor who somehow finds himself married to the executive. I do not say he will be unfaithful, but heaven pity the executive if it expects Borah to worry about the whole darn family.

As a matter of fact he regards it as his high duty to watch the executive with the utmost suspicion. The history of secret diplomacy in Europe has made a deep impression on him, and he believes that the wars and miseries of mankind are due chiefly to the irresponsible intrigues of diplomats. He has also a sublime faith that legislatures and popular majorities are in the nature of things pacific and just. It is the very essence of his philosophy that bad deeds are done in the dark, and that light brings righteousness. I have never detected the quiver of a doubt on his part that this is one of the eternal verities, but also I do not recall any attempt on his part to consider the weight of popular prejudice which beats upon a statesman who might wish to appease the Japanese or to deal rationally with debts and reparations. It is a fundamental fact about Borah that he accepts the dogma of open diplomacy at face value.

V

IT WILL BE a decisive fact in the immediate future of our foreign relations that Senator Borah looks upon the ancient prerogatives of the Senate as suited to the practice of open diplomacy. Other chairmen of the committee, Senator Lodge for example, have been jealous to maintain the rights of the Senate against the president, but they have been moved, if I read them correctly, by the inveterate desire of all men to hold and extend a vested right. But Mr. Borah is moved by a passion to thwart evil by publicity, and the powers of the Senate are for him a means to that end. He is more determined than Mr. Lodge ever was to make the Senate a major partner in diplomatic affairs, for Mr. Borah plays no favorites and cares nothing, where Mr. Lodge cared much, for the unity and glory of the Republican Party. Mr. Borah's insistence on the role of the Senate is inspired, therefore, by a faith that meant little to Mr. Lodge. It is a faith in the ultimate righteousness of an appeal to the people. If the senators were consulted and if the senators advised, Mr. Lodge was satisfied. He insisted that the president recognize the senators. Mr. Borah, on the other hand, conceives it to be the duty of the Senate to force the president to consult the whole electorate.

Thus Senator Borah is engaged in trying to turn the treaty-making powers of the Senate into the means to a very open popular diplomacy. The experiment will be well worth watching because surely there can be no doubt that with the increase of contact across frontiers, various interests within each nation are bound to play a larger part in the conduct of foreign policy. It has ceased to be possible for diplomacy to be in the sole keeping of the head of the state. The executive must obtain the advice and consent of many people if his engagements with a foreign nation are to be binding. The question is whether the Constitutional powers of the Senate under Article 2, Section 2, can be stretched to cover this new need.

They were not designed to make possible an open diplomacy. The authors of the Constitution certainly did not suppose that they were compelling the president to open up the whole conduct of foreign policy to popular discussion. *The Federalist* commends Article 2, Section 2, because it "provides that our negotiations for treaties shall have every advantage which can be derived from talents, information, integrity and deliberate investigation on the one hand, and from secrecy and dispatch on the other." In another place the writers of *The Federalist* argue that the House of Representatives is not fit to participate because "decision, secrecy and dispatch are incompatible with the genius of a body so variable and so numerous." It is plain that the authors of the Constitution thought that the president would consult in secret with a small body of men; there were only 26 senators at that time, and the president needed only to convince about 18 of them. The House which the fathers rejected as too variable and too numerous was then smaller than the present Senate. It consisted of only 65 members. President Washington himself tried once to consult the small Senate of that day about the treaty with the Creek Indians and had such an unpleasant time that he never tried it again. Later when the House asked him for information about the Jay Treaty, he refused, saying that "the nature of foreign relations requires caution and their success must often depend on secrecy."

While it is clear enough what the authors of the Constitution meant, they did not state what they meant very clearly. The phrase "advice and consent" is so vague that it left room for a large development of our constitutional practice. Thus by the beginning of the twentieth century the powers of the Senate had, at least in the opinion of Senator Lodge, grown to the point where the Senate virtually had the right to negotiate independently with a foreign power. The doctrine of Lodge is worth looking at here, for our hero, Mr. Borah, has adopted it and is making the fullest possible use of it.

Mr. Lodge felt that a little lecture on American constitutional law was in order, for Lord Lansdowne, then secretary of state for foreign affairs, had evinced a regrettable inability to understand the Senate. . . .

A treaty drawn by the president in agreement with a foreign power is still "inchoate," said Mr. Lodge; it is "a mere project for a treaty." And so a foreign power which sets out to make a treaty with the United States must deal first with the State Department at one end of Pennsylvania Avenue and then with another State Department at the other end. Lord Lansdowne must have found that very strange. He had not yet learned that a diplomatic affair with the United States is like a two-volume novel in which the hero marries the heroine at the end of the first volume and divorces her triumphantly at the end of the second.

In asserting these powers of the Senate, Mr. Lodge planted himself on the meaning of the Constitution. In the interpretation of this clause it is a case of each man his own oracle, for if one thing is clear it is that the Fathers had no very prophetic idea of how they meant Article 2, Section 2, to work. Hamilton wrote a paper on the subject for *The Federalist*, and the paper is one of the least illuminating he ever wrote. But in one clause of a sentence devoted to a very different subject he speaks of obtaining "sanction in the progressive stages of a treaty." Although this does not bear out Senator Lodge's notion that the Senate could "continue the negotiations" by itself, it does seem to say that the Senate was to advise and consent not merely on the completed treaty, but step by step in the negotiations.

VI

THE MORAL of it all is that the Constitution itself is so ambiguous that it could be stretched to cover any workable arrangement. The real difficulty for Mr. Borah or for anyone else who wishes to see the legislature play a serious part in diplomacy is that large bodies of men cannot conduct a negotiation or initiate a policy. As a general rule they can only approve or disapprove propositions presented to them. The Senate can accept or reject a treaty; it can even occasionally adopt amendments proposed by senators; it can make reservations. The Congress can declare war; it can appropriate money or refuse to appropriate money to carry out an international obligation. Yet these powers, great as they are, control only a very small area of diplomatic action. At the most they may be sufficient to compel the president to consider whether he can enlist the support of the legislature for the policies he is pursuing. The president is like a general with a somewhat mutinous army on his hands; he cannot be sure his troops will follow him. Occasionally his troops will run away from him. But whether his troops obey or disobey, they do not determine the strategy of the campaign. He determines the strategy in the light of the support he can muster.

The attempt of a legislature to control foreign policy is in the nature of things an attempt to make the tail wag the dog. Congress alone, for example, has the power to declare war. But the president has the power to make war and to put Congress in the position where it must either back him up or haul down the flag. The executive who believes a war is necessary can create a situation where Congress really has no choice. He can occupy ports, shoot off the cannon, and get himself embroiled so that no patriotic legislature will refuse to help him out. It is something of a fiction to say that Congress alone can declare war. It is nearer the truth to say that Congress has a theoretical right to decide whether a war which has already begun shall be continued. But Congress has no power to say how long the war shall be continued. For the president can make an armistice when he chooses.

The power of the Senate over treaties is no less elusive. In theory no covenant binding the action of the United States can be made without its consent; in fact every president makes decisions which are binding without the consent of the Senate. He may do this by exchanges of notes, by gentlemen's agreements, by the mere fact that when the president does one thing something else follows by the logic of necessity. The intervention of the Senate when formal treaties are presented to it occurs in the presence of a mountain of accomplished facts. The Senate can tinker a little with the text, but as a general practice it must take it or leave it. And even if the Senate takes the treaty, the real meaning of the treaty eludes the Senate because the power of interpretation and administration remains with the executive. "Whoever hath an absolute authority to interpret any written or spoken laws," said Bishop Hoadley, "it is he who is truly the law-giver to all intents and purposes.". . .

The effort of the Senate to control the conduct of foreign affairs is bound to be spasmodic, to be feeble as a general rule, but now and then powerfully obstructive. A continuous control in the present state of the world is out of the question. As long as the relations between great states remain essentially combative, until, if ever, their relations are reduced to established law and a formal, orderly, and leisurely procedure, the open, popular control of diplomacy which Mr. Borah desires will remain largely an aspiration. It is incompatible with the prevailing anarchy of heavily armed sovereign states. It is suited only to a pacific world in which there are no dangerous decisions to be made, in which any question can be debated and bungled without fatal damage in the rough and tumble of legislatures and elections. The internal peace of the United States is so profound that the methods of Congress are at the worst an inconvenience. But the peace of the world is so fragile that those same methods would convulse it in an unending agitation.

It is the fundamental paradox of Mr. Borah's career that he combines a passion for open diplomacy with a passionate objection to every step toward that world organization under which open diplomacy might ultimately become feasible. Unless he changes more than most men of his eminence change at his age, it is too much to expect that he will resolve that paradox. Mr. Borah is not the kind of man to subject himself to the labor of following through in a patient way the implications of his own ideal. He is a self-sufficient man with great confidence in the promptings of his own conscience. He shrinks instinctively from a train of thought which might compel him to revise certain of his passionate negations and from a course of action which it would be difficult to explain to large audiences. The definite pursuit of the ideal of open diplomacy would carry him into regions where he is not at home, into fields of cooperation which are unsuited to his temperament.

For he is a virtuoso who plays by ear. He is a powerful obstructor of good and of evil, always gallant and sometimes perverse. Amidst trimmers and place warmers he is a gadfly to the bureaucratic and the toplofty. He is an immense advertisement for the idea of open diplomacy. Like the universe and like the weather, the only thing to do about Borah is to accept him. You will find him very useful tomorrow, and you should not complain, then, if he leaves the confused relationship of the president and the Senate no less confused, and the anarchic relations of sovereign states no less anarchic. A man, even when by accident he becomes chairman of the Committee on Foreign Relations, does not change his character.

The Gathering Storm

THE NINETEEN THIRTIES

WHEN THE American stock market crashed in October 1929, shock waves reverberated throughout the global economy. Businesses went bankrupt, unemployment soared, and panicky governments dammed the free flow of capital with tariffs—a crisis chillingly evoked by Edwin F. Gay, one of the doyens of economic history, in his essay "The Great Depression." In 1932 America elected an energetic new president, Franklin Delano Roosevelt, who launched his New Deal series of economic revival measures.

The crisis of the liberal capitalist system paved the way for the twin rise of fascism and communism, the two new forms of totalitarianism that cast their shadows on the twentieth century. Under Stalin, the Soviet Union was becoming increasingly repressive, but Soviet ideologues disavowed any aggressive intentions. Indeed, Nikolai Bukharin, one of the Kremlin's most erudite polemicists, argued in "Imperialism and Communism" that only capitalist states could be truly imperialist. Within the borders of the Soviet Union, the forcible collectivization of agriculture in the 1930s triggered widescale famine and a vicious campaign against the peasants who clung to their traditional way of life. By the time Stalin finished settling scores with his political rivals—including Bukharin—in the Great Purges of 1934–38, the Soviet death toll lay in the millions. "A single death is a tragedy; a million deaths is a statistic," Stalin is supposed to have said.

On the other political extreme, Benito Mussolini's fascists had been running Italy since 1922, and fascist parties had become a staple of European politics. Writing from Il Duce's Italy, Benedetto Croce, the famed Italian philosopher, bravely attacked totalitarianism in "On Liberty," but Croce and his continental allies were clearly on the defensive. When the German Nazi Party staged a putsch in 1923 in Munich, it still seemed more farce than foreshadowing, but in the shadow of the Depression, the Nazis emerged as a major political force in Germany's 1930 elections. When the Nazis took the largest bloc of seats in the Reichstag in 1933, Adolf Hitler was made Germany's chancellor. The early warning about the totality of the Fuehrer's ruthlessness sounded by Heinrich Mann, the German novelist, in "Dictatorship of the Mind" proved all too accurate. Trumpeting the need for racial purity, Lebensraum, and a war against the Jews, Hitler assailed his neighbors and imprisoned his countrymen, hurling those he saw as enemies of the Volk into concentration camps.

The democracies reacted like deer caught in the headlights. In "Civilization on Trial," H. G. Wells, the great futurist, warned that "we are going to be tried out, and in a most extraordinary fashion. We are not ready for it." Still exhausted by the decimation of the Great War, Britain and France hoped that Hitler could be pacified. Across the Atlantic, American public opinion was still more concerned about recovering prosperity at home than about stopping aggression abroad. The Neutrality Act of 1935 forbade the United States from providing arms to a belligerent nation, whether aggressor or victim.

Aggressors multiplied throughout the decade. Imperialist Japan occupied Manchuria in 1931 and took Shanghai a year later. In 1935 Mussolini invaded Ethiopia, and the failure of the League of Nations' sanctions against Italy only highlighted the collapse of the Wilsonian collective security system. In 1936, in violation of Versailles, Germany reoccupied the demilitarized Rhineland, while General Francisco Franco's fascists plunged the imperiled Spanish republic into civil war. In 1937 Japanese troops slaughtered over 300,000 Chinese civilians during the rape of Nanking. In 1938 Hitler staged his *Anschluss* of Austria.

When Hitler demanded sections of Czechoslovakia with ethnic German populations, the democracies launched appeasement's last gasp. On his mission to Munich, British Prime Minister Neville Chamberlain traded the Sudetenland for Hitler's assurances that Britain and Germany would resolve their future disputes amicably. It was, Chamberlain told an anxious world, "peace for our time."

The Great Depression

Edwin F. Gay

JULY 1932

A RECENT statement by Mr. Justice Brandeis has been widely quoted. "The people of the United States," he said, "are now confronted with an emergency more serious than war. Misery is widespread, in a time, not of scarcity, but of overabundance. The long-continued depression has brought unprecedented unemployment, a catastrophic fall in commodity prices and a volume of economic losses which threatens our financial institutions."

The economic losses both of the world war and the present depression, in their full volume and extent, are incalculable, but it is not only of such losses that Mr. Justice Brandeis was speaking. The gravity of the present situation lies not merely in the widespread suffering, vast as that is, but in the questions it excites concerning the fundamental strength and character of our economic structure and in the series of decisions which must be made, indeed are now in process of making. These decisions are much more difficult than those of war. In war the chief problem is clearly set and calls for immediate action, unifying in its effect. In such a depression as this, the problem is infinitely complex, decisions are beset by doubt, action seems always too late or has effects contrary to what were expected, and disunion and disruption have spread as each centrifugal force, seeking to strengthen itself, weakens the whole. War stimulates the full expansion of productive energy, but the deep depression cripples every economic process and discourages even the most sanguine business leaders. There are many confusing prescriptions offered from all sides. But no one, however skilled, really knows the character of or the specific cure for what some practitioners diagnose as a wasting disease. Whether or not a phenomenon regularly recurring, though at unequal intervals and with varying intensity, may properly be called a disease is questionable. A continuous succession of wavelike fluctuations, each with its phases of rising business activity, boom, recession, and depression, may more properly be regarded as the result of the normal functioning of a competitive economy.

[69]

Multitudes of businessmen, each making his individual calculation of gain in a future market, but each affected by the contagious movement of contemporary business hopes or fears, unconsciously cooperate in creating the fluctuations known as business cycles. In this ebb and flow, however, there is more than the repeated concurrence of a mass of individual plans and expectations. Physical determinants are clearly present in other types of contemporary fluctuations, such as those affecting agriculture and the short seasonal swings. Monetary and other technological factors enter largely into the long secular trends. All the different types of fluctuations interact. It is possible, in the present instance, that a business cycle has been intensified by an agricultural cycle and by greater seasonal fluctuations and then prolonged by the impact of a longer downward-moving secular trend in prices. There are also to be considered the stresses and strains which may result when the normally uneven operation of the economic forces in the business cycle, never fully balanced, develops from time to time a state of acute disequilibrium. And, in addition to these and many other disturbing factors, come the irregular influences named by the economists, rather inadequately, as "random perturbations," such as cyclones, earthquakes, widespread visitations of disease, and wars. The economists find the analysis of business cycles no simple thing, and the present deep depression, transcending in depth and extent the usual amplitudes and intensities of business cycles, is still more difficult to explain.

It is generally recognized, however, that the world war has had serious effects upon the economic conditions of the postwar period, such as the depletion of manpower; the stimulus to overcapacity of some essential industries, including American agriculture; the forcing process in the industrial development of regions cut off from their former sources of supply and of the newly created states; the widespread monetary disorders; and the staggering burden of internal debts and foreign obligations. The world war left deep wounds, but they could be healed. As Sir Arthur Salter has just pointed out in his admirable book, *Recovery, the Second Effort,* the war—except in Russia—meant not the destruction but the dislocation of the economic structure. This seemed to be demonstrated by the remarkable economic recovery in the decade after the war, and especially after 1924, even in ravaged Europe. But now we are wondering whether this recovery was not simply a respite rather than a cure.

The range of the Great Depression is unprecedentedly wide. Past crises have affected many countries simultaneously; but, despite the growing economic international interdependence, even in previous major crises some important countries have been little affected. The timing of the business cycles as between countries has not been parallel, nor their incidence equal. At the close of 1929, when the crash came in the United States, about half the countries for which statistical evidence is available were already suffering a decline in prosperity. But thereafter the process continued, with brief deceptive pauses, until after the middle of 1931 the disastrous, deepening depression had become worldwide. The depression is also unprecedentedly deep. Experience as measured in statistics of prices, production, foreign and domestic trade, and unemployment shows nothing comparable in intensity. The United States has suffered bitterly during former depressions, notably in the years following 1837, and 1873, and 1893, but it then had free land to absorb its unemployed and an expanding European market for its increased agricultural production. During those former crises, banks failed and specie payments ceased to an extent which the present experience has not equalled, but this was the habitual behavior of a young and rapidly growing country. Finally, after the crisis of 1907, when the banks had again been prostrated, the Federal Reserve System was created to put an end to an intolerable weakness. Now, despite strong banks in the leading countries, despite a productive equipment in materials and men unmatched in the world's history, deep business depression is universal.

That the world war and the world depression are intimately linked, as fundamental cause and ultimate effect, is beginning to be realized. There are other cooperating causes of our present distress, some antedating the war and some coming in its wake; but the war accentuated the prior trends of change and was largely responsible for the later dislocations. The economists in 1930 at first looked for the familiar signs of a business cycle. There seemed in 1929 to be no such accumulation of inventory in the hands of producers as in 1920, but in the form of goods bought on credit, installment purchases, housing, and the like, a great inventory was being carried by consumers. In many lines of productive activity, both industrial and agricultural, it appeared that an excess capacity was facing a saturated market. "Cumulative disequilibria" of various sorts were seen to have strained the economic system: the increase in the consumer's spending power had not kept pace with the increase in productive power, the wage earner's income had not grown as rapidly as that of the entrepreneur, and the flow of savings toward investment in capital goods and in durable consumption goods was exceptionally great. The technological advance had been more rapid than the growth of the market demand for new or cheaper products, so that, despite the great mobility of the working population, there was a steady increase of unemployment. These and similar unbalancing elements, it was thought, went far to explain the break in the economic mechanism with its slackening business activity and increasing unemployment. But as the depression was prolonged and intensified through the first half of 1931, it became clear that changes of greater range and longer duration were operating than those ordinarily engendered by business cycles.

The economists looked farther afield. They noted the shift in monetary gold supply and the demonstrable alterations in the money markets of the world; the declining birth rate; the rise in the standard of living and the changes in habits of consumption tending to make the market more sensitive to fluctuations; the increasing mechanization which was revolutionizing agriculture and affecting many other industries; the development of large-scale organizations in industry, banking, and labor; and the spread of price agreements and market controls which tended to introduce dangerous rigidities into the flexible system of free competition.

Then came the collapse of the Austrian Kredit Anstalt in May 1931, the breakdown of the German financial system in June, England's abandonment of the gold standard in September, followed promptly by many other countries, the cessation of international lending, and the further and alarming deepening of depression everywhere. The factors producing business cycles and the changes in longtime trends have exerted their influence upon the depression, but the specialists in the study of business fluctuations, after arraying the factors and weighing those which are measurable, acknowledge that their accustomed methods of analysis are inadequate. A more incalculable force seems to be at work. The situation suggests that the credit economy, not alone of nations as separate units but of all, is involved; and that recovery demands both separate and common efforts.

"We have still inadequately realized," writes Sir Arthur Salter, "how deeply the foundations of the system of credit have been undermined." The world depression reveals many related causes at work, but it now is evident that the break in the stream of credit should be especially emphasized and carefully studied. The sapping process, undermining credit, goes back to the war, to the huge unproductive debts which it created and which, by the financial illusions engendered, have been continually extended. The war was fought with determination through four interminable years; and the confidence of all its participants was buoyed up, and in turn supported an enormous inflation of credit. The exaltation of war made possible the incredible toll it exacted. Unmindful of postwar consequences, the contestants piled mountainously high their demands upon the future and thus mobilized for war's exigent present the productive resources of the world. To the people of the United States especially, the war revealed possibilities of credit expansion which seemed boundless; the whole world shared in the illusion, but not so riotously in the exploitation of it. The military contribution of the United States in the war's concluding year was of decisive character, but the country's primary function was the furnishing of supplies, in the first two years paid for largely by shipments of gold from Europe and the repatriation of American securities and in the last two supported by great domestic credits, which financed the production of war materials both for the American armies and for their associates.

The war fervor, aided and inflamed by energetic organization, placed government bonds in the hands of millions of people who never before had possessed such instruments of credit. They were not thereby educated in the use of credit; they simply received a new vision of its possibilities. The basis was thus laid for the vast and credulous postwar market for credit which culminated in the portentous speculation of 1928 and 1929. Great enterprises learned that they could distribute their shares and bonds by direct sale to the public, and smaller enterprises were recapitalized by busy investment houses to float new securities in a national market canvassed by high-pressure bond salesmen. Despite the heavy inflow of gold to the United States, particularly during the first half of the decade, despite the easy money policy of the Federal Reserve Board, especially in 1927, and despite the large repayments by the United States Treasury of the principal of the domestic debt, prices of commodities did not rise. Instead, after 1924, they showed a slight tendency downward, in consonance probably with the more pronounced price-fall outside the United States. It was perhaps because the pressure for a rise was checked in this section of the elastic tissue of the price system that it burst forth with such redoubled vigor in the stock market. Here was presented the greatest scene in the history of speculation. Stock values were pyramided again and again as they soared to heights out of all rational relationship to earnings present or prospective. The mania spread in unexampled breadth; where millions had bought Liberty Bonds, tens of millions now were buying shares or speculating on margin at the new brokerage offices springing up everywhere.

Below these paper values, the easy credit was stimulating actual production. American economic progress during the postwar period was rapid but uneven. Certain regions, whose old staple industries or agricultural products were in competition with the new mechanization or with virgin land, lagged in the race; but the pace was set by relatively new industries like the electrical or chemical industries, with the giant automobile industry far in the lead both in methods of mass production and in volume of mass sales. The construction industry in all its branches, and the machine-tool industry, especially in its export trade, grew amazingly. Spending (though toward the close it showed signs of "sales resistance," even though reinforced by abundant consumers' credit) seemed on the whole to be holding its place with production. Public spending by governmental agencies—federal, state, and municipal—likewise mightily increased. The fructifying stream, attracted by high interest rates, overflowed in foreign loans, which in turn financed the growth in exports. Foreign states, towns, and business concerns, especially those of

Germany and Latin America, sought, or were sought by, the American investment houses and banks, until the total volume of private postwar loans surpassed, or on a net reckoning fully equalled, the public war loans.

All this was the work of credit, of which the war had taught the lesson of apparently unlimited expansion. Credit on the great scale is a modern invention, an instrument of immense power, comparable with the prime movers in the physical field for whose introduction through the Industrial Revolution it had prepared the way. Together these new powers are transforming the world. But the engineers of credit know far less about the limitations and control of their new organ than the engineers of steam and electricity do about theirs. Credit is a social force, operating upon masses of people through its own specialized institutions. It has become robust and resilient and yet sensitively flexible, adjusting itself to daily repeated shocks. Its outer limits of expansion and contraction are not ordinarily reached and tested, and hence in part the reason for our lack of scientific knowledge. Nevertheless, as historical experience if not yet economic theory has demonstrated, it has limits in both directions. Its essential form is that of a continuous stream of debts, constantly renewed, flowing where profitable enterprise beckons. Since these debts or advances rest upon a conglomerate of human estimates of future gains, some near and more certain, others distant and more speculative, wastage is inevitable, and so long as it is not excessive this does not check the stream. It flows confidently on and draws new volume from its watershed of supply.

The continuous and excessive waste of credit by unproductive use was initiated by the war and has been continued under the habit inherited from the war of drawing freely upon the future for the immediate enhancement of productive power and of living standards. Credit has been used in unprecedented volume, but it has also been abused, in a manner not indeed different in kind but enormously increased in degree as compared with earlier experiences. When finally . . . the *realisateurs* commenced to cash in on their paper gains, the swollen stream contracted, and for the first time the great body of investors became aware that it was fed by inadequate earnings. Then panics began. The domestic and foreign capital which had been drawn into the maelstrom by the lure of high call-rates was hastily withdrawn. The stream of American credit which had been diverted to the speculative market suddenly left the foreign debtors stranded, and their distress today adds to the depression. Abroad some of the unproductive debts cannot pay their interest; at home extravagantly invested funds, supplied by credit, fail to pay dividends or rent. Investors widely come to feel that the public trust, which credit implies, has been betrayed and their confidence abused. People complain of the paradox that poverty appears in the midst of abundance. It is no paradox; abundance is freighted on credit and credit stretched beyond its limits of safety must withdraw.

While America has been experiencing the elation and suffering of excessive overconfidence, bred from the war's extravagance and its aftereffects, Europe has not been immune. She was left shattered by the war. The monetary systems of combatants and neutrals were tottering. Some of these systems succumbed utterly; in the case of others, the fall was checked. But by the middle of the postwar decade, order had been restored, the bulk of the work of reconstruction seemed to have been accomplished, and Europe was turning hopefully to the modernization of her industries and to the redemption of her pledges, expressed or tacit, to make her lands fit for heroes to live in. The strong desire for social betterment, running from peasant land allotments to recreation facilities, was matched, on the part of peoples who had during the war seen money poured out like water, by a belief that a material improvement in the conditions of life was attainable. The same miraculous rock could be tapped again; and in fact the stream of credit did again flow. Furthermore, since the menace of social upheaval is a reality in Europe (where an example lies close on her eastern border), her rulers feel that measures of social amelioration are more than desirable: they are necessary. The debts for reconstruction added to the war debts were crushing, but in many countries they have been greatly alleviated by the devaluations of currency, shifting part of the loss to the *rentier* class and the recipients of fixed incomes. When the currencies had been restabilized, new hope made possible new credits.

But it now becomes apparent that the war left a legacy of fundamental insecurity to the continent of Europe. To the manifestly continuing political insecurity has been added a persistent undercurrent of economic insecurity, which has made itself felt in repeated emergencies and in various ways. The nervousness of European investors, great and small, has been shown in the more conspicuous episodes of the successive "flights" from the mark, the franc, or other currencies; it has been allayed for periods, but still has been instant to take alarm. Largely for this reason, the flow of capital from country to country has tended to be spasmodic and unpredictable; investors have sought security by shifting funds from one financial centre to another without primary regard to differences in interest rates. They have thus contributed to impede the quasi-automatic operation of the mechanism of foreign exchange which before the war, when security was taken for granted, affected national price levels and regulated the international movements of goods and gold.

In the quest for security, especially during the respite afforded by the relative improvement in economic conditions for a few years after 1925, many countries, anxious to stabilize their disordered currencies, adopted an equivalent for the gold standard. Their equivalent was the gold exchange standard which permitted them to place bills of exchange in their portfolios instead of gold bullion in their vaults. . . . By the end of 1931 a substantial part (probably a fifth) of the banking reserves of the world was in the exposed form of foreign exchange, the "cushion" of domestic circulating gold had everywhere disappeared, and about three-quarters of the world's monetary stock of gold had been so withdrawn as to intensify the downward movement of world commodity prices. Monetary security was sought, but on an unstable basis; and since England, the first establisher and maintainer of the gold standard, has departed from it, monetary insecurity and difficult experimentation with "managed" currencies have again returned.

The effort to maintain stability in the agitated postwar world has been the underlying motive for the renewal of the great movement not merely toward large-scale business organizations but toward combinations, cartels, and similar agreements for the maintenance of prices or the division and control of markets. The combination movement has been long-continued, for in industry it commenced its first great operations in the eighties and nineties of the last century, after the railroads had shown the way; it is worldwide; it is paralleled by an analogous growth of social organizations in many other fields, such as labor and agricultural and consumers' cooperatives; it shows variety, adaptiveness, and increasing strength; in short, it is an organic development of revolutionary importance. For it has begun to modify profoundly the system of free competition and the social attitudes which accompanied that blindly "automatic" system. . . . It seems apparent that this tendency toward a planned economy, already initiated each in its own sphere by a growing number of the great industries, sponsored governmentally by the necessities of the Great War, and now filling men's minds, should proceed further. It obviously faces great difficulties both in organization and in public control; and stability, if it is gradually attained, is likely to entail a slowing up of technical progress and a degree of social regimentation for which perhaps the public's mind is already being prepared. The process of readaptation of the economic system is likely to be long and full of unexpected disappointments, but the successes and failures of the various nations already experimenting with economic planning will be instructive. . . .

If in this outline of some of the economic consequences of the world war in their bearing on the world depression only cursory mention has been made of reparations and war debts, it is because they have become matter even more for political than for economic discussion. The two payments, while theoretically distinct, are in European opinion and practice so closely connected as to form practically one problem in two phases—receiving from

Germany in order to pay to the United States. Since the cessation of American lending to Germany and since the rise of nationalist propaganda, Germany has come passionately to believe, and her political leaders declare, that an end must be made of reparation payments. Indeed, it seems highly probable that no government could stand which proposed to continue these payments. In the interest not merely of European but of world appeasement and of the economic recovery which depends thereupon, some settlement must promptly be arrived at. An extended moratorium, which in any case must be granted, seems likely only to prolong the disquiet, not to allay it. France, pressed by her own economic insecurity, may prefer to take the best obtainable terms which Germany can now offer rather than run the risk of another Ruhr occupation and the even graver risk of thereby unsettling further an economic world already in peril. The United States, then, must come to grips with the related problem of the war debts. Will it prefer a radical revision of the debts to meet the radically changed position of the debtors, or will it prefer a futile and embittered altercation, charged with national animosities? A reasonable end to the debt problem would not, indeed, at once stop the world depression, but it would be a great step toward the appeasement which is necessary for recovery. The steady exacerbation of international feelings resulting from a settlement of reparations and debts which was not a settlement reveals in a clearer light the fundamental error of continuing the economic war after peace had been signed. It has only added continuously to postwar insecurity.

What has especially aggravated the European feeling about the war debts has been the American tariff. This has been held responsible for the relative decline in the imports from the European debtors to the United States. Supplementary causes may be found for the general decline in imports of European commodities into the United States, from the 48 percent of total imports in 1913 to the 30 percent of recent years. And there has been an offset, which should be taken into account, in the increase of expenditures by American tourists abroad. But the fact remains that the narrowly nationalistic policy of the United States, as exemplified again in the tariff of 1930—inexcusable from an economic point of view and definitely harmful from a broader national standpoint—has been one of the great complicating and accelerating factors in the cumulation of abnormal unbalances and rigidities which brought the world to the Great Depression.

A time must come when the United States as a powerful world state and a great creditor nation, hence vitally interested in world trade and world prosperity, will face the realities of its new position. It will realize that a policy of self-sufficiency is not only impossible, but that a policy which presupposes it to be possible is stultifying and impoverishing. To say, as one frequently heard it said, that because the value of American exports is less than ten percent of the total American production, we may therefore go our own way regardless of foreign trade or international responsibilities is to misinterpret the plain facts. The whole network of domestic prices and domestic credit in the United States is bound indissolubly with the system of world prices and with the stream of world credit. A dislocation anywhere in the fabric is now felt everywhere. The world war affirmed the international political responsibilities of the United States; the world depression demonstrates the economic interdependence of the United States with other states. It cannot be a hermit nation.

Imperialism and Communism

Nikolai Bukharin

JULY 1936

IT IS WELL known that people have sometimes talked prose without having the least idea what it is. This holds true not only of characters in French literature but also of professional politicians. Thus at the present time a regular epidemic of discussion is raging in certain sections of the capitalist press in the effort to find explanations for the acts of aggression which again threaten to rack the world with war. And they are being discovered in natural factors—territory, raw materials, growth of population. These are considered quite apart from the economic form of society and the political superstructure in which it finds expression. In this parlance, Germany, Italy, Japan are "nations without land." The natural growth of the population of these states necessarily leads to a hunt for new land and more raw materials. Here, according to this view, lie the roots of the future war. It is fate, historical destiny. And the only salvation lies in a redivision of territory.

A plan of this sort was proposed by the late Frank H. Simonds in an article entitled "The 'Haves' and 'Have-Nots'" in *The Fortnightly*. *The Economist* published detailed tables showing the distribution of land and raw materials among the various countries in order to prove Great Britain's right to the *status quo*. In France, the fascist proponents of a rapprochement with Germany at the expense of Soviet Ukraine are highly indignant over the vast territories of the Soviet Union and the comparative sparseness of its population. In Germany itself, imperialism is frankly proclaimed as the sacred right of "Aryans" suffocating for lack of "space" (*Volk ohne Raum*). Needless to say, the required "space" is sought in the Soviet Union, the government of which is moreover accused of continuing the foreign policy of the tsars. In Italy and Japan analogous theories have become the creed of the ruling classes, which preach them *ex professo*. The basis of all these arguments—though most of their authors are unaware of the fact—is the so-called theory of "Geopolitik," now particularly fashionable in fascist Germany. It is with this geopolitical "prose" that we shall commence our analysis.

I. "GEOPOLITICS" IN THEORY AND PRACTICE

. . . IN EFFECT, geopolitics flatly denies all history. Relatively constant factors such as territory, soil, climate (and racial attributes which biological sociologists also consider as constant) cannot serve to explain historical and social changes. "Politics" does not grow out of the "land" at all, but first and foremost out of economic relations. The "land" undoubtedly influences the historical process; but it does so primarily through the process of labor and through economics, and these in their turn exercise a decisive influence on politics. The territory and the racial attributes of the British Isles have changed very little since the nineties of the last century, and they cannot possibly be made to explain, let us say, Great Britain's rapid change from free trade to a high protective tariff. The existence of a foreign trade monopoly in the U.S.S.R. cannot be explained by the "Russian steppes" or by the so-called "Slavic soul." But Great Britain's change to a high protective tariff can very well be explained by the transition of her economic system to monopoly capitalism, with its trusts and syndicates; and the foreign trade monopoly in the U.S.S.R. can very easily be explained by the peculiarities of the socialist economic system, with its plan, and by the relationship of this system to the outside world. Arguments about space and territory *per se* remind one—if the adherents of these theories will excuse the remark—of people hunting for differential tariffs among crabs or for paper money on wheat fields.

But however ridiculous geopolitics is from the point of view of logic, it nevertheless plays a very active reactionary role *in practice*. It supplies an excuse for bellicose fascism, a justification for war and imperialism; it preaches new conquests and wars of intervention. The essence of the matter lies here, not in the quasi-moralistic poetized sophistry with which imperialists often veil their prose.

II. "PERPETUUM MOBILE" IN WARS

IN HIS article which I have already mentioned, the late Mr. Simonds, after sharply (and to a great extent correctly) criticizing the League of Nations, draws the conclusion that foreign territory and raw materials are indispensable to Germany, Italy, and Japan; that any attempt to persuade these countries to the contrary would be absurd; and that the League of Nations must adopt the rule of economic parity and make an equitable distribution of the world's resources of territory and raw materials. This will avert a world tragedy.

Indeed? But what will come of this plan objectively, that is, apart from the subjective intentions of its authors? Let us analyze this plan of the new "levellers."

First. Who are to be the *subjects* of this deal? Alas! These do not include such countries as Egypt or China or India. Nor do they include any of the small independent states like Czechoslovakia. The subjects of the deal are to be the biggest capitalist powers.

Second. Who are to be the *objects* of the deal? Apparently the U.S.S.R. and a number of small independent countries such as Lithuania (for the author of the scheme seeks to justify German fascist aspirations), China (for Japan's policy is similarly "justified"), and the colonies (Italy's policy also finds "justification" in this scheme). Thus in effect it is proposed: (1) to cut up the U.S.S.R.; (2) to destroy the independence of small countries such as Ethiopia; (3) to partition China; (4) to divide up the colonies again, like so much small coin thrown in to complete a bargain. In other words, the entire plan is aimed against (a) the workers (the U.S.S.R.); (b) the masses in densely populated China (i.e., the semi-colonies); (c) the colonial masses. *Cui prodest?* The biggest capitalist powers. Such is the scheme's "justice" and "morality."

Third. Let us assume that by some miracle or other the idea has been carried into effect. The great capitalist powers have divided up the spoils among themselves (the others, as we have seen, are *quantités négligeables*) on a "basic principle" of super-aristocratic world "parity." But what will happen the day after? That is the question.

It is not hard to answer. The mere fact that in different countries there are different levels of productive power, different quantities of skilled labor power, will lead to different results in the struggle for the world market. No amount of "autarchy" will save a country from having resort to this world market, the more so as the capitalist system will inevitably lead to overproduction. The search for new markets and spheres for capital investment will necessitate new redivisions of land and resources. And since tariff barriers, trusts, armies, and fleets will not disappear, the war song will break out afresh. Thus what is proposed is nothing more nor less than the continuing reproduction of wars, a *perpetuum mobile* of annihilating catastrophes. The picture is truly horrifying.

Fourth. Aside from all this, the plan recalls the verse about Roland's horse:

Nikolai Bukharin

Wunderschön war diese Stute,
Leider aber war sie tot.

It is just another Utopia. The more powerful groups of capitalists wielding state power will not surrender their colonies for the benefit of their poorer relatives. If Germany, Japan, and Italy cannot be persuaded to abandon their expansionist policy, then there is just as little expectation of philanthropy on the part of Great Britain, the United States, or France. As regards the workers of the U.S.S.R., they can see absolutely no reason for surrendering their common property to their bitterest class antagonists.

Fifth. Capitalist states might ask themselves whether this levelling scheme does not have in it the germs of what Japanese diplomats would call "dangerous thoughts." For mankind is divided not only horizontally into states, but also vertically into classes. (By the way, this idea of a redivision, and of a blow at the maxim "Beati possidentes," calls to mind the whole class which is made up of the "possidentes." Here, however, it is not a question of redividing the factories and distributing the machines among the workers but of common ownership of the means of production. And this is the course which history will take.)

III. WHAT IS IMPERIALISM?

SO WE MAY put the question as follows: Is the present tendency to violent expansion now being displayed so strikingly in Japan, Germany, and Italy a purely natural function of land and race, or is it a function of the social-economic system?

The question can be most easily considered by taking the example of Japan. The density of population in Japan is great. There is little land per capita. Emigration has always been very considerable. The German professor Paul Berkenkopf, in his recent work "Sibirien als Zukunftsland der Industrie," uses the very fact of overpopulation ("Druck der japanischen Übervölkerung") to explain Japanese imperialist expansion, assuming, however, that this expansion will proceed primarily in the direction of Australia and the Philippines. And thus it would seem that here as nowhere else the bare laws of geopolitics are the determining factor. But in that case how can we explain the crisis of overproduction? And how can we explain the paradox that this strange profusion of products is constantly impelling Japan's ruling classes to more intensive expansion? What becomes, then, of all the primitive argumentation that where there is little land, nothing to eat, and too many people, *ergo,* new territory is needed? It simply goes to pieces. Obviously the matter is not at all so simple. In reality, it is a bastard form of *fin de siècle* monopoly capitalism coupled with considerable survivals of feudal barbarism: savage exploitation of the workers and peasants, land-hunger on the part of the latter, exorbitantly high rents, poverty, and consequently low purchasing power of the masses—all leading to the paradox of plenty and poverty, over-production and the quest for new territories. And are not these things peculiar to capitalism as a whole? Is not the hunt for markets, coupled with overproduction and underconsumption, a characteristic feature of the special capitalist "mode of production?"

Or take Germany. We hear the chorus that it is absolutely essential for her to steal new territory from the U.S.S.R., since she, Germany, is starved for raw materials. We shall not speak here about the German war industry, which has swelled to gigantic proportions, which swallows up vast quantities of raw materials, and which does not in any way "grow" out of the properties of the German "soil." Nor shall we talk about the stocks of raw materials for war at the expense of consumption, nor about the sabotage on the part of the peasants. We only put the following elementary question: Why should not Germany *buy* raw materials from the U.S.S.R.? Does the latter want a high price? No, on the contrary. Many persons have shouted at the top of their voices that the U.S.S.R. is practising dumping—so favorable to the purchaser are the prices at which the U.S.S.R. has sold raw material. But German monopoly capital wants to have monopoly ownership of Ukrainian raw materials for military-economic autarchy, which in its turn is a weapon for further world struggle. "Territory," "space" (fascist philosophers have raised the category of "space" five heads higher than that of "time") do not produce any policy *by themselves*. It is definite social-historical conditions that lead to wars.

Mr. Simonds quoted Signor Mussolini's dictum: "For us Italians the choice is between foreign expansion and domestic explosion." And he added: "And that is why Italy and Germany, like Japan, are preparing for war." About Germany he spoke still more clearly: either a war of conquest, or communism.

Let us assume that this is so. But what does it signify? It simply signifies that communism can live without wars, whereas the other social form, capitalism, through the mouths of its own politicians and ideologists, declares: Better a war of conquest than communism. This only serves to corroborate the proposition that a war of conquest is a function of the social order, that it is not a nonhistorical category connected directly with geophysical and biological factors.

The structure of modern capitalism must be analyzed scientifically, soberly and without prejudice. The Italian fascists claim that there is no capitalism in Italy but a special kind of order which is neither capitalism nor socialism. Herr Hitler's followers declare that in their country they have national socialism. Mr. Araki and the other ideologists of Japanese aggression speak about the "imperial path," about Japan's peculiar traditions and her celestial mission: God himself points out definite strategic and tactical plans to Mr. Araki. Camouflage and juggling with words constitute one of the distinguishing features of profound social decadence. But fact remains fact. In none of the above-mentioned countries has one hair fallen from the head of the finance-capital oligarchy. Herr Fried, in his book *Das Ende des Kapitalismus*, painted a very graphic picture of this oligarchy. But Hitler's régime has left it in complete immunity; these oligarchs have only been converted (in words) into "leaders of industry" on the basis of "public service." If we recall that fascism's most outstanding philosopher, Spengler, considered the Hohenzollern Officers' Corps and the Prussian government officials as the epitome of "socialism," there is really no need for surprise. Has it not been said that "man was given a tongue to hide his thoughts?"

The same kind of camouflage is observable in another form even in capitalistic countries with democratic regimes. Not so long ago, for example, Mr. Thomas Nixon Carver, an indiscreet Pindar of "prosperity," proclaimed *urbi et orbi* that in the United States every worker is a capitalist. The subsequent spread of the crisis and of so-called "technical unemployment" have given a tragic refutation of this capitalist optimism.

What is in fact the real state of affairs? And why does this real state of affairs give rise to imperialist wars?

Since the eighties of the last century, as a result of the triumph of large-scale production and the centralization of capital, the form of capitalism has changed. From the previous stage of industrial capitalism, with its freedom of competition, its individualism, its principle of *laissez faire, laissez passer*, it entered the stage of monopoly capitalism (trusts, intergrowth of banking capital and industrial capital, monopoly prices). The partition of the world led to accentuated competition; to the policy of dumping (the losses incurred were compensated for by high monopoly prices in the home market); and to the system of a high protective tariff. In its turn, protectionism intensified the export of capital (in place of commodity exports, now hampered by tariff barriers). The monopolistic possession of markets, raw materials, and sphere of capital investment, together with the whole system of monopoly exploitation, tariffs, etc., based on the already accomplished partition of the so-called "freelands" (which meant putting an end to the principle of the Open Door), led capitalist competition on the world market to acquire more and more clearly the character of forcible pressure (*Machtpolitik*). The diminished possibilities of "peaceful penetration" were remedied by the brutal policy of armed force.

Accordingly, the state power of capital, its "interference" in economic life, acquires increased significance. We witness the militarization of the economic system and an extreme intensification of the tendency to economic autarchy, which is also important militarily and politically in determining the *Machtposition* in the arena of world struggle. Here the inner motive is represented by the interests of profit, which on the one hand maintain the purchasing power of the working masses at an extremely low level (even in Ricardo's day it was a well-known fact that profit stands in inverse proportion to wages) and which on the other hand continually force commodities and capital beyond the bounds of the given state, compelling a constant search for fresh markets, fresh sources of raw materials, and fresh spheres for capital investment. The greater the contradiction between the productive forces of capitalism and the mass impoverishment which is immanent in this system, the more intensive grows world competition, the more acute becomes the problem of war.

Imperialist war is an expression of the expansionist policy of monopoly capitalism. Such is the specific, historically limited significance of imperialist wars. On the one hand, monopoly capitalism acts as a check on the development of the productive forces (the decay of capitalism); on the other, it leads to catastrophes of the most devastating kind.

Thus not every sort of war, not even every predatory war, is an imperialist war. Slave-owning forms of society waged wars for slaves; feudal lords fought for land; merchants and traders fought for markets and for exploitation through trade and plunder ("Handel und Piraterie," as Goethe called it); and so forth. Imperialism wages wars to extend the domination of one country's finance capital, for the monopoly profits of trusts and banks. Its wars are universal (for the whole world is already divided up); its wars confront all mankind with the dilemma: either death or socialism. *Hic Rhodus! Hic salta!*

IV. IMPERIALISM AND THE U.S.S.R.

FROM THE ABOVE it will be clear how senseless it is to talk about the "imperialism" of the U.S.S.R., as is done *con amore* by fascist theoreticians and by "researchers" of the type of Herr von Kleinow. A phrase like "the imperialism of the U.S.S.R." is a contradiction in terms, like "dry water" or "square circles."

But it may be asked: Will not the U.S.S.R. pursue an aggressive policy, not in favor of finance capital but against it? Will it not fight for the expansion of socialism? Here again let us begin with an example.

As is well known, the empire of the tsars formerly occupied present territory of the Soviet Union, plus Poland, plus Finland, etc. It possessed even more territory and more "natural wealth" than does the U.S.S.R. But it was continually engaged in wars of conquest. On the eve of 1914 it dreamed of seizing Constantinople and the Dardanelles and of subjugating all Turkey, of seizing the whole of Galicia from Austria-Hungary, of dealing Germany a blow, and of concluding a trade agreement with her on onerous terms; and so on. What, under tsarism, drove not only the landlords but also the bourgeoisie (even before they had a share in the government) to these adventures? First and foremost, the weakness of the home market. The peasant was fleeced to the skin by the landlord; the worker's wages were meagre. Hence the policy which the tsar's minister Vyshnegradsky characterized in the words "We'll go hungry but we'll export." Hence the Far Eastern adventure—and the "Russo-Japanese War," during which, by the way, all sections of Russian society except the landlord aristocracy desired the tsarist government's defeat. Hence, too, Russia's participation in the world war, with a frenzied imperialist program (here the grain exporters played the biggest part).

Now let us take the U.S.S.R. One does not need to be a genius to observe that in the U.S.S.R. *the demand is not less but greater than the supply.* In our country we have a tremendously strong home market. Despite the enormous scale of production, there is a shortage of commodities; there are still too few goods on sale.

The socialist system contains within itself much greater possibilities for productive forces to develop, for labor to increase its productivity, and for technique to progress. But in the Soviet Union, be it noted, this cannot result either in unemployment or in overproduction. Our national economy is conducted not with a view to profits for a capitalist class, but to satisfy the requirements of the masses. This means that when production of necessary articles is increased, their consumption is proportionately raised and not lowered into the sea like Brazilian coffee. If completely superfluous articles are produced—a highly improbable contingency—corrections can be made in the production process itself. Under planned economy it is easy to redistribute the productive forces; they can be transferred to new sectors, engendering new requirements and supplying the masses with new lines of production. There will never be any threat of unemployment, and a universal rise in labor productivity will only lead to a growth of plenty, shorten the working day, and leave more scope for cultural development.

Thus the motive inherent in the very nature of the capitalist system, which begets surplus value and prevents its realization—the motive which is most glaringly manifested in the era of imperialism and impels the ruling classes to war—is reduced in a socialist society to absolute nonsense.

This was why beggarly tsarist Russia, where the "upper ten thousand" of landlords and bourgeois lived in splendor while the masses starved, pursued a policy of wars of conquest. And that is why the U.S.S.R., which is rapidly growing rich in the sense that well-being is spreading throughout the entire mass of the people while social wealth is concentrated in the hands of the socialist state, pursues an exactly opposite policy, the policy of peace. The U.S.S.R. is not interested in conquests in any direction whatever. But it is interested, very deeply and lastingly interested, in peace. What, then, remains of the celebrated argument that the U.S.S.R. "is continuing the policy of the tsars?"

There is another piece of geopolitical sophistry in circulation which goes more or less as follows. Fact remains fact: in 1914 Russia was in conflict with Japan in the Far East; in 1914–18 she was in conflict with Germany; the same thing is happening again, *mutatis mutandis,* and the fundamental geophysical laws are again breaking their way through all obstacles.

What is the reply to this piece of sophistry?

First, even the facts themselves are distorted. For example, in 1914 and the years following, Japan was in league with Russia against Germany; now Japan is in league with Germany against the U.S.S.R. The Japanese samurai have even been proclaimed oriental Prussians of Aryan extraction.

Second, the question must be stated more clearly. What, in effect, is under discussion? What we are discussing is not the mere fact of a conflict (for a conflict presupposes at least two parties—our object in this case not being to analyze the inner struggles of a Hamlet), but the policy of one party and the policy of another. After this logical dissection, the question becomes perfectly clear. In Japan power is in the hands of approximately the same classes as before, and Japan is continuing its policy of imperialist aggression, heading for war. The U.S.S.R. is not tsarist Russia and the radical change of the country's economic system demands an exactly opposite policy, the policy of peace. Nevertheless, war *may* break out, for the situation is not determined by the one-sided will to peace of the Soviets. War may be forced upon us. Contiguity of frontiers and territory certainly have an influence here, but not directly, and the war guilt will lie not with "the land" but with Japanese imperialism.

Finally, there is one other argument with which the opponents of the U.S.S.R. try to discredit Soviet foreign policy. It is trotted out regularly by Herr Hitler and his ideological agents. It runs, roughly speaking, as follows: National Socialism is based on "nationality" ("Volkstum," "Volksgemeinschaft"); its business is with the domestic, internal affairs of Germany; National Socialism is *national* socialism, and is not super- or supra-national. Accordingly, it never meddles in "other folks' affairs," but speaks exclusively *pro domo sua.* Conversely, Sovietism—bolshevism, communism—has a super- and supra-national orientation; it is an international force, dreaming of world domination; it is the *spiritus rector* of all sedition and unrest.

Clearly this argument is intimately connected with our theme.

First of all, a few words about the Germany of Herr Hitler. The German fascists, it is true, are idolaters of the fetish of so-called "race purity;" they even castrate those who are not pure Aryans and imprison people for the "crime" of sexual intercourse with non-Aryan men and women. They propagate economico-national autarchy, as a vessel containing the holy and precious body and blood of the "Nordic Aryan race." But it would be a childish absurdity to suppose that this leads to a policy of "noninterference." Quite the contrary. Fascist action is most energetic in all foreign countries. And this is easy to understand, for their very "national narrowness" is nothing more nor less than the clenching of the military-economic and ideological fist. Their orientation is towards world hegemony, entailing the crushing and enslavement of all other nations. No, to be sure, they are not internationalists. But they are potential nationalistic oppressors of all other nations (those of "low degree"). It is precisely from this point of view that the Nazis meddle in the internal affairs of all other states. It is worth knowing, for instance, that even in the case of the United States the Nazis count on the millions of citizens of German blood to act against the Anglo-Saxon and other elements. In fact, it is to fear of a German revolt that Herr Colin Ross ascribes the unfavorable attitude of Americans towards National Socialism. Setting out from the premise that "present-day America is tired and old, amazingly old" ("*das heutige Amerika ist müde und alt, erstaunlich alt*") the author threatens a national upheaval of millions of "self-knowing" Germans. Approximately the same arguments ("salvation" of the Ukraine or of the Volga Germans) are employed by Herr Rosenberg in his appeals for war against the U.S.S.R. It is thus quite futile for the Nazis to pose as offended children, occupied in the washing of purely domestic linen. That argument is mendacious.

However, *revenons à nos moutons*. Do we believe in the worldwide triumph of socialism? Of course we do. Moreover, we know for sure that this will undoubtedly come, as a result of the inner contradictions of capitalism, through the victory of the historically progressive forces within it. We know that our diagnosis and prognosis are scientific and exact. But does this mean that the U.S.S.R. should interfere in the affairs of other states or pursue a policy of conquest? Of course not. For the best "propaganda" of all is the very fact of the existence and uninterrupted development of the new economic relations and the new culture. It would be sheer stupidity to interrupt this process.

Hence it follows that not only from the economic but also from the purely political standpoint—not only from the standpoint of the U.S.S.R. proper but also from that of the ultimate worldwide victory of socialism—it is utterly senseless to think of a policy of war being adopted by the proletarian state. And as regards the "last days" and the "world rule of communism," history will settle this question. "*Que les destinées s'accomplissent!*". . .

V. THE SYSTEM OF PROLETARIAN STATES:
COMMUNISM AND WAR

NOW IT WILL be easy to answer the question as to whether wars between proletarian states will be possible—wars for markets, for raw materials, for spheres of capital investment—and whether wars will be possible under communism, i.e., in the subsequent stage of mankind's evolution, after it has already taken to socialism.

Basic actuating motives are represented by definite interests. The world economic system of the capitalist régime is broken up into "national" economic units with conflicting interests (we put the word "national" in quotation marks, for the term includes bourgeois states composing many nationalities). The most acute form of conflict in which this clash of interests finds expression is war between these states. War is a special form of capitalist competition, peculiar to the capitalist world as such. The question of relations between proletarian states is altogether different.

Logically: there is no clash of real interests between proletarian states whatsoever; on the contrary, their real interest is in maximum cooperation. From the very start this real interest is realized as the actuating motive of all activity, for it is commensurate with the whole system of rationally organized labor with the ideology of the revolutionary proletariat.

Genetically: the very process of the struggle waged by the proletarian states for their existence will knit them together in a still closer bond. There can be no doubt that after a certain stage of development, tremendously powerful centripetal tendencies will be revealed—tendencies toward a state union of proletarian republics.

Empirically: the experience of the U.S.S.R. fully confirms these considerations. Tsarist Russia collapsed as an integral whole, and in those parts where the bourgeoisie remained in power (Finland, Estonia, Lithuania, Poland), it has split apart and now forms mutually antagonistic elements (cf. Poland versus Lithuania). On the other hand, in those places where the workers were victorious they have joined the union of proletarian republics, united by a single economic plan and a centralized government but organized in a federation. The constituent nations have full rights, and their various cultures, national in form and socialist in content, are flourishing now as never before. This, of course, is far from being an accident; it is a manifestation of the most profound historical law, linked with a new social structure.

With the further flowering of proletarian states throughout the entire world, war will become unnecessary. War will be impossible in a system of unified communist society, where there are no classes and even—*horribile dictu*—no coercive state power nor armies. This society will really "turn swords into ploughshares" and release gigantic masses of energy for national creative work for the benefit of all mankind. If even the first historical phases of socialist development in our country have already produced such brilliant creative results as the Stakhanov movement and the heroic feats accomplished by our youth in all fields of culture, then what abundant sources of social wealth will pour forth in the splendid fraternal society of communism!

This, it will be said, is utopian. But we know very well that Aristotle was no fool, that he was one of the greatest men of all times. Yet he held that society was inconceivable without slaves. Not so long ago the planters of the Southern states held that Negroes are innate slaves. So today the bourgeois and their little "Aristotles" hold that society would be as inconceivable without war as without wage slavery and that the U.S.S.R. is a *lapsus historiæ*. Let them think so. *Qui vivra verra.*

Of Liberty

Benedetto Croce

OCTOBER 1932

BETWEEN the orderly Europe that we used to know and the distracted Europe of today is fixed the great gulf of the world war. We remember the old Europe with its riches, its flourishing trade, its abundance of goods, its ease of life, its bold sense of security; we see today the new Europe—impoverished, discouraged, crisscrossed with high tariff walls, each nation occupied solely with its own affairs, too distraught to pay heed to the things of the spirit and tormented by the fear of worse to come. Gone is the gay international society once the pride of Europe's capitals; extinct, or almost so, is the old community of thought, art, civilization. How many astounding changes there have been in frontiers and in political relationships! In the place of the Germany of the Hohenzollerns we see the German Republic; Austria-Hungary has been dismembered and cut up into new states; French sway has been reestablished over the provinces lost in 1870, and the Italian frontiers now include the unredeemed territories and extend to the Brenner; Poland has been reconstituted; Russia is ruled, not by the tsars but by the Soviets; and the United States has become a dominant factor in European policy.

Yet if we pass from externals to essentials and try to identify the controlling forces now at work, we soon discern that these two Europes, so dissimilar in appearance, have continuity and homogeneity. When we leave out superficial impressions and make a careful analysis, we detect the same characteristics in both, though in the Europe of today they have been exaggerated by the war. The same proclivities and the same spiritual conflicts are there, though aggravated by the general intellectual decay which was to be expected after a war which counted its victims by the millions, accustomed its survivors to violence, and destroyed the habit of critical, constructive, and concentrated mental labor.

Nationalistic and imperialistic impulses have seized the victorious nations because they are victors, and the vanquished because they are vanquished; while the new states add new nationalisms, new imperialisms to the list. Impatience with free institutions has led to open or masked dictatorships and, where dictatorships do not exist, to the desire for them. Liberty, which before the war was a faith, or at least a routine acceptance, has now departed from the hearts of men even if it still survives in certain institutions. In its place is an atavistic libertarism which more than ever ponders disorder and destruction, gives rein to extravagant impulses, and produces spectacular and sterile works. Indifferent and contemptuous, its followers scorn meditative and loving labor, labor with a reverent affection for the past and a courageous mastery of the future. They scorn actions which spring from the heart and speak to the heart, speculations which hold the germs of truth, history based on a realization of all that man has achieved by painful struggle, poetry which is beautiful.

Under the name of socialism, communism had already been introduced into the political life and institutions of Europe before the war. Now it has reappeared, crude and disruptive. Liberalism it ridicules as something naively moralistic. Like atavism, into which it often blends, this communism is a sterile thing that kills thought, religion, and art: seeking to subjugate them to its own purposes, it can only destroy them. All the distortions and decrepit sophistries of historical materialism have reappeared in the current opinions and theories of the day as if they were new and full of promise, although any man with a slight knowledge of criticism and the history of ideas passed judgment upon them long ago. They have taken on an air of novelty and modernness merely because, although originally introduced by Europe to Russia, they now come out of Russia; if anything they are more immature and shallow than ever; but in this age of unprecedented callowness and crudity, they gain unprecedented credence. Catholicism, moreover, which before the war sought to draw new strength from the forces of irrationalism and mysticism, has been gathering into its fold many weak and bewildered souls. Thus once again is heard that chorus of pessimism and decadence which echoed through prewar literature, this time announcing the decline of Western civilization and of the human race itself. According to these prophets, it is about to sink back to the level of beasts after having failed to reach the estate of man. . . .

And what practical moral is there for each of us in the fact that we cannot know the future? This: that we must take part in what is going on about us and not waste our forces in the contemplation of the unknowable, that we must act, to the degree that each of us can, as our conscience and duty command. Those who in disregard of the ancient admonition of Solon strive to understand and judge a life "before it is finished," and who lose themselves in conjecture and surmise, should be on their guard lest these digressions into the unknown prove a snare set by a bad demon to keep them from their goal.

Not "a history of the future" (as the old thinkers used to define prophecy), but a history of the past which is summed up in the present, is what we need for our work, for our action. And what we need most at the moment is to examine, or at least to review, those ideals which are generally accepted today. We must discover whether they contain the power to dissolve or surpass or correct the ideals which we ourselves hold; so that thereafter we may change or modify our ideals, and in any event reestablish them upon a surer, sounder foundation.

The ideal of a transcendental system of truth and, corollary to it, of a system of government from on high, exercised on earth by a vicar and represented by a church, has not yet acquired the intellectual proof which past ages found it to lack. Like all obvious statements, this one runs the risk of seeming ungenerous. Nonetheless, it is a fact that the spiritual impulse which has prompted many persons to return to Catholicism or to take refuge in it (or in similar if less venerable and authoritative havens) is merely a craving, amid the turmoil of clashing and changing ideals, for a truth that is fixed and a rule of life that is imposed from above. In some cases it may have no nobler basis than fear and renunciation, a childish terror in the presence of the perception that all truth is absolute and at the same time relative. But a moral ideal cannot conform to the needs of the discouraged and the fearful.

Nor can a moral ideal conform to the purposes of those who are drunk with action for action's sake; for action thus conceived leaves only nausea, a profound indifference toward all that has stirred the human race, and an incapacity for objective work. Humanity has drunk deep of nationalism and imperialism and the taste of them is already bitter as gall: *inveni amariorem felle.* Those who love action for its own sake still rage on. But where is their serenity of soul, their joy in life? The best of them are enveloped in gloom; the great mass of them are merely raw and stupid.

Communism, it is the fashion to claim, has passed from theory to practice and is being applied in Russia. But it is being practised not as communism but—in keeping with its inner contradiction—as a form of autocracy, as its critics had always predicted would be the case. Under it the people of Russia are denied even that faint breath of freedom which they managed to obtain under the autocracy of the tsars. The abolition of the state, that "transition from the régime of necessity to the régime of liberty" about which Marx theorized, has not taken place. Communism has not abolished the state—it could not and never will be able to do so—but, as irony would have it, has forged for itself one of the most oppressive state systems which it is possible to imagine. In saying this we are not trying to deny that perhaps there were circumstances which forced the Russian revolutionists to choose the course they did and no other. Neither do we wish to detract from the immensity of their endeavors to develop, under these circumstances, the productive forces of the country. Neither do we minimize the importance of the lessons to be learned from their endeavors or fail to admire the mystic enthusiasm, materialistic though it be, which inspires them and keeps them from sinking beneath the load which they have put on their own backs. It is this enthusiasm which gives them courage to trample on religion, thought, poetry, on everything in a word which we in the West revere as sacred or noble.

Nevertheless, the Russian communists have not solved, nor will their violent and repressive methods ever enable them to solve, the fundamental problem of human society, the problem of freedom. For in freedom only can human society flourish and bear fruit. Freedom alone gives meaning to life: without it life is unbearable. Here is an inescapable problem. It cannot be eliminated. It springs from the very vitals of things and stirs in the souls of all those countless human beings whom the communists are trying to control and reshape in accordance with their arbitrary concepts. And on the day that this problem is faced, the materialistic foundations of the Soviet structure will crumble and new and very different supports will have to be found for it. Then, even as now, pure communism will not be practised in Russia.

Outside of Russia this pseudo-communism has not gained much ground in spite of the fascination that always attaches to things remote in time and space—as the old adage has it, *maior e longinquo reverentia.* Two conditions present in Russia are indeed lacking in Western and Central Europe: the tsarist tradition and mysticism. Miliukov was not far from the truth when he wrote of Lenin some 12 or more years ago that "in Russia he was building on the solid foundations of the good old autocratic tradition, but that as far as other countries were concerned he was merely building castles in the air." Even if such experiments should develop in other parts of Europe, the fact that other countries differ so from Russia in religion, civilization, education, customs, traditions—in historical background, in short—would produce something quite new, whatever its name and appearance; or else, after an indeterminate period of blind groping and struggle, there would sooner or later emerge that liberty which is only another name for humanity.

For liberty is the only ideal which unites the stability that Catholicism once possessed with the flexibility which it could never attain, the only ideal which faces the future without proposing to mould it to some particular form, the only ideal that can survive criticism and give human society a fixed point by which from time to time to reestablish its balance. There are those who question the future of the ideal of freedom. To them we answer that it has more than a future: it has eternity. And today, despite the contempt and ridicule heaped upon it, liberty still endures in many of our institutions and customs and still exercises a beneficent influence upon them. More significant still, it abides in the hearts and minds of many noble men all over the world, men who though scattered and isolated, reduced to a small but aristocratic *res publica literaria,* still keep faith with it, reverently hallow its name, and love it more truly than ever they did in the days when no one denied or questioned its absolute sovereignty, when the mob proclaimed its glory and contaminated it with a vulgarity of which it is now purged.

And not only does freedom abide in such men, and not only does it exist and persist in the constitutions of many important countries and in institutions and customs. Its virtue is operative in things themselves and is gradually opening a way through many difficulties. We see it at work in the present wish for a truce in suspicions, a reduction in armaments, and a peaceful settlement among the nations of Europe. That this is true is apparent in the general feeling that somehow these nations must contrive to harmonize their plans and efforts if they are to retain not their political and economic supremacy only, but even their leadership as creators of civilization and the aptitudes for this unending task which they have acquired through centuries of labor and experience.

Disarmament and world peace are the only statesmanlike projects among the many put forward since the war which have not faded out or been dissipated; rather are they gaining ground from year to year and converting many who were once antagonistic or incredulous or faint-hearted. We are entitled to hope that they will not be allowed to fail but will be carried forward to fulfillment in the face of all opposition. It is true that the world war, which future historians may well regard as the *reductio ad absurdum* of nationalism, has embittered the relations of certain states as a result of an unjust and foolish peace treaty; but it also has made the peoples aware in their innermost consciousness that they have common virtues and defects, common strengths and weaknesses, that they share a common destiny, are inspired by the same affections, afflicted by the same sorrows, glory in the same patrimony of ideals. This explains why already in all parts of Europe we are witnessing the birth of a new consciousness, a new nationality—for nations are not, as has been imagined, data of nature but results of conscious acts, historical formations. Just as 70 years ago the Neapolitans and the Piedmontese decided to become Italians, not by abjuring their original nationality but by exalting and merging it in the new one, so Frenchmen and Germans and Italians and all the others will rise to becoming Europeans; they will think as Europeans, their hearts will beat for Europe as they now do for their smaller countries, not forgetting them but loving them the better.

This process of amalgamation is directly opposed to competitive nationalism and will in time destroy it entirely; meanwhile it tends to free Europe from the psychology of nationalism and its attendant habits of thought and action. If and when this happens, the liberal ideal will again prevail in the European mind and resume its sway over European hearts. . . .

In this new mental and moral atmosphere it will be imperative to take up again the so-called "social" problems. They are certainly not of recent making; thinkers and statesmen have struggled with them for centuries, dealing with them as they arose, case by case and in the spirit of the times. During the nineteenth century they were the object of deep attention and most heroic remedies and were dealt with in such a way as to improve greatly the conditions of the working classes, to raise their standards of living and to better their legal and moral status. "Planned" economy, as it is now being called, although it holds a foremost position in talk today is not essentially new; and the question cannot be seriously raised of finding a collective substitute for individual economy or free individual initiative, both of themselves necessary to human life and economic progress. Discussion can turn only on the proportions, great or small, to be assigned to one form of economic organization rather than to another, differing with different means, places, times, and other circumstances. This is primarily a question for technical experts and statesmen, who will have to devise solutions suitable to the times and favorable to an increase of wealth and its more equitable distribution. It is a question for experts and statesmen; but they will be unable to fulfill their function or attain their ends unless liberty be there to prepare and maintain the intellectual and moral atmosphere indispensable to labors so arduous, and to quicken the legal systems within which their duties must be performed.

Dictatorship of the Mind

Heinrich Mann

APRIL 1934

CONTROLLED ECONOMY has become familiar almost everywhere, but controlled thought is an innovation of the new dictatorships. The German dictatorship is perhaps unique in claiming nothing less than complete control over the whole intellectual and spiritual life of the nation. By comparison, thought and conscience are relatively free in Soviet Russia and in Fascist Italy; in fact, in these countries German writers can publish works which are suppressed in Germany on the grounds that they are liberal.

Controlled economy has proved to be too difficult a task for the Hitler dictatorship. It has gone back on its program of economic socialization, and its Four Year Plan remains only a promise. Despite subterfuges, there can no longer be doubt that nothing has been done for the middle classes. The only beneficiaries of the present gamble with the destinies of Germany, besides the members of the National Socialist Party, are the big industrialists, who gain by the strangling of the labor unions and who scent fresh profits in armaments. American democracy has established a greater degree of controlled economy than the boasted *totalitätsstaat*, which actually has reverted to a laissez-faire economy of 80 years ago.

The régime tries to make up for its impotence in economic matters by ceaseless interference in the intellectual and moral realm. It will tolerate neither opposition nor neutrality. Thought must be either National Socialist or it must not be; consequently it is the former, because it is easier to control men's minds than their interests. It is a regrettable fact that people living modestly by their talents or their brains can be brought into subjection much more easily than the monied classes. Great consideration has been shown to the latter in Germany, even when they happen to be Jews. The great department stores, which were to have been utterly destroyed, are still open and full of customers, and the Jewish owners no longer take the trouble to conceal their identities behind men of straw. Even the Ullsteins have succeeded in retaining part control of their publishing house, which is the most important in Germany. One of the directors of a large bank chose the moment when his coreligionists were being most outrageously persecuted to declare that he had never been molested. A banker descended from a Jewish family which has been distinguished for two hundred years has had himself declared an "Aryan."

However, if Einstein were rash enough to return to Germany, he could not count on such polite attentions. After all, he would be of no help in provisioning Germany for the next war. His personal fortune was slight and what there was has long since been confiscated. That method was obviously the most effective to adopt against intellectuals: their money was not protected by the chemical trusts and other groups of national importance. So we who live by our pens were promptly relieved of our bank accounts. Wishing to strike at liberty of thought, the authorities imagined that it was intimately bound up with the liberty to draw checks. They made a great mistake. The scholars who were driven from the universities and the writers who were threatened with being put in concentration camps did not come begging for mercy to those who were, temporarily, their masters. They accepted their lot, which was to suffer or to disappear. Many suicides occurred amongst the intellectuals, but they were mostly discreet, in the best of taste, not at all ostentatious. In taking leave of an existence which had lost all meaning for them, they were acting in just the same way as did those others to whom political or material ruin meant more than the will to live.

Of the professors and publicists sent to concentration camps, some were deliberate martyrs, others could not believe that they would be arrested simply because they had discharged their routine duties under the republican régime. They had not counted on being accused of corruption merely because they had eaten the bread of the republic. A certain actor who was very popular with radio audiences was punished for his popularity by six months' detention in one of the harshest camps. His mistake was in not having realized that popularity is an unpardonable crime in the eyes of the master minds who have monopolized, for their own ends and to their own advantage, every channel of publicity. It would have been wiser for him to go abroad. But he happened to be a sincere Protestant; he consulted only his conscience, and it had nothing with which to reproach him. Another prisoner, who even under the previous régime had paid dearly for his uncompromising pacifism, refused to seek safety in flight. Maybe he wished to set an example, in the hope of arousing the public conscience. But the list of victims was too long for his sufferings to have that result. Once a certain degree of violence has been reached and a sufficient number of atrocities have been committed, our sensibilities are dulled; we forget. People admit the facts but no longer judge them, since somehow or other they must live alongside those who are responsible for them. This particular victim will continue his futile martyrdom long after his very existence is forgotten.

Most of the intellectuals considered undesirable in Germany have neither chosen to die nor accepted the kind of life which their enemies had in store for them. They emigrated, and that in itself was bad enough. They now are undergoing the fate of all emigrés, which is not only poverty and loneliness, but lack of moral consideration. The average man has little respect for those whose cause has failed and who thereby are transformed from influential personalities into simple refugees. Moreover, the public is confused by the variegated crowd of refugees, many of whom, of course, find themselves where they are for reasons that have no connection with matters of principle. We must set to work to redeem our position by acting with complete sincerity and by not complaining too much. We are not too unfortunate. We retain one right, more precious than any other, the right to express our ideas freely. Our fellow-countrymen in Germany have forfeited that right, and it is not even certain that they would now know how to exercise it. One cannot submit with impunity to the system of controlled thought.

If some are emigrés in spite of themselves, often with little to recommend them, there also are others who left the country without being forced to do so. They are acknowledged "Aryans," war veterans, scholars and writers on the conservative side. They revolted against the suppression of freedom of thought. Too proud to take over the posts of persecuted colleagues, they followed them into exile, and their exodus continues. Every now and then some distinguished German professor leaves Germany to teach abroad, perhaps in a language which he has to learn for the purpose. Make no mistake, these departures are so many protests against the present régime. In extreme circumstances like the present, every act of the sort is a manifesto. The Nazis flattered themselves that they had in their favor one great poet, just one, whose mystic evocations seemed to justify the advent of the Third Reich. Once this Reich was established, the poet refused to recognize it in word or deed. He left the country, died abroad, and, in accordance with his wishes, was buried in foreign ground.

Anyone capable of moral humiliation would be discouraged by rebuffs of this kind, but they slide off the backs of people who are entirely preoccupied with the business of protecting their physical rule. Never have human beings been so deeply convinced of the single virtue of material facts. To them a nation is a race, determined zoologically, which can be modified at will by sterilization, outlawry, and other coercive measures. Similarly, thought becomes materialized in their hands and is simply a mechanism conveniently placed at the disposal of the strongest. Only official truths are admitted, and only such creative work as happens to serve the purpose of the authorities. Everything in the arts and sciences which contradicts or goes beyond the National Socialist doctrine is looked upon as nonexistent, simply by reason of the fact that the artists and thinkers concerned have left Germany. Having eliminated all opposition, the government is far from regretting the loss of eminent personalities which added to the permanent glory of the country. It is delighted to have to deal only with minds which are timid, with talents so mediocre that they can easily be directed. The method of selection is to ask all artists and writers to reply in writing to the two essential questions: Are you Aryan? Do you undertake to support the national government with all your strength? Anyone who refuses to sign immediately loses his public; there is no longer any audience in Germany to which he can address himself. The irreconcilables have been eliminated in advance; there remain only the weak and the mediocre to be dealt with, not to mention the shrewd who, after having made their way in a free régime, are quite prepared to profit from the methods of a dictatorship.

Having drawn up a list of the talents remaining available to them, the government then turned to the great problem of organizing them, hoping by lumping them into a mass to make up for the lack of individual distinction. As president of the Musical Union they even got Richard Strauss; and a former favorite of the German Republic, Gerhart Hauptmann, decided also to curry favor with the powers that be. I refuse to believe that these great masters have weak characters. I think, rather, that they have been accustomed for so long to seeing the national genius embodied in their persons that it seems to them impossible that they should not continue to represent it, no matter what the government happens to be. Apart from these two old men, who are too remote from actuality to be able to be very critical, the National Socialists have placed only second-raters at the head of their intellectual organizations. There are seven of these special unions, grouped in a General Cultural Union, presided over, as one might expect, by the minister of propaganda. German culture is now merely an instrument of propaganda, in the service of the government. It is entirely subordinated to the will of a single chief, named Goebbels. He is known today all over the world; but on his own, independently of the propaganda instruments of the party and the movement, he couldn't interest even a thousand readers in his plays and novels. As a matter of fact, it is not survivors like Hauptmann and Strauss who give the measure of German culture today. It is Goebbels. Having created nothing, he has at last propagandized himself into existence. When the party came to power, the victorious propagandist simply imposed himself upon a culture to which he had never contributed.

Further, the doctrine of the National Socialist Party does not admit individual thought or brilliant exceptions, which are the essence of real talent and superior intelligence. One must think as everybody thinks before confessing to gifts which are not everybody's. Moreover, if the minister of propaganda has to choose between a devoted mediocrity and a man of talent who is willing to make concessions, he will choose the former, though he pretends publicly to set great store by talent. His theory is that art cannot exist without talent, but that extremely individualistic talent creates an abyss between art and the nation. This preposterous theory was the subject of his inaugural speech before the Cultural Union. He informed his regimented audience that, before the advent of the Hitler government, the literary public had been rapidly dwindling, that the masses were becoming indifferent to literature. He conveniently forgot dozens of recent examples to the contrary. *All Quiet on the Western Front* sold a million copies in Germany alone. Thomas Mann's *Buddenbrooks* reached a sale of a million just in one cheap edition. As German is spoken by less than 60 million adults, these are high figures. German books were never read so widely as after the Weimar Republic came into existence. Democracy, by freeing the workers and by levelling classes, had served culture well by opening up its golden seams to millions who previously had been isolated from it.

Under the National Socialists, Germany has promptly lost the habit of reading. Partly this is because people have little time for it, being constantly occupied with manifestations in favor of the government, military night marches, and forced labor on behalf of a few people of wealth. Every German is conscripted for life. Never being alone for a minute, how can he think? Goebbels nevertheless expects him to be interested in a certain kind of literature, described as heroic romanticism. But these writings remain quite unknown to the general public. The nation to whom they are addressed is neither romantic nor heroic. It has been stuffed with lies but is not more romantic on that account. It has been steeped in violence and braggadocio, but that is far from heroism. A few victories fairly won and some spirit of sacrifice might help; but sacrificing others is not enough.

Obviously, the new National Socialist cultural system would not work without violent pressure on the unwilling. "If you refuse to buy our books, we shall compel you to, otherwise you will lose your job." That is how the author of *My Struggle,* who is also its publisher, and who besides has the advantage of being both chancellor and the owner of the chief newspaper in his party, speeds up the sales of the National Socialist bible. Radio owners have been sent to jail for deciding to give up their receiving sets because they could not stand hearing over and over again the speeches of the National Socialist leaders. The régime imposes its own press and will tolerate no other. Its aim is to keep the outer world from penetrating into Germany. Literature, drama, and moving pictures are strictly controlled. Only propagandist movies are now permitted, camouflaged, of course, if they are intended for export. The theatre has not yet received proper attention. As the playhouses are empty, it would be logical to compel the taxpayers to attend as a matter of duty and applaud the new romantico-heroic dramas.

The least resistance to all this comes from the youth. Always susceptible to irrational enthusiasm and appeals to collective action, the young men of Germany are the very basis of the dictatorship. They were the first to applaud it, and it rewards them by endlessly dwelling upon the inestimable value attributed to physical youth in certain epochs. Indeed, the ability to appeal to youth is clearly of the utmost value to leaders who are on bad terms with critical minds; they have nothing of that kind to fear from the young. Neither a critical sense nor common sense prevented the students from driving out professors who happened to be Jewish, democratic, or simply merely honest. Nor has it prevented them from taking bloody reprisals against their classmates who hold different ideas from theirs. From the beginning, the movement exploited the youths of less than 20 years. These swarmed in the streets whenever there was a demonstration against the republic or against freedom of thought. If thought is now controlled in Germany, instead of being free, it is chiefly the fault of the younger generation. They sing "We Are the Soldiers of the Future." It is hardly necessary to say that youths of 20 are always the soldiers of some future or other. But what future can lie before these German youths, already weighted down for all their lives by the injustices and contemptible actions they have committed?

That is one of the grave disadvantages of controlled thought. It has distorted the minds of whole generations of young folk, and it leaves them no time for learning. Indeed, students of National Socialist opinions have had to be granted special facilities at their examinations. So many scholars of great distinction have left the country that the world a few years hence seems destined to witness the mental decline of a nation which might have continued to be distinguished in all domains of scholarship and science, abstract as well as applied. Where would have been the world's chemical and mechanical inventions, its great industries, if men had not been able to think freely and work freely? And at the same time the spiritual springs of the nation are destroyed by lies and hypocrisy.

Another disadvantage of controlled thought is the absence of safety valves. These have all been closed. There is no criticism; there are no warnings. Catastrophes can approach unannounced. History has recorded, times without number, the dangers and degradations caused by the suppression of freedom of conscience. It is sad to see one generation of men going back on the moral conquests made by its predecessors. For a certain time, it is true, truth may be regarded as a mere matter of convention. But such truths are not the Truth, to which disinterested men will devote their lives. Nobody will be able to enjoy the immense experience of meeting face to face the perils of the Unknown by the exercise of the intellect. The delicious pains of creation will be unknown, since the artist is forbidden his own conception of humanity and must evoke only official visions. It will no longer be said that personality is the supreme happiness of man. The personality of a Goethe could never have been regimented by this régime of jealous, rancorous mediocrities.

They are powerfully entrenched and their capacity for harm is far from exhausted. They will last, and they will make the most of their opportunities before they disappear. But disappear they will, and free thought will survive them. On that score, too, history leaves no doubt. Though thought is persecuted, already it resists. The layman is still quiet; but the Christian churches are in revolt against the doctrine of racism. The churches do not recognize zoological races. They recognize only humanity, whose spiritual welfare has been put in their keeping. That welfare is also the concern of intellectuals, even though they are not so well organized as the clerics and are more exposed to worldly considerations. There will come the moment when they will realize their degradation and react against it. For the rest, Eternal Thought is in no wise affected by the abdication, forced or voluntary, of a few thousand intellectuals inside a certain set of frontier posts.

Civilization on Trial

H. G. Wells

JULY 1935

THE GAME of international politics impresses a lot of common men like myself as being based on false premises. In the issue of *Foreign Affairs* for April, I read an article which talks about "France" and the objectives of "Japan," and the purposes of "Russia," and what "Germany" intends to do. I have never been able to get over a certain skepticism about these matters. I can't succeed in translating nationalities into personalities. I can't make myself think of Japan as an individual who is plotting against Russia and who is preparing to form an alliance with Germany which would threaten Anglo-Saxon interests.

That sort of thing seems to me a romantic simplification of what is really happening in human affairs, and I think it leads to disastrous results. These might be avoided if we were more liberal and honest, if when we say, "Japan is going to do so-and-so," we said further, "What exactly is this Japan that is going to do so-and-so?" Japan is a vast country. The Japanese people have got certain foreign relationships, which they carry on through something which they call the Japanese Foreign Office. How long will it and its policies last? How far can we really believe that there is some simple thing called Japan which is malignant and patriotic and about to make an alliance with Germany?

And what is Germany, really? A mass of troubled persons who speak the German language and who are, I should think, in perhaps the most tragic position of any mass of intelligent people in the world. They have either got to repudiate their country or they have got to endure a grotesque sort of caricature of government by misrepresentation. Our foreign offices are going to deal with Germany as though it were an individual entity. But as a civilized man I continually try to see whether there is not a way of dealing with the civilized man in Germany and getting past that extraordinarily ugly Nazi mask which he has to wear because the alternative to the wearing of it would have meant submission to some foreign influence as dishonoring and even more humiliating.

Is there not a possibility that in the future we can get away from the idea that human affairs are necessarily shaped and controlled in foreign offices and embodied in what are called foreign policies? Is there not a broader, more general pattern of human civilization which we might possibly emphasize and bring into fuller operation than it is at this present time, in order to prevent this idiotic and unnecessary game of national antagonisms from culminating in war and possibly the destruction of civilization?

I was enormously impressed during my visit to the United States this past spring by the fact that because you Americans have too many natural resources you have not got a paradise. You have got millions of people with hands and brains idle, and you don't know what to do with them. At a rough guess, there are between three and four million young people in the United States who have no jobs, no compelling interest in life at all. You ask them to work short hours or no hours at all and to live on a dole. They think that they would be better off if they were dead. In England we are in the same case. We have got about two million young people, or more, and what have we got to give them? Nothing. What is the Nazi movement in Germany? What is fascism in Italy? Young men who have nothing to do. Hitler and Mussolini offer them, if nothing else, excitement and possible glory. Japan is coming up against the same problem.

I have no panacea to offer for that problem. It is the greatest problem in the world. Humanity has been accumulating energy at an enormous pace. In addition to manpower, it has brought in mechanical energy to an extraordinary extent. And now it doesn't know what to do with that surplus energy. Because it deals as it does with human relationships it cannot cash in on the surplus that it has achieved.

The surplus of energy which has accumulated in human affairs for several thousand years has been partially expended in building up the standards of life. But the most natural method of relief has been war. War is a kind of excretion of the human social body. The energy accumulates—and human intelligence is not adequate to the problem of how to utilize it. So it has to get rid of it again. The chief corrective has been war.

No country goes to war because it is poor; no country goes to war because it is weak and unhappy. A country goes to war because it is full of vigor, because it has a great mass of unemployed people, because it has materials at hand. War is an excretory product, and until the world discovers some other means of using its surplus energy, wars will go on.

The dogmatic doctrine known as communism offers no solution. Karl Marx misunderstood and perverted the philosophy of Robert Owen and the other idealistic socialists who looked for social betterment through collective action. Marx's theory of the inevitability of class warfare is one of the most pernicious things that ever happened to humanity. It is as bad as the idea of the inevitability of conflict between nations.

You Americans perhaps think that if Europe collapses into war you will be able to keep out of it. Many others, in England and elsewhere, have that same idea—to keep out of it. But I doubt that they can. The next war, if it spreads, and I think it is likely to spread, is going to mean the destruction of human civilization as we understand it.

Probably the greatest single body of mentality, so to speak, in the world today is the English-speaking community. I suppose that in the English-speaking community there are more people who read and write and talk than there are in any other community of thought in the world. Part of that community is in the United States, part is in Britain, and smaller parts are scattered about in Canada, South Africa, Australia, and so forth. It seems to me a most lamentable and astonishing thing that behind our common language we have not got a common idea of what we are going to attempt to do with the world in the years ahead.

It is obvious that we are going to be tried out, and in a most extraordinary fashion. We are not ready for it. We have allowed foreign offices with their technical points and legal definitions to elude us into the idea that here is an American community, here is a British community. And British bad manners and American suspicions have helped in keeping us apart. Is it not still possible for the English and the Americans to get a little closer together, to conceive some sort of common purpose, and to bring their common traditions into effective action in time to save the civilization of the world? Or shall we wait until, divided against ourselves, destruction comes upon the world through a general collapse into war?

In every community in the world there is a state of stress because of an extraordinary change from the insufficient productivity which ruled social life in the past to the present excessive productivity. In economics we speak of this as the economy of plenty replacing the economy of want. You in America have to work out that problem. All the world has to work out that problem.

Is it not possible for the English-speaking communities to begin getting together upon the answers to some of the financial riddles, the economic riddles, and the political riddles that paralyze us?

President Roosevelt told me when I saw him in Washington about something that has been happening on the border between the United States and Canada. At the eastern end of the border there has been a good deal of smuggling along the old side-roads, where it is easy for a truck or lorry to slip from one country into the other. To meet this situation the American government started an air patrol to watch these back roads, and the Canadians were going to start another, when some bright spirit, I don't know who it was, said, "Why have two services?" And what is happening now on the Canadian–United States border is that there is an air service which is looking for smugglers, and in the aeroplane sit a Canadian policeman and an American policeman, and that aeroplane can come down on either side of the border and make an arrest in the interest of Canada or in the interest of the United States.

Suppose someone saw the opportunity for this sort of thing on a larger scale. Suppose someone saw the possibility of having the United States fleet in the Pacific and the British fleet in the Atlantic, instead of having a British fleet in the Pacific and an American fleet in the Pacific, and a British fleet in the Atlantic and an American fleet in the Atlantic. Is it impossible? What makes it impossible? What divergence of purpose stands in the way?

Unless men can get outside their national limitations, and unless they can tackle economic and financial and monetary problems with something bigger than their national equipment, I think it is not a question of centuries but of decades before we see our civilization going down. And it will not be for the first time.

The problem is to make peace successful. If peace is not successful, if war intervenes, it will be due entirely to the fact that under existing conditions we are not able to utilize our surplus energy, to employ our idle hands, in any other way to make life satisfactory and interesting. Failing the release of energy that would come from making peace successful, we will collapse into war. The way to get rid of war is not by leagues. The energies for war go on accumulating just the same.

The only thing to do is to invent a successful form of peace. That means a new sort of life for human beings. The choice before us is war or a new world—a rational liberal collectivist world with an ever rising standard of life and an ever bolder collective enterprise, in science, in art, in every department of living. Because so far we have not shown the intellectual power and vigor to take the higher, more difficult way, because we have not had sense enough to discover what to do with our accumulation of social energy, is why at the present time we are drifting and sliding back towards destruction. If humanity fails, it will fail for the lack of organized mental effort and for no other reason.

War and Victory

THE NINETEEN FORTIES

❧WHEN GERMAN tanks thundered into Poland on September 1, 1939, the world was again at war. But the war this time was different—more mobile, more variegated, longer, and ultimately deadlier than even the Great War.

Europe unraveled quickly in the face of the renewed German drive for world power. Hitler and Stalin suspended their ideological hatred of each other to sign a nonaggression pact in August 1939. That year, Arnold J. Toynbee, the great British historian and a man who had some empathy for the dominant appeasement philosophy, called the Munich accord of 1938 "A Turning Point in History," but with a sinking feeling about where that turn might lead. The answer was not long in coming. As Hitler hurtled through Poland, Britain and France finally declared war on Nazi Germany.

Soon Europe lay under the German jackboot. The Nazi blitz devoured Denmark, Norway, France, Yugoslavia, and Greece, among others. But in 1941, Hitler made his fatal mistake: he launched Operation Barbarossa, the invasion of the Soviet Union. By year's end, both Moscow and Leningrad were under siege, but Bonaparte's old nemesis, the Russian winter, bogged down the German advance.

President Roosevelt watched as Europe burned, but he had won reelection in 1940 on a promise to keep America's boys out of Europe's wars. In America the mood was still one of disengagement and neutrality. Julien Benda, the great French philosopher, argued in his essay "Pacifism and Democracy" against one of the roots of isolationism, the widely held view that liberal disdain for the militarism of the Great War required pacifism. But in the end, it took the Japanese bombing of Pearl Harbor on December 7, 1941, to bring the United States into the war.

Though America's entry into the war was crucial, the tide was finally turned by the German defeat at Stalingrad and by Allied offensives in North

Africa that destroyed General Rommel's Afrika Korps. By May 1945, Mussolini's regime had collapsed, the Normandy invasion had succeeded, the Battle of the Bulge was won, and Adolf Hitler was dead, as were 6 million Jews and hundreds of thousands of other innocent civilians.

World War II was ended by one fateful decision. President Harry S Truman ushered in the nuclear age by using the newly invented atomic bomb against Japan. Hiroshima was followed by Nagasaki, which was followed by the emperor's unconditional surrender.

The world now stood on the brink of a new era. America began to build pillars for the postwar order—Bretton Woods, Dumbarton Oaks, the United Nations—but, as the legendary *New York Times* reporter James B. Reston records in "The Critic Turns Actor," Washington was still unaccustomed to its colossal position in world affairs. F.D.R. had hoped that the Soviet Union, along with Britain and China, would become one of the world's "four policemen." But his successor, the plain-spoken Truman, soon came to be gloomy about the chances of changing Soviet behavior. The Soviet Union remained a totalitarian state, and Stalin showed no inclination to disgorge the East European nations he had swallowed on the staggeringly costly Soviet march to Berlin. In March 1946, Winston Churchill famously warned that an "iron curtain" had descended across Europe.

The late 1940s saw the start of the moves and countermoves that would define global politics for the next four decades. The Soviets built their own atomic bomb. Washington announced the ambitious Marshall Plan to rebuild Western Europe, and in March 1947 the president unveiled the Truman Doctrine, calling for U.S. support for governments threatened by communist subjugation. "Reluctantly we have now come to understand that victory and peace are not synonymous," wrote Henry L. Stimson, the elder statesman who had been F.D.R.'s secretary of war, in his stirring "The Challenge to Americans." One war was over, but a new, colder war was just beginning.

A Turning Point in History

Arnold J. Toynbee

JANUARY 1939

THAT THE public events of September 1938 have been momentous is already a commonplace. They may mark a turning point not only in British history but in world history too. By the same token, our recent experiences have been so overwhelming that it is still very difficult to see them steadily and whole. One who looks at the new international situation from a British standpoint must first ask whether the line taken by Great Britain in 1938 marks a serious departure from the traditional line of British foreign policy.

The policy of Great Britain in the past towards Europe has been, like that of the United States, to confine her intervention in continental affairs to the minimum compatible with her own national interests as she sees them. The practical application of this fundamentally identical policy is, of course, governed by each country's particular geographical situation. The minimum to which the United States can safely reduce her intervention in Europe cannot be even approximated by an island that is separated from the continent by the mere breadth of the Channel rather than by the Atlantic. This difference has always compelled British isolationism to stop far short of American isolationism in practice. If British isolation from the continent has been relatively incomplete in the past, this difference between Great Britain's and America's respective situations is accentuated at the present time, when the Channel is no longer, while the Atlantic still is, an effective barrier against air attack.

In the past, what was the typical continental situation in which the British government and people felt themselves constrained to play a part in continental affairs? The policy of Great Britain towards Louis XIV, Napoleon, and William II seems to show that she has generally taken active steps, sooner or later, to join in resisting the domination of Europe by a single power when there has seemed to be a serious probability that this power would use its continental predominance in order to threaten the indepen-

[113]

dence of the British Isles and the security of British interests overseas. This qualification of the main statement is important, because there have been cases in which Great Britain has tolerated the continental predominance of some power that has manifestly harbored no designs against Great Britain herself. For an example we need look no further than to the British attitude towards the continental predominance of France between November 1918 and September 1938. Though Great Britain largely disapproved of French policy during this period, and made some perhaps rather feeble efforts to modify it, she never thought, during those years, of attempting to depose France from her postwar position. Another case, which comes nearer home to the present issue, is the attitude of Great Britain towards the advancement of Germany under the leadership of Bismarck. Great Britain took no decisive steps to prevent the rise of Prussia to dominance in Germany in 1864–71; indeed, British policy in regard to Denmark in 1864 displays a curiously close resemblance to the policy pursued in regard to Czechoslovakia in 1938.

Now that the postwar French domination on the continent has been brought to an end by the eventual resurgence of Germany, the question arises whether it has been replaced by a German domination; whether this German domination, if established, will prove to be different in character from the French; and finally whether, supposing that it does differ in character from the foregoing French régime, the new German domination will turn out to be of the kind against which Great Britain has always taken a stand in the past.

This is perhaps the fundamental question raised by what Great Britain did—or refrained from doing—in September. In coming to terms with Hitler at Munich, Great Britain and France went a long way, and maybe the whole way, towards giving him a free hand in Central and Eastern Europe— at least up to the western threshold of the Soviet Union. What can the German Führer make, and what will he wish to make, of this new opportunity? Will he be able now to establish a secure and lasting German predominance over that great tract of Europe that lies between the western frontier of the Soviet Union and the eastern frontier of France? If he does succeed in constructing a *Mittel-Europa* on a basis of German ascendancy, will he be tempted to use this large extension of German power as a means of making that power felt still further afield? And if he did one day use *Mittel-Europa* as a "jumping-off ground," in which direction would he move and how far would he aspire to go? Would he march eastwards overland into the Ukraine? Or would he seek to gain a reentry into that overseas world from which Germany was expelled as a result of the war of 1914–18 and the ensuing peace settlement? In the latter event, would he confine his ambitions within the limits of the colonial possessions of the West European powers, or would he try to extend his overseas operations to Latin America?

These questions may have been at issue not only in the September crisis; they may also be involved in British (and no doubt also in Russian and American) policy now, on the morrow of the Munich agreement, and in the future. The difficulty is that the momentous decisions which had, and have, to be taken in the light of these questions could not, and cannot, wait until the questions can be answered with any certainty. At present there are a number of possible alternative answers to each of them; and only the future course of events will reveal which answer hits the mark. This extreme uncertainty still clouds even the immediate question which the Munich agreement raises—the question, that is, of Germany's prospects in Central and Eastern Europe.

Can Germany now succeed in bringing her neighbors in Central, Eastern, and Southern Europe into a relationship with her in which they will minister to her power and serve her ends? In taking up this question at the present early stage, a British observer can do little more than set out the pros and cons.

The following points would seem to tell in Germany's favor.

First, within the circle of those European states whose populations come up to the highest standard of efficiency (as measured by education, technical ability, and material equipment), Greater Germany, with now nearly 80 million inhabitants, musters almost double the population of the next most populous European power and almost as large a population as Great Britain and France added together.

Secondly, Germany, in combination with her Italian partner in the Berlin-Rome Axis, now insulates France and Great Britain from everything on the continent that lies east of the eastern frontiers of the Reich and Italy. In wartime the Axis Powers would be able to cut Anglo-French communications with Eastern Europe and Russia, not only overland but also by sea via the Baltic (certainly) and via the Mediterranean (probably).

Thirdly, in the insulated area between the eastern frontiers of the two Axis powers and the western frontier of the Soviet Union, there are today a dozen small, young, and weak states, extending from Finland to Greece, which will henceforward have a hard struggle if they are to avoid the fate of falling under Germany's ascendancy strategically, politically, and economically.

In her relations with these neighbors, Germany now has so great a predominance of both military and economic power that she might be able to place them in a position in which their only chance of either security or prosperity would lie in cooperation with Germany on Germany's terms. As some of these nations have historic quarrels with one another, and as some of these quarrels have been perpetuated and embittered by the Peace Settlement of

1919, Germany might not find it difficult to play off her East European neighbors against one another: Czechoslovakia against Hungary, Hungary against Rumania, the Ukrainians against Poland, and perhaps even Jugoslavia against Italy. The minority situation in Italy and Poland today is not unlike that in Czechoslovakia before September. In each country there is both a German minority and one or more non-German minorities of a nationality which Germany might induce to make common cause with her, i.e., the Jugoslavs in Italy and the Ukrainians in Poland. This policy of setting her neighbors against one another could be pursued by Germany by way of support for the principle of national self-determination; and by liberating subject minorities she could weaken her stronger neighbors, while by respecting ethnic unities, as she seems now to be doing in Czechoslovakia, she would avoid driving any of these nationalities to complete despair and irreconcilable opposition to German ascendancy. If it is thus possible, as it seems to be, for Germany to gain most of her ends in Eastern Europe without ceasing to show substantial respect for national unity and autonomy, it would seem that she could in this way avoid arousing serious opposition.

Germany might also be able to find a common cause between herself and some of her East European neighbors in anti-Semitism, which is rife in Poland, Hungary, and Rumania as well as in Germany, and which now shows signs of breaking out in Czechoslovakia too. Another common interest to which she might successfully appeal in addressing herself to the people now in power in the East European countries is their desire for security from subversive movements from below. As the leader of an anti-Comintern front, Germany could present herself as the guarantor of the existing social and political order. In dealing with Italy and Poland, which would be the most restive of her associates, she might appeal to their common desire for colonial expansion. In order to consolidate her influence and control over Eastern Europe, Germany would no doubt make full use of the new technical facilities for propaganda and repression (e.g., the press, the cinema, the radio, the control over means of communication and discussion) which she is already using with such effect inside the Reich. In view of the dreadful nature of modern warfare at close range, together with the disparity of strength between Germany and even the strongest of her southern and eastern neighbors, these would be extremely reluctant to push to the point of armed conflict with Germany any resistance, either individual or collective, which they might attempt to make to the establishment of her ascendancy over them.

So much for the points in Germany's favor. But we can also see a number of obstacles to the establishment of German domination over Eastern Europe. . . .

It is questionable whether the German national temperament and political tradition (as seen in "Prussianism" as well as National Socialism) would be compatible with the establishment of German predominance in Central and Eastern Europe by the use of a minimum of force and a maximum of persuasion. Many of the arguments advanced in favor of German ability to control this area assume that Germany will in all cases be tactful and moderate; past history makes it very doubtful whether this condition can be fulfilled.

In estimating Germany's prospects in *Mittel-Europa*, we must also inquire into the solidity of the Berlin-Rome Axis. Manifestly Germany could not climb into the saddle in *Mittel-Europa* if the Axis were to give way beneath her feet. Italy today is in the unhappy position of being the weakest of the great powers in a world in which all great powers are on the verge of entering on an unlimited competition in rearmament. Will Italy's increasing relative weakness bind her more tightly than ever to her masterful German ally? Or will it drive her into some desperate effort to break loose, as a nominally equal partnership threatens to turn into a relationship rather resembling the present unequal relationship between Germany and Poland, or perhaps even that between Germany and the "new" Czechoslovakia?

It will be seen that, in trying to estimate Germany's prospect of establishing her ascendancy over Central, Eastern, and Southern Europe, we are groping in the realm of conjecture. At the present stage we can see some of the factors that tell respectively for Germany and against her, without being able to cast up the balance. In a situation of extreme uncertainty and obvious danger, it would, however, be imprudent for a country in the exposed position in which Great Britain finds herself today to shrink from reckoning with the more unpleasant and unfavorable of the alternative possibilities. Suppose, then, that Germany were to succeed, after all, in shaping to her purpose all that lies between France and Russia, Italy included; how would the two West European powers, Great Britain and France, stand in face of the new Central European Leviathan? A German-built and German-directed *Mittel-Europa*, in which more than 200 million efficient people of the white race would be organized under a single command for common purposes, would be a power of the order of politico-economic magnitude of the United States today and of the Soviet Union tomorrow (should no disaster overtake the Soviets in the meantime). In this new constellation of forces in Europe, what would be the outlook if there were a continuance of the present competition in armaments? We may hope to avert this calamity, but we cannot afford to ignore it. . . .

In September, after all, both the British and the French nations were willing in certain circumstances to go to war with Germany. There was a period of some days during which we believed that those circumstances were going to present themselves; war stared us in the face. Yet the inadequacy of our passive defenses did not drive us into dropping the "almost" out of our declared policy of "peace at almost any price." At the same time there can be no doubt that, if a similar crisis were to confront us at some future date after our passive defenses had been completed, we should be in a far better posture then than in September 1938 for dealing with the situation on its political and moral merits.

When we pass from the question of passive defense to that of active resistance, the prospects are much harder to assess; for active military strength is essentially competitive and relative; and a comparison between German and Anglo-French resources in this field is obscured by a number of unknown quantities. Our inquiry here almost reduces itself to a string of open questions. Are the metropolitan resources for the manufacture of armaments in Great Britain and France greater than those of Germany and Italy? Are the resources for the manufacture of armaments upon which Great Britain can draw overseas greater than those upon which Germany can draw in *Mittel-Europa*? It may be assumed that at present sea power helps Great Britain and hinders Germany in drawing resources from overseas. How far, however, has sea power been reduced by the development of aerial warfare? How far and how soon (if at all) could Germany, provided that she succeeded in dominating Europe, outbuild the British Navy while still retaining her predominance in the air and on land? Are the psychological factors favorable or adverse to Great Britain? Is a bigger return likely to be obtained from a system of regimentation or from one of voluntary service, assuming that both are developed to their fullest capacity? The question must also be asked how far Britain is prepared to go in the direction of regimentation if voluntary service should prove, on trial, to be incapable of competing with totalitarian methods.

Again, is Germany already approaching the point where she will be utilizing to the maximum her material and financial resources? And is she approaching the point where she will have made the fullest possible call upon the enthusiasm and the nervous energy of her people? Has Hitler, in securing satisfaction for German grievances, proportionately diminished the German people's willingness to go to war, or has he on the contrary increased his own prestige and given his people confidence for the pursuit of an aggressive policy? Is the division of opinion in Great Britain over the past and future conduct of foreign affairs likely to be as great a source of weakness as the latent opposition inside Germany and Italy to totalitarian methods of government?

Here again, we have run into a fog in which we cannot yet see beyond our noses. But taking together the two major problems of Germany's prospects of predominance in Central and southeastern Europe and the western powers' prospects of holding their own against her in the arms race, we can perhaps say that, in acquiescing in the Munich settlement, France and Britain avoided an immediate evil of appalling magnitude, for Europe as well as for themselves, at the price of accepting some very serious risks—which may or may not materialize in a future which is at present almost impenetrably veiled.

This raises the question of the reasons which made the peoples, as well as the governments, of Great Britain and France feel that the Munich terms represented the lesser of the two evils between which we had to choose.

The first and strongest reason was one which weighed with almost every man and woman in Great Britain and France during the crisis; and by implication this universal reason must be a simple one. While we had made up our minds to go to war if Herr Hitler insisted on imposing upon Czechoslovakia, by means of a military invasion, terms entirely dictated by Herr Hitler himself, there was perhaps no evil, short of that, which, to the minds of most of us, seemed greater than the evil of another European war under unprecedented moral and material conditions. The prospect of having one's wife and children, as well as oneself, massacred under one's own roof was one which the European householder had not had to look in the face since he had seen the last of the raids of the Vikings and the Magyars. In September 1938 that experience was nearly 1,000 years back in the past. "As safe as houses!" "The Englishman's house is his castle!" These proverbial phrases have an odd ring today.[1]

But the personal jeopardy to life, limb, and property was not the most appalling of the features which the prospect of a European war revealed. The individual, after all, has—or at any rate thinks, beforehand, that he has—a sporting chance of surviving even the most intensive aerial bombardment. The intolerable feature in the prospect was a disaster that was not a private probability but a public certainty. This certainty was that, if war did come, the things that we mean by "England," "France," and "Europe" would be destroyed beyond the possibility of restoration—not just the landscape and the buildings and the inhabitants, which could all, no doubt, at least theoretically, be replaced, but the invisible things of the spirit which are the essence of a community and a civilization. It has always been true that the spiritual ravages of war are more deadly than its material destructiveness. And when war

---

[1] An American or Canadian reader who wants to visualize to himself the meaning of air warfare between highly efficient powers in densely populated countries at point-blank range can assist his imagination by the simple device of plotting out, on a piece of tracing paper, a war map of Western Europe and then superimposing this on a peace map, drawn to the same scale, of the northeastern United States and the adjoining parts of Canada.

is keyed up—as it has been keyed up now—to a "totalitarian" pitch, it is the prospect of a "totalitarian" spiritual devastation that makes it morally almost impossible for civilized men and women to opt for war if there is any other alternative at all open to them. An acute personal realization of this prospect, in many millions of French and English souls, is the simple psychological explanation of the historical fact that, on their return home from Munich, Mr. Chamberlain and M. Daladier were welcomed by the general public with the same enthusiasm as were Herr Hitler and Signor Mussolini. At the moment of sudden relief there was even something like a European union of hearts, direct between people and people. The most striking outward manifestation of this astonishing psychological event was the German public's enthusiastic reception of the British prime minister.

The moral *impasse* with which the British and French peoples were confronted when they had to face the prospect of war with Germany in September 1938 comes to light in the question of the peace settlement. The peace settlement is the acid test of a war, since it is for the sake of achieving certain terms of peace that any war is fought; and, *ex hypothesi*, these terms must be of such supreme value and importance in the eyes of the belligerent as to make him feel that even a war is not too high a price to pay for obtaining them. This is eminently true if he is the citizen of a democratic state. For, in a democracy, the government can hardly venture to go to war unless it feels sure, in advance, that the people will be wholeheartedly behind it. Suppose then that in this autumn of 1938 war had broken out between Great Britain, France, the Little Entente, and the Soviet Union on the one side and Germany (with or without allies) on the other side; and suppose, further, that Germany had been defeated again, as completely as she was defeated in 1918; what would have been, this time, the Allied and associated powers' peace terms?

Should we, once again, have taken "national self-determination" for our watchword? In that case, we should have had, at the end of a victorious war, to impose on our ally Czechoslovakia, as her reward, that very cession of territories inhabited by alien minorities that is being imposed on her now, without a war, as her penalty for having had her frontiers drawn in the peace settlement of Paris on lines which were seriously at variance with the fundamental principle on which that imperfect peace settlement was professedly based. Or should we have maintained the *status quo?* But that would have meant getting the worst of both worlds. For *ex hypothesi* and *status quo,* as had been shown by nearly 20 years' experience of its working, neither squared with the principle of nationality nor on the other hand made Germany too weak to demand, at the sword's point, as she was actually demanding in September 1938, an application of the principle for her own benefit. As a matter of fact, it can be predicted almost with certainty that our peace terms would have been quite different from either of the two alternatives just suggested. For the character of peace terms is determined, as one knows, by the character of the antecedent war; and the European war of 1938 would have been dreadful beyond precedent and even beyond imagination. In all belligerent countries, almost everyone who was not a combatant would have become a refugee, and the refugees would have suffered the heavier casualties. In all countries the survivors' minds would have been rapidly reduced to one single fixed idea on the subject of peace terms: "If we win, then this time we must make it forever utterly impossible for the enemy to inflict this torment on us again." In this mood the victors would have imposed a Carthaginian peace. But of course we should have shuddered at the thought of such a peace settlement if we had contemplated it in advance before the bombing had begun. Short of contemplating anything of the kind, many of us who were acquainted with the nationality map of Czechoslovakia and with the political and economic situation in the German-inhabited districts of that state were feeling an acute moral discomfort at the notion of fighting for the balance of power in defiance of the principle of nationality. . . .

The principle of nationality—which first asserted itself in the modern world as a dynamic political force in 1775—has been steadily remaking the political map of the Old World, as well as the New World, ever since. In the nineteenth century it brought a Belgium, a Germany, and an Italy into existence. In the War of 1914–18 it broke up four great multinational empires in Eastern Europe. This wave has had, and still has, such an impetus that any statesmen or states that manage to ride it can be almost certain of being carried by it to triumph. It carried the Allied and associated powers to triumph in 1918; it has carried Germany to triumph in 1938. But how is it that, after 20 years, Herr Hitler has been able to steal President Wilson's thunder? The answer is that, in spite of our having made the armistice of November 1918 on the basis of the Fourteen Points, in the ensuing peace settlement we applied the principle of nationality for the benefit of every nation in Central and Eastern Europe with the exception of the three ex-enemy nations: the Germans, the Magyars, and the Bulgars. It is for the sake of getting that one-sided peace settlement rectified, by an application of the nationality principle for their own benefit too, that the Germans have accepted Hitler's leadership, or submitted to his tyranny, whichever way you prefer to put it. And by whichever name you do call Hitler, you cannot deny that he has fulfilled his mandate, however he may have acquired it, by "delivering the goods."

National unification is in fact being achieved in Central and Eastern Europe today by nations that, for the past 20 years, have been balked of it. This year ten million German ex-subjects of the defunct Hapsburg Monarchy have been incorporated into the German national state. Several hundred thousand Magyars, who were wrongfully detached from Hungary in 1921, are being restored to their mother country. Even the Ukrainians—who are the largest still wholly submerged nation in Europe—have at last secured home rule in that tiny corner of their vast patrimony that is known as "sub-Carpathian Ruthenia." These are all measures that ought to have been taken—and would have been taken, if our professed principles had been applied impartially—by "the Big Four" at Paris in 1919. Are we wholly to regret that a different "Big Four" have applied them belatedly in 1938 at Munich? In itself this surely cannot be a matter for regret; for nationality is commonly regarded as being a good principle as far as it goes. What we have to regret—and that most bitterly—is our failure to do justice all round at Paris in 1919; our subsequent failure to make good our sins of omission belatedly at any time within a subsequent period of nearly 20 years' grace; and, last and worst, the fact that, when we have at length acquiesced in justice being done in this particular respect at the fifty-ninth minute of the eleventh hour, our acquiescence wears the appearance of a capitulation, under an immediate threat of war, to a Nazi dictatorship.

An honest application of the principle of nationality was in any case bound to make Germany the strongest power in Europe for simple reasons that have been mentioned already. The Germans themselves are by far the most numerous nation in Europe, and they are flanked on the east by a bevy of nations which are conspicuously small and weak. For these two reasons in combination, a political map of Europe redrawn in accordance with the principle of nationality was bound to produce a *Mittel-Europa* under German hegemony. Part of the price of our sins of omission since the armistice of 1918 is that, instead of a democratic Germany entering into Germany's national heritage in 1920, this heritage has fallen to a Nazi Germany in 1938. Today Germany is the predominant power in Central and Eastern Europe, as sooner or later, seemingly, she was bound to be; but it is the tragedy of Europe, and of the whole world, that this now dominant Germany is not the Germany of Weimar but the Germany of Nuremberg. For when the principle of nationality is applied under a fanatical totalitarian régime, it ceases to be even approximately coincident with the more rational and more humane principle of self-determination. The measure of the difference is given by the number of non-Nazi German refugees for whom life in the Sudetenland has become impossible since September.

If a dominant Nazi Germany is the positive retribution for our sins, the negative retribution is the perhaps mortal sickness of the League of Nations. It is at first sight a paradoxical fact that a moment which sees the League to all appearance *in articulo mortis* should be the very moment that has also seen the practical realization, at long last, of two League principles which hitherto, unhappily, have been virtually dead letters. One of these principles is impartial justice for all. Well, we have got the principle of nationality in Central Europe applied to both sides equally at last, but the bitter irony is that nothing but the starkest power politics has availed to bring us to this, in itself desirable, result. The second League principle which has now at last secured application is that of "peaceful change." This autumn, populations amounting in the aggregate to as much as the total population of Ireland or Switzerland, and to more than the total population of Denmark or Norway, have been transferred from Czechoslovakian sovereignty to German, Hungarian, and Polish sovereignty without war. Though, of course, this has not been achieved without an extreme threat of war, it is nevertheless an unprecedented event; and it would be hard to say that it is not good. And yet the League seems to be dying of it. She is like a mother dying in childbirth because the birth is so long overdue.

Another ironical fact about the fate of the League is that the Japanese, Italian, and German hands that have struck the deadly blows share the blood-guiltiness with French, British, and American hands which have been professedly friendly. During the postwar years these American, British, and French hands held, between them, the destinies of the world in suspense. The three Western democratic great powers were then in a position to make the League's fortune if they chose. And what did they do? America abandoned the League in her infancy; France compromised the League by implicating her in a mischievous and futile system of anti-German power politics; while England—knowing that she ought both to guarantee France and to restrain her, yet not venturing to do either, and wishing that she might follow America into isolation, yet again not venturing to do that—has completed the discomfiture of the League by blowing alternately hot and cold, but almost always cold at the critical moments.

The worst of it is that the League is heir to the whole of our heritage of international cooperation; so that, if the League did die now, this heritage would be in mortal danger of perishing with her. It is true that the League is, in her most obvious aspect, an embodiment of President Wilson's ideas and that these ideas—at any rate in the form impressed upon them by the president's personal stamp—cannot lay claim to antiquity. But there are other aspects of the League which also catch a historian's eye. For instance, the League might be described alternatively as an instrument for "putting into commission" a rudimentary, but nevertheless genuine, *Pax Britannica*, based partly on naval power and partly on money power, which Great Britain maintained unaided, out of her own national resources, during the hundred years ending in 1914. This *Pax Britannica*, in its turn, was a very imperfect and belated substitute for a mediæval *Respublica Christiana* which was founded in the eleventh century by Pope Gregory VII and which went to pieces between the death of Pope Innocent III and the outbreak of the Reformation.

Today, perhaps more than at any other moment of history since our Western civilization emerged out of the Dark Ages, there is a crying need for some kind of world order. But if it is not to be a house built on the sands, this world order which we so urgently require must have some moral foundation. And what moral bond still holds between the armed, and ever more heavily arming, great powers of 1938? Common Christianity? Why, four of the great powers of the day—namely, Germany, Italy, Japan, and the Soviet Union—are avowedly dedicated to the worship of Leviathan, which is the most dangerous, as well as the most perverse, of the forms that idolatry can take. And the rest of us, if we are frank, will be constrained to confess that we honor our nominal Christianity more in the breach than in the observance. True religion may and will in the end win the hearts of mankind; but a work of conversion that must start almost from zero and that has the whole world for its field will necessarily take a proportionate length of time for its consummation. The establishment of some kind of world order is so urgent a need in an age of Leviathan worship and of bombing planes that mankind can hardly wait to see this need satisfied, as it might be ideally satisfied in the course of time, by the gradual triumph of Christianity.

The conversion of the modern world is therefore more likely to take place—like the conversion of the ancient world some 2,000 years back—within the framework of a provisional secular world order that will previously have been imposed by force, at the hands of some great pagan military power. As the history of the *Pax Romana* testifies, a world order of such pagan origin is unsatisfactory and ephemeral; but for a desperately urgent necessity, people will pay a heavy price. In Europe, at any rate, it seems not impossible that men and women, rather than see Europe perish, will now feel inclined to accept peace—as the Czechs have accepted it this autumn—in the form of a far-reaching submission to the harsh and brutal dictatorship that weighs, like a leaden cope, on the gigantic body of Germany.

There is one final string of questions which an Englishman today can hardly refrain from asking. In this crisis of human history, of which his own country has just felt the full force, what part are the non-European English-speaking peoples going to play? Is it true that a New World has been called into existence to redress the balance of the Old? Are the overseas countries now going to step into the breach and try to take a hand in building up our coming world order, in the hope of being able to give it, after all, something of their—and our—own democratic impress? Or are they going to recoil still further than at present into an isolation which can hardly avail to insulate them in the long run from that rising power in the Old World with which France and Great Britain, as well as Czechoslovakia, have already had to reckon? If a Greater Germany were eventually to make it her drill sergeant's mission to put the world in Prussian order by imposing on us all her *Pax Hitleriana,* what line would North America then take? Would she then seek, in Mr. Chamberlain's way, to come to terms with the Nazi power, or would she take Mr. Churchill's line of bidding Nazidom defiance? And if she, in her turn, found herself at grips with greater Germany, what then would be North America's attitude towards Great Britain? Would she think of British sea power as an asset to be preserved? Or of the British Empire as an entanglement to be avoided? These are burning questions for an English writer to ask and for American and Canadian readers to answer.

Pacifism and Democracy

Julien Benda

JULY 1941

IN ALL COUNTRIES there are democrats who maintain that a democratic state must, because it is democratic, refuse any kind of war—a war of defense just as much as a war of conquest. Their thesis is that a democracy must abstain from any international action which is liable to cause war. In short, it must be for peace at any price.

Those who take this position do not always say so frankly. They are embarrassed to admit that they refuse even a defensive war. They therefore claim that what is being presented to them as a defensive war is really an offensive war, planned by politicians or industrialists who expect to derive power or profits from having men kill one another. I once asked one of them whether he thought that the Greeks were right to have stood out against Xerxes rather than become his Helots. He did not reply. If he had stuck to his thesis he would have had to answer that they acted wrongly. Not long ago a citizen of a certain great democracy exclaimed: "This policy of our president means that we shall have war, and one out of every four of our sons will be killed." He should have been told that his own policy meant that all four of them risked becoming slaves. Maybe subconsciously he really preferred this prospect; but he probably would not have admitted it, even to himself.

Others are more outspoken. They endorse a slogan which a group of French socialists adopted a few years ago: "Servitude rather than war!" Or one that we used to hear from certain French intellectuals: "In our eyes *nothing* justifies war." In most cases this position is based simply on a desire to avoid fighting, camouflaged as well as possible under doctrinal reasons. The desire is normal enough, and especially today, when war has become the thing we know it to be and when the whole nation is involved in it. Sometimes, however, the position is based on sincere ideological convictions. Those who adopt it often are veterans of the last war. It is the position of these perfectly sincere people which we shall consider here, particularly the ones who maintain that the theory of peace at any price is an integral part of the definition of democracy.

DEMOCRACY'S "HIGHEST GOOD"

THE MISTAKE of thinking that peace at any price has anything to do with democracy comes from a confusion of essential values. It is imagined that democracy's paramount concern is human life, whereas it is human liberty. Human life deprived of liberty is worthless. Therefore the democrat, in order to preserve the advantages of democracy for his children, admits and sancti-fies the sacrifice of life. Over and over again in the course of history, democracy has proved this to be its supreme law. If our pacifists were consistent, they would have to condemn the French revolutionaries who were willing to shed human blood to win their liberties and the Americans who preferred war to remaining the servants of George III. As a matter of fact, some of them do. The question is how they can then pretend to be democrats.

They should meditate the words of George Washington, who was not a bad democrat. In his farewell address he weighed the advantages, in various circumstances, of neutrality and did not hesitate to say that "we may choose peace or war, as our interest, guided by justice, shall counsel." We shall be told in reply that war has become something very different from what it was in 1796. But the question of principle has not become different.

The mistake also arises from a confusion between the *fact* of war and the *love* of war. Democracy may accept the one and condemn the other. War may be imposed upon men who have no love for it whatsoever. The ideal of democracy is, certainly, to suppress the fact of war. But the effective way to attain this goal is to hold in check the people who worship war. This entails accepting the fact of war, under the democratic slogan "war on war."

SAVING PEACE AND ESTABLISHING PEACE

THERE IS A distinction, though it is scarcely ever made, between *saving* peace and *establishing* peace. To save peace is to ward off war in some particular moment of great excitement. There is no leading motive, no general idea. To establish peace is to act deliberately to prevent war in accordance with a thought-out plan, in a time when no particular fear of war exists because those who might wish to disturb the peace have been temporarily deprived of the power to do so. At Munich in 1938 the British and French ministers saved peace. We all know that they did not establish it. At Versailles, the victors of 1918 were in a position to establish peace, maybe because four years earlier they had been willing not to save it.

Two profoundly distinct conceptions of peace are here involved. According to one, peace is based on respect for contracts between nations and on sanctions against violators. This is the *legal* conception. The other, the *sentimental* conception, expects love between men to bring about peace, all idea of contracts or sanctions aside. The first conception puts justice before peace, or at least states that it is respect for justice which must bring peace. This is displeasing to the sentimentalists who, naturally, place love above justice. At the time of the Italo-Ethiopian war, the Archbishop of Canterbury startled some persons by declaring that he, a churchman, favored the use of sanctions against the aggressor. When told that sanctions were liable to cause war, he answered: "My ideal is not peace, but justice." He was only repeating the words of his divine Master: "I came not to send peace, but a sword," i.e., to make war against evil.

A few examples of the purely sentimental conception of peace might help my readers to measure its intellectual worth.

A famous author, I read recently, was visiting in the Engadine. As he stood looking at the landscape, he uttered some words which were much admired by the newspaperman who reported them. "Facing so much beauty," he said, "how is it possible not to think that men ought to love and not hate one another!" Laments of this sort seem to me quite childish. Men should be loved when they deserve to be loved, when they show justice and loyalty and respect for the rights of others. I am under no compulsion to love them when they violate elementary rules of moral conduct. Instead, I have to protect myself from them—even if, later on, I try to change them. Landscapes have nothing to do with it. . . .

Again, many of my readers probably saw a film depicting the wife of a German peasant who had been killed in the war giving a kind welcome to an escaped French prisoner. She lets him stay in her house several weeks and watches him depart with regret. The film's name, *Grande Illusion*, obviously was chosen to show the error of believing that war between nations implies hatred between peoples. But this question is not related to the question whether or not France in 1914 was right to resist the German invasion. . . .

NOT DEMOCRATS, BUT ANARCHISTS

ONE OF THE ways the absolute pacifists have of arguing is to challenge their opponents: "You call yourself a democracy, that is, a government of the people by the people, and yet you send me to war without consulting me, in spite of myself." Thus we find a character in Roger Martin du Gard's book *The Thibaults* declaring that if the French people had been consulted in 1914, 80 percent of them would have rejected war. This statement rests upon the hope—apparently justified, I must admit—that most men, even in most democracies, still have so little political education that, if consulted individually, they will refuse to make the sacrifices necessary for the preservation of the whole. Now it is arguable that no true democracy as yet exists—in the sense of being completely a government of the people and by the people. But is not the reason precisely because men find such difficulty in forgetting their individual conveniences in favor of the collective good? If they were consulted separately, how many citizens would offer spontaneously to pay taxes? Yet even "absolute democrats" probably admit that taxes are indispensable for the state.

"Absolute democrats" also contend not only that there should be a referendum on war, but that only those who voted "yes" should then have to go to war. This is a denial of national solidarity. Yet such people certainly accept some of the advantages of national solidarity. If they are civil servants, for example, they want to be paid salaries which some (perhaps many) of their fellow citizens might, if they were consulted, refuse to grant. If they are interested in art, they might find that many taxpayers, consulted in the same way, would veto appropriations to maintain the museums. The fact is that these intellectuals would be more truthful—or, let us say, more enlightened about their own natures—if instead of pretending to be pure democrats they called themselves pure individualists or pure anarchists.

Another sophistry often is uttered in the name of democracy. It consists in rejecting even a defensive war on the ground that it will require the surrender of full powers to the governing body and that this surrender will spell "the end of democracy." They forget that among the basic democratic principles it is formally inscribed that in exceptional circumstances a nation may grant full powers to the governing body. During its famous meeting of September 9, 1793, the Convention declared that it accepted the idea of dictatorship for times of crisis. This doctrine meant, of course, that popular control would be suspended only temporarily and that it would be restored as soon as the emergency had passed. "Revolutionary France," says the historian Mathiez, "would never have accepted the dictatorship of the Convention if she had not been convinced that victory was impossible without the suspension of her liberty."

Two occurrences in French history show democracy accepting dictatorial powers because it is necessary and discarding them as soon as the necessity is past—the rise and fall of Robespierre and the rise and fall of Clemenceau. The fall of each occurred when victory was at hand and the danger which the dictatorship had been created to repel seemed safely over. I say "seemed" because France was far from being out of danger on November 11, 1918, and it would have been better for the country if the war government had continued for a while longer.

FORCE, BUT FOR JUSTICE

THERE IS still another side to the argument of the "absolute democrats." They say that when democracy resorts to force it denies its essential character and becomes similar to the very systems which it affects to despise. This is a formalist argument. It forgets that one can inquire on whose behalf force is to be used. To use force on behalf of justice is not the same thing as to use it for aggression. This being so, the democratic system which uses force for justice cannot be assimilated to opposite systems which use force for aggression.

There also seems to be a widespread conception that democracy is a sort of celestial body, aloof and, by definition, scornful of mundane necessities of self-defense. This idea, like the total condemnation of force regardless of the purpose for which it is used, plays straight into the hands of those who wish to use force for aggression. It thus becomes itself an agent of immorality.

At the bottom of these erroneous conceptions of democracy we discern what some would call a Christian idea, namely that it is the fit and necessary lot of the righteous to be weak and to suffer. If the righteous ever becomes strong enough to demand justice, apparently he ceases, for this school of thought, to be righteous. If Socrates had resisted his executioners, for example, he would no longer symbolize righteousness. Carry the argument one step further, and it will be the executioners who, having become the victims, incarnate righteousness. This obviously was the sort of feeling which obsessed many persons in 1918, when a violent nation had at last been compelled to cease from violence and listen to reason.

In such matters, democratic doctrine, like the doctrine of one great school of Catholic thought, considers that the righteous are entitled to "the right of the sword" when they use it in a just cause and without regard for personal profit. Democracy merely remains true to its dogma when it reminds absolute pacifists that there are angels who go armed and that because Lohengrin draws his sword and strikes the felon down, he is not thereby any the less Lohengrin and has not become Attila.

Pascal said: "Justice without force is powerless." I should like to add: "It is essential for democracy that justice shall have power so long as there are men determined to ignore it." Contrary to those who pretend that, by very reason of its democratic principle, the democratic state must be deprived of arms, I contend that by very reason of its democratic principle it must be better armed than any other state in order that it may be respected by states which might otherwise be tempted to ignore justice and strike across its borders.

HOW ABSOLUTE PACIFISM EVADES THE ISSUE

TO BE consistent, nonresisters must accept the prospect that their country may be annihilated. André Gide wonders: "What would have happened in 1914 if France had offered no resistance to Germany?" Everyone knows what would have happened. When he says that France would have been invincible if she had used only spiritual force against Germany instead of opposing force to force, he forgets to inform his fellow citizens that there is nothing incompatible between the "invincibility" which he speaks of and the erasure of their country from the map.[1]

Others go even further and find that nonresistance to evil is a practical doctrine, the only one which will bring peace to the world. Tolstoi in his *Intimate Diary* says that when a wall stands up to blows it causes the aggression to continue, whereas if it gives in it "absorbs the movement" and causes it to stop. By analogy, war would be suppressed if people never resisted any group which was greedy to expand at their expense. Tolstoi omits, however, to tell us that in "absorbing the movement" the wall ceases to exist, that is to say, loses its life, which, oddly enough, it might wish to keep.

NON-INTERVENTION

IT IS absolutely contrary to the democratic ideal to watch from a distance, without interfering, while a strong nation crushes a weaker one and deprives it of its liberty. Non-intervention may be forced upon democracies because they happen not to be strong enough to give material help to the nation which is being abused and oppressed. But if they are true to themselves, they must deplore their weakness and inertia. To some extent they must feel disgraced, as a European minister felt disgraced when, in answer to a call for help from a small country whose independence was being threatened, he replied: "*Flere possumus, juvare non.*" To set up non-intervention as a principle, to feel almost proud of it, is to undermine democratic morality. Selfishness may be a necessity. It cannot be a democratic dogma.

A democracy which rejects the idea of intervention usually declares that it has adopted this attitude in order to "save peace." The truth is that its pas-

---

[1] "Journal," pp. 1320–21. The author adds that though Germany "could swallow France, she could not have digested her." There are no grounds for this assertion. Moreover, it is a most cruel experience merely to be swallowed.

siveness encourages the aggressor. He not only attacks the state which has appealed in vain for help, but some day he will perpetrate an act which even the laggard democracy cannot condone and which therefore causes war a second time. Thus the war of 1914 was brought on by the inertia of the democratic governments which did not care to interfere with Austria in Bosnia-Herzegovina in 1908. A statesman of one of the central empires told us in 1920: "It is you who were responsible for the war. You yielded to us for so many years that you led us to think that we could do anything with impunity." It is unnecessary to cite more recent examples.

It is not by accident that those who disturb the peace of the world are almost always the heads of autocratic states. A man who mocks ordinary standards of justice at home sees no reason to act differently abroad. For that reason democracy should be prepared to intervene within a foreign state when its head flagrantly violates the rights of his people. This is what Mr. Herbert Morrison, a member of the British Parliament, meant when he said on November 27, 1939: "We must cling to an ideal of government, whatever its actual form, as something which exists to serve peoples and not to dominate them; and we must remember that this is no mere internal question, since the governments which dominate at home are often the peace-breakers abroad." In the past few years the democracies have usually refrained from this kind of intervention. But their course has not been determined, as some would like to have us believe, out of regard for democratic principle, but simply because democracy has come to worship peace and quiet. So far as I know, there is no principle inscribed in its statutes providing for, or excusing, that form of worship.

OF "DEMOCRATIC ANTIMILITARISM"

ANOTHER ASPECT of the pacifist democracy which we are here discussing is that democrats often display a sort of systematic hostility to their country's military institutions. They haggle over the number of men there ought to be in the army, the number of years they should serve, how much money should be voted to cover their expenses. They claim that this "antimilitaristic" attitude suits the real spirit of democracy.

In a true democracy the military element should be subordinate to the civilian. Once this principle has been established, we need merely see to it that the military machine is powerful enough to perform its tasks and so to enable the democratic state to survive. One looks in vain through the great declarations of democratic principle, in any time or country, for a single text advocating a weak army. There are plenty of statements about the ideal future world in which this kind of institution will no longer be required. But there is no statement that makes weakness a virtue. Once again we find that an idea which never had any connection with democracy has been added to its concept and has falsified it.

We saw in France, a few years ago, what harm the doctrine of peace at any price can do to democracy. Its devotees maintained that the best defense against a neighbor's greed was disarmament. They even went so far as to advocate a general strike in case war came. Recently in several countries the enemies of democracy exploited the doctrine of peace at any price in order to prevent a war which, though necessary for the salvation of the state, menaced the interests of their particular class. In France men of this sort, who for years had berated the working class for their pacifism, suddenly found that same pacifism beautiful and called on labor to oppose the war which lay ahead.

Pacifism, in the sense I have described it here, is a parasite on democracy. It has nothing to do with democratic doctrine. Democracy must repudiate it.

The Critic Turns Actor

James B. Reston

OCTOBER 1945

THE UNITED STATES has changed overnight from the role of observer at international conferences to the role of leader. After sitting in the stalls for 25 years complaining about the play, the players, the music, and the general confusion, we have suddenly been shoved up on the stage and given the opportunity to help name the play, direct the music, and pick some (though definitely not all) of the players.

Fortunately, before the war ended, we had a little practice in the new role. We ran the Food and Agriculture Conference at Hot Springs, the first session of the UNRRA Council at Atlantic City, the Monetary and Financial Conference at Bretton Woods, the Civil Aviation Conference at Chicago, the preparatory security conference at Dumbarton Oaks, and the United Nations Security Conference at San Francisco.

Like all ingénues, we had our troubles. At Hot Springs we opened the play before either we or the cast were ready, and we surrounded the theater with military police and kept the critics out of hearing distance. At Bretton Woods, we were pretty good to the critics. We not only let them in to hear the play but let them wander around backstage where they could see the wheels and pulleys and all the professional tricks; but we didn't get all our own players together for a rehearsal before the opening night, and we neither prepared for enough guests nor had adequate facilities for those we expected.

At the Chicago Air Conference, the other players got the impression that we hogged the stage, gave out our own version of what was going on, and generally messed things up until, in the closing days, with astonishing abruptness, we fired our leading man (in this case Adolph Berle) and sent both the audience and some of the players home wondering if we were ever going to become professional.

Finally, at San Francisco, we got a good theater, learned our lines pretty well, struggled through a somewhat noisy and unruly first act, but came out in the end with more prestige and experience than we had had before.

As the location of these performances indicates—Hot Springs, Bretton Woods, Washington, Atlantic City, San Francisco—we have, of course, been touring the provinces. The big show is now coming on. The war is ended. The rehearsals are over. We are moving into the "big time." The action now will be concerned not with machinery but with life. Mistakes now will not simply mar the structure of an organization or affect the prestige of individuals or of nations; they will settle the question of life or death for millions.

What have we learned, first as observer and then as ingénue? What mistakes have we made which we might be able to correct? Might we not be able to use up our good players less prodigally? Where are we going in this new role?

II

WE HAVE learned, in part at least, some of the lessons of 1919. We have learned, for example, not to try to crowd too much into one big peace conference. The statesmen at Versailles tried to deal simultaneously with all the complex and controversial questions of boundaries, reparations, colonies, relief, and collective security. This time, even before we have called a peace conference, we have established our league of nations, set up an international bank and an economic and social council to deal with the economic causes of war, created an international relief organization, determined the principles which will guide our treatment of the defeated nations, and, with varying degrees of efficiency, created organizations to deal with food, labor, health, and social problems. In addition, we have reached an understanding with some of our Allies about certain boundaries—those of Poland and Finland, for example.

Secondly, we have learned how to recruit some of our players. We have achieved at least a basis for understanding among our two major political parties on the broad objectives of our foreign policy, and we have proved beyond any shadow of a doubt that McKinley's practice of taking representatives of the Senate along as members of the American delegation to international conferences was right and that Wilson's decision not to take them along undoubtedly helped lose him the necessary support of the United States Senate. . . .

We also sought and found other methods of insuring support for American action at these conferences in addition to seeking the aid of representatives of the United States Senate. For example, we learned that to take along to San Francisco as "consultants" the representatives of the most influential nonpolitical trade, religious, research, labor, and farm organizations also broadened the general understanding of the administration's policy and facilitated its acceptance. Their presence at San Francisco induced conviction, and their conviction produced support throughout the country which was reflected in the overwhelming ratification of the charter in the Senate.

These are points of advance which will be understood by our own people perhaps better than by nations which do not have our sharp separation between the authority of the legislative and executive branches of government. However, those of our Allies who remember what happened to the League of Nations under the two-thirds rule of the Senate will not be inclined to dismiss them as mere technicalities.

In other respects, too, we have shown progress in the conferences held in this country before the end of the war. For a nation which not only has no widely accepted tradition of civil service but which sometimes acts as if there were something distasteful about public service as such, we did remarkably well in getting together at San Francisco a secretariat capable of making all the complex physical arrangements for such a conference; and, after a slow start, this secretariat functioned extremely well in getting out the heavy paperwork of the conference. Also, we showed at both the Inter-American Conference in Mexico City late in the winter and at San Francisco in the spring a capacity for improvising and compromising in extremely difficult political situations.

But all this having been said, it must be added that it is not good enough, these days, to prove that we have done better than we did in 1919, that we have made progress in solving some of the domestic aspects of the conduct of our foreign affairs, and that we have retained our democratic capacity for improvising and compromising. For the problems confronting us now are obviously much more complex than they were in 1919, and we failed so miserably then and must do so much better this time that the comparison loses most of its meaning.

Furthermore, we have not learned all the lessons of the last peace conference; and some of the lessons that we have learned have been put to good use at some conferences and ignored at others; and sometimes, even in the same conference, we have carried out sound principles with regard to one important question and violated them with regard to the next. This needs to be illustrated because it is the heart of the problem and suggests certain points of interest for the future.

III

JUST BEFORE the Versailles Conference, some of the best minds in diplomacy tried to suggest a few simple rules of conduct, most of them dealing with the necessity of preparing for the conference in detail before it was called, arranging a careful agenda for it ahead of time, and sticking rigidly to that agenda. They are just as applicable now as they were then.

The French ambassador in Washington in 1919, M. Jusserand, for example, wrote a careful memorandum on this subject for the Supreme Council, in which he proposed that a set of preliminary terms be imposed on the defeated enemy, drew up a sort of priority list of problems facing the Big Four of that time, and prepared an agenda for the conference.

Even before M. Jusserand put his precise Latin mind to work on this problem, Sir Ernest Satow, one of the best authorities on diplomatic procedure of the day, wrote an admirable little book on the lessons of previous peace conferences for the British peace conference delegation, and urged them, above all things, to prepare carefully, to agree on the purpose and procedure of the conference, and to stick to their agreed formula. "Experience demonstrates," Sir Ernest wrote, "that, in order to ensure the success of a Congress or Conference, a distinct basis or bases ought to be agreed upon beforehand; and the greater the definiteness with which the main points of the basis are formulated beforehand, the greater is the likelihood of a general agreement being reached. In past history, when Congresses failed to attain a definite result, the failure was generally due to the ground not having been adequately prepared beforehand."

The Big Four rejected these suggestions, partly because they suffered from the great man's weakness for relying too much on his own abilities and partly because Mr. Wilson did not like M. Jusserand's curt, if accurate, description of the Fourteen Points. At any rate, when the conference was over, Colonel House, after long reflection, concluded that "the great fault of the political leaders was their failure to draft a plan of procedure."

It cannot be said that we have ignored this advice. The very fact that so many conferences were held before the fighting ended demonstrates the improvement in our preparation for this peace. Wilson wrote the first draft of the League Covenant after the last war while he was en route to Versailles, whereas first the Moscow Declaration and then the United Nations Charter began to be formulated by a special advisory committee in the State Department in 1942, and the Dumbarton Oaks proposals were published over six months before the end of the German war. Again, there was a preliminary conference of the major powers at Atlantic City to arrange a basis of agreement for the Bretton Woods Conference just such as had been suggested by Jusserand and Satow at the end of the last war. In other respects, also, the principle of careful preparation has been carried out by our public officials, often in collaboration with specialists from outside the government, recruited for the purpose.

But while conceding that preparation must always be a relative thing and that we have made great strides toward learning the lessons of past conferences, one must also admit that we certainly have not learned the lesson of the necessity of preparation as fully as we might. . . .

Improvisation was not perhaps as common at San Francisco as it appeared. Our delegation had not expected the Russians to raise the question of bringing in the Ukraine and White Russia as members of the Conference. President Roosevelt at Yalta had simply agreed to electing them eventually as members of the future world organization. We had agreed with the Latin American states, also, to keep the Argentine question out until the later stages of the conference. But in the circumstances of the moment, we decided to support Argentina's admission to the conference for a variety of reasons, some connected with the demands of Soviet Russia regarding the admission of the Ukraine and White Russia, some connected with the politics of this hemisphere, some connected with the prestige of our officials. Later, of course, we at least had the good judgment to wish that we had been more loyal to our original agenda than to the emotions of the moment.

On several occasions, no doubt, we have improvised successfully. There was, for example, no agreement before the San Francisco Conference on a trusteeship system for the new league of nations. One was worked out there, largely through the diligence of Harold Stassen; and while limited in many respects, it represents an advance over the old League mandate system.

But more often than not, when we have improvised the results have not been satisfactory. At San Francisco we improvised in the selection of committee chairmen, choosing them by country instead of as individuals. As a result, some of the committees worked well because the chairmen were excellent, while others were a tedious scramble. We foresaw the language problem at Bretton Woods, and consequently the proceedings there were conducted with a minimum of translations, and committees were able to function smoothly. But we went to San Francisco prepared to translate documents into three languages and finally decided to translate into five. This necessitated fundamental changes in the organization of the secretariat. We also agreed to translate all committee speeches not only into French but into Spanish as well, which turned the committee meetings into a series of prolonged translations and made deliberative study of questions extremely laborious. Some difficulty on this score cannot, of course, be avoided, but considering the technical efficiency of this country, there is nothing to prevent our doing what was done at Geneva, namely, having earphones at every committee chair and translators speaking from booths as the speaker addresses the committee. In this way, each member can plug in on the translator he wishes, and the tempo of the proceedings and the understanding of the delegates are improved.

At almost every one of the conferences held in this country, the problem of dealing with the press and radio correspondents has been improvised from one crisis to the next. It is a strange fact that the United States, which has elevated public relations into something between a science and philosophy, should find it so difficult to produce officials who can deal effectively with the press at an international conference. Yet it is generally conceded that this is a fact.

Admittedly, the problem presented is a tough one. Under our constitution the press is given a freedom which is little short of license. Certainly, too, it is true that we have our quota of reporters and commentators who either expect everything to be handed to them without any "digging" on their part or who find it more convenient (and unfortunately more profitable) to move in a realm of dogmatic opinion, unencumbered by too many ascertained facts.

At San Francisco it was also true that the sheer bulk of over fifteen hundred accredited "correspondents" was overwhelming and that the handling of them was a terrible responsibility. Many of them were merely there to see the San Francisco show through the courtesy of some benevolent publisher. Others represented official news agencies or government organs and consequently were "reporting" not so much to the public at home as to their officials and were asking questions not in order to seek the views of the speaker but to propagate the views of the principals to whom they themselves really were responsible.

But all this is merely another argument against improvising our press relations at international conferences. Our officials are well aware of the habits of American newspapermen. Yet they establish machinery to deal with the press as they would like it to be rather than as it is. Thus, they knew before the San Francisco conference started that the major decisions there would be taken in the meetings of the sponsoring nations. What they did not take account of was that because of this fact, the American press would concentrate on the meetings of the Big Five rather than on the committee and commission meetings of the conference, which dealt with major questions only after the Big Five had dealt with them in Secretary Stettinius' penthouse in the Fairmont Hotel. American officials thought the press should wait to report and comment on the decisions of the Big Five until they had been transmitted to the whole conference. They therefore did not make adequate provision to release information from the Big Five meetings. The consequence was, as any working reporter could have told them, that the news "leaked" out of the Big Five into the newspapers before it ever got to the rest of the Conference. The official press organization attached to the conference secretariat was very seldom the source of any real news.

Now some members of the press undoubtedly are inclined to underestimate the difficulties there would be in persuading the Russians, and even the British, to give out the news currently as it develops at international conferences. But it also seems to be true that our officials often cite those difficulties as an excuse for their own failure to work out an adequate press policy for the newspapers and the radio.

For example, at Dumbarton Oaks, Mr. Stettinius was persuaded that if he allowed the press to have any more access to the conference than they had (which was virtually none), the Russians would walk out—a view which, if true, does not bode well for the future of the security organization, but which, fortunately, few others who were at that conference support. At San Francisco, the press was promised a "liberal" policy. This turned out to be access to the plenary sessions, where nothing of great significance happened, and to the commission meetings, which did not meet until all the important decisions had been taken in the committee meetings. When the committee chairmen felt like it, of course, they would come down and report to the press on what had happened or, more accurately, on that part of the developments which they thought the reporters were entitled to know. The fact remains, however, that there really were two conferences going on at San Francisco: the conference of The Five and the conference of The Rest. The vital decisions were being taken in the meetings of the former, but as noted above, no adequate provision was made to advise the public regarding them.

Fortunately, even the regulations supporting the system of secrecy were improvised and finally broke down. When this happened and it was found— as it is almost always found—that the policy of secrecy breeds the very atmosphere of rumor and suspicion which officials seek to avoid, the system was finally modified and attempts were made to "leak out" to the reliable reporters some of the current developments of the conference.

The problem of determining what is said to the press of the world by governments with vastly different political and social systems is, of course, one of the most difficult the major Allies have to deal with. Volumes might be written about it. For the purposes of this article, only one or two observations need to be made.

The first is that unless the conference is held in a compound, as at Potsdam, the policy of secrecy does not work. It does not work because, at a full-dress conference, the information has necessarily to be very widely disseminated, and too many people do not believe in the policy of secrecy and do not abide by rules they consider unnecessary.

The second is that the problem will never be solved until the presence of the press is looked upon by the conference officials as an opportunity rather than a nuisance. Admittedly, delicate negotiations cannot be carried on in the headlines of the world's press; the London Poles were the last to try it and with melancholy results. But that does not mean that far more facts and background material on the matters under discussion cannot be released during conferences than is habitually the case. After all, on the general understanding of the people the success of these conferences will eventually depend.

The reason for some of the mistakes made at conferences is not difficult to find. In the first place, the planning for each conference has usually been done by a different official. In the case of Bretton Woods, the Treasury and the State Department fought for control; the planning for the Mexico City conference was done by the assistant secretary of state in charge of Latin American affairs; the preparations for San Francisco were in still different hands.

Thus, the promising American ingénue has not progressed from one play to the next, gathering experience and strength at each performance. What we have been doing is giving one group experience at one conference, then scattering it and calling in a new company for the next performance. This prodigal turnover of personnel in the American delegations is true not only at the level of civilian advisers and assistant secretaries but at the very top as well. Since the Dumbarton Oaks Conference ended, we are now operating through our third secretary of state. This means that another new team, minus a great deal of the experience picked up by other men in the past two years, will carry much of the burden in the forthcoming discussions and conferences, including the vital conferences of the five foreign secretaries at which the peace treaties with the vanquished enemy states are to be written.

The lessons of the conferences which have been held to date are nevertheless there to be observed, and they have just as much validity whether the team is old or new. One of these lessons is that, now that the fighting has ceased, these conferences furnish one of the major means by which we can hope to grope forward toward the necessary understanding between Russia and the West. Another lesson is that the difficulty of reaching an understanding with Russia only emphasizes the need for the most careful preparation before undertaking discussions with her. For it is already clear from our experience of the past two years that we cannot "explore" a question with the Russians as we can do with the British or the French. The Russian does not like to sit down and "think out loud" or "exchange views." He tends to look on this pleasant, if casual, Western habit with suspicion and thinks that we ought to come to conferences prepared to negotiate on the basis of a fixed policy, more or less as he thinks he does (though actually, of course, this doesn't always turn out to be the case).

We have made great progress since 1919. But it is not enough for us merely to be better now than we were then. The problems this time are so much more complex that any comparison with last time really has very little meaning. This time peace is not going to be decreed in a final peace conference. Peace will be attained, if attained it is, not by an act but through a process. Nor should the peace be planned, if it is to last, by a very few men, as was the case with the preparatory decisions taken at Casablanca, Teheran, Quebec, Yalta, and Potsdam. It should be thought through, with all the expert help available and all the careful documentation procurable, by the men who have to negotiate it; and it should be negotiated, with as full publicity as possible, by the men who will have to operate it. For the peace will be not an arrangement merely between governments but between peoples, and they must understand and support it if it is to last. These premises are accepted by most of our officials intellectually; they should be accepted by them as guides to action also.

The Challenge
to Americans

Henry L. Stimson

OCTOBER 1947

WE AMERICANS TODAY face a challenging opportunity, perhaps the greatest ever offered to a single nation. It is nothing less than a chance to use our full strength for the peace and freedom of the world. This opportunity comes when many of us are confused and unready. Only two years ago we triumphantly ended the greatest war in history. Most of us then looked forward eagerly to the relative relaxation of peace. Reluctantly we have now come to understand that victory and peace are not synonymous. Over large areas of the world we have nothing better than armed truce; in some places there is open fighting; everywhere men know that there is yet no stable settlement. Close on the heels of victory has loomed a new world crisis.

Particularly to Americans, the appearance of disquieting facts and possibilities has been upsetting. We are having our first experience of constant, full-scale activity in world politics. Other nations have lived for years as principals in the give-and-take of diplomacy. Until now we have been, except in wartime, on the fringe. It is no wonder that, when suddenly placed in the center of the alarms and excursions of international affairs, we are abnormally sensitive. And, of course, it does not help to find ourselves selected as chief target for the abuse and opposition of a very bad-mannered group of men who take their orders from the Kremlin. It is not surprising, then, that many of us are confused and unhappy about our foreign relations, and that some are tempted to seek refuge from their confusion either in retreat to isolationism or in suggested solutions whose simplicity is only matched by their folly. In the main, our difficulties arise from unwillingness to face reality.

It must be admitted that the elements of the new unrest appear to be unusually complex and trying. The war-shattered world must be rebuilt; the problem of atomic energy insistently demands solution; the present policy of

Russia must be frustrated. But it is my belief that the American people have it well within their power to meet and resolve all of these problems. The essential test is one of will and understanding. . . .

II

FIRST, AND most important, Americans must now understand that the United States has become, for better or worse, a wholly committed member of the world community. This has not happened by conscious choice; but it is a plain fact, and our only choice is whether or not to face it. For more than a generation the increasing interrelation of American life with the life of the world has outpaced our thinking and our policy; our refusal to catch up with reality during these years was the major source of our considerable share of the responsibility for the catastrophe of World War II.

It is the first condition of effective foreign policy that this nation put away forever any thought that America can again be an island to herself. No private program and no public policy, in any sector of our national life, can now escape from the compelling fact that if it is not framed with reference to the world, it is framed with perfect futility. This would be true if there were no such thing as nuclear fission and if all the land eastward from Poland to the Pacific were under water. Atomic energy and Soviet Russia are merely the two most conspicuous present demonstrations of what we have at stake in world affairs. The attitude of isolationism—political or economic—must die; in all its many forms the vain hope that we can live alone must be abandoned.

As a corollary to this first great principle, it follows that we shall be wholly wrong if we attempt to set a maximum or margin to our activity as members of the world. The only question we can safely ask today is whether in any of our actions on the world stage we are doing enough. In American policy toward the world there is no place for grudging or limited participation, and any attempt to cut our losses by setting bounds to our policy can only turn us backward onto the deadly road toward self-defeating isolation.

Our stake in the peace and freedom of the world is not a limited liability. Time after time in other years we have tried to solve our foreign problems with halfway measures, acting under the illusion that we could be partly in the world and partly irresponsible. Time after time our presidents and secretaries of state have been restrained, by their own fears or by public opinion, from effective action. It should by now be wholly clear that only failure, and its follower, war, can result from such efforts at a cheap solution.

We have fresh before us the contrary example of our magnificent success in wartime, when we have not stopped to count the cost. I have served as secretary of state in a time of frightened isolationism and as secretary of war in a time of brave and generous action. I know the withering effect of limited commitments, and I know the regenerative power of full action. I know, too, that America can afford it—as who does not know it, in the face of our record in the last seven years?

It is altogether fitting and proper, of course, that we should not waste our substance in activity without result. It is also evident that we cannot do everything we would like to do. But it would be shriveling timidity for America to refuse to play to the full her present necessary part in the world. And the certain penalty for such timidity would be failure.

The troubles of Europe and Asia are not "other people's troubles"; they are ours. The world is full of friends and enemies; it is full of warring ideas; but there are no mere "foreigners," no merely "foreign" ideologies, no merely "foreign" dangers, any more. Foreign affairs are now our most intimate domestic concern. All men, good or bad, are now our neighbors. All ideas dwell among us.

III

A SECOND principle, and one which requires emphasis as a necessary complement to any policy of full participation, is that we are forced to act in the world as it is, and not in the world as we wish it were or as we would like it to become. It is a world in which we are only one of many peoples and in which our basic principles of life are not shared by all our neighbors. It has been one of the more dangerous aspects of our internationalism in past years that too often it was accompanied by the curious assumption that the world would overnight become good and clean and peaceful everywhere if only America would lead the way. The most elementary experience of human affairs should show us all how naive and dangerous a view that is.

The most conspicuous present examples of this sort of thinking are to be found among those who refuse to recognize the strong probability that one of our great and powerful neighbor nations is at present controlled by men who are convinced that the very course of history is set against democracy and freedom, as we understand those words. A very large part of what I believe to be the mistaken thinking done by my friend Henry Wallace about Soviet Russia results simply from a good-hearted insistence that nobody can dislike us if we try to like them.

We have been very patient with the Soviet government and very hopeful of its good intentions. I have been among those who shared in these hopes and counseled this patience. The magnificent and loyal war effort of the Russian people and the great successful efforts at friendliness made during the war by President Roosevelt, gave us good reason for hope. I have believed—and I still believe—that we must show good faith in all our dealings with the Russians and that only by so doing can we leave the door open for Russian good faith toward us. I cannot too strongly express my regret that since the early spring of 1945—even before the death of Mr. Roosevelt—the Soviet government has steadily pursued an obstructive and unfriendly course. It has been our hope that the Russians would choose to be our friends; it was and is our conviction that such a choice would be to their advantage. But, for the time being, at least, those who determine Russian policy have chosen otherwise, and their choice has been slavishly followed by communists everywhere.

No sensible American can now ignore this fact, and those who now choose to travel in company with American communists are very clearly either knaves or fools. This is a judgment which I make reluctantly, but there is no help for it. I have often said that the surest way to make a man trustworthy is to trust him. But I must add that this does not always apply to a man who is determined to make you his dupe. Before we can make friends with the Russians, their leaders will have to be convinced that they have nothing to gain, and everything to lose, by acting on the assumption that our society is dying and that our principles are outworn. Americans who think they can make common cause with present-day communism are living in a world that does not exist.

They are not alone. An equal and opposite error is made by those who argue that Americans by strong-arm methods, perhaps even by a "preventive war," can and should rid the world of the communist menace. I cannot believe that this view is widely held. For it is worse than nonsense; it results from a hopeless misunderstanding of the geographical and military situation and a cynical incomprehension of what the people of the world will tolerate from *any* nation. Worst of all, this theory indicates a totally wrong assessment of the basic attitudes and motives of the American people. Even if it were true that the United States now had the opportunity to establish forceful hegemony throughout the world, we could not possibly take that opportunity without deserting our true inheritance. Americans as conquerors would be tragically miscast.

The world's affairs cannot be simplified by eager words. We cannot take refuge from reality in the folly of black-and-white solutions.

IV

IN DEALING with the Russians, both uncritical trust and unmitigated belligerence are impossible. There is a middle course. We do not yet know surely in what proportion unreasonable fears and twisted hopes are at the root of the perverted policy now followed by the Kremlin. Assuming both to be involved, we must disarm the fears and disappoint the hopes. We must no longer let the tide of Soviet expansion cheaply roll into the empty places left by war, and yet we must make it perfectly clear that we are not ourselves expansionist. Our task is to help threatened peoples to help themselves.

This is not easy. It is quite possible, indeed, that the blind reaction of some anticommunist governments may succeed to some extent in nullifying our labors. We must make every effort to prevent such a result. . . .

But our main answer to the Russians is not negative, nor is it in any sense anti-Russian. Our central task in dealing with the Kremlin is to demonstrate beyond the possibility of misunderstanding that freedom and prosperity, hand in hand, can be stably sustained in the Western democratic world. This would be our greatest task even if no Soviet problem existed, and to the Soviet threat it is our best response.

Soviet intransigence is based in very large part on the hope and belief that all noncommunist systems are doomed. Soviet policy aims to help them die. We must hope that time and the success of freedom and democracy in the Western world will convince both the Soviet leaders and the Russian people now behind them that our system is here to stay. This may not be possible; dictators do not easily change their hearts, and the modern armaments they possess may make it hard for their people to force such a change. Rather than be persuaded of their error, the Soviet leaders might in desperation resort to war, and against that possibility we have to guard by maintaining our present military advantages. We must never forget that while peace is a joint responsibility, the decision for war can be made by a single power; our military strength must be maintained as a standing discouragement to aggression.

I do not, however, expect the Russians to make war. I do not share the gloomy fear of some that we are now engaged in the preliminaries of an inevitable conflict. Even the most repressive dictatorship is not perfectly unassailable from within, and the most frenzied fanaticism is never unopposed. Whatever the ideological bases of Soviet policy, it seems clear that some at least of the leaders of Russia are men who have a marked respect for facts. We must make it wholly evident that a nonaggressive Russia will have nothing to fear from us. We must make it clear, too, that the Western noncommunist world is going to survive in growing economic and political stability. If we can do this, then slowly—but perhaps less slowly than we now believe— the Russian leaders may either change their minds or lose their jobs.

V

THE PROBLEM of Russia is thus reduced to a question of our own fitness to survive. I do not mean to belittle the communist challenge. I only mean that the essential question is one which we should have to answer if there were not a communist alive. Can we make freedom and prosperity real in the present world? If we can, communism is no threat. If not, with or without communism, our own civilization would ultimately fail.

The immediate and pressing challenge to our belief in freedom and prosperity is in Western Europe. Here are people who have traditionally shared our faith in human dignity. These are the nations by whose citizens our land was settled and in whose tradition our civilization is rooted. They are threatened by communism—but only because of the dark shadows cast by the hopelessness, hunger, and fear that have been the aftermath of the Nazi war. Communism or no communism, menace or no menace, it is our simple duty as neighbors to take a generous part in helping these great peoples to help themselves.

The reconstruction of Western Europe is a task from which Americans can decide to stand apart only if they wish to desert every principle by which they claim to live. And, as a decision of policy, it would be the most tragic mistake in our history. We must take part in this work; we must take our full part; we must be sure that we do enough. I must add that I believe we should act quickly. . . .

As we take part in the rebuilding of Europe, we must remember that we are building world peace, not an American peace. Freedom demands tolerance, and many Americans have much to learn about the variety of forms which free societies may take. There are Europeans, just as there are Americans, who do not believe in freedom, but they are in a minority, and . . . we shall not be able to separate the sheep from the goats merely by asking whether they believe in our particular economic and political system. Our cooperation with the free men of Europe must be founded on the basic principles of human dignity and not on any theory that their way to freedom must be exactly the same as ours. We cannot ask that Europe be rebuilt in the American image. If we join in the task of reconstruction with courage, confidence, and goodwill, we shall learn—and teach—a lot. But we must start with a willingness to understand.

The reconstruction of Western Europe is the immediate task. With it we have, of course, a job at home. We must maintain freedom and prosperity here. This is a demanding task in itself, and its success or failure will largely determine all our other efforts. If it is true that our prosperity depends on that of the world, it is true also that the whole world's economic future hangs on our success at home. We must go forward to new levels of peacetime production, and to do this we must all of us avoid the pitfalls of laziness, fear, and irresponsibility. Neither real profits nor real wages can be permanently sustained—and still less increased—by anything but rising production.

But I see no reason for any man to face the American future with any other feeling than one of confident hope. However grave our problems and however difficult their solution, I do not believe that this country is ready to acknowledge that failure is foreordained. It is our task to disprove and render laughable that utterly insulting theory. Our future does not depend on the tattered forecasts of Karl Marx. It depends on us.

VI

IN COUNSELING against policies which ignore the facts of the world as it is, I do not, of course, mean to argue that we can for a moment forget the nature of our final goal.

Lasting peace and freedom cannot be achieved until the world finds a way toward the necessary government of the whole. It is important that this should be widely understood, and efforts to spread such understanding are commendable. The riven atom, uncontrolled, can be only a growing menace to us all, and there can be no final safety short of full control throughout the world. Nor can we hope to realize the vast potential wealth of atomic energy until it is disarmed and rendered harmless. Upon us, as the people who first harnessed and made use of this force, there rests a grave and continuing responsibility for leadership in turning it toward life, not death.

But we cannot have world government or atomic control by wishing for them, and we cannot have them, in any meaningful sense, without Russia. If in response to our best effort there comes no answer but an everlasting "no," then we must go to work in other fields to change the frame of mind that caused that answer. We cannot ignore it.

It is a part of any practical policy that it must keep our principles out in the open. In the imperfect, veto-ridden United Nations there is now incarnate the hope of people everywhere that this world may become one in spirit as it is in fact. No misconceived idea of "realism" should induce us to ignore this living hope or abate in its pursuit. We should be foremost among those who seek to make the United Nations stronger; if the Russians will not help us, let them be forced to make their opposition clear. . . .

It must be our constant endeavor to conduct our policy with full and deep respect for our signed and ratified adherence to this new league which we have done so much to build. Our insistence upon world cooperation must be unremitting; only so can we deserve and win the confidence of those who, caring nothing for the politics of power, now see only the overriding need for peace. Both policy and principle bind us to the support of the United Nations.

VII

IT IS CLEAR, then, that in this country we are still free to maintain our freedom. We are called to an unprecedented effort of cooperation with our friends in every country. Immediately, we are called to act in the rebuilding of civilization in that part of the world which is closest to us in history, politics, and economics. We are required to think of our prosperity, our policy, and our first principles as indivisibly connected with the facts of life everywhere. We must put away forever the childishness of parochial hopes and un-American fears.

We need not suppose that the task we face is easy or that all our undertakings will be quickly successful. The construction of a stable peace is a longer, more complex, and greater task than the relatively simple work of war-making. But the nature of the challenge is the same. The issue before us today is at least as significant as the one which we finally faced in 1941. By a long series of mistakes and failures, dating back over a span of more than 20 years, we had in 1941 let it become too late to save ourselves by peaceful methods; in the end we had to fight. This is not true today. If we act now, with vigor and understanding, with steadiness and without fear, we can peacefully safeguard our freedom. It is only if we turn our backs, in mistaken complacence or mistrusting timidity, that war may again become inevitable.

How soon this nation will fully understand the size and nature of its present mission, I do not dare to say. But I venture to assert that in very large degree the future of mankind depends on the answer to this question. And I am confident that if the issues are clearly presented, the American people will give the right answer. Surely there is here a fair and tempting challenge to all Americans and especially to the nation's leaders, in and out of office.

A Cold War

THE NINETEEN FIFTIES

❧THE ALLIANCE THAT defeated Nazi Germany and Japan was made up of some of modern politics' strangest bedfellows. Churchill and Roosevelt had little choice but to cooperate with the Soviet Union to defeat the Axis. "If Hitler invaded Hell," Churchill said, "I would make at least a favorable reference to the Devil in the House of Commons." But with Hitler defeated, the two victorious giants began eyeing each other suspiciously over the ruins of Europe.

By the late 1940s the United States had decided that it had to adopt a strategy to contain Soviet power and expansion. The term *containment* was first coined in what is still the most important article *Foreign Affairs* has ever published, "The Sources of Soviet Conduct," which appeared in the July 1947 issue under the byline of "X." Its anonymous author was George F. Kennan, the brilliant State Department official who wrote the famous 1946 "long telegram" warning that the U.S.S.R. was intrinsically a hostile power. In the "X" article, Kennan prophetically urged the United States to counter Soviet ambitions in key regions until the Soviet regime eventually mellowed and was transformed.

First popularized by Walter Lippmann, the term *Cold War* entered the edgy vocabulary of the 1950s as a catchall for the complex of international tensions arising from the superpowers' competition. By 1950 the United States saw itself confronted by communist governments in both Beijing and Moscow. Hence North Korea's invasion of the south resoundingly confirmed one of Washington's greatest fears: that the Soviet Union would use proxies to export communism. When U.S. troops crossed the 38th parallel, the Chinese also entered the war. Chastened, Washington waited for the fighting to wane before accepting a June 1951 offer to begin cease-fire negotiations at Panmunjom.

America was now the leader of the free world, and fear of communism abroad fueled fear of communism at home, boosting McCarthyism and an arms race. Though it had assumed the awesome responsibilities of global leadership, the United States lacked a tradition of great power statesmanship. In "Reflections on American Diplomacy," a young Harvard professor named Henry A. Kissinger drew on lessons from European diplomacy to limn the dangers of coping with communist revolutionaries who did not accept the legitimacy of the international system. Albert Wohlstetter, a nuclear strategist and one of the Rand Corporation's "wizards of Armageddon," warned in "The Delicate Balance of Terror" that avoiding atomic calamity required painstakingly precise deterrence.

Meanwhile, the other superpower was also grappling with the Cold War. Stalin's successor, the rough-hewn Nikita Khrushchev, denounced Stalin's purges and loosened his domestic terror infrastructure, but there were limits to how much reform he was willing to tolerate. When the Hungarians tried to leave the Warsaw Pact in 1956, Soviet tanks drove them back into the fold. But the effects of Soviet rule were not merely political. Isaiah Berlin, an Oxford philosopher and perhaps the century's most eloquent exponent of liberalism, found deep historical roots for "The Silence in Russian Culture" under communism.

The rest of the planet had become an arena for the Cold War as well. With the Suez debacle underscoring the decline of the European imperial powers, the problems of what became known as the Third World received increased attention. In "The Realities in Africa," the great African-American intellectual W. E. B. Du Bois argued with characteristic force that European colonialism and racism could no longer be ignored. And Margaret Mead, the trailblazing anthropologist, cuttingly analyzed the tensions between the world's haves and have-nots in "The Underdeveloped and the Overdeveloped."

Throughout the Eisenhower administration, the world was worried about what the historian E. J. Hobsbawm called "the sort of accident which inevitably threatens those who skate long enough on sufficiently thin ice." It never came, and the 1950s wound down on a note of angst and listlessness, evoked by A. Whitney Griswold, the energetic president of Yale University, in his "Wormwood and Gall." But the decade ended with the election of the charismatic John F. Kennedy. With the 1960s came energy, youth, and activism—for better or worse.

The Sources of Soviet Conduct

X [George F. Kennan]

JULY 1947

THE POLITICAL personality of Soviet power as we know it today is the product of ideology and circumstances: ideology inherited by the present Soviet leaders from the movement in which they had their political origin, and circumstances of the power which they now have exercised for nearly three decades in Russia. There can be few tasks of psychological analysis more difficult than to try to trace the interaction of these two forces and the relative role of each in the determination of official Soviet conduct. Yet the attempt must be made if that conduct is to be understood and effectively countered.

It is difficult to summarize the set of ideological concepts with which the Soviet leaders came into power. Marxian ideology, in its Russian-communist projection, has always been in process of subtle evolution. The materials on which it bases itself are extensive and complex. But the outstanding features of communist thought as it existed in 1916 may perhaps be summarized as follows: (a) that the central factor in the life of man, the factor which determines the character of public life and the "physiognomy of society," is the system by which material goods are produced and exchanged; (b) that the capitalist system of production is a nefarious one which inevitably leads to the exploitation of the working class by the capital-owning class and is incapable of developing adequately the economic resources of society or of distributing fairly the material goods produced by human labor; (c) that capitalism contains the seeds of its own destruction and must, in view of the inability of the capital-owning class to adjust itself to economic change, result eventually and inescapably in a revolutionary transfer of power to the working class; and (d) that imperialism, the final phase of capitalism, leads directly to war and revolution.

The rest may be outlined in Lenin's own words: "Unevenness of economic and political development is the inflexible law of capitalism. It follows from this that the victory of Socialism may come originally in a few capitalist countries or even in a single capitalist country. The victorious proletariat of that country, having expropriated the capitalists and having organized Socialist production at home, would rise against the remaining capitalist world, drawing to itself in the process the oppressed classes of other countries."[1] It must be noted that there was no assumption that capitalism would perish without proletarian revolution. A final push was needed from a revolutionary proletariat movement in order to tip over the tottering structure. But it was regarded as inevitable that sooner or later that push be given.

For 50 years prior to the outbreak of the revolution, this pattern of thought had exercised great fascination for the members of the Russian revolutionary movement. Frustrated, discontented, hopeless of finding self-expression—or too impatient to seek it—in the confining limits of the tsarist political system, yet lacking wide popular support for their choice of bloody revolution as a means of social betterment, these revolutionists found in Marxist theory a highly convenient rationalization for their own instinctive desires. It afforded pseudo-scientific justification for their impatience, for their categoric denial of all value in the tsarist system, for their yearning for power and revenge and for their inclination to cut corners in the pursuit of it. It is therefore no wonder that they had come to believe implicitly in the truth and soundness of the Marxian-Leninist teachings, so congenial to their own impulses and emotions. Their sincerity need not be impugned. This is a phenomenon as old as human nature itself. It has never been more aptly described than by Edward Gibbon, who wrote in *The Decline and Fall of the Roman Empire*: "From enthusiasm to imposture the step is perilous and slippery; the demon of Socrates affords a memorable instance how a wise man may deceive himself, how a good man may deceive others, how the conscience may slumber in a mixed and middle state between self-illusion and voluntary fraud." And it was with this set of conceptions that the members of the Bolshevik Party entered into power.

Now it must be noted that through all the years of preparation for revolution, the attention of these men, as indeed of Marx himself, had been cen-

---

[1] "Concerning the Slogans of the United States of Europe," August 1915. Official Soviet edition of Lenin's works.

tered less on the future form which socialism[2] would take than on the necessary overthrow of rival power which, in their view, had to precede the introduction of socialism. Their views, therefore, on the positive program to be put into effect, once power was attained, were for the most part nebulous, visionary, and impractical. Beyond the nationalization of industry and the expropriation of large private capital holdings there was no agreed program. The treatment of the peasantry, which according to the Marxist formulation was not of the proletariat, had always been a vague spot in the pattern of communist thought; and it remained an object of controversy and vacillation for the first ten years of communist power.

The circumstances of the immediate post-revolution period—the existence in Russia of civil war and foreign intervention, together with the obvious fact that the communists represented only a tiny minority of the Russian people—made the establishment of dictatorial power a necessity. The experiment with "war communism" and the abrupt attempt to eliminate private production and trade had unfortunate economic consequences and caused further bitterness against the new revolutionary régime. While the temporary relaxation of the effort to communize Russia, represented by the New Economic Policy, alleviated some of this economic distress and thereby served its purpose, it also made it evident that the "capitalistic sector of society" was still prepared to profit at once from any relaxation of governmental pressure, and would, if permitted to continue to exist, always constitute a powerful opposing element to the Soviet régime and a serious rival for influence in the country. Somewhat the same situation prevailed with respect to the individual peasant who, in his own small way, was also a private producer.

Lenin, had he lived, might have proved a great enough man to reconcile these conflicting forces to the ultimate benefit of Russian society, though this is questionable. But be that as it may, Stalin, and those whom he led in the struggle for succession to Lenin's position of leadership, were not the men to tolerate rival political forces in the sphere of power which they coveted. Their sense of insecurity was too great. Their particular brand of fanaticism, unmodified by any of the Anglo-Saxon traditions of compromise, was too fierce and too jealous to envisage any permanent sharing of power. From the Russian-Asiatic world out of which they had emerged they carried with them a skepticism as to the possibilities of permanent and peaceful coexistence of rival forces. Easily persuaded of their own doctrinaire "rightness," they insisted on the submission or destruction of all competing power. Outside of the Com-

---

[2] Here and elsewhere in this paper "socialism" refers to Marxist or Leninist communism, not to liberal socialism of the Second International variety.

munist Party, Russian society was to have no rigidity. There were to be no forms of collective human activity or association which would not be dominated by the party. No other force in Russian society was to be permitted to achieve vitality or integrity. Only the party was to have structure. All else was to be an amorphous mass.

And within the party the same principle was to apply. The mass of party members might go through the motions of election, deliberation, decision, and action; but in these motions they were to be animated not by their own individual wills but by the awesome breath of the party leadership and the overbrooding presence of "the word."

Let it be stressed again that subjectively these men probably did not seek absolutism for its own sake. They doubtless believed—and found it easy to believe—that they alone knew what was good for society and that they would accomplish that good once their power was secure and unchallengeable. But in seeking that security of their own rule they were prepared to recognize no restrictions, either of God or man, on the character of their methods. And until such time as that security might be achieved, they placed far down on their scale of operational priorities the comforts and happiness of the peoples entrusted to their care.

Now the outstanding circumstance concerning the Soviet régime is that down to the present day this process of political consolidation has never been completed and the men in the Kremlin have continued to be predominantly absorbed with the struggle to secure and make absolute the power which they seized in November 1917. They have endeavored to secure it primarily against forces at home, within Soviet society itself. But they have also endeavored to secure it against the outside world. For ideology, as we have seen, taught them that the outside world was hostile and that it was their duty eventually to overthrow the political forces beyond their borders. The powerful hands of Russian history and tradition reached up to sustain them in this feeling. Finally, their own aggressive intransigence with respect to the outside world began to find its own reaction; and they were soon forced, to use another Gibbonesque phrase, "to chastise the contumacy" which they themselves had provoked. It is an undeniable privilege of every man to prove himself right in the thesis that the world is his enemy; for if he reiterates it frequently enough and makes it the background of his conduct he is bound eventually to be right.

Now it lies in the nature of the mental world of the Soviet leaders, as well as in the character of their ideology, that no opposition to them can be officially recognized as having any merit or justification whatsoever. Such opposition can flow, in theory, only from the hostile and incorrigible forces of dying capitalism. As long as remnants of capitalism were officially recognized as existing in Russia, it was possible to place on them, as an internal element, part of the blame for the maintenance of a dictatorial form of society. But as these remnants were liquidated, little by little, this justification fell away; and when it was indicated officially that they had been finally destroyed, it disappeared altogether. And this fact created one of the most basic of the compulsions which came to act upon the Soviet régime: since capitalism no longer existed in Russia and since it could not be admitted that there could be serious or widespread opposition to the Kremlin springing spontaneously from the liberated masses under its authority, it became necessary to justify the retention of the dictatorship by stressing the menace of capitalism abroad.

This began at an early date. In 1924 Stalin specifically defended the retention of the "organs of suppression," meaning, among others, the army and the secret police, on the ground that "as long as there is a capitalist encirclement there will be danger of intervention with all the consequences that flow from that danger." In accordance with that theory, and from that time on, all internal opposition forces in Russia have consistently been portrayed as the agents of foreign forces of reaction antagonistic to Soviet power.

By the same token, tremendous emphasis has been placed on the original communist thesis of a basic antagonism between the capitalist and socialist worlds. It is clear, from many indications, that this emphasis is not founded in reality. The real facts concerning it have been confused by the existence abroad of genuine resentment provoked by Soviet philosophy and tactics and occasionally by the existence of great centers of military power, notably the Nazi régime in Germany and the Japanese government of the late 1930s, which did indeed have aggressive designs against the Soviet Union. But there is ample evidence that the stress laid in Moscow on the menace confronting Soviet society from the world outside its borders is founded not in the realities of foreign antagonism but in the necessity of explaining away the maintenance of dictatorial authority at home.

Now the maintenance of this pattern of Soviet power, namely, the pursuit of unlimited authority domestically, accompanied by the cultivation of the semi-myth of implacable foreign hostility, has gone far to shape the actual machinery of Soviet power as we know it today. Internal organs of administration which did not serve this purpose withered on the vine. Organs which did serve this purpose became vastly swollen. The security of Soviet power came to rest on the iron discipline of the party, on the severity and ubiquity of the secret police, and on the uncompromising economic monopolism of the state. The "organs of suppression," in which the Soviet leaders had sought security from rival forces, became in large measure the masters of those whom they were designed to serve. Today the major part of the structure of Soviet power is committed to the perfection of the dictatorship and to the maintenance of the concept of Russia as in a state of siege, with the enemy lowering beyond the walls. And the millions of human beings who form that part of the structure of power must defend at all costs this concept of Russia's position, for without it they are themselves superfluous.

As things stand today, the rulers can no longer dream of parting with these organs of suppression. The quest for absolute power, pursued now for nearly three decades with a ruthlessness unparalleled (in scope at least) in modern times, has again produced internally, as it did externally, its own reaction. The excesses of the police apparatus have fanned the potential opposition to the régime into something far greater and more dangerous than it could have been before those excesses began.

But least of all can the rulers dispense with the fiction by which the maintenance of dictatorial power has been defended. For this fiction has been canonized in Soviet philosophy by the excesses already committed in its name; and it is now anchored in the Soviet structure of thought by bonds far greater than those of mere ideology.

II

SO MUCH FOR the historical background. What does it spell in terms of the political personality of Soviet power as we know it today?

Of the original ideology, nothing has been officially junked. Belief is maintained in the basic badness of capitalism, in the inevitability of its destruction, in the obligation of the proletariat to assist in that destruction and to take power into its own hands. But stress has come to be laid primarily on those concepts which relate most specifically to the Soviet régime itself: to its position as the sole truly socialist régime in a dark and misguided world, and to the relationships of power within it.

The first of these concepts is that of the innate antagonism between capitalism and socialism. We have seen how deeply that concept has become imbedded in foundations of Soviet power. It has profound implications for Russia's conduct as a member of international society. It means that there can never be on Moscow's side any sincere assumption of a community of aims between the Soviet Union and powers which are regarded as capitalist. It must invariably be assumed in Moscow that the aims of the capitalist world are antagonistic to the Soviet régime, and therefore to the interests of the peoples it controls. If the Soviet government occasionally sets its signature to documents which would indicate the contrary, this is to be regarded as a tactical manœuver permissible in dealing with the enemy (who is without honor) and should be taken in the spirit of *caveat emptor*. Basically, the antagonism remains. It is postulated. And from it flow many of the phenomena which we find disturbing in the Kremlin's conduct of foreign policy: the secretiveness, the lack of frankness, the duplicity, the wary suspiciousness, and the basic unfriendliness of purpose. These phenomena are there to stay, for the foreseeable future. There can be variations of degree and of emphasis. When there is something the Russians want from us, one or the other of these features of their policy may be thrust temporarily into the background; and when that happens there will always be Americans who will leap forward with gleeful announcements that "the Russians have changed," and some who will even try to take credit for having brought about such "changes." But we should not be misled by tactical manœuvers. These characteristics of Soviet policy, like the postulate from which they flow, are basic to the internal nature of Soviet power and will be with us, whether in the foreground or the background, until the internal nature of Soviet power is changed.

This means that we are going to continue for a long time to find the Russians difficult to deal with. It does not mean that they should be considered as embarked upon a do-or-die program to overthrow our society by a given date. The theory of the inevitability of the eventual fall of capitalism has the fortunate connotation that there is no hurry about it. The forces of progress can take their time in preparing the final *coup de grâce*. Meanwhile, what is vital is that the "socialist fatherland"—that oasis of power which has been already won for socialism in the person of the Soviet Union—should be cherished and defended by all good communists at home and abroad, its fortunes promoted, its enemies badgered and confounded. The promotion of premature, "adventuristic" revolutionary projects abroad which might embarrass Soviet power, in any way would be an inexcusable, even a counter-revolutionary act. The cause of socialism is the support and promotion of Soviet power, as defined in Moscow.

This brings us to the second of the concepts important to contemporary Soviet outlook. That is the infallibility of the Kremlin. The Soviet concept of power, which permits no focal points of organization outside the party itself, requires that the party leadership remain in theory the sole repository of truth. For if truth were to be found elsewhere, there would be justification for its expression in organized activity. But it is precisely that which the Kremlin cannot and will not permit.

The leadership of the Communist Party is therefore always right, and has been always right ever since in 1929 Stalin formalized his personal power by announcing that decisions of the Politburo were being taken unanimously.

On the principle of infallibility there rests the iron discipline of the Communist Party. In fact, the two concepts are mutually self-supporting. Perfect discipline requires recognition of infallibility. Infallibility requires the observance of discipline. And the two together go far to determine the behaviorism of the entire Soviet apparatus of power. But their effect cannot be understood unless a third factor be taken into account: namely, the fact that the leadership is at liberty to put forward for tactical purposes any particular thesis which it finds useful to the cause at any particular moment and to require the faithful and unquestioning acceptance of that thesis by the members of the movement as a whole. This means that truth is not a constant but is actually created, for all intents and purposes, by the Soviet leaders themselves. It may vary from week to week, from month to month. It is nothing absolute and immutable—nothing which flows from objective reality. It is only the most recent manifestation of the wisdom of those in whom the ultimate wisdom is supposed to reside, because they represent the logic of history. The accumulative effect of these factors is to give to the whole subordinate apparatus of Soviet power an unshakeable stubbornness and steadfastness in its orientation. This orientation can be changed at will by the Kremlin but by no other power. Once a given party line has been laid down on a given issue of current policy, the whole Soviet governmental machine, including the mechanism of diplomacy, moves inexorably along the prescribed path, like a persistent toy automobile wound up and headed in a given direction, stopping only when it meets with some unanswerable force. The individuals who are the components of this machine are unamenable to argument or reason which comes to them from outside sources. Their whole training has taught them to mistrust and discount the glib persuasiveness of the outside world. Like the white dog before the phonograph, they hear only the "master's voice." And if they are to be called off from the purposes last dictated to them, it is the master who must call them off. Thus the foreign representative cannot hope that his words will make any impression on them. The most that he can hope is that they will be transmitted to those at the top, who are capable of changing the party line. But even those are not likely to be swayed by any normal logic in the words of the bourgeois representative. Since there can be no appeal to common purposes, there can be no appeal to common mental approaches. For this reason, facts speak louder than words to the ears of the Kremlin; and words carry the greatest weight when they have the ring of reflecting, or being backed up by, facts of unchallengeable validity.

But we have seen that the Kremlin is under no ideological compulsion to accomplish its purposes in a hurry. Like the Church, it is dealing in ideological concepts which are of long-term validity, and it can afford to be patient. It has no right to risk the existing achievements of the revolution for the sake of vain baubles of the future. The very teachings of Lenin himself require great caution and flexibility in the pursuit of communist purposes. Again, these precepts are fortified by the lessons of Russian history: of centuries of obscure battles between nomadic forces over the stretches of a vast unfortified plain.

Here caution, circumspection, flexibility, and deception are the valuable qualities; and their value finds natural appreciation in the Russian or the oriental mind. Thus the Kremlin has no compunction about retreating in the face of superior force. And being under the compulsion of no timetable, it does not get panicky under the necessity for such retreat. Its political action is a fluid stream which moves constantly, wherever it is permitted to move, toward a given goal. Its main concern is to make sure that it has filled every nook and cranny available to it in the basin of world power. But if it finds unassailable barriers in its path, it accepts these philosophically and accommodates itself to them. The main thing is that there should always be pressure, unceasing constant pressure, toward the desired goal. There is no trace of any feeling in Soviet psychology that that goal must be reached at any given time.

These considerations make Soviet diplomacy at once easier and more difficult to deal with than the diplomacy of individual aggressive leaders like Napoleon and Hitler. On the one hand it is more sensitive to contrary force, more ready to yield on individual sectors of the diplomatic front when that force is felt to be too strong, and thus more rational in the logic and rhetoric of power. On the other hand it cannot be easily defeated or discouraged by a single victory on the part of its opponents. And the patient persistence by which it is animated means that it can be effectively countered not by sporadic acts which represent the momentary whims of democratic opinion but only by intelligent long-range policies on the part of Russia's adversaries— policies no less steady in their purpose, and no less variegated and resourceful in their application, than those of the Soviet Union itself.

In these circumstances it is clear that the main element of any United States policy toward the Soviet Union must be that of a long-term, patient but firm and vigilant containment of Russian expansive tendencies. It is important to note, however, that such a policy has nothing to do with outward histrionics: with threats or blustering or superfluous gestures of outward "toughness." While the Kremlin is basically flexible in its reaction to political realities, it is by no means unamenable to considerations of prestige. Like almost any other government, it can be placed by tactless and threatening gestures in a position where it cannot afford to yield even though this might be dictated by its sense of realism. The Russian leaders are keen judges of human psychology, and as such they are highly conscious that loss of temper and of self-control is never a source of strength in political affairs. They are quick to exploit such evidences of weakness. For these reasons, it is a *sine qua non* of successful dealing with Russia that the foreign government in question should remain at all times cool and collected and that its demands on Russian policy should be put forward in such a manner as to leave the way open for a compliance not too detrimental to Russian prestige.

III

IN THE light of the above, it will be clearly seen that the Soviet pressure against the free institutions of the Western world is something that can be contained by the adroit and vigilant application of counter-force at a series of constantly shifting geographical and political points, corresponding to the shifts and manœuvers of Soviet policy, but which cannot be charmed or talked out of existence. The Russians look forward to a duel of infinite duration, and they see that already they have scored great successes. It must be borne in mind that there was a time when the Communist Party represented far more of a minority in the sphere of Russian national life than Soviet power today represents in the world community.

But if ideology convinces the rulers of Russia that truth is on their side and that they can therefore afford to wait, those of us on whom that ideology has no claim are free to examine objectively the validity of that premise. The Soviet thesis not only implies complete lack of control by the West over its own economic destiny, it likewise assumes Russian unity, discipline, and patience over an infinite period. Let us bring this apocalyptic vision down to earth, and suppose that the Western world finds the strength and resourcefulness to contain Soviet power over a period of 10 to 15 years. What does that spell for Russia itself?

The Soviet leaders, taking advantage of the contributions of modern technique to the arts of despotism, have solved the question of obedience within the confines of their power. Few challenge their authority; and even those who do are unable to make that challenge valid as against the organs of suppression of the state.

The Kremlin has also proved able to accomplish its purpose of building up in Russia, regardless of the interests of the inhabitants, an industrial foundation of heavy metallurgy, which is, to be sure, not yet complete but which is nevertheless continuing to grow and is approaching those of the other major industrial countries. All of this, however, both the maintenance of internal political security and the building of heavy industry, has been carried out at a terrible cost in human life and in human hopes and energies. It has necessitated the use of forced labor on a scale unprecedented in modern times under conditions of peace. It has involved the neglect or abuse of other phases of Soviet economic life, particularly agriculture, consumers' goods production, housing, and transportation.

To all that, the war has added its tremendous toll of destruction, death, and human exhaustion. In consequence of this, we have in Russia today a population which is physically and spiritually tired. The mass of the people are disillusioned, skeptical, and no longer as accessible as they once were to the magical attraction which Soviet power still radiates to its followers abroad. The avidity with which people seized upon the slight respite accorded to the Church for tactical reasons during the war was eloquent testimony to the fact that their capacity for faith and devotion found little expression in the purposes of the régime.

In these circumstances, there are limits to the physical and nervous strength of people themselves. These limits are absolute ones, and are binding even for the cruelest dictatorship, because beyond them people cannot be driven. The forced labor camps and the other agencies of constraint provide temporary means of compelling people to work longer hours than their own volition or mere economic pressure would dictate; but if people survive them at all they become old before their time and must be considered as human casualties to the demands of dictatorship. In either case their best powers are no longer available to society and can no longer be enlisted in the service of the state.

Here only the younger generation can help. The younger generation, despite all vicissitudes and sufferings, is numerous and vigorous; and the Russians are a talented people. But it still remains to be seen what will be the effects on mature performance of the abnormal emotional strains of childhood which Soviet dictatorship created and which were enormously increased by the war. Such things as normal security and placidity of home environment have practically ceased to exist in the Soviet Union outside of the most remote farms and villages. And observers are not yet sure whether that is not going to leave its mark on the over-all capacity of the generation now coming into maturity.

In addition to this, we have the fact that Soviet economic development, while it can list certain formidable achievements, has been precariously spotty and uneven. Russian communists who speak of the "uneven development of capitalism" should blush at the contemplation of their own national economy. Here certain branches of economic life, such as the metallurgical and machine industries, have been pushed out of all proportion to other sectors of economy. Here is a nation striving to become in a short period one of the great industrial nations of the world while it still has no highway network worthy of the name and only a relatively primitive network of railways. Much has been done to increase efficiency of labor and to teach primitive peasants something about the operation of machines. But maintenance is still a crying deficiency of all Soviet economy. Construction is hasty and poor in quality. Depreciation must be enormous. And in vast sectors of economic life it has not yet been possible to instill into labor anything like that general culture of production and technical self-respect which characterizes the skilled worker of the West.

It is difficult to see how these deficiencies can be corrected at an early date by a tired and dispirited population working largely under the shadow of fear and compulsion. And as long as they are not overcome, Russia will remain economically a vulnerable, and in a certain sense an impotent, nation, capable of exporting its enthusiasms and of radiating the strange charm of its primitive political vitality but unable to back up those articles of export by the real evidences of material power and prosperity.

Meanwhile, a great uncertainty hangs over the political life of the Soviet Union. That is the uncertainty involved in the transfer of power from one individual or group of individuals to others.

This is, of course, outstandingly the problem of the personal position of Stalin. We must remember that his succession to Lenin's pinnacle of preeminence in the communist movement was the only such transfer of individual authority which the Soviet Union has experienced. That transfer took 12 years to consolidate. It cost the lives of millions of people and shook the state to its foundations. The attendant tremors were felt all through the international revolutionary movement, to the disadvantage of the Kremlin itself.

It is always possible that another transfer of preeminent power may take place quietly and inconspicuously, with no repercussions anywhere. But again, it is possible that the questions involved may unleash, to use some of Lenin's words, one of those "incredibly swift transitions" from "delicate deceit" to "wild violence" which characterize Russian history, and may shake Soviet power to its foundations.

But this is not only a question of Stalin himself. There has been, since 1938, a dangerous congealment of political life in the higher circles of Soviet power. The All-Union Congress of Soviets, in theory the supreme body of the party, is supposed to meet not less often than once in three years. It will soon be eight full years since its last meeting. During this period membership in the party has numerically doubled. Party mortality during the war was enormous; and today well over half of the party members are persons who have entered since the last party congress was held. Meanwhile, the same small group of men has carried on at the top through an amazing series of national vicissitudes. Surely there is some reason why the experiences of the war brought basic political changes to every one of the great governments of the West. Surely the causes of that phenomenon are basic enough to be present somewhere in the obscurity of Soviet political life, as well. And yet no recognition has been given to these causes in Russia.

It must be surmised from this that even within so highly disciplined an organization as the Communist Party there must be a growing divergence in age, outlook, and interest between the great mass of party members, only so recently recruited into the movement, and the little self-perpetuating clique of men at the top, whom most of these party members have never met, with whom they have never conversed, and with whom they can have no political intimacy.

Who can say whether, in these circumstances, the eventual rejuvenation of the higher spheres of authority (which can only be a matter of time) can take place smoothly and peacefully, or whether rivals in the quest for higher power will not eventually reach down into these politically immature and inexperienced masses in order to find support for their respective claims? If this were ever to happen, strange consequences could flow for the Communist Party: for the membership at large has been exercised only in the practices of iron discipline and obedience and not in the arts of compromise and accommodation. And if disunity were ever to seize and paralyze the party, the chaos and weakness of Russian society would be revealed in forms beyond description. For we have seen that Soviet power is only a crust concealing an amorphous mass of human beings among whom no independent organizational structure is tolerated. In Russia there is not even such a thing as local government. The present generation of Russians have never known spontaneity of collective action. If, consequently, anything were ever to occur to disrupt the unity and efficacy of the party as a political instrument, Soviet Russia might be changed overnight from one of the strongest to one of the weakest and most pitiable of national societies.

Thus the future of Soviet power may not be by any means secure as Russian capacity for self-delusion would make it appear to the men in the Kremlin. That they can keep power themselves, they have demonstrated. That they can quietly and easily turn it over to others remains to be proved. Meanwhile, the hardships of their rule and the vicissitudes of international life have taken a heavy toll of the strength and hopes of the great people on whom their power rests. It is curious to note that the ideological power of Soviet authority is strongest today in areas beyond the frontiers of Russia, beyond the reach of its police power. This phenomenon brings to mind a comparison used by Thomas Mann in his great novel *Buddenbrooks*. Observing that human institutions often show the greatest outward brilliance at a moment when inner decay is in reality farthest advanced, he compared the Buddenbrook family, in the days of its greatest glamour, to one of those stars whose light shines most brightly on this world when in reality it has long since ceased to exist. And who can say with assurance that the strong light still cast by the Kremlin on the dissatisfied peoples of the Western world is not the powerful afterglow of a constellation which is in actuality on the wane? This cannot be proved. And it cannot be disproved. But the possibility remains (and in the opinion of this writer it is a strong one) that Soviet power, like the capitalist world of its conception, bears within it the seeds of its own decay, and that the sprouting of these seeds is well advanced.

IV

IT IS CLEAR that the United States cannot expect in the foreseeable future to enjoy political intimacy with the Soviet régime. It must continue to regard the Soviet Union as a rival, not a partner, in the political arena. It must continue to expect that Soviet policies will reflect no abstract love of peace and stability, no real faith in the possibility of a permanent happy coexistence of the socialist and capitalist worlds, but rather a cautious, persistent pressure toward the disruption and weakening of all rival influence and rival power.

Balanced against this are the facts that Russia, as opposed to the Western world in general, is still by far the weaker party, that Soviet policy is highly flexible, and that Soviet society may well contain deficiencies which will eventually weaken its own total potential. This would of itself warrant the United States entering with reasonable confidence upon a policy of firm containment, designed to confront the Russians with unalterable counter-force at every point where they show signs of encroaching upon the interests of a peaceful and stable world.

But in actuality the possibilities for American policy are by no means limited to holding the line and hoping for the best. It is entirely possible for the United States to influence by its actions the internal developments, both within Russia and throughout the international communist movement, by which Russian policy is largely determined. This is not only a question of the modest measure of informational activity which this government can conduct in the Soviet Union and elsewhere, although that, too, is important. It is rather a question of the degree to which the United States can create among the peoples of the world generally the impression of a country which knows what it wants, which is coping successfully with the problems of its internal life and with the responsibilities of a world power, and which has a spiritual vitality capable of holding its own among the major ideological currents of the time. To the extent that such an impression can be created and maintained, the aims of Russian communism must appear sterile and quixotic, the hopes and enthusiasm of Moscow's supporters must wane, and added strain must be imposed on the Kremlin's foreign policies. For the palsied decrepitude of the capitalist world is the keystone of communist philosophy. Even the failure of the United States to experience the early economic depression which the ravens of the Red Square have been predicting with such complacent confidence since hostilities ceased would have deep and important repercussions throughout the communist world.

By the same token, exhibitions of indecision, disunity, and internal disintegration within this country have an exhilarating effect on the whole communist movement. At each evidence of these tendencies, a thrill of hope and excitement goes through the communist world; a new jauntiness can be noted in the Moscow tread; new groups of foreign supporters climb on to what they can only view as the band wagon of international politics; and Russian pressure increases all along the line in international affairs.

It would be an exaggeration to say that American behavior unassisted and alone could exercise a power of life and death over the communist movement and bring about the early fall of Soviet power in Russia. But the United States has it in its power to increase enormously the strains under which Soviet policy must operate, to force upon the Kremlin a far greater degree of moderation and circumspection than it has had to observe in recent years, and in this way to promote tendencies which must eventually find their outlet in either the break-up or the gradual mellowing of Soviet power. For no mystical, messianic movement—and particularly not that of the Kremlin—can face frustration indefinitely without eventually adjusting itself in one way or another to the logic of that state of affairs.

Thus the decision will really fall in large measure in this country itself. The issue of Soviet-American relations is in essence a test of the over-all worth of the United States as a nation among nations. To avoid destruction the United States need only measure up to its own best traditions and prove itself worthy of preservation as a great nation.

Surely, there was never a fairer test of national quality than this. In the light of these circumstances, the thoughtful observer of Russian-American relations will find no cause for complaint in the Kremlin's challenge to American society. He will rather experience a certain gratitude to a Providence which, by providing the American people with this implacable challenge, has made their entire security as a nation dependent on their pulling themselves together and accepting the responsibilities of moral and political leadership that history plainly intended them to bear.

Reflections on American Diplomacy

Henry A. Kissinger

OCTOBER 1956

"POLICY," wrote Metternich, the Austrian minister who steered his country through 39 years of crisis by a tour de force perhaps never excelled, "is like a play in many acts which unfolds inevitably once the curtain is raised. To declare then that the play will not go on is an absurdity. The play *will* go on either by means of the actors or by means of the spectators who mount the stage. . . . The crucial problem [of statesmanship], therefore, resides in the decision of whether to assemble the audience, whether the curtain is to be raised and above all in the intrinsic merit of the play."

There can be little doubt that the foreign policy of the United States has reached an impasse. For several years we have been groping for a concept to deal with the transformation of the Cold War from an effort to build defensive barriers into a contest for the allegiance of humanity. But the new Soviet tactics, coupled with the equally unassimilated increase in the destructive potential of the new weapons technology, have led to a crisis in our system of alliances and to substantial Soviet gains among the uncommitted peoples of the world.

It would be a mistake, however, to ascribe our difficulties to this or that error of policy or to a particular administration, although the present administration has not helped matters by its pretense of "normalcy." To return to Metternich's metaphor: It can be argued that our policy has reached an impasse because of our penchant for happy endings; the Soviet rulers have been able to use negotiations to their advantage because we insisted on reading from an old script. As in all tragedies, many of our problems have been produced in spite of our good intentions and have been caused, not by our worst qualities, but by our best. What is at issue, therefore, is not a policy but an attitude.

[170]

It is with this attitude and its consequences in the conduct of negotiations and our policy of alliances that this article seeks to deal.

II

IT IS understandable that a nation which for a century and a half had been preoccupied with its domestic affairs should seek to apply the pattern of these to international affairs. But the very success of the American experiment and the spontaneity of our social institutions have served to emphasize the dilemma faced at some stage by every country: how to reconcile its vision of itself with the vision of it as seen by others. To itself, a nation is an expression of justice, and the more spontaneous has been the growth of its social institutions the more this is true; for government functions effectively only when most citizens obey voluntarily, and they will obey only to the extent that they consider the demands of their rulers just. But to other nations, a state is a force to be balanced. This is inevitable because national strategy must be planned on the basis of the other side's capabilities and not merely a calculation of its intentions. There exists a double standard, therefore, in all foreign policy: internally, foreign policy is justified like all other policy in terms of an absolute standard; but abroad, what is defined as justice domestically becomes a program to be compromised by negotiation. If the institutions and values of the states comprising the international order are sufficiently similar, this incommensurability may not become apparent. But in a revolutionary period like the present, it affects profoundly relationships among states.

Foremost among the attitudes affecting our foreign policy is American empiricism and its quest for methodological certainty: nothing is "true" unless it is "objective" and it is not "objective" unless it is part of experience. This makes for the absence of dogmatism and for the ease of social relations on the domestic scene. But in the conduct of foreign policy it has pernicious consequences. Foreign policy is the art of weighing probabilities; mastery of it lies in grasping the nuances of possibilities. To attempt to conduct it as a science must lead to rigidity. For only the risks are certain; the opportunities are conjectural. One cannot be "sure" about the implications of events until they have happened, and when they have occurred it is too late to do anything about them. Empiricism in foreign policy leads to a penchant for *ad hoc* solutions; the rejection of dogmatism inclines our policymakers to postpone committing themselves until all facts are in; but by the time the facts are in, a crisis has usually developed or an opportunity has passed. Our policy is therefore geared to dealing with emergencies; it finds difficulty in developing the long-range program that might forestall them.

A symptom of our need for methodological certainty is the vast number of committees charged with examining and developing policy. The very multiplicity of committees makes it difficult to arrive at decisions in time. It tends to give a disproportionate influence to subordinate officials who prepare the initial memoranda, and it overwhelms our higher officials with trivia. Because of our cult of specialization, sovereign departments negotiate national policy among each other with no single authority able to take an overall view or to apply decisions over a period of time.[1] This results in a hiatus between grand strategy and particular tactics, between the definition of general objectives so vague as to be truistic and the concern with immediate problems. The gap is bridged only when a crisis forces the bureaucratic machinery into accelerated action, and then the top leadership has little choice but to concur in the administrative proposals. In short, we are trying to cope with political problems by administrative means.

The temptation to formulate policy administratively is ever present in a government organized, as ours is, primarily for the conduct of domestic affairs. But the spirit of policy and that of bureaucracy are fundamentally opposed. Profound policy thrives on creativeness; good administration thrives on routine—a procedure which can assimilate mediocrity. Policy involves an adjustment of risks; administration an avoidance of deviation. The attempt to formulate policy administratively leads to the acceptance of a standard which evaluates by mistakes avoided rather than by goals achieved. It is no accident that most great statesmen were opposed by the "experts" in their foreign offices, for the very greatness of the statesman's conception tends to make it inaccessible to those whose primary concern is with safety and minimum risk.

Our methodological doubt makes for vulnerability to Soviet maneuvers in two ways: on the one hand, every Soviet change of line is taken at least in part at face value, for we cannot be certain that the Soviets may not "mean" it this time until they have proved they do not; and they will try their best not to prove it until the tactic has served its purpose. On the other hand, we have found it difficult to adjust our tactics to new situations, so that we always tend to speak in the categories of the most recent threat but one. The paradoxical result is that we, the empiricists, appear to the world as rigid, unimaginative and even somewhat cynical, while the dogmatic Bolsheviks exhibit flexibility, daring, and subtlety. This is because our empiricism dooms us to an essentially reactive policy that improvises a counter to every Soviet

---

[1]This is true despite the National Security Council. Since the NSC is composed mainly of department heads overwhelmed with administrative responsibilities, all the pressures make for a departmental outlook and a concern with immediate problems.

move, while the Soviet emphasis on theory gives them the certainty to act, to maneuver, and to run risks. The very fact of action forces us to assume the risks of countermoves and absorbs our energies in essentially defensive maneuvers.

The willingness to act need not derive from theory, of course. Indeed, an overemphasis on theory can lead to a loss of touch with reality. In many societies—in Great Britain, for example—policy developed from a firmly held tradition of a national strategy. Throughout the nineteenth century it was a tenet of British policy that Antwerp should not fall into the hands of a major power. This was not backed by an elaborate metaphysics but simply by a tradition of British sea power whose requirements were so generally understood that they were never debated. It is the absence of a tradition of foreign policy which exaggerates the biases of our empiricism and makes it difficult to conduct our policy with a proper regard for the timing of measures. It causes us to overlook the fact that policy exists in time as well as in space, that a measure is correct only if it can be carried out at the proper moment. To be sure, our cumbersome administrative mechanism adds immeasurably to the problem. But in addition, our deliberations are conducted as if a course of action were eternally valid, as if a measure which might meet exactly the needs of a given moment could not backfire if adopted a year later. For this reason our policy lacks a feeling for nuance, the ability to come up with variations on the same theme, as the Soviets have done so effectively. We consider policymaking concluded when the National Security Council has come to a decision. And in fact, the process of arriving at a decision is so arduous and a reappraisal is necessarily so "agonizing" that we are reluctant to reexamine policies after they have outlived their usefulness.

But a written statement of policy is likely to amount to a truism; the real difficulty arises in applying it to concrete situations. And while we have often come up with the proper measures, we have not found it easy to adapt our approach to the requirements of the situation over a period of time. . . .

Another factor shaping our attitude toward foreign affairs is our lack of tragic experience. Though we have known severe hardships, our history has been notably free of disaster. Indeed, the American domestic experience exhibits an unparalleled success, of great daring rewarded and of great obstacles overcome. It is no wonder, therefore, that to many of our most responsible men, particularly in the business community, the warnings of impending peril or of imminent disaster sound like the Cassandra cries of abstracted "eggheads." For is not the attribute of the "egghead" his lack of touch with reality, and does not American reality show an unparalleled wealth coupled with an unparalleled growth?

There has been much criticism of Secretaries Humphrey and Wilson for their defense economies. But in fairness the psychological background of their decisions should be understood; despite all the information at their disposal, they simply cannot believe that in the nuclear age the penalty for miscalculation may be national catastrophe. They may know in their heads, but they cannot accept in their hearts, that the society they helped to build could disappear as did Rome or Carthage or Byzantium, which probably seemed as eternal to their citizens. These characteristics make for an absence of a sense of urgency, a tendency to believe that everything can be tried once and that the worst consequence mistakes can have is that we may be forced to redouble our efforts later on. The irrevocable error is not yet part of the American experience.

Related to this problem is our reluctance to think in terms of power. To be sure, American expansion both economic and geographical was not accomplished without a judicious application of power. But our Calvinist heritage has required success to display the attribute of justice. Even our great fortunes, however accumulated, were almost invariably held to impose a social obligation; the great foundation is after all a peculiarly American phenomenon. As a nation, we have used power almost shamefacedly as if it were inherently wicked. We have wanted to be liked for our own sakes and we have wished to succeed because of the persuasiveness of our principles rather than through our strength. Our feeling of guilt with respect to power has caused us to transform all wars into crusades and then to apply our power in the most absolute terms. We have rarely found intermediary ways to apply our power, and in those cases we have done so reluctantly.

But international relations cannot be conducted without an awareness of power relationships. To be sure, the contemporary evolution cannot be managed merely by an exercise of force. But unless we maintain at least an equilibrium of power between us and the Soviet bloc, we will have no chance to undertake any positive measures. And maintaining this equilibrium may confront us with some very difficult choices. We are certain to be confronted with situations of extraordinary ambiguity such as civil wars or domestic coups. Every successful Soviet move makes our moral position that much more difficult: Indochina was more ambiguous than Korea; the Soviet arms deal with Egypt more ambiguous than Indochina; the Suez crisis more ambiguous than the arms deal. There can be no doubt that we should seek to prevent such occurrences. But once they have occurred, we must find the will to act and to run risks in a situation which permits only a choice among evils. While we should never give up our principles, we must also realize that we cannot maintain our principles unless we survive.

Consistent with our reluctance to think in terms of power has been our notion of the nature of peace. We assume that peace is the "normal" pattern of relations among states, that it is equivalent to a consciousness of harmony, that it can be aimed at directly as a goal of policy. These are truisms rarely challenged in our political debate. Both major political parties maintain that they work for a lasting peace, even if they differ about the best means of attaining it. Both make statements which imply that on a certain magic day, perhaps after a four-power conference, "peace will break out."

No idea could be more dangerous. To begin with, the polarization of power in the world would give international relations a degree of instability even if there were no ideological disagreement, and the present volatile state of technology is likely to compound this sense of insecurity. Moreover, whenever peace—conceived as the avoidance of war—has become the direct objective of a power or a group of powers, international relations have been at the mercy of the state willing to forego peace. No statesman can entrust the fate of his country entirely to the continued good will of another sovereign state, if only because the best guarantee for the will remaining good is not to tempt it by too great a disproportion of power. Peace, therefore, cannot be aimed at directly; it is the expression of certain conditions and power relationships. It is to these relationships—not to peace—that diplomacy must address itself.

It is obviously to the interest of the Soviet Union to equate peace with a state of good feeling unconnected with power relationships or past usurpations, for such an attitude ratifies all its gains since World War II. By the same token, it is to the interest of the United States to leave no doubt that the tension of the Cold War was produced not only by the intransigence of the Soviet tone but also by the intransigence of their measures. As long as the Soviets can give the impression that conciliatory statements by themselves are a symptom of peaceful intentions, they can control the pace of negotiations and gain the benefits of the advocacy of peace without paying any price for its achievement. If the Soviets are given the privilege of initiating negotiations when it suits their purpose and of breaking them off without any penalty, diplomacy will become a tool of Soviet propaganda. And the variety of Soviet maneuvers will in time erode the cohesion of the free world.

III

WITH THIS WE have reached one of the major problems confronting current American diplomacy: the changed nature of negotiations in a revolutionary political order. An international order, the basic arrangements of which are accepted by all the major powers, may be called "legitimate"; a system which contains a power or group of powers which refuses to accept either the arrangements of the settlement or the domestic structure of the other states is "revolutionary." A legitimate order does not make conflicts impossible; it limits their scope. Wars may arise, but they will be fought in *the name* of the existing system, and the peace will be justified as a better expression of the agreed arrangements. In a revolutionary order, on the other hand, disputes do not concern adjustments within a given framework, but the framework itself.

There can be little doubt that we are living through a revolutionary period. On the physical plane, the power of weapons is out of balance with the objectives for which they might be employed; as a result, at a moment of unparalleled strength we find ourselves paralyzed by the implications of our own weapons technology. On the political plane, many of the newly independent powers continue to inject into their international policies the revolutionary fervor that gained them independence. On the ideological plane, the contemporary ferment is fed by the newly awakened hopes and expectations of hitherto inarticulate peoples and by the rapidity with which ideas can be communicated. And the Soviet bloc, eager to exploit all dissatisfactions for its own ends, has given the present situation its revolutionary urgency.

This is true despite the conciliatory statements of the Twentieth Party Congress. For "peaceful coexistence" was not advanced as an acceptance of the *status quo*. On the contrary, it was justified as the most efficient offensive tactic, as a more effective means to subvert the existing order. The Soviet leaders gave up neither the class struggle with its postulate of irreconcilable conflict, nor the inevitable triumph of communism with its corollary of the dictatorship of the proletariat. To be sure, war was held to be no longer inevitable, but only because soon the U.S.S.R. would possess preponderant strength. Should the policy of "peaceful coexistence" prove less fruitful than expected, we can look for other tactics. "In the world from now on," Mao has said, "neutrality is only a word for deceiving people."

These have been hard lessons to come by. Lulled by a century and a half of comparative tranquillity and without experience with disaster, we have been reluctant to take at face value the often-repeated Soviet assertion that they mean to smash the existing framework. We have tended to treat Soviet protestations as if their intent were merely tactical—as if the U.S.S.R. overstated its case for bargaining purposes or were motivated by specific grievances to be assuaged by individual concessions. There is a measure of pathos in our effort to find "reasonable" motives for the Soviets to cease being Bolshevik: the opportunity to develop the resources of their own country, the unlimited possibilities of nuclear energy or of international trade. We reveal thereby a state of mind which cannot come to grips with a policy of unlimited objectives. Our belief that an antagonist can be vanquished by the persuasiveness of argument, our trust in the efficacy of the process of negotiation, reflect the dominant role played in our diplomacy by the legal profession and their conception of diplomacy as a legal process.

But the legal method cannot be applied in a revolutionary situation, for it presupposes a framework of agreed rules within which negotiating skill is exercised. It is not the process of negotiation as such which accounts for the settlement of legal disputes, but a social environment which permits that process to operate. This explains why conciliatory American statements have so often missed their mark. To the Soviets, the key to their ultimate triumph resides in their superior understanding of "objective" forces and of the processes of history.[2] Even when they accept the "subjective" sincerity of American statesmen, they still believe them powerless to deal with the "objective" factors of American society which will ultimately produce a showdown. Conciliatory American statements will appear to the Soviet leaders either as hypocrisy or stupidity, ignorance or propaganda. It is therefore futile to seek to sway Soviet leaders through logical persuasion or by invocations of abstract justice. Soviet statesmen consider conferences a means to confirm an "objective" situation. A Soviet diplomat who wishes to make concessions can justify them at home only if he can demonstrate that they resulted from a proper balancing of risks.

In short, diplomacy has a different function in a revolutionary international order. In a legitimate order, diplomacy seeks to compromise disagreements in order to perpetuate the international system. Adjustments occur because agreement is itself a desirable goal, because of a tacit agreement to come to an agreement. In a revolutionary order, on the other hand, adjustments have primarily a tactical significance: to prepare positions for the next test of strength. Negotiations in a legitimate order have three functions: to formulate by expressing agreements or discords in a manner that does not open unbridgeable schisms; to perpetuate by providing a forum for making concessions; to persuade by stating a plausible reason for settlement. But in a revolutionary period, most of these functions have changed their purpose: diplomats can still meet, but they cannot persuade, for they have ceased to speak the same language. Instead, diplomatic conferences become elaborate stage plays which seek to attach the uncommitted to one or the other of the contenders.

---

[2]There is no little exasperation in the Soviet replies to our repeated assertion that a change of tactics on their part implies a surrender of Marxism. Khrushchev has said (September 17, 1955), "If anyone believes that our smiles involve abandonment of the teaching of Marx, Engels, and Lenin, he deceives himself poorly. Those who wait for that must wait until a shrimp learns to whistle."

Nothing is more futile, therefore, than to attempt to deal with a revolutionary power by ordinary diplomatic methods. In a legitimate order, demands once made are negotiable; they are put forward with the intention of being compromised. But in a revolutionary order, they are programmatic; they represent a claim for allegiance. In a legitimate order, it is good negotiating tactics to formulate maximum demands because this facilitates compromise without loss of essential objectives. In a revolutionary order, it is good negotiating tactics to formulate minimum demands in order to gain the advantage of advocating moderation. In a legitimate order, proposals are addressed to the opposite number at the conference table. They must, therefore, be drafted with great attention to their substantive content and with sufficient ambiguity so that they do not appear as invitations to surrender. But in a revolutionary order, the protagonists at the conference table address not so much one another as the world at large. Proposals here must be framed with a maximum of clarity and even simplicity, for their major utility is their symbolic content. In short, in a legitimate order, a conference represents a struggle to find formulae to achieve agreement; in a revolutionary order, it is a struggle to capture the symbols which move humanity.

The major weakness of U.S. diplomacy has been the insufficient attention given to the symbolic aspect of foreign policy. Our positions have usually been worked out with great attention to their legal content, with special emphasis on the step-by-step approach of traditional diplomacy. But while we have been addressing the Soviets, they have been speaking to the people of the world. With a few exceptions we have not succeeded in dramatizing our position, in reducing a complex negotiation to its symbolic terms. In major areas of the world the Soviets have captured the "peace offensive" by dint of the endless repetition of slogans that seemed preposterous when first advanced but which have become common currency through usage. The power which has added 150 million people to its orbit by force has become the champion of anticolonialism; the state which has developed slave labor as an integral part of its economic system has emerged in many parts of the world as the champion of human dignity. Neither regarding German unity nor Korea nor the satellite orbit have we succeeded in mobilizing world opinion. But Formosa has become a symbol of American intransigence and our overseas air bases a token of American aggressiveness. We have replied to every Soviet thrust like a pedantic professor sure of his righteousness; but the world is not moved by legalistic phrases, at least in a revolutionary period. This is not to say that negotiation should be conceived as mere propaganda; only that by failing to cope adequately with their psychological aspect, we have given the Soviets unnecessary opportunities.

As a result, the international debate is carried on almost entirely in the categories and at the pace established by the Soviets; the world's attention is directed toward the horror of nuclear weapons but not toward the fact of aggression which would unleash them. The Soviets negotiate when a relaxation of tension serves their purpose, and they break off negotiations when it is to their advantage, without being forced to shoulder the onus for the failure. We were right to agree to the summit conference and the subsequent meeting of the foreign ministers. But it was not necessary to permit the Four-Power meetings to become an effort to turn the Soviets respectable; or for the president to give the Soviet Union a certificate of good conduct by assuring Bulganin he believed in his peaceful intentions. Nor was it wise to let the Soviet leaders build up a distinction between the president and the rest of the United States government, so that any increase in tensions will be ascribed to the fact that the president succumbed to the pressures of his advisors or to the operation of the "objective" factors of the U.S. economy or to a change of administration. Because of our inability to raise the negotiations above the commonplace, they were conducted in a never-never land where a Soviet smile was considered to outweigh the fact of the perpetuated division of Germany and where problems were evaded simply by denying that they existed.

IV

BUT COULD we have carried our allies and the uncommitted along on a different policy? Perhaps the best way to approach a discussion of our system of alliances is to analyze the historical role of coalitions. In the past, coalitions have generally been held together by a combination of three motivations: (1) To leave no doubt about the alignment of forces and to discourage aggression by assembling superior power—this in effect is the doctrine of collective security. (2) To provide an obligation for assistance. Were the national interest unambiguous and unchangeable, each power would know its obligations without any formal pact. But the national interest fluctuates within limits; it must be adapted to changing circumstances. An alliance is a form of insurance against contingencies, an additional weight when considering whether to go to war. (3) To legitimize the assistance of foreign troops or intervention in a foreign country.

An alliance is effective, then, to the extent that its power appears formidable and its purpose unambiguous. If an alliance is composed of too many disparate elements or if its members pursue too varying aims, it will not survive a real test. The legal obligation by itself will not suffice if the coalition has no common purpose or is incapable of giving its purpose a military expression. The French system of alliances between the two wars, however imposing on paper, could not survive the conflicting interests of its components and its lack of a unifying military doctrine. It is not the fact of alliance which deters aggression but the application it can be given in any concrete case.

If we examine the structure of the present system of alliances created by the United States, we discover that most of the historic conditions for coalitions no longer apply or apply in a different sense. From the point of view of power relationships, none of our alliances, save NATO, adds to our effective strength. And NATO is in difficulty because we cannot give it a military doctrine which makes sense to our NATO partners. Our interest in the alliance is twofold: (a) to prevent Eurasia from being controlled by a hostile power, because if the United States were confined to the Western Hemisphere it could survive, if at all, only through an effort inconsistent with what is now considered the American way of life; (b) to add to our overall strength vis-à-vis the U.S.S.R. by obtaining overseas facilities, particularly air bases. Our empiricist bias has, however, caused us to place these objectives in the framework of a specific threat—that of overt Soviet military aggression—and to look at this threat only in terms of the total strategic relationship between us and the Soviet bloc. In these terms, Eurasia is protected not by our capability for local defense, but by our strategic superiority in an all-out war, and we have therefore tended to justify our alliances because of the overseas air bases they afford us.

An alliance is useless, however, unless it expresses a mutuality of interest between the partners. Our military policy is increasingly based on a strategy of "revenge," the objective of which is to retaliate with greater destruction than we suffer. But in all situations short of all-out war (and perhaps even then), deterrence is produced not by a capability to inflict *disproportionate* losses, but a capability to inflict losses *unacceptable* in relation to specific objectives in dispute. The Soviet successes in the postwar period demonstrate that in certain circumstances even an inferior retaliatory capability can produce deterrence. Despite our strategic superiority we refused to intervene in Indochina or expand the war in Korea, because Korea and Indochina did not seem "worth" an all-out war and because we had inadequate alternative capabilities to make the Soviet calculus of risks seem unattractive. An all-out strategy, moreover, not only increases our own inhibitions but runs counter to a coalition policy. Our allies realize that in all-out war they will add to our effective strength only by supplying facilities; they see no significance in a military contribution of their own. As long as our military doctrine threatens to transform every war into an all-out war, our system of alliances will be in jeopardy.

Our policies have, moreover, been inhibited by the notion of collective security drawn from the lessons of the 1930s, when a united front might well have deterred Hitler, and by our historical bias in favor of federal structures.

We base our coalitions on the assumption that unless all allies resist any aggression anywhere, no effective resistance is possible at all. But this notion of collective security has the paradoxical result of paralyzing the partner capable of resisting alone. For governments hard pressed to act in areas of direct concern to them cannot be brought to run risks outside that area, so that the effort to obtain NATO support in Asia tends to undermine the cohesiveness of NATO in Europe. Even within the purely regional alliances, the combinations of purposes are extremely various. Pakistan desires arms more for their effect on India than for the protection they afford against the U.S.S.R. or China; Iraq is interested in the Baghdad Pact primarily for the military advantages it gives over Saudi Arabia and Egypt. And in neither SEATO nor the Baghdad Pact are we associated with partners with whom we share the degree of common purpose conferred by the cultural heritage that we share with our European allies.

The problems of our system of alliances can be summed up under two headings: either the alliances add little to our effective strength or they do not reflect a common purpose, or both. In such circumstances a system of collective security leads in fact to a dilution of purpose and to an air of unreality in which the existence of an alliance, and not the resolution behind it, is considered the guarantee of security. Thus, we speak of plugging gaps in defenses as if a treaty instrument were itself a defense. We will not be able to overcome these difficulties until we develop a new approach to our coalition policy, above all until we set less ambitious goals. We must confine our alliances to the purposes we and our allies share.

But can such a coalition policy be developed? The implications of the growing Soviet nuclear capability would seem to impose a measure of harmony between the interest of the United States in an overall strategy and our allies' concern with local defense. For with the end of our immunity from nuclear attack, the nature of deterrence has altered. A deterrent is effective only to the degree that it is plausible, and as the Soviet nuclear stockpile grows, our willingness to run the risk of an all-out war for any objective save a direct attack on the continental United States will diminish. In such a situation, deterrence with respect to the issues most likely to be in dispute is above all achieved by a capability for local defense. In the face of the horrors of thermonuclear war, it is in our interest to seek to defend Eurasia by means other than all-out war: to devise a strategy which will allow us to inflict the minimum amount of damage consistent with deterrence. The justification for our alliances, therefore, is less that they add to our over-all strength than that they give us an opportunity to apply our power subtly and with less fearful risks.

From the military point of view, our alliances should be conceived as devices to organize local defense and our assistance as a means to make local defense possible. We should make clear to our allies that their best chance of avoiding thermonuclear war resides in our ability to make local aggression too costly. They should understand that they cannot avoid their dilemma by neutrality or surrender, for if we are pushed out of Eurasia they will bring on what they fear most. Confined to the Western Hemisphere, we would have no choice but to fight an all-out war. To be sure, the Soviets have skillfully fomented neutralism by giving the impression that local resistance must inevitably lead to all-out war. But the Soviets can be no more interested than we in total war; the fear of thermonuclear extinction would provide a powerful sanction against expanding a conflict.

The corollary to a regional system of alliances, however, is willingness on our part to act alone if the over-all strategic balance is imperiled. None of our allies, with the exception of Great Britain, has the capability or the willingness to act outside its own geographical area. To ask them to do so will only undermine the domestic position of already weak governments and demoralize them further. It will lead to subterfuges and to the dilution of common action behind the form of joint communiqués. We have to face the fact that only the United States is strong enough domestically and economically to assume worldwide responsibilities and that the attempt to obtain the prior approval by all our allies of our every step will lead not to common action but to inaction. To be sure, whenever there exists a community of purpose, as for example with Great Britain in the Middle East and perhaps in Southeast Asia, we should concert our efforts. But we must reserve the right to act alone, or with a regional grouping of powers, if our strategic interest so dictates. We cannot permit the Soviets to overturn the balance of power for the sake of allied unity, for whatever the disagreement of our allies on specific measures, their survival depends on our unimpaired strength.

The military point of view must not supply the sole motivation for our system of alliances, however. In fact, in many areas, particularly those newly independent, our emphasis on the military factor is the cause of our failure to develop a sense of common purpose. We are undoubtedly right in our belief in the Soviet menace. But revolutions are not logical, and the Asian revolution is interested more in internal development than in foreign affairs. Our insistence that they focus some of their energies outward appears to them as an irritating interruption of their primary concern and lends color to Soviet peace offensives. Moreover, the military contribution of both the Baghdad Pact and SEATO does not compensate for the decision of Egypt and India to stand apart and for the domestic pressures these instruments generated in some of the signatory countries.

The primary function of these pacts is to draw a line across which the U.S.S.R. cannot move without the risk of war and to legitimize intervention by the United States should war break out. But the line could have been better drawn by a unilateral declaration. Behind this shield we could then have concentrated on the primary problem of creating a sense of common purpose by emphasizing shared objectives, primarily by striving for the grouping of powers to assist in economic development. . . . As these political groupings gain in economic strength, their own interest would dictate a more active concern for common defense; at least it would provide the economic base for a meaningful defense. A powerful grouping of states on the Russian borders is against the interests of the Soviet Union regardless of whether the purpose of this grouping is primarily military. And by the same token, such a grouping is desirable from the American point of view even if it does not go along with our every policy.

The problem of the uncommitted states cannot be solved, however, merely by an economic grouping of powers. It is related to the whole U.S. posture. Anti-Americanism is fashionable today in many parts of the globe. As the richest and most powerful nation, we are the natural target for all frustrations. As the power which bears the primary responsibility for the defense of the free world, we are unpopular with all who are so preoccupied with the development of their own countries that they are unwilling to pay sufficient attention to foreign threats. We should, of course, seek to allay legitimate grievances, but we would be wrong to take every criticism at face value. Many of our most voluble critics in Southeast Asia would be terrified were our military protection suddenly withdrawn. Nehru's neutrality is possible, after all, only as long as the United States remains strong. A great deal of anti-Americanism hides a feeling of insecurity both material and spiritual. Popularity is a hopeless mirage in a situation which is revolutionary precisely because old values are disintegrating and millions are groping for a new orientation. For this reason, it is impossible to base policy solely on an inquiry into what people desire; a revolutionary situation is distinguished by its dissatisfactions, which join in protest against the existing order but can propose no clear substitute. This is the reason why most revolutions have been captured by a small minority which could give a sense of direction to popular resentments. In the uncommitted areas popularity may therefore be less important than respect.

In its relations with the uncommitted, the United States must develop not only a greater compassion but also a greater majesty. The picture of high American officials scurrying to all quarters of the globe to inform themselves on each crisis as it develops cannot but make an impression of uncertainty. The nervousness exhibited in our reactions to Soviet moves must contrast unfavorably with what appears to be the deliberate purposefulness of the Soviets. Moreover, for understandable reasons, many of the uncommitted na-

tions are eager to preserve the peace at almost any price. Because of what appears to them as vacillation and uncertainty, they choose in every crisis to direct pressure against us as the more malleable of the two superpowers. To the
degree that we can project a greater sense of purpose, some of these pressures
may be deflected on the Soviet bloc. A revolution like Egypt's or even India's
cannot be managed by understanding alone; it also requires a readiness on
our part to bear the psychological burden of difficult decisions.

V

WE THUS return to our original problem: the adequacy of American attitudes for dealing with the present crisis. This is above all a problem of leadership. For nations learn only by experience; they "know" only when it is too
late to act. But statesmen must act *as if* their intuition were already experience, as if their aspiration were truth. The statesman is, therefore, like one of
the heroes of classical tragedy who has had an intuition of the future, but
who cannot transmit it directly to his fellowmen and who cannot validate its
"truth." This is why statesmen often share the fate of prophets, that they are
without honor in their own country, and that their greatness is usually apparent only in retrospect when their intuition has become experience. The
statesman must be an educator; he must bridge the gap between a people's
experience and his vision, between its tradition and its future. In this task his
possibilities are limited. A statesman who too far outruns the experience of
his people will not be able to sell his program at home; witness Wilson. A
statesman who limits his policy to the experience of his people will doom
himself to sterility; witness French policy since World War I.

One of the crucial challenges confronting a society is therefore the capacity to produce a leadership group capable of transcending the experience
of that society. And here our sudden emergence as the major power in the
free world presents particular difficulties. The qualities of our leadership
groups were formed during the period when our primary concerns were domestic. Politics was considered a necessary evil, and the primary function of
the state was the exercise of police powers. Neither education nor incentives
existed for our leadership groups to think in political or strategic terms. This
was compounded by our empiricism with its cult of the expert and its premium on specialization. The two groups which are most dominant in the
higher levels of government, industry and the law, can serve as an illustration.
The rewards in industry, particularly large-scale industry, are for administrative competence; they therefore produce a tendency to deal with conceptual
problems by administrative means, by turning them over to committees of
experts. And the legal profession, trained to think in terms of discrete indi-

vidual cases, produces a penchant for *ad hoc* decisions and a resistance to the "hypothetical cases" inherent in long-range planning. Our leadership groups are therefore better prepared to deal with technical than with conceptual problems, with economic than with political issues. Projected on the Washington scene, they often lack the background to cope with a developing political and strategic situation: each problem is dealt with "on its merits," a procedure which emphasizes the particular at the expense of the general and bogs down planning in a mass of detail. The absence of a conceptual framework makes it difficult for them even to identify our problems or to choose effectively among the proposals and interpretations with which our governmental machinery is overloaded.

This explains many postwar Soviet successes. Whatever the qualities of Soviet leadership, its training is eminently political and conceptual. Reading Lenin or Mao or Stalin, one is struck by the emphasis on the relationship between political, military, psychological, and economic factors, the insistence on finding a conceptual basis for political action and on the need for dominating a situation by flexible tactics and inflexible purpose. And the internal struggles in the Kremlin ensure that only the most iron-nerved reach the top. Against the Politburo, trained to think in general terms and freed of problems of day-to-day administration, we have pitted leaders overwhelmed with departmental duties and trained to think that it was a cardinal sin to transgress on another's field of specialization. To our leaders, policy is as a series of discrete problems; to the Soviet leaders it is an aspect of a continuing political process. As a result, the contest between us and the Soviets has had many of the attributes of any contest between a professional and an amateur: even a mediocre professional will usually defeat an excellent amateur, not because the amateur does not know what to do, but because he cannot react sufficiently quickly or consistently. Our leaders have not lacked ability, but they have had to learn while doing and this has imposed too great a handicap.

To be sure, many of the shortcomings of our leadership groups reflect the very qualities which have made for the ease of relationships in American society. The condition for our limited government has been the absence of basic social schisms, the regulation of many concerns not by government fiat but by "what is taken for granted." A society can operate in this fashion only if disputes are not pushed to their logical conclusions and if disagreements are blunted by the absence of dogmatism. And in fact the fear of seeming dogmatic permeates our social scene. Most opinions are introduced with a disclaimer which indicates that the proponent is aware of their contingency and also that he claims no superior validity for his own conclusions. This produces a preference for decisions by committee, because the process of conversation permits disagreements to be discovered most easily and adjustments made before positions have hardened. Our decision-making process is therefore geared to the pace of conversation; even departmental memoranda on which policy decisions are ultimately based are written with an eye to eventual compromise and not with the expectation that any one of them will be accepted in its entirety.

It would be wrong to be too pessimistic. No one would have believed when World War II ended that the United States would assume commitments on such a worldwide scale. Our shortcomings are imposing only because of the magnitude of the threat confronting us. Moreover, the performance of the United States, for all its failings, compares favorably with that of the other nations of the non-Soviet world. Our difficulties in foreign policy are therefore only a symptom—and by no means the most obvious—of an inward uncertainty in the free world. To be sure, democracies by the nature of their institutions cannot conduct policy as deviously, change course as rapidly, or prepare their moves as secretly as dictatorships. But the crisis of the non-Soviet world is deeper. The tragic element in foreign policy is the impossibility of escaping conjecture; after the "objective" analysis of fact there remains a residue of uncertainty about the meaning of events or the opportunities they offer. A statesman can often escape his dilemmas by lowering his sights; he always has the option to ignore the other side's capabilities by assuming it has peaceful intentions. Many of the difficulties of the non-Soviet world have been the result of an attempt to use the element of uncertainty as an excuse for inaction. But certainty in foreign policy is conferred at least as much by philosophy as by fact; it derives from the imposition of purpose on events.

This is not to say that we should imitate Soviet dogmatism. A society can survive only by the genius that made it great. But we should be able to leaven our empiricism with a sense of urgency. And while our history may leave us not well enough prepared to deal with tragedy, it can teach us that great achievement does not result from a quest for safety. Even so, our task will remain psychologically more complex than that of the Soviets. As the strongest and perhaps the most vital power of the free world, we face the challenge of demonstrating that democracy is able to find the moral certainty to act without the support of fanaticism and to run risks without a guarantee of success.

The Delicate Balance of Terror

Albert Wohlstetter

JANUARY 1959

THE FIRST SHOCK administered by the Soviet launching of sputnik has almost dissipated. The flurry of statements and investigations and improvised responses has died down, leaving a small residue: a slight increase in the schedule of bomber and ballistic missile production, with a resulting small increment in our defense expenditures for the current fiscal year; a considerable enthusiasm for space travel; and some stirrings of interest in the teaching of mathematics and physics in the secondary schools. Western defense policy has almost returned to the level of activity and the emphasis suited to the basic assumptions which were controlling before sputnik.

One of the most important of these assumptions—that a general thermonuclear war is extremely unlikely—is held in common by most of the critics of our defense policy as well as by its proponents. Because of its crucial role in the Western strategy of defense, I should like to examine the stability of the thermonuclear balance which, it is generally supposed, would make aggression irrational or even insane. The balance, I believe, is in fact precarious, and this fact has critical implications for policy. Deterrence in the 1960s is neither assured nor impossible but will be the product of sustained intelligent effort and hard choices, responsibly made. As a major illustration important both for defense and foreign policy, I shall treat the particularly stringent conditions for deterrence which affect forces based close to the enemy, whether they are U.S. forces or those of our allies, under single or joint control. I shall comment also on the inadequacy as well as the necessity of deterrence, on the problem of accidental outbreak of war, and on disarmament.

II. THE PRESUMED AUTOMATIC BALANCE

I EMPHASIZE that requirements for deterrence are stringent. We have heard so much about the atomic stalemate and the receding probability of war which it has produced that this may strike the reader as something of an exaggeration. Is deterrence a necessary consequence of both sides having a nuclear delivery capability, and is all-out war nearly obsolete? Is mutual extinction the only outcome of a general war? This belief, frequently expressed by references to Mr. Oppenheimer's simile of the two scorpions in a bottle, is perhaps the prevalent one. It is held by a very eminent and diverse group of people—in England by Sir Winston Churchill, P. M. S. Blackett, Sir John Slessor, Admiral Buzzard, and many others; in France by such figures as Raymond Aron, General Gallois, and General Gazin; in this country by the titular heads of both parties as well as almost all writers on military and foreign affairs, by both Henry Kissinger and his critic, James E. King, Jr., and by George Kennan as well as Dean Acheson. Mr. Kennan refers to American concern about surprise attack as simply obsessive; and many people have drawn the consequence of the stalemate as has Blackett, who states: "If it is in fact true, as most current opinion holds, that strategic air power has abolished global war, then an urgent problem for the West is to assess how little effort must be put into it to keep global war abolished." If peace were founded firmly on mutual terror, and mutual terror on symmetrical nuclear capabilities, this would be, as Churchill has said, "a melancholy paradox"; nonetheless, a most comforting one.

Deterrence, however, is not automatic. While feasible, it will be much harder to achieve in the 1960s than is generally believed. One of the most disturbing features of current opinion is the underestimation of this difficulty. This is due partly to a misconstruction of the technological race as a problem in matching striking forces, partly to a wishful analysis of the Soviet ability to strike first.

Since sputnik, the United States has made several moves to assure the world (that is, the enemy, but more especially our allies and ourselves) that we will match or overmatch Soviet technology and, specifically, Soviet offense technology. We have, for example, accelerated the bomber and ballistic missile programs, in particular the intermediate-range ballistic missiles. The problem has been conceived as more or better bombers—or rockets; or sputniks; or engineers. This has meant confusing deterrence with matching or exceeding the enemy's ability to strike first. Matching weapons, however, misconstrues the nature of the technological race. Not, as is frequently said, because only a few bombs owned by the defender can make aggression fruitless, but because even many might not. One outmoded A-bomb dropped from an obsolete bomber might destroy a great many supersonic jets and ballistic missiles. To deter an attack means being able to strike back in spite of it. It means, in other words, a capability to strike second. In the last year or two there has been a growing awareness of the importance of the distinction between a "strike-first" and a "strike-second" capability but little, if any, recognition of the implications of this distinction for the balance of terror theory.

Where the published writings have not simply underestimated Soviet capabilities and the advantages of a first strike, they have in general placed artificial constraints on the Soviet use of the capabilities attributed to them. They assume, for example, that the enemy will attack in mass over the Arctic through our Distant Early Warning line, with bombers refueled over Canada—all resulting in plenty of warning. Most hopefully, it is sometimes assumed that such attacks will be preceded by days of visible preparations for moving ground troops. Such assumptions suggest that the Soviet leaders will be rather bumbling or, better, cooperative. However attractive it may be for us to narrow Soviet alternatives to these, they would be low in the order of preference of any reasonable Russians planning war.

III. THE QUANTITATIVE NATURE OF THE PROBLEM AND THE UNCERTAINTIES

IN TREATING Soviet strategies it is important to consider Soviet rather than Western advantage and to consider the strategy of both sides quantitatively. The effectiveness of our own choices will depend on a most complex numerical interaction of Soviet and Western plans. Unfortunately, both the privileged and unprivileged information on these matters is precarious. As a result, competent people have been led into critical error in evaluating the prospects for deterrence. Western journalists have greatly overestimated the difficulties of a Soviet surprise attack with thermonuclear weapons and vastly underestimated the complexity of the Western problem of retaliation.

One intelligent commentator, Richard Rovere, recently expressed the common view: "If the Russians had ten thousand warheads and a missile for each, and we had ten hydrogen bombs and ten obsolete bombers, . . . aggression would still be a folly that would appeal only to an insane adventurer." Mr. Rovere's example is plausible because it assumes implicitly that the defender's hydrogen bombs will with certainty be visited on the aggressor; then the damage done by the ten bombs seems terrible enough for deterrence, and any more would be simply redundant. This is the basis for the common view. The example raises questions, even assuming the delivery of the ten weapons. For instance, the targets aimed at in retaliation might be sheltered, and a quite modest civil defense could hold within tolerable limits the damage done to such city targets by ten delivered bombs. But the essential point is that the weapons would not be very likely to reach their targets. Even if the bombers were dispersed at ten different points, and protected by shelters so blast resistant as to stand up anywhere outside the lip of the bomb crater—even inside the fire ball itself—the chances of one of these bombers surviving the huge attack directed at it would be on the order of one in a million. (This calculation takes account of the unreliability and inaccuracy of the missile.) And the damage done by the small minority of these ten planes that might be in the air at the time of the attack, armed and ready to run the gauntlet of an alert air defense system, if not zero, would be very small indeed compared to damage that Russia has suffered in the past. For Mr. Rovere, like many other writers on this subject, numerical superiority is not important at all.

For Joseph Alsop, on the other hand, it is important, but the superiority is on our side. Mr. Alsop recently enunciated as one of the four rules of nuclear war: "The aggressor's problem is astronomically difficult; and the aggressor requires an overwhelming superiority of force." There are, he believes, no fewer than 400 SAC bases in the NATO nations alone and many more elsewhere, all of which would have to be attacked in a very short space of time. The "thousands of coordinated air sorties and/or missile firings," he concludes, are not feasible. Mr. Alsop's argument is numerical and has the virtue of demonstrating that at least the relative numbers are important. But the numbers he uses are very wide of the mark. He overestimates the number of such bases by a factor of more than ten, and in any case, missile firings on the scale of a thousand or more involve costs that are by no means out of proportion, given the strategic budgets of the great powers. Whether or not thousands are needed depends on the yield and the accuracy of the enemy missiles, something about which it would be a great mistake for us to display confidence.

Perhaps the first step in dispelling the nearly universal optimism about the stability of deterrence would be to recognize the difficulties in analyzing the uncertainties and interactions between our own wide range of choices and the moves open to the Soviets. On our side we must consider an enormous variety of strategic weapons which might compose our force and, for each of these, several alternative methods of basing and operation. These are the choices that determine whether a weapons system will have any genuine capability in the realistic circumstances of a war. . . .

The difficulty of describing in a brief article the best mixture of weapons for the long-term future beginning in 1960, their base requirements, their potentiality for stabilizing or upsetting the balance among the great powers, and their implications for the alliance is not just a matter of space or the constraint of security. The difficulty in fact stems from some rather basic insecurities. These matters are wildly uncertain; we are talking about weapons and vehicles that are some time off, and even if the precise performances currently hoped for and claimed by contractors were in the public domain, it would be a good idea to doubt them. . . .

Some of the complexities can be suggested by referring to the successive obstacles to be hurdled by any system providing a capability to strike second, that is, to strike back. Such deterrent systems must have (a) a stable, "steady-state" peacetime operation within feasible budgets (besides the logistic and operational costs, there are, for example, problems of false alarms and accidents). They must have also the ability (b) to survive enemy attacks, (c) to make and communicate the decision to retaliate, (d) to reach enemy territory with fuel enough to complete their mission, (e) to penetrate enemy active defenses, that is, fighters and surface-to-air missiles, and (f) to destroy the target in spite of any "passive" civil defense in the form of dispersal or protective construction or evacuation of the target itself.

Within limits the enemy is free to use his offensive and defensive forces so as to exploit the weaknesses of each of our systems. He will also be free, within limits, in the 1960s to choose that composition of forces which will make life as difficult as possible for the various systems we might select. It would be quite wrong to assume that we have the same degree of flexibility or that the uncertainties I have described affect a totalitarian aggressor and the party attacked equally. A totalitarian country can preserve secrecy about the capabilities and disposition of his forces very much better than a Western democracy. And the aggressor has, among other enormous advantages of the first strike, the ability to weigh continually our performance at each of the six barriers and to choose that precise time and circumstance for attack which will reduce uncertainty. It is important not to confuse our uncertainty with his. Strangely enough, some military commentators have not made this distinction and have founded their certainty of deterrence on the fact simply that there are uncertainties. . . .

IV. THE DELICACY OF THE BALANCE OF TERROR

THE MOST important conclusion is that we must expect a vast increase in the weight of attack which the Soviets can deliver with little warning and the growth of a significant Russian capability for an essentially warningless attack. As a result, strategic deterrence, while feasible, will be extremely difficult to achieve, and at critical junctures in the 1960s we may not have the power to deter attack. Whether we have it or not will depend on some difficult strategic choices as to the future composition of the deterrent forces as well as hard choices on its basing, operations, and defense.

Manned bombers will continue to make up the predominant part of our striking force in the early 1960s. None of the popular remedies for their defense will suffice—not, for example, mere increase of alertness (which will be offset by the Soviets' increasing capability for attack without significant warning), nor simple dispersal or sheltering alone or mobility taken by itself, nor a mere piling up of interceptors and defense missiles around SAC bases. . . .

On the other hand, it would be unwise to look for miracles in the new weapons systems, which by the mid-1960s may constitute a considerable portion of the United States force. After the Thor, Atlas, and Titan, there are a number of promising developments. The solid-fueled rockets, Minuteman and Polaris, promise in particular to be extremely significant components of the deterrent force. Today they are being touted as making the problem of deterrence easy to solve and, in fact, guaranteeing its solution. But none of the new developments in vehicles is likely to do that. For the complex job of deterrence, they all have limitations. The unvaryingly immoderate claims for each new weapons system should make us wary of the latest "technological breakthroughs." Only a very short time ago the ballistic missile itself was supposed to be intrinsically invulnerable on the ground. It is now more generally understood that its survival is likely to depend on a variety of choices in its defense.

It is hard to talk with confidence about the mid and late 1960s. A systematic study of an optimal or a good deterrent force which considered all the major factors affecting choice and dealt adequately with the uncertainties would be a formidable task. In lieu of this, I shall mention briefly why none of the many systems available or projected dominates the others in any obvious way. My comments will take the form of a swift run-through of the characteristic advantages and disadvantages of various strategic systems at each of the six successive hurdles mentioned earlier.

The first hurdle to be surmounted is the attainment of a stable, steady-state peacetime operation. Systems which depend for their survival on extreme decentralization of controls, as may be the case with large-scale dispersal and some of the mobile weapons, raise problems of accidents, and over a long period of peacetime operation this leads in turn to serious political problems. Systems relying on extensive movement by land, perhaps by truck caravan, are an obvious example; the introduction of these on European roads, as is sometimes suggested, would raise grave questions for the governments of some of our allies. Any extensive increase in the armed air alert will increase the hazard of accident and intensify the concern already expressed among our allies. Some of the proposals for bombardment satellites may involve such hazards of unintended bomb release as to make them out of the question.

The cost to buy and operate various weapons systems must be seriously considered. Some systems buy their ability to negotiate a given hurdle—say, surviving the enemy attack—only at prohibitive cost. Then the number that can be bought out of a given budget will be small and this will affect the relative performance of competing systems at various other hurdles, for example, penetrating enemy defenses. Some of the relevant cost comparisons, then, are between competing systems; others concern the extra costs to the enemy of canceling an additional expenditure of our own. For example, some dispersal is essential, though usually it is expensive; if the dispersed bases are within a warning net, dispersal can help to provide warning against some sorts of attack, since it forces the attacker to increase the size of his raid and so makes it more liable to detection as well as somewhat harder to coordinate. But as the sole or principal defense of our offensive force, dispersal has only a brief useful life and can be justified financially only up to a point. For against our costs of construction, maintenance, and operation of an additional base must be set the enemy's much lower costs of delivering one extra weapon. And, in general, any feasible degree of dispersal leaves a considerable concentration of value at a single target point. For example, a squadron of heavy bombers costing, with their associated tankers and penetration aids, perhaps $500 million over five years might be eliminated, if it were otherwise unprotected, by an enemy intercontinental ballistic missile costing perhaps $16 million. After making allowance for the unreliability and inaccuracy of the missile, this means a ratio of some ten for one or better. To achieve safety by *brute* numbers in so unfavorable a competition is not likely to be viable economically or politically. However, a viable peacetime operation is only the first hurdle to be surmounted.

At the second hurdle—surviving the enemy offense—ground alert systems placed deep within a warning net look good against a manned bomber attack, much less good against intercontinental ballistic missiles, and not good at all against ballistic missiles launched from the sea. In the last case, systems such as the Minuteman, which may be sheltered and dispersed as well as alert, would do well. Systems involving launching platforms which are mobile and concealed, such as Polaris submarines, have particular advantage for surviving an enemy offense.

However, there is a third hurdle to be surmounted—namely that of making the decision to retaliate and communicating it. Here, Polaris, the combat air patrol of B-52s, and in fact all of the mobile platforms—under water, on the surface, in the air, and above the air—have severe problems. Long-distance communication may be jammed, and most important, communication centers may be destroyed.

At the fourth hurdle—ability to reach enemy territory with fuel enough to complete the mission—several of our short-legged systems have operational problems such as coordination with tankers and using bases close to the enemy. For a good many years to come, up to the mid-1960s in fact, this will be a formidable hurdle for the greater part of our deterrent force. The next section of this article deals with this problem at some length.

The fifth hurdle is the aggressor's long-range interceptors and close-in missile defenses. To get past these might require large numbers of planes and missiles. (If the high cost of overcoming an earlier obstacle—using extreme dispersal or airborne alert or the like—limits the number of planes or missiles bought, our capability is likely to be penalized disproportionately here.) Or getting through may involve carrying heavy loads of radar decoys, electronic jammers, and other aids to defense penetration. For example, vehicles like Minuteman and Polaris, which were made small to facilitate dispersal or mobility, may suffer here because they can carry fewer penetration aids.

At the final hurdle—destroying the target in spite of the passive defenses that may protect it—low-payload and low-accuracy systems, such as Minuteman and Polaris, may be frustrated by blast-resistant shelters. For example, 5 half-megaton weapons with an average inaccuracy of 2 miles might be expected to destroy half the population of a city of 900,000, spread over 40 square miles, provided the inhabitants are without shelters. But if they are provided with shelters capable of resisting overpressures of 100 pounds per square inch, approximately 60 such weapons would be required; and deep rock shelters might force the total up to over a thousand.

Prizes for a retaliatory capability are not distributed for getting over one of these jumps. A system must get over all six. I hope these illustrations will suggest that assuring ourselves the power to strike back after a massive thermonuclear surprise attack is by no means as automatic as is widely believed.

In counteracting the general optimism as to the ease and, in fact, the inevitability of deterrence, I should like to avoid creating the extreme opposite impression. Deterrence demands hard, continuing, intelligent work, but it can be achieved. The job of deterring rational attack by guaranteeing great damage to an aggressor is, for example, very much less difficult than erecting a nearly airtight defense of cities in the face of full-scale thermonuclear surprise attack. Protecting manned bombers and missiles is much easier because they may be dispersed, sheltered, or kept mobile, and they can respond to warning with greater speed. Mixtures of these and other defenses with complementary strengths can preserve a powerful remainder after attack. Obviously not all our bombers and missiles need to survive in order to fulfill their mission. To preserve the majority of our cities, intact, in the face of surprise attack is immensely more difficult, if not impossible. (This does not mean that the aggressor has the same problem in preserving his cities from retaliation by a poorly protected, badly damaged force. And it does not mean that *we* should not do more to limit the extent of the catastrophe to our cities in case deterrence fails. I believe we should.) Deterrence, however, provided we work at it, is feasible, and what is more, it is a crucial objective of national policy.

What can be said, then, as to whether general war is unlikely? Would not a general thermonuclear war mean "extinction" for the aggressor as well as the defender? "Extinction" is a state that badly needs analysis. Russian casualties in World War II were more than 20 million. Yet Russia recovered extremely well from this catastrophe. There are several quite plausible circumstances in the future when the Russians might be quite confident of being able to limit damage to considerably less than this number—if they make sensible strategic choices and we do not. On the other hand, the risks of not striking might at some juncture appear very great to the Soviets, involving, for example, disastrous defeat in peripheral war, loss of key satellites with danger of revolt spreading—possibly to Russia itself—or fear of an attack by ourselves. Then, striking first, by surprise, would be the sensible choice for them, and from their point of view the smaller risk.

It should be clear that it is not fruitful to talk about the likelihood of general war without specifying the range of alternatives that are pressing on the aggressor and the strategic postures of both the Soviet bloc and the West. Deterrence is a matter of comparative risks. The balance is not automatic. First, since thermonuclear weapons give an enormous advantage to the aggressor, it takes great ingenuity and realism at any given level of nuclear technology to devise a stable equilibrium. And second, this technology itself is changing with fantastic speed. Deterrence will require an urgent and continuing effort.

V. THE USES AND RISKS OF BASES CLOSE TO THE SOVIETS

IT MAY NOW be useful to focus attention on the special problems of deterrent forces close to the Soviet Union. First, overseas areas have played an important role in the past and have a continuing though less certain role today. Second, the recent acceleration of production of intermediate-range ballistic missiles and the negotiation of agreements with various NATO powers for their basing and operation have given our overseas bases a renewed importance in deterring attack on the United States—or so it would appear at first blush. Third, an analysis can throw some light on the problems faced by our allies in developing an independent ability to deter all-out attack on themselves, and in this way it can clarify the much agitated question of nuclear sharing. Finally, overseas bases affect in many critical ways, political and economic as well as military, the status of the alliance.

At the end of the last decade, overseas bases appeared to be an advantageous means of achieving the radius extension needed by our short-legged bombers, of permitting them to use several axes of attack, and of increasing the number of sorties possible in the course of an extended campaign. With the growth of our own thermonuclear stockpile, it became apparent that a long campaign involving many reuses of a large proportion of our bombers was not likely to be necessary. With the growth of a Russian nuclear-delivery capability, it became clear that this was most unlikely to be feasible.

Our overseas bases now have the disadvantage of high vulnerability. Because they are closer than the United States to the Soviet Union, they are subject to a vastly greater attack by a larger variety as well as number of vehicles. With given resources, the Soviets might deliver on nearby bases a freight of bombs with something like 50 to 100 times the yield that they could muster at intercontinental range. Missile accuracy would more than double. Because there is not much space for obtaining warning—in any case, there are no deep-warning radar nets—and since most of our overseas bases are close to deep water from which submarines might launch missiles, the warning problem is very much more severe than for bases in the interior of the United States.

As a result, early in the 1950s the U.S. Air Force decided to recall many of our bombers to the continental United States and to use the overseas bases chiefly for refueling, particularly poststrike ground refueling. This reduced drastically the vulnerability of U.S. bombers and at the same time retained many of the advantages of overseas operation. For some years now SAC has been reducing the number of aircraft usually deployed overseas. The purpose is to reduce vulnerability and has little to do with any increasing radius of SAC aircraft. The early B-52 radius is roughly that of the B-36; the B-47, roughly that of the B-50 or B-29. In fact the radius limitation and therefore the basing requirements we have discussed will not change substantially for some time to come. We can talk with comparative confidence here, because the U.S. strategic force is itself largely determined for this period. Such a force changes more slowly than is generally realized. The vast majority of the force will consist of manned bombers, and most of these will be of medium range. *Some* U.S. bombers will be able to reach *some* targets from *some* U.S. bases within the 48 states without landing on the way back. On the other hand, some bomber-target combinations are not feasible without pretarget landing (and are therefore doubtful). The Atlas, Titan, and Polaris rockets, when available, can of course do without overseas bases (though the proportion of Polaris submarines kept at sea can be made larger by the use of submarine tenders based overseas). But even with the projected force of aerial tankers, the greater part of our force, which will be manned bombers, cannot be used at all in attacks on the Soviet Union without at least some use of overseas areas.

What of the bases for Thor and Jupiter, our first intermediate-range ballistic missiles? These have to be close to the enemy, and they must of course be operating bases, not merely refueling stations. The Thors and Jupiters will be continuously in range of an enormous Soviet potential for surprise attack. These installations therefore reopen, in a most acute form, some of the serious questions of ground vulnerability that were raised about six years ago in connection with our overseas bomber bases. The decision to station the Thor and Jupiter missiles overseas has been our principal public response to the Russian advances in rocketry and perhaps our most plausible response. Because it involves our ballistic missiles, it appears directly to answer the Russian rockets. Because it involves using European bases, it appears to make up for the range superiority of the Russian intercontinental missile. And most important, it directly involves the NATO powers and gives them an element of control.

There is no question that it was genuinely urgent not only to meet the Russian threat but to do so visibly, in order to save the loosening NATO alliance. Our allies were fearful that the Soviet ballistic missiles might mean that we were no longer able or willing to retaliate against the Soviet Union in case of an attack on them. We hastened to make public a reaction which would restore their confidence. This move surely appears to increase our own power to strike back and also to give our allies a deterrent of their own, independent of our decision. It has also been argued that in this respect it merely advances the inevitable date at which our allies will acquire "modern" weapons of their own and that it widens the range of Soviet challenges which Europe can meet. But we must face seriously the question whether this move will in fact assure either the ability to retaliate or the decision to attempt it, on the part of our allies or ourselves. And we should ask at the very least whether further expansion of this policy will buy as much retaliatory power as other ways of spending the considerable sums involved. Finally, it is important to be clear whether the Thor and Jupiter actually increase the flexibility or range of response available to our allies.

One justification for this move is that it disperses retaliatory weapons and that this is the most effective sanction against the thermonuclear aggressor. The limitations of dispersal have already been discussed, but it remains to examine the argument that overseas bases provide *widespread* dispersal, which imposes on the aggressor insoluble problems of coordination.

There is of course something in the notion that forcing the enemy to attack many political entities increases the seriousness of his decision, but there is very little in the notion that dispersal in several countries makes the problem of destruction more difficult in the military sense. Dispersal does not require separation by the distance of oceans—just by the lethal diameters of enemy bombs. And the task of coordinating bomber attacks on Europe and the eastern coast of the United States, say, is not appreciably more difficult than coordinating attacks on our east and west coasts. In the case of ballistic missiles, the elapsed time from firing to impact on the target can be calculated with high accuracy. Although there will be some failures and delays, times of firing can be arranged so that impact on many dispersed points is almost simultaneous—on Okinawa and the United Kingdom, for instance, as well as on California and Ohio. Moreover, it is important to keep in mind that these far-flung bases, while distant from each other and from the United States, are on the whole close to the enemy. To eliminate them, therefore, requires a smaller expenditure of resources on his part than targets at intercontinental range. For close-in targets he can use a wider variety of weapons carrying larger payloads and with higher accuracy.

The seeming appositeness of an overseas-based Thor and Jupiter as an answer to a Russian intercontinental ballistic missile stems not so much from any careful analysis of their retaliatory power under attack as from the directness of the comparison they suggest: a rocket equals a rocket, an intercontinental missile equals an intermediate-range missile based at closer range to the target. But this again mistakes the nature of the technological race. It conceives the problem of deterrence as that of simply matching or exceeding the aggressor's capability to strike first. A surprising proportion of the debate on defense policy has betrayed this confusion. Matching technological developments are useful for prestige, and such demonstrations have a vital function in preserving the alliance and in reassuring the neutral powers. But propaganda is not enough. The only reasonably certain way of maintaining a reputation for strength is to display an actual power to our friends as well as our enemies. We should ask, then, whether further expansion of the current programs for basing Thor and Jupiter is an efficient way to increase American retaliatory power. If overseas bases are considered too vulnerable for manned bombers, will not the same be true for missiles?

The basis for the hopeful impression that they will not is rather vague, including a mixture of hypothetical properties of ballistic missiles in which perhaps the dominant element is their supposedly much more rapid, "push-button" response. What need to be considered here are the response time of such missiles (including decision, preparation, and launch times) and how they are to be defended.

The decision to fire a missile with a thermonuclear warhead is much harder to make than a decision simply to start a manned aircraft on its way, with orders to return to base unless instructed to continue to its assigned target. This is the "fail-safe" procedure practised by the U.S. Air Force. In contrast, once a missile is launched, there is no method of recall or deflection which is not subject to risks of electronic or mechanical failure. Therefore, such a decision must wait for much more unambiguous evidence of enemy intentions. It must and will take a longer time to make and is less likely to be made at all. Where more than one country is involved, the joint decision is harder still, since there is opportunity to disagree about the ambiguity of the evidence, as well as to reach quite different interpretations of national interest. On much less momentous matters the process of making decisions in NATO is complicated, and it should be recognized that such complexity has much to do with the genuine concern of the various NATO powers about the danger of accidentally starting World War III. Such fears will not be diminished with the advent of IRBMs. In fact, widespread dispersion of nuclear armed missiles raises measurably the possibility of accidental war.

Second, it is quite erroneous to suppose that by contrast with manned bombers the first IRBMs can be launched almost as simply as pressing a button. Countdown procedures for early missiles are liable to interruption, and the characteristics of the liquid oxygen fuel limits the readiness of their response. Unlike JP-4, the fuel used in jet bombers, liquid oxygen cannot be held for long periods of time in these vehicles. In this respect such missiles will be *less* ready than alert bombers. Third, the smaller warning time available overseas makes more difficult any response. This includes, in particular, any active defense, not only against ballistic missile attacks but, for example, against low-altitude or various circuitous attacks by manned aircraft.

Finally, passive defense by means of shelter is more difficult, given the larger bomb yields, better accuracies, and larger forces available to the Russians at such close range. And if the press reports are correct, the plans for IRBM installations do not call for bomb-resistant shelters. If this is so, it should be taken into account in measuring the actual contribution of these installations to the West's retaliatory power. Viewed as a contribution to deterring all-out attack on the United States, the Thor and Jupiter bases seem unlikely to compare favorably with other alternatives. If newspaper references to hard bargaining by some of our future hosts are to be believed, it would seem that such negotiations have been conducted under misapprehensions on both sides as to the benefits to the United States.

But many proponents of the distribution of Thor and Jupiter—and possibly some of our allies—have in mind not an increase in U.S. deterrence but the development of an independent capability in several of the NATO countries to deter all-out attack against themselves. This would be a useful thing if it can be managed at supportable cost and if it does not entail the sacrifice of even more critical measures of protection. But aside from the special problems of joint control, which would affect the certainty of response adversely, precisely who their legal owner is will not affect the retaliatory power of the Thors and Jupiters one way or the other. They would not be able to deter an attack which they could not survive. It is curious that many who question the utility of American overseas bases (for example, our bomber bases in the United Kingdom) simply assume that, for our allies, possession of strategic nuclear weapons is one with deterrence.

There remains the view that the provision of these weapons will broaden the range of response open to our allies. In so far as this view rests on the belief that the intermediate-range ballistic missile is adapted to limited war, it is wide of the mark. The inaccuracy of an IRBM requires high-yield warheads, and such a combination of inaccuracy and high yield, while quite appropriate and adequate against unprotected targets in a general war, would scarcely come within even the most lax, in fact reckless, definition of limited war. Such a weapon is inappropriate for even the nuclear variety of limited war, and it is totally useless for meeting the wide variety of provocations that are well below the threshold of nuclear response. In so far as these missiles will be costly for our allies to install, operate, and support, they are likely to displace a conventional capability that might be genuinely useful in limited engagements. More important, they are likely to be used as an excuse for budget cutting. In this way they will accelerate the general trend toward dependence on all-out response and so will have the opposite effect to the one claimed.

Nevertheless, if the Thor and Jupiter have these defects, might not some future weapon be free of them? Some of these defects, of course, will be overcome in time. Solid fuels or storable liquids will eventually replace liquid oxygen, reliabilities will increase, various forms of mobility or portability will become feasible, accuracies may even be so improved that such weapons can be used in limited wars. But these developments are all years away. In consequence, the discussion will be advanced if a little more precision is given such terms as "missiles" or "modern" or "advanced weapons." We are not distributing a generic "modern" weapon with all the virtues of flexibility in varying circumstances and of invulnerability in all-out war. But even with advances in the state of the art on our side, it will remain difficult to maintain a deterrent, especially close in under the enemy's guns.

It follows that, though a wider distribution of nuclear weapons may be inevitable, or at any rate likely, and though some countries in addition to the Soviet Union and the United States may even develop an independent deterrent, it is by no means inevitable or even very likely that the power to deter all-out thermonuclear attack will be widespread. This is true even though a minor power would not need to guarantee as large a retaliation as we in order to deter attack on itself. Unfortunately, the minor powers have smaller resources as well as poorer strategic locations. Mere membership in the nuclear club might carry with it prestige, as the applicants and nominees expect, but it will be rather expensive, and in time it will be clear that it does not necessarily confer any of the expected privileges enjoyed by the two charter members. The burden of deterring a general war as distinct from limited wars is still likely to be on the United States and therefore, so far as our allies are concerned, on the military alliance.

There is one final consideration. Missiles placed near the enemy, even if they could not retaliate, would have a potent capability for striking first by surprise. And it might not be easy for the enemy to discern their purpose. The existence of such a force might be a considerable provocation and in fact a dangerous one in the sense that it would place a great burden on our deterrent force which more than ever would have to guarantee extreme risks to the attacker—worse than the risks of waiting in the face of this danger. When not coupled with the ability to strike in retaliation, such a capability might suggest—erroneously, to be sure, in the case of the democracies—an intention to strike first. If so, it would tend to provoke rather than to deter general war.

I have dealt here with only one of the functions of overseas bases: their use as a support for the strategic deterrent force. They have a variety of important military, political, and economic roles which are beyond the scope of this paper. Expenditures in connection with the construction or operation of our bases, for example, are a form of economic aid and, moreover, a form that is rather palatable to the Congress. There are other functions in a central war where their importance may be very considerable, and their usefulness in a limited war might be substantial.

Indeed nothing said here should suggest that deterrence is in itself an adequate strategy. The complementary requirements of a sufficient military policy cannot be discussed in detail here. Certainly they include a more serious development of power to meet limited aggression, especially with more advanced conventional weapons than those now available. They also include more energetic provision for active and passive defenses to limit the dimensions of the catastrophe in case deterrence should fail. For example, an economically feasible shelter program might make the difference between 50 million survivors and 120 million survivors.

But it would be a fatal mistake to suppose that because strategic deterrence is inadequate by itself it can be dispensed with. Deterrence is not dispensable. If the picture of the world I have drawn is rather bleak, it could nonetheless be cataclysmically worse. Suppose both the United States and the Soviet Union had the power to destroy each other's retaliatory forces and society, given the opportunity to administer the opening blow. The situation would then be something like the old-fashioned Western gun duel. It would be extraordinarily risky for one side *not* to attempt to destroy the other, or to delay doing so, since it not only can emerge unscathed by striking first but this is the sole way it can reasonably hope to emerge at all. Evidently such a situation is extremely unstable. On the other hand, if it is clear that the aggressor too will suffer catastrophic damage in the event of his aggression, he then has strong reason not to attack, even though he can administer great damage. A protected retaliatory capability has a stabilizing influence not only in deterring rational attack, but also in offering every inducement to both powers to reduce the chance of accidental war.

The critics who feel that deterrence is "bankrupt" sometimes say that we stress deterrence too much. I believe this is quite wrong if it means that we are devoting too much effort to protect our power to retaliate; but I think it is quite right if it means that we have talked too much of a strategic threat as a substitute for many things it cannot replace.

VI. DETERRENCE, ACCIDENTS, AND DISARMAMENT

UP TO NOW I have talked mainly about the problem of deterring general war, of making it improbable that an act of war will be undertaken deliberately, with a clear understanding of the consequences, that is, rationally. That such deterrence will not be easy to maintain in the 1960s simply expresses the proposition that a surprise thermonuclear attack might *not* be an irrational or insane act on the part of the aggressor. A deterrent strategy is aimed at a rational enemy. Without a deterrent, general war is likely. With it, however, war might still occur.

In order to reduce the risk of a rational act of aggression, we are being forced to undertake measures (increased alertness, dispersal, mobility) which, to a significant extent, increase the risk of an irrational or unintentional act of war. The accident problem is serious, and it would be a great mistake to dismiss the recent Soviet charges on this subject as simply part of the war of nerves. In a clear sense the great multiplication and spread of nuclear arms throughout the world, the drastic increase in the degree of readiness of these weapons, and the decrease in the time available for the decision on their use must inevitably raise the risk of accident. . . .

There are many sorts of accidents that could happen. There can be electronic or mechanical failures of the sort illustrated by the B-47 and Nike mishaps; there can be aberrations of individuals, perhaps quite low in the echelon of command; there can be miscalculations on the part of governments as to enemy intent and the meaning of ambiguous signals. Not all deterrent strategies will involve the risk of accident equally. One of the principles of selecting a strategy should be to reduce the chance of accident, wherever we can, without a corresponding increase in vulnerability to a rational surprise attack. This is the purpose of the "fail-safe" procedures for launching SAC.

These problems are also relevant to the disarmament question. The Russians, exploiting an inaccurate United Press report which suggested that SAC started en masse toward Russia in response to frequent radar "ghosts," cried out against these supposed Arctic flights. The United States response, and its sequels, stated correctly that such flights had never been undertaken except in planned exercises and would not be undertaken in response to such unreliable warning. We pointed out the importance of quick response and a high degree of readiness in the protection of the deterrent force. The nature of the fail-safe precaution was also described.

We added, however, to cap the argument, that if the Russians were really worried about surprise attack they would accept the president's "open skies" proposal. This addition, however, conceals an absurdity. Aerial photography would have its uses in a disarmament plan—for example, to check an exchange of information on the location of ground bases. However, so far as surprise is concerned, an "open skies" plan would have direct use only to discover attacks requiring much more lengthy, visible, and unambiguous preparations than are likely today. The very readiness of our own strategic force suggests a state of technology which outmodes the "open skies" plan as a counter to surprise attack. Not even the most advanced reconnaissance equipment can disclose an intention from 40,000 feet. Who can say what the men in the blockhouse of an ICBM base have in mind? Or, for that matter, what is the final destination of training flights or fail-safe flights starting over the Pacific or North Atlantic from staging areas?

The actions that need to be taken on our own to deter attack might usefully be complemented by bilateral agreements for inspection and reporting and, possibly, limitation of arms and of methods of operating strategic and naval air forces. But the protection of our retaliatory power remains essential; and the better the protection, the smaller the burden placed on the agreement to limit arms and modes of operation and to make them subject to inspection. Reliance on "open skies" alone to prevent surprise would invite catastrophe and the loss of power to retaliate. Such a plan is worthless for discovering a well-prepared attack with ICBMs or submarine-launched missiles or a routine mass training flight whose destination could be kept ambiguous. A tremendous weight of weapons could be delivered in spite of it.

Although it is quite hopeless to look for an inspection scheme which would permit abandonment of the deterrent, this does not mean that some partial agreement on inspection and limitation might not help to reduce the chance of any sizable surprise attack. We should explore the possibilities of agreements involving limitation and inspection. But how we go about this will be conditioned by our appreciation of the problem of deterrence itself.

The critics of current policy who perceive the inadequacy of the strategy of deterrence are prominent among those urging disarmament negotiations, an end to the arms race, and a reduction of tension. This is a paramount interest of some of our allies. The balance of terror theory is the basis for some of the more lighthearted suggestions: if deterrence is automatic, strategic weapons on one side cancel those of the other, and it should be easy for both sides to give them up. So James E. King, Jr., one of the most sensible writers on the subject of limited war, suggests that weapons needed for "unlimited" war are those which both sides can most easily agree to abolish, simply because "neither side can anticipate anything but disaster" from their use. "Isn't there enough stability in the 'balance of terror'," he asks, "to justify our believing that the Russians can be trusted—within acceptable limits—to abandon the weapons whose 'utility is confined to the threat or conduct of a war of annihilation'?"

Indeed, if there were no real danger of a rational attack, then accidents and the "*n*th" country problem would be the only problems. As I have indicated, they are serious problems and some sorts of limitation and inspection agreement might diminish them. But if there is to be any prospect of realistic and useful agreement, we must reject the theory of automatic deterrence. And we must bear in mind that the more extensive a disarmament agreement is, the smaller the force that a violator would have to hide in order to achieve complete domination. Most obviously, "*the abolition* of the weapons necessary in a general or 'unlimited' war" would offer the most insuperable obstacles to an inspection plan, since the violator could gain an overwhelming advantage from the concealment of even a few weapons. The need for a deterrent, in this connection too, is ineradicable.

VII. SUMMARY

ALMOST EVERYONE seems concerned with the need to relax tension. However, relaxation of tension, which everyone thinks is good, is not easily distinguished from relaxing one's guard, which almost everyone thinks is bad. Relaxation, like Miltown, is not an end in itself. Not all danger comes from tension. To be tense where there is danger is only rational.

What can we say then, in sum, on the balance of terror theory of automatic deterrence? It is a contribution to the rhetoric rather than the logic of war in the thermonuclear age. The notion that a carefully planned surprise attack can be checkmated almost effortlessly, that, in short, we may resume our deep pre-sputnik sleep, is wrong, and its nearly universal acceptance is terribly dangerous. Though deterrence is not enough in itself, it is vital. There are two principal points.

First, deterring general war in both the early and late 1960s will be hard at best and hardest both for ourselves and our allies wherever we use forces based near the enemy.

Second, even if we can deter general war by a strenuous and continuing effort, this will by no means be the whole of a military, much less a foreign policy. Such a policy would not of itself remove the danger of accidental outbreak or limit the damage in case deterrence failed; nor would it be at all adequate for crises on the periphery.

A generally useful way of concluding a grim argument of this kind would be to affirm that we have the resources, intelligence, and courage to make the correct decisions. That is, of course, the case. And there is a good chance that we will do so. But perhaps, as a small aid toward making such decisions more likely, we should contemplate the possibility that they may *not* be made. They *are* hard, *do* involve sacrifice, *are* affected by great uncertainties, and concern matters in which much is altogether unknown and much else must be hedged by secrecy; and, above all, they entail a new image of ourselves in a world of persistent danger. It is by no means *certain* that we shall meet the test.

The Silence in
Russian Culture

Isaiah Berlin

OCTOBER 1957

ONE OF THE most arresting characteristics of modern Russian culture is its acute self-consciousness. There has surely never been a society more deeply and exclusively preoccupied with itself, its own nature and destiny. From the 1830s until our own day, the subject of almost all critical and imaginative writing in Russia is Russia. The great novelists, and a good many minor novelists too, as well as the vast majority of the characters in Russian novels, are continuously concerned not merely with their purposes as human beings or members of families or classes or professions, but with their condition or mission or future as Russians, members of a unique society with unique problems. This national self-absorption is to be found among novelists and playwrights of otherwise very different outlooks. An obsessed religious teacher like Dostoevsky; a didactic moralist like Tolstoy; an artist regarded in the West as being dedicated to timeless and universal psychological and aesthetic patterns like Turgenev; a "pure" unpolitical writer, careful not to preach, like Chekhov, are all, and throughout their lives, crucially concerned with the "Russian problem." Russian publicists, historians, political theorists, writers on social topics, literary critics, philosophers, theologians, poets, first and last, all without exception and at enormous length, discuss such issues as what it is to be a Russian; the virtues, vices, and destiny of the Russian individual and society; but above all the historic role of Russia among the nations; or, in particular, whether its social structure—say, the relation of intellectuals to the masses or of industry to agriculture—is *sui generis,* or whether, on the contrary, it is similar to that of other countries, or perhaps an anomalous, or stunted, or an abortive example of some superior Western model.

From the 1880s onward, a vast, now unreadably tedious, mass of books, articles, pamphlets began to flood upon the Russian intelligentsia, mostly concerned to prove either that Russia is destined to obey unique laws of its own—so that the experience of other countries has little or nothing to teach it—or, on the contrary, that its failures are entirely due to an unhappy dissimilarity to the life of other nations, a blindness to this or that universal law which governs all societies and which Russians ignore at their peril. The writers of Western countries, as often as not, produce their works of art or learning or even day-to-day comment (even in America where there exists similar self-consciousness, though not on so vast a scale) without necessarily tormenting themselves with the question whether their subject matter has been treated in its right historical or moral or metaphysical context. In Russia, at any rate since the second half of the nineteenth century, the reverse obtained. There, no serious writer could think of taking a step without concerning himself with the question whether his work was appropriately related to the great ultimate problems, the purposes of men on earth. The duty of all those who claimed to have the insight to understand, and the moral courage to face, their personal or social or national condition was always the same: in the first place to relate the relevant problems to the path which the given society (i.e., Russian; and only after that, human) was inexorably pursuing (if one was a determinist), or should be pursuing (if one thought one had freedom of choice), at the particular historical (or moral or metaphysical) stage of its development.

No doubt the Romantic doctrines, particularly in Germany, with their emphasis on the unique historical missions of different groups of men—Germans, or industrialists, or poets—which dominated European literature and journalism in the 1830s and 1840s, are partly responsible for this pervasive Russian attitude. But it went further in Russia than elsewhere. This was partly due to the fact that the effective advance of Russia to the center of the European scene (after the Napoleonic wars) coincided with the impact of the Romantic movement; it derived partly from a sense of their own cultural inferiority, which made many educated Russians painfully anxious to find a worthy part of their own to play—worthy, above all, of their growing material power in a world that was apt to look down upon them, and cause them to look down upon themselves, as a dark mass of benighted barbarians ruled by brutal despots and good only for crushing other freer, more civilized peoples. Again there may be, as some writers maintain, a strong craving for teleological and indeed eschatological systems in all societies influenced by Byzantium or by the Orthodox Church—a craving that the Russian priesthood, lacking as it conspicuously did the intellectual resources and tradition of the Western churches, could not satisfy, at any rate in the case of the better educated and critically inclined young men.

Whatever the truth about its origins, the state of mind of virtually all

Russian intellectuals in the nineteenth and early twentieth centuries (there were some exceptions) was dominated by the belief that all problems are interconnected and that there is some single system in terms of which they are all in principle soluble; moreover, that the discovery of this system is the beginning and end of morality, social life, education; and that to abandon the search for it in order to concentrate upon isolated or personal ends, say, the pursuit of knowledge, or artistic creation, or happiness, or individual freedom for their own sakes, is willful, subjective, irrational, egoistic, an immoral evasion of human responsibility. This attitude is characteristic not merely of the left-wing Russian intelligentsia, but of the outlook of civilized Russians of all shades of political opinion, spread widely both in religious and in secular, in literary and in scientific circles. Almost any philosophical system that affected to give a comprehensive answer to the great questions found a marvellously, indeed excessively, enthusiastic welcome among these eager, overresponsive, idealistic, impeccably consistent, sometimes only too rigorously logical thinkers.

And the systems were not slow in arriving. First came German historicism, particularly in its Hegelian form, which conceived of history as the essential, indeed the only genuine science. True, Hegel looked on the Slavs with contempt as "unhistorical" and declared that (like the "extinct" Chinese civilization) they had no part to play in the march of the human spirit. This part of Hegel was quietly ignored, and adequate room made in the universal schema for the Slavs in general and (on the authority of Hegel's formidable rival, Schelling) for the Russians in particular. After the infatuation with Schiller, Fichte, Hegel and other German Idealists came a similar faith in French social prophets—Saint-Simon, Fourier, and their many disciples and interpreters, who offered cut-and-dried "scientific" plans of reform or revolution for which some among their Russian disciples, with their will to believe in literal inspiration, were ready to lay down their lives. This was followed by many another *Lebensphilosophie,* inspired by Rousseau, by Comtian positivism, Darwinism, neomediævalism, anarchism, which in Russia went far beyond their Western prototypes. Unlike the West where such systems often languished and declined amid cynical indifference, in the Russian Empire they became fighting faiths, thriving on the opposition to them of contrary ideologies—mystical monarchism, Slavophil nostalgia, clericalism, and the like; and under absolutism, where ideas and daydreams are liable to become substitutes for action, ballooned out into fantastic shapes, dominating the lives of their devotees to a degree scarcely known elsewhere. To turn history or logic or one of the natural sciences—biology or sociology—into a theodicy; to seek, and affect to find, within them solutions to agonizing moral or religious doubts and perplexities; to transform them into secular theologies—

all that is nothing new in human history. But the Russians indulged in this process on a heroic and desperate scale, and in the course of it brought forth what today is called the attitude of total commitment, at least of its modern form.

Over a century ago Russian critics denounced European civilization for its lack of understanding. It seemed to them characteristic of the morally desiccated, limited thinkers of the West to maintain that human activities were not all necessarily interconnected with each other—that what a man did as a writer was one thing and what he did as a citizen was another; that a man might be a good chemist and yet maltreat his family or cheat at cards; that a man might compose profound music and yet hold stupid or immoral political views that were no business of the critics or of the public. This notion of life, according to Russians of almost all shades of opinion, was artificial and shallow and flew to pieces before the deeper insight of the all-embracing view, according to which the life of individuals and the life of their institutions were one and indivisible. Every faculty and element in the individual were in a state of constant interplay; a man could not be one thing as a painter and another as a citizen, honest as a mathematician and false as a husband; it was impossible to draw frontiers between any aspects of human activity, above all between public and private life. Any attempt to insulate this or that area from the invasion of outside forces was held to be founded upon the radical fallacy of thinking that the true function and purpose of a human being does not penetrate every one of his acts and relationships—or worse still, that men had, as men, no specific function or purpose at all. It followed that whatever most fully embodies this ultimate total human purpose—the state, according to the Hegelians; an élite of scientists, artists, and managers, according to the followers of Saint-Simon or Comte; the church, according to those who leaned towards ecclesiastical authority; an elected body of persons embodying the popular or national will, according to democrats or nationalists; the class designated by "history" to free itself and all mankind, according to socialists and communists—this central body had a right to invade everything. The very notion of the inviolability of persons, or of areas of life, as an ultimate principle was nothing but an effort to limit, to narrow, to conceal, to shut out the light, to preserve privilege, to protect some portion of ourselves from the universal truth—and therefore the central source of error, weakness and vice.

The doctrine that there is one truth and one only, which the whole of one's life should be made to serve, one method, and one only, of arriving at it, and one body of experts alone qualified to discover and interpret it—this ancient and familiar doctrine can take many shapes. But even in its most idealistic and unworldly forms, it is, in essence, totalitarian. Even those critical versions of it which permit doubts about the nature of the central truth, or about the best method of its discovery, or the title of its preachers, allow none about the right and the duty, once it is established, to make everyone and everything obey it; they allow no intrinsic virtue to variety of opinion or conduct as such; indeed, the opposite. For there can be no more than one truth, one right way of life. Only vice and error are many. Consequently, when Marxism finally came to Russia in the 1870s and 1880s, it found an almost ideal soil for its seeds.

II

MARXISM CONTAINED all the elements which the young *révoltés* in Russia were looking for. It claimed to be able to demonstrate the proper goals of human existence in terms of a pattern of history of which there was "scientific" proof. The moral and political values which it preached could, so it claimed, be determined "objectively," that is to say, not in terms of the subjective and relative and unpredictable attitudes of different individuals or classes or cultures, but in terms of principles which, being "founded" on the "objective behavior of things," were absolute and alone led to the salvation and liberation of all men to the degree to which they were rational. It preached the indissoluble oneness of men and institutions. It claimed, just as the eighteenth-century French philosophers had in effect claimed, that all real, that is to say soluble, problems were fundamentally technological; that the ends of man—what human beings could be and, if they knew their true interests, would necessarily want to be—were given by the new scientific picture of the universe. The only problem was how to realize these ends. This was not a moral or political problem but a technical task: that of finding and using the right means for the "demonstrably" valid, universal goal; a problem of engineering.

Stalin's famous and most revealing phrase about intellectuals as "engineers of human souls" was faithfully derived from Marxist premises. The duty of intellectuals was to elucidate the correct social goals on the basis of a "scientific" analysis of society and history; and then, by means of education, or "conditioning," so to attune the minds of their fellow citizens that they grasped demonstrated truths and responded accordingly, like the harmonious constituents of a properly regulated and efficiently functioning mechanism. The simile which Lenin used in one of his most famous statements of political doctrine—*State and Revolution*—according to which the new free society, liberated from the coercion of one class by another, would resemble a factory or workshop in which the workers did their jobs almost out of mechanical habit, was a piece of imagery drawn from this technocratic view of human life. The watchwords were efficiency, tidiness, security, freedom for the good to do what they wanted; this last being necessarily one and the same goal for all those who were rational and knew the truth, not freedom to do anything whatever, but only what is right—the only thing which any rational being can wish to do—that which alone will make for true, everlasting universal happiness. This is an old Jacobin doctrine, and indeed much older—in its essentials as old as Plato. But no one, perhaps, had believed it quite so naively or fanatically in any previous age.

During the decade that followed the October Revolution, these principles—the moral and metaphysical foundations of totalitarianism—were genuinely accepted, at any rate by some among the Communist leaders. Whatever the personal shortcomings of Trotsky or Zinoviev or Bukharin or Molotov or the heads of the secret police, and perhaps even of Stalin at this stage, there is no reason for doubting the sincerity or depth of their convictions or principles. A great many disagreements arose, of course, but they were concerned not with ends but with means; when they went sufficiently far they were stigmatized as deviations. Thus Trotsky thought that there was a danger of a too-well-entrenched bureaucracy which would function as a brake—like all vested interests—upon the progress of the revolution, which needed agents who were more imaginative, more bloody, bold, and resolute—men not tempted to stop halfway on the path of the world revolution. The so-called workers' opposition objected to the concentration of authority in the hands of the Central Committee of the Communist Party and wanted more equality and more democratic control exercised by workers' organizations. The right-wing deviationists thought that overrapid collectivization of agriculture would produce a degree of economic dislocation, pauperization, and ruin likely to be more damaging to the Soviet economy than the adoption of a slower pace in the harsh process of liquidating peasant property and its defenders, together with other so-called survivals of the capitalist régime, and advocated a less urgent tempo and milder measures. There were disagreements as to how far the army might be used in the regimentation of industry. There were memorable disagreements about foreign policy and the policy towards communists abroad.

The acutest of all disagreements occurred, perhaps, on the cultural front: there were those who thought that any "slap in the face" (as it used to be called) to the bourgeois culture of the West, in whatever form—aggressive futurism and modernism in the arts, for example, or any violent revolt against tradition—was *eo ipso* an expression of Bolshevism, in so far as it was a blow at the Western establishment, lowered its morale, and undermined its moral and aesthetic foundations. A good deal of experiment, sometimes bold and interesting, at other times merely eccentric and worthless, occurred at this time in the Soviet Union in the guise of cultural warfare against the encircling capitalist world. This was the "Cultural Bolshevism," particularly popular in Germany, against which communist policy later so sternly set its face. For one thing the audacities of the cultural Bolsheviks were, as might be expected, the personal acts of individual artists and therefore found little favor in the eyes of those members of the party for whom communism meant belief in the task of creating a specifically proletarian culture by means of collective action and for whom the aberrations of the *avant-garde* poets, painters, and producers were merely so much individualist eccentricity—an *outré* and decadent perversion of the very bourgeois civilization which the revolution was out to destroy. Lenin, be it noted, disliked all forms of modernism intensely: his attitude to radical artistic experiment was bourgeois in the extreme. But he made no attempt to enforce his aesthetic views, and under the benevolent patronage of the commissar of education, Lunacharsky, a failed critical playwright but a sincere opponent of open barbarism, the controversies continued unabated. There were splits within factions: the champions of "proletarian" culture could not agree on whether it was to be produced by individual men of gifts who distilled within themselves the aspirations of the proletarian masses, actual and potential, acting, as it were, as their mouthpieces or rather megaphones; or whether, as the extremer ideologists proclaimed, individuals as such had no part at all to play in the new order, for the art of the new collectivist society must itself be collective. These latter in effect believed that works of art must be written collectively by groups, and criticism—reviews, essays, directives—by squads of critics, bearing collective responsibility for their work, each member being an anonymous component of a social whole. Again, some maintained that the business of proletarian art was to present the new reality in an intenser form, to heighten it if necessary by the inventions of the socialism-impregnated imagination; others thought that the business of artists was strictly utilitarian: to help with the making of communist society by documentary reportage of the new life: the building of factories, collective farms, power stations; the destruction of the old installations; the production of the essentials of the socialist economy—tractors, combines, uniform food, identical clothing, mass-produced houses, books— above all, good, happy, uncomplicated, standard human beings.

One could go on to multiply examples; the point I wish to make is that these "programmatic" controversies were, in the first place, genuine; that is to say, the contending parties, on the whole, believed what they were saying, and the disagreements between them could justly be described as real differences in the interpretation of an accepted Marxist doctrine. Moreover they were, to some degree, carried on in public; and, most important of all, they were differences not about ends but about means. The ends had become universally accepted since the opponents and doubters had been eliminated or silenced. The intransigence of the Comintern in dealing with foreign communist and still more socialist parties and the merciless heresy hunts probably derived, for the most part, from the honest belief that these parties might compromise on the central truth—on the dogma of what constituted the desired society—or else that they had chosen, or might choose, paths that could lead away, however imperceptibly at first, from these sacred and undisputed goals.

It was its own conception of itself that divided Bolshevism so sharply from its parent, Western Marxism, a conception which made it not merely a set of political or social or economic beliefs or policies, but a way of life, all penetrating and compulsory, controlled absolutely by the party or the Central Committee of the party in a way for which little authority can be found even in the most extreme pronouncements of Marx or Engels. This was the "tsarism in reverse," which Herzen in the early 1950s had gloomily and accurately predicted that communism in Russia would become and which it owes primarily to the personality of Lenin himself. No doubt the conditions of Russian life, which molded both him and it, in part created the need for religious certainty and messianic doctrine which Marxism provided. But the authoritarian element is among Lenin's specific contributions—the conception of the party as a sect ruled ruthlessly by its elders and demanding from its members the total sacrifice upon its altar of all that they most cherished (material goods, moral principles, personal relationships), the more defiant and horrifying to tender-minded morality the better. It was this streak of stony fanaticism enlivened by a sardonic humor and vindictive trampling upon the liberal past that unnerved some of Lenin's socialist colleagues and attracted such disciples as Stalin and Zinoviev.

It was part and parcel of this vision of the millennium, disguised as a rational doctrine, to ignore the fact that as a scientific theory, claiming to be able to explain and predict social and economic change, Marxism had, by the beginning of the twentieth century, been decisively refuted by events in ways which have been described too often and too fully to be worth recapitulation. In the West, efforts to save the theory from intellectual bankruptcy, some orthodox, some heretical, were from time to time made by conscientious socialists and others. In Russia this was, by and large, not required. In Russia, especially after the October Revolution, Marxism had become a metaphysics, professedly resting on an analysis of history but stubbornly ignoring all awkward facts, designed by force or persuasion to secure conformity to a set of dogmatic propositions with its own esoteric, half-intelligible terminology, its own "dialectical" techniques of argument, its own clear and rigid *a priori* notions of what men and society must, at whatever cost, be made to be.

One of the most striking differences between the Soviet Union and the West was (and is) that in Russia those who were defeated in these internal Soviet controversies were liable from the very beginning of the régime—even before the official beginning of the terror—to be at best silenced, at worst punished or executed. Yet even these Draconian measures did not make the controversies less real. Indeed they had the opposite effect—the fact that the fruit of victory was power, and of defeat elimination, added an element of violent excitement to the duels in which the antagonists had so much to lose or win. I do not mean to assert that all or even the majority of those engaged in these febrile and perilous controversies were persons of integrity or moved by disinterested motives; a great deal of ruthless or desperate fighting for position or survival, with little regard for the professed principles of Marxism, was evident enough in Russia in the 1920s. But at least some sort of wage was paid by vice to virtue; the protagonists in these struggles still felt traditionally obliged to advance some kind of theoretical justification for their conduct, and since some of them seemed to believe deeply in what they said, the issues were at times matters of genuine principle. This was most obviously the case on the "cultural front," which has at all times yielded the most reliable symptoms of what was going on in other spheres of Soviet life. Moreover, among the controversialists, men of remarkable gifts and temperament were to be found, and their attitudes, whether honest or opportunist, were those of exceptional human beings. Lunacharsky, Vorovsky, Averbakh were not, by any possible standard, critics of the first water, but they possessed a genuine revolutionary eloquence; Bukharin, Trotsky, Radek were as thinkers negligible, but one of them was a man of genius, and the others were at the very least gifted agitators. And among the creative writers and artists, there still were some figures of the first rank who had not emigrated or had returned. This alone made the 1920s memorable, not only in Russian history but in Russian culture.

To all this Stalin put an abrupt end, and a new phase began.

III

THE IDEOLOGICAL policy of Stalin's régime is a fascinating topic, deserving separate study to itself, which no one has yet attempted seriously and towards which I should like only to make one or two suggestions.

Once it had become clear to Stalin and his henchmen that an early world revolution was not to be expected and that the doubtless inevitable fulfillment of Marxist prophecies in the capitalist world might take place at a time and in ways very different from those which the earlier, more optimistic founding fathers had prophesied, he concentrated upon three interconnected purposes. Firstly, the perpetuation of the Bolshevik régime, and in particular of those of its leaders who were prepared to accept his own authority. Secondly, the maintenance and increase of Soviet power—political, economic, and military—in a hostile world, by every possible means short of those entailing a radical change in the Soviet system itself. And thirdly, the elimination of all factors, whether at home or abroad, likely to jeopardize either of these two central purposes, whether or not such elimination was consistent with Marxism, socialism, or any other ideological attitude.

Stalin has at times been compared to Napoleon. It is, on the whole, a fanciful and misleading comparison. Stalin did not suppress or pervert the Bolshevik Revolution as Napoleon "liquidated" the Jacobins. There never was a Thermidor (still less a Brumaire) in the Russian Revolution: neither in the mid-1920s (where Trotsky naturally placed it), nor after the assassination of Kirov, nor after the death of Stalin. But there is something also in this analogy that is illuminating. To ask whether Stalin was a faithful Marxist or even a faithful Leninist is like asking whether Napoleon believed in the ideals or ideas of the French Revolution. Napoleon was sufficiently a child of the revolution to be instinctively opposed to everything connected with the prerevolutionary régime and to wish to come to terms with some of its survivals solely for limited periods and for reasons of expediency. Just as Napoleon took it for granted that the relics of feudalism in Europe were doomed beyond recall, that the dynastic principle was not worth respecting, that nationalism was a force that must be used, that centralization and uniformity were policies favorable to his rule, and the like, so it may be assumed that Stalin was Marxist and Leninist enough to believe that capitalism was inescapably doomed to be destroyed by its own "internal contradictions," although it might here and there engage in a desperate struggle for survival, whether it realized this or not and however useless such a struggle might be. Similarly Stalin probably accepted the tactical corollary that wherever such "contradictions" reached an acute stage, those who wished to survive and inherit the earth must seek to exacerbate these critical situations and not to palliate them; whereas in situations where these contradictions had not yet reached a critical point, the path of prudence on the part of the members of the new society, i.e., the communists, was not to promote premature risings but to bore from within and concentrate on Popular Fronts and Trojan horses of various kinds. It is clear that he genuinely believed that the future of human society was inevitably collectivist and not individualist; that the power of religion and the churches was collapsing; that control of economic power was more important (i.e., capable of effecting greater changes or stopping them) than, say, nationalist sentiment or political power; and in all these respects he was, of course, a true, if exceedingly crude follower of Marx. But if it be asked whether he was a Marxist in the sense in which Lenin undoubtedly was one—i.e., of believing that as the result of the dreadful birth pangs, a new world would be born in which men would in some sense be freer than before, capable of developing their faculties on a vastly more productive scale, living in a world without wars, starvation, and oppression, it seems doubtful whether he troubled himself with such questions any more than the Emperor Napoleon reflected about the ultimate validity of any of the ideals of the French Revolution. And, to his intellectual credit be it said, Stalin paid little enough regard—even by way of lip service—to the many utopian elements in Lenin's outlook.

It is, perhaps, a second point of similarity with Napoleon that Stalin firmly grasped a truth which perhaps Napoleon was the first among secular rulers fully to realize and act upon, namely that discussion of ideas—disputes about issues apparently remote from politics, such as metaphysics or logic or aesthetics—was, by promoting the critical spirit, in principle more dangerous to despotic régimes engaged in a struggle for power than belief in any form of authoritarianism. Napoleon's open hostility to the *idéologues*—the empiricists and positivists of his day—is well known. He openly preferred the implacable legitimist and ultramontane Bonald, who abused him and would have no truck with him, to the politically mild and conformist liberal, Destutt de Tracy. Similarly Stalin, when he felt himself securely in power, decided to put an end to all ideological controversy as such in the Soviet Union. He did this by proclaiming one school to be victorious over all others (it does not historically matter which). The new directive was that the business of the intelligentsia—writers, artists, academics, and so forth—was not to interpret, argue about, analyze, still less develop or apply in new spheres, the principles of Marxism, but to simplify them, adopt an agreed interpretation of their meaning, and then repeat and ingeminate and hammer home in every available medium and on all possible occasions the selfsame set of approved truths. The new Stalinist values were similar to those proclaimed by Mussolini: loyalty, energy, obedience, discipline. Too much time had been wasted in controversy, time which could have been spent in promoting enforced industrialization or educating the new Soviet man. The very notion that there was an area of permissible disagreement about the interpretation of even unquestioned dogma created the possibility of insubordination; this, beginning indeed in spheres remote from the centers of power—say, musical criticism or linguistics—might spread to more politically sensitive areas and so weaken the drive for economic and military power for which no sacrifice was too great or too immoral. The celebrated Marxist formula—the unity of theory and practice—was simplified to mean a set of quotations to justify officially enunciated policies. The methods taken to suppress the least symptom of independence on the part of even the most faithful Stalinist intellectuals (let alone so-called deviationists or unreconstructed relics of older dispensations)—and, let it be added, the success of these methods—are a phenomenon without parallel in the recorded history of human oppression.

The result has been a long blank page in the history of Russian culture. Between 1932 and, say, 1945 or indeed 1955, it would not be too much to say that—outside natural science—scarcely any idea or piece of critical writing of high intrinsic value was published in Russia and hardly any work of art—scarcely anything genuinely interesting or important in itself and not merely as a symptom of the régime or of the methods practiced by it, that is to say, as a piece of historical evidence.

This policy was, perhaps, chiefly due to Stalin's personal character. He was a half-literate member of an oppressed minority, filled with resentment against superior persons and intellectuals of all kinds, but particularly against those articulate and argumentative socialists whose dialectical skill in the realm of theory must have humiliated him often both before the revolution and after it, and of whom Trotsky was only the most arrogant and brilliant representative. Stalin's attitude towards ideas, intellectuals, and intellectual freedom was a mixture of fear, cynical contempt, and sadistic humor that took the form (a touch of Caligula) of discovering to what grotesque and de-grading postures he could reduce both the Soviet and foreign members of his cowering congregation. After his death this policy has on occasion been defended by his heirs on the ground that when an old world is being destroyed and a new world brought into being, the makers and breakers cannot be expected to have time for the arts and letters, or even ideas, which must, at any rate for the moment, suffer what befalls them without protest.

It is interesting to ask how such absolute subservience, and for so long a period, could have been secured on the part of an intelligentsia which had after all not merely contributed the very term to the languages of Europe, but had itself played so prominent and decisive a role in bringing about victory of the revolution. Here was a body of persons the blood of whose martyrs had been the seed of the entire revolutionary movement, a body to which Lenin, far more than Marx, had assigned a leading role in the task of subverting the old order and of keeping the new one going; and yet, when it was crushed, not a mouse stirred: a few indignant voices abroad, but inside the Soviet Union silence and total submission. Mere intimidation, torture, and murder should not have proved sufficient in a country which, we are always told, was not unused to just such methods and had nevertheless preserved a revolutionary underground alive for the better part of a century. It is here that one must acknowledge that Stalin achieved this by his own original contributions to the art of government—inventions that deserve the attention of every student of the history and practice of government.

IV

THE FIRST invention has been called by Mr. Utis "the artificial dialectic." It is well known that according to the systems of Hegel and of Marx, events do not proceed in direct causal sequence but by means of a conflict of forces—of thesis and antithesis—ending in a collision between them, and a Pyrrhic victory, in the course of which they eliminate each other, and history takes "a leap" to a new level, where the process, called dialectical, begins once again. Whatever may be the validity of this theory in any other sphere, it has a very specific applicability to revolutionary situations.

As every student of the subject must know, the principal practical problem before those who have successfully brought off a large-scale revolution is how to prevent the resultant situation from collapsing into one of two opposed extremes. The first—let us, following Mr. Utis, call it Scylla—is reached when the zealots of the revolution, observing that the new world which the revolution was meant to create has somehow not yet come to pass, seek for explanations, culprits, scapegoats; blame it on criminal weakness or treachery on the part of this or that group of their agents or allies; declare the revolution in mortal peril and start a witch hunt which presently develops into a terror, in the course of which various groups of revolutionaries tend to eliminate each other successively, and social existence is in danger of losing the minimum degree of cohesion without which no society can continue to be. This process tends to be checked by some form of counterrevolution, which is brought on by a desperate effort on the part of the majority, whose security is threatened, to preserve itself and achieve stability, an instinctive social recoil from some imminent-looking collapse. This is what occurred during the great French Revolution, to some extent during the Commune of 1871, in some parts of Eastern Europe in 1918, and it might have occurred in 1848 had the extreme left-wing parties begun to win. The mounting spiral of terror was, in fact, what Trotsky was suspected of wishing to promote.

The opposite extreme—Charybdis—is subsidence into a weary indifference, when the original impetus of the revolution begins after a time to ebb and people seek a respite from the terrible tension of the unnatural life to which they have been exposed, they seek relief, comfort, normal forms of life; and the revolution slides by degrees into the ease, *Schlamperei*, moral squalor, financial chicanery, and general corruption of the kind which marked, for example, the French Directoire; or else subsides into some conventional dictatorship or oligarchy, as had happened so often in Latin America and elsewhere. The problem for the makers of the revolution, therefore, is how to keep the revolution going without falling foul of either the Scylla of utopian fanaticism or the Charybdis of cynical opportunism.

Stalin should be credited with having discovered and applied a method which did, in fact, solve this particular problem in a certain sense. Theoretically, history or nature (as interpreted by Hegel or Marx) should, by pursuing its own dialectical process, cause these opposites to collide at the crucial stage, forcing reality to ascend a creative spiral instead of collapsing into one-sided forms of bankruptcy. But since history and nature evidently tend to nod, man must from time to time come to the aid of these impersonal agencies. The government, as soon as it sees signs of the fatal hankering after the fleshpots of the older life, must tighten the reins, intensify its propaganda, exhort, frighten, terrorize, if need be make examples of as may conspicuous backsliders as may be required to stop the rout. Malingerers, comfort-lovers, doubters, heretics, other "negative elements" are eliminated. This is the "thesis." The rest of the population, duly chastened, dominated by terror rather than hope or desire for gain or faith, throws themselves into the required labors, and the economy bounds forward for a while. But then the élite of the revolutionary purists, the fanatical terrorists, the simon-pure heart of the party, who must be genuinely convinced of the sacred duty of cutting off the rotten branches of the body politic, inevitably go too far. If they did not, if they could stop in time, they would not have been the kind of people to perform the task of inquisition with the desperate zeal and ruthlessness required; hypocrites, half-believers, moderates, opportunists, men of cautious judgment or human feeling are of no use for this purpose, for they will, as Bakunin had warned long ago, compromise halfway. Then the moment arrives when the population, too terrorized to advance, or too starved, becomes listless, downs tools, and efficiency and productivity begin to drop off; this is the moment for clemency. The zealots are accused of having gone too far, they are accused of oppressing the people, and—always a popular move— they are in their turn publicly disciplined, that is, in Stalin's heyday, purged and executed. Some small increase of freedom is allowed in remote fields, say, that of literary criticism or poetry or archæology, nothing so near the center of things as economics or politics. This is the "antithesis." The people breathe again; there is optimism, gratitude, talk of the wisdom of their rulers now that their eyes have been opened to the "excesses" of their unfaithful servants, hope of further liberties, a thaw; production leaps up; the government is praised for returning to some earlier, more tolerant ideal; and a relatively happier period ensues.

This once more leads to the inevitable relaxation of tension, slackening of discipline, lowering of productive effort. Once more there is (the new thesis) a call for a return to ideological purity, for the reestablishment of fundamental principles and loyalties, for the elimination of the parasitical saboteurs, self-seekers, drones, foreign agents, enemies of the people who have in some way managed to creep into the fold. There is a new purge, a new spurt of ideological fanaticism, a new crusade, and the heads of the counterrevolutionary hydra (the new antithesis) have to be cut off once again.

In this way the population is, as it were, kept perpetually on the run, its development proceeds by a zigzag path, and individual self-preservation depends on a gift for perceiving at which precise moment the central authority is about to order a retreat or an advance and a knack for swiftly adjusting oneself to the new direction. Here timing is all. A miscalculation, due to inertia or political insensitiveness or, worse still, political or moral conviction, causing one to linger too long on a road that has been condemned, must almost always, particularly if persisted in, mean disgrace or death.

It cannot be denied that by this deliberate policy of carefully timed purges and counterpurges of various intensities, of contraction and expansion, Stalin did manage to preserve in being a system that cannot be actively approved or felt to be natural by most of those concerned and indeed to keep it going for a longer period than that for which any other revolution has, thus far, managed to survive. There is a full discussion of the method in the article by Mr. Utis already cited. Although, as the author there maintains, the method, to be successful, requires the master hand of its inventor, it appears to have survived him. Despite the grave shocks to the system caused by the struggle for power among Stalin's successors, the emergence into the open of conflicts and factions, the risings of oppressed peoples in the West totally unforeseen in Moscow, what Mr. Utis calls the "artificial dialectic" appears to be functioning still. The succession, in strict sequence, during the last five years, of "liberal" and repressive moves by the Soviet rulers, both at home and abroad, although no longer conducted with the virtuosity (or the deep personal sadism) of Stalin, has too much regularity of pattern to be unintended. The hypothesis advanced by the author to explain only Stalin's own methods of government seems to fit his successors.

The method is an original political invention, and Stalin deserves full credit for it. One of its deliberate by-products has been the total demoralization of what is still in the U.S.S.R. called the intelligentsia—persons interested in art or in ideas. Under the worst moments of tsarist oppression, there did, after all, exist some areas of wholly free expression; moreover, one could always be silent. This was altered by Stalin. No areas were excluded from the party's directives; and to refuse to say what had been ordered was insubordination and led to punishment. "Inner emigration" requires the possibility of the use of one's mind and means of expression at least in neutral ways. But if one's chances of sheer survival have been made dependent on continuous active support of principles or policies which may seem absurd or morally abhorrent; and if, moreover, the whole of one's mental capacity is taxed by the perpetual need to chart one's course in fatally dangerous waters, to maneuver from position to position, while one's moral fiber is tested by the need to bow one's head low not to one but to many capricious, unpredictably changing divinities, so that the least inattention, slackness, or error costs one dear—then there is less and less possibility of thinking one's own thoughts or of escaping into an inner citadel in which one can remain secretly heterodox and independent and know what one believes. Stalin went further. He forbade more than a minimum degree of official intercommunication between one academic faculty and another, between laboratory and institute, and successfully prevented the growth of any center of intellectual authority, however humble and obedient, however fraudulent and obscurantist. No priesthood of dialectical materialism had been allowed to arise, because no discussion of theoretical issues was permitted; the business of the Academy of Sciences or the Institute of Red Professors or the Marx-Engels Institute was to quote Marx in supporting Stalin's *acts:* the *doctrine* he, or some other member of the Politburo (certainly not a professor), would supply for himself.

Where there is an official church or college of augurs, with its own privileges and mysteries, there is a relatively fenced-off area, with walls within which both orthodoxy and heresy can flourish. Stalin set himself to repress ideas as such—at a very high cost, be it added, not merely in terms of the basic education of Soviet citizens (not to speak of disinterested intellectual activity, "pure" research and so on), but even in the useful and applied sciences which were gravely handicapped by the lack of freedom of discussion and suffered an abnormally high admixture of adventurers, charlatans, and professional informers. All this was effective in stifling every form of intellectual life to a far greater degree than was realized by even the most hostile and pessimistic observers to the West, or, for that matter, by communist parties outside the Soviet orbit. To have created such a system is a very striking achievement on Stalin's part, whose importance should not be underrated. For it has crushed the life out of what once was one of the most gifted and productive societies in the world. At any rate for the time being.

V

THERE IS YET a second consequence of this system which is worthy of remark, namely that most of the standard vices so monotonously attributed by Marxists to capitalism are to be found in their purest form only in the Soviet Union itself. Most readers of this journal will be familiar with such stock Marxist categories as capitalist exploitation, the iron law of wages, the transformation of human beings into mere commodities, the skimming off of surplus value by those who control the means of production, the dependence of the ideological superstructure on the economic base, and other communist phrases. But where do these concepts best apply?

Economic exploitation is a phenomenon familiar enough in the West; but there is no society in which one body of men is more firmly, systematically and openly "exploited" by another than the workers of the Soviet Union by their overseers. True, the benefits of this process do not go to private employers or capitalists. The exploiter is the state itself, or rather those who effectively control its apparatus of coercion and authority. These controllers—whether they act as party officials or state bureaucrats or both—act far more like the capitalists of Marxist mythology than any living capitalists in the West today. The Soviet rulers really do see to it that the workers are supplied with that precise minimum of food, shelter, clothing, entertainment, education, and so forth that they are thought to require in order to produce the maximum quantity of the goods and services at which the state planners are aiming. The rest is skimmed off as surplus value far more conveniently and neatly than it can ever have been detached in the unplanned West. Wages are regulated in the most "iron" way possible—by the needs of production. Economic exploitation here is conducted under laboratory conditions not conceivable in Western Europe or America.[1] It is again in the Soviet Union that official professions of "ideology"—principles, slogans, ideals—correspond least to actual practice. It is there, too, that some intellectuals can most truly be described as lackeys (some sluggish and reluctant, others filled with a kind of cynical delight and pride in their own virtuosity) of the ruling group. It is there, far more obviously than in the West, that ideas, literature, works of art act as "rationalizations" or smoke screens for ruthless deeds, or means of escape from the contemplation of crimes or follies, or as an opium for the masses. It is there that the state religion—for that is what the dead and fossilized "dialectical materialism" of the official Soviet philosophers has, in effect, more or less avowedly become—is nothing but a consciously used weapon in the war against the enemy, within and without and lays no claim to "objective" truth.

The materialist theory of history teaches us that the primary factors that determine the lives of individuals and societies are economic, namely, the relationships of human beings in the productive system; while such cultural

---

[1] Mr. Milovan Djilas corroborates this forcibly in his book, *The New Class* (New York: Praeger, 1957). Whether the system is to be called state capitalism (the state being anything but a democracy) or a "degenerate workers' state" or a naked autocracy is a question of the most appropriate label. The facts themselves are not in doubt.

phenomena as their religious, ethical, and political ideas, their judicial and political institutions, their literature, arts, scientific beliefs, and so forth belong to various tiers of the "superstructure," that is, are determined by—are a function of—the "base." This celebrated and justly influential doctrine, embodying as it does a great deal that is new, important, illuminating, and by now very widely accepted, has, nevertheless, never been easy to fit in detail to any given society or period of history in the past. Every attempt to apply it narrowly[2] always encountered too many exceptions: if these were to be explained away, they usually had to be stretched till the theory became too vague or encrusted with too many qualifications to retain any utility. But it holds only too faithfully of Soviet society. There it is absolutely clear to everyone what is part of the base and what is part of the superstructure. Writers and architects can have no illusions about which level of the pyramid they constitute. Economic, military, and other "material" needs really do wholly determine—because they are deliberately made to determine—ideological phenomena, and not vice versa. It is not nature nor history that has produced this situation, but a piece of highly artificial engineering, by which Stalin and his officials have transformed the Russian empire.

It is an extraordinary irony of history that categories and concepts invented to describe Western capitalism should turn out to fit most closely its mortal enemy. But this is scarcely an accident, a *lusus historiae*. Every student of the Russian Revolution knows that the issue that divided the Bolsheviks most deeply from the orthodox Marxists—the Mensheviks—was the practicability of an immediate transition to socialism. The Mensheviks maintained that according to any interpretation of Marx, genuine socialism could be established only in a society which had reached a high degree of industrialization—where the organized proletariat formed the majority of the population and was, through the working of the "inexorable" and mounting "contradictions" of economic development, in a position to "expropriate the expropriators" and initiate socialism. No one could maintain that this stage had yet been reached in the Russian empire. But the Bolsheviks, mainly under Trotsky's inspiration, claimed that instead of semipassively waiting for capitalism (a bourgeois republic) to do the job, leaving the workers insufficiently protected from the free play of "history," "nature," etc., this process could be con-

---

[2] Say, to demonstrate that the writings of Thomas Love Peacock could not possibly have arisen save in the economic conditions of early nineteenth-century England; and that these in their turn made some such writings as those of, let us say, Aldous Huxley (or others like him) quite inevitable a century later.

trolled by a proletarian dictatorship; Russia could be made to go through the stages demanded by the "dialectic of history" under hothouse conditions regulated by the Communist Party. This was to be the famous "transitional" period of the dictatorship of the proletariat—the artificial or controlled equivalent of "natural" capitalist development in the West: two roads leading equally to full-blown communism, but the Russian corridor less painful because not left to the vagaries of "nature" but planned by men in control of their own fate owing to their possession of the "scientific" weapon of Marxist theory and able, therefore, to "shorten the birth pangs" by a well-executed revolution. If, like Lenin, one begins with fanatical faith in the truth of the Marxist analysis of history, the fact that it does not too well fit even the capitalist West, which it was designed to describe, will make little difference. If the pattern does not correspond to the facts, the facts must be made to tally with the pattern. There was relatively little capitalism, and a feeble proletariat, in Russia in 1917. But the dialectic of history cannot be cheated. Unless Marxism rested on a gigantic fallacy, there *could* be no salvation without the equivalent of the capitalist phase. Hence the corresponding phenomena had to be synthetically produced—made to emerge by artificial means.

This can sometimes be done with success, as in Japan, for example. But the Japanese followed the light of reason and experience. They modernized themselves by the methods that seemed to work best, without being chained to a dogmatic theory. They achieved their purpose not without brutalities, but rapidly and with spectacular success. This course was not open to Lenin and his followers. They were compelled by their fidelity to the Marxist classics to subordinate their practical judgment to the demands of theory: the social and economic development of Russia had to proceed by fixed steps whose order was laid down by the Marxist manuals. This created fantastic handicaps that were overcome at a terrible human cost. Russia *had* to go through phases which, according to Marx, Western capitalism passed during and after its industrial revolution. Russian reality had to be altered to resemble a model constructed, not too competently, to account for the progress of a society very unlike itself. A society was vivisected, as it were, to fit a theory which began life as no more than the explanation of its evolution. Something which began as descriptive became normative: a theory intended to account for the development and behavior of Western Europe in the nineteenth century had been turned into a blueprint for Eastern Europe in the twentieth.

Actions founded upon errors of social observation do not necessarily end badly. There is, for all to see, that part of American constitutional development which was inspired by Montesquieu's mistaken interpretation of British political theory and practice. Lenin's error proved more costly. Russia was precipitated into unheard-of horrors of industrialization largely because

Marx had drawn a dark picture of Western capitalism and said that no society could escape something analogous. The imposition of the Bolshevik system upon an economically retarded country is a unique and monstrous monument to the power of a few men's wills and their sovereign contempt for history and empirical evidence; and a bloodcurdling interpretation of the Unity of Theory and Practice.

VI

FACED WITH crises and the possibility of collapse, Lenin executed a partial retreat. And his successors, under the pressure of events, substituted various practical makeshifts and realistic devices and policies in place of the extravagant utopian design which dominates Lenin's thinking. Nevertheless, the violent break with reality that is at the heart of the Bolshevik Revolution can evidently not be eliminated without causing the régime to collapse; at any rate no serious attempt to do so has ever been made. For this reason Soviet society is not, in the normal sense, a civil society at all.

The purpose of normal human societies is in the first place to survive; and after that, to satisfy what Mill called "the deepest interests of mankind," that is to say, to satisfy at any rate a minimum number of men's normal desires after their basic needs are satisfied—say, for self-expression, happiness, freedom, justice. Any government which realizes these values to a reasonable degree is held to fulfill its function. These are not the principal ends of Soviet society or of its government. Conditioned by its revolutionary origins, it is organized to achieve objectives, to respond to challenges, win victories. Like a school, a team of players, still more like an army on the march, it is a specialized institution designed for specific purposes that must be made explicit to its members by the leaders. Soviet life is constructed to strive for goals. It makes little difference what the particular goals may be—military or civil, the defeat of the enemy within or without, or the attainment of industrial objectives—announced goals there must be, if Soviet society is to continue to be. The leaders understand this well, and whether or not they are to be regarded as prisoners of their own system, they know that they must continue to exhort their subjects to greater and greater endeavors if they are to avoid the disintegration of the régime. They are in the position of army commanders in a war, who realize that unless their troops see a minimum amount of active service, the discipline, the esprit de corps, the continued existence of the armies as fighting units cannot be guaranteed.

The leaders of the Soviet Union, for all we know, may by now be secretly hankering after the peaceful existence, to abandon the exiguous splendors and unending cruelties and miseries of the régime and subside into "normal" existence. If they harbor any such desires, they know that in the short run, at least, this is not practicable. For Soviet society is organized not for happiness, comfort, liberty, justice, personal relationships, but for combat. Whether they wish it or not, the drivers and controllers of this immense train cannot now halt it or leap from it in mid-course without risk of destruction. If they are to survive and above all remain in power, they must go on. Whether they can replace parts of it while it is moving, and so transform it (themselves) into something less savage, less dangerous to themselves and mankind, remains to be seen. At any rate that must be the hope of those who do not think war inevitable.

In the meanwhile this caricature of *dirigisme* has discredited the tradition of social idealism and liquidated the intelligentsia connected with it, perhaps more decisively than unaided persecution could have done. Nothing destroys a minority movement more effectively than the official adoption and inevitable betrayal and perversion of its ends by the state itself. There are cases where nothing succeeds less well than success.

The Realities in Africa

European Profit or Negro Development?

W. E. B. Du Bois

JULY 1943

IN MODERN TIMES two great world movements have hinged on the relation of Africa to the other continents: the African slave trade, which transferred perhaps ten million laborers from Africa to America and played a major role in the establishment of capitalism in England and Europe based on sugar and cotton, and the partitioning of Africa after the Franco-Prussian War which, with the Berlin Conference of 1884, brought colonial imperialism to flower.

The primary reality of imperialism in Africa today is economic. Since 1884 there has been invested in that continent a sum larger than the total gold reserve of the British Empire and France in 1939. Due to this investment, there were exported annually from Africa, just before the present war, $700 million worth of products. And this valuation of African exports is abnormally low, since in a market controlled by the manufacturers the labor cost is depressed so as to yield high profit; the potential value of African raw materials runs into the billions.

These, then, are the two facts to keep in mind in our discussions of the future of Africa—that in the nineteenth century the African trade in men changed to a trade in raw materials and that thenceforth the political domination which insured monopoly of raw materials to the various contending empires was predicated on the exploitation of African labor inside the continent. The integration of Africa into the world economic organization since the Industrial Revolution has been of far greater significance than social scientists like to admit. A quite natural reticence regarding the immense extent of the slave trade fostered the tendency to treat that question as an incidental moral lapse which was overshadowed and atoned for by the abolitionist crusade of 1800–60. But an understanding of the economic background of that crusade is basic to the correct interpretation of the twentieth century and its two world wars.

In the eighteenth century England became the great slave-trading nation of the world and made America a land of chattel slavery. But in the nineteenth century England appears as the emancipator, who stopped the slave trade at great cost, abolished slavery in her own territories, and stimulated the reaction against Negro slavery throughout the world. How do these attitudes harmonize? The rise of liberal and philanthropic thought in the latter part of the eighteenth century accounts, of course, for no little of the growth of opposition to slavery and the slave trade; but it accounts for only a part of it. Other and dominant factors were the diminishing returns of the African slave trade itself, the bankruptcy of the West Indian sugar economy through the Haitian Revolution, the interference of Napoleon, and the competition of Spain. Without this pressure of economic forces, Parliament would not have yielded so easily to the abolition crusade. Moreover, new fields of investment and profit were being opened to Englishmen by the consolidation of the empire in India and by the acquisition of new spheres of influence in China and elsewhere. In Africa, British rule was actually strengthened by the antislavery crusade, for new territory was annexed and controlled under the aegis of emancipation. It would not be right to question for a moment the sincerity of Sharpe, Wilberforce, Buxton, and their followers. But the moral force they represented would have met with greater resistance had it not been working along lines favorable to English investment and colonial profit.

There followed a brief but interesting period of readjustment. For a while after the triumph of the abolition movement the idea was fairly widespread in England that Africa was to be allowed its own development so long as trade was free. . . . But soon the investing countries realized that strong political control in African and Asiatic colonies would result in such a monopoly of labor and raw material as to insure magnificent profits. The slave trade and slavery would not only be unnecessary; they were actually a handicap to profitable investment.

The process of strengthening control over the people of Africa was therefore developed in the name of stopping the slave trade and abolishing slavery. For a while, English philanthropy and English imperialism seemed to have found one of those preestablished harmonies in economic life upon which Bentham and the Physiocrats had loved to expatiate. Increased trade and stable government in Africa was going to be the best way of civilizing the natives and lifting them toward self-government. Philanthropy, guided by men like Livingstone, envisaged the raising of the status of black labor in

Africa as not only compatible with industrial profit, but practically synonymous with it. It was equally clear that unless there was political domination of these colonies to insure a virtual monopoly of material and labor, the colonial investment there would not be secure. The almost complete partition of Africa followed, settling in the hands of England a vast colonial empire and yielding to France and to Germany less valuable but nevertheless large imperial domains.

A technique of domination was gradually developed. Physical force backed by superior firearms was used in the Sudan. In South Africa, economic pressure was applied by land monopoly, supplemented by a head tax which meant compulsory labor. A caste system of Negroes subordinated to whites was widely instituted but to some extent modified by cultural segregation, sometimes called "Indirect Rule," by which the cultural integrity of African tribes was within limits permitted for local government, but their economic activities guided by the interests of investment in the hands of the governing country. Just as European peasants did not get a cent of compensation for the three and a half million acres of common land taken from them between 1801 and 1831, so in the Union of South Africa the natives who formed 80 percent of the population came to possess only 8 percent of the land. In Kenya 3 million natives are confined today to 50,000 square miles of the poorest land; the best land has been given to Europeans, often at a nominal price, in estates so large that they can only be cultivated by hired labor. Again and again forced labor has been legalized in Kenya; and it is legal today. Labor in the mines of South Africa was long removed only a step from serfdom, and labor conditions there now allow a native wage of $15 a month. In the Belgian Congo and French Equatorial Africa there has been a sordid history of cruelty, extermination, and exploitation.

We must not blink the fact that in the past it has been profitable to a mother country to possess colonies. One sometimes hears that colonies represent a sort of philanthropic enterprise. The colonial system is commended for whatever education and social services it has given to the natives and is not blamed if these social services have been miserably inadequate as compared to the need. The fact is that so far as government investment is concerned, the money which Great Britain, France, Portugal, and Germany *as governments* have invested in Africa has yielded small returns in taxes and revenues. But this governmental investment and its concomitant political control have been the basis upon which private investors have built their private empires, being thus furnished free capital by home taxation; and while the mass of people in the mother country have been taxed and often heavily for this governmental gift abroad, the private capitalist who has invested in the colonies has reaped not only interest from his own investment but returns from investments which he did not make and which are protected by armies and navies which he only partially supported. Immense sums have been derived from raw material and labor whose price has been depressed to a minimum while the resulting goods processed in the mother country are sold at monopoly prices. The profits have not been evenly distributed at home; but the net return to the white races for their investment in colored labor and raw material in Africa has been immense. That, very briefly, is the fundamental fact of the situation which confronts us in Africa today.

II

FOR CONVENIENCE we refer to "Africa" in a word. But we should remember that there is no one "Africa." There is in the continent of Africa no unity of physical characteristics, of cultural development, of historical experience, or of racial identity. . . .

Berbers of North Africa are usually classed as "white" peoples; Abyssinians are now and then declared not to be Negroes; but on the whole, all Africans, save recent white European immigrants and their offspring, are classed among the peoples of the earth who are inferior in status and in kind.

This decree of inferiority is not based on scientific study—indeed the careful anthropological and social study of Africa has only just begun. Again we must come back to dollars, pounds, marks, and francs. The judgment on Africa was rendered on economic grounds (although, of course, pseudoscientific dogma were adduced to bolster it). Liberal thought and violent revolution in the eighteenth and early nineteenth centuries shook the foundations of a social hierarchy in Europe based on unchangeable class distinctions. But in the nineteenth and early twentieth centuries the Color Line was drawn as at least a partial substitute for this stratification. Granting that all white men were born free and equal, was it not manifest—ostensibly after Gobineau and Darwin, but in reality after James Watt, Eli Whitney, Warren Hastings, and Cecil Rhodes—that Africans and Asiatics were born slaves, serfs, or inferiors? The real necessity of this fantastic rationalization was supplied by the demands of modern colonial imperialism. The process of exploitation that culminated in the British, French, and German empires before the First World War turned out to be an investment whose vast returns depended on cheap labor, under strict political control, without too much interference from mawkish philanthropy.

Philanthropy has fought stout battles for a liberalization of imperialistic rule in the past. The focus of those battles has usually been the question of education of the peoples of Africa; it was the difference of opinion on this issue which awoke philanthropy from its dream of foreordained harmony be-

tween the cohorts of Christianity and business. The painful question inevitably arose: to what degree should native people be allowed an education,
in view of the fact that educated men do not make cheap and docile laborers?
Sharp disputes took place between missionaries and administrative officials
over the missionaries' plans for schools and for the training of skilled artisans,
civil servants, and professional men such as physicians. In some cases, at least,
the insistence of the missionaries was so great that government was forced to
yield.

The cultural possibilities of the African native are undeniable. It is admitted even in South Africa today that the native is not being kept out of
skilled labor because he is incapable. And his capacity for political self-rule is
shown by the success of the native states of the West Coast, the Bunga of the
Transkei, and other such experiments. Missionaries, travellers, and now many
government agents agree that it would be possible to place centers of education in Africa which would in a few generations train an intelligentsia capable eventually of taking fairly complete charge of the social development of
the continent. . . .

Cutting across this whole question comes the issue of the use of Negroes
in war. The Civil War in the United States was fought with the help of
200,000 black troops with a growing possibility of enlisting a majority of the
slaves; and their use made further slavery unthinkable. The First World War
was fought with the help of black troops which France brought to Europe to
ward off annihilation; the blacks of French West Africa were armed on a
large scale and became an effective fighting force in Europe. Europe
protested—the English in South Africa as well as the Germans in Europe. If
armed natives were going to be used in European disputes, would not native
colonial revolt be only matter of years? . . .

Unless this question of racial status is frankly and intelligently faced, it
will become a problem not simply of Africa but of the world. More than the
welfare of the blacks is involved. As long as there is in the world a reservoir of
cheap labor that can raise necessary raw materials, and as long as arrangements can be made to transport these raw materials to manufacturing countries, this body of cheap labor will compete directly or indirectly with
European labor and will be often substituted for European labor. This situation will increase the power of investors and employers over the political organization of the state, leading to agitation and revolt within the state on the
part of the laboring classes and to wars between states which are competing
for domination over these sources of profit. And if the fiction of inferiority is
maintained, there will be added to all this the revolt of the suppressed races
themselves, who, because of their low wages, are the basic cause of the whole
situation.

The world war of 1914–18 was caused in part by the German demand for a larger share in the domination over labor and in the exploitation of raw materials in Asia and Africa. An important aspect of the world war of 1939 is the competition for the profit of Asiatic labor and materials—competition in part between European countries, in part between those countries and Japan. Submerged labor is revolting in the East Indies, Burma, and India itself. It would be a grave mistake to think that Africans are not asking the same questions that Asiatics are: "Is it a white man's war?"

The social development of Africa for the welfare of the Africans, with educated Africans in charge of the program, would certainly interfere with the private profits of foreign investment and would ultimately change the entire relationship of Africa to the modern world. Is the development of Africa for the welfare of Africans the aim? Or is the aim a world dominated by Anglo-Saxons, or at least by the stock of white Europe? If the aim is to keep Africa in subjection just as long as possible, will this not plant the seeds of future hatreds and more war?

III

ONE WOULD think that Africa, so important in world trade and world industrial organization and containing at least 125 million people, would be carefully considered today in any plan for postwar reconstruction. This does not seem to be the case. When we examine the plans which have been published we find either no mention of Africa or only vague references. In President Roosevelt's "four freedoms" speech in January 1941, he did not seem to be thinking of Africa when he mentioned freedom of speech, freedom from want, and freedom from fear. . . . The eight points of the Atlantic Charter were so obviously aimed at European and North American conditions that Winston Churchill frankly affirmed this to be the case, although he was afterward contradicted by President Roosevelt. The proposals which have been made by publicists like Clarence Streit and Henry Luce imply a domination of the world by English-speaking peoples, with only passing consideration of black folk. Only in the recent report on "The Atlantic Charter and Africa from an American Standpoint," by the Committee on Africa, the War, and Peace Aims is a more realistic attitude toward Africa manifest. The committee insists . . . "that Africa still represents the largest undeveloped area in the world, with mineral deposits, agricultural land, waterpower, forest and wild life, resources of importance, all of which are decreasing in value because of careless or reckless use or exploitation; and that these resources need development for its own defense and welfare."

The largest undeveloped area in the world! Is that phrase, spoken frankly by a body particularly conscious of African problems, the clue to the reticence of the other postwar statements on the subject of Africa? I do not mean to be unduly pessimistic; but realism demands that we face the fact that after this war the United Nations will be almost irresistibly tempted to consider Africa from an industrial and commercial point of view as a means of helping pay war costs and reestablishing prosperity.

If the treatment of Africa in postwar planning begins or ends here, the results will be tragic. One can see in all these postwar plans—although often, I know, the implication is not intentional or even suspected—the persistence of the old pattern of thought: the white man's need of African labor and raw materials and the assumption that these must be cheap in order to yield maximum profits. Above all, and most tragically, appears the assumption that the only problem so far as Africa is concerned is that the various dominating nations of the world must henceforth be treated equitably in sharing the material and the labor.

The memorable phrase of the First World War, the German demand for "a place in the sun," meant that Germany demanded metals, vegetable oils, fibres, and foods from Africa on equal terms with England, either by pooling or preferably by dividing up Africa's land, labor, and resources afresh. To return to such a plan after a generation of indecision, after another ghastly war, and in a period bursting with the components of still another and vaster war would be blindness indeed. Yet this is precisely what many have in mind. If the rivalry of dominant European nations for colonial profit can be composed by a more equitable distribution of raw materials and labor, they say, then peace will be assured in the world. When they say nothing about the aspirations of the peoples of Africa themselves, what they are actually saying is that peace will be assured if we will all merely return to the eighteenth century.

IV

THE FIRST National Congress of British West Africa met in Accra, capital of the Gold Coast Colony, in mid-March 1920. The congress, composed of delegates from Nigeria, the Gold Coast, Sierra Leone, and Gambia, drafted a memorial to His Majesty the King which is a worthy and remarkable document:

> In presenting the case for the franchise for the different colonies composing British West Africa, namely, the Gambia, Sierra Leone, the Gold Coast and Nigeria, it is important to remember that each of these colonies is at present governed under the Crown Colony System. By that is meant that

the power of selecting members for the legislative councils is in the Governor of each colony and not dependable upon the will of the people through an elective system. In the demand for the franchise by the people of British West Africa, it is not to be supposed that they are asking to be allowed to copy a foreign institution. On the contrary, it is important to notice that the principle of electing representatives to local councils and bodies is inherent in all the systems of British West Africa. According to African institutions every member of a community belongs to a given family with its duly accredited head, who represents that family in the village council, naturally composed of the heads of the several families. Similarly in a district council the different representatives of each village or town would be appointed by the different villages and towns, and so with the Provincial Council until, by the same process, we arrive at the Supreme Council, namely, the State Council, presided over by the Paramount Chief. . . .

The Congress presses for the appointment of duly qualified and experienced legal men to judicial appointments in British West Africa no matter how high the emolument might be. It also presses for the appointment of African barristers of experience, many of whom as jurists and legislative councillors are found along the West Coast, to appointments on the judicial bench as well as other judicial appointments. The Congress contends that there are African legal men of experience capable of holding any judicial office in British West Africa. . . .

It must be remembered that this clear and concise demand for elementary democratic rights among the black people of British West Africa was drafted by native-born Africans of Negro descent. . . .

Beside this document, now, place a statement made in 1923 by the white settlers of Kenya. It is the voice of triumphant commercialism, formulating a racial philosophy for the modern world:

It has been shown that the Black Race possesses initiative but lacks constructive powers, characteristics which justify Lugard's judgment that for the native African "the era of complete independence is not yet visible on the horizon of time." The controlling powers may, therefore, aim at advancing the black race as far along the road of progress as its capacity allows, without misgivings that the success of their endeavours will lead to a demand for their withdrawal, entailing loss of prestige and trade. The development of British territories in Africa opens up a vista of commercial expansion so endless that calculated description is difficult. The bare facts are that the area of these territories is 4,000,000 square miles, as compared with India's 1,900,000; that India's overseas trade is about £350,000,000, and British Africa's (excluding Egypt) is about £292,000,000; that the non-self-governing territories, whose total area is 2,628,498 square miles, already produce an overseas trade of £76,500,000, although their development can hardly be said to have begun; that the average fertility and mineral wealth of their soil are at least equal to those of any other great land mass; that they hold an intelligent fast-breeding native population of about 60 millions, waiting for guidance to engage in the production of the raw materials of industry and foodstuffs; and that white settlement coöperating with the native populations does stimulate production many hundreds of times, and does bring about a demand for manufactured articles out of all proportion to its numerical strength.

Here, then, is the African question: European profit—or Negro development? There is no denying that the training of an African intelligentsia implies most difficult problems—the problem of preserving rather than destroying the native cultural patterns and all the problems that come with inexperienced social leadership. The point is that the decision in these matters must not be left to those interested primarily in financial gain, or to white people alone. If there is to be real Negro development there must be created some organ of international trusteeship, and the native intelligence of Africa must be represented on the guiding boards. Can we expect Europe and America to approach this question in a way that promises a solution? We could not expect it under ordinary circumstances; but the circumstances today are not ordinary.

If I were to try to state summarily the objectives of postwar planning for Africa, looking toward the achievement of the world peace which we all so deeply feel must follow this world war, I would say first that it is necessary to renounce the assumption that there are a few large groups of mankind called races, with hereditary differences shown by color, hair, and measurements of the bony skeleton which fix forever their relations to each other and indicate the possibilities of their individual members. There is no proof that persons and groups in Africa are not as capable of useful lives and effective progress as peoples in Europe and America.

I would say, second, that we must repudiate the more or less conscious feeling, widespread among the white peoples of the world, that other folk exist not for themselves, but for their uses to Europe; that white Europe and America have the right to invade the territory of colored peoples, to force them to work and to interfere at will with their cultural patterns, while demanding for whites themselves a preferred status and seriously and arbitrarily restricting the contacts of colored folk with other and higher culture. The most dangerous excuse for this situation is the relation between European capital and colored labor involving high profit, low wages, and cheap raw material. It places the strong motive of private profit in the foreground of our interracial relations, while the greater objects of cultural understanding and moral uplift are pushed into the background.

I would say, third, that it must be agreed that in Africa the land and the natural resources belong primarily to the native inhabitants. The necessary capital for the development of Africa's resources should be gradually and increasingly raised from savings of the African natives which a higher wage and a just incidence of taxation would make possible. I would say, fourth, that a systematic effort must be begun to train an educated class among the natives, and that class must be allowed to express its opinions and those opinions be given due weight. And I would say, finally, that political control must be taken away from commercial and business interests owned and conducted in the foreign nations which dominate the continent and this control be vested provisionally in an international mandates commission.

These, in simplest form, are the proposals for the future which correspond to the present realities in Africa.

The Underdeveloped
and the Overdeveloped

Margaret Mead

OCTOBER 1962

THIS PAIR of phrases sums up the new, conflicting, and contradictory assumptions that underlie the highly unsatisfactory climate of opinion in today's world. The use of the word "underdeveloped" in connection with a country implies that the most significant dimension of measurement in the world today is standard of living and that standard of living should be measured in terms of those indices that are inextricably linked with industrialization. Countries that are unindustrialized and depend primarily on agriculture and other primary industries are poor. Countries that are industrialized are rich. Richness and poverty are unequivocal terms. They relate to a single scale and provide one set of measurements in accordance with which all countries can be placed.

Economists grant that the problem of weighting is a difficult one. It is perfectly clear that, in a country in which 90 percent of the population can raise little more food than they need for their own consumption, very little will be left over to satisfy other and more complicated needs. If, for example, there is just enough extra food to take to a nearby market to sell for the few things that must be bought there—salt, candles, tea or coffee, tobacco, woven cloth—and the sellers always walk to market, then when bicycles are introduced, there will be no funds to buy them unless a change takes place. But in a relatively rich underdeveloped country like old Bali, where food was plentiful and there was a large surplus which could be spent on cremations, it was possible to cut down on cremations and to buy bicycles instead. When this happens, the standard of living is said to be higher. The culture has been impoverished and the country is not yet developed, but a first step in development has been taken—at cultural expense only. But where, as in most underdeveloped countries, the population lives at the subsistence level without a surplus of any kind, where the only source of animal protein is the ox or the pig consumed at a feast, the desire to own a bicycle can be realized only at the expense of something that is absolutely essential to subsistence as well as to a full and rewarding life. So, once the people of any country have learned to want manufactured objects that they cannot buy out of an existing surplus, because there is no such surplus, they are immediately defined by themselves and others as underdeveloped and therefore poor.

The term "underdeveloped" is used technically to place a country in terms of industrialization, real and potential, on a scale which implies that industrial development can, should, and will take place. The term "poor," however, is not used to place a country on a continuum of technical change. It is used rather to describe its relative consumption position—or the relative consumption position of the majority of its citizens—in comparison with other countries. Poor can mean not knowing where the next meal is coming from, as it does for many of the urban poor, or it can mean not being able to buy a bicycle, a jeep, or a truck. It has no absolute connotation, in this context.

A group of primitive Eskimo, caught between winter and summer, their snow house melting above their heads but the time not yet come when summer hunting and fishing have brought in new supplies of food, or, at the opposite season, caught by the terrible autumnal storms that for days on end make hunting impossible, sitting together starving and the lamps gone out for lack of oil, until in desperation some hunter braves the storm and the punishing supernaturals—these people can be described as in danger of death but not as poor. They had the same equipment as the other Eskimo for meeting the harsh realities of their environment. They knew how to build snow houses; they had dogs, sleds, harpoons, soapstone lamps, bone needles, clothes of skin and fur. In those desperate situations when, in order to stay alive, they had to eat their dogs and then had to go on living without the means to make a living, they might be considered unfortunate. Or a man who, for some reason, had no wife to cook for him and dress his skins might be considered temporarily unfortunate. But these losses were potentially retrievable. His misfortune was a temporary lack of equipment or the lack of a working partner as compared with his fellow Eskimo. For an isolated individual or family group, the lack might well be fatal; in other circumstances recoupment was possible. In the early days of contact, Europeans in the Arctic had to adopt Eskimo equipment in order to survive; the Eskimo were not then, by comparison, poor. But later, when modern equipment suitable for the Arctic was developed, the Eskimo did become poor in comparison with Europeans.

Poverty appears only when some people are organized into groups from which they themselves have no means of escape or of self-betterment, because of ignorance, or government regulation, or lack of a culturally derived belief that escape is possible. So they are immobilized and do without necessities that others have, or they do without some of the luxuries that others have. Moreover, the more egalitarian the society, the more important is the concept of poverty. Where only the chief or the feudal lord lives in a large house and all other men in houses which are small and mean, the distinction is not between richness and poverty but between privilege and absence of privilege in a system based on rank or caste or class. But when it is possible for a majority of the population to have some given thing—a tin roof, a well, a pump, inside plumbing, a donkey, a team of horses, two teams of horses, a bicycle, a tractor, a truck, a station wagon—then the smaller number who cannot acquire it do not regard themselves, and are not regarded by others, as members of a different or a lesser breed. Instead they come to feel, and others come to feel, that they are simply poor.

While the term "underdeveloped" implies occupation of a place on a continuum that is defined in terms of technological per capita capacity to produce, the term "poor" implies placement at the bottom of the scale of consumption, having less than others—less, usually, than most others. When the two ideas are combined, and emphasis is laid on the relative presence or absence of technical productive capacity, all this is changed.

In older discussions of the condition of the poor, the poor at home or abroad, it was emphasized that it would do little good to divide up the riches of the wealthy few in an attempt to alleviate the poverty of the myriads of poor. Then it was possible for the rich to sit at overweighted tables while the poor pressed their noses against the windows in envious contemplation. If the rich were generous in a time of famine or flood, if they built hospitals or endowed schools so that a few more individuals could escape from misery, they could go their way without too bad a conscience. However wealth was rationalized—as the reward of individual effort or parental effort, as the necessary support of high birth—it was necessarily only for the few; the fortunate should be individually generous and should improve their position in heaven. If they did so, they had no special reason to feel guilty; they could enjoy their wealth.

But acceptance of the assumption that technological development is possible for all and, therefore, that improvement of consumption is possible for all meant that it was no longer morally acceptable to let the majority of the peoples of the world live in poverty. From an economy of scarcity—in which, if one person got more, someone else got less and no redistribution of the rubies and emeralds of the rich could, in the long run, help more than a handful of beggars—we have moved, by definition, to an economy of plenty. Riches are no longer somebody's disproportionate, though legitimate, share of a scarce supply; poverty is no longer the consequence of someone else having a large proportion of the existing supply. Stated simply, as between the peoples of the world, poverty is the consequence of being underdeveloped. According to this doctrine, wealth is not given but is produced and every country is capable of an ever-rising rate of production; therefore, poverty, defined as the present state of low consumption of most of the peoples of the world, is remediable. A people need not be poor; development will cure their poverty.

Systematic change from the older to the newer position has difficulties, but there is a further complication. For, in the present position, poverty is defined in two different ways—relative and absolute. In the relative sense, poverty is defined as having less than others. In the absolute sense, there is a minimum standard below which no human beings should fall; when this minimum standard is attained by all the peoples of the world, when the now developed nations have helped the underdeveloped countries to develop, then everyone will be well off. This complication, arising from the discrepant definitions of poverty as relative and as absolute, is as seldom worked out in discussions about countries as it is in relief situations in the United States, where the relief agency attempts to meet standards of nutrition, medical care, shelter, and so on, on an absolute scale of health and decency, while the recipients of relief experience profound and humiliating poverty on a relative standard.

A further consequence of the confusion between these two definitions of poverty is the effect it has on the planning and expectations of countries that are, by definition, rich. By implication, "closing the gap" between underdeveloped and developed countries means that the developed countries are, in fact, developed (or, as Myrdal puts it, are "now developed") and, essentially, should develop no further; that is, the standard of living should rise no further. Instead, such countries should use the surplus that could go into further development to "close the gap" by supplying the undeveloped countries with capital already accumulated in the rich countries through the sweat and toil of the poor of other generations.

If, on the contrary, the rich countries continue to develop their already enormous productive capacities for their own use, and existing discrepancies in birth rates are maintained, then the underdeveloped countries will become poorer, relative to the rich countries, but poverty in the other sense—the absolute sense—will also result, i.e., deprivation of basic subsistence goods.

Thus advocacy of "closing the gap" includes, implicitly, a demand that developed countries should either arrest consumption or arrest the motivating force in their productive development—the desire for a rising consumption standard.

A second very widely accepted assumption is that our capacity—based on our tremendous command of technology—to feed, clothe, shelter, educate, and medicate the peoples of the world should be shared among the peoples of the world seen not as individual human beings with human needs, but as citizens of nation-states. The vision that no one need be hungry or cold, illiterate and ignorant, or suffer from an illness for which there is a cure coincided with the contemporary implementation of ideals of self-determination, especially for colonial peoples. Both are aspects of anticolonialism, as an ethic and as a political tool which has been exploited in the Cold War and by ambitious local leaders, hungry for power.

So, on the one hand, our new conception of technical development is geared to a twentieth-century understanding of the relationship between technology, productivity, and the determination and satisfaction of minimal human needs. But on the other hand, our conception of how these needs are to be met is geared to an obsolescent conception of what nation-states, of whatever size, shape, resources, population, and so on, can accomplish as full, complete, and sufficient units for the implementation of new forms of satisfaction of human needs. The focus is not on hungry *people*, wherever they may be, but on underdeveloped *countries*, which should be able to feed, clothe, and educate their citizens. The combination of these two ethics—the right of human beings to the satisfaction of their basic needs and the right to national autonomy of any group of people who have come to regard themselves as a group because of the institution of colonialism or the accidents of political treaties—has resulted in an extraordinary degree of obfuscation.

For centuries the lack of equal resources, natural or man-made, has been compensated for by migration of some kind. The poor peasant went to the city or another country, or worked as a coolie overseas. Younger sons of the landed gentry or the wealthy went abroad to make their fortune. Inlanders went to sea. Opportunity was conceived of as localized and people as movable within a region, within a country, between nations or areas of the world. But today, possibly in reaction to the stress of millions of refugees—people who left their homes unwillingly—we have created a new right, the right to stay at home under one's own apple tree and have light industry brought to one's own backyard. This implication of bringing development to underdeveloped countries has gone almost unnoticed. Americans have been subjected to so much compulsory moving since the beginning of World War II, and have developed such a phobia about shifting their children from one school to another, that it seems to them a quite reasonable demand that everyone should be allowed to stay in his own country and have the comforts of civilization brought within his reach. Moreover, various fortuitous circumstances attendant on the wars and revolutions of the twentieth century have effectively obscured some of the serious consequences of taking the position that it is the right of every *nation*, new or old, rich or poor, large or small, no matter where located or how technically competent, to be developed and to become, if not rich, at least as well off as every other nation, with as high a standard of living for its people and as large and as conspicuous marks of national prestige in the way of embassies, airlines, armies, and so on.

Today the idea of the nation-state as the unit of development is the more easily supported because a very important part of the planning for underdeveloped nations has been done by those who come from small developed nation-states, in which state intervention and planning for a welfare state are already far advanced. If extensive intervention by government has made it possible for such countries as Sweden, Switzerland, Denmark, Norway, Holland, Belgium, West Germany, and the United Kingdom to maintain an optimum standard of living, then government appears to be the appropriate instrument for benevolent economic change; the welfare of peoples is thought of as inextricably related to activities of government; and the focus is on the nation-state—which has a government—as the appropriate unit in developing the means of improving the well-being of a people.

Thus, just at the moment in history when most of the paraphernalia of the nation-state, postulated on the political protection of citizens whose economic lot it was powerless to ameliorate, is becoming obsolete (for it can no longer protect its citizens, and their economic lot can be more efficiently ameliorated in larger or smaller units), the nation-state has been transformed into a highly valued and highly inefficient instrument for the equalization of opportunity and the optimization of the good life. At a time when there is a crying need for transnational organizations, whether it be for the sharing of scarce or unevenly distributed natural resources, the eradication of disease, or the use of scarce intellectual resources, most of the efforts of the world have gone into the construction of mechanisms that are not transnational but intergovernmental.

In a new nation the poverty of its people and the prestige of its day- or month- or year-old national identity become intertwined. The poverty of the people represents a moral claim on the conscience of the world, which can be enforced in political terms, manipulated for political purposes, sometimes promoting but more often defeating the satisfaction of the very needs in the name of which the manipulation is done. While Germaine Tillion pled for the maintenance of the tie between France and Algeria for the sake of the hungry people of Algeria, political considerations made this impossible. In China, millions are on the verge of starvation and there is urgent need for materials and tools essential for mere subsistence. Yet to supply them, under present circumstances, would mean crossing a national boundary and, in addition, crossing an ideological line defined by the Cold War and breaching mainland China's new inviolability. Coupled with our enormously enhanced ability to feed the peoples of the world, technically, is a definite crippling of our ability to do so organizationally. While valid in themselves, the arguments in favor of national pride, self-determination, autonomy, and dignity essentially fail to recognize—even as they have been used to decry bilateral aid and to promote internationally organized aid—the ways in which nation-states, all nation-states, have become economically and technically irrelevant. There are two continuous reminders of the irrelevancy of the old borders, as lines drawn on the ground. One is our technical ability to feed the peoples of the world, disregarding boundaries; the other is the presence of the satellites of the United States and the Soviet Union, circling overhead.

II

IN THE context of the foregoing discussion, the term "overdeveloped" is anomalous. If technical development is good because it produces a higher standard of living, how can there be an overdeveloped country? It should be recognized that the phrase has been used most frequently to undo the damage done by placing all countries on a single scale. The term was brought into use collaboratively by members of underdeveloped and more developed countries, acting out of patriotism, ambition, or humanitarianism. Only by playing up the underdeveloped state of the underdeveloped countries, by calling them poor, did it seem possible to create the climate of opinion that was being sought. But when this resulted in a single scale, on which all countries could be set up in a hierarchy, it became clear that a low position—on a scale of development—was necessarily invidious and odious. The underdeveloped countries wanted to gain every benefit from having their position so defined; especially they wanted high priority in every form of economic aid. At the same time the inappropriate association between economic need and national prestige meant that it was insulting to be called underdeveloped. With a display of the kind of good manners by which a hostess, to put at ease the guest who has dropped a plate, proceeds to break a platter, internationalists, guilty over colonialism and preventable human suffering on the one hand, and their own conspicuous, wasteful consumption on the other, responded to the touchiness of members of less industrialized countries by calling the old, rich, industrialized countries "overdeveloped." Seen simply in these terms, it is a piece of good manners in rather poor taste.

But the term overdeveloped also permits several questions to be raised about what is the position of industrialized countries in a world which has been reorganized in accordance with preindustrial ideas of nationalism. Are they, for example, overdeveloped in terms of overconsumption? This judgment is expressed in the accusation that enough paper is wasted every day in the United States to provide the newsprint necessary to save freedom in some new country. Or it is said that the power wasted in the average electrified home would be enough to bring food and water to a village of several hundred people, or that by eliminating the duplication of radios and television sets in American homes, a great many villages could be supplied with modern communications. In these terms, can a country like the United States be said to have passed the point of optimum development? This question, in turn, can lead to the advocacy either of arrest or of curtailment of standards of consumption in the developed nations—or at least to a growing fear that other nation-states will not long tolerate their have-not position vis-à-vis the have nations.

But those who use the term overdeveloped may go even further. They may point to indices of social disorganization in those industrial countries in which political democracy and welfare-state organization have gone further than elsewhere—the indices of crime, delinquency, suicide, divorce, alcoholism, and homicide. These are the current costs of overdevelopment—of becoming rich without abolishing poverty, however high the level of that poverty is in comparison with the poverty of the average Indian or Mestizo resident of a Latin American city or an average resident of Calcutta.

Furthermore, use of the term raises the question of whether the continuum of technical development, which is assumed to be a good thing, may not in fact be something which should not be pursued indefinitely or something which should not be pursued at all, or at least so single-mindedly. It emphasizes the price paid by human beings in industrial countries—both the price paid by those who suffer in their own person through neglect that leads to crime, alcoholism, family disorganization, and so on, and the price paid by the apparent beneficiaries of industrialization through lack of space, leisure, and privacy and through the exchange of peace of mind for a greater number of material possessions. It stresses the values of a preindustrial (or just possibly a postindustrial) form of society, in which standard of living may be seen as having optimum but not maximum value. It refocuses attention on the values of other countries of the world, poor only by a recent definition of what is the right of a nation-state, and stresses values which are intangible. Coupled with an emphasis on the intangibles of faith and a delight in life, there may be, as in Theobald's work, a sophisticated recognition of how difficult it is to transform the motivations of people who have worked all their lives for what they regard as enough into a restless quest for more, because this is part of their newly acquired sense of national identity.

In fact, the world has been maneuvered into a situation which is not technically, economically, or politically feasible. The association of national identity with industrial development is no less ridiculous on a world scale than it would be on a national scale if some group of developers (in the United States, for example) were to say: Every town in the United States, of whatever size, location, or composition, needs a modern factory that can give steady employment to five hundred people and will adjust constructively to changes in world demand. We will lend you the money to build it, supply you with the name of a distributor who will provide you with the equipment, lend you more money if you get in trouble, and control the world market so that your product will always be salable. It is up to you to decide whether the unit of control is to be an unincorporated borough or a section of a metropolitan area, etc. It is also up to you to decide whether the board of managers is to be composed of the DAR, the Chamber of Commerce, ten elementary school-teachers, the fire department, a local of an international union, the top ten percent of the senior class in high school, a representative sample of families who have lived in the area for a hundred years, Catholics, Baptists, Jehovah's Witnesses, a random selection of engineers educated at MIT, former employees of the FBI, at least ten percent American Indians, and so on. We want you to have a high standard of living. We are sure that a manufacturing plant will make it possible for you to improve your health and your educational facilities and to share in the general benefits of an affluent society. But, the developers would have to add, be certain that all this, however you organize it, will result in support of our political position and will not help our rivals. All other considerations—technical, economic, and social—are to be subordinated to this end. It is true we and our political rivals agree that you must have a series of benefits in the way of food, housing, medical care, education, and security; there is no argument about this. And of course you are free to choose the size and shape of the unit within which you want to work. What really is at stake is that in doing this you stay on our side. But our aim is for you as a community—regardless of whether you are a village, a city, or a suburban housing development—to catch up with the highest standard of living that can be shown to exist anywhere.

In effect, the idea of worldwide economic development on a single scale is a case where our ethic for human welfare and human dignity has outrun our ethic for group relevance, where political rivalry, in terms of the 1960s, still permits an efflorescence of economically irrelevant units within which economic development is expected to occur.

What we need urgently today is a set of new propositions which are congruent, one with the other:

1. The technical skills and resources exist; no one in the world need be hungry or cold, unclothed, uneducated, or unmedicated. Standards can be set below which no people anywhere should be allowed to fall. What help is

needed to bring their living standard up to the minimum can be introduced in ways that are appropriate, whether by the export of natural resources; by migration, immigration, or resettlement; regional planning or worldwide organization.

2. The nation-state, which historically was concerned primarily with warding off attack and with attacking others, is an imperfect unit for the administration of human welfare and is an even more imperfect one for the administration of economic development. There is a need for a new kind of nationhood within which every people may find dignity and take responsibility in certain ways for their fellow citizens and in other ways for all other peoples.

3. Any single scale of development is invidious and leads inevitably to conflict, humiliation, and hurt pride. Our present roster of nations has in common only nationhood; in other respects the widest discrepancies exist—in size, age, wealth, tradition, degree of internal homogeneity, natural resources, rate of growth, racial composition, legal practice, level of skill. So it is important to phrase nationhood in terms of what a nation can accomplish in the way of assigning dignity, responsibility, and recognized worldwide status to all peoples of this planet. Citizenship, so phrased, is independent of age, sex, size, intelligence, experience, wealth, beauty, past glory, or future expectations. Any attempt to alter this position, in regard to individual citizenship, would—and should—be opposed with vigor. Yet we are allowing the world to drift toward a position in which all nations will fail to find the dignity they seek if, as is now the case, nationhood is joined to planning for economic development in inappropriate ways. Single-scale development, under these circumstances, will inevitably result in a hierarchy of citizenship as well as of nations.

We need to develop a new framework within which to meet people's basic needs and all world-relevant needs, i.e., for transportation, communications, currency, the allocation of medical supplies, and so on. All these should be dealt with in other than national or simple intergovernmental frameworks. Simultaneously, those countries which are now called underdeveloped could be encouraged to develop their own distinctive identities within the modern world, to cherish their local languages while all children also learned a world language, to develop their own architecture, their own poetry, their own style of life.

With the development of new contexts, it would immediately become apparent that there is nowhere an "overdeveloped" country. The price paid, in delinquency, crime, suicide, and disorganization, by those who live in politically democratic, industrialized countries, is high because they themselves have failed to realize their own economic potential. This in turn hinders the development of a worldwide viable economy.

Nations are, and should be, different from one another. Units of economic development should meet technical, not national, criteria. What we need to work out is a series of overlapping structures which are so acephalous that it will be as difficult for any member to destroy them as it will be unprofitable for any member to withdraw.

Wormwood and Gall

An Introspective Note on American Diplomacy

A. Whitney Griswold

OCTOBER 1960

LAST SPRING AND early summer events transpired on the international stage which, if not finally judged to have been disastrous, must certainly be recorded as among the most disconcerting in the annals of American diplomacy. However we may look upon them now, whatever the consequences to which they may have led or may yet lead, the U-2 incident, the wreck of the summit conference, the Tokyo riots, the collapse of the disarmament conference, and the Cuban crisis constituted a series of immediate setbacks to our foreign policy of such gravity as to cause serious doubts about the conduct of that policy at home and among both friendly and neutral nations abroad. They made it look as though President Eisenhower's personal odyssey in the cause of peace had ended in failure and American leadership of the free nations in that cause had faltered. Hopes for an armistice or an easement of tension in the cold war were dashed, and the conflict was resumed with furious intensity over the Arctic, in Cuba, and in the Congo.

As these events followed one another in rapid succession, they gave rise to increasingly troubled feelings and reflections. The stoning of Vice President Nixon in South America two years ago came vividly to mind. What was happening? Had these things been stage-managed from Moscow? Or did they spring from deeper and more complicated sources? Were they evidence of inadequacy in our own diplomacy? Such were the questions Americans asked themselves as they absorbed their almost daily installments of sensation and shock during the weeks leading up to the national nominating conventions.

Many answers have been given to those questions without, however, allaying the doubts and uncertainties which prompted them. Official explanations of the U-2 flight were so incoherent and self-contradictory that they became as much of an embarrassment as the ill-fated flight itself. The full reason why such a hazardous risk was run so close to a conference on which such prolonged, laborious, and elaborate preparations had been expended and in which, rightly or wrongly, so many hopes had been invested, will probably not be known for some time. Neither will the full reason for the subsequent behavior of Khrushchev, who began by making the most of a legitimate grievance handed to him on a silver platter and ended by consuming both grievance and platter in such an egregious display of rage and histrionic self-righteousness as to leave little doubt that he had been out to break up the conference no matter what happened. Why? Had he moved farther toward the West than his military colleagues or the Chinese would tolerate? Or was he subjecting us to the hot-and-cold Pavlov treatment in the hope of reducing us to docility like the famous dogs? Instead of producing answers, the questions merely reproduced themselves.

The mood engendered in many Americans by these events was one of chagrin. It was not unnatural, perhaps, for a nation that has but recently arrived at man's estate in international affairs and had such enormous and unaccustomed responsibilities thrust upon it to feel rueful about some of the things it has experienced in its new role. We have, I think, learned to recognize communist gall for what it is, and though we do not like its taste, we do not allow it to upset us. But when, as has happened during the past two years, this is augmented by waves of anti-American feelings, demonstrations, and manifestations of hostile sentiments in nations dependent upon us in varying measure for economic aid or military protection (or both) and avowedly friendly to our aims, wormwood is mixed with the gall. Savoring the bitter mixture we say to ourselves, we are damned if we don't and damned if we do. After the First World War we were damned for not staying with the peace. Now, after the Second World War, we are damned because we are staying with the peace. A quarter century ago we were denounced as isolationists. Now the slogan is, Yankees go home. As communist propaganda this is one thing. As a reflection of what may be independent national feelings, it is quite another.

We are obliged to face the possibility that it is indeed the latter, without taking refuge in self-pity or thoughts of the ingratitude of friends. For we cannot go home. As shown by the history of our participation in Far Eastern affairs beginning with the writing of the Open Door notes, isolationism was dying for half a century before it finally expired at Pearl Harbor in 1941. Strong as its historical sources had been—traditional, sociological, geographical, or political—they had dried up. The part we played in organizing the United Nations and have continued to play as a member; the Truman Doctrine, the Marshall Plan, NATO and SEATO; the Korean War; the nomination of President Eisenhower in 1952, and the present platforms of both political parties—these and other events should suffice as proof on both sides of the Iron Curtain of the fundamental change that has taken place in our national outlook and politics. We are forced to stay with the peace by the imperatives of the nuclear age. We therefore have no choice but to master our emotions and examine intellectually the nature of the forces arrayed against us.

II

THE MOST obvious and easiest to identify of these forces is the Soviet government and the tactics it employs in the Cold War. But, as I have already implied, this is not the only force, and even it is complex in nature. Is it more Russian than it is communist or more communist than it is Russian? Did Khrushchev mean what he said about peaceful coexistence in the pages of this magazine last October, or was he merely throwing dust in our eyes while preparing new Cold War offensives? Which is more significant to us, Khrushchev's speech at Bucharest last June in which he apparently broke with the Chinese once and for all on peaceful coexistence with the West, or subsequent Russian tirades against us over the RB-47, Cuba, and the Congo? Possible answers to these questions lead off in many different directions, too many and too different to be boxed up in any such simplified formula as capitalism versus communism or to admit of the equally simplified explanation that every reverse we have experienced in international affairs was caused by Khrushchev pulling a lever.

Undoubtedly Russia's advance in satellites and missiles, whether or not it is as great in relation to our own as critics of the Eisenhower administration aver, has been great enough to bring about some shift in the balance of power; and this in turn has influenced the calculations of some of our allies. On the other hand, the aggressive tactics of the Chinese may have caused a compensating shift among some of the neutral nations. The Tokyo riots were not a conclusive test of either hypothesis. Too many noncommunists took part in them; and the horror of nuclear warfare, the seeming contradiction between the treaty and the prohibition against war in the Japanese Constitution—both of which we had sponsored—and revulsion at the parliamentary tactics of the Kishi government were, in the view of many rioters, perfectly good Japanese rather than Russian reasons for doing so.

It is of course much easier to be wise after the event than it was before it. But two conclusions about the Tokyo riots seem inescapable. The first is that in both origin and nature they turned out to be very much more complicated than a communist plot directed from Moscow. The second is that because this complexity was not fully understood by us, it cost us another diplomatic setback which might have been avoided.

Does this mean, as some critics have held, that the president should not go traveling abroad on visits of state? I do not think so. There is a time for the president to travel and a time for him not to travel, and it is up to his own judgment and that of his advisers to determine which is which. What the Tokyo experience argues in this regard is that diplomacy is an exacting, full-time profession with a functional purpose as vital to the United States in the space age as it was to the Greeks who started it, to the Italian states which organized it as a profession in the fifteenth century, and as it has been to all the nations, including the United Nations, that have practiced it since those times; and that while personal visits by heads of state may assist in the performance of that function, they can also interfere with it and they can never replace it. Diplomacy is supposed to keep things in a negotiable state. By investing in the process the final authority and national prestige attached to the office of the president, whether it be a summit conference or in a visit of state, we run the risk of freezing what ought to be kept fluid before it is ready to be frozen, of assuming attitudes we did not mean to assume, of manœuvring ourselves into uncomfortable positions from which we cannot budge. There are times when such a risk is worth taking. Summit conferences may be forced upon us by the fact that in Soviet Russia we are dealing with a totalitarian state which can negotiate to any purpose only through its head. But the risk should never be taken without recognizing that it is a risk and never in substitution for the systematic formulation and conduct of policy that are the functional as well as the traditional responsibilities of the Department of State. As to visits of state, showmanship is not statesmanship and parades are not plebiscites. After the cheering has died away, warm feelings and pleasant memories of the visitor soon fade unless they are sustained by well-thought-out policy on the basis of which constructive decisions can be made about what to do next.

III

IF WE HAVE failed to convince Japan or Cuba or any other free nation of the validity of our foreign policy, the possibility exists that it is because we have failed to give that policy the force and direction it needs. By force I mean the force of conviction, and by direction, a clear view of the principles on which the policy is based and the ends it is intended to accomplish. Could it be that some of both have been lost in the administrative ant hills in which our foreign policy is defined and the intricate filtration system through which it must pass before it can be executed? The president with his staff of special assistants, the National Security Council, the Council of Economic Advisers, the Central Intelligence Agency, the Joint Chiefs of Staff, the International Cooperation Administration, the Development Loan Fund, the Export-Import Bank, the Atomic Energy Commission, and the National Aeronautics and Space Agency are but some of the agencies directly concerned with the making of foreign policy, in addition to the Department of State with its staff of nearly 35,000 officers and employees. In such organizational redundancy, the grass roots from which national aims in a democracy are supposed to spring and the goals of policy into which those aims must be translated may become too widely separated; the computer may be too complicated for the programming, the programming too complicated for the user.

In an age of organization and in a nation with a passion for it, perhaps all this organization is to be expected. But is it wise and is it necessary? It is not for me or any other layman to say just how many men are needed to carry out a given technical assignment within the universal scope of our international commitments and responsibilities or what the sum of all such technical personnel requirements should be. This is a fast-moving age of scientific and technological revolution which produces (and requires) many experts of many sorts. Conceivably we need more, rather than fewer, men than are at present employed by the Foreign Service, the International Cooperation Administration, the United States Information Agency, and all other operating staffs and agencies in the field. But when it comes to the goals toward which the efforts of these technicians are to be directed, the fundamental conception and definition of the policy without which they will be the blind leading the blind, wisdom is at an even greater premium than technical knowledge and facts; and wisdom has a tendency to shun crowds. The present foreign policy of the United States needs to be enriched by creative ideas as much as does American art or American music. Creative ideas are seldom produced by conferences or committees. There is one maxim attributed to Lenin, the wisdom of which transcends its origin. It is: Reduce the membership and strengthen the party. This might well be applied to the sprawling, many-headed colossus that now directs our foreign affairs.

At the same time the grass roots need tending. The American electorate has hardly begun to acquire the knowledge of its foreign affairs that should go with its responsibilities. I use the word *knowledge* broadly to include understanding as well as information. Too often foreign problems are reduced to the metaphor of the prize ring: "Lodge hits back at Gromyko" and "Let's stand up and slug it out toe-to-toe with Khrushchev." Granted that the whole subject of foreign affairs is inherently complex and that the more it involves military considerations and the more military considerations depend upon scientific data, the more esoteric it becomes. This is no reason for the layman to wash his hands of it. On the contrary, it is a reason for him to improve his knowledge so as to be able to give the policymaker discriminating support or to register intelligent dissent in moments of decision.

Yet we are woefully deficient in the means of acquiring such knowledge. Outside of our larger cities—and inside many of them—foreign news receives meagre treatment in the press; and in our educational system as a whole, in relation to the present responsibilities of the United States, the academic map of the world is almost as primitive as the maps of Columbus. The press has a great void to fill; the academic map must be redrawn to include nations and civilizations—heretofore known only to explorers, missionaries, and professional diplomats—which man's skill and man's fate have brought together with us in a realm of common experience. The obligation of our educational system, particularly of our colleges and universities, does not stop with the study of these nations and peoples. It includes the devising of ways for them to study us—for their professional apprentices, above all, their teachers, to spend part of their apprenticeship in our institutions of higher learning, as we have long since been accustomed to do in the universities of Britain and the Continent. This, incidentally, holds true for Europe as well as for Asia and Africa. . . .

It may never be possible to close this gap altogether, but it can be narrowed and bridged. American society is more gregarious than the British, and our college curriculum is less highly specialized than in the English universities of which C. P. Snow writes. Nevertheless, the gap exists here also, and in the direct interest of the foreign policy of the United States the colleges and universities must put forward their best efforts to close it. Not least of their advantages in this task is the tradition of a university as a community of scholars in which knowledge is shared rather than bottled up and monopolized. They are called upon now to revive that tradition and put to its service all the ingenuity and resources at their command, so that we may not only be competent in science and technology but also able to understand more perfectly their meaning and relationship to the other arts by which we live.

IV

THE MOST disturbing of all thoughts inspired by recent events—more disturbing even than the thought that the sacrifices we made in the Korean War and the billions of dollars we have spent in aid of the free and uncommitted nations should hang in precarious balance in the scales of world opinion—is our suspicion today that on the one hand we are not gauging the independent aims and interests of those nations as clearly as we should and on the other that they may not see ours as clearly as they should. Do the aims and interests of those nations form or correspond to any consistent pattern according to which our policy should be more closely shaped?

It is a common complaint of the professional diplomatist engaged in his day-to-day tasks in the field that he cannot see the woods for the trees. As he works away, more often than not with great industry and competence, he suffers for want of a grand design within which he can feel his labors are leading to some constructive conclusion or goal. It is at this point that the policymaker must come to his assistance, and the electorate and the educational system must come to the aid of the policymaker. Have they done so? When Vice President Nixon was stoned in South America, it was said that this was not such a bad thing after all because it taught us the importance of understanding and keeping up with what was going on in that part of the world. How much it may have taught us and how much we have yet to learn remain to be seen. In the Castro revolution, for example, we are dealing with economic and social forces that had become clearly visible in Cuba a decade ago. Similarly, the Tokyo riots took our officials unawares in a country in which we had had unusual opportunities for firsthand observation and study.

It would be rash indeed to suggest that these events were entirely and exactly predictable and equally rash to attribute them wholly or even mainly to the machinations of Khrushchev. Perhaps it will help us to see and understand them and others like them more clearly if we take into fuller account the five distinct yet simultaneous and interrelated revolutionary forces that common knowledge tells us have been and are at work in the world. The first of these is a scientific revolution, the second is an industrial revolution, the third is the communist revolution, and the fourth is a revolutionary movement toward national independence. The fifth is a restiveness on the part of the younger generation which is evident in almost all countries and reaches revolutionary intensity and proportions in some.

The Cold War is neither the cause of these revolutions nor the result of them, though it happens to be going on at the same time and is, of course, fed by one of them, namely, the communist. If we would keep the well-known fact of the existence of these revolutions more clearly in mind day in and day out, and if we would ask ourselves whether or how any of them or any combination of them may be affecting each specific situation of national concern, public opinion might gain perspective and our diplomacy might be caught off-guard less often.

The scientific revolution caused by recent discoveries about the nature of energy, space, time, and matter is the greatest and most far-reaching in its effects since the scientific revolution of the seventeenth century. The Industrial Revolution, to which the earlier scientific discoveries gave rise in the eighteenth century and grew mightily in the nineteenth, has been spreading through the world ever since. The scientific revolution of our time has infused it with new forces—electronics, automation, atomic power—and thereby is accelerating its spread. In heretofore unindustrialized countries such as India, China, Indonesia, and the African nations, changes in human society are in prospect, if not already begun, which will have more momentous social, economic, and political effects than any that have taken place since man turned from hunting to agriculture. Because nations are similarly affected by the scientific and the industrial revolutions, it might be supposed that they would be drawn together by them. So they might be were it not for the communist revolution, which exploits the gap between the backward and more highly developed peoples and the virulent nationalism that often accompanies the move toward independence.

The scientific revolution did not start the communist revolution. The Industrial Revolution did not start it. Its prophet, Marx, rested his case on industrial data that were in process of rapid change while he wrote and obsolete when he had finished his writing. Marx put a doctrinaire interpretation on the Industrial Revolution and promised all who accepted his doctrine the complete "scientific" rationalization of that revolution in economic and social terms. That promise has never been made good. In most countries it has died a-borning; claims to have fulfilled it have been made in others where the rationalizing has been done and enforced by absolute dictatorial authority. The very fact of coercion belies the pretension of scientific inevitability. On the other hand, where the industrial revolution has been permitted to develop in conditions of greater freedom, the evils predicted by Marx have not ensued. It has steadily improved rather than worsened the conditions of labor. Marx proclaimed the communist revolution as the final evolutionary phase of a highly industrialized society. Instead, it has taken root only in underdeveloped agrarian societies.

Of all five revolutionary forces, the restiveness of youth, which seems the most familiar, is perhaps the least well understood. . . .

There is more to this force than the normal friction between the generations. There is something in the minds of young people today which they themselves have not been able to make wholly articulate and not all the behavioral sciences have succeeded in bringing out fully into the light. Exactly what that is lies beyond my scope and perhaps my competence to explain. Suffice it to recognize it as a subject of profound significance to our diplomacy and to offer three thoughts which may shed some light upon it.

The first thought is that youth is far more disillusioned with war than most of its elders—who think that they too are disillusioned with it—realize. With this disillusionment goes a disbelief in the old concepts of patriotism and codes of chivalry that used to find their ultimate fulfillment and sanction in war. Yet patriotism is not dead, and youth still feels the primal urge to fight. The Great Deterrent wrings the last drop of glamor, even of honor, out of war, but does not stop our young men from fighting in Korea; or serving the armed forces of their country with courage and devotion; or, at high school age, fighting one another in gangs for the sole purpose of proving their courage to themselves; or, as college students, withdrawing into the symbolic rebellion of the beatnik, or actively contesting or rioting against any and all semblances of authority. Where there is plenty of freedom and the living is good, they riot at jazz festivals. Where there is not plenty of freedom and the living is precarious, they riot to overthrow the government. One thing that gives continuity to these actions is their thoughts about war. In Japan, for example, when noncommunist students were asked what they were thinking about when they joined in the Tokyo riots, they are said to have replied, "the day the sky turned red and our house burned down." I am sure that in the American and English riots, touched off by jazz rather than by treaties of alliance, the same feelings and thoughts about war (though we might have to probe more deeply to discover them)—the same skepticism, mistrust, and unbelief concerning everything and everyone connected with war—were present in the minds of the rioters as were present in the minds of those in Tokyo.

A second thought about the restiveness of the younger generation relates particularly to the underdeveloped and emergent nations. In these it is only the younger generation that has received any education in our sense of the word. Because of previous conditions the educational opportunity has passed the older generation by. As this opportunity now brings knowledge of the world flooding into these countries, that knowledge will fill only one set of receptacles. This means that, to the degree that political stability depends upon the balancing weight of age and experience, there will be less and less political stability.

Even in countries like our own, mastery of the scientific and industrial revolutions—if they are ever to be mastered—is going to the rising generation; and the pace of those revolutions is handing the future to that generation more rapidly and more completely than most of us realize. This brings me to my third thought about its restiveness. This restiveness is not to be understood purely by its more obvious symptoms. Underlying it is a more accurate knowledge of the physical world and a potentially more intelligent disposition of its human affairs than any which have preceded them. Knowledge turns into power. The forms that power will take will depend upon the way in which the United States, the free nations, and the emergent nations respond to the educational challenge that confronts them all.

This much is certain: the five revolutionary forces which I have cited, and which are often treated or taken for granted as being one and the same thing, are neither one and the same thing nor yet the ineluctable, deterministic results of one another, but separate and distinct things which can, and often do, move in different combinations and directions. There is scope for nations to react to these five forces, and to others that might be added, such as hunger and fear, in a multiplicity of ways. A better understanding of the forces would not only give us a clearer idea of the general direction our foreign policy should take but a firmer grasp of the concrete situations to which it is applied.

V

THERE REMAINS the possibility that we may not have given the world an accurate impression of our own national character and aims. In this regard what we do about ourselves counts for much more than what we say about ourselves. As it is, the free and neutral nations know several things about us which, though our statesmen may not have turned them to immediate advantage, should be decided assets to our diplomacy in the long run; and I suspect that the Russians know these things, too. One is that, whatever else our failings and shortcomings, we are poor dissemblers, more accustomed to blurting out the truth than to keeping state secrets. We believe that the truth is on our side and will prevail. Another is that no other nation in history has ever achieved such power and used it with such forbearance in its international relations. Another is that the spirit which produced the charters of free government and individual liberty in our Constitution and its Bill of Rights, and which now supports those principles in the United Nations, is stronger than any disposition to feel sorry for ourselves because we are misunderstood or to withdraw into ourselves because of diplomatic reverses. Again, American capitalism bears no more resemblance to the communist picture of it than Abraham Lincoln does to Karl Marx (or, for that matter, than the present Russian industrial state to the one that Marx prophesied). No nation has created as productive an economy as ours; none provides so many opportunities and so much freedom for human talent to find its natural outlet. These truths can be denied, but not successfully in the long run.

When the free nations examine the record, they must conclude, too, that we are not imperialists. We never were imperialists. Our tentative, highly self-conscious, highly imitative adventures in imperialism at the turn of the century were short-lived and ended in remorse. As far as concerns China, now our principal accuser in this respect, we have always been anti-imperialist. During the entire history of our relations with China, as the record plainly shows, we have defended her territorial and administrative integrity. This was the fundamental principle around which our whole Far Eastern policy was built. The Russians know (though it is convenient for them to forget it) that it saved them the maritime provinces of Siberia. The nations on both sides of the Iron Curtain should know, finally, that we are not merely the leader of a defensive alliance but rather a participant in a common effort on the part of free nations and nations emerging into freedom to build a community of peace, in which mankind may emancipate itself from hunger and disease and improve its standard of living, as modern science and technology have now, for the first time in history, made universally possible.

Much has been said during this presidential campaign about the image of America and how to improve it. To begin with, we must have a good original. On this subject I think no one has spoken more wisely than the French economist Turgot, who in 1778, shortly after the Battle of Saratoga and the alliance with France had ensured the success of our struggle for independence, wrote to his English friend Dr. Richard Price about the American people as follows:

> This people is the hope of the human race. It may become the model. It ought to show the world by facts, that men can be free and yet peaceful, and may dispense with the chains in which tyrants and knaves of every color have presumed to bind them, under pretext of the public good. The Americans should be an example of political, religious, commercial, and industrial liberty. The asylum they offer to the oppressed of every nation, the avenue of escape they open, will compel governments to be just and enlightened; and the rest of the world in due time will see through the empty illusions in which policy is conceived. But to obtain these ends for us, America must secure them to herself.

These prophetic words point to a fundamental principle which we neglect at our peril: that is, the continuity between domestic and foreign policy. Granted that the communists have done everything in their power to deface our national portrait and poison the minds of its beholders. But if the rest of the world cannot see in us all that we should like them to see, the main reason is because we cannot see it in ourselves, no matter how often or how hard we stare in the mirror. The mirror cannot create; it can only reflect, and what is not there will not be reflected. In the domestic realm we have unfinished social and economic business of grave importance on our hands. It is itemized in the platforms of both parties. One way to strengthen our foreign policy is to get on with that business. This is not the responsibility of our diplomacy. It is our responsibility *to* our diplomacy.

The Quagmire of Vietnam

THE NINETEEN SIXTIES

⅋THE AMERICAN DESCENT into Vietnam remains both a logical outgrowth of Cold War trends and a baffling testament to the march of folly.
John Kenneth Galbraith, President Kennedy's ambassador to India, once
archly asked who in the administration was responsible for picking out countries as strategic. In fact, it was the entire Kennedy administration that assumed that the defense of South Vietnam was a vital U.S. interest. Starting
in a limited way in the 1950s under Dwight D. Eisenhower, the United States
began to assume France's old role as guardian of the ancien regime in Indochina. Eisenhower invoked the domino theory to argue that if Vietnam fell
to communism, all of Southeast Asia might topple. The involvement deepened dramatically under Kennedy and his successor, Lyndon B. Johnson. It
scarcely occurred to Washington that America might meet the same fate as
France did against Ho Chi Minh's determined guerrillas.

Fearful of the domestic costs of a communist victory in Southeast Asia,
Kennedy used Vietnam as a showcase for American might, know-how, and
swagger. He began by sending military "advisers" to teach the South Vietnamese to defend themselves. In the face of Vietcong advances, Washington
soon introduced support troops and napalm bombings. By the time Kennedy
was assassinated in 1963, there were over 16,000 U.S. troops in Vietnam.

Lyndon Johnson also feared looking soft on communism. In August
1964, Johnson used the attack on a U.S. ship in the Gulf of Tonkin to win a
blank check from Congress to carry the war to the north. More cautious
voices were ignored, including that of Hans J. Morgenthau, one of the
founders of the realist school of international relations, who argued early on
in "To Intervene or Not to Intervene" that American interventions needed to
be based on a hard-headed calculus of national interest and probability of
success. By 1967 there were 436,000 American troops in Indochina. It was to

no avail. After the Vietcong's surprising show of strength in the Tet offensive of January 1968, even Defense Secretary Robert McNamara, the steely technocrat who was the war's architect, could scent defeat and resigned. His successor, Clark M. Clifford, who laid out the gripping story of his mounting opposition to the war in "A Viet Nam Reappraisal," also came to see Vietnam as a tragic blunder. The war led into the youth rebellion of the 1960s and spawned an antigovernment radicalism complete with marches, demonstrations, and sit-ins. The tone and content of the antiwar movement were deplored by many, as epitomized by the neoconservative intellectual Irving Kristol's "American Intellectuals and Foreign Policy," which argued that the nation's elites were irresponsible, abusive, and unhelpful to a world power. In the end, as David Halberstam put it, despite his domestic ambitions, Johnson would enter the history books as a war president, and not a very good one at that.

Richard M. Nixon won the presidency in 1968 by promising that he had a secret plan to end the war. His national security adviser would be Henry A. Kissinger, whose "The Viet Nam Negotiations," published mere months before his appointment, warned cannily that traditional American strategies were ill-equipped to cope with Ho's guerrillas. Kissinger was concerned that U.S. credibility would be battered further by too precipitous a retreat from Vietnam and proposed a policy of "Vietnamization" that sought to return control of the war to the South Vietnamese and enable the United States to make a not entirely graceless exit. But along the way, Nixon and Kissinger added a sideshow in Cambodia, which the United States invaded in 1970 to cut Vietcong supply lines. Public opinion soured further with the expansion of the war into Laos, the killing of four antiwar protestors at Kent State, and the revelation of the My Lai massacre. While the administration began its famous opening to China in 1972, Nixon ordered the "carpet bombing" of the North as the last offensive before Hanoi and Washington finally came to terms. Without the United States to assist, the Saigon government collapsed in 1975, with the communists renaming the former southern capital Ho Chi Minh City. Fifty-eight thousand Americans had died, millions of Vietnamese were killed, Cambodia was ravaged by the Khmer Rouge, and America was divided as never before; but America's longest war was finally over.

To Intervene or
Not To Intervene

Hans J. Morgenthau

APRIL 1967

INTERVENTION IS AS ancient and well-established an instrument of foreign policy as are diplomatic pressure, negotiations, and war. From the time of the ancient Greeks to this day, some states have found it advantageous to intervene in the affairs of other states on behalf of their own interests and against the latters' will. Other states, in view of their interests, have opposed such interventions and have intervened on behalf of theirs.

It is only since the French Revolution of 1789 and the rise of the nation-state that the legitimacy of intervention has been questioned. Article 119 of the French Constitution of 1793 declared that the French people "do not interfere in the domestic affairs of other nations and will not tolerate interference by other nations in their affairs." This declaration ushered in a period of interventions by all concerned on the largest possible scale. For a century and a half afterwards, statesmen, lawyers, and political writers tried in vain to formulate objective criteria by which to distinguish between legitimate and illegitimate intervention. The principle of nonintervention was incorporated into the textbooks of international law, and statesmen have never ceased to pay lip service to it. In December 1965, the United Nations General Assembly adopted a "Declaration on the Inadmissibility of Intervention in the Domestic Affairs of States and the Protection of their Independence and Sovereignty," according to which "no state has the right to intervene, directly or indirectly, for any reason whatever, in the internal or external affairs of any other state . . ." and "no state shall organize, assist, foment, finance, incite or tolerate subversive, terrorist or armed activities directed toward the violent overthrow of another state, or interfere in civil strife in another state." Yet again we are witnessing throughout the world activities violating all the rules laid down in this declaration.

[265]

Both the legal commitments against intervention and the practice of intervention serve the political purposes of particular nations. The former serve to discredit the intervention of the other side and to justify one's own. Thus the principle of nonintervention, as formulated at the beginning of the nineteenth century, sought to protect the new nation-states from interference by the traditional monarchies of Europe. For the main instrument of the Holy Alliance, openly proclaimed in the treaty establishing it, was intervention. Thus, to give only two examples among many, Russia tried to intervene in Spain in 1820, and actually intervened in Hungary in 1848, in order to oppose liberal revolutions. Great Britain opposed these interventions because it was opposed to the expansion of Russian power. Yet it intervened on behalf of nationalism in Greece and on behalf of the conservative status quo in Portugal because its interests seemed to require it.

What we have witnessed since the end of the Second World War thus appears as a mere continuation of a tradition which was well established in the nineteenth century. There is nothing new either in the contemporary doctrine opposing intervention or in the pragmatic use of intervention on behalf of the interests of individual nations. What Great Britain and Russia were doing in the nineteenth century, the United States and the Soviet Union seem to be doing today. Thus, to cite again two spectacular examples among many, the Soviet Union intervened in Hungary in 1956 as Russia had done in 1848, and the United States intervened in Cuba at the beginning of the 1960s as it had done in the first decades of the century. Yet there are fundamental differences between the interventions of the past and those of the present. Five such differences have significantly altered the techniques of contemporary intervention, have drastically reduced the traditional legal significance of the consent of the state intervened against, and have affected in a general way the peace and order of the world.

First, the process of decolonization, which started after the Second World War and is now almost completed, has more than doubled the number of sovereign nations. Many if not most of these new nations are not viable political, military, and economic entities; they are lacking in some if not all of the prerequisites of nationhood. Their governments need regular outside support. Thus France subsidizes its former colonies in Africa; all the major industrial nations extend economic and financial aid to the new ones, and the United States, the Soviet Union, and China do so on a competitive basis.

What makes this aid a lever for intervention is the fact that in most cases it is not just an advantage which the new nations can afford to take or leave, but a condition for their survival. The Indian economy, for example, would collapse without outside support, and in consequence the Indian state itself would probably disintegrate. Large masses of Egyptians would starve without the outside supply of food. What is true of these two ancient and relatively well-developed nations is of course true of most of the new nations which are nations within their present boundaries only by virtue of the accidents of colonial policy: the supplier of foreign aid holds the power of life and death over them. If a foreign nation supplies aid it intervenes; if it does not supply aid it also intervenes. In the measure that the government must depend on foreign aid for its own and its nation's survival it is inevitably exposed to political pressures from the supplying government. Many of the recipient governments have been able to minimize or even neutralize these political pressures by keeping open alternative sources of foreign aid and by playing one supplying government against the other. Some nations, such as Egypt, have developed this technique into a fine and highly successful art.

Second, our age resembles the period of history after the Napoleonic Wars, when the theory of nonintervention and the practice of intervention flourished, in that it is a revolutionary age. Many nations, new and old, are threatened by revolution or are at one time or another in the throes of it. A successful revolution frequently portends a new orientation in the country's foreign policy, as it did in the Congo, Cuba, and Indonesia. Thus the great powers, expecting gains or fearing disadvantages from the revolution, are tempted to intervene on the side of the faction favoring them. This is particularly so when the revolution is committed to a communist or anticommunist position. Thus China has almost indiscriminately intervened throughout the world on behalf of subversive movements, very much in the manner in which the Bolshevist government under Lenin and Trotsky tried to promote world revolution. In many nations, the United States and the Soviet Union oppose each other surreptitiously through the intermediary of governments and political movements. It is at this point that the third new factor comes into play.

Of all the revolutionary changes that have occurred in world politics since the end of the Second World War, none has exerted a greater influence upon the conduct of foreign policy than the recognition on the part of the two superpowers, armed with a large arsenal of nuclear weapons, that a direct confrontation between them would entail unacceptable risks; for it could lead to their mutual destruction. Both have recognized that a nuclear war fought against each other would be a suicidal absurdity. Thus they have decided that they must avoid a direct confrontation. This is the real political and military meaning of the slogan of "peaceful coexistence."

Instead of confronting each other openly and directly, the United States and the Soviet Union have chosen to oppose and compete with each other surreptitiously through the intermediary of third parties. The internal weakness of most new and emerging nations requiring foreign support and the revolutionary situation in many of them give the great powers the opportunity of doing so. Thus, aside from competing for influence upon a particular government in the traditional ways, the United States and the Soviet Union have interjected their power into the domestic conflicts of weak nations, supporting the government or the opposition as the case may be. While one might think that on ideological grounds the United States would always intervene on the side of the government and the Soviet Union on the side of the opposition, it is characteristic of the interplay between ideology and power politics, to which we shall turn in a moment, that this has not always been so. Thus the Soviet Union intervened in Hungary in 1956 on the side of the government, and the United States has been intervening in Cuba on the side of the opposition. The Soviet slogan of support for "wars of national liberation" is in truth an ideological justification of Soviet support for that side in a civil conflict in which the Soviet Union happens to have an interest. In the Congo, the United States and the Soviet Union have switched their support from the government to the opposition and back again according to the fortunes of a succession of civil wars.

While contemporary interventions serving national power interests have sometimes been masked by the ideologies of communism and anticommunism, these ideologies have been an independent motivating force. This is the fourth factor which we must consider. The United States and the Soviet Union face each other not only as two great powers which in the traditional ways compete for advantage. They also face each other as the fountainheads of two hostile and incompatible ideologies, systems of government and ways of life, each trying to expand the reach of its respective political values and institutions and to prevent the expansion of the other. Thus the Cold War has not only been a conflict between two world powers but also a contest between two secular religions. And like the religious wars of the seventeenth century, the war between communism and democracy does not respect national boundaries. It finds enemies and allies in all countries, opposing the one and supporting the other regardless of the niceties of international law. Here is the dynamic force which has led the two superpowers to intervene all over the globe, sometimes surreptitiously, sometimes openly, sometimes with the accepted methods of diplomatic pressure and propaganda, sometimes with the frowned-upon instruments of covert subversion and open force.

These four factors favoring intervention in our time are counteracted by a fifth one, which in a sense compensates for the weakness of the nations intervened in. Having just emerged from a colonial status or struggling to emerge from a semicolonial one, these nations react to their dependence on outside support with a fierce resistance to the threat of "neocolonialism." While they cannot exist without support from stronger nations, they refuse to exchange their newly won independence for a new dependency. Hence their ambivalent reaction to outside intervention. They need it and they resent it. This ambivalence compels them to choose among several different courses of action. They can seek support from multiple outside sources, thereby canceling out dependence on one by dependence on the other. They can alternate among different sources of support, at one time relying on one, and at another time relying on another. Finally, they can choose between complete dependence and complete independence, either by becoming a client of one of the major powers or by forswearing outside support altogether.

This ambivalence of the weak nations imposes new techniques upon the intervening ones. Intervention must either be brutally direct in order to overcome resistance or it must be surreptitious in order to be acceptable, or the two extremes may be combined. Thus the United States intervened in Cuba in 1961 through the proxy of a refugee force, and the Soviet Union intervened in Hungary in 1956 by appointing a government which asked for its intervention.

II

WHAT FOLLOWS from this condition of intervention in our time for the foreign policies of the United States? Four basic conclusions can be drawn: the futility of the search for abstract principles, the error of anticommunist intervention per se, the self-defeating character of antirevolutionary intervention per se, and the requirement of prudence.

First, it is futile to search for an abstract principle which would allow us to distinguish in a concrete case between legitimate and illegitimate intervention. This was so even in the nineteenth century when intervention for the purpose of colonial expansion was generally regarded to be legitimate and when the active players on the political stage were relatively self-sufficient nation-states, which not only were not in need of intervention but actually were opposed to it as a threat to their existence. If this was so then, it stands to reason that in an age when large segments of whole continents must choose between anarchy and intervention, intervention cannot be limited by abstract principles, let alone effectively outlawed by a United Nations resolution.

Let us suppose that nation A intervenes on behalf of the government of nation B by giving it military, economic, and technical aid on the latter's request, and that the government of B becomes so completely dependent upon A as to act as the latter's satellite. Let us further suppose that the local opposition calls upon country C for support against the agents of a foreign oppressor and that C heeds that call. Which one of these interventions is legitimate? Country A will of course say that its own is and C's is not, and vice versa, and the ideologues on both sides will be kept busy justifying the one and damning the other. This ideological shadowboxing cannot affect the incidence of interventions. All nations will continue to be guided in their decisions to intervene and their choice of the means of intervention by what they regard as their respective national interests. There is indeed an urgent need for the governments of the great powers to abide by certain rules according to which the game of intervention is to be played. But these rules must be deduced not from abstract principles, which are incapable of controlling the actions of governments, but from the interests of the nations concerned and from their practice of foreign policy reflecting those interests. . . .

The interventions of the United States in Cuba, the Dominican Republic, and Viet Nam, as well as others less spectacular, have been justified as reactions to communist intervention. This argument derives from the assumption that communism everywhere in the world is not only morally unacceptable and philosophically hostile to the United States, but is also detrimental to the national interests of the United States and must therefore be opposed on political as well as moral and philosophic grounds. I shall assume for the purposes of this discussion that, as a matter of fact, communist intervention actually preceded ours in all these instances and shall raise the question as to whether our national interest required our counterintervention.

Ten or twenty years ago, this question could have been answered in the positive without further examination. For then communism anywhere in the world was a mere extension of Soviet power, controlled and used for the purposes of that power. Since we were committed to the containment of the Soviet Union, we were also committed to the containment of communism anywhere in the world. However, today we are faced not with one monolithic communist bloc controlled and used by the Soviet Union, but with a variety of communisms, whose relations with the Soviet Union and China change from country to country and from time to time and whose bearing upon the interests of the United States requires empirical examination in each concrete instance. Communism has become polycentric, that is to say, each communist government and movement, to a greater or lesser extent, pursues its own national interests within the common framework of communist ideology and institutions. The bearing which the pursuit of those interests has upon the interests of the United States must be determined in terms not of communist ideology but of the compatibility of those interests with the interests of the United States.

Subjecting our interventions in Cuba, the Dominican Republic, and Viet Nam to this empirical test, one realizes the inadequacy of the simple slogan "stop communism" as the rationale of our interventions. While this slogan is popular at home and makes but minimal demands upon discriminating judgment, it inspires policies which do either too much or too little in opposing communism and can provide no yardstick for a policy which measures the degree of its opposition by the degree of the communist threat. Thus on the one hand, as part of the settlement of the missile crisis of 1962, we pledged ourselves not to intervene in Cuba, which is today a military and political outpost of the Soviet Union and the fountainhead of subversion and military intervention in the Western Hemisphere, and as such directly affects the interests of the United States. On the other hand, we have intervened massively in Viet Nam, even at the risk of a major war, although the communist threat to American interests from Viet Nam is at best remote and in any event is infinitely more remote than the communist threat emanating from Cuba. . . .

This type of intervention against communism per se naturally tends to blend into intervention against revolution per se. Thus we tend to intervene against all radical revolutionary movements because we are afraid lest they be taken over by communists, and conversely we tend to intervene on behalf of all governments and movements which are opposed to radical revolution, because they are also opposed to communism. Such a policy of intervention is unsound on intellectual grounds for the reasons mentioned in our discussion of contemporary communism; it is also bound to fail in practice.

Many nations of Asia, Africa, and Latin America are today in a prerevolutionary stage, and it is likely to be only a matter of time until actual revolution will break out in one or another of these nations. The revolutionary movements which will then come to the fore are bound to have, to a greater or lesser degree, a communist component; that is, they risk being taken over by communism. Nothing is simpler, both in terms of intellectual effort and, at least initially, practical execution, than to trace all these revolutions to a common conspiratorial source, to equate all revolutionary movements with world communism, and to oppose them with indiscriminate fervor as uniformly hostile to our interests. The United States would then be forced to intervene against revolutions throughout the world because of the ever-present threat of a communist takeover and would transform itself, in spite of its better insight and intentions, into an antirevolutionary power per se.

Such a policy of intervention might succeed if it had to deal with nothing more than isolated revolutionary movements which could be smothered by force of arms. But it cannot succeed, since it is faced with revolutionary situations all over the world; for even the militarily most powerful nation does not have sufficient usable resources to deal simultaneously with a number of acute revolutions. Such a policy of indiscriminate intervention against revolution is bound to fail not only with regard to the individual revolution to which it is applied but also in terms of its own indiscriminate anticommunism. For the very logic which would make us appear as the antirevolutionary power per se would surrender to communism the sponsorship of revolution everywhere. Thus anticommunist intervention achieves what it aims to prevent: the exploitation of the revolutions of the age by communism.

In truth, the choice before us is not between the status quo and revolution or even between communist and noncommunist revolution, but between a revolution hostile to the interests of the United States and a revolution which is not hostile to these interests. The United States, far from intervening against revolutions per se, has therefore to intervene in competition with the main instigators of revolution—the Soviet Union, communist China, and Cuba—on behalf of revolution. This intervention should serve two alternative aims: first, to protect the revolution from a communist takeover, and second, if we should fail in this, to prevent such a communist revolution from turning against the interests of the United States. Such a policy, substituting the yardstick of the American national interest for that of anticommunism, would obviously form a complete reversal of the positions which we have taken in recent years and of which our interventions in Viet Nam and the Dominican Republic are the recent prime examples.

If this analysis of our policy of intervention is correct, then we have intervened not wisely but too well. Our policy of intervention has been under the ideological spell of our opposition to communism and potentially communist-led revolutions. Yet while this ideological orientation has continued to determine our policy of intervention, the Soviet Union has continued to pay lip service to support for "wars of national liberation" but has in practice relegated these wars to a secondary place in the struggle for the world. . . .

One factor which cannot have failed to influence the Soviet Union in toning down its ideological commitment to intervention has been the relative failure of ideological intervention. The United States, China, and Cuba have joined the Soviet Union in the experience of that failure. The new and emerging nations have been eager to reap the benefits of intervention, but have also been very anxious not to be tied with ideological strings to the intervening nation. After making great efforts, expending considerable resources, and running serious risks, the participants in this worldwide ideological competition are still approximately at the point from which they started: measured against their ambitions and expectations, the uncommitted third of the world is still by and large an ideological no-man's-land.

This experience of failure is particularly painful, and ought to be particularly instructive, for the United States. For we have intervened in the political, military, and economic affairs of other countries to the tune of far in excess of $100 billion, and we are at present involved in a costly and risky war in order to build a nation in South Viet Nam. Only the enemies of the United States will question the generosity of these efforts, which have no parallel in history. But have these efforts been wise? Have the commitments made and risks taken been commensurate with the results to be expected and actually achieved? The answer must be in the negative. Our economic aid has been successful in supporting economies which were already in the process of development; it has been by and large unsuccessful in creating economic development where none existed before, largely because the moral and rational preconditions for such development were lacking. Learning from this failure, we have established the theoretical principle of concentrating aid upon the few nations which can use it rather than giving it to the many who need it. While this principle of selectivity is sound in theory, its consistent practical application has been thwarted by the harsh political and military realities which may require economic aid which is economically not justified, as well as by political and military considerations derived from the ideological concerns discussed above.

This principle of selectivity must be extended to the political and military sphere as well. We have come to overrate enormously what a nation can do for another nation by intervening in affairs—even with the latter's consent. This overestimation of our power to intervene is a corollary of our ideological commitment, which by its very nature has no limit. Committed to intervening against communist aggression and subversion anywhere, we have come to assume that we have the power to do so successfully. But in truth, both the need for intervention and the chances for successful intervention are much more limited than we have been led to believe. Intervene we must where our national interest requires it and where our power gives us a chance to succeed. The choice of these occasions will be determined not by sweeping ideological commitments nor by blind reliance upon American power but by a careful calculation of the interests involved and the power available. If the United States applies this standard, it will intervene less and succeed more.

The Viet Nam Negotiations

Henry A. Kissinger

JANUARY 1969

THE PEACE NEGOTIATIONS in Paris have been marked by the classic Viet-namese syndrome: optimism alternating with bewilderment; euphoria giving way to frustration. The halt to the bombing produced another wave of high hope. Yet it was followed almost immediately by the dispute with Saigon over its participation in the talks. The merits of this issue aside, we must realize that a civil war which has torn a society for 20 years and which has involved the great powers is unlikely to be settled in a single dramatic stroke. Even if there were mutual trust—a commodity not in excessive supply—the com-plexity of the issues and the difficulty of grasping their interrelationship would make for complicated negotiations. Throughout the war, criteria by which to measure progress have been hard to come by; this problem has con-tinued during the negotiations. The dilemma is that almost any statement about Viet Nam is likely to be true; unfortunately, truth does not guarantee relevance.

The sequence of events that led to negotiations probably started with General Westmoreland's visit to Washington in November 1967. On that oc-casion, General Westmoreland told a Joint Session of Congress that the war was being won militarily. He outlined "indicators" of progress and stated that a limited withdrawal of American combat forces might be undertaken begin-ning late in 1968. On January 17, 1968, President Johnson, in his State of the Union address, emphasized that the pacification program—the extension of the control of Saigon into the countryside—was progressing satisfactorily. Sixty-seven percent of the population of South Viet Nam lived in relatively secure areas; the figure was expected to rise. A week later, the Tet offensive overthrew the assumptions of American strategy.

What had gone wrong? The basic problem has been conceptual: the ten-dency to apply traditional maxims of both strategy and "nation building" to a situation which they did not fit.

[274]

American military strategy followed the classic doctrine that victory depended on a combination of control of territory and attrition of the opponent. Therefore, the majority of the American forces were deployed along the frontiers of South Viet Nam to prevent enemy infiltration and in the central highlands where most of the North Vietnamese main-force units—those units organized along traditional military lines—were concentrated. The theory was that defeat of the main forces would cause the guerrillas to wither on the vine. Victory would depend on inflicting casualties substantially greater than those we suffered until Hanoi's losses became "unacceptable."

This strategy suffered from two disabilities: (a) the nature of guerrilla warfare: (b) the asymmetry in the definition of what constituted unacceptable losses. A guerrilla war differs from traditional military operations because its key prize is not control of territory but control of the population. This depends, in part, on psychological criteria, especially a sense of security. No positive program can succeed unless the population feels safe from terror or reprisal. Guerrillas rarely seek to hold real estate; their tactic is to use terror and intimidation to discourage cooperation with constituted authority.

The distribution of the population in Viet Nam makes this problem particularly acute. Over 90 percent of the population live in the coastal plain and the Mekong Delta; the central highlands and the frontiers, on the other hand, are essentially unpopulated. Eighty percent of American forces came to be concentrated in areas containing less than four percent of the population; the locale of military operations was geographically removed from that of the guerrilla conflict. As North Vietnamese theoretical writings never tired of pointing out, the United States could not hold territory and protect the population simultaneously. By opting for military victory through attrition, the American strategy produced what came to be the characteristic feature of the Vietnamese war: military successes that could not be translated into permanent political advantage. (Even the goal of stopping infiltration was very hard to implement in the trackless, nearly impenetrable jungles along the Cambodian and Laotian frontiers.)

As a result, the American conception of security came to have little in common with the experience of the Vietnamese villagers. American maps classified areas by three categories of control, neatly shown in various colors: government, contested, and Viet Cong. The formal criteria were complicated, and depended to an unusual extent on reports by officers whose short terms of duty (barely 12 months) made it next to impossible for them to grasp the intangibles and nuances which constitute the real elements of control in the Vietnamese countryside. In essence, the first category included all villages which contained some governmental authority; "contested" referred to areas slated to be entered by governmental cadres. The American notion of security was a reflection of Western administrative theory; control was assumed to be in the hands of one of the contestants more or less exclusively.

But the actual situation in Viet Nam was quite different; a realistic security map would have shown few areas of exclusive jurisdiction; the pervasive experience of the Vietnamese villager was the ubiquitousness of both sides. Saigon controlled much of the country in the daytime, in the sense that government troops could move anywhere if they went in sufficient force; the Viet Cong dominated a large part of the same population at night. For the villagers, the presence of government during the day had to be weighed against its absence after dark, when Saigon's cadres almost invariably withdrew into the district or provincial capitals. If armed teams of administrators considered the villages unsafe at night, the villagers could hardly be expected to resist the guerrillas. Thus, the typical pattern in Viet Nam has been dual control, with the villagers complying with whatever force was dominant during a particular part of the day.

The political impact of this dual control was far from symmetrical, however. To be effective, the government had to demonstrate a very great capacity to provide protection; probably well over 90 percent. The guerrillas' aim was largely negative: to prevent the consolidation of governmental authority. They did not need to destroy all governmental programs; indeed in some areas, they made no effort to interfere with them. They did have to demonstrate a capability to punish individuals who threw in their lot with Saigon. An occasional assassination or raid served to shake confidence for months afterward.

The North Vietnamese and Viet Cong had another advantage, which they used skillfully. American "victories" were empty unless they laid the basis for an eventual withdrawal. The North Vietnamese and Viet Cong, fighting in their own country, needed merely to keep in being forces sufficiently strong to dominate the population after the United States tired of the war. We fought a military war; our opponents fought a political one. We sought physical attrition; our opponents aimed for our psychological exhaustion. In the process, we lost sight of one of the cardinal maxims of guerrilla war: the guerrilla wins if he does not lose. The conventional army loses if it does not win. The North Vietnamese used their main forces the way a bullfighter uses his cape—to keep us lunging in areas of marginal political importance.

The strategy of attrition failed to reduce the guerrillas and was in difficulty even with respect to the North Vietnamese main forces. Since Hanoi made no attempt to hold any territory, and since the terrain of the central highlands cloaked North Vietnamese movements, it proved difficult to make the opposing forces fight except at places which they chose. Indeed, a considerable majority of engagements came to be initiated by the other side; this enabled Hanoi to regulate its casualties (and ours) at least within certain limits. The so-called "kill-ratios" of United States to North Vietnamese casualties became highly unreliable indicators. Even when the figures were accurate they were irrelevant, because the level of what was "unacceptable" to Americans fighting thousands of miles from home turned out to be much lower than that of Hanoi fighting on Vietnamese soil.

All this caused our military operations to have little relationship to our declared political objectives. Progress in establishing a political base was excruciatingly slow; our diplomacy and our strategy were conducted in isolation from each other. President Johnson had announced repeatedly that we would be ready to negotiate, unconditionally, at any moment, anywhere. This, in effect, left the timing of negotiations to the other side. But short of a complete collapse of the opponent, our military deployment was not well designed to support negotiations. For purposes of negotiating, we would have been better off with 100 percent control over 60 percent of the country than with 60 percent control of 100 percent of the country.

The effort to strengthen Saigon's political control faced other problems. To be effective, the so-called pacification program had to meet two conditions: (a) it had to provide security for the population; (b) it had to establish a political and institutional link between the villages and Saigon. Neither condition was ever met: impatience to show "progress" in the strategy of attrition caused us to give low priority to protection of the population; in any event, there was no concept as to how to bring about a political framework relating Saigon to the countryside. As a result, economic programs had to carry an excessive load. In Viet Nam—as in most developing countries—the overwhelming problem is not to *buttress* but to *develop* a political framework. Economic progress that undermines the existing patterns of obligation—which are generally personal or feudal—serves to accentuate the need for political institutions. One ironic aspect of the war in Viet Nam is that, while we profess an idealistic philosophy, our failures have been due to an excessive reliance on material factors. The communists, by contrast, holding to a materialistic interpretation, owe many of their successes to their ability to supply an answer to the question of the nature and foundation of political authority.

The Tet offensive brought to a head the compounded weaknesses—or, as the North Vietnamese say, the internal contradictions—of the American position. To be sure, from a strictly military point of view, Tet was an American victory. Viet Cong casualties were very high; in many provinces, the Viet Cong infrastructure of guerrillas and shadow administrators surfaced and could be severely mauled by American forces. But in a guerrilla war, purely military considerations are not decisive: psychological and political factors loom at least as large.

On that level the Tet offensive was a political defeat in the countryside for Saigon and the United States. Two claims had been pressed on the villages. The United States and Saigon had promised that they would be able to protect an ever larger number of villages. The Viet Cong had never made such a claim; they merely asserted that they were the real power and presence in the villages, and they threatened retribution upon those who collaborated with Saigon or the United States.

As happened so often in the past, the Viet Cong made their claim stick. Some 20 provincial capitals were occupied. Though the Viet Cong held none (except Hué) for more than a few days, they were there long enough to execute hundreds of Vietnamese on the basis of previously prepared lists. The words "secure area" never had the same significance for Vietnamese civilians as for Americans, but if the term had any meaning, it applied to the provincial and district capitals. This was precisely where the Tet offensive took its most severe toll. The Viet Cong had made a point which far transcended military considerations in importance: there are no secure areas for Vietnamese civilians. This has compounded the already great tendency of the Vietnamese population to await developments and not to commit itself irrevocably to the Saigon government. The withdrawal of government troops from the countryside to protect the cities and the consequent increase in Viet Cong activity in the villages even in the daytime have served to strengthen this trend. One result of the Tet offensive was to delay—perhaps indefinitely—the consolidation of governmental authority, which in turn is the only meaningful definition of "victory" in guerrilla warfare.

For all these reasons, the Tet offensive marked the watershed of the American effort. Henceforth, no matter how effective our actions, the prevalent strategy could no longer achieve its objectives within a period or with force levels politically acceptable to the American people. This realization caused Washington, for the first time, to put a ceiling on the number of troops for Viet Nam. Denied the very large additional forces requested, the military command in Viet Nam felt obliged to begin a gradual change from its peripheral strategy to one concentrating on the protection of the populated areas. This made inevitable an eventual commitment to a political solution and marked the beginning of the quest for a negotiated settlement. Thus the stage was set for President Johnson's speech of March 31, which ushered in the current negotiations.

THE ENVIRONMENT OF NEGOTIATIONS

OF COURSE, the popular picture that negotiations began in May is only partially correct. The United States and Hanoi have rarely been out of touch since the American commitment in Viet Nam started to escalate. Not all these contacts have been face to face. Some have been by means of public pronouncements. Between 1965 and 1968, the various parties publicly stated their positions in a variety of forums: Hanoi announced Four Points, the NLF put forth Five Points, Saigon advanced Seven Points, and the United States—perhaps due to its larger bureaucracy—promulgated Fourteen.

These public pronouncements produced a fairly wide area of apparent agreement on some general principles: that the Geneva Accords could form the basis of a settlement, that American forces would be withdrawn ultimately, that the reunification of Viet Nam should come about through direct negotiation between the Vietnamese, that (after a settlement) Viet Nam would not contain foreign bases. The United States has indicated that three of Hanoi's Four Points are acceptable.

There is disagreement about the status of Hanoi's forces in the South; indeed, Hanoi has yet to admit that it has forces in the South—though it has prepared a "fallback position" to the effect that North Vietnamese forces in the South cannot be considered "external." The role of the NLF is equally in dispute. Saigon rejects a separate political role for the NLF; the NLF considers Saigon a puppet régime. There is no agreement about the meaning of those propositions which sound alike or on how they are to be enforced.

In addition to negotiations by public pronouncements, there have been secret contacts which have been described in many books and articles. It has been alleged that these contacts have failed because of a lack of imagination or a failure of coordination within our government. (There have also been charges of deliberate sabotage.) A fair assessment of these criticisms will not be possible for many years. But it is clear that many critics vastly oversimplify the problem. Good will may not always have been present; but even were it to motivate all sides, rapid, dramatic results would be unlikely. For all parties face enormous difficulties. Indeed, the tendency of each side to overestimate the freedom of maneuver of the other has almost certainly increased distrust. It has caused Hanoi to appear perversely obstinate to Washington and Washington to seem devious to Hanoi.

Both the Hanoi government and the United States are limited in their freedom of action by the state of mind of the population of South Viet Nam, which will ultimately determine the outcome of the conflict. The Vietnamese people have lived under foreign rule for approximately half of their history. They have maintained a remarkable cultural and social cohesion by being finely attuned to the realities of power. To survive, the Vietnamese have had to learn to calculate—almost instinctively—the real balance of forces. If negotiations give the impression of being a camouflaged surrender, there will be nothing left to negotiate. Support for the side which seems to be losing will collapse. Thus, all the parties are aware—Hanoi explicitly, for it does not view war and negotiation as separate processes; we in a more complicated bureaucratic manner—that *the way* negotiations are carried out is almost as important as *what* is negotiated. The choreography of how one enters negotiations, what is settled first, and in what manner is inseparable from the substance of the issues.

Wariness is thus imposed on the negotiators; a series of deadlocks is difficult to avoid. There are no "easy" issues, for each issue is symbolic and therefore in a way prejudges the final settlement. On its merits, the debate about the site of the conference—extending over a period of four weeks in April and May—was trivial. Judged intellectually, the four weeks were "wasted." But they did serve a useful function: they enabled the United States to let Saigon get used to the idea that there *would* be negotiations and to maintain that it retained control over events. It would not be surprising if Hanoi had a similar problem with the NLF.

The same problem was illustrated by the way the decision to stop the bombing was presented. Within 24 hours after announcement of the halt, both Hanoi and Saigon made statements of extraordinary bellicosity, which, taken literally, would have doomed the substantive talks about to begin. But their real purpose was to reassure each side's supporters in the South. Saigon especially has had a difficult problem. It has been pictured by many as perversely stubborn because of its haggling over the status of the NLF. However, to Saigon, the status of the NLF cannot be a procedural matter. For South Viet Nam it has been very nearly the central issue of the war. Washington must bear at least part of the responsibility for underestimating the depth and seriousness of this concern.

The situation confronted by Washington and Hanoi internationally is scarcely less complex. Much of the bitter debate in the United States about the war has been conducted in terms of 1961 and 1962. Unquestionably, the failure at that time to analyze adequately the geopolitical importance of Viet Nam contributed to the current dilemma. But the commitment of 500,000 Americans has settled the issue of the importance of Viet Nam. For what is involved now is confidence in American promises. However fashionable it is to ridicule the terms "credibility and prestige," they are not empty phrases; other nations can gear their actions to ours only if they can count on our steadiness. The collapse of the American effort in Viet Nam would not mollify many critics; most of them would simply add the charge of unreliability to the accusation of bad judgment. Those whose safety or national goals depend on American commitments could only be dismayed. In many parts of the world—the Middle East, Europe, Latin America, even Japan—stability depends on confidence in American promises. Unilateral withdrawal, or a settlement which unintentionally amounts to the same thing, could therefore lead to the erosion of restraints and to an even more dangerous international situation. No American policymaker can simply dismiss these dangers.

Hanoi's position is at least as complicated. Its concerns are not global; they are xenophobically Vietnamese (which includes, of course, hegemonial ambitions in Laos and Cambodia). But Hanoi is extraordinarily dependent on the international environment. It could not continue the war without foreign material assistance. It counts almost as heavily on the pressures of world public opinion. Any event that detracts from global preoccupations with the war in Viet Nam thus diminishes Hanoi's bargaining position. From this point of view, the Soviet invasion of Czechoslovakia was a major setback for Hanoi.

Hanoi's margin of survival is so narrow that precise calculation has become a way of life; caution is almost an obsession. Its bargaining position depends on a fine assessment of international factors—especially of the jungle of intracommunist relations. In order to retain its autonomy, Hanoi must maneuver skillfully between Peking, Moscow, and the NLF. Hanoi has no desire to become completely dependent on one of the communist giants. But since they disagree violently, they reinforce Hanoi's already strong tendency toward obscurantist formulations. In short, Hanoi's freedom of maneuver is severely limited.

The same is true of the Soviet Union, whose large-scale aid to Hanoi makes it a semi-participant in the war. Moscow must be torn by contradictory inclinations. A complete victory for Hanoi would tend to benefit Peking in the struggle for influence among the communist parties of the world; it would support the Chinese argument that intransigence toward the United States is, if not without risk, at least relatively manageable. But a defeat of Hanoi would demonstrate Soviet inability to protect "fraternal" communist countries against the United States. It would also weaken a potential barrier to Chinese influence in Southeast Asia and enable Peking to turn its full fury on Moscow. For a long time, Moscow has seemed paralyzed by conflicting considerations and bureaucratic inertia.

Events in Czechoslovakia have reduced Moscow's usefulness even further. We would compound the heavy costs of our pallid reaction to events in Czechoslovakia if our allies could blame it on a quid pro quo for Soviet assistance in extricating us from Southeast Asia. Washington therefore requires great delicacy in dealing with Moscow on the Viet Nam issue. It cannot be in the American interest to add fuel to the already widespread charge that the superpowers are sacrificing their allies to maintain spheres of influence.

This state of affairs would be enough to explain prolonged negotiations progressing through a series of apparent stalemates. In addition, a vast gulf in cultural and bureaucratic style between Hanoi and Washington complicates matters further. It would be difficult to imagine two societies less meant to understand each other than the Vietnamese and the American. History and culture combine to produce almost morbid suspiciousness on the part of the Vietnamese. Because survival has depended on a subtle skill in manipulating physically stronger foreigners, the Vietnamese style of communication is indirect and, by American standards, devious—qualities which avoid a total commitment and an overt test of strength. The fear of being made to look foolish seems to transcend most other considerations. Even if the United States accepted Hanoi's maximum program, the result might well be months of haggling while Hanoi looked for our "angle" and made sure that no other concessions were likely to be forthcoming.

These tendencies are magnified by communist ideology, which defines the United States as inherently hostile, and by Hanoi's experience in previous negotiations with the United States. It may well feel that the Geneva Conferences of 1954 and 1962 (over Laos) deprived it of part of its achievements on the battlefield.

All this produces the particular negotiating style of Hanoi: the careful planning, the subtle, indirect methods, the preference for opaque communications which keep open as many options as possible toward both foe and friend (the latter may seem equally important to Hanoi). North Viet Nam's diplomacy operates in cycles of reconnaissance and withdrawal to give an opportunity to assess the opponent's reaction. This is then followed by another diplomatic sortie to consolidate the achievements of the previous phase or to try another route. In this sense, many contacts with Hanoi which seemed "abortive" to us probably served (from Hanoi's point of view) the function of defining the terrain. The methods of Hanoi's diplomacy are not very different from Viet Cong military strategy and sometimes appear just as impenetrable to us.

If this analysis is correct, few North Vietnamese moves are accidental; even the most obtuse communication is likely to serve a purpose. On the other hand, it is not a style which easily lends itself to the sort of analysis at which we excel: the pragmatic, legal dissection of individual cases. Where Hanoi makes a fetish of planning, Washington is allergic to it. We prefer to deal with cases as they arise, "on their merits." Pronouncements that the United States is ready to negotiate do not guarantee that a negotiating position exists or that the U.S. government has articulated its objectives.

Until a conference comes to be scheduled, two groups in the American bureaucracy usually combine to thwart the elaboration of a negotiating position: those who oppose negotiations and those who favor them. The opponents generally equate negotiations with surrender; if they agree to discuss settlement terms at all, it is to define the conditions of the enemy's capitulation. Aware of this tendency and of the reluctance of the top echelon to ex-

pend capital on settling disputes which involve no immediate practical consequences, the advocates of negotiations cooperate in avoiding the issue. Moreover, delay serves their own purposes in that it enables them to reserve
freedom of action for the conference room.

Pragmatism and bureaucracy thus combine to produce a diplomatic style
marked by rigidity in advance of formal negotiations and excessive reliance
on tactical considerations once negotiations start. In the preliminary phases,
we generally lack a negotiating program; during the conference, bargaining
considerations tend to shape internal discussions. In the process, we deprive
ourselves of criteria by which to judge progress. The overconcern with tactics
suppresses a feeling for nuance and for intangibles.

The incompatibility of the American and North Vietnamese styles of
diplomacy produced, for a long time, a massive breakdown of communication—especially in the preliminary phases of negotiation. While Hanoi was
feeling its way toward negotiations, it bent all its ingenuity to avoid clear-cut,
formal commitments. Ambiguity permitted Hanoi to probe without giving
away much in return; Hanoi has no peers in slicing the salami very thin. It
wanted the context of events rather than a formal document to define its
obligations, lest its relations with Peking or the NLF be compromised.

Washington was unequipped for this mode of communication. To a government which equates commitments with legally enforceable obligations,
Hanoi's subtle changes of tense were literally incomprehensible. In a press
conference in February 1968, President Johnson said, "As near as I am able to
detect, Hanoi has not changed its course of conduct since the very first response it made. Sometimes they will change 'will' to 'would' or 'shall' to
'should,' or something of the kind. But the answer is all the same." A different kind of analysis might have inquired why Hanoi would open up a channel for a meaningless communication, especially in the light of a record of
careful planning which made it extremely unlikely that a change of tense
would be inadvertent.

Whatever the might-have-beens, Hanoi appeared to Washington as devious, deceitful, and tricky. To Hanoi, Washington must have seemed, if not
obtuse, then cannily purposeful. In any event, the deadlock produced by the
difference in negotiating style concerned specific clauses less than the philosophical issue of the nature of an international "commitment" or the meaning
of "trickery.". . .

CEASE-FIRE AND COALITION GOVERNMENT

SUBSTANTIVE negotiations confront the United States with a major conceptual problem: whether to proceed step by step, discussing each item "on its

merits," or whether to begin by attempting to get agreement about some ultimate goals.

The difference is not trivial. If the negotiations proceed step by step through a formal agenda, the danger is great that the bombing halt will turn out to be an admission ticket to another deadlock. The issues are so interrelated that a partial settlement foreshadows the ultimate outcome and therefore contains all of its complexities. Mutual distrust and the absence of clarity as to final goals combine to produce an extraordinary incentive to submit all proposals to the most searching scrutiny and to erect hedges for failure or bad faith.

This is well illustrated by two schemes which public debate has identified as suitable topics for the next stage of negotiations: cease-fire and coalition government.

It has become axiomatic that a bombing halt would lead—almost automatically—to a cease-fire. However, negotiating a cease-fire may well be tantamount to establishing the preconditions of a political settlement. If there existed a front line with unchallenged control behind it, as in Korea, the solution would be traditional and relatively simple: the two sides could stop shooting at each other, and the cease-fire line could follow the front line. But there are no front lines in Viet Nam; control is not territorial; it depends on who has forces in a given area and on the time of day. If a cease-fire permits the government to move without challenge, day or night, it will amount to a Saigon victory. If Saigon is prevented from entering certain areas, it means in effect partition, which, as in Laos, tends toward permanency. Unlike Laos, however, the pattern would be a crazy quilt, with enclaves of conflicting loyalties all over the country.

This would involve the following additional problems: (1) It would lead to an intense scramble to establish predominant control before the cease-fire went into effect. (2) It would make next to impossible the verification of any withdrawal of North Vietnamese forces that might be negotiated; the local authorities in areas of preponderant communist control would doubtless certify that no external forces were present and impede any effort at international inspection. (3) It would raise the problem of the applicability of a cease-fire to guerrilla activity in the noncommunist part of the country; in other words, how to deal with the asymmetry between the actions of regular and of guerrilla forces. Regular forces operate on a scale which makes possible a relatively precise definition of what is permitted and what is proscribed; guerrilla forces, by contrast, can be effective through isolated acts of terror difficult to distinguish from normal criminal activity.

There would be many other problems: who collects taxes and how, who enforces the cease-fire and by what means. In other words, a tacit de facto cease-fire may prove more attainable than a negotiated one. By the same token, a formal cease-fire is likely to predetermine the ultimate settlement and tend toward partition. Cease-fire is thus not so much a step toward a final settlement as a form of it.

This is even more true of another staple of the Viet Nam debate: the notion of a coalition government. Of course, there are two meanings of the term: as a means of legitimizing partition, indeed a disguise for continuing the civil war; or as a "true" coalition government attempting to govern the whole country. In the first case, a coalition government would be a facade with noncommunist and communist ministries in effect governing their own parts of the country. This is what happened in Laos, where each party in the "coalition government" wound up with its own armed forces and its own territorial administration. The central government did not exercise any truly national functions. Each side carried on its own business—including civil war. But in Laos, each side controlled contiguous territory, not a series of enclaves as in South Viet Nam. Too, of all the ways to bring about partition, negotiations about a coalition government are the most dangerous because the mere participation of the United States in talking about it could change the political landscape of South Viet Nam.

Coalition government is perhaps the most emotionally charged issue in Viet Nam, where it tends to be identified with the second meaning: a joint Saigon-NLF administration of the entire country. There can be no American objection, of course, to direct negotiations between Saigon and the NLF. The issue is whether the United States should be party to an attempt to *impose* a coalition government. We must be clear that our involvement in such an effort may well destroy the existing political structure of South Viet Nam and thus lead to a communist takeover.

Some urge negotiations on a coalition government for precisely this reason: as a face-saving formula for arranging the communist political victory which they consider inevitable. But those who believe that the political evolution of South Viet Nam should not be foreclosed by an American decision must realize that the subject of a coalition government is the most thankless and tricky area for negotiation *by outsiders.*

The notion that a coalition government represents a "compromise" which will permit a new political evolution hardly does justice to Vietnamese conditions. Even the noncommunist groups have demonstrated the difficulty Vietnamese have in compromising differences. It is beyond imagination that parties that have been murdering and betraying each other for 25 years could work together as a team giving joint instructions to the entire country. The image of a line of command extending from Saigon into the countryside is hardly true of the noncommunist government in Saigon. It would be absurd in the case of a coalition government. Such a government would possess no authority other than that of each minister over the forces he controlled either through personal or party loyalty.

To take just one example of the difficulties: communist ministers would be foolhardy in the extreme if they entered Saigon without bringing along sufficient military force for their protection. But the introduction of communist military forces into the chief bastion of governmental strength would change the balance of political forces in South Viet Nam. The danger of a coalition government is that it would decouple the noncommunist elements from effective control over their armed forces and police, leaving them unable to defend themselves adequately.

In short, negotiations seeking to impose a coalition from the outside are likely to change markedly and irreversibly the political process in South Viet Nam—as Vietnamese who believe that a coalition government cannot work quickly choose sides. We would, in effect, be settling the war on an issue least amenable to outside influence, with respect to which we have the least grasp of conditions and the long-term implications of which are most problematical.

This is not to say that the United States should resist an outcome freely negotiated among the Vietnamese. It does suggest that any negotiation on this point by the United States is likely to lead either to an impasse or to the collapse of Saigon.

WHERE DO WE GO FROM HERE?

PARADOXICAL as it may seem, the best way to make progress where distrust is so deep and the issues so interrelated may be to seek agreement on ultimate goals first and to work back to the details to implement them.

This requires an analysis of the strengths and weaknesses of both sides. Hanoi's strength is that it is fighting among its own people in familiar territory, while the United States is fighting far away. As long as Hanoi can preserve some political assets in the South, it retains the prospect of an ultimately favorable political outcome. Not surprisingly, Hanoi has shown a superior grasp of the local situation and a greater capacity to design military operations for political ends. Hanoi relies on world opinion and American domestic pressures; it believes that the unpopularity of the war in Viet Nam will ultimately force an American withdrawal.

Hanoi's weaknesses are that superior planning can substitute for material resources only up to a point. Beyond it, differences of scale are bound to become significant and a continuation of the war will require a degree of foreign assistance which may threaten North Viet Nam's autonomy. This Hanoi has jealously safeguarded until now. A prolonged, even if ultimately victorious war might leave Viet Nam so exhausted as to jeopardize the purpose of decades of struggle.

Moreover, a country as sensitive to international currents as North Viet Nam cannot be reassured by recent developments. The Soviet invasion of Czechoslovakia removed Viet Nam as the principal concern of world opinion, at least for a while. Some countries heretofore critical of the United States remembered their own peril and their need for American protection; this served to reduce the intensity of public pressures on America. Hanoi's support of Moscow demonstrated the degree of Hanoi's dependence on the U.S.S.R.; it also may have been intended to forestall Soviet pressures on Hanoi to be more flexible by putting Moscow in Hanoi's debt. Whatever the reason, the vision of a Titoist Viet Nam suddenly seemed less plausible—all the more so as Moscow's justification for the invasion of Czechoslovakia can provide a theoretical basis for an eventual Chinese move against North Viet Nam. Finally, the Soviet doctrine according to which Moscow has a right to intervene to protect socialist domestic structures made a Sino-Soviet war at least conceivable. For Moscow's accusations against Peking have been, if anything, even sharper than those against Prague. But in case of a Sino-Soviet conflict, Hanoi would be left high and dry. International crises threatening to overshadow Viet Nam in successive years—the Middle East in 1967; Central Europe in 1968—thus may have convinced Hanoi that time is not necessarily on its side.

American assets and liabilities are the reverse of these. No matter how irrelevant some of our political conceptions or how insensitive our strategy, we are so powerful that Hanoi is simply unable to defeat us militarily. By its own efforts, Hanoi cannot force the withdrawal of American forces from South Viet Nam. Indeed, a substantial improvement in the American military position seems to have taken place. As a result, we have achieved our minimum objective: Hanoi is unable to gain a military victory. Since it cannot force our withdrawal, it must negotiate about it. Unfortunately, our military strength has no political corollary; we have been unable so far to create a political structure that could survive military opposition from Hanoi after we withdraw.

The structure of the negotiation is thus quite different from Korea. There are no front lines with secure areas behind them. In Viet Nam, negotiations do not ratify a military status quo but create a new political reality. There are no unambiguous tests of relative political and military strength. The political situation for both sides is precarious—within Viet Nam for the United States, internationally for Hanoi. Thus it is probable that neither side can risk a negotiation so prolonged as that of Panmunjom a decade and a half ago. In such a situation, a favorable outcome depends on a clear definition of objectives. The limits of the American commitment can be expressed in two propositions: first, the United States cannot accept a military defeat or a change in the political structure of South Viet Nam brought about by external military force; second, once North Vietnamese forces and pressures are removed, the United States has no obligation to maintain a government in Saigon by force.

American objectives should therefore be (1) to bring about a staged withdrawal of external forces, North Vietnamese and American, (2) thereby to create a maximum incentive for the contending forces in South Viet Nam to work out a political agreement. The structure and content of such an agreement must be left to the South Vietnamese. It could take place formally on the national level. Or, it could occur locally on the provincial level where even now tacit accommodations are not unusual in many areas such as the Mekong Delta.

The details of a phased, mutual withdrawal are not decisive for our present purposes and, in any case, would have to be left to negotiations. It is possible, however, to list some principles: the withdrawal should be over a sufficiently long period so that a genuine indigenous political process has a chance to become established; the contending sides in South Viet Nam should commit themselves not to pursue their objectives by force while the withdrawal of external forces is going on; in so far as possible, the definition of what constitutes a suitable political process or structure should be left to the South Vietnamese, with the schedule for mutual withdrawal creating the time frame for an agreement.

The United States, then, should concentrate on the subject of the mutual withdrawal of external forces and avoid negotiating about the internal structure of South Viet Nam for as long as possible. The primary responsibility for negotiating the internal structure of South Viet Nam should be left for direct negotiations among the South Vietnamese. If we involve ourselves deeply in the issue of South Viet Nam's internal arrangements, we shall find ourselves in a morass of complexities subject to two major disadvantages. First, we will be the party in the negotiation least attuned to the subtleties of Vietnamese politics. Second, we are likely to wind up applying the greater part of our pressure against Saigon as the seeming obstacle to an accommodation. The result may be the complete demoralization of Saigon, profound domestic tensions within the United States, and a prolonged stalemate or a resumption of the war.

Whatever the approach, the negotiating procedure becomes vital; indeed, it may well determine the outcome and the speed with which it is achieved.

Tying the bombing halt to Saigon's participation in the substantive discussions was probably unwise—all the more so as Hanoi seems to have been prepared to continue bilateral talks. The participation of Saigon and the NLF raised issues about status that would have been better deferred; it made a discussion of the internal structure of South Viet Nam hard to avoid. Nevertheless, the principles sketched above, while now more difficult to implement, can still guide the negotiations. The tension between Washington and Saigon can even prove salutary if it forces both sides to learn that if they are to negotiate effectively they must confront the fundamental issues explicitly.

As these lines are being written, the formula for resolving the issue of Saigon's participation in the conference is not yet clear. But the general approach should be the same whatever the eventual compromise. . . .

To be sure, Saigon, for understandable reasons, has consistently refused to deal with the NLF as an international entity. But if Saigon understands its own interests, it will come to realize that the procedure outlined here involves a minimum and necessary concession. The three-tiered approach gives Saigon the greatest possible control over the issues that affect its own fate; direct negotiations between the United States and the NLF would be obviated. A sovereign government is free to talk to any group that represents an important domestic power base without thereby conferring sovereignty on it; it happens all the time in union negotiations or even in police work.

But why should Hanoi accept such an approach? The answer is that partly it has no choice; it cannot bring about a withdrawal of American forces by its own efforts, particularly if the United States adopts a less impatient strategy—one better geared to the protection of the population and sustainable with substantially reduced casualties. Hanoi may also believe that the NLF, being better organized and more determined, can win a political contest. (Of course, the prerequisite of a settlement is that both sides think they have a chance to win or at least to avoid losing.) Above all, Hanoi may not wish to give the United States a permanent voice in internal South Vietnamese affairs, as it will if the two-sided approach is followed. It may be reinforced in this attitude by the belief that a prolonged negotiation about coalition government may end no more satisfactorily from Hanoi's point of view than did the Geneva negotiations over Viet Nam in 1954 and Laos in 1962. As for the United States, if it brings about a removal of external forces and pressures, and if it gains a reasonable time for political consolidation, it will have done the maximum possible for an ally—short of permanent occupation.

To be sure, Hanoi cannot be asked to leave the NLF to the mercy of Saigon. While a coalition government is undesirable, a mixed commission to develop and supervise a political process to reintegrate the country—including free elections—could be useful. And there must be an international presence to enforce good faith. Similarly, we cannot be expected to rely on Hanoi's word that the removal of its forces and pressures from South Viet

Nam is permanent. An international force would be required to supervise access routes. It should be reinforced by an electronic barrier to check movements.

A negotiating procedure and a definition of objectives cannot guarantee a settlement, of course. If Hanoi proves intransigent and the war goes on, we should seek to achieve as many of our objectives as possible unilaterally. We should adopt a strategy which reduces casualties and concentrates on protecting the population. We should continue to strengthen the Vietnamese army to permit a gradual withdrawal of some American forces, and we should encourage Saigon to broaden its base so that it is stronger for the political contest with the communists, which sooner or later it must undertake.

No war in a century has aroused the passions of the conflict in Viet Nam. By turning Viet Nam into a symbol of deeper resentments, many groups have defeated the objective they profess to seek. However we got into Viet Nam, whatever the judgment of our actions, ending the war honorably is essential for the peace of the world. Any other solution may unloose forces that would complicate prospects of international order. A new administration must be given the benefit of the doubt and a chance to move toward a peace which grants the people of Viet Nam what they have so long struggled to achieve: an opportunity to work out their own destiny in their own way.

American Intellectuals and Foreign Policy

Irving Kristol

JULY 1967

A RECENT LETTER to *The New York Times*, complaining about the role of the academic community in opposing President Johnson's Viet Nam policy, argued that "it is not clear why people trained in mathematics, religion, geology, music, etc., believe their opinions on military and international problems should carry much validity." And the letter went on: "Certainly they [the professors] would oppose unqualified Pentagon generals telling them how to teach their course."

One can understand this complaint; one may even sympathize with the sentiments behind it. The fact remains, however, that it does miss the point. For the issue is not intellectual competence or intellectual validity—not really, and despite all protestations to the contrary. What is at stake is that species of power we call moral authority. The intellectual critics of American foreign policy obviously and sincerely believe that their arguments are right. But it is clear they believe, even more obviously and sincerely, that *they* are right—and that the totality of this rightness amounts to much more than the sum of the individual argument.

An intellectual may be defined as a man who speaks with general authority about a subject on which he has no particular competence. This definition sounds ironic, but is not. The authority is real enough, just as the lack of specific competence is crucial. An economist writing about economics is not acting as an intellectual, nor is a literary critic when he explicates a text. In such cases, we are witnessing professionals at work. On the other hand, there is good reason why we ordinarily take the "man of letters" as the archetypical intellectual. It is he who most closely resembles his sociological forbear and ideal type: the sermonizing cleric.

Precisely which people, at which time, in any particular social situation,

are certified as "intellectuals" is less important than the fact that such certifi-
cation is achieved—informally but indisputably. And this process involves
the recognition of the intellectual as legitimately possessing the prerogative
of being moral guide and critic to the world. (It is not too much of an exaggeration to say that even the clergy in the modern world can claim this prerogative only to the extent that it apes the intellectual class. It is the "writing
cleric," like the "writing psychoanalyst," who achieves recognition.) But there
is this critical difference between the intellectual of today and the average
cleric of yesteryear: the intellectual, lacking in otherworldly interests, is committed to the pursuit of temporal status, temporal influence, and temporal
power with a single-minded passion that used to be found only in the highest
reaches of the Catholic Church. Way back in 1797, Benjamin Constant observed that "in the new society where the prestige of rank is destroyed, we—
thinkers, writers, and philosophers—should be honored as the first among all
citizens." The only reason Constant did not say "we intellectuals" is that the
term had not yet come into common usage.

It is simply not possible to comprehend what is happening in the United
States today unless one keeps the sociological condition and political ambitions of the intellectual class very much in the forefront of one's mind. What
we are witnessing is no mere difference of opinion about foreign policy or
about Viet Nam. Such differences of opinion do exist, of course. Some of the
most articulate critics believe that the United States has, through bureaucratic inertia and mental sloth, persisted in a foreign policy that, whatever its
relevance to the immediate postwar years, is by now dangerously anachronis-
tic. They insist that the United States has unthinkingly accepted world
responsibilities which are beyond its resources and that, in any case, these responsibilities have only an illusory connection with the enduring national interest. These men may be right; or they may be wrong. But right or wrong,
this debate is largely irrelevant to the convulsion that the American intellectual community is now going through—even though occasional references
may be made to it, for credibility's sake. One does not accuse the president of
the United States and the secretary of state of being "war criminals" and
"mass murderers" because they have erred in estimating the proper dimensions of the United States' overseas commitments. And it is precisely accusations of this kind that are inflaming passions on the campus, and which are
more and more coming to characterize the "peace movement" as a whole.

What we are observing is a phenomenon that is far more complex in its
origins and far-reaching in its implications. It involves, among other things,
the highly problematic relationship of the modern intellectual to foreign affairs, the basic self-definition of the American intellectual, the tortured connections between American liberal ideology and the American imperial

republic, and the role of the newly established academic classes in an affluent society. Above all, it raises the question of whether democratic societies can cope with the kinds of political pathologies that seem to be spontaneously generated by their very commitment to economic and social progress.

II

NO MODERN NATION has ever constructed a foreign policy that was acceptable to its intellectuals. True, at moments of national peril or national exaltation, intellectuals will feel the same patriotic emotions as everyone else, and will subscribe as enthusiastically to the common cause. But these moments pass, the process of disengagement begins, and it usually does not take long for disengagement to eventuate in alienation. Public opinion polls generally reveal that the overwhelming majority of ordinary citizens, at any particular time, will be approving of their government's foreign policy; among intellectuals, this majority tends to be skimpy at best, and will frequently not exist at all. It is reasonable to suppose that there is an instinctive bias at work here, favorable to government among the common people, unfavorable among the intellectuals.

The bias of the common man is easy to understand: he is never much interested in foreign affairs; his patriotic feelings incline him to favor his own government against the governments of foreigners; and in cases of international conflict, he is ready to sacrifice his self-interest for what the government assures him to be the common good. The persistent bias of intellectuals, on the other hand, requires some explaining.

We have noted that the intellectual lays claim—and the claim is, more often than not, recognized—to moral authority over the intentions and actions of political leaders. This claim finds concrete rhetorical expression in an ideology. What creates a community of intellectuals, as against a mere aggregate of individuals, is the fact that they subscribe—with varying degrees of warmth, or with more or less explicit reservations—to a prevailing ideology. This ideology permits them to interpret the past, make sense of the present, outline a shape for the future. It constitutes the essence of their rationality, as this is directed toward the life of man in society.

Now, it is the peculiarity of foreign policy that it is the area of public life in which ideology flounders most dramatically. Thus, while it is possible—if not necessarily fruitful—to organize the political writings of the past 300 years along a spectrum ranging from the ideological "left" to the ideological "right," no such arrangement is conceivable for writings on foreign policy. There is no great "radical" text on the conduct of foreign policy—and no great "conservative" text, either. What texts there are (e.g., Machiavelli,

Grotius, in our own day the writings of George Kennan and Hans Morgenthau) are used indifferently by all parties, as circumstance allows.

And we find, if we pursue the matter further, that the entire tradition of Western political thought has very little to say about foreign policy. From Thucydides to our own time, political philosophy has seen foreign affairs as so radically affected by contingency, fortune, and fate as to leave little room for speculative enlightenment. John Locke was fertile in suggestions for the establishment and maintenance of good government, but when it came to foreign affairs he pretty much threw up his hands: "What is to be done in reference to foreigners, depending much upon their actions and the variation of designs and interests, must be left in great part to the prudence of those who have this power committed to them, to be managed by the best of their skill for the advantage of the Commonwealth."

The reasons why this should be so are not mysterious. To begin with, the very idea of "foreign policy" is so amorphous as to be misleading. As James Q. Wilson has pointed out, it is not at all clear that a State Department can have a foreign policy in a meaningful sense of that term—i.e., one "policy" that encompasses our economic, military, political, and sentimental relations with nations neighborly or distant, friendly or inimical. Moreover, whereas a national community is governed by principles by which one takes one's intellectual and moral bearings, the nations of the world do not constitute such a community and propose few principles by which their conduct may be evaluated. What this adds up to is that ideology can obtain exasperatingly little purchase over the realities of foreign policy—and that intellectuals feel keenly their dispossession from this area. It is not that intellectuals actually believe—though they often assert it—that the heavy reliance upon expediency in foreign affairs is intrinsically immoral. It is just that this reliance renders intellectuals as a class so much the less indispensable: to the extent that expediency is a necessary principle of action, to that extent the sovereignty of intellectuals is automatically circumscribed. It is only where politics is ideologized that intellectuals have a pivotal social and political role. To be good at coping with expediential situations you don't have to be an intellectual—and it may even be a handicap.

It is this state of affairs that explains the extraordinary consistencies of intellectuals on matters of foreign policy, and the ease with which they can enunciate a positive principle, only in the next breath to urge a contrary action. So it is that many intellectuals are appalled at our military intervention in Southeast Asia, on the grounds that, no matter what happens there, the national security of the United States will not be threatened. But these same intellectuals would raise no objection if the United States sent an expeditionary force all the way to South Africa to overthrow apartheid, even though

South Africa offers no threat to American security. So it is, too, that intellectual critics are fond of accusing American foreign policy of neglecting "political solutions" in favor of crude military and economic action—thereby demonstrating their faith that, if foreign policy were suffused with sufficient ideological rationality, it would dissolve the recalcitrance that mere statesmen encounter. And when the statesman candidly responds that he is coping, not with problems, but with an endless series of crises, and that he really has no way of knowing beforehand what "solution," if any, is feasible, he is simply reinforcing the intellectual's conviction that the managers of foreign affairs are, if not more wicked than he is, then certainly more stupid. Usually, he will be willing to think they are both.

Charles Frankel has written that "international affairs are peculiarly susceptible to galloping abstractions" and has stressed that "intellectuals, more than most other groups, have the power to create, dignify, inflate, criticize, moderate or puncture these abstractions." In the event, intellectuals rarely moderate or puncture but are diligent in inflation. Abstractions are their life's blood, and even when they resolutely decide to become "tough-minded" they end up with an oversimplified ideology of Realpolitik that is quite useless as a guide to the conduct of foreign affairs and leads its expounders to one self-contradiction after another. But the important point is not that intellectuals are always wrong on matters of foreign policy—they are not, and could not possibly be, if only by the laws of chance. What is striking is that, right or wrong, they are so often, from the statesman's point of view, irrelevant. And it is their self-definition as ideological creatures that makes them so.

III

IN THE United States, this ideological self-definition has taken on a very special form, and the relation of the American intellectual to foreign policy has its own distinctive qualities. Just how distinctive may be gathered from asking oneself the following question: Is it conceivable that American intellectuals should *ever* disapprove of *any* popular revolution, anywhere in the world—whatever the express or implicit principles of this revolution? One can make this question even sharper: Is it conceivable for American intellectuals ever to approve of their government suppressing, or helping to frustrate, any popular revolution *by poor people*—whatever the nature or consequences of this revolution? The answer would obviously have to be in the negative; and the implications of this answer for American foreign policy are not insignificant. This policy must work within a climate of opinion that finds the idea of a *gradual* evolution of traditional societies thoroughly uninteresting—which, indeed, has an instinctive detestation of all traditional societies as being inherently unjust and an equally instinctive approval, as being inherently righteous, of any revolutionary ideology which claims to incorporate the people's will.

As a matter of fact, even though official policy must obviously be based on other considerations, the makers of policy themselves find it nearly impossible to escape from this ideological framework. The State Department, for example, is always insisting that the United States is a truly revolutionary society, founded on revolutionary principles and offering a true revolutionary promise—as contrasted with the communists' spurious promises. The intellectual critics of American foreign policy deny that any such revolutionary intention or program exists—but think it ought to. There are precious few people in the United States who will say aloud that revolutionary intentions are inconsistent with a prudent and responsible foreign policy of a great power. Oddly enough, to hear this point made with some urgency these days, one has to go to the Soviet Union.

The American intellectual tradition has two profound commitments: to "ideals" and to "the people." It is the marriage of these two themes that has made the American mind and given it its characteristic cast—which might be called *transcendentalist populism*.

The "transcendentalist" theme in American thought is linked to a disrespect for tradition, a suspicion of all institutionalized authority, an unshakable faith in the "natural" (what once was called "divine") wisdom of the sincere individual, an incorruptible allegiance to one's own "inner light." The American intellectual sees himself as being in perpetual "prophetic confrontation" with principalities and powers. (That very phrase, "prophetic confrontation," has lately been used by Hans Morgenthau to define the proper stance of the intellectual vis-à-vis his government's policies.) Tell an American intellectual that he is a disturber of the intellectual peace, and he is gratified. Tell him he is a reassuring spokesman for calm and tranquillity, and he will think you have made a nasty accusation.

This transcendentalist "protestantism" of the American intellectual derives from the history of American Protestantism itself—as does his near-mystical celebration of "the people." Indeed, the two themes have evolved as part of one historical process, which has been concisely described by the historian, Russell B. Nye:

> From the mid-18th century to the mid-19th in American thought . . . the accepted version of the individual's power to grasp and interpret God's truth underwent a complete change—from Calvin's dependence on the Bible . . . to Deism's grant to man of equal sovereignty in a universe of reason, to Channing's transfer of sovereignty from Bible and church to man, and finally to the *self*-reliance of Emerson, Parker, and Thoreau. The lines of

thought moved from Mather's distrust of man, to Jefferson's qualified confidence in him, to Emerson's and Jackson's deep and abiding faith in his capacity to find out and act upon divine truth.

This evolution, which might be called the democratization of the spirit, has created an American intellectual who is at one and the same time (a) humble toward an idealized and mythical prototype of the common man (if the people have a quasi-ecclesiastical function, to oppose them in any consistent way partakes of heresy) and (b) arrogant toward existing authority, as presumptively representing nothing but a petrified form of yesteryear's vital forces. It has also had a peculiar effect upon the politics of American intellectuals, which is more often than not a kind of transcendentalist politics, focusing less on the reform of the polity than on the perfection and purification of self in opposition to the polity. Just as the intellectual opposition to slavery in the 1830s and 1840s paid little attention to the reform of particular institutions but focused primarily on the need for the individual to avoid being compromised and contaminated by this general evil, so in the 1960s what appears most to torment our academic intellectuals is the morality of their own actions—whether they should cooperate with Selective Service, accept government contracts, pay taxes, etc. At both times, the issue of individual, conscientious "civil disobedience" has become acute. It is instructive to note that though the British Labor Party bitterly opposed British imperialism for over five decades, its opposition never took any such form. This is some measure of the difference between a political tradition and one that transcends mere politics.

The United States, to be sure, does have its own political tradition. And though the American intellectual tradition has suffused all areas of American life, it has never completely overwhelmed the political. This latter, mainly the creation of American Whiggery, is incarnated in our major institutions and finds its literary expression in such documents as the Constitution, the Federalist Papers, some presidential addresses, judicial decisions, etc. This tradition is still very much alive in our law schools and helps explain why these schools play so singular a role in our political life. But among intellectuals it has never enjoyed much favor, being thought to be inherently conservative and nondemocratic. The American intellectual of today is far more comfortable listening to a "protest folk song"—the truly indigenous art form of transcendental populism—than he is listening to a grave and solemn debate over a matter of policy. Witness the way in which the one genre has overwhelmed the other in the "teach-in."

Precisely what an American intellectual does *not* believe was most elegantly expressed by Sir Thomas More, in the discussion of an intellectual's obligation in his *Utopia*:

If evil persons cannot be quite rooted out, and if you cannot correct habitual attitudes as you wish, you must not therefore abandon the commonwealth. . . . You must strive to guide policy indirectly, so that you make the best of things, and what you cannot turn to good, you can at least make less bad. For it is impossible to do all things well unless all men are good, and this I do not expect to see for a long time.

There have been, of course, some American intellectuals who have followed Sir Thomas More's direction. For their efforts and pains, they have been subjected to the scorn and contempt of the intellectual community as a whole. (Arthur Schlesinger, Jr., Eric Goldman, and John Roche could provide us with eloquent testimony on this score.) This community, unlike Sir Thomas More, is quite convinced that all men are indeed good and that any such modest and compromising involvement with political power can represent only a corruption of the spirit.

IV

THE TRANSFORMATION of the American republic into an imperial power has sharply exacerbated the relations between the intellectual and the makers of foreign policy. The term "imperial power" is merely a synonym for "great power" and is not necessarily the same thing as "imperialistic" power. But there would seem to be a gain in clarity, and a diminution of humbug, in insisting on the use of the more provocative phrase. There are a great many people who appear to think that a great power is only the magnification of a small power, and that the principles governing the actions of the latter are simply transferrable—perhaps with some modification—to the former. In fact, there is a qualitative difference between the two conditions, and the difference can be summed up as follows: a great power is "imperial" because what it does *not* do is just as significant, and just as consequential, as what it does. Which is to say, a great power does not have the range of freedom of action—derived from the freedom of inaction—that a small power possesses. It is entangled in a web of responsibilities from which there is no hope of escape; and its policymakers are doomed to a strenuous and unquiet life, with no prospect of ultimate resolution, no hope for an unproblematic existence, no promise of final contentment. It is understandable that these policymakers should sometimes talk as if some particular redirection of policy, of any great power, is capable of terminating the tensions inherent in this imperial condition. But it is foolish for us to believe them; and it is even more foolish for them to believe themselves. It is no accident that all classical political philosophers, and all depicters of utopia, have agreed that, to be truly happy, a human community should be relatively small and as isolated as possible from foreign entanglements.

Indeed, this utopian ideal is a major historic theme of American foreign policy, being at the root of what we call "isolationism." And so long as the United States was not a great power, it was not entirely utopian. The American republic, until the beginning of the twentieth century, was genuinely isolationist, and isolationism made both practical and idealistic sense. Practical sense, because the United States was geographically isolated from the main currents of world politics. Idealistic sense, because the United States could feel—and it was no illusion—that it served as a splendid and inspiring example to all believers in popular government everywhere and that this exemplary role was more important than any foreign actions it might undertake, with the limited resources at its command. True, at the same time that the United States was isolationist, it was also expansionist. But there is no necessary contradiction between these two orientations, even though some modern historians are shocked to contemplate their coexistence. Most of the territories that the United States coveted, and all that were acquired, prior to the Civil War, were thinly populated—there was no subjugation of large, alien masses. And the intent of this expansion was always to incorporate such territories into the United States on absolutely equal terms, not to dominate them for any reasons of state. The idea of "manifest destiny" was therefore easily reconcilable to the isolationist idea. This reconciliation became troublesome only when expansion threatened to disturb the regional balance of power within the republic. . . .

In the end, of course, "manifest destiny" did write an end to American isolationism, by establishing the material conditions for the emergence of the United States as a great power. But the isolationist idea, or at least crucial aspects of it, survived—not simply as some kind of "cultural lag," but by reason of being so intimately conjoined to "the American way of life," and to the American intellectual creed. This way of life insisted upon the subordination of public policy to private, individual needs and concerns. It had little use for the idea of military glory, which Abraham Lincoln called "that attractive rainbow that rises in showers of blood—that serpent's eye that charms to destroy." It was intensely patriotic but allergic to all conceptions of national *grandeur.* The United States was tempted to a brief fling at European-style imperialism under Presidents McKinley and Theodore Roosevelt, but found the experience disagreeable, and that enterprise was gradually liquidated. When the American democracy entered World War I, it was in no imperial frame of mind. On the contrary, the whole point of the Wilsonian "crusade" was to rid the world of imperial politics. One can almost say that this crusade was a penultimate outburst of the isolationist spirit, in that its goal was a happy, self-determined existence for all the individuals on this earth—*une vie à l'Américaine*—without further cruel violations of it by international power politics.

The disillusionment consequent upon this crusade prepared the way for the United States to enter history as an imperial power. To be sure, its most immediate effect was to stimulate a purely geographic isolationism that was shot through with streaks of xenophobia. But this attitude simply could not withstand the pressure of events and the insistent demands of world realities. In retrospect, the spectacle of the United States entering World War II has an almost dreamlike, fatalistic quality. There was never, prior to Pearl Harbor, any literal threat to the national security of the United States. And there was no popular enthusiasm, except among a small if influential group of "internationalists," for the United States' accepting responsibility for the maintenance of "world order." It all just seemed inescapable, and the alternative—retiring into a Fortress America—just too unmanly. The dominant mood was resignation, tinged with outrage at the Japanese bombardment of American soil. And resignation—sometimes sullen, sometimes equable—has remained the dominant popular mood ever since.

Strangely enough, this resigned acceptance of great-power responsibilities by the American people has been accompanied by a great unease on the part of the intellectuals. It is strange, because one had expected the reverse of this situation. During the two postwar decades, many commentators expressed doubt whether the American people could sustain the frustrations and sacrifices inherent in an imperial role. Such doubts were given point by the upsurge of extremist sentiments associated with the late Senator McCarthy and unquestionably incited by popular resentment at the Korean War. But Korea can now be seen to have been a kind of baptism-by-fire; and the war in Viet Nam has been borne with greater patience than might have been expected. It is not a popular war—how could it be?—but the general feeling is that it has to be endured. It is among the intellectuals—including some of the aforementioned commentators—that extreme dissatisfaction, sometimes extremist dissatisfaction, is rife. It is among American intellectuals that the isolationist ideal is experiencing its final, convulsive agony.

Though this dissatisfaction affects only a minority, it is nevertheless a most serious matter. It is much to be doubted that the United States can continue to play an imperial role without the endorsement of its intellectual class. Or, to put it more precisely: since there is no way the United States, as the world's mightiest power, can avoid such an imperial role, the opposition of its intellectuals means that this role will be played out in a domestic climate of ideological dissent that will enfeeble the resolution of our statesmen and diminish the credibility of their policies abroad.

What is to be done? It is always possible to hope that this intellectual class will come to realize that its traditional ideology needs reformation and revision. It is even possible to argue plausibly that, in the nature of things, this is "historically inevitable." One can go so far as to say that, on intellectual grounds alone, this intellectual class will feel moved to desist from the shrill enunciation of pieties and principles that have little relevance to the particular cases our statesmen now confront and to help formulate a new set of more specific principles that will relate the ideals which sustain the American democracy to the harsh and nasty imperatives of imperial power. All of this is possible. But one must add that none of these possibilities is likely to be realized in the immediate or even near future.

It is unlikely for two reasons. The first is that the burden of guilt such a process would generate would be so great as to be insupportable. It took three centuries to create the American intellectual as we know him today; he is not going to be recreated in one generation. He is committed in the most profound way to a whole set of assumptions and ideas that are rooted in the "isolationist" era of American history, and he cannot depart from these assumptions and ideals without a terrible sense of self-betrayal. Our State Department may find it necessary, if disagreeable, to support military dictatorships in certain countries, at certain times. It is hard to see our intellectuals swallowing this necessity. They might agree in the abstract that alternatives are not available. They might even grant to certain dictatorships the kind of dispensation that is often extended to heathens by an otherwise dogmatic orthodoxy. But they will gag at extending such a dispensation to "our" dictators—this would be too subversive of the dogmas by which they define their existence as a class. The furthest that American intellectuals can go toward coping with the realities of imperial power is to erect a double standard that undermines the moral basis of American diplomacy.

Secondly, this crisis of the intellectual class in the face of an imperial destiny coincides with an internal power struggle within the United States itself. Our intellectuals are moving toward a significant "confrontation" with the American "establishment" and will do nothing to strengthen the position of their antagonist. Which is to say that the American intellectual class actually has an interest in thwarting the evolution of any kind of responsible and coherent imperial policy. Just what this interest is, and what this confrontation involves, we are only now beginning to discern. Behind the general fog that the ideology of dissent generates, the outlines of a very material sociological and political problem are emerging.

V

IT HAS ALWAYS been assumed that as the United States became a more highly organized national society, as its economy became more managerial, its power more imperial, and its populace more sophisticated, the intellectuals would move inexorably closer to the seats of authority—would, perhaps, even be incorporated en masse into a kind of "power élite." Many writers and thinkers—and not only on the political left—have viewed this prospect with the greatest unease, for it seemed to them to threaten the continued existence of intellectuals as a critical and moral force in American life.

Well, it has happened here—only, as is so often the case, it is all very different from what one expected. It is true that a small section of the American intellectual class has become a kind of permanent brain trust to the political, the military, the economic authorities. These are the men who commute regularly to Washington, who help draw up programs for reorganizing the bureaucracy, who evaluate proposed weapons systems, who figure out ways to improve our cities and assist our poor, who analyze the course of economic growth, who reckon the cost and effectiveness of foreign aid programs, who dream up new approaches to such old social problems as the mental health of the aged, etc., etc. But what has also happened, at the same time, is that a whole new intellectual class has emerged as a result of the explosive growth, in these past decades, of higher education in the United States. And these "new men," so far from being any kind of élite, are a mass—and have engendered their own mass movement.

As a matter of courtesy and habit, one refers to these professors as "intellectuals." Some of them, of course, are intellectuals, in the traditional sense of the term. The majority unquestionably are not—no population, no matter how elevated, could produce *that many* intellectuals. Professor Robert Nisbet, as shrewd an observer of the academic scene as we have, has estimated that "at the present time not less than sixty percent of all academics in the universities in this country have so profound a distaste for the classroom and for the pains of genuine scholarship or creative thought that they will seize upon anything . . . to exempt themselves respectably from each."

In most instances, whether a man these days ends up a college professor or, say, a social worker or a civil servant is largely a matter of chance. Nevertheless, this academic mass has taken over not only the political metaphysics of the American intellectual, but also his status and prerogatives. Americans have always had a superstitious, if touching, faith in the importance of education. And the American people have quickly conceded to the professoriat of our affluent society the moral authority that intellectuals have always claimed as their peculiar endowment.

Now, this new intellectual class, though to outsiders appearing to be not at all badly off, is full of grievance and resentment. It feels discriminated against—opinion polls reveal that professors, especially in the social sciences and humanities, invariably tend drastically to underestimate the esteem in which public opinion (and, more particularly, the opinion of the business community) holds them. It feels underpaid; you'll not find any credence on the campus for the proposition (demonstrably true) that the salaries of professors do not compare unfavorably with the salaries of bank executives. It feels put upon in all sorts of other familiar ways. The symptoms are only too typical: here is a new class that is "alienated" from the established order because it feels that this order has not conceded to it sufficient power and recognition.

The politics of this new class is novel in that its locus of struggle is the college campus. One is shocked at this—we are used to thinking that politics ought not to intrude on the campus. But we shall no doubt get accustomed to the idea. Meanwhile, there is going to be a great deal of unpleasant turbulence. The academic community in the United States today has evolved into a new political constituency. College students, like their teachers, are "new men" who find the traditional student role too restrictive. Students and faculty therefore find it easy to combine their numbers and their energies for the purpose of social and political action. The first objective—already accomplished in large measure—is to weaken control of the administration and to dispossess it of its authoritative powers over campus activities. From this point the movement into politics proper—including elections—is about as predictable as anything can be.

Just what direction this movement into politics will follow, it is too early to say with certainty. Presumably, it will be toward "the left," since this is the historical orientation of the intellectual class as a whole. It is even possible that the movement will not be calmed until the United States has witnessed the transformation of its two-party system to make room for a mass party of the ideological left, as in most European countries—except that its "grass roots" will be on the campus rather than in the factory. But what is certain is that the national prestige and the international position of the United States are being adversely affected by this *sécession des clercs*. Imperial powers need social equilibrium at home if they are to act effectively in the world. It was possible to think, in the years immediately after World War II, that the United States had indeed achieved this kind of equilibrium—that consensus and equipoise at home would permit our statesmen to formulate and pursue a coherent foreign policy. But the "academic revolution" of the 1950s and 1960s raises this issue again, in a most problematic and urgent way.

VI

THOUGH THERE is much fancy rhetoric, pro and con, about "the purpose of American foreign policy," there is really nothing esoteric about this purpose. The United States wishes to establish and sustain a world order that (a) ensures its national security as against the other great powers, (b) encourages other nations, especially the smaller ones, to mold their own social, political, and economic institutions along lines that are at least not repugnant to (if not actually congruent with) American values, and (c) minimizes the possibility of naked, armed conflict. This is, of course, also the purpose of the foreign policies of such other great powers as Soviet Russia and Maoist China. Nor could it be otherwise, short of a fit of collective insanity on the part of the governing classes of these powers. Without the conflict, tension, and reconciliation of such imperial purposes, there would be no such thing as "foreign affairs" or "world politics," as we ordinarily understand these terms.

But for any imperial policy to work effectively—even if one means by that nothing more than doing the least possible mischief—it needs intellectual and moral guidance. It needs such guidance precisely because, in foreign affairs, one is always forced to compromise one's values. In the United States today, a relative handful of intellectuals proffers such guidance to the policymaker. But the intellectual community en masse, disaffected from established power even as it tries to establish a power base of its own, feels no such sense of responsibility. It denounces, it mocks, it vilifies—and even if one were to concede that its fierce indignation was justified by extraordinary ineptitude in high places, the fact remains that its activity is singularly unhelpful. The United States is not going to cease being an imperial power, no matter what happens in Viet Nam or elsewhere. It is the world situation—and the history which created this situation—that appoints imperial powers, not anyone's decision or even anyone's overweening ambition. And power begets responsibility—above all, the responsibility to use this power responsibly. The policymaker in the United States today—and, no doubt, in the other great powers, too—finds this responsibility a terrible burden. The intellectuals, in contrast, are bemused by dreams of power without responsibility, even as they complain of moral responsibility without power. It is not a healthy situation; and, as of this moment, it must be said that one cannot see how, or where, or when it will all end.

A Viet Nam Reappraisal

The Personal History of One Man's View
and How It Evolved

Clark M. Clifford

JULY 1969

VIET NAM REMAINS unquestionably the transcendent problem that confronts our nation. Though the escalation has ceased, we seem to be no closer to finding our way out of this infinitely complex difficulty. The confidence of the past has become the frustration of the present. Predictions of progress and of military success, made so often by so many, have proved to be illusory as the fighting and the dying continue at a tragic rate. Within our country, the dialogue quickens and the debate sharpens. There is a growing impatience among our people, and questions regarding the war and our participation in it are being asked with increasing vehemence.

Many individuals these past years have sought to make some contribution toward finding the answers that have been so elusive. It is with this hope in mind that I present herewith the case history of one man's attitude toward Viet Nam, and the various stages of thought he experienced as he plodded painfully from one point of view to another, and another, until he arrived at the unshakable opinion he possesses today.

Views on Viet Nam have become increasingly polarized as the war has gone on without visible progress toward the traditional American military triumph. There remain some who insist that we were right to intervene militarily and, because we were right, we have no choice but to press on until the enemy knuckles under and concedes defeat. At the other extreme, and in increasing numbers, there are those who maintain that the present unsatisfactory situation proves that our Viet Nam policy has been wrong from the very beginning. There are even those who suggest that our problems in Viet Nam

[305]

cast doubt on the entire course of American foreign policy since World War II. Both schools share a common and, as I see it, an erroneous concept. They both would make military victory the ultimate test of the propriety of our participation in the conflict in Southeast Asia.

I find myself unable to agree with either extreme. At the time of our original involvement in Viet Nam, I considered it to be based upon sound and unassailable premises, thoroughly consistent with our self-interest and our responsibilities. There has been no change in the exemplary character of our intentions in Viet Nam. We intervened to help a new and small nation resist subjugation by a neighboring country—a neighboring country, incidentally, which was being assisted by the resources of the world's two largest communist powers.

I see no profit and no purpose in any divisive national debate about whether we were right or wrong initially to become involved in the struggle in Viet Nam. Such debate at the present time clouds the issue and obscures the pressing need for a clear and logical evaluation of our present predicament, and how we can extricate ourselves from it.

Only history will be able to tell whether or not our military presence in Southeast Asia was warranted. Certainly the decisions that brought it about were based upon a reasonable reading of the past three decades. We had seen the calamitous consequences of standing aside while totalitarian and expansionist nations moved successively against their weaker neighbors and accumulated a military might which left even the stronger nations uneasy and insecure. We had seen in the period immediately after World War II the seemingly insatiable urge of the Soviet Union to secure satellite states on its western periphery. We had seen in Asia itself the attempt by open invasion to extend communist control into the independent South of the Korean Peninsula. We had reason to feel that the fate averted Korea through American and United Nations military force would overtake the independent countries of Asia, albeit in somewhat subtler form, were we to stand aside while the communist North sponsored subversion and terrorism in South Viet Nam.

The transformation that has taken place in my thinking has been brought about, however, by the conclusion that the world situation has changed dramatically and that American involvement in Viet Nam can and must change with it. Important ingredients of this present situation include the manner in which South Viet Nam and its Asian neighbors have responded to the threat and to our own massive intervention. They also include internal developments both in Asian nations and elsewhere and the changing relations among world powers.

The decisions which our nation faces today in Viet Nam should not be made on interpretations of the facts as they were perceived 4 or 5 or 15 years ago, even if, through compromise, a consensus could be reached on these interpretations. They must instead be based upon our present view of our obligations as a world power; upon our current concept of our national security; upon our conclusions regarding our commitments as they exist today; upon our fervent desire to contribute to peace throughout the world; and, hopefully, upon our acceptance of the principle of enlightened self-interest.

But these are broad and general guidelines, subject to many constructions and misconstructions. They also have the obvious drawback of being remote and impersonal.

The purpose of this article is to present to the reader the intimate and highly personal experience of one man, in the hope that by so doing there will be a simpler and clearer understanding of where we are in Viet Nam today, and what we must do about it. I shall go back to the beginning and identify, as well as I can, the origins of my consciousness of the problem, the opportunities I had to obtain the facts, and the resulting evolution of what I shall guardedly refer to as my thought processes.

II

ALTHOUGH I HAD served President Truman in the White House from May 1945 until February 1950, I do not recall ever having had to focus on Southeast Asia. Indochina, as it was then universally known, was regarded by our government as a French problem. President Truman was prompted from time to time by the State Department to approve statements that seemed to me to be little more than reiterations of the long-standing American attitude against "colonialism." If any of those provoked extensive discussion at the White House, I cannot recall. For the next decade, I watched foreign affairs and the growing turbulence of Asia from the sidelines as a private citizen, increasingly concerned but not directly involved.

In the summer of 1960, Senator John Kennedy invited me to act as his transition planner and later as liaison with the Eisenhower administration in the interval between the election and January 20, 1961. Among the foreign policy problems that I encountered at once was a deteriorating situation in Southeast Asia. Major-General Wilton B. Persons, whom President Eisenhower had designated to work with me, explained the gravity of the situation as viewed by the outgoing administration. I suggested to the president-elect that it would be well for him to hear President Eisenhower personally on the subject. He agreed, and accordingly General Persons and I placed Southeast Asia as the first item on the agenda of the final meeting between the outgoing and the incoming presidents. This meeting, held on the morning of January 19, 1961, in the Cabinet Room, was attended by President Eisenhower,

Secretary of State Christian Herter, Secretary of Defense Thomas Gates, Secretary of the Treasury Robert Anderson, and General Persons. President-elect Kennedy had his counterparts present: Secretary of State–designate Dean Rusk, Secretary of Defense–designate Robert McNamara, Secretary of the Treasury–designate Douglas Dillon, and me.

At President-elect Kennedy's suggestion, I took notes of the important subjects discussed. Most of the time, the discussion centered on Southeast Asia, with emphasis upon Laos. At that particular time, January 1961, Laos had come sharply into focus and appeared to constitute the major danger in the area.

My notes disclose the following comments by the President:

> At this point, President Eisenhower said, with considerable emotion, that Laos was the key to the entire area of Southeast Asia.
>
> He said that if we permitted Laos to fall, then we would have to write off all the area. He stated we must not permit a Communist take-over. He reiterated that we should make every effort to persuade member nations of SEATO or the International Control Commission to accept the burden with us to defend the freedom of Laos.
>
> As he concluded these remarks, President Eisenhower stated it was imperative that Laos be defended. He said that the United States should accept this task with our allies, if we could persuade them, and alone if we could not. He added, "Our unilateral intervention would be our last desperate hope in the event we were unable to prevail upon the other signatories to join us."

That morning's discussion, and the gravity with which President Eisenhower addressed the problem, had a substantial impact on me. He and his advisers were finishing eight years of responsible service to the nation. I had neither facts nor personal experience to challenge their assessment of the situation, even if I had had the inclination to do so. The thrust of the presentation was the great importance to the United States of taking a firm stand in Southeast Asia, and I accepted that judgment.

On an earlier occasion, in speaking of Southeast Asia, President Eisenhower had said that South Viet Nam's capture by the communists would bring their power several hundred miles into a hitherto free region. The freedom of 12 million people would be lost immediately and that of 150 million in adjacent lands would be seriously endangered. The loss of South Viet Nam would set in motion a crumbling process that could, as it progressed, have grave consequences for us and for freedom.

As I listened to him in the Cabinet Room that January morning, I recalled that it was President Eisenhower who had acquainted the public with

After the First World War, the world looked to President Woodrow Wilson for leadership. Wilson, seen here *(right)* with British Prime Minister David Lloyd George *(left)* and French Prime Minister Georges Clemenceau in 1919 in Paris during the peace negotiations, tried unsuccessfully to establish a new world order.

FOREIGN AFFAIRS

The first issue of *Foreign Affairs,* published in September 1922, included essays by Czechoslovakian Prime Minister Eduard Benes on Eastern Europe, Archibald Cary Coolidge (writing under the pseudonym "K") on Bolshevism, and a then-obscure lawyer named John Foster Dulles on the Allies' debts.

COUNCIL ON FOREIGN RELATIONS

Foreign Affairs' founding editor, Archibald Cary Coolidge, the eminent Harvard scholar of Russian studies and a distant relative of President Calvin Coolidge. He edited the magazine until his death in 1928.

COUNCIL ON FOREIGN RELATIONS

Hamilton Fish Armstrong, Coolidge's managing editor, took over the editorship in 1928 and retired 44 years later in 1972. *Foreign Affairs* still bears the stamp of this extraordinary tenure.

Elihu Root, Theodore Roosevelt's secretary of state, helped found the League of Nations and won the Nobel Peace Prize in 1912. He wrote the lead essay in *Foreign Affairs'* first issue.

Nikolai Bukharin, seen here in 1929, was regarded as the most "liberal" of the leaders of the Russian Revolution. Eight years after this photo was taken, he was arrested during Stalin's purges and shot dead.

W. E. B. Du Bois, a sociologist, historian, and activist, was a founder of the National Association for the Advancement of Colored People. Du Bois wrote eloquently against European imperialism, often in the pages of *Foreign Affairs*.

Arnold J. Toynbee, the legendary British scholar, seen with an abridgment of his ten-volume magnum opus, *A Study of History*.

H. G. Wells, the British science fiction novelist and commentator, seen in 1933 examining a stack of one of his many best-sellers.

President Franklin D. Roosevelt congratulates Henry L. Stimson after the latter's swearing-in as secretary of war in 1940. The veteran Republican statesman had held the same job under William Howard Taft and had also been Herbert Hoover's secretary of state.

George F. Kennan, the author of the "X" article. Kennan's pseudonymous essay "The Sources of Soviet Conduct" ran in *Foreign Affairs* in 1947 while its author was director of the State Department's policy planning staff. The article, still the most influential ever to appear in *Foreign Affairs*, coined the term "containment" and laid out the fundamentals of America's Cold War strategy.

Hans J. Morgenthau, a professor at the University of Chicago and one of the founders of the realist school of international relations. His classic *Politics Among Nations* was used to train a generation of postwar strategists.

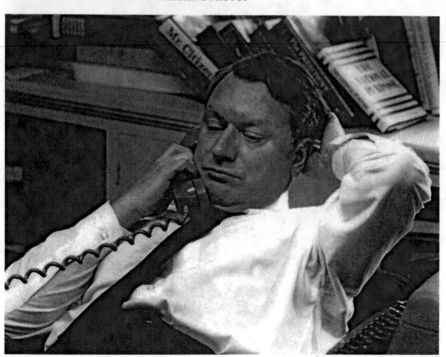

James B. Reston, photographed by Henri Cartier-Bresson at his desk in 1969, was one of the pillars of *The New York Times*. A two-time winner of the Pulitzer Prize, Scotty Reston served as the *Times'* Washington bureau chief, diplomatic correspondent, columnist, and executive editor.

Walter Lippmann, photographed here by Henri Cartier-Bresson, was the pre-eminent columnist of his day and one of America's dominant public intellectuals.

Margaret Mead, the American anthropologist, did groundbreaking field research on Oceania and was curator of ethnology at the American Museum of Natural History in New York.

Two young men underneath the globe they would one day help shape: Zbigniew Brzezinski *(left)*, later national security adviser to President Carter, and Henry A. Kissinger, who would serve as national security adviser to President Nixon and as secretary of state to Presidents Nixon and Ford, at a 1965 meeting at the Council on Foreign Relations.

In January 1961, President-elect John F. Kennedy drops in at the Cambridge, Massachusetts, home of his future aide, Harvard history professor Arthur Schlesinger, Jr. One of the nation's preeminent public intellectuals, Schlesinger would also write the Pulitzer Prize–winning *A Thousand Days* on his friend's brief presidency.

President Lyndon B. Johnson with Clark M. Clifford, who became secretary of defense in 1968—and quickly concluded that the Johnson administration's Vietnam policy had been a tragic mistake.

William P. Bundy, the editor of *Foreign Affairs* from 1972 to 1984. Bundy also served in the Johnson administration, as head of the State Department's Far Eastern Affairs division.

William F. Buckley, Jr., the founder of *National Review* and modern American conservatism as an intellectual force.

Foreign Affairs entered American pop culture briefly with this cameo in the Cold War's defining film, *Dr. Strangelove.*

William G. Hyland, *Foreign Affairs'* editor from 1984 to 1992, shows Soviet leader Mikhail Gorbachev a copy of the journal's first issue, with underlining and notes by V. I. Lenin.

Aleksandr Solzhenitsyn, the dissident novelist and winner of the Nobel Prize, boards a train during his return to Russia after 20 years of exile abroad.

In "The Clash of Civilizations?" Samuel P. Huntington, a renowned political scientist and currently one of Harvard's University Professors, predicted that the post–Cold War era would be marked by cultural conflicts.

Lee Kuan Yew, who ruled Singapore for 31 years and turned it into one of the world's economic power-houses, cautions that Asia will not adopt Western democratic values even as it exceeds Western growth rates.

the phrase "domino theory" by using it to describe how one country after another could be expected to fall under communist control once the process started in Southeast Asia.

In the spring of 1961, I was appointed to membership on the president's Foreign Intelligence Advisory Board. In this capacity, I received briefings from time to time on affairs in Asia. The information provided the board supported the assessment of the previous administration, with which President Kennedy concurred. "Withdrawal in the case of Viet Nam," President Kennedy said in 1961, "and in the case of Thailand could mean the collapse of the whole area." He never wavered. A year later, he said of Viet Nam: "We are not going to withdraw from that effort. In my opinion, for us to withdraw from that effort would mean a collapse not only of South Viet Nam but Southeast Asia. So we are going to stay there." I had no occasion to question the collective opinion of our duly chosen officials.

After President Johnson took office, our involvement became greater, but so did most public and private assessments of the correctness of our course. The Tonkin Gulf resolution was adopted by the Congress in 1964 by a vote of 504 to 2. The language was stern: "The United States is, therefore, prepared, as the President determines, to take all necessary steps, including the use of armed force, to assist any member or protocol state of the Southeast Asia Collective Defense Treaty requesting assistance in defense of its freedom."

When decisions were made in 1965 to increase, in very substantial fashion, the American commitment in Viet Nam, I accepted the judgment that such actions were necessary. That fall, I made a trip to Southeast Asia in my capacity as chairman of the Foreign Intelligence Advisory Board. The optimism of our military and Vietnamese officials on the conduct of the war, together with the encouragement of our Asian allies, confirmed my belief in the correctness of our policy. In the absence at the time of indications that Hanoi had any interest in peace negotiations, I did not favor the 37-day bombing halt over the Christmas 1965–New Year 1966 holiday season. I felt such a halt could be construed by Hanoi as a sign of weakness on our part.

In 1966 I served as an adviser to President Johnson at the Manila Conference. It was an impressive gathering of the chiefs of state and heads of government of the allied nations; it reassured me that we were on the right road and that our military progress was bringing us closer to the resolution of the conflict.

In the late summer of 1967, President Johnson asked me to go with his special assistant, General Maxwell Taylor, to review the situation in South Viet Nam and then to visit some of our Pacific allies. We were to brief them on the war and to discuss with them the possibility of their increasing their troop commitments. Our briefings in South Viet Nam were extensive and encouraging. There were suggestions that the enemy was being hurt badly and that our bombing and superior firepower were beginning to achieve the expected results.

Our visits to the allied capitals, however, produced results that I had not foreseen. It was strikingly apparent to me that the other troop-contributing countries no longer shared our degree of concern about the war in South Viet Nam. General Taylor and I urged them to increase their participation. In the main, our plea fell on deaf ears.

Thailand, a near neighbor to South Viet Nam, with a population of some 30 million, had assigned only 2,500 men to South Viet Nam and was in no hurry to allocate more.

The president of the Philippines advised President Johnson that he preferred we not stop there because of possible adverse public reaction. The Philippines, so close and ostensibly so vulnerable if they accepted the domino theory, had sent a hospital corps and an engineer battalion to Viet Nam, but no combat troops. It was also made clear to President Johnson that they had no intention of sending any combat personnel.

South Korea had the only sizable contingent of Asian troops assisting South Viet Nam, but officials argued that a higher level of activity on the part of the North Koreans prevented their increasing their support.

Disappointing though these visits were, I had high hopes for the success of our mission in Australia and New Zealand. I recalled that Australia, then with a much smaller population, had been able to maintain well over 300,000 troops overseas in World War II. They had sent only 7,000 to Viet Nam. Surely there was hope here. But Prime Minister Holt, who had been fully briefed, presented a long list of reasons why Australia was already close to its maximum effort.

In New Zealand, we spent the better part of a day conferring with the prime minister and his cabinet, while hundreds of students picketed the Parliament building carrying signs bearing peace slogans. These officials were courteous and sympathetic, as all the others had been, but they made it clear that any appreciable increase was out of the question. New Zealand at one time had 70,000 troops overseas in the various theaters of World War II. They had 500 men in Viet Nam. I naturally wondered if this was their evaluation of the respective dangers of the two conflicts.

I returned home puzzled, troubled, concerned. Was it possible that our assessment of the danger to the stability of Southeast Asia and the western Pacific was exaggerated? Was it possible that those nations which were neighbors of Viet Nam had a clearer perception of the tides of world events in 1967 than we? Was it possible that we were continuing to be guided by judgments that might once have had validity but were now obsolete? In short, although I still counted myself a staunch supporter of our policies, there were nagging, not-to-be-suppressed doubts in my mind.

These doubts were dramatized a short time later back in the United States when I attended a dinner at the White House for Prime Minister Lee Kuan Yew of Singapore. His country, which knew the bitterness of defeat and occupation in World War II, had declined to send any men at all to Viet Nam. In answer to my question as to when he thought troops might be sent, he stated he saw no possibility of that taking place because of the adverse political effect in Singapore.

Accordingly, I welcomed President Johnson's San Antonio speech of September 30, 1967, with far greater enthusiasm than I would have had I not so recently returned from the Pacific. I felt it marked a substantial step in the right direction because it offered an alternative to a military solution of the lengthy and costly conflict. Allied bombing of North Viet Nam had by now assumed a symbolic significance of enormous proportions and the president focused his attention on this. The essence of his proposal was an offer to stop the bombing of North Viet Nam if prompt and productive peace discussions with the other side would ensue. We would assume that the other side would "not take advantage" of the bombing cessation. By this formula, the president made an imaginative move to end the deadlock over the bombing and get negotiations started.

I, of course, shared the universal disappointment that the San Antonio offer evoked no favorable response from Hanoi, but my feelings were more complex than those of mere disappointment. As I listened to the official discussion in Washington, my feelings turned from disappointment to dismay. I found it was being quietly asserted that, in return for a bombing cessation in the North, the North Vietnamese must stop sending men and matériel into South Viet Nam. On the surface, this might have seemed a fair exchange. To me, it was an unfortunate interpretation that—intentionally or not—rendered the San Antonio formula virtually meaningless. The North Vietnamese had more than 100,000 men in the South. It was totally unrealistic to expect them to abandon their men by not replacing casualties and by failing to provide them with clothing, food, munitions, and other supplies. We could never expect them to accept an offer to negotiate on those conditions.

III

IN MID-JANUARY 1968, President Johnson asked me to serve as Secretary of Defense, succeeding Secretary McNamara, who was leaving to become president of the World Bank. In the confirmation hearing before the Senate Armed Services Committee on January 25, I was asked about the San Antonio formula. The interpretation I gave was in accord with President Johnson's intense desire to start negotiations, and it offered a possibility of acceptance which I was convinced did not exist with the extreme and rigid interpretations that so concerned me. I said that assumed that the North Vietnamese would "continue to transport the normal amount of goods, munitions, and men to South Viet Nam" at the levels that had prevailed prior to our bombing cessation. This was my understanding of what the president meant by "not take advantage."

The varying interpretations of the San Antonio formula raised in my mind the question as to whether all of us had the same objective in view. Some, it seemed, could envision as satisfactory no solution short of the complete military defeat of the enemy. I did not count myself in this group. Although I still accepted as valid the premises of our Viet Nam involvement, I was dissatisfied with the rigidities that so limited our course of action and our alternatives.

I took office on March 1, 1968. The enemy's Tet offensive of late January and early February had been beaten back at great cost. The confidence of the American people had been badly shaken. The ability of the South Vietnamese government to restore order and morale in the populace, and discipline and esprit in the armed forces, was being questioned. At the president's direction, General Earle G. Wheeler, Chairman of the Joint Chiefs of Staff, had flown to Viet Nam in late February for an on-the-spot conference with General Westmoreland. He had just returned and presented the military's request that over 200,000 troops be prepared for deployment to Viet Nam. These troops would be in addition to the 525,000 previously authorized. I was directed, as my first assignment, to chair a task force named by the president to determine how this new requirement could be met. We were not instructed to assess the need for substantial increases in men and matériel; we were to devise the means by which they could be provided.

My work was cut out. The task force included Secretary Rusk, Secretary Henry Fowler, Under Secretary of State Nicholas Katzenbach, Deputy Secretary of Defense Paul Nitze, General Wheeler, CIA Director Richard Helms, the president's special assistant, Walt Rostow, General Maxwell Taylor, and other skilled and highly capable officials. All of them had had long and direct experience with Vietnamese problems. I had not. I had attended various meetings in the past several years and I had been to Viet Nam three times, but it was quickly apparent to me how little one knows if he has been on the periphery of a problem and not truly in it. Until the day-long sessions of early March, I had never had the opportunity of intensive analysis and fact-finding. Now I was thrust into a vigorous, ruthlessly frank assessment of our situation by the men who knew the most about it. Try though we would to stay with the assignment of devising means to meet the military's requests, fundamental questions began to recur over and over.

It is, of course, not possible to recall all the questions that were asked nor all the answers that were given. Had a transcript of our discussions been made—one was not—it would have run to hundreds of closely printed pages. The documents brought to the table by participants would have totalled, if collected in one place—which they were not—many hundreds more. All that is pertinent to this essay are the impressions I formed, and the conclusions I ultimately reached in those days of exhausting scrutiny. In the colloquial style of those meetings, here are some of the principal issues raised and some of the answers as I understood them:

"Will 200,000 more men do the job?" I found no assurance that they would.

"If not, how many more might be needed—and when?" There was no way of knowing.

"What would be involved in committing 200,000 more men to Viet Nam?" A reserve call-up of approximately 280,000, an increased draft call, and an extension of tours of duty of most men then in service.

"Can the enemy respond with a buildup of his own?" He could and he probably would.

"What are the estimated costs of the latest requests?" First calculations were on the order of $2 billion for the remaining four months of that fiscal year, and an increase of $10 to $12 billion for the year beginning July 1, 1968.

"What will be the impact on the economy?" So great that we would face the possibility of credit restrictions, a tax increase, and even wage and price controls. The balance of payments would be worsened by at least half a billion dollars a year.

"Can bombing stop the war?" Never by itself. It was inflicting heavy personnel and matériel losses, but bombing by itself would not stop the war.

"Will stepping up the bombing decrease American casualties?" Very little, if at all. Our casualties were due to the intensity of the ground fighting in the South. We had already dropped a heavier tonnage of bombs than in all the theaters of World War II. During 1967, an estimated 90,000 North Vietnamese had infiltrated into South Viet Nam. In the opening weeks of 1968, infiltrators were coming in at three to four times the rate of a year earlier, despite the ferocity and intensity of our campaign of aerial interdiction.

"How long must we keep on sending our men and carrying the main burden of combat?" The South Vietnamese were doing better, but they were not ready yet to replace our troops and we did not know when they would be.

When I asked for a presentation of the military plan for attaining victory in Viet Nam, I was told that there was no plan for victory in the historic

American sense. Why not? Because our forces were operating under three major political restrictions: The president had forbidden the invasion of North Viet Nam because this could trigger the mutual assistance pact between North Viet Nam and China; the president had forbidden the mining of the harbor at Haiphong, the principal port through which the North received military supplies, because a Soviet vessel might be sunk; the president had forbidden our forces to pursue the enemy into Laos and Cambodia, for to do so would spread the war, politically and geographically, with no discernible advantage. These and other restrictions which precluded an all-out, no-holds-barred military effort were wisely designed to prevent our being drawn into a larger war. We had no inclination to recommend to the president their cancellation.

"Given these circumstances, how can we win?" We would, I was told, continue to evidence our superiority over the enemy; we would continue to attack in the belief that he would reach the stage where he would find it inadvisable to go on with the war. He could not afford the attrition we were inflicting on him. And we were improving our posture all the time.

I then asked, "What is the best estimate as to how long this course of action will take? Six months? One year? Two years?" There was no agreement on an answer. Not only was there no agreement, I could find no one willing to express any confidence in his guesses. Certainly, none of us was willing to assert that he could see "light at the end of the tunnel" or that American troops would be coming home by the end of the year.

After days of this type of analysis, my concern had greatly deepened. I could not find out when the war was going to end; I could not find out the manner in which it was going to end; I could not find out whether the new requests for men and equipment were going to be enough, or whether it would take more and, if more, when and how much; I could not find out how soon the South Vietnamese forces would be ready to take over. All I had was the statement, given with too little self-assurance to be comforting, that if we persisted for an indeterminate length of time, the enemy would choose not to go on.

And so I asked, "Does anyone see any diminution in the will of the enemy after four years of our having been there, after enormous casualties, and after massive destruction from our bombing?"

The answer was that there appeared to be no diminution in the will of the enemy. This reply was doubly impressive, because I was more conscious each day of domestic unrest in our own country. Draft card burnings, marches in the streets, problems on school campuses, bitterness, and divisiveness were rampant. Just as disturbing to me were the economic implications of a struggle to be indefinitely continued at ever-increasing cost. The dollar was already in trouble, prices were escalating far too fast, and emergency controls on foreign investment imposed on New Year's Day would be only a prelude to more stringent controls, if we were to add another $12 billion to Viet Nam spending—with perhaps still more to follow.

I was also conscious of our obligations and involvements elsewhere in the world. There were certain hopeful signs in our relations with the Soviet Union, but both nations were hampered in moving toward vitally important talks on the limitation of strategic weapons so long as the United States was committed to a military solution in Viet Nam. We could not afford to disregard our interests in the Middle East, South Asia, Africa, Western Europe, and elsewhere. Even accepting the validity of our objective in Viet Nam, that objective had to be viewed in the context of our overall national interest and could not sensibly be pursued at a price so high as to impair our ability to achieve other, and perhaps even more important, foreign policy objectives.

Also, I could not free myself from the continuing nagging doubt left over from that August trip, that if the nations living in the shadow of Viet Nam were not now persuaded by the domino theory, perhaps it was time for us to take another look. Our efforts had given the nations in that area a number of years following independence to organize and build their security. I could see no reason at this time for us to continue to add to our commitment. Finally, there was no assurance that a 40 percent increase in American troops would place us within the next few weeks, months, or even years in any substantially better military position than we were in then. All that could be predicted accurately was that more troops would raise the level of combat and automatically raise the level of casualties on both sides.

And so, after these exhausting days, I was convinced that the military course we were pursuing was not only endless, but hopeless. A further substantial increase in American forces could only increase the devastation and the Americanization of the war and thus leave us even further from our goal of a peace that would permit the people of South Viet Nam to fashion their own political and economic institutions. Henceforth, I was also convinced, our primary goal should be to level off our involvement, and to work toward gradual disengagement.

IV

TO REACH A conclusion and to implement it are not the same, especially when one does not have the ultimate power of decision. It now became my purpose to emphasize to my colleagues and to the president that the United States had entered Viet Nam with a limited aim—to prevent its subjugation by the North and to enable the people of South Viet Nam to determine their own future. I also argued that we had largely accomplished that objective. Nothing required us to remain until the North had been ejected from the South and the Saigon government had been established in complete military control of all South Viet Nam. An increase of over 200,000 in troop strength would mean that American forces would be twice the size of the regular South Vietnamese Army at that time. Our goal of building a stronger South Vietnamese government and an effective military force capable of ultimately taking over from us would be frustrated rather than furthered. The more we continued to do in South Viet Nam, the less likely the South Vietnamese were to shoulder their own burden.

The debate continued at the White House for days. President Johnson encouraged me to report my findings and my views with total candor, but he was equally insistent on hearing the views of others. Finally, the president, in the closing hours of March, made his decisions and reported them to the people on the evening of the 31st. Three related directly to the month's review of the war. First, the president announced he was establishing a ceiling of 549,500 in the American commitment to Viet Nam; the only new troops going out would be support troops previously promised. Second, we would speed up our aid to the South Vietnamese armed forces. We would equip and train them to take over major combat responsibilities from us on a much accelerated schedule. Third, speaking to Hanoi, the President stated he was greatly restricting American bombing of the North as an invitation and an inducement to begin peace talks. We would no longer bomb north of the Twentieth Parallel. By this act of unilateral restraint, nearly 80 percent of the territory of North Viet Nam would no longer be subjected to our bombing.

I had taken office at the beginning of the month with one overriding immediate assignment—responding to the military quest to strengthen our forces in Viet Nam so that we might prosecute the war more forcefully. Now my colleagues and I had two different and longer-range tasks—developing a plan shifting the burden to the South Vietnamese as rapidly as they could be made ready and supporting our government's diplomatic efforts to engage in peace talks.

To assess the rate of progress in the first task, I went to Viet Nam in July. I was heartened by the excellent spirit and the condition of our forces, but I found distressingly little evidence that the other troop-contributing countries or the South Vietnamese were straining to relieve us of our burdens. Although there had been nominal increases in troop contributions from Australia and Thailand since the preceding summer, the Philippines had actually withdrawn several hundred men. The troop-contributing countries were bearing no more of the combat burden; their casualty rates were actually falling.

As for South Vietnamese officials, in discussion after discussion, I found them professing unawareness of shortcomings in such matters as troop training, junior officer strength, and rate of desertions. They were, I felt, too complacent when the facts were laid before them. I asked Vice President Ky, for example, about the gross desertion rate of South Vietnamese combat personnel that was running at 30 percent a year. He responded that it was so large, in part, because their men were not paid enough. I asked what his government intended to do. He suggested that we could cut back our bombing, give the money thus saved to the Saigon government, and it would be used for troop pay. He was not jesting; his suggestion was a serious one. I returned home oppressed by the pervasive Americanization of the war: we were still giving the military instructions, still doing most of the fighting, still providing all the matériel, still paying most of the bills. Worst of all, I concluded that the South Vietnamese leaders seemed content to have it that way.

The North had responded to the president's speech of March 31, and meetings had begun in Paris in May. It was, however, a euphemism to call them peace talks. In mid-summer, substantive discussions had not yet begun. Our negotiators, the able and experienced Ambassador Averell Harriman and his talented associate, Cyrus Vance, were insisting that the Saigon government be a participant in the talks. Hanoi rejected this. President Johnson, rightly and understandably, refused to order a total bombing halt of the North until Hanoi would accept reciprocal restraints. Hanoi refused. With this unsatisfactory deadlock, the summer passed in Paris.

In Viet Nam, American casualty lists were tragically long, week after week. The enemy was not winning but, I felt, neither were we. There were many other areas in the world where our influence, moral force, and economic contributions were sorely in demand and were limited because of our preoccupation with our involvement in Southeast Asia.

I returned from a NATO meeting in Bonn on Sunday evening, October 13, to find a summons to a White House meeting the following morning. There had been movement in Paris. There were no formal agreements, but certain "understandings" had been reached by our negotiating team and the North Vietnamese. At last the North had accepted the participation of the South in peace talks. We would stop all bombing of North Viet Nam. Substantive talks were to start promptly. We had made it clear to Hanoi that we could not continue such talks if there were indiscriminate shelling of major cities in the South or if the demilitarized zone were violated so as to place our troops in jeopardy.

The president outlined the situation to his advisers. We spent a day of hard and full review. The Joint Chiefs of Staff were unanimous in stating that the bombing halt under these circumstances was acceptable. The State Department was authorized to report to Saigon that we had won a seat at the conference table for the Saigon government and to request the earliest possible presence of their delegation in Paris. I felt a sense of relief and hope; we were started down the road to peace.

These feelings were short-lived. The next three weeks were almost as agonizing to me as March had been. The cables from Saigon were stunning. The South Vietnamese government, suddenly and unexpectedly, was not willing to go to Paris. First one reason, then another, then still another were cabled to Washington. As fast as one Saigon obstacle was overcome, another took its place. Incredulity turned to dismay. I felt that the president and the United States were being badly used. Even worse, I felt that Saigon was attempting to exert a veto power over our agreement to engage in peace negotiations. I admired greatly the president's ability to be patient under the most exasperating circumstances. Each day ran the risk that the North might change its mind and that months of diligent effort at Paris would be in vain; each day saw a new effort on his part to meet the latest Saigon objection.

To satisfy himself that the bombing halt would neither jeopardize our own forces nor those of our allies, the president ordered General Creighton W. Abrams back from South Viet Nam for a personal report. Finally, on October 31, President Johnson announced that the bombing of North Viet Nam would cease, peace talks would begin promptly, and Saigon was assured of a place at the conference table. However, it took weeks to get the Saigon government to Paris and still additional weeks to get their agreement on seating arrangements.

By the time the various difficulties had been resolved, certain clear and unequivocal opinions regarding the attitude and posture of the Saigon government had crystalized in my mind. These opinions had been forming since my trip to South Viet Nam the preceding July.

The goal of the Saigon government and the goal of the United States were no longer one and the same, if indeed they ever had been. They were not in total conflict but they were clearly not identical. We had largely accomplished the objective for which we had entered the struggle. There was no longer any question about the desire of the American people to bring the Viet Nam adventure to a close.

As Ambassador Harriman observed, it is dangerous to let your aims be escalated in the middle of a war. Keep your objectives in mind, he advised, and as soon as they are attained, call a halt. The winning of the loyalty of villagers to the central government in Saigon, the form of a postwar government, who its leaders should be, and how they are to be selected—these were clearly not among our original war objectives. But these were the precise areas of our differences with the Saigon government.

As Saigon authorities saw it, the longer the war went on, with the large-scale American involvement, the more stable was their régime, and the fewer concessions they would have to make to other political groupings. If the United States were to continue its military efforts for another two or three years, perhaps the North Vietnamese and the Viet Cong would be so decimated that no concessions would be needed at all. In the meantime, vast amounts of American wealth were being poured into the South Vietnamese economy. In short, grim and distasteful though it might be, I concluded during the bleak winter weeks that Saigon was in no hurry for the fighting to end and that the Saigon régime did not want us to reach an early settlement of military issues with Hanoi.

The fact is that the creation of strong political, social, and economic institutions is a job that the Vietnamese must do for themselves. We cannot do it for them, nor can they do it while our presence hangs over them so massively. President Thieu, Vice President Ky, Prime Minister Huong, and those who may follow them have the task of welding viable political institutions from the 100 or more splinter groups that call themselves political parties. It is up to us to let them get on with the job. Nothing we might do could be so beneficial or could so add to the political maturity of South Viet Nam as to begin to withdraw our combat troops. Moreover, in my opinion, we cannot realistically expect to achieve anything more through our military force, and the time has come to begin to disengage. That was my final conclusion as I left the Pentagon on January 20, 1969.

V

IT REMAINS my firm opinion today. It is based not only on my personal experiences, but on the many significant changes that have occurred in the world situation in the last four years.

In 1965, the forces supported by North Viet Nam were on the verge of a military takeover of South Viet Nam. Only by sending large numbers of American troops was it possible to prevent this from happening. The South Vietnamese were militarily weak and politically demoralized. They could not, at that time, be expected to preserve for themselves the right to determine their own future. Communist China had recently proclaimed its intention to implement the doctrine of "wars of national liberation." Khrushchev's fall from power the preceding October and Chou En-lai's visit to Moscow in November 1964 posed the dire possibility of the two communist giants working together to spread disruption throughout the underdeveloped nations of the world. Indonesia, under Sukarno, presented a posture of implacable hostility toward Malaysia and was a destabilizing element in the entire Pacific picture. Malaysia itself, as well as Thailand and Singapore, needed time for their governmental institutions to mature. Apparent American indifference to developments in Asia might, at that time, have had a disastrous impact on the independent countries of that area.

During the past four years, the situation has altered dramatically. The armed forces of South Viet Nam have increased in size and proficiency. The political situation there has become more stable, and the governmental institutions more representative. Elsewhere in Asia, conditions of greater security exist. The bloody defeat of the attempted communist coup in Indonesia removed Sukarno from power and changed the confrontation with Malaysia to cooperation between the two countries. The governments of Thailand and Singapore have made good use of these four years to increase their popular support. Australia and New Zealand have moved toward closer regional defense ties, while Japan, the Republic of Korea, and Taiwan have exhibited a rate of economic growth and an improvement in living standards that discredit the teachings of Chairman Mao.

Of at least equal significance is the fact that, since 1965, relations between Russia and China have steadily worsened. The schism between these two powers is one of the watershed events of our time. Ironically, their joint support of Hanoi has contributed to the acrimony between them. It has brought into focus their competition for leadership in the communist camp. Conflicting positions on the desirability of the peace negotiation in Paris have provided a further divisive factor. In an analogous development, increased Soviet aid to North Korea has made Pyongyang less dependent on China. The Cultural Revolution and the depredations of the Red Guards have created in China a situation of internal unrest that presently preoccupies China's military forces. The recent border clashes on the Ussuri River further decrease the likelihood that China will, in the near future, be able to devote its attention and resources to the export of revolution.

These considerations are augmented by another. It seems clear that the necessity to devote more of our minds and our means to our pressing domestic problems requires that we set a chronological limit on our Vietnamese involvement.

A year ago, we placed a numerical limit on this involvement and did so without lessening the effectiveness of the total military effort. There will, undeniably, be many problems inherent in the replacement of American combat forces with South Vietnamese forces. But whatever these problems, they must be faced. There is no way to achieve our goal of creating the conditions that will allow the South Vietnamese to determine their own future unless we begin, and begin promptly, to turn over to them the major responsibility for their own defense. This ability to defend themselves can never be developed so long as we continue to bear the brunt of the battle. Sooner or later, the test must be whether the South Vietnamese will serve their own country sufficiently well to guarantee its national survival. In my view, this test must be made sooner, rather than later.

A first step would be to inform the South Vietnamese government that we will withdraw about 100,000 troops before the end of this year. We should also make it clear that this is not an isolated action, but the beginning of a process under which all U.S. ground combat forces will have been withdrawn from Viet Nam by the end of 1970. The same information should, of course, be provided to the other countries who are contributing forces for the defense of South Viet Nam.

Strenuous political and military objections to this decision must be anticipated. Arguments will be made that such a withdrawal will cause the collapse of the Saigon government and jeopardize the security of our own and allied troops. Identical arguments, however, were urged against the decisions to restrict the bombing on March 31 of last year and to stop it completely on October 31. They have proven to be unfounded. There is, in fact, no magic and no specific military rationale for the number of American troops presently in South Viet Nam. The current figure represents only the level at which the escalator stopped.

It should also be noted that our military commanders have stated flatly since last summer that no additional American troops are needed. During these months the number of South Vietnamese under arms in the government cause has increased substantially, and we have received steady reports of their improved performance. Gradual withdrawal of American combat troops thus not only would be consistent with continued overall military strength, but also would serve to substantiate the claims of the growing combat effectiveness of the South Vietnamese forces.

Concurrently with the decision to begin withdrawal, orders should be issued to our military commanders to discontinue efforts to apply maximum military pressure on the enemy and to seek instead to reduce the level of combat. The public statements of our officials show that there has as yet been no change in our policy of maximum military effort. The result has been a continuation of the high level of American casualties, without any discernible impact on the peace negotiations in Paris.

While our combat troops are being withdrawn, we would continue to provide the armed forces of the Saigon government with logistic support and with our air resources. As the process goes on, we can appraise both friendly and enemy reactions. The pattern of our eventual withdrawal of noncombat troops and personnel engaged in airlift and air support can be determined on the basis of political and military developments. So long as we retain our air resources in South Viet Nam, with total air superiority, I do not believe that the lessening in the military pressure exerted by the ground forces would permit the enemy to make any significant gains. There is, moreover, the possibility of reciprocal reduction in North Vietnamese combat activity.

Our decision progressively to turn over the combat burden to the armed forces of South Viet Nam would confront the North Vietnamese leaders with a painful dilemma. Word that the Americans were beginning to withdraw might at first lead them to claims of victory. But even these initial claims could be expected to be tinged with apprehension. There has, in my view, long been considerable evidence that Hanoi fears the possibility that those whom they characterize as "puppet forces" may, with continued but gradually reduced American support, prove able to stand off the communist forces.

As American combat forces are withdrawn, Hanoi would be faced with the prospect of a prolonged and substantial presence of American air and logistics personnel in support of South Viet Nam's combat troops, which would be constantly improving in efficiency. Hanoi's only alternative would be to arrange, tacitly or explicitly, for a mutual withdrawal of all external forces. In either eventuality, the resulting balance of forces should avert any danger of a bloodbath which some fear might occur in the aftermath of our withdrawal.

Once our withdrawal of combat troops commences, the Saigon government would recognize, probably for the first time, that American objectives do not demand the perpetuation in power of any one group of South Vietnamese. So long as we appear prepared to remain indefinitely, there is no pressure on Saigon to dilute the control of those presently in positions of power by making room for individuals representative of other nationalist elements in South Vietnamese society.

Accordingly, I anticipate no adverse impact on the Paris negotiations from the announcement and implementation of a program of American withdrawal. Instead, I would foresee the creation of circumstances under which true bargaining may proceed among the Vietnamese present in Paris. Unquestionably, the North Vietnamese and the National Liberation Front would do so in the hope that any political settlement would move them toward eventual domination in South Viet Nam. But their hopes and expectations necessarily will yield to the political realities, and these political realities are, in the final analysis, both beyond our control and beyond our ken. Moreover, they are basically none of our business. The one million South Vietnamese in the various components of the armed forces, with American logistics, airlift and air support, should be able, if they have the will, to prevent the imposition by force of a Hanoi-controlled régime. If they lack a sense or a sufficiency of national purpose, we can never force it on them.

In the long run, the security of the Pacific region will depend upon the ability of the countries there to meet the legitimate growing demands of their own people. No military strength we can bring to bear can give them internal stability or popular acceptance. In Southeast Asia, and elsewhere in the less developed regions of the world, our ability to understand and to control the basic forces that are at play is a very limited one. We can advise, we can urge, we can furnish economic aid. But American military power cannot build nations, any more than it can solve the social and economic problems that face us here at home.

This, then, is the case history of the evolution of one individual's thinking regarding Viet Nam. Throughout this entire period it has been difficult to cling closely to reality because of the constant recurrence of optimistic predictions that our task was nearly over, and that better times were just around the corner, or just over the next hill.

We cannot afford to lose sight of the fact that this is a limited war, for limited aims and employing limited power. The forces we now have deployed and the human and material costs we are now incurring have become, in my opinion, out of all proportion to our purpose. The present scale of military effort can bring us no closer to meaningful victory. It can only continue to devastate the countryside and to prolong the suffering of the Vietnamese people of every political persuasion.

Unless we have the imagination and the courage to adopt a different course, I am convinced that we will be in no better, and no different, a position a year from now than we are today.

At current casualty rates, 10,000 more American boys will have lost their lives.

We should reduce American casualties by reducing American combat forces. We should do so in accordance with a definite schedule and with a specified end point.

Let us start to bring our men home—and let us start *now*.

An Age of Limits

THE NINETEEN SEVENTIES

✇AFTER THE TUMULT of Vietnam, the 1970s proved to be an introspective, angst-ridden decade. Nixon and Kissinger, now secretary of state, introduced a policy of détente with Moscow and sought to shift the global balance of power through their famous rapprochement with China, the other communist superpower. But the aftereffects of Vietnam—the loss of national purpose, the self-doubt, the deterioration of alliances—still lingered, as evoked by Hamilton Fish Armstrong, the longtime editor of *Foreign Affairs*, in his heartfelt valedictory essay, "Isolated America."

Further shocks were in store. In 1971, Nixon unhinged much of the postwar Bretton Woods monetary system by declining to provide gold for dollars of countries running balance-of-payments surpluses. In "A Monetary System for the Future," Richard N. Cooper, a Harvard economist, saw this move as leading to unstable currency swings and proposed as an ambitious solution a global currency. The Middle East was plunged again into war in 1973, which was followed by the mid-1970s oil crisis. The seemingly unstoppable U.S. economy sank into stagflation—inflation plus unemployment. To add to the gloom, a series of vicious attacks by Palestinian terrorists, including the murder of 11 Israeli athletes at the 1972 Munich Olympics, left Americans glued to their televisions in horror. As the historian David Fromkin noted in "The Strategy of Terrorism," such horror was precisely the point; in the age of Marshall McLuhan, the psychological reaction of the viewer counts as much as the act of political murder itself.

Richard Nixon resigned in August 1974 over the Watergate scandals. Gerald Ford, the heir to the Nixon-Kissinger era of realpolitik, was succeeded in 1977 by Jimmy Carter. The new president promised to restore morality to U.S. foreign policy by pushing vigorously for human rights.

The resultant collision of high-mindedness with geopolitical realities made for four years of confusion in U.S. diplomacy. In "Human Rights and the American Tradition," Arthur Schlesinger, Jr., the historian and Kennedy aide, praised Carter for his renewed emphasis on one of the United States' noblest legacies; in "Human Rights and Foreign Policy: A Proposal," William F. Buckley, Jr., the conservative pundit, took a more jaundiced view, urging overeager would-be Wilsonians not "to mix business with displeasure."

But the issue that truly haunted the 1970s was the Middle East. Carter won his one major triumph by midwifing the 1978 Camp David peace accords between Israel and Egypt. Indeed, as Fouad Ajami, a Middle East expert, argued in "The End of Pan-Arabism," Egyptian President Anwar al-Sadat's 1977 visit to Jerusalem marked an historic shift away from the dream of a mythical united Arab nation and toward a normal state system. But turmoil erupted again in 1979 when the Ayatollah Khomeini's Shiite fundamentalist followers removed the linchpin of America's regional strategy by sweeping the despotic shah of Iran from power and overran the U.S. embassy in Tehran, taking 52 Americans hostage. During the hostage crisis, America became, in the words of the historian Warren I. Cohen, "Gulliver tormented by the Lilliputians." To compound Carter's woes, the president's hopes for a rapprochement with Moscow were dashed in December 1979 when Soviet tanks invaded Afghanistan, ending the decade with White House rhetoric that recalled the chilliest days of the Cold War.

Isolated America

Hamilton Fish Armstrong

OCTOBER 1972

SEVENTY-FIVE YEARS ago, Archibald Cary Coolidge, who later became the first editor of *Foreign Affairs*, wrote a book with a theme and title entirely novel at that time, *The United States as a World Power.* In it he made the first attempt to define the new role in the world then rapidly being assumed by the United States. He remarked that all nations divide mankind into two categories—themselves and everybody else. And he said that Americans would be just as prone as others to cherish the pleasing belief that they had grown great by their own virtues and the favor of a kindly Providence, whereas the progress of other states was marked by unscrupulous rapacity; hence, they would demand that American statesmen keep sharp watch lest nefarious foreigners take advantage of their good nature and honest simplicity. The accuracy of Mr. Coolidge's analysis was corroborated before long by the alacrity with which the American people accepted the idea that they had come into World War I altruistically, in order to make the world safe for democracy ("American" democracy); and again by their readiness to suppose that President Wilson and his advisers at Paris had been bamboozled by wily European statesmen. The latter conception was promoted by American isolationists who depicted the League of Nations as a naive and useless affair and a trap to involve us in Old World power politics.

The war in Vietnam has been the longest and in some respects the most calamitous war in our history. It has rent the American people apart, spiritually and politically. It is a war which has not been and could not be won, a war which was pushed from small beginnings to an appalling multitude of horrors, many of which we have become conscious of only by degrees. The methods we have used in fighting the war have scandalized and disgusted public opinion in almost all foreign countries.

Not since we withdrew into comfortable isolation in 1920 has the prestige of the United States stood so low. Following Harding's sweeping victory

[329]

and his announcement that Wilson's League was "now deceased," the League of Nations passed out of the minds of most Americans. Having won the war for their allies, as they put it, Americans considered that they were entitled to attend to their own affairs exclusively. The world was stunned. The United States had won glory by turning the tide of battle in Europe and moral stature by sponsoring, through President Wilson, a program for organizing the peace that the world craved. In their disillusionment, Europeans did not forget America's achievements in the war or minimize what the American Relief Administration and other organizations continued to do in feeding the starving and restoring the wreckage in devastated regions. But something was gone from the picture that the world had formed in wartime of Americans; their adventurousness, their willingness to take risks had disappeared. There were Americans, too, who felt that the American dream had paled and who had twinges of conscience that their country was taking no part in the endeavor to make a new war less likely.

Efforts were made before long to demonstrate that the United States was on the side of peace even though it would not share the alleged risks of becoming a member of the League of Nations. One effort was made in Coolidge's administration, the second in Hoover's. In the summer of 1928 Secretary of State Kellogg took part in negotiating what became the Pact of Paris, the purpose of which was, in the popular phrase, to "outlaw war." It aimed to establish peace by fiat and was acceptable to the U.S. Senate because its signatories were not committed to take any concrete action to prevent aggression. It was harmless except to the extent that it led the American public to suppose that something effective had been done to compensate for the refusal to participate in the League. A second effort to show that the United States was on the side of peace was made by Secretary of State Stimson in January 1932. The League had been struggling vainly to find means to curb the Japanese invasion of Manchuria. Stimson sought to back up the effort by committing the United States to a policy of not recognizing the fruits of aggression. The plan was well intentioned, but its effect in slowing the Japanese invasion was nil.

This was not a period in which the United States was influential in world affairs. Materially, it was a Great Power in capital letters; morally, its greatness did not shine. When the Great Depression overwhelmed the United States, as all nations, Roosevelt's spectacular measures of reform gave the American people hope and trust again, but there was little energy left to think about the troubles and dangers of others. The European landscape was black. A new arms race set in. Hitler's advent was a portent of what was to come. Roosevelt made an effort to have the Neutrality Act amended so that the United States need not, by insisting on its rights as a neutral, break a blockade set up by members of the League against an aggressor; the possibility that it would recognize a blockade would be a powerful deterrent to aggression. The Senate refused.

Through the interwar years, the picture of the United States in the eyes of the world remained much as it had been after the Senate killed the proposal to join the League, refused to ratify the Treaty of Versailles, and rejected the Tripartite Pact which promised France protection against fresh German attack and which she had accepted as a substitute for seizing territorial guarantees of her own on the Rhine. Nor did it ratify the Protocol of the World Court. American policy was looked upon as quirky and unpredictable.

II

IN THE FIRST issue of *Foreign Affairs*, Elihu Root expressed a fairly obvious fact in picturesque language: "When foreign affairs were ruled by autocracies or oligarchies the danger of war was in sinister purpose. When foreign affairs are ruled by democracies the danger of war will be in mistaken beliefs." It is notable that Mr. Root, having in mind the collapse of four great autocracies following the First World War, referred to autocracies in the past tense, an error of which we soon became aware.

Since the United States is not an autocracy nor is it an oligarchy in the formal meaning of that term, the Vietnam War did not originate in what Mr. Root called sinister purpose. Did it, then, originate in mistaken beliefs? If we did indeed start down the road to war unwittingly and in ignorance, and if we failed to notice the points at which our leaders went wrong in time to curb or deflect them from a doomed failure, what are the characteristics of our society which account for our having been left in such a pitiable situation?

Discussions of the issues raised by these questions, indeed the discussion of all the problems of American foreign relations, are being carried on today in a denatured terminology. The rhetoric of good words and high ideals is everywhere heard; but the opponents of selfish or provincial attitudes are at a disadvantage which they did not face formerly and do not altogether recognize now. The words used to express the highest aspirations have become shopworn. Calls to duty or endeavor like those uttered 50 years ago by Woodrow Wilson today sound hollow and meretricious. The phrases have been used and abused too long.

It was in that period of American public euphoria, misleadingly called "normalcy," that *Foreign Affairs* was founded. Its purpose was not to promote specific policies, however laudable, but to increase the interest of the American public in foreign policy as such and stimulate their consciousness that they were an integral part of a world society and had a concern for its welfare as a whole. To anyone who had a share in that enterprise, there seems to be a similarity in the situation then and now. Actually, however, the forces at work are very different. The risk today is not that the American people may become isolationist; the reality is that the United States is being isolated.

In these conditions, an attempt to write other than cynically about the present situation of the United States seems bound to be an exercise in futility. Yet the attempt must be made. Unless we evaluate and not merely enumerate the elements in our society as they condition the quality of our foreign policy, we shall not make progress in changing what we feel is wrong with it. And wrong it must have been. Not, in the experience of the present writer, since the Harding era when we denied our enlightened self-interest and retreated from responsibility in our foreign relationships, while confessing to scandal and tawdry commercialism at home, has the world had such a poor opinion of us. American principles, which sometimes were characterized as naive but in general were respected as sincere and humane, now are freely called hypocritical and self-serving; the weight of American material and military power, looked to in the past as a mainstay of world stability, is now mistrusted and feared.

III

ONCE AGAIN in the Second World War, the United States saved Western civilization. The victory won, it took the lead in forming the United Nations, and the Senate voted membership in it almost unanimously. It is now one of the two superpowers, unassailable in nuclear strength. Nevertheless, its political power is less than its material power, and its prestige is tarnished.

Our methods of fighting the Vietnam War are what have chiefly fanned world opinion against us. But there are other causes of resentment too. Radical changes in the structure of our foreign policy undertaken recently without notice to friends and allies have strengthened a feeling that American policies are conceived for American purposes only. Gratitude for the immense sums given for foreign aid since the war, and especially for the help given Europe in the Marshall Plan, has largely evaporated. Just as the war has sharpened all our internal conflicts, so it has accentuated foreign criticism of American civilization and intensified the resentment of foreign governments that the United States seems more and more to ignore their political interests and economic needs.

In the summer of 1971, President Nixon announced without warning that his national security adviser, Henry Kissinger, had been secretly consulting with Premier Chou En-lai in Peking and that he himself was planning a visit there shortly. A month later, he announced that he had unpegged the dollar from gold and ordered a ten percent surcharge on imports; this our allies considered contrary to international agreement. These actions, and to a lesser degree the later announcement that the president also planned to visit Moscow, confirmed the feeling in many foreign offices that American policy was erratic and egocentric.

The president's goal was to come to live-and-let-live terms with two great nations that had long sought to undermine our position in the world and that were hostile to our social and political system. His grand hope was to end the remnants of the Cold War with Soviet Russia and make progress toward curtailing the arms race; and to open contacts with the People's Republic of China, with which we had no diplomatic relations and with which we had once come close to war on behalf of our protégé Taiwan. The objectives were admirable, provided the endeavor did not involve sacrificing friendships and alliances with peoples with whom we had had close ties, some of them traditional and in a sense sentimental, some economic and commercial, some rooted in similar concepts of constitutional government, democracy, and freedom. In his preoccupation with methods of attaining the goal, and in his excitement as he seemed to near it, the president lost sight of the proviso. The result was a chaotic situation. The stability of the monetary system was further undermined, with our NATO allies among those most adversely affected. Canada, an essential friend and neighbor, Japan, the rising power in East Asia, and India, the largest Asian democracy, were alienated. . . .

Our isolation from other peoples is the reverse of 50 years ago; today we are the object, not the subject.

IV

OUR AGE FINDS it convenient to simplify everything. "Know thyself," a difficult proposition, is supplanted by "Know everybody," not "everybody" as diverse types but as a single prototype—glands, psyches, behavioral reactions, and all. That we take refuge in generality is not surprising. Our society has become so complex that the multiplicity of its individual problems overwhelms us. To save our self-respect, we turn from the un-understandable particular to the perhaps understandable general.

What is called for is a resolute attempt at complication, as the events detailed above indicate. Interactions must be understood as well as facts. Science and technology are adding to the world's problems, not solving them. Something better than a hit-or-miss relationship must be established between the knowledge amassed by scientists in a multitude of fields and the decision-making processes of those who guide political action. How are discoveries in physics to be related to population trends, urban blight, television addiction, substitutes for standard nutritional resources? The answers will not come out of a computer, because judgment as to utility and aesthetic choice cannot be fed in along with the facts. Robert Oppenheimer once said to me that physics had become so recondite that the formulae that demonstrate one scientist's conclusions often remain intelligible only to himself. How, then, is a statesman knowing nothing of science to choose between alternative recommendations regarding, say, the development of ballistic missiles, presented to him by scientific advisers who may not know possible variations in fundamental factors involved?

Those who watched the negotiators at the Paris Peace Conference of 1919 struggle to find a realistic and usable pattern of the events that were transforming the world around them, and so to act to forestall new tragedy, redeem promises, and justify hopes, were conscious that the leaders assembled there, men on the whole of unusual caliber and in some cases unusual idealism, were unable to come to grips individually with more than a single fraction of the problems they faced. Single minds could not encompass such complexities. Since then the condensation of time and space has magnified the complexities and made each component problem more immediate.

This ought to temper our criticism of our leaders as we look back at the remnants of half-understood policies and stumbling actions that strew the path of our involvement in Vietnam. It does not make us feel a need, however, to be lenient in our judgment where they disguised disasters in clichés or cloaked the miseries of millions of refugees, harried hither and yon under a rain of bombs, under comfortable terms like "resettlement" and "reeducation."

It must be made less likely—for it can never be made impossible—for American leaders again to take the country into war unawares. Proposed legislation to limit executive power to conduct an undeclared war by requiring the president to obtain congressional approval of his action within 30 days is misleading; in 30 days a war will have achieved a momentum of its own and will have introduced complications in relations with third powers that neither the public nor Congress will know how to limit or terminate. And of course no domestic legislation can prevent foreign attack, nuclear or otherwise. The prescription for reform is not written in specific terms. If we assume that mistaken beliefs, in Mr. Root's terms, have been responsible for the failure of the American democracy to curb actions of its leaders that are leading to war, the prescription is stunningly large, and recovery can come only slowly as a result of a multitude of actions that could give our country a sense of direction again.

The direction is not backward, in nostalgia, to the virtues of our forefathers, except that we will draw from them an adventurous spirit and in that spirit will answer the question "What is wrong?" with the answer they gave, "Let's do something about it." The direction is forward, to recognize and accept the present ills of our society and to set about curing them—by rehumanizing ourselves, by readopting civility as a part of good behavior, by recognizing that history can inform the future, by encouraging the growth of élites in many fields, not in order to copy them snobbishly but to set intellectual standards to which everyone may in some degree aspire, by asserting that aesthetics is an essential element in art, by reestablishing learning as opening doors to choice, by leavening the mediocrity of our culture with snatches of unorthodoxy, by welcoming diversity of opinion as an essential element of strength in a democracy.

Is this a dream? The crudeness brought by the mechanization of modern life says, yes it is. But science need not be against us, nor need we be against science. Almost 40 years ago Newton D. Baker wrote in *Foreign Affairs:* "The triumph of science in the material world encourages us to do some laboratory work with the human spirit. A peaceful world would have been less amazing to George Washington than wireless telegraphy. We must not think too well of atoms at the expense of thinking too ill of men." If we accept that adjuration, we may recover our self-confidence and self-respect and regain for our nation the standing in the world's estimation it once possessed.

The Strategy of Terrorism

David Fromkin

JULY 1975

THE GRIM EVENTS at the Athens airport on August 5, 1973, were in a sense symbolic. Dreadfully real to those who were involved, the occurrences of that day also transcended their own reality, somewhat as myths do, epitomizing an entire aspect of contemporary existence in one specific drama.

When the hand grenades were hurled into the departure lounge and the machine gunners simultaneously mowed down the passengers waiting to embark for New York City, it seemed incomprehensible that so harmless a group should be attacked. The merest glance at their hand luggage, filled with snorkels and cameras, would have shown that they had spent their time in such peaceful pursuits as swimming, sunbathing, and snapping photos of the Parthenon.

The raid had been undertaken on behalf of an Arab Palestine. Yet the airport passengers had done the Arabs no harm. Their journey had only been to Greece. Palestine had nothing to do with them; it was another country, across the sea, and its problems were not of their making. Moreover, Athens was a capital friendly to the Arab cause—as was Paris, the scene of more recent airline attacks.

Similar incidents have occurred with terrible frequency throughout the 1960s and 1970s. The generations that have come to maturity in Europe and America since the end of the Second World War have asked only to bask in the sunshine of a summertime world; but increasingly they have been forced instead to live in the fearful shadow of other people's deadly quarrels. Gangs of politically motivated gunmen have disrupted everyday life, intruding and forcing their parochial feuds upon the unwilling attention of everybody else.

True, other ages have suffered from crime and outrage, but what we are experiencing today goes beyond such things. Too small to impose their will by military force, terrorist bands nonetheless are capable nowadays of causing enough damage to intimidate and blackmail the governments of the world. Only modern technology makes this possible—the bazooka, the plastic

[336]

bomb, the submachine gun, and perhaps, over the horizon, the nuclear mini-bomb. The transformation has enabled terrorism to enter the political arena on a new scale and to express ideological goals of an organized sort rather than mere crime, madness, or emotional derangement as in the past.

Political terrorism is a distinctive disorder of the modern world. It originated as a term and, arguably, as a practice, less than two centuries ago and has come into the spotlight of global conflict in our lifetime. Whereas both organized and irregular (or guerrilla) warfare began with the human race, political terrorism emerged as a concept only in 1793. As a political strategy, it is both new and original; and if I am correct, its nature has not yet fully been appreciated.

Of course nobody can remain unaware of the upsurge of global terrorism that has occurred in recent years. But the novelty of it has not been perceived. Force usually generates fear, and fear is usually an additional weapon. But terrorism employs the weapon of fear in a special and complicated sort of way.

II

THE DISASSOCIATION of fear from force in the context of organized politics emerged first in the Reign of Terror, the episode (1793–94) during the history of revolutionary France from which the English and French words for terrorism derive. The terrorists in question were, of course, Robespierre and his satellites, St. Just and Couthon. Sitting as a faction in the Committee of Public Safety, their accusations of treason sent victims to the guillotine in droves. By the mere threat of accusation against their fellow committee members, they used the entire committee, thus united, in order to dominate the National Convention and the other public bodies of the French republic. . . .

Robespierre had coerced a nation of 27 million people into accepting his dictatorship. His followers sent many thousands either to jail or to their deaths; one scholar's estimate is 40,000 deaths and 300,000 arrests. Yet when retribution came and Robespierre and his group of supporters were executed, it turned out that in all there were only 22 of them.

Of course it is not meant to suggest that this is the whole story of the French Terror. Yet what emerges most strongly from any account of these events is the dramatic disparity between the objective weakness of the Robespierre faction, whose numbers were few and whose military resources were limited, and their immense subjective power, which allowed them to kill, imprison, or control so many. There was no need to fear the triumvirs other than the fact that other people feared them and therefore would execute their orders. Their power was unreal; it was an illusionist's trick. No citadels had to be stormed, no armies had to be crushed, in order to overthrow them. If the public ignored what they said, then the terrorists went back to being political nobodies. Their dictatorship vanished in an instant when Robespierre and his colleagues were prevented from reaching the speakers' platform on 9 Thermidor.

In the end, the terrorists overreached themselves, and men saw through them and stood up to them. Then—and only then—it became clear that France had never had anything to fear from them other than fear itself.

III

PERHAPS THE closest parallel to Robespierre's method was that followed by the late Senator Joseph McCarthy in 1950–54. Like Robespierre, McCarthy claimed to have lists of traitors whose names he would not immediately reveal, and many did his will in order to avoid being accused by him of treason or of lack of patriotism. And, like Robespierre's, his power stopped when he went too far and Joseph Welch, his Fouché, stood up to him on television. But McCarthy never seized supreme power in the country, nor did his accusations send people to the guillotine. In that sense it can be said that Robespierre has had no successors.

Since his time, in fact, political terrorism has become especially notorious in a different cause from that in which Robespierre used it. It has been used to destroy governments rather than to sustain them. This changed the way in which many people thought of it as a political strategy and how they viewed its adherents. As revolutionaries, terrorists have come to seem romantic figures to many. Their life of dangers and disguises, risks and betrayals, conspiracies and secret societies, exerted a powerful fascination. As torn and tormented characters, they provided authors with the stuff of which complex and interesting novels can be made.

Though the terrorists seemed romantic, until recently they also seemed ineffective. Until the Irish Treaty of 1921, they scored no significant political successes. The most famous of the terrorist groups up to that time was the Terrorist Brigade of the Russian Socialists-Revolutionists; and not merely did they fail to change the tsarist government in the ways in which they desired, they also failed to pick up the pieces when it was overthrown by others. Plekhanov, Lenin, Trotsky, and the other Russian disciples of Marx had seen more clearly in placing their emphasis on mass organization rather than on individual terrorism. The Bolsheviks came to power by winning the metropolitan workmen, the sailors of the Baltic fleet, and the soldiers to their side. Organization proved to be the key to victory. It was not individual gunmen but armed masses who seized power in Russia. Revolution, like war, is the strategy of the strong; terrorism is the strategy of the weak.

It is an uncertain and indirect strategy that employs the weapon of fear in a special sort of way in which to make governments react. Is fear an effective method? Is fright any kind of weapon at all? What can terrorists hope to accomplish by sowing fear? How can it help their side to vanquish its opponents? Clearly it can do so in many ways. Fright can paralyze the will, befuddle the mind, and exhaust the strength of an adversary. Moreover, it can persuade an opponent that a particular political point of view is taken with such deadly seriousness by its few adherents that it should be accommodated, rather than suffering casualties year after year in a campaign to suppress it.

All of these elements came together, for example, in the struggle that led to the independence of southern Ireland. It is difficult to disentangle the role of terrorism in this achievement from the other elements that were involved, for the Irish also had put in motion what was, in effect, a guerrilla warfare campaign. Moreover, the Liberal members of the coalition that then governed the United Kingdom had a political commitment that went back more than a quarter of a century to the cause of Irish Home Rule. Yet there can be little doubt that terrorism played a major role in causing Britain to tire of the struggle.

Terrorism can also make heroes out of gunmen, and thereby rally popular support to their cause. The problem this creates for them is that when the time comes to make the compromises necessary in order to negotiate the terms of their victory, the glamour wanes and, with it, the political support. Michael Collins was a romantic figure who captured the imagination of all Ireland as long as he was an outlaw; but when he sat down to make peace, he was seen by many in a much different light. As he signed the Irish Treaty of 1921 on Britain's behalf, Lord Birkenhead remarked to Collins, "I may have signed my political death-warrant tonight"; to which Collins replied, "I may have signed my actual death-warrant." Eight months later Michael Collins lay dead on an Irish roadway with a bullet through his head.

Just as it can make gangsters into heroes, terrorist provocations can also make policemen into villains. The Black-and-Tans who fought the Irish revolutionists were, in an objective sense, so successful at repression that Michael Collins told an English official afterward, in regard to the July 1921 peace negotiations: "You had us dead beat. We could not have lasted another three weeks." Yet Black-and-Tan methods made the cause of repression so odious that Britain was induced to choose another course of action.

Brutality is an induced governmental response that can boomerang. It is this ability to use the strength of repression against itself, in many different ways, that has enabled terrorist strategies to succeed in many situations that have, rightly or wrongly, been described as colonialist in the modern world.

IV

SOPHISTICATED approaches have been developed along these lines. One of these was explained to me and to others at a meeting in New York City sometime in 1945 by one of the founders of the Irgun Zvai Leumi, a tiny group of Jewish militants in what was then the British-mandated territory of Palestine. His organization had no more than 1,000 or 1,500 members, and it was at odds with the Palestinian Jewish community almost as much as it was with the mandatory regime. Yet he proposed to combat Great Britain, then a global power whose armed forces in the Second World War numbered in the millions, and to expel Great Britain from Palestine.

How could such a thousand-to-one struggle be won? To do so, as he explained it, his organization would attack property interests. After giving advance warning to evacuate them, his small band of followers would blow up buildings. This, he said, would lead the British to overreact by garrisoning the country with an immense army drawn from stations in other parts of the world. But postwar Britain could not afford financially to maintain so great an army either there or anywhere else for any extended period of time. Britain urgently needed to demobilize its armed forces. The strain would tell; and eventually economic pressure would drive the Attlee-Bevin government either to withdraw from Palestine or else to try some reckless and possibly losing gamble in an effort to retrieve the situation.

It can be argued that such is in fact what happened. Of course Britain might have withdrawn anyway, at some other time or for some other reason. But that is really beside the point, for the Irgun wanted independence then and there, in order to open up the country to refugees from Hitler's Europe. They got what they wanted when they wanted it by doing it in their own way.

There were two flaws in the Irgun strategy. It would have failed had the British not reacted to the destruction of buildings as they were expected to do. If instead they had done nothing at all, maintained only a modest military garrison, and sent for no reinforcements, all that would have happened would have been that a few more buildings would have been blown up and the owners would have collected the insurance money and would have rebuilt them; and the Irgun would have proved a failure.

In the second place, the plan of attacking property without hurting people proved to be unrealistic. Accidents inevitably occur when violence is unleashed. Almost a hundred persons were killed when the Irgun blew up the King David Hotel in Jerusalem. According to the plan, they should have been evacuated before the blast, but in actual life people misunderstand, or their telephone line is busy, or somebody forgets to give them the message in time. Moreover, terrorism generates its own momentum, and before long the killing becomes deliberate. The bloodshed caused by the Irgun isolated it politically and alienated the rest of the Palestinian Jewish community. The British failed to perceive or exploit this situation. But Ben-Gurion did; in 1948 he made use of it to crush the Irgun, for the Israeli army might have been unwilling to carry out orders to attack those unloading the Irgun ship the *Altalena* if the Irgun had not used up its political credit before then by the taking of too many lives.

Yet despite its flaws, the strategy was sufficiently ingenious so that the Irgun played a big part in getting the British to withdraw. Its ingenuity lay in using an opponent's own strength against him. It was a sort of jujitsu. First the adversary was made to be afraid, and then, predictably, he would react to his fear by increasing the bulk of his strength, and then the sheer weight of that bulk would drag him down. Another way of saying this is that the Irgun, seeing that it was too small to defeat Great Britain, decided, as an alternative approach, that Britain was big enough to defeat itself.

V

IN THE 1950s, the nationalist rebel group in Algeria developed yet another method of using the strength of an occupying power against itself. Their method was to induce that strength to be used as a form of persuasion.

For in Algeria the whole question was one of persuasion. The problem initially faced by the miniscule band of Algerian nationalists that called itself the National Liberation Front (or, in its French initials, FLN) was that Algeria at that time had little sense of national identity. Its population was not homogeneous; and the Berbers, the Arabs, and the settlers of European descent were peoples quite different from one another. The name and separate existence of Algeria were only of recent origin. For most of recorded history, Algeria had been no more than the middle part of North Africa, with no distinct history of its own. Legally it was merely the southern part of France. The French had treated Morocco and Tunisia as protectorates, with separate identities, but not Algeria, which was absorbed into France herself. With sarcasm, Frenchmen used to reply to Americans who urged independence for Algeria by saying that, on the same basis, the United States should set Wisconsin free or give back independence to South Carolina.

It was a jibe that went to the heart of the matter. Colonial empires were coming to an end in the 1950s and 1960s. If Algeria was a nation, then inevitably it would be set free to govern itself. Only if it were genuinely a part of France could it continue to be ruled from Paris. All depended, therefore, on whether the indigenous population could be convinced by the French government that Algeria was not a separate country or upon whether they could be persuaded by the FLN to change their minds so as to think of themselves as a nation.

The FLN strategy of terrorism addressed itself to this central and decisive issue. By itself, as has been said, terror can accomplish nothing in terms of political goals; it can only aim at obtaining a response that will achieve those goals for it. What the FLN did was to goad the French into reacting in such a way as to demonstrate the unreality of the claim that there was no distinct Algerian nation. Unlike the Irgun, the FLN did not set out to campaign merely against property; it attacked people. It used random violence, planting bombs in marketplaces and in other crowded locations. The instinctive French reaction was to treat all persons of non-European origin as suspects; but, as Raymond Aron was to write, "As suspects, all the Muslims felt excluded from the existing community." Their feeling was confirmed when, in the middle 1950s, the authorities further reacted by transferring the French army units composed of Muslim Algerian troops out of Algeria and into mainland France and replacing them in Algeria by European troops. By such actions they showed in the most unmistakable way that they regarded no Algerians as Frenchmen except for the European settlers. They spoke of we and us, and of they and them, and did not realize that their doing so meant the end of Algérie Française.

Thus the French conceded the issue of the war at its very outset. They threw away the potential support of Muslim Algeria because they were skeptical of the possibility that it could be obtained. From that moment the conclusion of the conflict was foregone. Once the sympathies of the population had shifted to its side, the FLN was able to outgrow mere terrorism and to organize a campaign of guerrilla warfare. It also was enabled to appeal to world sympathies on behalf of a people fighting for its freedom. From the French point of view, all had become hopeless; for no amount of force can keep an unwilling population indefinitely in subjection. Even though the FLN had written the script, the French, with suicidal logic, went ahead to play the role for which they had been cast.

The FLN success was therefore a special case. It required a particular kind of opponent. It could not be duplicated in other circumstances and conditions.

VI

REVOLUTIONIST-TERRORISTS of the last decade have failed to perceive the special characteristics of the colonialist situation that facilitated success for Irish, Irgun, and Algerian terrorists. They have tried to apply the strategy of terrorism in situations that are essentially different. This has been true, for example, of extremist groups seeking to overthrow liberal-pluralistic regimes during the 1960s. Their theory has been that their terrorist attacks would force hitherto liberal regimes to become repressive, a change which in turn would alienate the masses, thus setting the stage for revolution. But it has not worked out that way in practice. In the United States, for example, terrorist bomb attacks have not led to any change at all in the form of government, much less to a transformation of America into a police state. . . .

Other revolutionary groups have taken a somewhat different approach. They have argued that liberal democracies are already police states. Thus, the object of revolutionary terrorist action should be to reveal this hidden reality to the population at large. Unthinking reaction by the authorities to terrorist provocation would accomplish the desired result. Thus the aim of terrorism would be to trick the government into taking off its mask.

In open societies such as Great Britain and the United States, the liberal democratic features have proved to be a face and not a mask: there is nothing to take off, and the strategy failed because its factual premise proved to be untrue.

In closed societies, the strategy has been to show that authoritarian regimes are actually impotent despite their outward show of virility. In such circumstances, supposedly, by demonstrating that the public authorities are powerless to enforce law and order, a campaign of terror can cause a government to collapse; but the flaw in the theory is that the terrorists usually are not strong enough to take its place. Either some more broadly based group will seize power, or else, as in Argentina, private groups will take the law into their own hands and retaliate in kind against murder and extortion, so that society relapses into a semianarchic state of reprisals and blood feuds, where terrorists are buried with their victims.

VII

IT IS AGAINST this background that Arab Palestinian terrorism has seized the attention of the contemporary world. It is aimed at Israel; it is aimed at the Arabs who live within Israel; and it is aimed at the world outside. It is, in other words, a mixed strategy. Each of its mixed aspects has to be considered separately. All that Arab terrorism can accomplish in the land that has been promised to so many is to frighten and to threaten the Arab inhabitants of Israel in order to keep them from cooperating with the Israeli authorities. Israel itself, however, cannot be terrorized into disappearing of its own accord; yet removing Israel from the map has long been the proclaimed goal of the Arab terrorist movement.

Terrorism can be employed more successfully in colonialist situations than in Palestine because a colonial power suffers the disadvantage of fighting the battle away from its own base, and also because a colonial power, having a country of its own to which it can withdraw, is under no compulsion to fight to the bitter end. The Israelis, though termed colonialist by the Arabs, are fighting on home territory, and they have no other country to which they can withdraw; they fight with their backs to the sea. They can be goaded into a self-defeating reaction, but unless they permit that to happen, nothing can be done to their domestic public opinion that is likely to destroy them. The Arab terrorists therefore have turned elsewhere and have attacked the arteries of world transportation in hopes that a world indifferent to the merits of the Arab-Israeli dispute will turn against the Israelis in order to end the annoyance of a disrupted airline service.

In doing so they have strayed across a frontier and into the eerie world of Mr. McLuhan, and they have transformed terrorism into a form of mass communication—but communication aimed at the whole world and not, as in the case of Algeria, mostly at the indigenous population. Theirs is a campaign that needs publicity in order to succeed, and therefore they have come to operate within the ambit of contemporary public relations and communications arts: the world of cinema, camp fashion, and pop art, in which deadlines and prime time are the chief realities and in which shock value is the chief virtue. If audiences throughout the world react with horror, and turn against the political cause in whose name so many innocent people have been harmed and killed, the strategy will have backfired. So far they have not done so and it has not done so.

It is a corruption of the human spirit for which all political sides are responsible. The left-wing journalist Paul Johnson wrote an article some months back arguing that left-wing movements are as much at fault as anybody else for accepting the murder of the innocent as a legitimate means for the pursuit of political ends. He quoted the sixteenth-century humanist Castellio, "who was lucky to escape burning by both Catholics and Protestants, and who pointed out in his tract for toleration, *Whether Heretics Are To Be Persecuted?*, that no certitude of righteousness justifies violence: 'To kill a man is not to defend a doctrine, it is to kill a man'." Appalled at the welcome accorded by the United Nations to the leader of the Arab terrorists, Johnson wrote that, "Step by step, almost imperceptibly, without anyone being aware that a fatal watershed has been crossed, mankind has descended into the age of terror."

VIII

IF THIS IS an age of terror, then it has become all the more important for us to understand exactly what it is that terrorism means. Terrorism, as has been seen, is the weapon of those who are prepared to use violence but who believe that they would lose any contest of sheer strength. All too little understood, the uniqueness of the strategy lies in this: that it achieves its goal not through its acts but through the response to its acts. In any other such strategy, the violence is the beginning and its consequences are the end of it. For terrorism, however, the consequences of the violence are themselves merely a first step and form a stepping-stone toward objectives that are more remote. Whereas military and revolutionary actions aim at a physical result, terrorist actions aim at a psychological result.

But even that psychological result is not the final goal. Terrorism is violence used in order to create fear; but it is aimed at creating fear in order that the fear, in turn, will lead somebody else—not the terrorist—to embark on some quite different program of action that will accomplish whatever it is that the terrorist really desires. Unlike the soldier, the guerrilla fighter, or the revolutionist, the terrorist therefore is always in the paradoxical position of undertaking actions the immediate physical consequences of which are not particularly desired by him. An ordinary murderer will kill somebody because he wants the person to be dead, but a terrorist will shoot somebody even though it is a matter of complete indifference to him whether that person lives or dies. He would do so, for example, in order to provoke a brutal police repression that he believes will lead to political conditions propitious to revolutionary agitation and organization aimed at overthrowing the government. The act of murder is the same in both cases, but its purpose is different, and each act plays a different role in the strategies of violence.

Only an understanding of the purpose for which such an act is undertaken can enable us to know the nature of the act. When Julius Caesar was murdered in the Roman Senate, it was an assassination of the traditional sort, intended to eliminate a specific figure from the political scene; but had he been killed there by the representative of a subversive sect, intent on plunging his dagger into the first Roman leader he encountered in order to provoke a certain political response from the Senate, it would instead have been an act of political terrorism.

It is because an action of the same sort may be undertaken by two different groups with two quite different ends in view that terrorism is so often confused with guerrilla warfare, for terrorists and guerrillas often seem to be doing the same sorts of things. Both of them, for example, often sabotage transportation facilities. When T. E. Lawrence led his classic guerrilla warfare campaign against Turkish rule in Arabia, he systematically dynamited railway tracks and bridges. Lawrence's strategy was later explained by Winston Churchill as follows: "The Turkish armies operating against Egypt depended upon the desert railway. This slender steel track ran through hundreds of miles of blistering desert. If it were permanently cut the Turkish armies must perish." And Lawrence therefore rode on camel-back across the sands to destroy the enemy army by blowing up its transportation facilities. In recent years those who say that they wish to destroy the state of Israel have also blown up transportation facilities in the Arab desert; in this case, jet airplanes belonging to civil aviation companies. Yet if thereby they were to permanently cut the airline networks of TWA or BOAC, they would not cause the Israeli army to perish. Indeed the fate of such civil aviation companies is a matter of indifference to the terrorists. Lawrence the guerrilla leader attacked a railway because he wanted to destroy it, whereas Arab terrorists attack an airline even though they do not want to destroy it.

The distinction is of more than academic importance. The French lost their empire over Algeria when they mistook terrorism for guerrilla warfare. They thought that when the FLN planted a bomb in a public bus, it was in order to blow up the bus, whereas the real FLN purpose in planting the bomb was not to blow up the bus, but to lure authorities into reacting by arresting all the non-Europeans in the area as suspects.

The terrorist is like a magician who tricks you into watching his right hand while his left hand, unnoticed, makes the switch. It is understandable that the French authorities in Algeria became totally obsessed by the need to stamp out criminal attacks, but it was fatal to their policy to do so, for the violent attacks were merely a subsidiary issue. The tiny FLN band of outlaws could have blown up every bus in all of Algeria and never won a convert to their cause of independence. Failing to understand the strategy of terrorism, the French did not see that it was not the FLN's move, but rather the French countermove, that would determine whether the FLN succeeded or failed.

It may be the case that the current Israeli policy of attacking Arab terrorist bases in southern Lebanon is another example of concentrating too much attention on preventing terrorist actions and too little attention on foiling terrorist purposes. The Israeli policy is certainly understandable on many grounds, and valid arguments can be adduced in its support; but the weakening of an essentially benevolent Lebanese government, as well as the further estrangement of world opinion, are results of the Israeli raids into Lebanon that may outweigh the value of using that particular approach to the problem of combating terrorism.

For the Israelis, threatened by enemies outside of their society, the problem is an enormously difficult one. For societies threatened only by enemies from within, it is considerably less so. The very wickedness of terrorism makes it a vulnerable strategy in such a society. Other strategies sometimes kill the innocent by mistake. Terrorism kills the innocent deliberately; for not even the terrorist necessarily believes that the particular person who happens to become his victim deserves to be killed or injured. It is horrifying not merely because of the deed that is done but also because at first the deed seems pointless. If you want to make war on the United States on behalf of Puerto Rican independence, why blow up a historic tavern in New York's financial district? What has Fraunces Tavern got to do with Puerto Rico? Why not attack the alleged forces of occupation in Puerto Rico instead? If you opposed by force and violence the continuation of U.S. aid to South Vietnam, why threaten to destroy the Smithsonian Institution? What had its plant collections and its ichthyological specimens to do with American policy in Southeast Asia? The destruction seems so purposeless that it is a natural reaction to turn on those who perpetrate it in hatred and in anger.

The tragedies that befall great public figures can sometimes seem to have been deserved; but when a man on the street is killed at random on behalf of a cause with which he had nothing to do, it is a different matter and provokes a different reaction. In a homogeneous society, at any rate, it leads to a reaction against the terrorism, and it renders it vulnerable to a campaign that politically isolates it in order to physically destroy it, for the nature of the attacks tends to demonstrate that terrorists are enemies of the people rather than merely of the government. It is for this reason that Che Guevara, as a theoretician and practitioner of guerrilla warfare, warned against the strategy of terrorism, arguing that it hinders "contact with the masses and makes impossible unification for actions that will be necessary at a critical moment."

Even in the international arena, terrorist movements are vulnerable when their actions alienate support. This was tacitly recognized by the Palestine Liberation Organization (PLO) when on January 29, 1975, it announced that henceforth it had decided to treat hijacking of airplanes, ships, or trains as crimes and would impose death penalties on hijackers if their actions led to the loss of life. Whether the PLO will indeed abandon its campaign of terror against international transportation remains to be seen. Yet the declaration of its intention to do so is in itself significant, for it suggests a realization that a point has arrived when a public identification with terrorist activity will harm rather than help. This is because terrorism is so much more evil than other strategies of violence that public opinion sometimes can be rallied against it.

Indeed, in view of its inherent weakness, it is remarkable how many political successes have been scored by the strategy of terrorism in the last few decades. Its success seems to be due in large part to a miscomprehension of the strategy by its opponents. They have neglected the more important of the two levels on which terrorism operates. They have failed to focus on the crucial issue of how the manner in which they, as opponents, respond affects the political goals of the terrorists. Discussion instead has centered on the criminal justice aspects of the question: prevention and punishment.

Much has been written, for example, about the technological defenses that have been developed or could be developed against terrorism in order to prevent it from occurring. This can be a highly useful line of approach, as the successful use of electronic surveillance devices at airports seems to have demonstrated. It may even be advisable to require that any new technologies that are developed from time to time should incorporate some sort of internal defense against attack, much as environmentalists argue that pollution control devices should be incorporated in equipment and its cost charged to the manufacturers. Yet no technology is perfect, and there will always be somebody who will manage to slip by any defenses that can be created.

Prevention of terrorism in nontechnological ways scarcely merits discussion. Perhaps one day the social sciences will teach us how to drain the swamps of misery in which hatred and fanaticism breed, but at the moment that day seems far distant. The hollow formalism of the law offers, if anything, even less help. Ingenious schemes for new international tribunals and procedures have been proposed, and they completely miss the point. The manifest unwillingness of many governments to use existing legal remedies against terrorism shows that the real problem is the lack of a will and not the lack of a way. . . .

The overriding questions are not legal or technological; they are philosophical and political. Terrorism is the indirect strategy that wins or loses only in terms of how you respond to it. The decision as to how accommodating or how uncompromising you should be in your response to it involves questions that fall primarily within the domain of political philosophy.

IX

THOSE WHO are the targets of terrorism—and who are prepared to defend themselves by doing whatever is necessary in order to beat it—start with a major advantage. The advantage is that success or failure depends upon them alone. Terrorism wins only if you respond to it in the way that the terrorists want you to, which means that its fate is in your hands and not in theirs. If you choose not to respond at all, or else to respond in a way different from that which they desire, they will fail to achieve their objectives.

The important point is that the choice is yours. That is the ultimate weakness of terrorism as a strategy. It means that, though terrorism cannot always be prevented, it can always be defeated. You can always refuse to do what they want you to do.

Whether to pay the price of defeating terrorism is increasingly going to be a major question in our time. The answer is relatively easy in most kidnapping and ransom situations: experience has shown that blackmailers and extortionists usually are encouraged to try it again if you give in to their demands the first time. So, if you can do so, you should accept the consequences, however terrible, of standing firm in order to avoid an infinite sequence of painful events.

But the price of doing so is constantly rising, as technology increases the range and magnitude of horrible possibilities. Terrorist outrages, when they occur, are bound to become more deadly. Increasingly, we will be under pressure to abridge our laws and liberties in order to suppress the terrorists. It is a pressure that should be resisted.

In our personal lives we sometimes have to choose between these alternatives: whether to live a good life or whether to live a long life. Political society in the years to come is likely to face a similar choice. An open society such as ours is especially vulnerable to terrorist violence, which seems to threaten us with ever more dreadful and drastic fates. Have we the stoicism to endure nonetheless? Will we be tempted to abandon our political and moral values? Will we be willing to go on paying an ever higher price in order to defeat the terrorists by refusing to respond in the way they want us to?

Of course it would make things easier if terrorism simply would go away. It seems unlikely to do so. The weapons are at hand, and they probably will be used, for terrorism will never cease until the day when the Old Man of the Mountain loses his last disciple. The old man was grand master of the sect called the Assassins (hashish-ins) because of the hashish which he gave them. The old man, according to Marco Polo, used to drug his young disciples and transport them while they were asleep to his secret pleasure garden, persuading them when they awoke in it that it was paradise itself. Drugging them again, he would transport them back to the everyday world while they slept. Never afterward did they doubt that their master could and would reward them with eternal paradise after death if they did his killing for him while they were alive. And so they did do his killing for him.

If anything, the modern world seems to breed more and more votaries of this peculiar sect. They seem to thrive and multiply everywhere in the world, bomb or machine gun in hand, motivated by political fantasies and hallucinations, fully convinced that their slaughter of the innocent will somehow usher in a political millennium for mankind. "*Voici le temps des* ASSASSINS," as Rimbaud wrote in the dawn of the industrial age; and we do indeed live in the time of the assassins.

The End of Pan-Arabism

Fouad Ajami

WINTER 1978/79

POLITICAL IDEAS MAKE their own realities. Often in defiance of logic, they hold men and are in turn held by them, creating a world in their own image, only to play themselves out in the end, shackled by routine problems not foreseen by those who spun the myth, or living past their prime and ceasing to move people sufficiently. Or, political ideas turn to ashes and leave behind them a trail of errors, suffering, and devastation.

An idea that has dominated the political consciousness of modern Arabs is nearing its end, if it is not already a thing of the past. It is the myth of pan-Arabism, of the *Umma Arabiyya Wahida Dhat Risala Khalida,* "the one Arab nation with an immortal mission." At the height of its power, pan-Arabism could make regimes look small and petty: disembodied structures headed by selfish rulers who resisted the sweeping mission of Arabism and were sustained by outside powers that supposedly feared the one idea that could resurrect the classical golden age of the Arabs. As historian Bernard Lewis summed it up little more than a decade ago, allegiance to the state was "tacit, even surreptitious," while Arab unity was "the sole publicly acceptable objective of statesmen and ideologues alike." What this meant was that states were without sufficient legitimacy. Those among them that resisted the claims of pan-Arabism were at a disadvantage—their populations a fair target for pan-Arabist appeals, their leaders to be overthrown and replaced by others more committed to the transcendent goal. Now, however, *raison d'état,* once an alien and illegitimate doctrine, is gaining ground. Slowly and grimly, with a great deal of anguish and of outright violence, a "normal" state system is becoming a fact of life.

No great idea passes from the scene without screams of anguish, protests of true believers, and assertions by serious analysts that the idea still stands—battered, transformed, but standing nonetheless—and debate about the vitality of pan-Arabism continues, for it is still far from accepted that the idea has

been eclipsed. Writing in the July 1978 *Foreign Affairs,* Walid Khalidi reaf-
firmed the vitality of the pan-Arabist idea. He observed that the Arab system
is "first and foremost a 'Pan' system. It postulates the existence of a single
Arab Nation behind the facade of a multiplicity of sovereign states. . . . From
this perspective, the individual Arab states are *deviant* and *transient* entities;
their frontiers illusory; their rulers interim caretakers or obstacles to be removed." Before the "super-legitimacy" of pan-Arabism, the legitimacy of the
Arab states "shrinks into irrelevance." In such a system, "explicit or transpar-
ent *raison d'état* is heresy." What is normal for others is abnormal in the Arab
world. Since Arab states are really deviant entities, which in time will pass
from the scene, they are to be constrained in what they do for statehood.
Nothing less than a pan-Arab superstate will do.

A second view is that of Mohamed Hassanein Heikal, once the propaga-
tor of Nasserist ideology and today one of the bearers of the myths—in President Sadat's pejorative description, one of the high priests of the Nasserist
temple. Heikal, who once made the distinction between Egypt as a state and
Egypt as a revolution, and who defended the right of the "Arab revolution" to
interfere in the internal affairs of Arab countries, now grudgingly concedes
that the state has triumphed over the aspirations of pan-Arabism. He has re-
counted a conversation he had with Secretary of State Kissinger during the
latter's shuttle diplomacy in the Middle East in which he told Mr. Kissinger
that Egypt was not merely a state on the banks of the Nile, but the embodiment of "an idea, a tide, a historical movement." To this Mr. Kissinger is reported to have said that he himself could not deal with latent intangible
forces, or negotiate with an idea.

The Sadat diplomacy—of which Mr. Heikal is a critic—seemed to sustain the Kissingerian view. The idea that Heikal once brandished in the face
of Nasser's rivals has lost its lure and power. Everyone, laments Heikal, rec-
ognizes that "the idea, the tide, the historical movement" is absent and that
the party sitting across the negotiating table is the Egyptian state with its
limited frontiers, resources, and calculable interests.

Heikal has reiterated this view that the Arab system is on the defensive,
that "it has been forced to retreat in disarray," in this journal. Egypt, "for so
long the mainstay of the Arab system," has opted out of it; the opportunity
afforded by the October War of 1973 to put the system on solid foundations
was lost, with the fault presumably in the decision-maker's judgment. Faith
intrudes, however, for Heikal ends on an upbeat note. The Arab system may
suffer a temporary setback, but it could bounce back (presumably when the
Egyptian decision-maker sees the error of his ways), because the Arab world
possesses a vitality that makes "the real constituency of any Arab leader the
Arab world as a whole." Once again, the leader's constituency does not end

with the boundaries of his state: even when the idea is violated, it still possesses sanctity and recuperative power.

The story of pan-Arabism's retreat goes deeper than Sadat's policy. And, to be sure, it has nothing to do with Mr. Kissinger's diplomacy, for whatever the carrots and sticks in his bag, Mr. Kissinger could not remake Arab history or defeat a compelling idea. The willingness of the Egyptian state to be more like other states—to negotiate for itself—had nothing to do with Mr. Kissinger's diplomatic tactics, but was rather the result of changes and transformations within Arab politics itself. Reason of state had already begun to prevail in inter-Arab affairs, and pan-Arabism had lost its hold over the popular imagination several years before Kissinger appeared on the scene with a distinct preference for an "Egyptian solution" and an aversion to dealing with "historical movements."

II

PAN-ARABISM'S retreat began in 1967 after the Six Day War, which marked the Waterloo of pan-Arabism. In the immediate aftermath of the war there was no competing system of legitimacy—in fact, very little if any legitimacy remained in Arab politics as a whole. The regimes had survived, but the defeat had dishonored practically all of them and had devastated, in particular, the pan-Arabists in Cairo and Damascus. No regime could have gone its separate way then. The "radical" regime in Cairo would capitulate to the will of the oil states led by Saudi Arabia, but the oil states would not press their victory too far or too hard. The military defeat was sustained directly by the armies of Egypt, Syria, and Jordan—for all practical purposes and in terms of inter-Arab politics, by Egypt—but the defeat had underlined the vulnerability of the Arab system of states, the bankruptcy of the Arab order and its guardians, whether radical or conservative. The champions of pan-Arabism were defeated in the Arab system; the idea had lost its magic. Yet particular states were still captives of a status quo erected by the defeat, which they could neither undo nor indefinitely live with.

Opportunity to break out of that situation and to assert reason of state would arise with the October War. The irony is that the war which Mr. Heikal and others looked at as an opportunity to revive the Arab system was precisely the event that would enable reason of state to challenge the then feeble but still venerated pretensions of pan-Arabism. The logic that triumphed in October 1973 was not the pan-Arabist one held up by Nasser and the Baath, it was the more limited notion of solidarity preferred by those states that had long opposed pan-Arabism. What President Sadat was to do subsequently was read the results of October 1973—more accurately perhaps,

to use the results—and to stake out a large territory of independent prerogative for Egypt and himself. What might have been an Egyptian temptation
between 1967 and 1973, particularly under President Sadat in the second half
of that period, could be done in the aftermath of the October War because it
was only after that war that the man at the helm of the Egyptian state was in
command. The "honor" of the state had been redeemed. Egypt's sacrifices
and what Mr. Sadat called "the size of the victory" on the Egyptian-Israeli
front—presumably larger than it was on the Syrian-Israeli front, as it had
been nonexistent on the Jordanian and Palestinian front—would be used to
legitimate break with the Arab system.

Times had changed; so had the leader in charge. Whatever his frustrations with the Arab system—and they were plentiful—Nasser was too much
a captive of that system to break with it in the same manner and to the same
degree as Sadat. Given his personal makeup, his history, the constituency he
had acquired, and the images he had manipulated, the best Nasser could do
was moderate his policies and set the stage for someone less tied to the policies of the past. Even in defeat Nasser was still a pan-Arab hero: his victories
lay in the Arab system, for after 1967 there was very little left in Egypt to
point to with much pride. . . .

Anwar Sadat had never excited a pan-Arab audience and had never been
a hero. But if he lacked the hero's stature, he also lacked the hero's reputation
and was free of the chains that tie heroes to their great deeds. If anything, Sadat would find it a bit gratifying—and this is only human—to slay the myth
of his predecessor, a man he had once known as an equal and who had managed to rise above Sadat and other colleagues to heroic proportions in no
small part through the love and devotion of people in distant Arab capitals.
Sadat could hope to compete with his predecessor in Egypt proper, but in the
Arab world his predecessor was larger than life. Perhaps in Sadat's "Egyp-
tianness" there is a desire of sorts to move from Nasser's shadow into a
smaller arena where his predecessor is more subject to errors and to a normal,
more tangible audit.

With the pan-Arab hero out of the way, the conservative Arab states
would find it easier to deal with his successor, a less ambitious man, more accepting of boundaries and ideological differences. That is why Sadat could
enlist those states in a joint endeavor like the October War, a feat which
Nasser might never have been able to accomplish. That Sadat would eventually go further down the road of autonomy than the limits preferred by the oil
states is one of the supreme ironies of recent Arab politics. Where the oil
states once feared Egypt's meddlesome politics, they lived to experience the
fear of her disengagement from pan-Arab responsibilities. The threat that
once emanated from her radicalism and pan-Arabism receded; a new threat

came from her separate and independent nationalism. Of all the Arab states, Egypt is the largest, the most politically stable, the most legitimate within her boundaries. This enabled Egypt to give pan-Arabism concrete power, and then, when she tired of it, to turn inward. The oil states had wanted from Egypt an abandonment of the pan-Arabist ideology and acceptance of the logic of the state system, and they got that. What Sadat's diplomacy was to show was that states—or, more precisely and aptly, the leaders of states— could read their interests differently and independently.

III

SADAT'S DIPLOMACY was the most dramatic illustration of the weakness of pan-Arabism and objectively the most important, if only because Egypt had been, as Mr. Heikal rightly states, "the mainstay of the Arab system." But throughout the preceding decade there had been other "revolts," other "separatist" attacks against the monolithic pan-Arab doctrine. It is only within the context of those other attacks that the Sadat diplomacy can be correctly situated in Arab politics.

The Palestinians launched the first post-1967 attack against pan-Arabism. Given their predicament, their economic and political dependence upon the Arab states and their lack of a territorial base, theirs had to be a different kind of attack. But there was no doubt that those who rallied around Yasir Arafat and George Habash in the aftermath of the Six Day War had given up on pan-Arabism—the first group in the name of Palestinian nationalism, the second in the name of social revolution. The duel that raged between the Palestinians and the Nasserites from early 1968 until Nasser's death in 1970 was in essence a fight about the independent rights of Palestinian nationalism. If the Arab states could not protect themselves against Israel, let alone do something for the Palestinians, then the latter were to construct their own independent politics. In the final analysis, it was Arafat's brand of nationalism, with its pledge of nonintervention in the internal affairs of Arab countries, that found its way into the organized Arab state system, rather than George Habash's revolution. Arafat's narrow focus on Palestinian nationalism and his avoidance of social and ideological issues were in keeping with the new tenor of Arab politics, and that is why Arafat's course found a reasonable measure of support in Riyadh: in his strict Palestinian nationalism, there was an acceptance of reason of state. That acceptance was not applicable to the two "sanctuaries," Jordan and Lebanon, hence the two civil wars in which the Palestinians came to be involved.

Another crack in the pan-Arab edifice was the virtual end of the Baath Party, the pan-Arab party that took seriously its mission of bringing about the one Arab nation. A shell called the Baath remains, and it claims power in both Iraq and Syria, home to the Baath in the post-World War II years, but President Hafez al-Assad is cut of different cloth. A cautious member of a minority sect, he harbors no illusions about Arab unity and is probably the first leader in modern Syrian history to make peace with Syria's national situation and to accept the limitations of geography and resources. Since his rise to power in 1970, he has managed to rid Syria of a great deal of its romanticism and extremism and to move it to the center of Arab politics. . . .

The threat of a partitioned Lebanon is yet another serious challenge to pan-Arabism in a decade of setbacks. This challenge comes from an area that never accepted the idea of Arabism but made a peculiar kind of peace with it, namely, Christian Lebanon. As long as the Arabists accepted Lebanon's unique identity and situation, Lebanon could find its role and place in the "Arab family" as a link between the Arabs and the West: as a place for those who played and lost in the game of politics and needed a place to write their memoirs or plot their return to power; as a playground for Saudis and Kuwaitis who wished to escape the climate and puritanism of their own countries; as a banking haven for Syrians who wanted to flee from the politics and intrigues of the military and the economic irresponsibility of would-be socialists. Lebanon, so it was believed, could have it both ways: live off the Arab world yet think of itself as a piece of the Occident. Arabism was far away; one could pay homage to it and go about the business of trading, publishing, smuggling, banking.

This worked as long as the Arab-Israeli conflict was removed from Lebanon's soil—a situation that changed after 1970, when the Palestinians, expelled from Jordan, made their political home in Lebanon. Then the glib, superficial Arabism of Lebanon met a test it was destined to fail. The leaders in the Christian community who had known the Arab system and made their peace with it lost to those for whom Arabism and Islam were synonymous and who believed in their own cultural supremacy and the backwardness of the Arabs. Convinced that they were being abandoned by the West (they too had heard of the "decline of the West"), resentful of the post-October 1973 wealth and prominence of the Muslim Arab states, losing control over a country that had gotten too "Palestinianized" and radicalized for their taste, aware that the demographic facts were shattering the myth of Christian majority, the Maronites would do what would have been unthinkable yesterday: after a brief reliance on a Syrian connection, they opted for a break with the Arab system—an alliance with Israel and a full commitment to partition.

Through it all, the advocates of partition would be helped by the obvious culpability of the Arab states, which had exported the "sacred Arab cause"— the Palestinian issue—onto Lebanese soil. In other words, the least Arab of countries, as well as the weakest militarily, was to bear the brunt of full Israeli retaliation and to accept a parallel and competing system of authority. Sincere or not, the Palestinian slogan of nonintervention in the internal affairs of Arab countries was harder to practice than to preach. With Israel more than willing and able to retaliate for raids into her territory, the Lebanese formula would unravel. The gift of an enlarged Lebanon bequeathed by the French turned into a nightmare, and the Maronite militias took up arms, first to defeat the leftist Palestinian/Muslim alliance and then, a little later, to try to carve out their own state, bidding farewell to the pleasantries of "Arab brotherhood." They were now willing to state what had been their conviction for quite some time: that they think of themselves as a different breed; that they are apart from the Arab world, not geographically but culturally of a different world. The Syrian army may win a confrontation or two, but what must be honestly and candidly dealt with is a bid for partition and creation of a sovereign Maronite state. If anything, Syrian assaults steel the will of the militias and silence those in the Christian community who still believe that things could be managed with a slightly reformed version of the old status quo.

IV

. . . A SOCIAL scientist at Kuwait University has supplied us with important evidence substantiating the demise of pan-Arabism and suggesting the shape of things to come. Taking a sample of students from practically all Arab countries, he administered a questionnaire to nearly 500 undergraduates at Kuwait University with the aim of ascertaining their views on pan-Arabism, family, state, and religion. What he found was a remarkable assertion of Islamic sentiment and of patriotism associated with particular Arab states—in other words, the vacuum left behind as a result of the demise of pan-Arabism is being filled by religious belief on one level and by loyalty to the state on another. His data led him to conclude that the discussions of "one Arab nation" and "Arab brotherhood" are myths and exhausted slogans.

This shift in belief corresponds to concrete changes in the distribution of power in the Arab system. Power has shifted to the state (Saudi Arabia) that has long been a foe of pan-Arabism and has traditionally seen itself as a guardian of the *turath*, the heritage, or Islam, to be more precise. Muslim universalism is a safer doctrine than the geographically more limited but politically more troublesome idea of pan-Arabism; the "48 Muslim countries and 700 million Muslims" is a safe and distant symbol, giving a semblance of "super-legitimacy" without posing a threat to reason of state. Summit conferences like the one held in Lahore in 1974 and institutions like the Islamic Economic Conference appeal to those who wish to speak of the resurrection of Islam without shackling the power of the state. No one wants to unite Saudi Arabia and Bangladesh, Indonesia and the United Arab Emirates. The only challenge that Islamic sentiment might pose would come from far below the world of state elites, where a militant, popular kind of Islam may reject— as it does in Iran, and to a lesser extent in Egypt—the world view and preferences of state elites. But that, at least in the Arab context, is a different problem from the disruptive doctrine of pan-Arabism, for it is a challenge contained within the boundaries of the state.

V

THE BOUNDARIES of Arab states have been around now for nearly six decades. It is not their existence which is novel, but their power and legitimacy—the power (as much as that power exists in the modern state system) to keep pan-Arab claims at bay and effectively to claim the loyalty of those within. They are no longer as "illusory and permeable" as they used to be. The states that lie within them are less "shy" about asserting their rights, more normal in the claims that they make.

The Arabs who had once seemed whole—both to themselves and to others—suddenly look as diverse as they had been all along. The differences, smothered over by ideology and by a universalistic designation, can in no way be ignored or suppressed. Indeed, the more they are blanketed over by a thin veneer of superficial universalism, the more dangerous they become, if only because they create resentment on the part of those who do not feel the designation and who judge that Arabism places them at a disadvantage—that is, it used to ask some of them to fight and die while others did not, or to use their territory as sanctuary for guerrilla raids while others were safely insulated by cease-fire lines and U.N. troops, or to pay for the economic inefficiency and large populations of sister states.

The Arab system of states will have to search for a new equilibrium, for a more limited and perhaps more workable system, because concrete and irreversible changes have already taken place to make interstate boundaries harder and more legitimate. Six factors that enabled pan-Arabism to slight boundaries and to play havoc with sovereignty are either things of the past or are undergoing fundamental metamorphosis:

1. The universalism of pan-Arabism derived to a considerable extent from the universalism of the Ottoman Empire, of which the Arab states had been a part for four centuries. In other words, scholars, officials, and officers slipped from one universalist system into another. It was an understandable response to the nationalism of the Young Turks: if the Turks

were a nation, so too were the Arabs. But whatever unity was lent to the Arab society by the universalism of the Ottoman system now belongs to the past. The Ottoman experience has been committed to history, and six decades after its collapse it is becoming a fading memory.

2. Arab nationalism rested on the power and popularity of the pamphlet and the book; it was conceived and spread by intellectuals, mostly those in exile. From Europe, where publicists like Neguib Azoury, Shakib Arslan, and later Michel Aflaq of the Baath Party conceived their ideas, the distinctions among Arabs seemed negligible, almost nonexistent. It was theory written from afar by theorists concerned with and consumed by large-scale distinctions between rival and whole civilizations.

Now the power of intellectuals is waning, with a definite backlash in the Arab world against the written word and intellectuals. The beneficiaries are either men of affairs schooled in the hard knocks of politics—a Hafez Assad rather than Michel Aflaq—or development-oriented elites. In contrast to the literary intellectuals who dominated the early stage of Arab nationalism, the new elite is a more sober, less grandiose group—less likely to emphasize the abstractions of Arab unity, more sensitive to the realities on the ground or more committed to specific tasks. A nationalism that fails to create a political order cannot withstand the dissolution of its creed, and the intellectuals were temperamentally unfit to create such a concrete order. It is one thing to polemicize about the "one nation" and its metaphysical base, but quite another to erect it on the ground.

3. The anticolonialism of the mandate years lent a great deal of unity to the Arab system, as an entire generation was traumatized by what they saw as the Arabs' betrayal by the West. The Balfour Declaration and the Sykes/Picot agreement made their imprint on a large number of Arab nationalists, wherever they were, and forged a strong bond of unity among officials, publicists, and officers who thought in terms of the Arab and the West.

However, what we observed of the Ottoman Empire pretty much applies as well to the anti-Westernism of the mandate years. Britain and France, the two powers whose deeds and diplomacy haunted and traumatized a generation of nationalists, have been cut down to size; they made their last stand in the Suez affair, and since then their diplomacy has, on the whole, been sympathetic to the Arab states. London is no longer a hostile capital where diplomatic schemes are hatched against the Arabs; in fact, it has become familiar and accessible, with whole sections that have been "Arabized." The British, once resented and admired masters, now covet Arab investments and worry about the penetration of their society by Arab capital. France has become synonymous with Charles de Gaulle: an admired symbol of nationalism and, from 1962 onward, a "friend" of the Arab states. Beyond this, there has been a subtle and steady "growing up," a realization by Arabs that they have no monopoly on trauma, so to speak, that they are not the only ones whose ambitions have been thwarted and to whom history has dealt a raw deal or two. Worldly success in the aftermath of October 1973 is to a great extent responsible for this shift.

4. There was a mobile, trans-state elite that moved from one Arab state to another; they knew and understood one another, and their horizons transcended the boundaries of a single state. They "believed implicitly in the existence of an Arab nation: in schools, in barracks, in the Ottoman parliament, in exile in Cairo, and in the Sharifian forces they had come to know each other and acquired the ease of discourse which possession of a common language and a common education gives." Some of these men formed the nucleus of the group that rallied around the Hashemite Prince Faisal as he came out of the Arabian Peninsula to be crowned in Syria and later (having been driven out of Damascus by the French) to rule over Iraq.

That mobile structure of dynasts, officers, officials, and scholars has by now been replaced by more "parochial" elites as the usual complex of bureaucratic interests has developed in each of the Arab states. The change may be best captured by comparing the leading Arab dynasty in the early and middle parts of this century to the leading dynasty today. The Hashemites thought of the Arab world as their domain. They ruled in the peninsula and, with the help of the British, established monarchies in Damascus (Prince Faisal's short-lived Arab kingdom), Transjordan, and Iraq. Of all that, a modest throne remains in Jordan where a skilled but hemmed-in monarch tries his best to survive and to reconcile conflicting claims and pressures. Today's leading royal house, the Saudi family, is committed to its own sovereignty in the blessed (materially and spiritually) piece of land it has. The victory of the more "local" Ibn Saud over the "pan-Arab" Sharif Hussein half a century ago may have been the first victory (albeit of a dynastic/tribal kind) for reasons of state over the more grandiose ambitions of pan-Arabism. Below the dynastic level, the same shift in favor of parochial elites is equally evident in the usual occupations that states generate. To be sure, technocrats, teachers, and skilled workers migrate in large numbers from the populated Arab states to the richer oil states, but these are people who migrate for a living and are content to leave power to the host governments.

5. The Palestine defeat in 1948 was seen as an injury to the pride and integrity of the entire Arab world—not strictly as a Palestinian defeat, but as a pan-Arab one. The creation of Israel was a deeply wounding and traumatizing experience, a symbol of Arab weakness and backwardness, a reminder that whatever the Arabs were in the past, whatever their old glories and achievements, they were now in decline, at the mercy of others, no longer sovereign in their own region. Having vowed to undo the "shame" of the defeat, it became difficult for any state to take itself out of the conflict.

The unity forced onto the Arab world by the Arab-Israeli conflict has eroded—perhaps less dramatically than in other areas, but eroded nonetheless. Whatever the future shape of the conflict between the Arab states and Israel, the Sadat diplomacy has dragged the Arabs—with great numbers of them shouting, objecting, feeling violated and betrayed—into the modern game of states. The conflict is no longer about Israel's existence, but about its boundaries; and in inter-Arab affairs, the leading military state has for all appearances rejected the inter-Arab division of labor that assigned it the principal obligation for a pan-Arab cause.

6. Finally, from 1956 (after Suez) until Nasser's death in 1970, or until the 1967 defeat, the power of pan-Arabism derived from the power of charismatic leadership. Prior to the emergence of Nasser as a pan-Arab savior, the idea had been an elite endeavor of publicists, intellectuals, and a few officers. Nasser would take the theories and the emotions to the masses, give pan-Arabism its moment in the sun, and then its tragic end in 1967.

The politics of charisma, however, have passed from the scene. T. E. Lawrence once expressed a stereotype about the Arabs that has managed to stick: "Arabs," he said, "could be swung on an idea as on a cord. . . . Without a creed they could be taken to the four corners of the world (but not to heaven) by being shown the riches of the earth and the pleasures of it, but if on the road, led in this fashion, they met the prophet of an idea, who had nowhere to lay his head and who depended for his food on charity and birds, then they would all leave their wealth for his inspiration." Today the idea and the prophet are gone: the man who could in a speech excite youth in West Beirut, Amman, and Baghdad against their governments is no longer there, and this has contributed to the normalization of the Arab state system.

The circumstances that produced the ebb of Nasserist charisma may be *sui generis,* but the end of Nasserism is a piece of a bigger puzzle. It is the end of that stage of Third World history represented by men like Nasser, Nehru,

Sukarno, Nkrumah—dreamers who sought what one of them, Nkrumah, described as the "kingdom of politics." In that kingdom they sought answers to questions of identity and self-worth, dabbled in dreams and intangibles, but their politics were bound to come to an end, for the sort of nationalist fervor they embodied triumphs for a moment but cannot last forever.

The exhaustion of the nationalist fervor generally signals a coming to the fore of economic issues and demands, of problems that do not lend themselves to solo performances, to the magic touch of charisma. Less colorful leaders, whose links to the nationalist struggle are often tenuous, are the ones who have to satisfy the new needs. With defeat in 1967, charisma turned to ashes, and the conservative oil states made their financial help contingent upon a new style and kind of politics. The romantic phase of nationalism is over, then, as it falls upon the second generation to accomplish the technical and often grim tasks of governance. Anwar al-Sadat's recent autobiography, *In Search of Identity*, is really the last of its kind. The next time an Egyptian head of state writes an autobiography, I suspect that identity will not be the principal thread; he may have to name it "In Search of Productivity" or something similarly routine. Whoever he turns out to be, he may well be envious that one of his predecessors "philosophized" about revolution, while the other talked of identity.

VI

WHETHER THE Arabs like it or not, what they are left with and what they increasingly must acknowledge is a profound fragmentation of the Arab existential and political crisis. We know the themes and memories that lent unity to their consciousness and history: one language, the classical golden age of Islam, the decline of the Muslim order, the universalism of the Ottoman Empire, the yearning for independence, the traumas of being initiated into an international system in which they were not full participants, the Palestine defeat, the Six Day War, and finally October 1973. Particular regimes and leaders aside, Arab states are stuck with one another, and the shared themes and concerns could conceivably provide a basis for a working regional order—or, if pushed too far, for disaster and continuous discord.

The shared themes and concerns must not obscure the fragmentation. There is no longer a collective Arab crisis, and there is no use pretending that it exists. To illustrate, let me briefly sketch the separate and quite different dilemmas of several populations in the Arab world.

In Egypt, the serious life-and-death issue is economic, and the main struggle is for human worth and dignity in a crowded, economically pressed society. For a young educated Saudi, Kuwaiti, or Libyan, the sky is the limit:

huge projects to run, European vacations, investments, offers from foreign businessmen and people with all kinds of schemes, dreams, and gadgets. For a young and equally skilled and educated Egyptian, the overwhelming reality he has to deal with is unemployment or a dead-end job in a sluggish bureaucracy and the impossible dream of making ends meet, the nightmare of finding and affording an apartment in Cairo, where rentals have gone sky-high thanks in part to the abundance of petrodollars. Is there a mystery to the frustration of the young Egyptian, his suspicion that he must go to Sinai and face Israeli arms while others talk of pan-Arabism in London and Paris? Is this not the reality that President Sadat so masterfully evoked when he spoke of "nightclub revolutionaries"? The wealthy Arab states have been somewhat helpful to Egypt, but Egypt's economic needs are staggering, and it is these needs and grievances that enabled the Egyptian president to do what he did on the foreign policy front.

Whether Sadat's diplomacy stands or falls, it will do so on its own merit, judged in terms of what it will or will not do for Egypt; charges of treason, or tribunals against Sadat by Iraq or Libya, will be to no avail. But foreign policy can be a ruler's escape, and victories and virtuoso performances are easier to pull off in distant places than at home. The noted Egyptian analyst Lewis Awad has recently argued that much of what Nasser did in foreign policy was sheer escapism. The same temptation may again present itself, this time by irrelevant talk about threats in the Horn of Africa, challenging the Soviet Union, and the like. For Egypt, the real threat is at home: a huge population that must be fed and educated; a decaying capital; an overcrowded society that must seek an economic role in the surrounding region and must therefore avoid too sharp a break with its neighbors.

The Fertile Crescent offers a striking contrast to the Egyptian case. There, the crisis is political; it is a crisis of political legitimacy, of taming political passions, of finding a framework that satisfies the aspirations for self-determination. Lebanon and the Palestinian question are the two outstanding political problems, and barring some unforeseen solutions to both, that area is destined to suffer more of the bloodshed and violence that have become its lot.

Without a territorial base of their own, the Palestinians would still have it within their power to disrupt the Arab system of states. This power derives not only from their presence in Lebanon and Jordan and their influence in Kuwait, but also from their appeal to an overwhelming body of opinion throughout the Arab world that wants what it thinks an appropriate resolution to the Palestinian question: self-determination for the Palestinians. Both historical-emotional factors and the cold logic of reason of state overlap here, for it is believed that the best way of taming Palestinian radicalism is to contain the Palestinians within their own state, either autonomous or linked to

Jordan, and that only then will the Arab system of states be effectively normalized.

The Palestinians, too, have come to see it this way. Whereas it was once heresy to speak of an independent Palestinian state—after all, Palestine was supposed to be part of a larger Arab entity—the Palestinians have come to realize that they too require the normalcy of statehood. Their view has come to converge with the recognition of most Arab states that their own reason of state vis-à-vis Palestinian claims is best served by the Palestinians acquiring their own territory with all the responsibilities such a process usually entails. This explains President Sadat's insistence during the Camp David negotiations on a linkage between an Egyptian settlement and a framework for the West Bank and Gaza Strip, and it explains as well Saudi Arabia's cautious response to the summit. . . .

In the oil states, there are the problems of managing great wealth and then of setting that wealth and what it builds next to the violence and instability of the Fertile Crescent and the poverty of Egypt. Saudi Arabia, the leading oil state, understands what John C. Campbell calls the "political fragility" that lies beneath its prosperity. Having helped exorcise the area of Nasserism, the Saudis were willing to deploy the oil weapon in the October War, to subsidize the two Arab combatants, and when the war was over, to try to keep them together. Their distinct preference is for a "moderate" Arab system of states based on a reasonable measure of consensus. . . .

Above and beyond particular foreign policy decisions, the oil states will continue to experience the difficulties of living in a militarized, impoverished part of the world, as well as the dreams and possibilities spawned by great wealth. They can help their neighbors and try to buy a reasonable measure of stability, but they cannot remake or keep the entire region afloat, tame all its passions, deal with all its grievances. They can influence other Arab states but cannot dictate their policies because they have difficulty "converting" the medium of power they have—money—into other assets. This was most poignantly demonstrated by President Sadat's margin for maneuverability in his dealings with Saudi Arabia. "Petro-power" has more sway in Arab life than it did a decade or two ago, but it is a vulnerable kind of power; with the logic of numbers and demography so heavily stacked against it, it needs allies, protection, and a great deal of subtlety and caution.

For quite some time—if only because of pan-Arabism's noise and refusal to play by the rules of the game of states—a view prevailed in the West and among some of the Arabs that if pan-Arabism were to subside, all would be well. States would be left to undertake what states undertake within their boundaries; the conflict with Israel would be resolved, or at least transformed and made more like other conflicts, less lethal, less resistant to resolution.

There is a great deal of merit to that view, but the politics of states can also kill, can dislocate, destabilize, and erupt into turmoil and violence. With economic development approximating a new *raison d'état,* states can lose their legitimacy because they fail to deliver the goods—not intangibles such as identity, but tangibles such as jobs, education, and food.

In a world of states we cannot be sanguine about saying that a state system has been normalized. The state next door may move in, not in the name of something lofty and metaphysical like pan-Arabism, but, again, for something more tangible—to preempt the dangers of an unstable state next door (Syria and Lebanon) or to avert the troubles of an erratic leader and to annex a wealthy neighbor at the same time (Egypt and Libya). Counter-elites and young officers may rebel, not in the name of pan-Arabism, but because they have a better cure for the ailment of the state. And in a situation of that kind, "betrayal" of obligations to other states could be a convenient justification for a political game that remains dangerous and deadly.

There are plenty of things to work out and fight over in the Arab system of states: the "responsibility" of the rich states; the "rights" of the poor states; the usual struggle for primacy and advantage among the resourceful and skilled states; the quest for self-determination on the part of the Palestinians; the restoration of civil order and legitimacy in Lebanon; the struggle of the most economically pressed, yet preeminent Arab state for economic solvency and viability. The passing of pan-Arabism means just that: the end of one set of troubles. Normalization of the Arab system, on the whole positive and overdue, brings in its train its own troubles, inflicts its own wounds, commits its own errors.

A Monetary System
for the Future

Richard N. Cooper

WINTER 1984

IN THIS FORTIETH anniversary year of the international monetary conference at Bretton Woods, New Hampshire, there have been numerous but vague calls for a new Bretton Woods conference to improve our international monetary system, which, if not actually ailing, at least leaves many participants uneasy and discomfited. Much of the discomfort relates to the large and burdensome external debt that has accumulated around the world, but much also goes beyond debt to the underlying monetary arrangements among countries.

Are international monetary arrangements stable? Are they likely to survive over a considerable period of time, such as a couple of decades? My answer is negative. Dissatisfaction with the very short-run and year-to-year movements in real exchange rates, combined with technological developments which will lead to further integration of the world economy, will sooner or later force a change of existing arrangements. Unless that alteration is carefully managed, it will take the form of defensive, insulating measures involving restrictions on international transactions, both trade and finance. That would be politically divisive and economically costly.

A new Bretton Woods conference is wholly premature. But it is not premature to begin thinking about how we would like international monetary arrangements to evolve in the remainder of this century. With this in mind, I suggest a radical alternative scheme for the next century: *the creation of a common currency for all of the industrial democracies, with a common monetary policy and a joint Bank of Issue to determine that monetary policy.* Individual countries would be free to determine their fiscal policy actions, but those would be constrained by the need to borrow in the international capital market. Free trade is a natural but not entirely necessary complement to these macroeconomic arrangements.

[365]

This suggestion, outlined in the following pages, is far too radical for the near future. It could, however, provide a "vision" or goal that can guide interim steps in improving international monetary arrangements and by which we can judge the evolution of national economic policy. . . .

II

BRETTON WOODS. The system that emerged from the Bretton Woods Conference 40 years ago had five key structural features:

First, it consciously provided a great deal of freedom for national economic policy to pursue national economic objectives, with the objective of assuring full employment, price stability, economic growth, and so forth. The Bretton Woods agreement was produced in the same climate of opinion which resulted in the White Paper on Employment Policy in the United Kingdom, the Employment Act of 1946 in the United States, and comparable legislation or statements of national policy in other countries, deriving directly from the experience of the 1930s and from a determination that that experience should never be repeated.

Second, the Bretton Woods system stipulated that exchange rates between currencies should be fixed. It was taken for granted that fixed exchange rates were desirable against the turbulent background of flexible exchange rates that prevailed in the early 1920s and again briefly in the early 1930s.

Third, currencies should be convertible one into another for international trade in goods and services, including travel. Again, that stipulation was against the background of extensive use of exchange controls by Nazi Germany during the 1930s and the tight wartime restrictions on trade and payments levied by many countries, which the Bretton Woods architects considered desirable to end as quickly as possible.

These three features taken together—autonomy of national policies, fixed exchange rates, and convertibility of currencies—were in conflict with one another. Countries could not frame their national economic policies independently and still maintain fixed exchange rates and currency convertibility except by luck and coincidence. That potential conflict was recognized by the Bretton Woods architects, who therefore added two further features.

Fourth, provision was made for medium-term international lending to cover balance-of-payments deficits that might result temporarily from the combination of the first three features. A new institution, the International Monetary Fund (IMF), was created as a channel for this new lending.

Fifth, countries were allowed, and in time came to be encouraged, to alter their exchange rates if it became clear that imbalances in payments were not temporary in nature. In other words, if a "fundamental disequilibrium" emerged, the exchange rate was to be changed by a discrete amount, with international agreement, in recognition that such imbalances would be inappropriate to finance indefinitely.

These then were the basic features of the Bretton Woods system. Interestingly, there was no provision in the system for secular growth in international reserves beyond a somewhat ambiguous provision permitting what was called a "uniform change in par values": that is to say, a deliberate rise in the price of gold. It was implicitly assumed that new gold production taken into monetary reserves would be sufficient to provide for adequate growth. In the event, the U.S. dollar came to provide for the needed liquidity, as well as emerging as the currency of intervention in a regime in which some operating medium was necessary to assure that exchange rates remained fixed. . . .

As it emerged—though not as it was designed—the Bretton Woods system might be said to have involved a bargain between the United States and the rest of the world: the United States would maintain domestic economic stability, and other countries would fix their currencies to the dollar and would accumulate their reserves in gold-convertible dollars. After a relatively brief period of postwar redistribution of the world's monetary gold stock, they would not actually convert their dollars into gold. Under this bargain, other countries would import economic stability from the United States. If a country got out of line with the world norm, it would have to change the par value of its currency. In turn, the United States did not have to be as concerned as other countries about how it financed a balance-of-payments deficit. Indeed, the very notion of a balance-of-payments deficit was an ambiguous one for the United States under these circumstances, although that did not keep the Commerce Department from publishing figures which it called the "deficit" for many years.

A second characteristic of this arrangement was that the dollar was overvalued relative to what it would have been without steady accretion of dollars in the reserves of other countries. That feature permitted some export-led growth by the rest of the world that would not have taken place under different monetary arrangements, under which American products would have been somewhat more competitive in world markets.

In this view of the world, the United States broke its part of the bargain in the late 1960s by inflating too much in connection with the Vietnam War and the Great Society programs. Some Europeans thought that the United States was inflating too much even in the early 1960s. On this point, they would not have found much agreement from Americans. Indeed, disagreement over U.S. policy in the early 1960s indicated one of the weaknesses of the supposed bargain, namely dispute around the world over what exactly represented economically stabilizing behavior by the United States.

The structure of the Bretton Woods system had two intrinsic flaws in it, so that it would have broken down sooner or later even without the burst of U.S. inflation in the late 1960s. First, the gold convertibility of the dollar was bound to become increasingly doubtful as dollar liabilities rose over time relative to the U.S. gold stock. To halt the accumulation of foreign-held dollar reserves would have stifled growth of the world economy. Yet to allow the accumulation to continue would have gradually undermined the foundation of the system. Professor Robert Triffin of Yale University pointed out this dilemma as early as 1959. A new international reserve asset, IMF-issued Special Drawing Rights—aptly described as paper gold at the time—was finally created in the late 1960s as a long-run substitute for the dollar, thus offering a solution to the dilemma. But the solution came too late. This part of the system broke down in 1971, when President Nixon indefinitely suspended gold convertibility of the dollar. Two points are worth noting in passing. The first is that the U.S. dollar was the only currency that was convertible into gold, even though the Bretton Woods agreement was formally symmetrical with regard to all currencies. The second is that countries continued to accumulate dollars in their international reserves even after gold convertibility of the dollar was suspended.

The second flaw in the Bretton Woods system was its reliance on discrete changes in exchange rates to correct imbalances in payments. Once a disequilibrium persisted long enough to be "fundamental" rather than temporary in nature, it was clear to everyone, and the system thus produced the celebrated one-way option for currency speculation. Since the remedy to a fundamental disequilibrium was a jump in the value of the currency, speculators could move into or out of the currency at relatively low cost when they thought the jump would occur and take their gains after it occurred. It is interesting to note that the Bretton Woods architects had appreciated this problem, at least in principle, and to remedy it had stipulated that currencies should be convertible for current account transactions, but not for capital account transactions. The possibility was envisioned that countries might maintain controls on capital flows, and indeed countries were even enjoined to help other countries maintain and enforce their capital controls. So capital controls were in principle allowed under the Bretton Woods system, and indeed in a certain sense they were required by the internal logic of the system.

This feature of the system did not anticipate the enormous changes both in the nature of trade and in international capital movements that would take place over time. With improved and cheaper communications, it became easy to move capital through telegraphic transfers around the world at relatively low cost. In addition, many firms, especially American firms, began to invest heavily abroad in the 1950s and 1960s, so that many intracorporate transactions became international in nature. Finally, international trade gradually evolved away from traditional commodity trade toward special order and long-lead-time manufactures in which payments for trade and credit terms become inextricably mixed. For all of these reasons, it became increasingly difficult to separate capital from current account transactions and to maintain control on capital transactions.

The movement of funds that was associated with anticipated discrete changes in exchange rates became quite enormous and greatly complicated the management of domestic economic policies. In many countries, they threatened the autonomy of domestic national policy, which was to have been preserved by the Bretton Woods system. For example, Germany in 1969 experienced a 25 percent increase in its money supply in a single week due to the inflow of speculative funds across the foreign exchanges and to the requirement that Germany maintain a fixed exchange rate for the mark in terms of other currencies.

In truth, the free movement of capital is incompatible with a system of exchange rates that are occasionally changed by consequential amounts and in a predictable direction. This part of the Bretton Woods system broke down definitively in 1973, although the breakdown started in 1970 when Canada allowed its currency to float.

The U.S. inflation of the late 1960s resulted in large dollar outflows in the early 1970s that strained the Bretton Woods system to the breaking point. But it should be clear by now that this was only the proximate cause of the breakdown of the Bretton Woods system. The intrinsic flaws in the system would have come to the surface sooner or later, in response to one strain or another. They happened to come to the fore in 1971–73.

It is worth remarking that the breakdown of the Bretton Woods system was only partial. The International Monetary Fund is an important survivor, both as a lender and as a forum for managing the international monetary system. The convertibility of currencies and the continuing autonomy of national economic policies—both features of the Bretton Woods architecture—are still taken as desiderata in a well-functioning international monetary system. It is a measure of the success of that system that we take them for granted. It was the exchange rate features of the system that broke down and the psychologically important but technically tenuous link to the historic gold standard via the gold convertibility of the leading currency.

III

PRESENT ARRANGEMENTS. For the past decade, the world has permitted a variety of exchange rate arrangements, but in practice with a much higher degree of flexibility than prevailed under the Bretton Woods system. This "non-system" has served the world economy rather well during a turbulent decade. It is true that the overall economic performance during the past decade, whether measured in terms of inflation rates or growth rates or unemployment rates, has been far inferior to what it was during the 1950s and 1960s. But it probably would have been even worse if governments had tried to maintain the Bretton Woods system through the period. In view of the large disturbances which the world economy has undergone, an attempt to maintain fixed but adjustable exchange rates would almost certainly have required a much higher degree of restrictions over both capital and current transactions than in fact prevailed. Thus exchange rate flexibility helped to preserve a relatively open trading and financial system.

During the decade, movable exchange rates have generally corrected for differences in national inflation rates, as economists predicted they would. But the movements in exchange rates have gone beyond that and affected "real" exchange rates as well—that is, competitiveness as measured by the relative prices at which the goods of one country on the average trade against the goods of another.

An evaluation of the period as a whole is complicated and difficult. Many of the movements in real exchange rates followed textbook predictions, responding to imbalances in current accounts or to dramatic changes in resource endowments (such as the discovery of North Sea oil), or they followed divergent movements in aggregate demand. But some of the movements in real exchange rates have not followed textbook patterns, and even when they have, they have often been viewed as unwelcome disturbances by some countries, especially following the sharp depreciation of the U.S. dollar in 1978 and again following the sharp appreciation of the dollar in 1981 and 1982. Perhaps for this reason, most countries of the world in fact have not allowed their currencies to float. Rather, they have fixed the value of their currencies against something—against another currency, or a basket of currencies, or in the case of the European Monetary System, against one another. Thus it is not entirely accurate to characterize current arrangements as involving floating exchange rates. In practice, the exchange rates of several major currencies—the U.S. dollar, the Japanese yen, the British pound, the Canadian dollar—do float more or less freely, but other currencies do not float, although they have shown greater flexibility than they would have under a Bretton Woods regime.

Movements in some key bilateral exchange rates, such as the dollar–deutsche mark rate, have shown sharp short-run variations on occasion during the past decade, which were not keyed to fundamental economic developments in any obvious way. There have been occasional weeks of average daily variations in excess of three percent. Why such great variability? In some respects foreign currency holdings are like any other financial asset whose current price reflects all the information available that may have a bearing on its future value. New information may then affect market prices (in this instance exchange rates) sharply as the "market" reappraises the future in the light of new information.

This analogy to stock prices helps to explain the abruptness of some movements in exchange rates. But it hardly helps to explain month after month of sharp variability, up and down. Much "new" information, in a longer perspective, is in fact only noise, whose bearing on the price in question can reasonably be expected to be reversed in the near if not immediate future, especially since trade can eventually be expected to respond to persistent movements in exchange rates.

Abrupt up-and-down shifts in exchange rates may not, by themselves, greatly affect trade and production, since they should reasonably be expected to be reversed soon if they are not clearly linked to more fundamental economic developments. The added uncertainty about what an exchange rate will be when a transaction is completed will, however, undoubtedly discourage trade and investment for export to some extent.

The main difficulty with flexible exchange rates is that another influence is also at work, which can transmute the influence of noisy news into larger changes in exchange rates than otherwise would take place. It is the presence of crowd or bandwagon effects in the trading community. Few know how to interpret the news. Many use a movement in the exchange rate itself as a source of information about market sentiment. To avoid being left behind, dealers jump on the bandwagon, thus pushing the exchange rate further in the direction it tended to go initially. Expectations feed on expectations.

When this process is operating, even those who suspect the exchange rate has gone too far still have an interest in holding their investments so long as the prospect for further gain outweighs the probability of reversal. Thus a secondary judgment, oriented toward market dynamics, is superimposed on the reassessment based on the new information and may come to dominate the movement in exchange rates for a time. This would not be troublesome if there were no real economic consequences. But in some periods, expectations about the "fundamentals" may be so weakly held that the rate can be dominated by purely market dynamics for periods measured in weeks or months. When that is so, the exchange rate may in turn affect new information, such as price indexes, increases which the public interprets as "inflation." Or it may set in motion urgent steps to avoid risks, as when multinational firms move to protect their quarterly balance sheets (at the expense of the operating earnings of the firms). So a vicious circle may temporarily be set in motion. And this vicious circle may aggravate inflation rates and hence inflationary expectations, or it may divert management attention away from real long-term investment to short-term balance-sheet considerations. In either case an unnecessary and avoidable element of instability is introduced into national economies.

Two features of present exchange rate arrangements will not be satisfactory over the long run. First, movements in real exchange rates have major effects on national economies, effects which are often unwelcome. Yet movements in real exchange rates cannot be easily controlled by use of the usual instruments of national economic policy because the determinants of exchange rates are diverse and complex. The result is that at any moment the influence of policy actions on exchange rates is uncertain. Portfolio decisions with respect to financial assets play a key role in the short-run determination of exchange rates, yet the influence of policy actions on portfolio decisions, via expectations, is uncertain. This marks a substantial contrast with the influence of policy actions on the aggregate demand for goods and services, where the linkages with policy are clearer. Despite this, we have not to date been able to eliminate the so-called business cycle. Unpredictable movements in real exchange rates, and unpredictable responses of real exchange rates to government action, greatly aggravate the problem of macroeconomic management.

Second, under a regime of flexible exchange rates there is a temptation, hence some tendency, to manipulate the exchange rate for national purposes. This can be done either to fight inflation, since monetary tightening produces an immediate reward—at the expense of other countries, so long as others do not respond in kind—in terms of a reduced inflation rate brought about by an appreciated currency. Or it can be used to combat unemployment, when expansionary monetary policy depreciates the currency—again, in general, at the expense of other countries. Of course, the new configuration of exchange rates may be satisfactory to all or most countries, but that would be a coincidence. Ordinarily these represent self-centered national actions which simply pass the problem either of inflation or of unemployment to other countries. Members of the IMF have a general responsibility to avoid such manipulation of exchange rates, and the IMF has a general responsibility for surveillance over exchange rate practices, with the aim of preventing such practices. But surveillance really has not gotten off the ground, and it is not clear under today's arrangements what the IMF can really do, for example, when a Sweden deliberately depreciates its currency in order to increase output and employment, or when a United States achieves a substantial reduction in its inflation rate through a policy of tight money which has greatly appreciated the dollar against other currencies.

Just as present exchange rate arrangements are not really sustainable over the long run, neither are present arrangements for the creation of reserves. The principal reserve medium today is a national currency, the U.S. dollar, dependent in large part for its supply on the policies of the United States. This has been accepted, more or less grudgingly, because it has worked reasonably well and there is no clear feasible alternative. But it leaves a deep sense of uneasiness around the world, even when the United States in the judgment of others is relatively well behaved; and the uneasiness grows dramatically when in such periods as 1970–71 and 1978 and 1981–82 the rest of the world, or parts of it, believe the United States is not well behaved.

Moreover, as the United States shrinks in relation to the rest of the world, as it is bound to do, the intrinsic weaknesses of reliance on the U.S. dollar will become more apparent, especially in the United States, where the possible reaction of foreign dollar-holders will become an ever greater constraint on U.S. monetary policy. The United States is bound to shrink relative to the rest of the world, not because it is doing badly, but because the rest of the world may be expected to do well. The natural growth in the labor force and the rate of capital accumulation are both higher in many parts of the world than they are in the United States. Furthermore, technologically lagging countries can reduce the technological gap between themselves and the United States, which operates on the frontiers of modern technology. Thus the simple arithmetic of economic growth will insure a gradual relative decline of the United States, for instance from about one-fourth of gross world product at present to around one-sixth 25 years from now if the United States grows on average at three percent a year and the rest of the world grows on average at five percent a year, both plausible numbers.

In short, the present set of monetary arrangements, while not in any immediate danger of collapse from its intrinsic features, as distinguished from some external event, is not stable in the long run. It is not a durable system. It must evolve into something else.

But what will or should it evolve into? One possibility is that the frustrations arising from the sense of loss of national control will lead to significant attempts to reassert national control by sharply reducing the openness and permeability of national economies to external influences. The move to flexible exchange rates can itself be interpreted as such a response, since countries enjoyed even less control, especially as regards monetary policy, under a system of fixed exchange rates with high capital mobility. But we have now learned that flexible exchange rates, while they offer some degree of greater national autonomy, do not effectively insulate national economies from external influences, and indeed in some instances may even exacerbate the impact of external influences on national economic developments. So the frustrations at loss of national control continue, and alleviating them requires much stronger insulating material than flexible exchange rates alone provide. It would probably involve a reversion to extensive use of restrictions over capital movements. And since capital transactions cannot be effectively separated from current transactions, there would be a tendency to extend restrictions to current transactions as well.

IV

FUTURE ARRANGEMENTS. I suggest a different possible evolution of international monetary arrangements that attempts to deal with the intrinsic problems with present arrangements that render them unstable in the long run. First, let us go forward 25 years, to the year 2010. That is far enough ahead so that developments that are completely unrealistic in the next five or ten years can be contemplated. But it is not so far ahead that we cannot really contemplate them at all.

By 2010 the populations and labor forces of the modern industrial economies will of course be larger than they are today, but the labor force engaged in manufacturing production in today's OECD (Organization for Economic Cooperation and Development) countries will probably have declined. Manufacturing is likely to go the way that agriculture has already gone, with a declining share of the labor force able to produce all of the material goods that the rest of society needs. Real incomes per capita will be over 50 percent higher than they are today. The world will be very electronic. Thus not only will large-scale financial transactions take place virtually instantaneously to any part of the world—we are close to that situation today—but even retail transactions in financial services and in goods can take place electronically. That is, householders will be able to purchase information regarding taxation, investments, retirement possibilities, or education by consulting electronic catalogues and information sources in their own homes. Even goods will be able to be purchased by inspecting them on a television screen, placing the order electronically, and having them delivered in a relatively short period of time. English will become even more widespread as the language of commerce.

With higher real incomes and lower relative prices for long-distance transportation, much more travel will take place than occurs today. Reliable, high-speed and low-cost communications over the globe will permit management control of production locations in many places. Lower transportation costs (relative to the price of other goods and services) will encourage trade. These factors taken together are likely to result in greater possibilities for substitution of geographic locations, not only in manufacturing production but also in many services. Thus, real movements in exchange rates will be highly disruptive of profits, production, and employment in any particular location.

Yet financial factors will still dominate the determination of exchange rates in the short run. In view of the greater sensitivity of production to changes in real exchange rates, governments must reduce arbitrary movements in real exchange rates in order to maintain an open trading system. With widespread information and low transaction costs, an adjustable peg system of exchange rates that requires occasional discretionary movements in market exchange rates is not likely to be tenable—indeed, did not prove to be tenable even under the technological conditions prevailing in the 1960s.

These various considerations lead me to conclude that *we will need a system of credibly fixed exchange rates* by that time if we are to preserve an open trading and financial system. Exchange rates can be most credibly fixed if they are eliminated altogether, that is, if international transactions take place with a single currency. But a single currency is possible only if there is in effect a single monetary policy and a single authority issuing the currency and directing the monetary policy. How can independent states accomplish that? They need to turn over the determination of monetary policy to a supranational body, but one which is responsible collectively to the governments of the independent states. There is some precedent for parts of this type of arrangement in the origins of the U.S. Federal Reserve System, which blended quite separate regions of the country and banks subject to diverse state banking jurisdictions into a single system, paralleling the increasingly national financial market. Similarly, we will need a world monetary system that parallels the increasingly global financial market. It will probably not be possible, even within the time scale envisaged here, to have a truly global Bank of Issue. But that will not be necessary either, and it may be possible to have a Bank of Issue which serves a more limited group of democratic countries and which can serve as the core of an international system.

The Monetary Authority. The tasks, the instruments, and the decision-making structure of the Bank of Issue could look something like the following:

—The governing board would be made up of representatives of national governments, whose votes would be weighted according to the share of the national GNP in the total gross product of the community of participating nations. This weighting could be altered at five-year intervals to allow for differences in growth rates.

—The task of the monetary authority would be to stabilize the macroeconomic environment and to avoid or mitigate liquidity crises by acting as a lender of last resort, just as national central banks do today. The debate on the relative weights to be attached to output and employment as opposed to price stabilization, and on how monetary policy should actually be managed, could continue just as it does at present, without prejudice.

—The Bank of Issue would accomplish its tasks by engaging in open market operations in which it issued the new currency for the securities of member countries. It could also engage in rediscount operations, whereby it extended claims against itself in exchange for acceptable paper at the initiative of banks within the system, subject to its own acquiescence in those initiatives.

The Bank of Issue need not engage in detailed regulation of the banks throughout the system covered by the new currency. That could be left in the hands of national regulators. It would, however, probably want to issue guidelines—minimum standards—to be followed by national regulators and to maintain enough surveillance over banks to be sure of itself when it was called upon to act as a lender of last resort.

In the first instance, open market operations by the Bank of Issue could be distributed among the securities of national governments in proportion to their voting weight (i.e., their GNP share), but over time this limitation would probably cease to be necessary as financial markets evolved and securities issued by many national governments became virtually perfect substitutes one for another. In any case, the Bank of Issue's holdings of national government securities could be altered from GNP shares via the rediscounting facility, as needed.

Seigniorage in this system would automatically be distributed to national governments as their securities were purchased by the Bank of Issue, thereby giving them the purchasing power to buy goods and services. In addition, the Bank of Issue would run profits from its interest earnings, and those could be distributed from time to time to national governments on the basis of their voting shares.

The currency of the Bank of Issue could be practically anything. Most natural would be an evolution from the present U.S. dollar, making use of the extensive dollar-based worldwide markets. But if that were not politically acceptable, it could be a synthetic unit that the public would have to get used to, just as it had to get used to the metric system when that replaced numerous national systems. The key point is that monetary control—the issuance of currency and of reserve credit—would be in the hands of the new Bank of Issue, not in the hands of any national government, no matter what the historical origin of the new currency happened to be.

National Economic Policy. The publics of the industrial democracies have placed high expectations on their national governments for economic management. Here governments are being asked to pass monetary policy to a supranational agency, the actions of which they can influence but not determine, taken one by one. Would national governments be giving up all of their macroeconomic control? The answer to this question is negative, since they could still pursue fiscal policy at the national level. What they would be giving up is monetary financing of budget deficits beyond their prorated allocation from jointly agreed open market operations. In particular, they could not engage in inflationary finance to reduce the real value of outstanding currency and debt at the national level, although the requisite majority could do so at the international level. To finance budget deficits, therefore, it would be necessary to go to the capital market. But under the envisaged circumstances there would no doubt be a very high degree of capital mobility among participants, since all securities would be denominated in a single, widely used currency. Of course, the influence of national fiscal actions on national aggregate demand would be limited by leakages abroad through demand for imports and, at the outer limits, by the extent to which individual governments could barrow in the capital market.

Governments could also use their fiscal powers to attract internationally mobile firms by means of tax holidays or other fiscal incentives. These practices have already emerged as a new form of fiscal action both within countries (e.g., industrial development bonds issued by individual states within the United States) and between countries. With internationally mobile capital, these practices may indeed succeed in generating local employment in "depressed" areas without necessarily resulting in a misallocation of resources, as the burden of taxation is shifted to relatively immobile residents. Nonetheless, if these practices became too competitive among nations, they might want to put some collectively agreed limits on them and even allow special differentiation under some circumstances, e.g., when unemployment rates were higher than some agreed norm.

One old-fashioned policy instrument for encouraging local investment and employment is the use of tariffs to discriminate against foreign goods. It would be logical if this single currency regime were accompanied by free trade, just as the dollar area within the United States is accompanied by free trade. That would also be consistent with the collaborative political spirit that would be required for the single currency regime to be established. Free trade would insure one market in goods as well as in financial instruments. The scheme would be quite workable also with modest tariffs, at below the levels that now generally prevail among industrialized countries. But the exact nature of the commercial regime is beyond the scope of this article.

How the Regime Would Work. Governments could determine the balance between their expenditures and taxes as they do now, but beyond their prorated share of the Bank of Issue's open market purchases and profits, they would have to borrow on the capital market to cover any budget deficits. Market access would be determined by a market assessment of the probability of repayment, which would assuredly be high within a plausible range of budgetary behavior. Both receipts and expenditures would be made in the common currency, as would the borrowing. Each country could set its own course independently, with no need for formal coordination of fiscal policy. Financial markets would "coordinate" to some extent, via interest rates, since if all governments decided to borrow heavily at once, in a period in which private demands for credit were also high, interest rates would rise and that would induce greater caution in borrowing. But the larger countries would certainly find it useful to exchange information on intentions with respect to future actions, so that each of them could take the prospective actions of others into account. This exchange would no doubt evolve over time into an iterative process that was hardly distinguishable from coordination, although in the end each country would be free to act as it saw fit.

Monetary policy would be set for the community as a whole by a board of governors, who in practice would probably be finance ministers. No single country would be in control. A weighted majority of the governors would decide the principles both to govern monetary policy (e.g., how much weight to give to monetary magnitudes as opposed to other economic variables in framing monetary policy) and with respect to actual operations. The governors in turn would be accountable to legislatures. The Bank of Issue would have a certain autonomy by virtue of not being beholden to any single legislative or executive authority. Thus it could not be manipulated for particular electoral reasons. On the other hand, its actions would be determined by a majority of officials who would be individually accountable to legislatures or executives, so that if a (weighted) majority of them desired a shift in policy, it would occur.

Balance-of-payments adjustment within this regime would be as easy, or as difficult, as it is between regions of the United States or any other large country today. The adjustment would be automatic, except insofar as it was cushioned by capital inflows induced by fiscal actions. Automatic balance-of-payments adjustment sometimes leads to unemployment, as following a shift in demand away from the products of a particular region or country. Fiscal policy in its various forms could be used to cushion such unemployment. In addition, my guess is that there would be considerable net immigration into the present industrial democracies by early in the next century, and the distribution of that flow of migrants would provide considerable flexibility to the labor force in the region as a whole.

This one-currency regime is much too radical to envisage in the near future. But it is not too radical to envisage 25 years from now, and indeed some such scheme, or its functional equivalent, will be necessary to avoid retrogression into greater reliance on barriers to international trade and financial transactions. Moreover, it is useful to have a vision to provide guidance for the steps that may be feasible in the near future. Some idea of where we would like to get to provides a sense of direction for the next steps.

V

NEXT STEPS. The idea of a single currency is so far from being politically feasible at present—in its call for a pooling of monetary sovereignty—that it will require many years of consideration before people become accustomed to the idea. But the economic effect can be gradually approximated by giving greater weight to exchange rates in framing national monetary policy. Many countries—all those with fixed or semi-fixed rates—of course already do this. This injunction therefore applies mainly to the United States, Canada, Japan, the United Kingdom, and the members of the European Monetary System taken as a group. If monetary policy were governed in such a way as to limit wide swings in key exchange rates, this would tend also to reduce fluctuations in real exchange rates. This result could be accomplished by adoption of one or another of the formal schemes that have been proposed from time to time, such as the target zone, whereby countries undertake to confine market movements of the exchange rate within a specified band centered on a target rate, which target can if necessary be altered from time to time. The European Monetary System is a variant of such a scheme, with central rates being subject to periodic renegotiation as they become questionable. Seven changes in central rates have been made in the period since 1979, and generally the changes have been sufficiently small so that market exchange rates were not immediately affected or were affected only modestly.

It may not be possible to reach international agreement on a formal scheme for exchange rate management. But the process of official discussion of such schemes, each particular one of which is subject to defects under some circumstances, will apprise officials of the possibilities for accomplishing the principal objective, viz., to reduce undue fluctuations in real exchange rates. Thus launching a move toward "reform" of exchange rate arrangements may fail in the sense that no formal scheme is agreed on but still succeed in its underlying purpose of establishing a more or less shared view of what exchange rates should be at a given time and a consensus to work toward keeping market rates within the neighborhood of the consensus rates.

What is also necessary is some consultation among major countries on the overall "tone" of monetary policy. This is a politically difficult step and cannot be taken overtly any time soon, since each nation has its formal system of decision making and channels of responsibilities for determining monetary policy. However, the same result can be accomplished informally, centered around discussion of exchange rate management, for which there seems to be a widespread desire, especially in business circles. . . .

A key question concerning the new Bank of Issue is what countries should participate in its management, use its currency, and forswear national monetary policy. We have come to think of the international monetary system, centered on the IMF with its 146 members, as a global system, albeit excluding most communist countries and Switzerland. That was certainly the conception at Bretton Woods, even though most of the early negotiation had been between the Americans and the British. That was also the spirit of the times at Bretton Woods, when the wartime allies placed their hopes for a better world in the United Nations organization and its functional affiliates.

But there is serious question about whether one world money is either necessary or desirable. And it is certainly not feasible within our generous 25-year time frame. It is not feasible for two reasons. First, it is highly doubtful whether the American public, to take just one example, could ever accept that countries with oppressive autocratic regimes should vote on the monetary policy that would affect monetary conditions in the United States. I believe that the same reservations would obtain in other democratic societies. For such a bold step to work at all, it presupposes a certain convergence of political values as reflected in the nature of political decision making and the basic trust and confidence to which those give rise.

Second, countries with different values, circumstances, and systems of governance are bound to introduce into negotiations leading toward a common Bank of Issue elements which are of greater interest to them, thus broadening the agenda for negotiation and rendering impossible an already difficult negotiation. For both reasons the proposal should be undertaken in the first instance by the United States, Japan, and the members of the European Community. This group represents the core of the monetary system at present and for some time to come. Other democracies would be free to join if they wished and if they were willing to undertake the commitments involved, but no one should be obliged to join. Very likely many countries would find it attractive in the early stages not to join, but nonetheless to peg their currencies to the SDR or whatever was the unit of account of the Bank of Issue. They would retain some monetary freedom, however, which members had given up. Some countries would also be reluctant to give up the seigniorage from currency issue, which can be consequential where currency still bears a high ratio to GNP.

In short, there would be an inner club accepting higher responsibilities but open to additional members who met the requirements and of value even to nonmembers by providing a stable monetary environment against which to frame their economic policies. But this arrangement would mark a formal break with the universalism that governs the de jure if not the de facto structure of the Bretton Woods system today.

Human Rights and the American Tradition

Arthur Schlesinger, Jr.

AMERICA AND THE WORLD 1978

NOTHING THE CARTER administration has done has excited more hope, puzzlement, and confusion than the effort to make human rights a primary theme in the international relations of the United States. Observers, watching the human rights initiative stumble from one contradiction to another, have announced its demise at regular intervals. Yet the campaign has plainly touched exposed nerves around the planet; it reverberates from Moscow, Santiago, and Kampala to Peking; and after two uncertain years, it remains a vital if problematic strain in American foreign policy. It therefore seems appropriate to attempt an interim assessment of the human rights initiative: its origins, its ambiguities, its achievements, its perils, its prospects.

II

HUMAN RIGHTS—roughly the idea that all individuals everywhere are entitled to life, liberty, and the pursuit of happiness on this earth—is a relatively modern proposition. Political orators like to trace this idea to religious sources, especially to the so-called Judeo-Christian tradition. In fact the great religious ages were notable for their indifference to human rights in the contemporary sense—not only for their acquiescence in poverty, inequality, and oppression, but for their addiction to slavery, torture, wartime atrocities, and genocide.

Christianity, for example, assigned to earthly misery an honored and indispensable role in the drama of salvation. The trials visited on mankind in this world were conceived as ordained by the Almighty in order to test and train sinful mortals. From the religious perspective, nothing that might take place on earth mattered in comparison to what must take place hereafter. The world was but an inn at which humans spent a night on their voyage to eternity, so what difference could it make if the food was poor or the bed uncomfortable?

No doubt the idea of natural rights has classical antecedents, among, for example, the Stoics. But humanitarianism—the notion that natural rights have immediate, concrete, and universal application—is a product of the last four centuries. Tocqueville persuasively attributed the humanitarian ethic to the rise of the idea of equality. In aristocratic societies, he wrote, those in the upper caste hardly believed that their inferiors "belong to the same race." When medieval chroniclers "relate the tragic end of a noble, their grief flows apace; whereas they tell you at a breath and without wincing of massacres and tortures inflicted on the common sort of people." Tocqueville recalled the "cruel jocularity" with which the intelligent and delightful Madame de Sévigné, one of the most civilized women of the seventeenth century, described the breaking on a wheel of an itinerant fiddler "for getting up a dance and stealing some stamped paper." It would be wrong, Tocqueville observed, to suppose that Madame de Sévigné was selfish or sadistic. Rather, she "had no clear notion of suffering in anyone who was not a person of quality."

But the age of equality, Tocqueville suggested, vastly increased the number of people who saw each other as equals. That equality was the source of the new mood of "general compassion" was proved by the contrast between the way white Americans treated themselves and the way they treated their slaves. "The same man who is full of humanity toward his fellow creatures when they are at the same time his equals becomes insensible to their afflictions as soon as the equality ceases. His mildness should therefore be attributed to the equality of conditions rather than to civilization and education."

The ethic of humanitarianism came into its own in the eighteenth century. Since religion had traditionally rejected the notion that people had a right to earthly happiness, early human rights formulations, as with Voltaire and later in the French Revolution, had a markedly antireligious cast. Only later, as religion itself succumbed to the new ethic and began to see the Kingdom of God as attainable within history, could the claim be made that the Judeo-Christian tradition commanded the pursuit of happiness in this world. The basic human rights documents—the American Declaration of Independence and the French Declaration of the Rights of Man—were written by political, not by religious, leaders.

III

THE UNITED STATES was founded on the proclamation of "unalienable" rights, and human rights ever since have had a peculiar resonance in the

American tradition. Nor was the application of this idea to foreign policy an innovation of the Carter administration. Americans have agreed since 1776 that the United States must be the beacon of human rights to an unregenerate world. The question has always been how America is to execute this mission.

John Quincy Adams discussed the American choice in his famous Fourth of July address in 1821. "Wherever the standard of freedom and independence has been or shall be unfurled," Adams said,

> there will her heart, her benedictions and her prayers be But she goes not abroad, in search of monsters to destroy. She is the well-wisher to the freedom and independence of all. She is the champion and vindicator only of her own. She will commend the general cause by the countenance of her voice, and the benignant sympathy of her example. She well knows that by once enlisting under other banners than her own, were they even the banners of foreign independence, she would involve herself beyond the power of extrication, in all the wars of interest and intrigue, of individual avarice, envy, and ambition, which assume the colors and usurp the standard of freedom. The fundamental maxims of her policy would insensibly change from *liberty* to *force*. . . . She might become the dictatress of the world. She would no longer be the ruler of her own spirit.

In 1847 Albert Gallatin, the last survivor among the great statesmen of the early republic, made the same point. "Your mission," he told his countrymen, "was to be a model for all other governments and for all other less-favored nations, to adhere to the most elevated principles of political morality, to apply all your faculties to the gradual improvement of your own institutions and social state, and *by your example* to exert a moral influence most beneficial to mankind" [emphasis added].

Then in December 1849, Senator Lewis Cass of Michigan, who had been Jackson's secretary of war and in 1848 the Democratic presidential candidate and who later became Buchanan's secretary of state, introduced a resolution instructing the Foreign Relations Committee to inquire into the "expediency" of suspending diplomatic relations with Austria. Cass intended this as the national response to the bloody suppression by Austrian and Russian troops of the Hungarian Revolution of 1848—"atrocious acts of despotism," Cass said, "by which human liberty and life have been sacrificed." Louis Kossuth, the president of the short-lived Hungarian republic, soon visited the United States, pointing out in powerful speeches the anomaly that, while Americans talked endlessly about their mission of liberty, they declined "to take any active part in the regulation of the condition of the outward world." Yet, if the American destiny was what "you all believe it to be, then, indeed, that destiny can never be fulfilled by acting the part of passive spectators and by this very passivity granting a charter to ambitious czars to dispose of the condition of the world." Americans, Kossuth said, trusted so much "to the operative power of your institutions and of your example that they really believe they will make their way throughout the world by their moral influence. . . . I have never yet heard of a despot who had yielded to the moral influence of liberty."

Cass's resolution and Kossuth's challenge confronted Americans with the question of how they were to fulfill the mission of human rights. John Parker Hale, a Free Soil Democrat from New Hampshire, opened the debate. "Aching and throbbing hearts," he said ironically, "[had] been waiting, and watching, and agonizing for just such a day as that when the Government shall . . . express its sympathies for the millions who are under the heel of power." But if the Hungarian repression were indeed a moral question, Hale thought, the resolution should speak, not of the "expediency" of suspending relations with Austria but the "duty." Cass, however, had assured the Senate that American trade with Austria was negligible, thus making it "quite clear to the country that they can let off a good deal of indignation, and that it will cost them but very little." Was this the way to treat a moral question? Imagine the American minister in Turkey, where Kossuth had now fled, trying to cheer the Hungarian refugees by telling them "that the Senate of the great American Republic are inquiring, this very day, how much it will cost to utter a little indignation in their behalf?"

The future historian, Hale said, might start off his chapter about these times:

> At the commencement of this year, the American Senate, the highest legislative body of the world, the wisest, greatest, and most magnanimous people that ever lived or ever will live, forgetting and neglecting the trifling local affairs which concerned their own limits, constituted themselves into a high court, and proceeded to try the nations of the earth for "atrocious acts of despotism."

Hale hoped that the historian could go on to say that the United States proceeded "to try, not some few second-rate Powers with but little commerce, and whom it would cost but little to deal with, but that they took the empire of Russia first, and tried her." After all, Russian arms had overcome Kossuth. "I will not consent to sit in judgment upon Austria, until we have passed judgment upon some of these larger criminals. I am not willing that our action should be like that of small nets which catch the small fishes but let the great ones go."

What Cass proposed, Hale continued, was "that we erect ourselves into a high court of indignation! We are to arraign at our bar the nations of the earth, and they are to pass in trial before us, and we are to pass judgment upon them." An excellent principle—but why stop with Austria? I want to try the tsar of Russia, Hale said, not just for what he did in Hungary but "for what he had done long ago in sending those unfortunate exiles to Siberian snows. . . . I want them to know that the American Senate have sympathies also for them. . . . I want to try him for his agency in the partition of Poland. . . . When we have done this, we shall show that we are governed by no pusillanimous motives in expressing our indignation against a weaker Power." And "when we have tried Russia, let us not stop there. I think we ought to arraign . . . England for the manner in which she tried Smith O'Brien and the Irish patriots. . . . I want to go to India, and to try England for the oppressions, the cruelties, and the wars that she waged there."

If the principle was good, Hale said, it should be applied impartially. "After we have got through with Russia and England, I want . . . France to be placed at the bar. . . . I want to go to Algiers and to inquire what France has done there. . . . Then, sir, while the court is in session . . . I want to try Spain. . . . Let us show that we are in earnest, and not merely showing off our indignation where there is no power of resentment, and where it will not be likely to cost us anything."

And, after we have passed judgment on the nations of Christendom and "they lie writhing in an agony of mortification at our feet," then let us "go from these high places down before the bar, and plead ourselves." For in "the capital of the Model Republic . . . within sight of the flag of freedom that floats over our heads . . . men are to be bought, and women are to be bought, and kept at twenty-five cents per day, until ready to be transported to some other market." The principle of the Cass resolution—"that liberty is [man's] God-given right, and the oppression that takes it from him by man is a wrong"—ought to begin at home.

Henry Clay, then in the twilight of his career, joined the debate. He was struck by the "incongruity" between Cass's premises and his remedy. Cass had discoursed about the "enormities of Austrian despotism," but his conclusion was only to recall "a little chargé d'affaires that we happen to have at Vienna. Why, the natural conclusion would be to declare war immediately against Austria." But was it really sensible to close the door of intercourse with Austria? Why not send a distinguished American to Vienna to plead quietly on behalf of the Hungarians? And why not "bring forward some original plan for affording succor and relief to the exiles of Hungary?"

In any event, Clay said, the Cass resolution asks us to judge foreign nations "as their conduct may be found to correspond with our notion and judgment of what is right and proper in the administration of human affairs." It assumes "the right of interference in the internal affairs of foreign nations. . . . But where is to be the limit?" You may say to Spain that unless it abolishes the Inquisition, to Turkey that unless it abolishes polygamy, the United States will cease all intercourse with you. "Where, again I ask, are we to stop? Why should we not interfere in behalf of suffering Ireland? Why not interfere in behalf of suffering humanity wherever we may find it?" Let the Senate reflect, Clay warned, that in going down this road, we may "open a new field of collision, terminating perhaps in war, and exposing ourselves to the reaction of foreign Powers, who, when they see us assuming to judge of their conduct, will undertake in their turn to judge of our conduct."

IV

THIS ANCIENT DEBATE serves as a reminder of what small progress America has made since the 31st Congress in resolving the question of the national mission. Cass's resolution showed the profound and admirably uncontrollable American impulse to demonstrate sympathy for suffering people in other lands. The response by Hale and Clay expressed doubts that still persist: Is the point of foreign policy to discharge moral indignation or to produce real changes in a real world? May quiet diplomacy not be more effective in international persuasion than public denunciation? Must not the United States, when it invokes human rights, apply the principle across the board and not just to small and weak countries? May not intervention on behalf of human rights jeopardize other national interests and increase the danger of war? In any event, by what authority do we interfere in the internal affairs of foreign countries? Should all nations be expected to embrace the American conception of human rights? Does not the habit of passing judgment on foreign states nourish national self-righteousness? Should not a human rights crusade perhaps begin at home?

Cass's resolution failed. Yet the questions raised by his appeal nagged the national conscience. After the Civil War, President Grant observed in his first annual message that while Americans sympathized "with all people struggling for liberty . . . it is due to our honor that we should abstain from enforcing our views upon unwilling nations and from taking an interested part, without *invitation*, in the quarrels . . . between governments and their subjects." Nonetheless, both Congress and the executive thereafter condemned assaults on human rights abroad—the persecution of Jews in Russia, Eastern Europe, and the Levant; the massacre of Armenians in Turkey; the oppression of the Irish; "the cruel treatment of State prisoners in Siberia." Justification presumably lay in the doctrine of humanitarian intervention. "Although we . . . as a rule scrupulously abstain from interfering, directly or indirectly, in the public affairs" of the Austro-Hungarian Empire, Secretary of State Hamilton Fish informed the American minister in Vienna in 1872, the persecution of Jews in Moldavia and Wallachia was so "inhuman" as to impart to the situation "a cosmopolitan character, in the redress of which all countries, governments, and creeds are alike interested." Twenty years later Secretary of State James G. Blaine told the Russian Minister of Foreign Affairs that, while the American government "does not assume to dictate the internal policy of other nations . . . nevertheless, the mutual duties of nations require that each should use its power with a due regard for the result which its exercise produces on the rest of the world."

The pressures of conscience, reinforced by ethnic lobbies fearful for relatives in the homeland, injected human rights into foreign affairs so regularly in these years that Theodore Roosevelt in 1904 felt impelled to issue a warning. No shrinking violet when it came to the assertion of American power in the world, T.R. nonetheless cautioned Congress:

> Ordinarily it is very much wiser and more useful for us to concern ourselves with striving for our own moral and material betterment here at home than to concern ourselves with trying to better the condition of things in other nations. We have plenty of sins of our own to war against, and under ordinary circumstances we can do more for the general uplifting of humanity by striving with heart and soul to put a stop to civic corruption, to brutal lawlessness and violent race prejudices here at home than by passing resolutions about wrongdoing elsewhere.

Despite T.R.'s effort to recall his countrymen to the older tradition of doing good by example rather than by interference, the conviction grew in the bloody twentieth century that crimes against humanity indeed had "a cosmopolitan character" and were humanity's business. Wilsonianism gave this view general blessing, though Wilson cast the issue in terms of national self-determination. But the conception of an international interest in *individual* rights was evolving. The eighth Conference of American States (1938) produced resolutions in "defense of human rights." Franklin Roosevelt's Four Freedoms (1941) applied specifically to people, not to nations. Roosevelt also extended the conception to cover not only freedom of speech and worship, but freedom from want ("economic understandings which will secure to every nation a healthy peacetime life for its inhabitants") and freedom from fear (that is, of military aggression). F.D.R.'s third freedom, supplemented by his Economic Bill of Rights (1944), soon flowered into the idea of social and economic rights to be sought along with traditional "Bill-of-Rights" rights.

The "Declaration by United Nations" (1942) called for "complete victory" in order, among other things, "to preserve human rights"; and the U.N. Charter (1945) pledged member nations to joint and separate action to promote "human rights." Three years later the U.N. General Assembly adopted the Universal Declaration of Human Rights. This lengthy document included both "civil and political rights" and "economic, social and cultural rights," the second category designed to please states that denied their subjects the first. The declaration was followed by a series of subsidiary conventions and covenants. As David Owen, the present British foreign secretary, has accurately noted, these documents, "though usually passed by large majorities, normally had no perceptible impact on the protection of human rights in any part of the world." Yet standards solemnly declared, even if unobserved, live on to supply ammunition to those who thereafter demand observance.

The idea of human rights, like nearly everything else, was caught up in the Cold War. The democratic states assailed the communist world for its abuse of civil and political rights; the communist world assailed the democratic states for their neglect of social and economic rights. Human rights began to emerge as a theme in American foreign policy in this context; thus Kennedy in his inaugural address spoke of a new generation of Americans "unwilling to witness or permit the slow undoing of those human rights to which this nation has always been committed." But human rights were also seen as an object of détente; thus Kennedy asked at American University in 1963: "Is not peace, in the last analysis, basically a matter of human rights?" "Since human rights are indivisible," Kennedy told the United Nations two months before Dallas, "this body cannot stand aside when those rights are abused and neglected by any member state."

Vietnam interrupted Washington's movement toward human rights as a major theme of foreign policy. The case for American intervention spoke of national self-determination rather than individual rights; it would not, in any case, have been easy for a state engaged in mass destruction to allege a consuming interest in human rights. The issue lay dormant in Washington even after American forces left Vietnam in 1973. Henry Kissinger's diplomacy made a virtue of the de-ideologization of foreign relations. A policy aiming at the manipulation of the balance of power doubtless contained an inner bias in favor of governments that could deliver their nations without having to worry about political opposition or a free press. In any event, the United States in these years embraced without visible disgust governments both of the authoritarian Right (Greece, Portugal, Brazil, Chile) and of the totalitarian Left (Russia, China, Rumania, Yugoslavia).

What forced the human rights issue on the world was the courage of the dissenters in the Soviet Union. Sakharov, Solzhenitsyn, the Medvedevs, and the rest of those intrepid men embodied the challenge to the democratic conscience that Kossuth and the heroes of 1848 had embodied a century earlier. The initial response to this challenge came not at all from Washington but from the governments of Western Europe, especially Britain and France, and resulted in the celebrated Basket Three of the Helsinki Final Act, with its manifold human rights provisions. In 1975 and 1976 many Americans denounced Helsinki—among them, Jimmy Carter.

But the dominance of realpolitik in the Kissinger years frustrated those in the Wilsonian tradition who felt that American foreign policy should be founded on ideals. It frustrated equally those in the school of F.D.R. who did not doubt that foreign policy must be founded on national interest but considered ideals an indispensable constituent of American power. Official indifference to the Soviet dissidents, symbolized by President Ford's refusal in mid-1975 to receive Solzhenitsyn, seemed to reveal a moral vacuum at the center of American foreign policy.

Congress meanwhile undertook to force the human rights issue on the executive. It used its legislative power to forbid or restrict economic or military aid to countries that engaged "in a consistent pattern of gross violations of internationally recognized human rights." It denied aid to a long list of erring countries by name. In the case of the Soviet Union, it demanded change in Soviet emigration practices as a condition for export credits and for the extension of most-favored-nation trade status. It required the State Department to submit annual reports on the state of human rights in more than a hundred countries.

Congressional pressure soon affected Foggy Bottom. "If the Department did not place itself ahead of the curve on this issue," Deputy Secretary of State Robert Ingersoll warned Secretary Kissinger in 1974, "Congress would take the matter out of the Department's hands." In 1975 the department established an Office of Humanitarian Affairs. But the secretary doubted that human rights had a serious place in foreign policy. Informed that the American ambassador to Chile had raised human rights issues with the military dictatorship, he said, "Tell Popper to cut out the political science lectures." And if human rights were in any sense an object of policy, the secretary was sure that quiet diplomacy, not public exhortation and punitive action, was the way to promote them—a view that received a measure of vindication when Jewish migration from the Soviet Union sharply declined after the passage of the Jackson-Vanik amendment. Congressional pressure continued to rise nevertheless. Eventually it affected the secretary himself. In 1976 Kissinger pronounced human rights "centrally important . . . one of the most compelling issues of our time."

V

BY 1977 THE world was well prepared for new human rights initiatives. Up to this point Washington had lagged badly behind. But the new president, in a remarkable display of leadership, seized the standard of human rights and succeeded in presenting it to the world as if it had been American property all along. He was able to do this because the time was ripe and because the cause fulfilled the old American conviction of having a mission to the world.

It is not altogether clear how Carter personally came to human rights. The phrase does not appear in the chapter on foreign policy in his memoir *Why Not the Best?* (1975). Nor was the issue prominent in his presidential campaign. On occasion, indeed, he seemed to be moving in the opposite direction. He criticized not only the Helsinki Agreement but the whole philosophy of intervention. "Our people have now learned," he told the Foreign Policy Association in June 1976, "the folly of our trying to inject our power into the internal affairs of other nations." At the same time, he had a general feeling, as he wrote in *Why Not the Best?* that "our government's foreign policy has not exemplified any commitment to moral principles," that foreign policy must rest on the same moral standards "which are characteristic of the individual citizens," and that "there is only one nation in the world which is capable of true leadership among the community of nations, and that is the United States." "We cannot look away," he added in Washington on September 8, 1976, "when a government tortures people, or jails them for their beliefs, or denies minorities fair treatment or the right to emigrate."

The future historian will have to trace the internal discussions during the interregnum that culminated in the striking words of the inaugural address: "Because we are free we can never be indifferent to the fate of freedom elsewhere. . . . Our commitment to human rights must be absolute." (Carter also said that the United States had a special obligation "to take on those moral duties which, when assumed, seem invariably to be in our own best interests." The irony appears to have been unconscious.)

One can surmise that the president-elect, seeking to give American foreign policy a moral force and content it had lacked in the Nixon years, arrived at human rights as the perfect unifying principle. This principle tapped the most acute contemporary concerns as well as the finest American traditions. It promised to restore America's international moral position, so sadly eroded by Vietnam, Watergate, support of dictatorships, CIA assassination plots, etc. It promised also to restore a domestic consensus behind foreign policy. The doctrine gratified both cold warriors, who wanted to indict the communist world, and idealists, who saw human rights as the only basis for lasting peace.

So the campaign was launched with appropriate pyrotechnics—a presidential letter to Sakharov, a White House meeting with Vladimir Bukovsky; brave declarations of human rights principle. But it soon ran into trouble. The idea, critics were quick to point out, had not been "thought through." Perhaps this was just as well. Had the new president confided the idea to the

State Department for analysis, there very likely would have been no human rights campaign at all. Confronted by new departures, bureaucracies customarily feel that risks outweigh opportunities. Sometimes changes can be wrought in government only when a president, by publicly committing the government to a new course, forces the bureaucracy to devise new policies. Truman's Point Four and Kennedy's Alliance for Progress are other examples.

Yet the failure to think the initiative through led Carter, then and later, to make the promotion of human rights sound a little too easy. He would have been wiser to admit the difficulties of converting principle into policy. "When I began to speak out for human rights," David Owen recently remarked, ". . . I warned that there was a price to pay, and that the price was a little inconsistency from time to time. If I had to make that comment again, I would no longer say a *little* inconsistency, I would say a *very great deal* of inconsistency." The questions that John P. Hale and Henry Clay had raised long before against Lewis Cass returned to bedevil the Carter administration. "Administration Still Groping to Define 'Human Rights'," read the headline in *The Washington Post* three months after the inauguration.

Two weeks later Secretary of State Vance made a valiant and judicious essay at definition. Speaking at the University of Georgia Law School, he distinguished three categories of human rights: the right to be free from government violation of the integrity of the person (an adaptation of F.D.R.'s freedom from fear); the right to the fulfillment of vital needs as for food, shelter, health care, and education (freedom from want); and the right to civil and political liberties (F.D.R.'s other two freedoms). In pursuing these rights, Vance warned, we must recognize "the limits of our power and of our wisdom," avoid "a rigid, hubristic attempt to impose our values on others," and reject the illusion that "a call to the banner of human rights will bring sudden transformations in authoritarian societies. We have embarked on a long journey." But Vance did not really try to deduce a policy from the principle, saying enigmatically that "there may be disagreement on the priorities these rights deserve."

Disagreement on the priorities was indeed unceasing. Diplomats objected when the human rights campaign threatened arms control negotiations or political relationships. Admirals and generals objected when it imperiled cherished military bases and alliances. Treasury officials estimated that foreign policy restrictions cost the economy up to ten billion dollars a year, thereby increasing the trade deficit. Businessmen objected when the campaign hurt exports. Carter himself, the presumed number one human rights crusader, was soon to be found visiting authoritarian nations, selling them arms, and saluting their leaders. His human rights policy, it appeared, was entirely compatible with effusive support for the shah of Iran, with an egregious letter of commendation to Somoza in Nicaragua, with the possible recognition of Vietnam and Cuba. Washington was fearless in denouncing human rights abuses in countries like Cambodia, Paraguay, and Uganda, where the United States had negligible strategic and economic interests; a good deal less fearless toward South Korea, Saudi Arabia, Yugoslavia, and most of black Africa; increasingly circumspect about the Soviet Union; totally silent about China.

By mid-1978 Solzhenitsyn could speak sarcastically of bureaucrats who exploded in "anger and inflexibility . . . when dealing with weak government and weak countries" but became "tongue-tied and paralyzed when they deal with powerful governments." "Unless standards of human rights are seen to be applied uniformly and neutrally to all nations regardless of the nature of their regimes or the size of their armaments," Senator Moynihan of New York sternly said, "unless this is done it will quickly be seen that it is not human rights at all which are invoked . . . but simply arbitrary political standards dressed up in the guise of human rights."

VI

THE CAMPAIGN—it could not be termed a policy—raised other problems. There was the question of its impact on the Soviet Union. "What we are now facing," Georgi Arbatov, the Kremlin's house Americanologist, told an English interviewer in November 1978, "is a consistent effort of interference in the internal affairs of the Soviet Union and an attempt to inflict harm on some of our institutions. It is waged in a way that would have produced a serious uproar in the United States if we'd done what you've done toward us." This was, of course, a ridiculous complaint from the representative of a country that for more than half a century had consistently tried to interfere in American internal affairs and to inflict harm on American institutions (and especially ridiculous in view of the fact, well known to Arbatov, that such interference had long since produced "a serious uproar" in the United States). Still, if Americans would recall how they felt about Soviet subversion, they might understand that this was precisely the way the Soviet government felt about the human rights campaign. Nor could anyone doubt that the campaign, pursued *à outrance*, would strike at the very foundation of the Soviet order.

The deterioration of Soviet-American relations during 1977 alarmed those who believed that the ultimate human right was the right to be alive and, therefore, that the prevention of nuclear war was the overriding issue for mankind and the condition for the promotion of all other human rights. Carter's campaign, French President Giscard d'Estaing observed in the summer of 1977, "has compromised the process of détente." The Soviet resentment, for some utterly mysterious reason, astonished Carter himself; he spoke in June 1977 of the "surprising adverse reaction in the Soviet Union to our stand on human rights." But he accepted it as a fact of life and moderated his campaign accordingly, thereby raising the virtuous wrath of those who had seen the campaign primarily as a means of reviving the Cold War.

There was the question, too, of the impact on the United States. America was once again erecting itself into a "high court of indignation." But what was America to sit in judgment upon the world? A born-again president might have remembered Matthew 7:2–3: "And why beholdest thou the mote that is in thy brother's eye, but considerest not the beam that is in thine own eye?" As John P. Hale had reminded the Senate in 1850 of the slave markets in the District of Columbia, so latter-day critics asked whether the United States ought not, before setting forth to reform the world, secure human rights for black, red, and brown citizens, for the targets of the FBI and the CIA, for the victims of muggers in the streets. How could the government invoke Helsinki's Basket Three while it denied visas to Soviet trade unionists and diplomats—and granted one to Ian Smith? How dared it lecture Fidel Castro about human rights after having spent a number of years trying to murder him?

An even more difficult question was involved—the question urged by Henry Clay when he wondered about American presumption in supposing that all nations were morally bound to accept our own conception of what was "right and proper" in human affairs. Was it reasonable, asked the Iranian ambassador to the United Nations, "to expect from developing countries in Asia, Africa, and Latin America to apply overnight your high standards when most of them are still grappling with problems of food, education, health, employment, etc.?" Was not the whole concept of political and civil rights ethnocentric and culture-bound and therefore the American determination to cram it down the throats of the world an adventure in cultural imperialism? "Those Americans who profess to know with such certainty what other people want and what is good for them in the way of political institutions," wrote George Kennan, "would do well to ask themselves whether they are not actually attempting to impose their own values, traditions, and habits of thought on peoples for whom these things have no validity and no usefulness."

Observers commented on the "holier-than-thou" attitude discernible in the Washington human rights bureaucracy—a condescension toward lesser breeds summed up in the odious remark an unnamed official made to Elizabeth Drew of *The New Yorker:* "I think that the mulish world has noticed the two-by-four." And as the British historian Sir Herbert Butterfield reminds us, "Moral indignation corrupts the agent who possesses it and is not calculated to reform the man who is the object of it." Little has done more harm to human affairs than illusions on the part of leaders and of nations of their infallibility. Reinhold Niebuhr has warned of "a deep layer of Messianic consciousness in the mind of America" and of "the depth of evil to which individuals and communities may sink particularly when they try to play the role of God in history." The human rights campaign led even pro-American Europeans to worry about rekindled messianism across the Atlantic and to recall, as Countess Marion Dönhoff put it, that "foreign policy based on moral values, as espoused by Wilson and Dulles, did not make the world noticeably more moral. On the contrary it led to dead ends and catastrophes."

VII

IN SHORT ORDER the human rights campaign was hailed before a high court of indignation of its own and readily convicted of hypocrisy, double standards, undermining détente, undermining stalwart anticommunist allies, of cultural imperialism, racism, messianism, and so on. It is little wonder that the initiative, buffeted by intractable circumstance, by plausible criticism, and by quarrels among its original supporters over its emphases, came to seem so selective, intermittent, and riddled with contradiction that it chronically threatened to disappear altogether. One writer entitled an article on the subject in mid-1978 "A Crusade Quickly Cancelled."

Yet the criticism, however plausible, may also have been exaggerated. To all-or-nothing demands of the Solzhenitsyn-Moynihan sort, Patricia Derian, assistant secretary of state for human rights and humanitarian affairs, made persuasive response:

> We candidly recognize that diversity of cultures and interests and different stages of economic and political maturity make it essential to treat each country on the merits of its own situation. It would be impossible to pursue our human rights objectives in precisely the same way for all countries, and silly to try.

Of course the double standard was inherent in the situation. Not only were other nations in varying stages of maturity, but the promotion of human rights could not in any case be the supreme goal of foreign policy, the object to which all else was to be subordinated. A nation's fundamental interest must be self-preservation; and, when national security and the promotion of human rights came into genuine conflict, national security had to prevail—though this was not at all to say that the national security bureaucracy was anywhere near to being the infallible expositor of national security. Human rights, in the nature of foreign policy, could only be one of several contending national interests.

As for the impact on the Soviet Union, this was perhaps exaggerated. It was often said that the 1977 crackdown on dissidents was a response to the human rights campaign. Prominent dissidents themselves disagreed. Viewed in retrospect, the crackdown was more probably a response to the effect that dissidence was having within the Soviet Union and would have taken place whether or not Washington had let loose on human rights.

The campaign unquestionably infuriated the Russians. But the Soviet response was tactical rather than strategic, and even the tactics were confused. Part of the time Soviet representatives responded with bluster. They claimed before the U.N. Human Rights Commission that the communist system protected individual freedoms to a "qualitatively unprecedented level," that any Soviet citizens may express opinions that "may not coincide with the Soviet outlook," and that there has "never been any case in which a healthy person has been interned in a psychiatric asylum: this is absolutely impossible." At the same time, they have compromised their old line that the discussion of individual cases represents an intervention in internal affairs by themselves raising American human rights cases in international forums. "The more the Russians take up western cases," as the London *Times* recently noted, "the less they can legitimately complain when the west does the same."

The future of détente would depend on other factors than human rights—unless cold warriors in the Senate succeeded in using human rights to block a new SALT agreement. (And, if they attempted this, they would be rejecting the counsel of leading Soviet dissenters. "I emphasize the priority of the disarmament issue within the overall complex of détente aims," Sakharov said in his statement of July 15, 1978. "I emphasize the practical necessity for an independent decision of current problems in the disarmament area and international security.") Arbatov, crabbing about human rights in November 1978, did *not* say, as he carefully said when considering the possibility of a Chinese-American axis, "Then the whole situation would look different to us. . . . Then there is no place for détente." Plainly, the Russians prefer the discomfiture of living with the human rights campaign to the danger of a break with the United States and a Chinese-American alliance.

The impact on the United States was exaggerated also. In practice, the human rights campaign turned out to be notably less than a crusade. Moreover, intercession into the affairs of countries that mistreat their own citizens now had a more solid foundation in international law than simply the old doctrine of humanitarian intervention. The U.N. Charter and succeeding international documents ended finally the idea that human rights were solely a matter of domestic jurisdiction.

Nor was it by any means certain that concern for human rights was a form of cultural imperialism. If the assertion that such rights were universal, and not merely the local prejudice of Caucasian societies bordering the North Atlantic, might imply racial arrogance, the limitation of these rights to a few white nations might imply racial arrogance as well. Did the relativists mean that nonwhite peoples were incapable of appreciating due process, personal liberty, and self-government? History certainly suggested that democracy has worked best in the North Atlantic orbit, but democratic aspiration could not be so easily localized. "Human rights," a distinguished former Philippine senator told Americans with understandable irritation, "are not a western discovery." India, for all its religious and linguistic divisions, its poverty and its illiteracy, had voted emphatically in early 1977 for a return to democracy.

The case of China was to the point. So far as one could tell, there was probably more intellectual freedom in the Soviet Union under Khrushchev and Brezhnev than in China under Mao. The American government, however, was far more zealous in preaching human rights to Moscow than to Peking. Why? American officials used to explain that, since there was "no visible constituency for it within the country," the regime was not at a stage where anything could be done about it. Perhaps they supposed there was no constituency for abstruse historical reasons—the Confucian tradition, the concern with the collective rather than with the individual good, and so on. But by 1978 Amnesty International had issued a telling report portraying the sweep of political repression in China; and Peking wall posters proclaimed, "We cannot tolerate that human rights and democracy are only slogans of the western bourgeoisie, and [that] the eastern proletariat only needs dictatorship." Another poster: "As Chinese citizens, we think that truth is universal and that the soul of mankind, human rights, is not limited by national boundaries or geography." The poster was signed "The Human Rights Group."

Perhaps human rights were less culture-bound than some Americans, in an excess either of humility or vanity, liked to believe. In the end, the answer to the question whether political and civil rights are local or universal depends on one's view of man. Over the long run, this historian finds it hard to believe that the instinct for political and civil freedom is confined to the happy few in the North Atlantic littoral.

VIII

BY THE END of 1978 it appeared that, even if the crusade was dead, the campaign was here to stay, at least for the life of the Carter administration. Human rights was now institutionalized as a claimant agency in American foreign policy decisions. Foreign assistance took account of the condition of human rights in cases where strategic considerations were not deemed over-riding. . . . A long list of countries were denied aid or permitted it under se-vere restrictions: Cuba, Vietnam, Cambodia, Chile, Argentina, Uganda, Mozambique, Ethiopia, Paraguay, and others. The American government opposed loans by international financial institutions to countries flagrantly violating human rights. American embassies became human rights watch of-fices around the world. The repeated resurrections of the campaign in the face of premature obituaries demonstrated both the genuine continuity of the administration's concern and, even more, the issue's underlying vitality.

For all its vulnerabilities, the campaign had significantly altered the in-ternational atmosphere. It had placed human rights on the world's agenda—and on the world's conscience. It had given heart to brave men and women fighting for their rights around the planet. It had encouraged the release of political prisoners in Indonesia, South Korea, the Philippines, Brazil, Cuba, and other countries, amnesty in Poland, a peaceful change of administration in the Dominican Republic. It had placed the burden of proof within the American government on those who wanted to embrace despots. And by ex-erting pressure, however unevenly, for human rights, the American govern-ment had also significantly altered the world's theory of the United States as a rampant capitalist power bent on global economic hegemony. . . .

Can the United States do more than it has done to induce other govern-ments to stop abusing their people? If a strong prima facie case can be made against military assistance to countries that trample on political and civil rights, the case for the termination of economic assistance is sometimes less clear. Why should people already poor and oppressed be punished further be-cause of the iniquity of their governments? In most cases the denial of Amer-ican assistance would not cause a government whose survival depends on repression to change its policies of control. Moreover, once inserted into bi-lateral relations, human rights invites unseemly bargaining—the release of political prisoners, for example, in exchange for a credit from the Export-Im-port Bank.

The more the United States presses human rights as a unilateral initia-tive, the more it risks becoming a high court of indignation. One hopes that the administration will ponder the point made by American statesmen from John Quincy Adams to Theodore Roosevelt that, save in extreme cases, we can probably do more for human rights by example at home than by inter-vention abroad. One would wish, too, for more systematic self-scrutiny of our own motives. Not every American who invokes human rights these days re-ally cares all that much about human rights per se. Cold warriors, who showed no interest in the fate of human rights under Greek colonels or

Chilean generals, hope to use the issue in order to block a SALT II agreement. Protectionists seize the issue in order to stop the import into the United States of competitive Latin American products such as sugar and cotton. Nor has the United States been willing to join any international authority that would engage in external scrutiny of our practices. This fear lies behind the continued resistance to those toothless wonders, the U.N. conventions and covenants. While it may be arresting to hear our president proclaim that "no force on earth" can separate us from the commitment "to enhance human rights," we would be wise to rid ourselves of the messianic illusion that the United States is the only nation "capable of true leadership among the community of nations."

IX

THE LIMITS of a unilateral American role in reforming the world are plain—and raise the question of the multilateralization of the human rights campaign. But the U.N. General Assembly's concern for human rights is evidently exhausted by contemplation of South Africa, Israel, and Chile. Even Cambodia and Uganda have thus far escaped rebuke. And the U.N. Human Rights Commission is an imposture, its members nurtured, in the words of Murray Kempton, "in the libertarian atmosphere of countries like Bulgaria, Iran, . . . and the Soviet Union." Even Uganda is a member. . . .

The Conference on Security and Cooperation in Europe, established under the Helsinki Agreement, provides another forum for the promotion of human rights. The first follow-up meeting (held, ironically, in Yugoslavia, a nation celebrated for the high quality of its political prisoners) gave the democracies an opportunity to challenge the communist states on their failure to give effect to Basket Three. By responding with specific allegations of Western violations, the communist states themselves legitimized the issue for international debate. Though the meeting adjourned without agreement, it conducted an effective review of the post-Helsinki record. The communists neither walked out nor declined the next meeting to be held in Madrid in 1980.

It would be a mistake, however, to expect drastic transformations to come out of Madrid. It may well be that, given the existing balance of values as well as power in world affairs, human rights cannot be pushed much further in the sphere of government-to-government relations. The next phase of the campaign is likely to gather its force outside government. One side effect of the Carter administration's campaign has been to leave the impression that human rights is essentially a matter among states. Yet when states push human rights, their motives are always, and rightly, suspect. The "moral duties" assumed by governments, in Carter's unfortunate but accurate phrase in his inaugural address, seem "invariably" to be in their own "best interests." Politicization is not necessarily the best destiny for human rights.

X

THE MORAL duties of human rights rest just as strongly on nongovernmental as on governmental bodies. Amnesty International, the International League for the Rights of Man, and the International Commission of Jurists have of course performed notable work. A special obligation rests, I would think, on professional associations. Many political prisoners are professionals themselves. When they are arrested, sent to labor camps or insane asylums, tortured, murdered, their professional colleagues around the world have the obligation to rally to their defense. So the National Academy of Sciences spoke out for Sakharov, Shcharansky, and other Soviet scientists; so the American Psychiatric Association protested the arrest of Alexander Podrabinek after the publication of his book on the confinement of Soviet dissenters to insane asylums; so the World Psychiatric Association condemned the political misuse of psychiatry in the Soviet Union and elsewhere; so PEN, the Authors League, and the Association of American Publishers have protested the suppression of cultural freedom.

It is singular that American scientists and psychiatrists have been far more sensitive to human rights issues than American political scientists and historians. The American Political Science Association, after righteously declining to meet in Chicago because Illinois had not ratified the Equal Rights Amendment, could find no human rights obstacle to participating in the 1979 meeting of the International Political Science Association in Moscow. The American Historical Association watched the persecution of Soviet historians—Amalrik, Medvedev, Solzhenitsyn (whose *Gulag Archipelago* is a historical work), Valentyn Moroz—without a word of objection or regret.

The conventional argument against protests is that they antagonize orthodox Soviet political scientists and historians without helping the dissenters. Yet experience has shown that it is precisely the spotlight of international concern that exerts restraining effect on arbitrary government. "The most frightening thing that can happen to a person," Mihajlo Mihajlov, the dissident Yugoslav writer, has noted, "is to be forgotten in prison." Amalrik has testified that it plays "a very important part in terms of moral support to know that one is known and well-known. . . . The Soviet authorities do react quite sensitively to western public opinion." "It must be understood," Solzhenitsyn himself has said, "that the East is not at all indifferent to protests from Western society. On the contrary it mortally fears them—and only them." E. P. Thompson, the historian of the English working class, commented: "Solzhenitsyn has asked us to shout once more. And we must, urgently, meet his request. . . . We must make it clear again, without equivocation, that we uphold the right of Soviet citizens to think, communicate, and act as free, self-activating people; and that we utterly despise the clumsy police patrols of Soviet intellectual and social life."

The American Historical Association did not shout, or even whisper. Instead, it took part in the Third U.S.-U.S.S.R. Historians' Colloquium in Moscow in November 1978 and secured a grant from the National Endowment for the Humanities for two U.S.-U.S.S.R. conferences on quantitative history in 1979 and 1980, thereby expressing its solidarity with the historians the regime approves rather than with those the regime persecutes. I write all this with intense shame for my profession.

To regard human rights as simply an issue among states is a form of cop-out. Nor, I would emphasize, should professional concern be confined to the abuse of human rights in the communist world. Since professional associations need not balance competing national interests, they can speak without constraint about the persecution of their colleagues in all countries. The promotion of human rights depends in the end on the individual commitment of men and women in free societies. "Nothing is more disgusting," said Emerson, "than the crowing about liberty by slaves, as most men are, and the flippant mistaking for freedom of some paper preamble like a Declaration of Independence or the statute right to vote, by those who have never dared to think or to act." In the end, it is on the strength of this spirit, applied primarily at home and secondarily and carefully abroad, that the success of the American mission depends.

Human Rights and Foreign Policy: A Proposal

William F. Buckley, Jr.

WINTER 1980/81

The Soviets in Geneva [to negotiate SALT II] never even hinted at
the Kremlin's resentment of the Carter human rights policy, and
the Americans were equally careful not to echo their Government's criticism of Soviet human rights abuses. Unaware of this
rule, a newcomer to the U.S. team brought up the dissidents in an
informal tête-à-tête with his Russian opposite number. When he
reported the exchange later in a "memcon," his superiors told him
never again to mix business with displeasure.

— *Time* Magazine, May 21, 1979,
a special report on the history of the
negotiation of the SALT II treaty.

. . . WE ARE ALL agreed that the movement for human rights, politically
expressed, is quite new; that U.S. involvement in that movement has been
uneven; that the advent of the United Nations Covenant on Human Rights
slightly altered the juridical international picture; that the Soviet Union came
recently to a policy of manipulating the West's campaign for human rights;
that the Vietnam War brought on a general disillusionment with American
idealism; that the realpolitik of Nixon-Kissinger generated first congressional
resistance and then, through candidate and later President Jimmy Carter, executive resistance to adjourn official U.S. concern for human rights. And, of
course, everyone knows that Mr. Carter's human rights policy is now in
shambles. This is the case, in my judgment, not because of executive ineptitude, but because of morphological problems that can't be met without an organic division of responsibility.

[402]

II

ALTHOUGH THE very idea of human "rights" is firmly rooted in biblical injunction, which asserts a metaphysical equality ("Thou shalt love thy neighbor as thyself") and enjoins altruism ("Inasmuch as ye have done it unto one of the least of these my brethren, ye have done it unto me"), biblical insights made little political progress over the centuries in which church and state joined in accepting, and even underwriting, civil class distinctions at the extreme of which were self-assured kings and self-abnegating slaves, never mind that the political phenomenon never challenged, let alone diluted, the theological conviction that both kings and slaves would eventually answer to the same divine tribunal.

Human rights, including a measure of political rights, were asserted and to a degree explicated in the documents that led to, and flowered from, the American and French Revolutions. The Bill of Rights and the Declaration of the Rights of Man enumerated individual rights which the state might not impinge upon, save by due process. The respect paid to these rights by sponsoring governments varied with the vicissitudes of the historical season, an ambivalence by no means outdated. Negro slaves in America coexisted with the Bill of Rights; the Reign of Terror in France with the Declaration of the Rights of Man; Gulag with Helsinki. There are few surviving commentators, let alone historians, who are inclined to defend the proposition that the articulation of a human right leads to its realization.

In short, though inchoately an ancient idea, human rights are a relatively new political objective and, as often as not, only a nominal political objective.

The United States has had cyclical romances with the notion of responsibility for the rights of extranationals, an insight also biblical in origin ("Am I my brother's keeper?" asked Cain, who, having drawn the wrong conclusion, slew Abel), cosmopolitanized by John Donne's resonant assertion that we are, as individuals, involved in mankind. Professor Schlesinger nicely summarizes the episode involving Louis Kossuth, driven from Hungary by the Austrians during the repression following the convulsions of 1848. There were those in Congress who came close to advocating a punitive expedition against Austria; others considered lesser sanctions; but, all in all, Congress engaged in a feisty bout of moral indignation. The prevailing voice, however, was Henry Clay's. His argument was in two parts, the first that the United States, with its fitful record, uneasily judged the delinquencies of other nations; the other, that condemning Austria while ignoring such conspicuous transgressors on human rights as Turkey, Spain, Great Britain (yes, Great Britain!), and Russia, was simply . . . eccentric.

Several years before Professor Schlesinger reminded us of it, George Kennan, in his exasperation over the Vietnam War, had called attention to the tranquilization of rambunctious American idealism by Secretary of State John Quincy Adams, delivered, appropriately enough, on the Fourth of July (in 1821). "Wherever the standard of freedom and independence has been or shall be unfurled," Adams said, "there will be America's heart, her benedictions, and her prayers. But she goes not abroad in search of monsters to destroy. She is the well-wisher to the freedom and independence of all. She is the champion and vindicator only of her own."

The rhetorical exaltation of what is still known as Wilsonianism reached its apogee in the inaugural address of President John F. Kennedy. It is painful to repeat those ingenuous strophes, so dissonant to the ear after the Vietnam War, but a narrative of U.S. attitudes toward human rights abroad is simply incomplete without them. We will, declared the freshly anointed President, "pay any price, bear any burden, meet any hardship, support any friend, oppose any foe, to assure the survival and the success of liberty."

Did Mr. Kennedy, in uttering those words, recognize the *weight* of the responsibility he was assuming on behalf of the United States? The answer is that he *gloried* in that responsibility: "In the long history of the world, only a few generations have been granted the role of defending freedom in its hour of maximum danger. I do not shrink from this responsibility—I welcome it."

Was this pure bombast? Or was the listener entitled to assume that the new president had actually given thought to the practical consequences of his words? "The energy, the faith, the devotion which we bring to this endeavor will light our country and all who serve it—and the glow from that fire can truly light the world." A few months later that glow lit up the Bay of Pigs, but by no means the world, or even the Capitol steps from which these quixotic—potvaliant?—words had been spoken.

In short, U.S. involvement in the movement to universalize human rights has been episodic, but even early on, it evidenced an inchoate disjunction between the power to affirm and the power to dispose.

Yet the scaffolding on which President Kennedy had spoken was not insubstantial. There were the Fourteen Points of Woodrow Wilson, which he coupled to his antecedent crusade to make the world "safe for democracy." There came then, in 1941, Franklin D. Roosevelt's Four Freedoms. These—in passing—were significant for transmuting human rights into something much more than the negative injunctions on government activity conveyed in the Bill of Rights. F.D.R. did not exactly discover, but he and Winston Churchill gave declamatory voice to, positive but not readily achievable obligations of government: something called Freedom from Want, which seven years later gave birth to about 30 importunate children (e.g., "Everyone has the right . . . to free choice of employment") in the Universal Declaration and related documents—children who, for the most part, have lived unhappily ever since. But while Woodrow Wilson and Franklin Roosevelt and John F. Kennedy were merely American presidents, giving voice to an erratic, yet progressively universalist, statement of American idealism, the birth of the United Nations and the subscription by member states to its charter gave near-universal codification to the notion of the obligation of the state to acknowledge the human rights of its own citizens and hinted at the mutual obligation of states to ensure each other's fidelity to these obligations. Because the charter itself—and this before the ensuing elaboration in the Universal Declaration and other comments—committed its members to "reaffirm faith in fundamental human rights."

In short, the United Nations transformed human rights into something of an official international paradigm and began to suggest an obligation by member states to modify their foreign policy accordingly.

The Universal Declaration's International Covenant on Civil and Political Rights and on Economic, Social, and Political Rights were announced on September 26, 1973, as having been ratified by the Presidium of the Supreme Soviet and thus under the Soviet Constitution became the supreme law of the land. The Soviet ratification aroused little popular notice. To this day there is no universally accepted explanation for Soviet timing. Probably it had to do with the Soviet Union's efforts to ingratiate itself with those European countries with which, two years later, it concluded the Final Act of the Conference on Security and Cooperation in Europe (Helsinki Accords). "Basket Three" of this pact became the most emphatic juridical validation of certain individual rights in Soviet history. The Universal Declaration, after 25 years of desuetude, had become, for most nations, mere liturgy; safe, therefore, to ratify without giving rise to international expectations. Basket Three was widely held to be the indispensable moral quid pro quo by the Soviet Union to the Helsinki Accords that gave the Soviet Union what it had wanted for so long, namely, de jure recognition of the postwar frontiers. To have accepted Basket Three while ignoring the Universal Declaration would have posed problems for Soviet negotiators.

As it happened, most of the Soviet citizens who undertook actively to monitor compliance by the Soviet Union with the terms of Basket Three are in jail, psychiatric hospitals, exile; or mute. Their Czechoslovakian counterparts have been tried, convicted, and sent to jail.

In short, the Soviet Union in due course recognized the necessity to cope with, and therefore manipulate, the human rights dimension as an aspect of its own foreign policy.

III

NOBODY KNOWS exactly what impelled Jimmy Carter to seize on human rights as the touchstone of U.S. foreign policy. Mr. Carter's opposition to the Vietnam War could be classified as ritualistic: i.e., he was not one of its early critics. Now the U.S. venture in Vietnam has been disgraced by most moralists, which is to say less than that it has been disgraced by history. Its relevance here is that Jimmy Carter on several occasions spoke ill of it. In his acceptance speech at Madison Square Garden upon being nominated for president, he spoke of it as an "immoral" war. At Notre Dame University in 1977, he stated that our "inordinate fear of communism" led us to the "intellectual and moral poverty" of the Vietnam War. Senator Daniel Patrick Moynihan's comment is here relevant not merely for the job it does of effective contention, but in shedding light on the confused provenance of Jimmy Carter's stated redirection of U.S. foreign policy with emphasis on human rights. Moynihan said, "This causal connection can . . . be challenged. Some of us said at the time that the enterprise was doomed because it was misconceived and mismanaged. Are we to say now—in this, echoing what our enemies say of us—that it was also wrong or immoral to wish to resist the advance of totalitarian communism?"

Carter's reference to Vietnam, together with Moynihan's demurral, catapult us into the awful complication posed by the Vietnam War, coming on the heels of the attempted liberation of Cuba. The *moral* disavowal of the Vietnam War took us a long way toward the Platonization of the spirit of our concern for human rights. Elizabeth Drew reminds us that Jimmy Carter came to the whole subject of human-rights-as-an-integral-part-of-foreign-policy in a haphazard way—not to be compared, say, with the evolution of Lincoln's structured approach to slavery. In an address to the Foreign Policy Association in New York in 1976, Carter said that "we . . . can take the lead in . . . promoting basic global standards of human rights,"—a statement that might have been made, and has been, by an orator in the United Nations. But by the time he reached his inaugural address, he was speaking of his commitment to human rights as "absolute."

The opposition to the war in Vietnam did more than implicitly to disavow any generic responsibility by the United States to resist totalitarian aggression in such terms as had been advanced by President Kennedy. So bitter was the opposition to the war that it was transmuted in some quarters into a tacit disavowal of the modus operandi of American culture, recalling Henry Clay's arguments against U.S. moral effrontery. The process began by stressing the imperfections of our ally Ngo Dinh Diem; went on to the immorality of our military procedures (napalm, bombing); and ended by concluding that the United States was so tainted that there was nothing really to say about the superiority of our own society over that against which we had set out to defend the South Vietnamese.

The effect of this self-denigration must be supposed to have had a great impact on the perception of the People's Republic of China. Barbara Tuchman, for instance, came back from China to write a paean on Mao Zedong, conceding only perfunctorily that, to be sure, there were certain "negative aspects," which, however, "fade in relative importance" alongside the accomplishments of the regime. . . . One must conclude that the hectic enthusiasm for a society that observed not a single provision of the U.S. Bill of Rights must have reflected the low opinion of the United States, its paraphernalia of rights notwithstanding, that prevailed among the most intense critics of the Vietnam War.

In brief: the retreat from Vietnam was not merely a disavowal of Wilsonianism as a foreign policy, but a disavowal of Wilsonianism as metaphor. Who is to say that the society that grants such liberties as we grant, and is nevertheless so rotten, is necessarily to be preferred over such a society as Ho Chi Minh and Mao Zedong created, without human rights, to be sure, but otherwise so wholesome? Surely utopia lies somewhere beyond the rights of Coca Cola to operate—or even of the Bill of Rights to guarantee individual inviolability in the face of social *force majeure?* Although the intellectual community is retreating from its position on Mao Zedong ever so slowly, indeed one might say *pari passu* with the retreat of the present rulers of China from idolization of Mao, it is doing so. The events in Cambodia and the phenomenon of the boat people have likewise injured the perception of North Vietnam as a kind of godfatherly presence in Indochina. The prominence given to Carter's position on human rights was a reaction to the radical ideological egalitarianism brought on by the Vietnam War—the criticism whose base was, in effect, "Who says we-all are better off than them-all?"

During these years (1969–76) our foreign policy was given over to the balance-of-power politics of Nixon, Kissinger, and Ford. Critics of the war became hard investigators of executive military and paramilitary procedures. Of all things, the CIA under Kennedy (leave aside the tangentially relevant question whether at his instructions) apparently expressed a velleity (it cannot have been more than that) to assassinate Cuba's Fidel Castro; failing which, to make his beard fall off; failing which, to contrive to give him laughing gas or whatever, that would activate in the middle of one of his speeches (one wonders, what would be the resulting difference?). The investigators learned that the U.S. government had intervened, however indirectly, to help those in Chile who resisted President Salvador Allende. And of course, we continued our alliances with random dictators, in South Korea, in the Philippines, in Iran and Pakistan; all over. President Carter, joining the critics even as he plunged headlong into his crusade for human rights, summed it all up at Notre Dame a few months into his presidency by saying that "our inordinate fear of communism" had driven us (the president at this point was referring to preceding administrations) "to embrace any dictator who joined us in our fear."

The political right, meanwhile, staggered from a succession of shocks absorbable only because their longtime attachment to Richard Nixon appeased their strategic misgivings (how could *he* betray the cause?). The first of these was the triumphant opening to Beijing. Whatever its usefulness as strategy, a public that had been brought up to believe that Mao Zedong combined the vices of the theoretician Lenin and the executioner Stalin saw their champion on television toasting the health of Mao in the Great Hall of the People and returning to Washington to give personal testimony to "the total belief" of the Chinese leaders in "their system of government." A few months later Nixon was off to Moscow, where he participated openly, indeed effusively, in the apparent *Gemütlichkeit,* with leaders who were simultaneously provisioning the North Vietnamese who were continuing their workaday slaughter of American soldiers in Vietnam.

Then, in the summer of 1975, Solzhenitsyn came to Washington—and President Gerald Ford, on the advice of Henry Kissinger, declined to receive him. The impurity of that gesture resonated in the consciousness of those who felt that morality had at least a symbolic role to play in foreign policy.

Two events give historic importance to the second of the three debates between President Gerald Ford and candidate Jimmy Carter. The subject was foreign policy, and the Carter entourage were anxious that their candidate not give the impression of being too soft to cope with the Soviet Union, too good-natured, too manipulable. It is reported that Zbigniew Brzezinski advised the candidate to revise his position on the Helsinki Accords, which he had theretofore merely criticized as giving the Soviet Union legal standing in Eastern Europe. Why not go soft on the treaty, which was popular in Europe and in much of the United States, and bring up the Soviet Union's failure to live up to its obligations under Basket Three? "According to a number of witnesses, it was in San Francisco that Carter first heard of Basket Three—a term that in the course of the debate he dropped on what must have been a puzzled nation, as if he had been familiar with it for some time." On the same program in which candidate Carter showed a deft familiarity with an outstanding, if already forlorn, mechanism designed to protect certain rights of citizens living under Soviet domination, the president of the United States announced that Eastern Europe was free of "Soviet domination." The questioner, Max Frankel of *The New York Times,* could no more believe his ears than the millions of listeners and thought it a slip of the tongue, asking the question one more time: "I'm sorry, could I just follow—did I understand you to say, sir, that the Russians are not using Eastern Europe as their own sphere of influence in occupying most of the countries there and making sure with their troops that it is a communist zone?" President Ford answered emphatically, "I don't believe, Mr. Frankel . . . that the Poles consider themselves dominated by the Soviet Union."

In a single broadcast, Jimmy Carter had shown himself sensitive to human rights and to Soviet infidelity to a treaty commitment, while his opponent gave the impression that he was not even aware that a whole people were being routinely deprived of their rights. It is a subjective judgment that Gerald Ford's gaffe, alongside Carter's thrust, affected the outcome of the election. In any event, Carter did win, and human rights, as U.S. policy, were back in the saddle, though reconciliations that were to prove impossible lay ahead.

In short, realpolitik crowded out human rights during the Kissinger years, but the momentum of the criticism of the Vietnam War drove critics to superordinate the right of the sovereign nation (e.g., Chile, Cuba) over any responsibility by the United States to frustrate totalitarianization. Jimmy Carter detected, in his random emphasis on human rights, a popular political response that issued from (a) conservatives affronted by the collapse of the social face of diplomatic anticommunism and (b) liberals who felt that the denigration of human rights in the tidal wave of anti-Americanism required reconsideration.

IV

ANOTHER REASON for Executive assertiveness in the matter of human rights was the mounting activity of Congress, motivated once again by the momentum that had been generated against Executive unaccountability during the Vietnam War. Inevitably, a branch of government losing power to other branches of government attempts to redress the balance. The lesion of power to Congress during 1969–76, expressed in such legislation as the Cooper-Church Amendment and the War Powers Act (measures designed to limit the power of the Executive to take the country into protracted military engagements like Vietnam), had the effect on the Executive that daily calisthenics by a contender would have on a prospective competitor. Professor Schlesinger quotes Deputy Secretary of State Robert Ingersoll, warning Kissinger in 1974, "If the Department did not place itself ahead of the curve on this issue [human rights], Congress would take the matter out of the Department's hands."

Indeed Congress had been busy. A profusion of human rights legislation began with the passage of the Amendment to the Foreign Assistance Act of 1973, multiplying enormously the scattered bits of law enacted previously. . . .

Now all this legislation is at once a comprehensive assertion of U.S. interest in human rights, and an invitation to philosophical and diplomatic chaos. It reflects most of the weaknesses of our public policy in its practical deviousness and in the selective indignation it encourages. Congress has ruled that no economic assistance may be extended to any country engaged in gross violations of "internationally recognized" human rights—"unless such assistance will directly benefit the needy people in such country." It is difficult to imagine a situation in which economic assistance, particularly in kind, would not in fact help needy people or fail so to represent itself. The act goes on to require of the State Department a yearly report, one that would take into account the probings of relevant international organizations on the status of human rights within all countries receiving assistance.

The legislation is interesting in that there isn't (to my knowledge) any record of any congressional review of assistance given to a delinquent country which actually led to the official congressional conclusion that such assistance was illegal on the grounds that (a) the country was a gross violator of human rights, while (b) U.S. aid did not in fact help needy people. The impact of the yearly reports is, then—assuming the president elects not to act on them—purely psychological: to hold in obloquy those nations that are gross violators of human rights. To let them, so to speak, twist slowly, slowly in the wind of moral displeasure, even if their stomachs are full. All this figures substantially in the conclusions to which I have been drawn, below. A second, and perverse, feature of the annual report is that it tends to highlight the villainies of countries to which we routinely give aid. Since we do not give aid to the communist countries, they are officially exempted from the annual pathological examinations—an interesting means of achieving immunity. . . .

The Jackson-Vanik Amendment—denying most-favored-nation treatment to countries that deny their citizens the right or opportunity to emigrate—is the most celebrated of the congressional human rights enactments. Although clearly aimed at one country (the Soviet Union) for the benefit of one class of aspirant-emigrés (Jews), the language is generically drawn. The amendment, by the way, preserves the usual waiver granted to the president under specified circumstances. The Soviet Union objected violently to its passage, cancelled a trade negotiation and, after the bill's passage, retaliated by reducing the number of Jews to whom it issued exit visas. Henry Kissinger and Richard Nixon have on more than one occasion cited the Jackson-Vanik Amendment and its consequences as clear evidence that "quiet diplomacy" works better than legislation when the objective is an actual change in policy rather than moral rodomontade.

In brief: the encyclopaedic intervention by Congress into the international human rights market has by practical necessity needed to provide for executive waiver. But the residual effect is to encourage specific pressures against (a) countries of less than critical strategic importance; and (b) countries without U.S. constituencies sufficient to exert effective influence on the U.S. government. The resulting mix is ineffective in respect of the enhancement of human rights and unedifying in respect of a consistent regard for human rights.

V

ALTHOUGH President Carter, as we have seen, had been generally bland on the subject of human rights, he was a tiger by the time of his inaugural address: "Our commitment to human rights must be absolute." The real problem, of course, is where to fix our commitment to human rights on this side of absoluteness.[1] President Carter's inaugural address presaged the ensuing chaos. For a while there was great excitement. However short-lived, it was breath-catching. In a few days Jimmy Carter actually answered a letter addressed to him by Andrei Sakharov. A few weeks after that he contrived to meet and shake hands (no photographs) with the valiant Vladimir Bukovsky, among the most illustrious of Soviet dissidents. The Soviet Union exploded. Within a year, the United States ambassador to the United Nations Human Rights Commission in Geneva was being privately instructed by President Carter's secretary of state *under no circumstances* even to mention the name of Yuri Orlov, who had just been packed off to jail for the crime of monitoring Soviet noncompliance with the provisions of the Helsinki Accords' Basket Three, which candidate Carter had castigated the Soviet Union for failure to live up to. Jimmy Carter was crestfallen, the great Human Rights Band laid down its instruments, and everyone has been struggling ever since plausibly to give the theme of our policy on human rights.

An attempt to say what is operative U.S. policy in respect of human rights requires a survey of the behavior of the principal executive of U.S. for-

---

[1] The President is plagued by verbal imprecision. It does not really mean anything at all to say that one's commitment to human rights "must be absolute." Since it *cannot* be absolute (an absolute commitment would require us to declare war against China and the Soviet Union, just to begin with), then it has to be something less than absolute.

eign policy. President Carter's position is best attempted not by reasoning a priori from his general commitment ("absolute") to human rights, but a posteriori from his actions. Almost immediately it transpired that the State Department bureaucracy was apprehensive about the impact of Carter's human rights declarations on concrete questions being negotiated or prospectively in negotiation. The military, in pursuit of its own concerns for U.S. security, was similarly troubled. The State Department and the disarmament folk feared that an antagonized Soviet Union would behave more militantly at the bargaining table. The military was quite unwilling to trade Subic Bay in the Philippines for a moral boycott of President Marcos. An opportunity arose for President Carter to begin to make critical distinctions. Fogbound, he did not do so.

In a speech delivered March 25, 1964 in the Senate, Senator William Fulbright, at the time chairman of the Senate Foreign Relations Committee, made a useful distinction, even if he went too far with it: "Insofar as a nation is content to practice its doctrines within its own frontiers, that nation, however repugnant its ideology, is one with which we have no proper quarrel." That distinction is geopolitically appealing. Thus in 1965, to guard against what President Johnson perceived as the threat of a communization of the Dominican Republic (it is immaterial whether the threat was real or fancied), we landed armed forces in the Dominican Republic. The western half of Hispaniola had been for eight years under the domination of a murderous Haitian doctor who routinely practiced all the conventional barbarities on his people and not a few unconventional ones. It did not occur to us to send the marines (as once we had done during this century, though our motives were eclectic) to put down Papa Doc—tacit recognition of the intuitive cogency of Fulbright's doctrine. . . .

But President Carter not only failed to remark Fulbright's distinction, he agitated to blur it. "I have never had an inclination to single out the Soviet Union as the only place where human rights are being abridged," he said at his press conference of February 23, 1977. And again on March 24 at a press conference, "I've tried to make sure that the world knows that we're not singling out the Soviet Union for abuse or criticism." By June, he was sounding defensive. Not only had the phrase become formulaic ("We've not singled out the Soviet Union for criticism"), he went on to say exactly the opposite of what all his rhetoric required: "and I've never tried to inject myself into the internal affairs of the Soviet Union. I've never made the first comment that personally criticized General Secretary Brezhnev."

Human rights everywhere was the president's theoretical objective. And so it remained, even if there were to be no more letters to Sakharovs or visits with Bukovskys. He clung tenaciously to his theoretical position: "I've worked day and night to make sure that a concern for human rights is woven through everything our government does, both at home and abroad," he said at a press conference at the end of his first year in office (December 15, 1977); and one year later, commemorating the 30th anniversary of the adoption of the Universal Declaration of Human Rights (December 6, 1978), he pronounced, "As long as I am president, the government of the United States will continue, throughout the world, to enhance human rights. No force on Earth can separate us from that commitment." . . .

But the president, although he summoned the necessary discipline to restrain himself from criticism, found it difficult to avoid diplomatic hyperbole. Arriving in Warsaw on December 30, 1977, he greeted the communist proconsul Gierek with the astonishing news that Poland was a "partner in a common effort against war and deprivation." He recalled that at the end of World War I, Herbert Hoover ("a great American") "came to Poland to help you ease the suffering of an independent Poland. Circumstances were different and the struggle was long, but Hoover said, and I quote, 'If history teaches us anything, it is that from the unquenchable vitality of the Polish race, Poland will rise again from these ashes.' And," said Carter—jubilantly?—"his prediction came true." These words were perfectly congruent with the picture of Poland described during the famous debate by Gerald Ford. They would not have needed changing if it had happened that during the week before Carter's touchdown in Warsaw, Poland had suddenly wrested its independence from the Soviet Union. The press did not have long to wait. Later in the day:

> Q. During the presidential debates, in a celebrated exchange, President Ford claimed that Eastern Europe was not under Soviet domination. And you replied, "Tell it to the Poles." Well, now that you're here, is it your view that this domination will continue almost into perpetuity, or do you see a day when Poland may be actually free?

The president replied that "our nation is committed to the proposition that all countries would be autonomous . . . and . . . free of unwanted interference and entanglements with other nations. . . . I think . . . it's a deep commitment of the vast majority of the Polish people, a desire and a commitment not to be dominated."

> Q. You don't deny that they are dominated here?
> A. I think I've commented all I wish on that subject.

Four months later, on April 12, 1978, President Carter welcomed President Ceausescu of Rumania to the White House. At the ceremony, Carter announced that "the people of the United States are honored by having as our guest a great leader of a great country." And he went on to say, "Our goals are also the same, to have a just system of economics and politics, to let the people of the world share in growth, in peace, in personal freedom." In Civil Liberties, Freedom House gives a rating of six to Rumania (seven is the lowest rating). In its Ranking of Nations by Political Rights, it gives Rumania a seven.

In greeting Yugoslav President Tito (March 7, 1978), Carter said: "Perhaps as much as any other person, he exemplifies in Yugoslavia the eagerness for freedom, independence, and liberty that exists throughout Eastern Europe and indeed throughout the world." Freedom House on Yugoslavia: Civil Liberties, five; Political Rights, six.

It was not until April 21, 1978 that Carter got around to criticizing Cambodia. When he did, he called it the world's "worst" violator of human rights. "America," he said, "cannot avoid the responsibility to speak out in condemnation of the Cambodian government, the worst violator of human rights in the world today." America, through its president, precisely *had* avoided the responsibility to speak out in condemnation of the Cambodian government about whose practices as much was known by the end of 1975 as by the spring of 1978.

In brief: by his own example as president, and by the letdown that followed his exalted rhetoric on the subject, Mr. Carter, with some help from the 93rd Congress, has reduced the claims of human rights in U.S. foreign policy to an almost unparalleled state of confusion.

VI

MY PROPOSAL is to separate two questions. The first is: How do human rights fare in a given country? The second: What should the United States do about it? It is the commingling of the two that has brought forth existing confusions and distortions. The question whether we collaborate with the Soviet Union in order to avoid a world war is unrelated to any commitment a civilized nation ought to feel to human rights. Although the avoidance of a world war and the safety of the American state are primary objectives, the ethical imperative requires us as a nation, journeying through history, regularly to remark the brutality of the Soviet system—even if we make no commitment, thereby, to do anything concrete to mitigate those conditions.

On the whole we are better off stating, at all those international conferences, what it is we believe that sovereign states owe to their citizens in the way of recognizing individual rights—and let it go at that—than to collaborate in rituals of efficacy which we know will be without operative meaning. By the same token a constant encephalophonic reading, uninfluenced by distractions of diplomatic concern, of the condition of human rights in a given country, to the extent that this can be accomplished (the difficulty in ascertaining these conditions obviously varies) gives a gyroscopic steadiness of judgment which is the enemy of hypocrisy, dissimulation, and such other inventions as have disfigured the idealism of the human rights movement.

Congress should repeal existing legislation on the question of human rights (although, because of the loopholes, it would not really need to do so in order to promulgate the commission described below). It should then establish a Commission on Human Rights composed of a chairman and four members, with provisions for a staff of a dozen persons (approximately the size of the staff of the assistant secretary of state for human rights and humanitarian affairs). For symbolic reasons primarily, but also for practical reasons, the commission should not be affiliated with the Department of State. It might plausibly be affiliated with the judiciary or perhaps even with the Department of Justice. What matters most is that its mandate should be distinctive, unrelated to policymaking, whether by the executive or the legislative branches of government. . . .

The mandate would most severely restrict the commission's public role to the reporting of factual conditions: never to the recommendation of policy. Policy would continue to issue from Congress and the Executive. The commission would report publicly, once a year, to the president and to Congress—in the nature of the event, to the world—on the condition of human freedom in every country, using the Universal Declaration of the United Nations as the paradigm. . . .

VII

IT SHOULD BE unnecessary to explain that the existence of a United States Commission on Human Rights could not constitutionally deprive either Congress or the Executive of powers that inhere in those institutions. No one has the power to tell the president he should not make a fool of himself on landing in Warsaw—he would still be free to do so. But the silent, yet omnipresent, countenance of the Commission on Human Rights, with its lapidary findings on the condition of human rights in Poland, would make it less likely that the president, in pursuit of diplomacy, would traduce idealism. Congress can vote to deny arms or soybeans or *Saturday Night Fever* to any country Congress chooses to punish or victimize or bully or wheedle; but the existence of the commission, with its findings, would provide certain coordinates that might guard against such caprice as nowadays tends to disfigure country-specific legislation.

And—viewed from the other end—for the wretched of the earth, in their prisons, with or without walls, in the torture chambers, in the loneliness they feel as they weigh the distortions of diplomacy, there would be something like: a constant. A commission mute while the United States collaborates with Stalin in pursuit of Hitler, or Mao in pursuit of Brezhnev, but resolutely unwilling to falsify the record of Josef Stalin or Mao Zedong in their treatment of their own people.

"The great enemy of clear language is insincerity," Orwell wrote, in the same essay in which he lamented that "in our time, political speech and writing are largely the defense of the indefensible." To say the truth—says Solzhenitsyn—is the single most important thing of all. Politicians cannot always say the truth and pursue policies organic to their profession. But the saying of the truth about human rights, as distinguished from the superordination of human rights over all other concerns, is not incompatible with the mechanics of foreign policy.

Finally the question is asked: Would such a commission, with its yearly findings, its reports to the nation, its testimony before Congress, its international broadcast of its findings—would it enhance human rights? It is quite impossible to assert that it would do so—or that it would not do so. With the best will in the world, Wilsonianism succeeded in making the world most awfully unsafe for democracy. But as mentioned earlier, there is an encouraging survival, through it all, of the idea of the inviolable individual, and that idea needs watering, not only by the practice of human rights at home, but by the recognition of their neglect abroad. It is a waste of time to argue the inefficacy of telling the truth, the telling of which is useful for its own sake.

The Collapse of Communism

THE NINETEEN EIGHTIES

&PRESIDENT RONALD REAGAN famously called the Soviet Union an "evil empire." But Reagan's tone was mild compared to that of Aleksandr Solzhenitsyn, the legendary Soviet dissident author, whose "Misconceptions About Russia Are a Threat to America" combined a blistering jeremiad against Soviet communism with a warning to the West to abandon any thoughts of détente. President Reagan, elected in 1980, continued and expanded Carter's post-Afghanistan military build-up, sent American troops to Grenada and Lebanon, proposed a new "Star Wars" missile shield, and backed anticommunist insurgents in Nicaragua, Angola, Cambodia, and Afghanistan. The Cold War seemed once again to be heating up.

In fact, Reagan presided over the last battle of the Cold War. After the death of a series of indistinguishably gray general secretaries, in 1985 the cardinals of the Kremlin finally anointed a young apparatchik named Mikhail Gorbachev. A year earlier, Richard Pipes, a historian and Reagan adviser, analyzed the condition of the Soviet system in "Can the Soviet Union Reform?" and suggested that internal reform was Moscow's only feasible option. And sure enough, the new Soviet leader undertook a bold series of reforms known as glasnost (openness) and perestroika (restructuring), which resulted—intentionally and unintentionally—in the collapse of Soviet communism and, indeed, the collapse of the Soviet Union itself. Gorbachev's attempts to save Marxism-Leninism by reforming it—through attempts to modernize his stagnant Brezhnevite economy and political system and reorder Moscow's ties with the West—quickly snowballed out of his control.

The end came with dizzying speed. In 1989, as the world watched in astonishment, Soviet troops were withdrawing from Afghanistan and from Eastern Europe. Gorbachev warned his Warsaw Pact allies that he would not intervene to save them. In Poland, the Solidarity labor movement swept to power. Budapest decided to let refugees fleeing East Germany cross Hungary to reach their truncated land's western, democratic half. In November, the Berlin Wall came down. The tide swept through Eastern Europe—epitomized by the Czech velvet revolution led by a modern philosopher king, Vaclav Havel, the Prague playwright turned president. Only in Romania did the revolution of 1989 turn violent. Within a year, the division of Europe had been undone and the Iron Curtain lifted. Germany was reunified in 1990 and became part of NATO. In August 1991, a motley array of Kremlin die-hards staged a ham-handed coup, but opposition rallied around Russian President Boris Yeltsin, and Gorbachev was returned to power. But the writing was on the walls. The Baltic states declared independence and bolted from the Soviet Union, followed promptly by its other 12 constituent republics. The Communist Party itself was banned. Finally, on December 31, 1991, the Soviet Union landed where Trotsky had vowed capitalism would: in the dustbin of history. The demise of the U.S.S.R. was put beautifully into historical perspective by George F. Kennan—"X" himself—in "Communism in Russian History." But in "The Cold War and Its Aftermath," Zbigniew Brzezinski, Carter's national security adviser, warned that the dangers of further fragmentation and the pains of transition to a free-market economy in Russia were not to be underestimated. The post–Cold War world would live in less fear of nuclear war, but new uncertainties, ethnic tensions, insecurities, and struggles would mark the new world order.

Misconceptions About Russia Are a Threat to America

Aleksandr Solzhenitsyn

SPRING 1980

ANYONE NOT HOPELESSLY blinded by his own illusions must recognize that the West today finds itself in a crisis, perhaps even in mortal danger. One could point to numerous particular causes or trace the specific stages over the last 60 years which have led to the present state of affairs. But the ultimate cause clearly lies in 60 years of obstinate blindness to the true nature of communism.

I am not concerned here with those who cherish, glorify, and defend communism to this day. To such people I have nothing to say. Yet there are many others who are aware that communism is an evil and menace to the world, but who have nevertheless failed to grasp its implacable nature. And such individuals, in their capacities as policy advisers and political leaders, are even now committing fresh blunders which will inevitably have lethal repercussions in the future.

Two mistakes are especially common. One is the failure to understand the radical hostility of communism to mankind as a whole—the failure to realize that communism is irredeemable, that there exist no "better" variants of communism; that it is incapable of growing "kinder," that it cannot survive as an ideology without using terror, and that, consequently, to coexist with communism on the same planet is impossible. Either it will spread, cancer-like, to destroy mankind, or else mankind will have to rid itself of communism (and even then face lengthy treatment for secondary tumors).

The second and equally prevalent mistake is to assume an indissoluble link between the universal disease of communism and the country where it first seized control—Russia. This error skews one's perception of the threat and cripples all attempts to respond sensibly to it, thus leaving the West disarmed. This misinterpretation is fraught with tragic consequences; it is imperiling every nation, Americans no less than Russians. One will not have to await the coming of future generations to hear curses flung at those who have implanted this misapprehension in the public awareness.

I have written and spoken at length about the first of these errors, and in so doing have aroused considerable skepticism in the West, but agreement seems to be increasing with the passage of time and as the lessons of history are assimilated.

The present essay is mainly devoted to the second fallacy.

II

To BEGIN WITH, there is the careless and inaccurate use of the words "Russia" and "Russian" in place of "U.S.S.R." and "Soviet." (There is even a persistent emotional bias against the former: "Russian tanks have entered Prague," "Russian imperialism," "Never trust the Russians" as against "Soviet achievements in space" and "the triumphs of the Soviet ballet.") Yet it ought to be clear that these concepts are not only opposites, but are *inimical.* "Russia" is to the Soviet Union as a man is to the disease afflicting him. We do not, after all, confuse a man with his illness; we do not refer to him by the name of that illness or curse him for it.

After 1917 the state as a functioning whole—the country with its government, policies, and armed forces—can no longer be referred to as "Russia." It is inappropriate to apply the word "Russian" to the present authorities in the U.S.S.R., to its army, or to its future military successes and regimes of occupation throughout the world, even though the official language in each case might be Russian. (This is equally true of both China and Vietnam, only in their case no equivalent of the word "Soviet" is available.) A certain American diplomat recently exclaimed: "Let Brezhnev's Russian heart be run by an American pacemaker!" Quite wrong! He should have said "Soviet heart." Nationality is determined not by one's origins alone, but also by the direction of one's loyalties and affections. A Brezhnev who has connived at the ruin of his own people in the interests of foreign adventures has no Russian heart. All that his ilk have done—to destroy the national way of life and to pollute nature, to desecrate national shrines and monuments, and to keep the people in hunger and poverty for the last 60 years—shows that the communist leaders are alien to the people and indifferent to its suffering. (This is equally true of the ferocious Khmer Rouge, the Polish functionary who may have been reared by a Catholic mother, the young communist activist, taskmaster over a group of starving coolies, or the stolid Georges Marchais with his Kremlin-like exterior—each has turned his back on his own nationality and has embraced inhumanity.)

For present-day purposes, the word "Russia" can serve only to designate an oppressed people which is denied the possibility of acting as one entity, or to denote its suppressed national consciousness, religion, and culture. Or else it can point to a future nation liberated from communism.

There was no such confusion in the 1920s when progressive Western opinion exulted over bolshevism: the object of its enthusiasm was then named "Soviet" outright. During the tragic years of the Second World War, the concepts "Russian" and "Soviet" seem to have merged in the eyes of the world (a cruel error, which is discussed below). And with the coming of the Cold War, the animosities generated were then directed principally toward the word "Russian." The effects are being felt to this day; in fact, new and bitter accusations have in recent years been leveled against all things "Russian."

III

THE AMERICAN reader receives his information about, and forms his understanding of, Russian history and the present-day Soviet Union chiefly from the following sources: American scholars (historians and Slavists), American diplomats, American correspondents in Moscow, and recent émigrés from the U.S.S.R. (I am not including Soviet propaganda publications, to which less credence is given lately, or the impressions of tourists, which, thanks to the skillful efforts of Intourist, remain altogether superficial.)

When American historical scholarship is confronted with the paucity of Soviet sources and with their Marxist distortion, then, for all its apparently unlimited scope and freedom from prejudice, it often unwittingly adopts the procrustean framework provided by official Soviet historiography and, under the illusion of conducting independent research, involuntarily duplicates the approach and sometimes even the methodology of Soviet scholarship, in imitation of which it then duly skirts certain hidden and carefully hushed-up topics.

It is sufficient to recall that until the most recent times the very existence of the Gulag Archipelago, its inhuman cruelty, its scope, its duration, and the sheer volume of death it generated, were not acknowledged by Western scholarship. To take a further example, the mighty outbreaks of spontaneous popular resistance to communism in our country between 1918 and 1922 have been quite disregarded by scholars in the West, and where they have been noted, they are termed "banditry," in line with Soviet parlance (for example, by Moshe Lewin). In overall evaluations of Soviet history, we still encounter the raptures with which "progressive" public opinion in Europe greeted the "dawning of a new life," even as the terrorism and destruction of 1917–21 were at their height in our country. And to this day many American academics seriously refer to "the ideals of the revolution," when in fact these "ideals" manifested themselves from the very first in the murder of millions of people.

Nor has Russia's distant past been spared the distorting effects of fervent radical thought in the West. In recent years American scholarship has been noticeably dominated by a most facile, one-dimensional approach, which consists in explaining the unique events of the twentieth century, first in Russia and then in other lands, not as something peculiar to communism, not as a phenomenon new to human history, but as if they derived from primordial Russian national characteristics established in some distant century. This is nothing less than a racist view. The events of the twentieth century are explained by flimsy and superficial analogies drawn from the past. While communism was still the object of Western infatuation, it was hailed as the indisputable dawning of a new era. But ever since communism has had to be condemned, it has been ingeniously ascribed to the age-old Russian slave mentality.

This interpretation currently enjoys wide support, since it is so advantageous to many people: if the crimes and vices of communism are not inherent to it but can be attributed entirely to the traditions of old Russia, then it follows that there exists no fundamental threat to the Western world; the rosy vistas of détente are preserved, together with trade and even friendship with communist countries, thereby ensuring continued comfort and security for the West; Western communists are freed from incrimination and suspicion ("they'll do a better job; theirs will be a really good communism"); and a burden falls from the conscience of those liberals and radicals who lent so much of their fervor and their assistance to this bloody regime in the past.

Scholars of this persuasion treat the history of the old Russia in a correspondingly peremptory manner. They permit themselves the most arbitrary selection of phenomena, facts, and persons and accept unreliable or simply false versions of events. Even more striking is their almost total disregard for the spiritual history of a country which has been in existence for a thousand years, as though (as Marxists argue) this has had no bearing upon the course of its material history. It is regarded as essential when studying the history and culture of China, or Thailand, or any African country, to feel some respect for the distinctive features of that culture. But when it comes to the thousand years of Eastern Christianity in Russia, Western researchers by and large feel only astonishment and contempt: why ever did this strange world, an entire continent, persistently reject the Western view of things? Why did it refuse to follow the manifestly superior path of Western society? Russia is categorically condemned for every feature which distinguishes her from the West.

Richard Pipes' book *Russia Under the Old Regime* may stand as typical of a long series of such pronouncements that distort the image of Russia. Pipes shows a complete disregard for the spiritual life of the Russian people and its view of the world—Christianity. He examines entire centuries of Russian history without reference to Russian Orthodoxy and its leading proponents (suffice to say that St. Sergius of Radonezh, whose influence upon centuries of Russian spiritual and public life was incomparably great, is not once mentioned in the book, while Nil Sorsky is presented in an anecdotal role). Thus, instead of being shown the living being of a nation, we witness the dissection of a corpse. Pipes does devote one chapter to the Church itself, which he sees only as a civil institution and treats in the spirit of Soviet atheistic propaganda. This people and this country are presented as spiritually underdeveloped and motivated, from peasant to tsar, exclusively by crude material interests. Even within the sections devoted to individual topics, there is no convincing, logical portrayal of history, but only a chaotic jumble of epochs and events from various centuries, often without so much as a date. The author willfully ignores those events, persons, or aspects of Russian life which would not prove conducive to his thesis, which is that the entire history of Russia has had but a single purpose—the creation of a police state. He selects only that which contributes to his derisive and openly hostile description of Russian history and the Russian people. The book allows only one possible conclusion to be drawn: that the Russian nation is anti-human in its essence, that it has been good for nothing throughout its thousand years of history, and that as far as any future is concerned it is obviously a hopeless case. Pipes even bestows upon Emperor Nicholas I the distinction of having invented totalitarianism. Leaving aside the fact that it was not until Lenin that totalitarianism was ever actually implemented, Mr. Pipes, with all his erudition, should have been able to indicate that the idea of the totalitarian state was first proposed by Hobbes in his *Leviathan* (the head of the state is there said to have dominion not only over the citizens' lives and property, but also over their *conscience*). Rousseau, too, had leanings in this direction when he declared the democratic state to be "unlimited sovereign" not only over the possessions of its citizens, but over their *person* as well. . . .

There are two names which are repeated from book to book and article to article with a mindless persistence by all the scholars and essayists of this tendency: Ivan the Terrible and Peter the Great, to whom—implicitly or explicitly—they reduce the whole sense of Russian history. But one could just as easily find two or three kings no whit less cruel in the histories of England, France, or Spain, or indeed of any country, and yet no one thinks of reducing the complexity of historical meaning to such figures alone. And in any case, no two monarchs can determine the history of a thousand-year-old nation. But the refrain continues. Some scholars use this technique to show that communism is possible only in countries with a "morally defective" history, others in order to remove the stigma from communism itself, laying the blame for its incorrect implementation upon Russian national characteristics. Such a view was voiced in a number of recent articles devoted to the centenary of Stalin's birth, for instance in a piece by Professor Robert C. Tucker.

Tucker's short but vigorous article is astounding: surely this must have been written 25 years ago! How can a scholar and student of politics persist to this day in misunderstanding so fundamentally the phenomenon of communism? We are confronted yet again with those familiar, never-fading ideals of the revolution, which the despicable Stalin ruined by ignoring Marx in favor of the abominable lessons of Russian history. Professor Tucker hastens to salvage socialism by suggesting that Stalin was not, after all, a *genuine* socialist! He did not act in accordance with Marxist theories, but trod in the footsteps of that wearisome pair, Ivan the Terrible from the sixteenth century and Peter the Great from the eighteenth. The whole Stalin era, we are to believe, is a *radical reversion* to the former tsarist era, and in no wise represents a consistent application of Marxism to contemporary realities; indeed, far from carrying on the Bolshevik cause, Stalin contributed toward its destruction. Modesty prevents me from asking Professor Tucker to read at least the first volume of *The Gulag Archipelago,* and better still all three. But perhaps that would refresh his memory of how the communist police apparatus, which would eventually grind up some 60 million victims, was set up by Lenin, Trotsky, and Dzerzhinsky, first in the form of the Cheka, which had unlimited authority to execute unlimited numbers of people without trial; how Lenin drew up in his own hand the future Article 58 of the Criminal Code, on which the whole of Stalin's Gulag was founded; and how the entire Red Terror and the repression of millions of peasants were formulated by Lenin and Trotsky. *These* instructions, at least, Stalin carried out conscientiously, albeit only to the extent of his limited intellectual abilities. The only respect in which he ventured to depart from Lenin was his destruction of the Communist Party leadership for the purpose of strengthening his own power. But even here he was merely enacting a universal law of vast and bloody revolutions, which invariably devour their own creators.

In the Soviet Union it used to be said with good reason that "Stalin is Lenin today," and indeed the entire Stalin period is a direct continuation of the Lenin era, only more mature in terms of its results and its long uninterrupted development. No "Stalinism" has ever existed, either in theory or in practice; there was never any such phenomenon or any such era. This concept was invented after 1956 by intellectuals of the European Left as a way of salvaging the "ideals" of communism. And only by some evil figment of the imagination could Stalin be called a "Russian nationalist"—this of the man who exterminated 15 million of the best Russian peasants, who broke the back of the Russian peasantry and thereby of Russia herself, and who sacrificed the lives of more than 30 million people in the Second World War, which he waged without regard for less profligate means of warfare, without grudging the lives of the people.

Just what "model" could Stalin have seen in the former, tsarist Russia, as Tucker has it? Camps there were none; the very concept was unknown. Long-stay prisons were very few in number, and hence political prisoners—with the exception of terrorist extremists, but including all the Bolsheviks—were sent off to exile, where they were well fed and cared for at the expense of the state, where no one forced them to work, and from whence any who so wished could flee abroad without difficulty. But even if we consider the number of nonpolitical prisoners at forced labor in those days, we find that it amounted to less than one ten-thousandth of the population of Gulag. All criminal investigations were conducted in strict compliance with established law, all trials were open, and defendants were legally represented. The total number of secret police operatives in the whole country was less than that presently available to the KGB of the Ryazan oblast alone; secret police departments were located only in the three major cities, and even there surveillance was weak, and anyone leaving the city limits immediately escaped observation. In the army there was no secret intelligence or surveillance whatsoever (a fact which greatly facilitated the February Revolution), since Nicholas II considered any activity of this type an insult to his army. To this we may add the absence of special border troops and fortified frontiers and the complete freedom to emigrate.

In their presentation of prerevolutionary Russia, many Western historians succumb to a persistent but fallacious tradition, thereby to some extent echoing the arguments of Soviet propaganda. Before the outbreak of war in 1914, Russia could boast of a flourishing manufacturing industry, rapid growth, and a flexible decentralized economy; its inhabitants were not constrained in their choice of economic activities, significant progress had been made in the field of workers' legislation, and the material well-being of the peasants was at a level which has never been reached under the Soviet regime. Newspapers were free from preliminary political censorship (even during the war), there was complete cultural freedom, the intelligentsia was not restricted in its activity, religious and philosophical views of every shade were tolerated, and institutions of higher education enjoyed inviolable autonomy. Russia, with her many nationalities, knew no deportations of entire peoples and no armed separatist movements. This picture is not merely dissimilar to that of the communist era but is in every respect its direct antithesis. Alexander I had even entered Paris with his army, but he did not annex an inch of European soil. Soviet conquerors never withdraw from any lands on which they once have set foot—and yet these are viewed as cognate phenomena! The "bad" Russia of old never loomed ominously over Europe, still less over America and Africa. She exported grain and butter, not arms and instructors in terrorism. And she collapsed out of loyalty to her Western allies, when Nicholas II prolonged the senseless war with Wilhelm instead of saving his country by concluding a separate peace (like Sadat today). Western animosity toward the former Russia was aroused by Russian revolutionaries in emigration, who propounded crude and simplistic views inspired by their political passions; these were never counterbalanced by responses or explanations from Russia, since no one there had any conception of the role of "agitation and propaganda." When, for example, on January 9, 1905, tragic events culminated in the death of about a hundred people during a St. Petersburg demonstration (no one was arrested), this came to be regarded as an inerasable stigma, a shameful episode which amply characterizes Russia. Yet the Soviet Union is not constantly reproached for the 17th of June, 1953, when 600 demonstrators in Berlin were killed in cold blood and 50,000 more arrested. Indeed, such episodes seem to inspire respect for Soviet strength: "We must seek a common language."

Somehow, over the years, the friendship which existed between Russia and the young, newly formed United States in the eighteenth century has been forgotten. Hostility toward Russia gained ground from the early twentieth century on. We are still witnessing its consequences today. But today these are much more than just remote sentiments; they threaten to lead the entire Western world into a fatal error.

IV

WITH AMERICAN scholars demonstrating such a fundamental misunderstanding of Russia and the U.S.S.R., the blunders perpetrated by politicians come as less of a surprise. Although they are ostensibly men of action, their heads are ever under the sway of current theories and their hands shackled by the exigencies of the moment.

Only the combined effect of these factors can account for the notorious resolution on the "captive nations" (PL 86–90), passed by the U.S. Congress on July 17, 1959, and subsequently renewed: the manifest culprit, the U.S.S.R., is nowhere identified by name; world communism is referred to as "Russian"; Russia is charged with the subjugation of mainland China and Tibet and the Russians are denied a place on the roll of oppressed nations (which includes the nonexistent "Idel-Ural" and "Cossackia").

Ignorance and misunderstanding have clearly spread far beyond this one resolution.

Many present and former U.S. diplomats have also used their office and authority to help enshroud Soviet communism in a dangerous, explosive cloud of vaporous arguments and illusions. Much of this legacy stems from such diplomats of the Roosevelt school as Averell Harriman, who to this day assures gullible Americans that the Kremlin rulers are peace-loving men who just happen to be moved by heartfelt compassion for the wartime suffering of their Soviet people. (One need only recall the plight of the Crimean Tatars, who are still barred from returning to the Crimea for the sole reason that this would encroach upon Brezhnev's hunting estates.) In reality the Kremlin leadership is immeasurably indifferent to and remote from the Russian people, a people whom they have exploited to the point of total exhaustion and near extinction and whom, when the need arises, they will mercilessly drive to destruction in their millions.

By means of his essays, public statements, and words of advice, all of which are supposedly rooted in a profound understanding of Soviet life, George Kennan has for years had a major detrimental influence upon the shape and direction of American foreign policy. He is one of the more persistent architects of the myth of the "moderates" in the Politburo, despite the fact that no such moderates have ever revealed themselves by so much as a hint. He is forever urging us to pay greater heed to the Soviet leaders' pronouncements and even today finds it inconceivable that anyone should mistrust Brezhnev's vigorous denials of aggressive intent. He prefers to ascribe the seizure of Afghanistan to the "defensive impulses" of the Soviet leadership. Many Western diplomats have abandoned painstaking analysis in favor of incurable self-delusion, as we can see in such a veteran of the political arena as Willy Brandt, whose "Ostpolitik" is suicidal for Germany. Yet these ruinous ventures are the very ones honored with Nobel Prizes for Peace.

I would note here a tendency which might be called the "Kissinger syndrome," although it is by no means peculiar to him alone. Such individuals, while holding high office, pursue a policy of appeasement and capitulation, which sooner or later will cost the West many years and many lives, but immediately upon retirement the scales fall from their eyes and they begin to advocate firmness and resolution. How can this be? What caused the change? Enlightenment just doesn't come that suddenly! Might we not assume that they were well aware of the real state of affairs all along, but simply drifted with the political tide, clinging to their posts?

Long years of appeasement have invariably entailed the surrender of the

West's positions and the bolstering of its adversary. Today we can assess on a global scale the achievement of the West's leading diplomats after 35 years of concerted effort: they have succeeded in strengthening the U.S.S.R. and Communist China in so many ways that only the ideological rift between those two regimes (for which the West can take no credit) still preserves the Western world from disaster. In other words, the survival of the West already depends on factors which are effectively beyond its control.

These diplomats still fall back on their precarious assumptions about an imaginary split within the Soviet Politburo between nonexistent "conservatives" and "liberals," "hawks" and "doves," "right" and "left," between old and young, bad and good—an exercise of surpassing futility. Never has the Politburo numbered a humane or peace-loving man among its members. The communist bureaucracy is not constituted to allow men of that caliber to rise to the top—they would instantly suffocate there.

Despite all this, America continues to be fed a soothing diet of fond hopes and illusions. Hopes have been expressed of a split in the Politburo, with one particular version claiming that it was not in fact Brezhnev who occupied Afghanistan! Or else leading experts have offered the fancy that "the U.S.S.R. will meet its Vietnam," be it in Angola, Ethiopia, or Afghanistan. (These experts and their readers may rest assured that the U.S.S.R. is at present quite capable of gobbling up five more such countries, swiftly and without choking.) And again and again we are asked to set our hopes on détente despite the trampling of yet another country. (There is indeed no cause for alarm here, for even after Afghanistan the Soviet leaders will be only too happy to restore détente to the status quo ante—an opportunity for them to purchase all that they require in between acts of aggression.)

It goes without saying that America will never understand the U.S.S.R. or fully grasp the danger it poses by relying on information from diplomats such as these.

But politicians of that ilk have lately been reinforced by recent émigrés from the Soviet Union, who have set about actively promoting their own spurious "explanation" of Russia and the U.S.S.R. There are no outstanding names among them, yet they earn prompt recognition as professors and Russian specialists thanks to their sure sense of the kind of evidence that will find favor. They are persistent, outspoken, and repetitious contributors to the press of many countries, and the more or less concerted line which they take in their articles, interviews, and even books may be briefly summed up as follows: "collaboration with the communist government of the U.S.S.R., and war on Russian national consciousness."

While these individuals were still in the U.S.S.R., they generally served the communist cause in various institutes, or were even actively employed for a number of years in the mendacious communist press, without ever voicing opposition. Then they emigrated from the Soviet Union on Israeli visas, without actually going to Israel (the Israelis term them "dropouts"). Having reached their destinations in the West, they immediately proclaimed themselves experts on Russia, on her history and national spirit, and on the life of the Russian people today—something which they could not so much as observe from their privileged positions in Moscow.

The most energetic of these new informants do not even blame the Soviet system for the 60 million lives it destroyed or reproach it for its militant atheism. They condone its wholesale repression, while proclaiming Brezhnev a "peacemaker" and openly urging that the communist regime in the U.S.S.R. be given maximum support as the "lesser evil," the best alternative open to the West. Yet they simultaneously accuse the Russian national movement of this same kind of collaboration. The significance of the current spiritual processes in Russia is seriously misrepresented to the West. Western public opinion is being encouraged to respond with fear and even hatred to any revival in Russian national awareness, a sentiment which has been crushed almost to extinction by 60 years of communist power; in particular, contrived and disingenuous attempts have been made to link that revival with the government's calculated encouragement of anti-Semitism. For this purpose Soviet people are portrayed as nothing but a herd of sheep, utterly incapable of forming their own conclusions about their fate over the last 60 years or of understanding the cause of their poverty and suffering, entirely dependent upon official explanations from the communist leaders, and hence quite content to accept the anti-Semitic excuses which the government foists upon them. (In actual fact, the average Soviet citizen has a far shrewder understanding of the inhuman nature of communism than has many a Western essayist and politician.)

Several of these émigrés also indulge in rather uninformed digressions into earlier periods of Russian history, in close conformity with the above-mentioned myopic school of American historiography. . . .

Given that a hostile and distorted portrayal of old Russia has been a tradition in American historical scholarship, seeds such as these are capable of bearing poisonous fruit.

The efforts of these tendentious informants have been supplemented and reinforced over the last year by a number of articles written by American journalists and in particular by the Moscow correspondents of American newspapers. The gist of these articles is more of the same: the grave threat which any rebirth of Russian national consciousness is said to pose to the West; an unabashed blurring of distinctions between Russian Orthodoxy and anti-Semitism (when it is not explicitly claimed that the two are identical, they are obtrusively juxtaposed in consecutive phrases and paragraphs); finally there is the extraordinary theory according to which the rising forces of national and religious consciousness and the declining, cynical communist leaders have but a single dream—to merge together into some sort of "New Right." The only puzzling question is what has been stopping them from doing just that for all these years? Who is there to forbid it? The truth of the matter is that religious and national circles in the U.S.S.R. have been systematically persecuted with the full force of the criminal code.

At first glance one is struck by how closely accounts by émigré informants and by free American correspondents coincide: if two independent sources report one and the same thing, then there must surely be something to it. But one must take into account the circumstances under which all Western correspondents have to operate in the Soviet Union: authentic Soviet life, especially life in the provinces and in the rural districts, is hidden from their view by an impenetrable wall; any trips they make out of the city are purely cosmetic, and are carefully stage-managed by the KGB; moreover, it is extremely hazardous for ordinary Soviet people in the provinces to engage in conversation with a foreigner, other than at the KGB's behest. Typical is Robert Kaiser's admission that in the four years he spent as Moscow correspondent of *The Washington Post* he had heard no mention whatever of the massive Novocherkassk uprising of 1962! The Western correspondent relies for his information upon the following: a careful screening of the vacuous and sterile official Soviet press; off-the-record comments and speculations gleaned from Western diplomats (the sources coincide!); and chance encounters with middle-level representatives of the Soviet elite (but as human material this is too shoddy and unreliable to merit serious attention). Their chief source, however, is the conversations they have with those few Muscovites who have already irrevocably violated the ban on fraternizing with foreigners; usually these are representatives of the same Moscow circles to which the aforementioned émigré informants once belonged. They are the chief source of information used in strident doom-laden articles about the worldwide menace of Russian nationalism. And this is how some anonymous anti-Semitic leaflet in a Moscow gateway is taken up by the Western press and invested with universal significance. But it also explains why the sources so often agree: an image of the world is formed in accordance with its reflection in a single splinter of glass. In physics this is known as systematic instrument error. . . .

Only this absence of informed opinion can account for the warped view that the main problem in the U.S.S.R. today is that of emigration. How can the problems of any major country be reduced to the issue of who is allowed to depart from it? Here and there in the Russian provinces (Perm was a recent example) strikes involving many thousands of starving workers have been dispersed by force of arms (paratroops have even had to be dropped onto the factory roof)—but is the West alert enough to note all this and to react to it? And what of the far-reaching process which is now underway in Russia and which is scheduled for completion in 10–15 years, a process threatening the very survival of the Russian people? It aims at nothing less than the final destruction of the Russian peasantry: huts and villages are being razed, peasants are being herded together in multistoried settlements on the industrial model, links with the soil are being severed; national traditions, the national way of life, even apparently the Russian landscape and the national character—all are disappearing forever. And the reaction of the meager Western news media to this murderous communist onslaught on the very soul of our people? *They have not so much as noticed it!* In the first revolution (1917–20) Lenin's curved dagger slashed at the throat of Russia. Yet Russia survived. In the second revolution (1929–31) Stalin's sledgehammer strove to pound Russia to dust. Yet Russia survived. The third and final revolution is irrevocably underway, with Brezhnev's bulldozer bent on scraping Russia from the face of the earth. And at this moment, when Russian nationhood is being destroyed without pity, the Western media raise a hue and cry about the foremost threat to the world today—Russian national consciousness . . .

V

MOSCOW IS NOT the Soviet Union. Ever since the early 1930s, general living standards in the capital have been artificially boosted above the national level—by plundering the rest of the populace, particularly in rural areas. (The same is partially true of Leningrad and of certain restricted scientific settlements.) Thus for more than half a century the population of Moscow has had its diet artificially augmented and has been artificially maintained at a psychological level quite unlike that of the pillaged country at large. (The Bolsheviks learned the lesson of 1917, when the February Revolution broke out in hungry Petrograd.) As a result Moscow has come to be a special little world, poised somewhere between the U.S.S.R. and the West: in terms of material comfort it is almost as superior to the rest of the Soviet Union as the West is superior to Moscow. However, this also means that any judgments based on Moscow experiences must be significantly corrected before they may be applied to Soviet experience in general. Authentic Soviet life is to be seen only in provincial towns, in rural areas, in the labor camps, and in the harsh conditions of the peacetime army.

For my part, I spent the entire 55 years of my Soviet life in the remoter areas of the U.S.S.R., never enjoying the privileges of residence in the capital.

I can thus draw upon my experiences without having to make any such correction, and my comments will consequently pertain not to Moscow, but to the country as whole.

To begin with, the West's vision has been obscured by the false cliché according to which the Russians are the "ruling nationality" of the U.S.S.R. They are no such thing and never have been at any time since 1917. For the first 15 years of Soviet power it fell to the Russians, Ukrainians, and Byelorussians to bear the crippling, devastating blow of communism (the declining birth rates of recent years have their roots in that period), and in the process their upper classes, clergy, cultural tradition, and intelligentsia, as well as the main food-producing section of the peasantry, were wiped out almost without trace. The finest names of the Russian past were outlawed and reviled, the country's history was systematically vilified, churches were obliterated in their tens of thousands, towns and streets were renamed in honor of executioners—a practice to be expected only of armies of occupation. But as the communists felt more firmly in control, they dealt similar blows to each of the remaining national republics in turn, acting on a principle equally dear to Lenin, Hitler, and the common thug: always crush your enemies one by one. Thus in the U.S.S.R. there simply was no "ruling nationality": the communist internationalists never had need of one. The decision to retain Russian as the official language was purely mechanical; one language after all had to serve in this capacity. The sole effect of this use of Russian has been to defile the language; it has not encouraged Russians to think of themselves as masters: just because a rapist addresses his victim in her own language, this does not make it any less of a rape. And the fact that from the end of the 1930s the communist leadership came to be increasingly composed of men of Russian and Ukrainian origin did absolutely nothing to raise those nations to hegemony. The same law operates throughout the world (in China, too, and in Korea): to cast in one's lot with the communist leadership is to repudiate not only one's own nation, but humankind itself.

But the bigger sheep yields more fleece, and so throughout the Soviet period it has been the RSFSR which has borne the main brunt of economic oppression. Fearing an outbreak of national resistance, the authorities were a little more cautious in applying economic measures to the other national republics. The inhuman *kolkhoz* system was installed everywhere; nevertheless, the profit margin on a hundredweight of oranges in Georgia was incomparably more favorable than that on a hundredweight of Russian potatoes harvested with greater expenditure of labor. Each of the republics was exploited without mercy, but the ultimate degree of exploitation was reached in the RSFSR, and today the most poverty-stricken rural areas of the U.S.S.R. are the Russian villages. The same is true of Russian provincial towns, which have not seen meat, butter, or eggs for decades and which can only dream of even such simple fare as macaroni and margarine.

Subsistence at such an abysmally low level—for half a century!—is leading to a biological degeneration of the people, to a decline in its physical and spiritual powers, a process that is intensified by mind-numbing political propaganda, by the violent eradication of religion, by the suppression of every sign of culture, by a situation where drunkenness is the only form of freedom, where women are doubly exhausted (by working for the state on an equal footing with men and also in the home, without the aid of domestic appliances), and where the minds of its children are systematically robbed. Public morality has declined drastically, not due to any inherent failing in the people, but because the communists have denied it sustenance, both physical and spiritual, and have disposed of all those who could provide spiritual relief, above all the priesthood.

Russian national consciousness today has been suppressed and humiliated to an extraordinary degree by all that it has endured and continues to endure. It is the consciousness of a man whose long illness has brought him to the point of death and who can dream only of rest and recuperation. The thoughts and aspirations of a family in the depths of Russia are immeasurably more modest and timid than the Western correspondent can possibly gather from his leisurely Moscow chats. This is how their thoughts run: if only the petty local communist despot would somehow quit his uncontrolled tyranny, if only they could get enough to eat for once, and buy shoes for the children, and lay in enough fuel for the winter; if only they could have sufficient space to live even two to a room; if only a church would be opened within a hundred miles of where they live; if only they weren't forbidden to baptize their children and bring them up knowing right from wrong; and if only they could get father away from the bottle.

And it is *this* yearning on the part of the Russian hinterland to rise and live like men, not beasts, to regain some portion of religious and national consciousness, which the West's glib and garrulous informants today label "Russian chauvinism" and the supreme threat to contemporary mankind, a menace greater by far than the well-fed dragon of communism whose paw is already raised, bristling with tanks and rockets, over what remains of our planet. It is *these* unfortunates, this mortally ill people helpless to save itself from ruin, who are credited with fanatical messianism and militant nationalism!

This is just a phantom to scare the gullible. The simple love of one's mother country, an inborn feeling of patriotism, is today branded "Russian nationalism." But no one can possibly incite to militant nationalism a country which for 50 years has not even had enough bread to eat. It is not the average Russian who feels compelled to hold other nations captive, to keep Eastern

Europe encaged, to seize and arm far-off lands; this answers only the malignant needs of the Politburo. As for "historical Russian messianism," this is contrived nonsense: it has been several centuries since any section of the government or intelligentsia influential in the spiritual life of the country has suffered from the disease of messianism. Indeed, it seems inconceivable to me that in our sordid age any people on earth would have the gall to deem itself "chosen."

All the peoples of the Soviet Union need a long period of convalescence after the ravages of communism, and for the Russian people, which endured the most violent and protracted onslaught of all, it will take perhaps 150 or 200 years of peace and national integrity to effect a recovery. But a Russia of peace and national integrity is inimical to the communist madness. A Russian national reawakening and liberation would mark the downfall of Soviet, and with it of world, communism. And Soviet communism is well aware that it is being abrogated by the Russian national consciousness. For those who genuinely love Russia, no reconciliation with communism has ever been possible or ever will be.

That is why communism has always been most ruthless of all in its treatment of Christians and advocates of national rebirth. In the early years this meant wholesale execution; later the victims were left to rot in the camps. But to this very day the persecution continues inexorably: Vladimir Shelkov was done to death by 25 years in the camps, Ogurtsov has already served 13 years and Osipov 12; this winter the completely apolitical "Committee for the Defense of Believers' Rights" was smashed; the independent priests, Father Gleb Yakunin and Father Dimitri Dudko, have been arrested, and the members of Ogorodnikov's Christian seminar have all been hauled off to prison. The authorities make no attempt to hide the fact that they are crushing the Christian faith with the full force of their machinery of terror. And at this moment, when religious circles in the U.S.S.R. are being persecuted with such unmitigated ferocity—how fine and edifying it is to hear Russian Orthodoxy reviled by the Western press!

The present anti-Russian campaign by those who provide the West with its information is beginning to flourish even in the foremost American newspapers and journals, and it is of the greatest value and comfort to Soviet communism (although I do not wish to insist that the whole campaign is necessarily Soviet-inspired).

For the West, on the other hand, this campaign stands the facts on their head, inducing it to fear its natural ally—the oppressed Russian people—and to trust its mortal foe, the communist regime. The West is persuaded to send this regime lavish aid, which it so badly needs after half a century of economic bankruptcy.

VI

BUT EVEN A humbled, defeated, and despoiled nation continues to exist physically, and the aim of the communist authorities (whether in the U.S.S.R., in China, or in Cuba) is to force the people to serve them unfailingly as a work force or, if need be, as a fighting force. However, when it comes to war, communist ideology has long since lost all its drawing power in the U.S.S.R.; it inspires no one. The regime's intention is thus obvious: to take that same Russian national sentiment which they themselves have been persecuting and to exploit it once more for their new war, for their brutal imperialistic ambitions; indeed to do so with ever greater frenzy and desperation as communism grows ideologically moribund, in a bid to derive from national sentiments the strength and fortitude they lack. This is certainly a real danger.

The informants discussed earlier see this danger, indeed they recognize nothing *but* this danger (rather than the true aspirations of the national spirit). Hence, at their bluntest they abuse us in advance as chauvinists and fascists, while at their most circumspect they argue as follows: since you can see that any religious and national renascence of the Russian people may be exploited by the Soviet authorities for their own vile purposes, you must renounce not only this renascence but any national aspirations whatever.

But then the Soviet authorities also try to exploit the Jewish emigration from the U.S.S.R. in order to fan the flames of anti-Semitism, and not without success. ("See that? They're the only ones allowed to escape from this hell, and the West sends goods to pay for it!") Does it follow that we are entitled to advise Jews to forego the quest for their spiritual and national origins? Of course not. Are we not all entitled to live our natural life on the earth and to strive toward our individual goals, without heed for what others may think or what the papers may write, and without worrying about the dark forces that may attempt to exploit those goals for their own ends?

And why should we speak only about the future? We have our recent past to draw on. In 1918–22 throughout Russia, throngs of peasants with pitchforks (and even in some recorded cases bearing only icons) marched in their thousands against the machine guns of the Red Army; in bolshevism they saw a force inimical to their very existence as a nation. And in their thousands they were slaughtered.

And what of 1941–45? It was then that communism first succeeded in saddling and bridling Russian nationalism: millions of lives were affected and it took place in full view of the rest of the world; the murderer saddled his half-dead victim but in America or Britain no one was appalled; the whole Western world responded with unanimous enthusiasm, and "Russia" was forgiven for all the unpleasant associations her name aroused and for all past sins and omissions. For the first time she became the object of infatuation and applause (paradoxically, even as she ceased being herself), because this saddle horse was then saving the Western world from Hitler. Nor did we hear any reproaches about this being the "supreme danger," although that is in fact precisely what it was. At the time the West refused even to entertain the thought that the Russians might have any feelings other than communist ones.

But what were the real feelings of the peoples under Soviet dominion? Here is how it was. June 22, 1941, had just reverberated into history, Old Man Stalin had sobbed out his bewildered speech, and the entire working population of adult age and of whatever nationality (not the younger generation, cretinized by Marxism) held its breath in anticipation: Our bloodsuckers have had it! We'll soon be free now. This damned communism is done for! Lithuania, Latvia, and Estonia gave the Germans a jubilant welcome. Byelorussia, the Western Ukraine, and the first occupied Russian territories followed suit. But the mood of the people was demonstrated most graphically of all by the Red Army: before the eyes of the whole world it retreated along a 2,000-kilometer front, on foot, but every bit as fast as motorized units. Nothing could possibly be more convincing than the way these men, soldiers in their prime, voted with their feet. Numerical superiority was entirely with the Red Army, they had excellent artillery and a strong tank force, yet back they rolled, a rout without compare, unprecedented in the annals of Russian and world history. In the first few months some three million officers and men had fallen into enemy hands!

That is what the popular mood was like—the mood of peoples some of whom had lived through 24 years of communism and others but a single year. For them the whole point of this latest war was to cast off the scourge of communism. Naturally enough, each people was primarily bent not on resolving any European problem, but on its own national task—liberation from communism.

Did the West see this catastrophic retreat? It could not do otherwise. But did it learn any lessons from it? No; blinded by its own pains and anxieties, it has failed to grasp the point to this very day. Yet if it had been unflinchingly committed to the principle of *universal* liberty, it should not have used Lend-Lease to buy the murderous Stalin's help and should not have strengthened his dominion over nations which were seeking their own freedom. The West should have opened an independent front against Hitler and crushed him by *its own* efforts. The democratic countries had the strength to achieve this, but they grudged it, preferring to shield themselves with the unfortunate peoples of the U.S.S.R.

After 24 years of terror, no amount of persuasion could have enabled communism to save its skin by saddling Russian nationalism. But as it turned out (deprived of outside information in the hermetically sealed communist world, we had no way of anticipating this) another, similar scourge was bearing down on us from the West, one, moreover, with its own special antinational mission: to annihilate the Russian people in part and to enslave the survivors. And the first thing the Germans did was to restore the collective farms (whose members had scattered in all directions) in order to exploit the peasantry more efficiently. Thus the Russian people were caught between hammer and anvil; faced with two ferocious adversaries, they were bound to favor the one who spoke their own language. Thus was our nationalism forced to don the saddle and bridle of communism. At a stroke communism seemed to forget its own slogans and doctrines, remaining deaf to them for several years to come; it forgot Marxism, whereas phrases about "glorious Russia" never left its lips; it even went so far as to restore the Church—but all this lasted only until the end of the war. And so our victory in this ill-starred war served only to tighten the yoke about our necks.

But there was also a Russian movement that sought a third path: attempting to take advantage of this war and in spite of the odds to liberate Russia from communism. Such men were in no sense supporters of Hitler; their integration into his empire was involuntary, and in their hearts they regarded only the Western countries as their allies (moreover they felt this sincerely, with none of the duplicity of the communists). For the West, however, anyone who wanted to liberate himself from communism in that war was regarded as a traitor to the cause of the West. Every nation in the U.S.S.R. could be wiped out for all the West cared, and any number of millions could die in Soviet concentration camps, just as long as it could get out of this war successfully and as quickly as possible. And so hundreds of thousands of these Russians and Cossacks, Tatars and Caucasian nationals were sacrificed; they were not even allowed to surrender to the Americans but were turned over to the Soviet Union, there to face reprisals and execution.

Even more shocking is the way the British and American armies surrendered into the vengeful hands of the communists hundreds of thousands of peaceful civilians, convoys of old men, women, and children, as well as ordinary Soviet POWs and forced laborers used by the Germans—surrendered them against their will, and even after witnessing the suicide of some of them. And British units shot, bayonetted, and clubbed these people who for some reason did not wish to return to their homeland. Yet more amazing still is the fact that not only were none of these British and American officers ever punished or reprimanded, but for almost 30 years the free, proud, and unfettered press of these two countries unanimously and with studied innocence kept its silence about their governments' act of treachery. For 30 years not a single honest pen presented itself! Surely this is the most astonishing fact of all! In this single instance the West's unbroken tradition of publicity suddenly failed. Why?

At the time, it seemed more advantageous to buy off the communists with a couple of million foolish people and in this way to purchase perpetual peace.

In the same way—and without any real need—the whole of Eastern Europe was sacrificed to Stalin.

Now, 35 years later, we can sum up the cost of this wisdom: the security of the West today is solely dependent upon the unforeseen Sino-Soviet rift.

VII

THE SELFISH and ruinous mistake that the West committed during World War II has since been repeated time and time again, always in the fervent hope of avoiding a confrontation with communism. The West has done its utmost to ignore communist mass murder and aggression. It promptly forgave East Berlin (1953) as well as Budapest and Prague. It hastened to believe in the peaceful intentions of North Korea (which will yet show its true worth) and in the nobility of North Vietnam. It has allowed itself to be shamefully duped over the Helsinki agreement (for which it paid by recognizing forever all the communist takeovers in Europe). It seized on the myth of a progressive Cuba (even Angola, Ethiopia, and South Yemen have not sufficed to disenchant Senator McGovern) and put its faith in the alleged key to salvation represented by Eurocommunism. It solemnly participated in the interminable sessions of the sham Vienna Conference on European Disarmament. And after April 1978, it tried for two years not to notice the seizure of Afghanistan. Historians and future observers will be amazed and at a loss to explain such cowardly blindness. Only the appalling Cambodian genocide has exposed to the West the depth of the lethal abyss (familiar to us, who have lived there for 60 years), but even here, it seems, the Western conscience is already becoming inured and distracted.

It is high time for all starry-eyed dreamers to realize that the nature of communism is one and the same the whole world over, that it is everywhere inimical to the national welfare, invariably striving to destroy the national organism in which it is developing before moving on to destroy adjacent organisms. No matter what the illusions of détente, no one will ever achieve a stable peace with communism, which is capable only of voracious expansion. Whatever the latest act in the charade of détente, communism continues to wage an incessant ideological war in which the West is unfailingly referred to as the enemy. Communism will never desist from its efforts to seize the world, be it through direct military conquest, through subversion and terrorism, or by subtly undermining society from within.

Italy and France are still free, but they have already allowed themselves to be corroded by powerful communist parties. Every human being and any society (especially a democracy) tries to hope for the best, this is only natural. But in the case of communism there is simply nothing to hope for: no reconciliation with communist doctrine is possible. The alternatives are either its complete triumph throughout the world or else its total collapse everywhere. The only salvation for Russia, for China, and for the entire world lies in a renunciation of this doctrine. Otherwise the world will face inexorable ruin.

The communist occupation of Eastern Europe and East Asia will not come to an end; indeed, there is an imminent danger of a takeover in Western Europe and many other parts of the world. The prospects for communism in Latin America and Africa have already been clearly demonstrated; in fact any country that is not careful can be seized. There is of course the hope that things will turn out differently: that the communist aggressors will ultimately fail, like all aggressors in the past. They themselves believe that their hour of world conquest has arrived and, scenting victory, they unwittingly hasten—to their doom. But to achieve such an outcome in a future war would cost mankind billions of casualties.

In view of this mortal danger, one might have thought that American diplomatic efforts would be directed above all toward reducing the threatening might of these imperialistic "horsemen," to ensuring that they will never again succeed in bridling the national feelings of any country and drawing upon the vitality of its people. Yet this path has not been followed; in fact, the opposite course of action has been pursued.

American diplomacy over the last 35 years presents a spectacle of sorry bumbling. The United States, only recently the dominant world power, the victor in World War II and the leader in the United Nations, has seen a steady, rapid, and often humiliating erosion of its position at the United Nations and in the world at large. It has continually declined vis-à-vis the U.S.S.R.: a process which even its Western allies have come to condone. Things have reached the point where American senators make apologetic visits to Moscow in order to ensure that the debates in the Senate are not taken amiss in the Kremlin. The whole thrust of American diplomacy has been directed to postponing any conflict, even at the cost of progressively diminishing American strength.

The lesson of World War II is that only desperate, pitiless circumstances can bring about any cooperation between communism and the nation it has enslaved. The United States has not learned this lesson: the Soviet and Eastern European governments have been treated as the genuine spokesmen of the national aspirations of the peoples they have subjugated, and the false representatives of these regimes have been dealt with respectfully. This amounts to a rejection—in advance, and in a form most detrimental to American interests—of any future alliance with the oppressed peoples, who are thereby driven firmly into the clutches of communism. This policy leaves the Russian and the Chinese people in bitter and desperate isolation—something the Russians already tasted in 1941.

In the 1950s an eminent representative of the postwar Russian emigration submitted to the U.S. administration a project for coordinating the efforts of Russian anticommunist forces. The response was formulated by a high-ranking American official: "We have no need of any kind of Russia, whether future or past." A conceited, mindless, and suicidal answer as far as American interests are concerned. The world has now come to the point where without the rebirth of a healthy, national-minded Russia, America itself will not survive, since all would be annihilated in the bloody clash. In that struggle it would be ruinous for America to fail to distinguish, in theory and in practice, between the communist aggressors and the peoples of the U.S.S.R. so tragically drawn into the conflict. It would be disastrous to fight "the Russians" instead of communism and thereby force a repetition of 1941, when the Russians will again grasp at freedom and find no helping hand.

The day-to-day implementation of current American foreign policy has served to support this perverse and pernicious surrender of the Russian national consciousness to its communist taskmaster. And now, after 35 years of failure, American diplomacy has gambled on another shortsighted, unwise—indeed mad—policy: to use China as a shield, which means in effect abandoning the national forces of China as well and driving them completely under the communist yoke. (In the interests of this policy it was even deemed acceptable to contribute Taiwan as a down payment.)

This act of betrayal is a blow to the national feelings of both Chinese *and* Russians. ("America is openly supporting our totalitarian oppressors and equipping them against us!")

I hardly dare ask where that leaves the principles of democracy. Where is the vaunted respect for the freedom of all nations? But even in purely strategic terms this is a shortsighted policy: a fateful reconciliation of the two communist regimes could occur overnight, at which point they could unite in turning against the West. But even without such a reconciliation, a China armed by America would be more than a match for America.

The strategic error of not realizing that the oppressed peoples are allies of the West has led Western governments to commit a number of irreparable blunders. For many years they could have had free access to the oppressed people via the airwaves. But this means was either not used at all or else used incompetently. It would have been an easy matter for America to relay television broadcasts to the Soviet Union via satellite, but it was easier still to abandon this project after angry protests from the Soviet regime (which knows what to fear). It goes without saying that this medium would require a proper appreciation for the needs and intellectual concerns of the suffering people to whom it is addressed. And it also goes without saying that offensive commercial broadcasts are not what is needed—this would merely be an affront to the hungry viewers and would be worse than nothing.

The defective information about the U.S.S.R. that reaches America brings about a mutual lack of communication, and as a result Americans too find it difficult to understand what they look like from the other side. A case in point is the Russian section of the Voice of America, which seems to go out of its way to repel the thoughtful Russian listener from any understanding of America, to alienate his sympathies and even to shock and distress him.

The West is incapable of creating balanced and effective broadcasts to the Soviet Union precisely because information about the U.S.S.R. is received in the West in skewed and distorted form. The Russian section of the Voice of America, with its large staff and considerable budget, serves American interests poorly, in fact frequently does them great disservice. Apart from news and topical political commentary, hours of the daily program are filled with trite and inconsequential drivel which can do nothing but irritate the hungry and oppressed millions of listeners whose paramount need is to be told the truth about their own history. . . .

But this is not the worst of it: at times the Voice of America dances to the tune called by the communist regime or indeed becomes indistinguishable from a Moscow radio station. A recent broadcast apropos of Tito's illness announced that there was also "joyful news" to report from Yugoslavia: in the days of their leader's illness, thousands of citizens are eagerly joining the party! Is this really any different from the insulting Leninist-Stalinist drivel that blares forth every day from Soviet loudspeakers? Such a broadcast can only cause Soviet listeners to doubt the mental competence of those who transmit it. And the religious program almost completely excludes Orthodox services, which are what Russian listeners most need, deprived as they are of churches. In the meager time slot available to religion as a whole, Orthodoxy is curtailed (as it is curtailed in the U.S.S.R.) because it is "a religion uncharacteristic of the U.S.A." This may be so, but it is surely characteristic of Russia! And the broadcast *is* conducted in Russian.

If we add to this the fact that the broadcasts are presented in a language difficult to acknowledge as Russian (replete with crude grammatical errors, poor syntax, inadequate enunciation, and misplaced stress), then it is fair to conclude that every reasonable effort has been made to turn away Russian listeners from this radio station.

This is an inept utilization of the mightiest weapon that the United States possesses to create mutual understanding (or even an alliance) between America and the oppressed Russian people.

It is true that other Western Russian-language radio stations have similar defects. The BBC, too, shows a marked eagerness not to offend communist sensibilities and a superficial understanding of the Russian people of today; this leads to an inability to select what is genuinely important for its listeners, and many valuable hours of broadcasting time are taken up with worthless and irrelevant twaddle.

VIII

FOR THE multinational human mass confined today within the boundaries of the Soviet Union, there are only two possibilities: either a brutally imperialistic development of communism, with the subjugation of countries in many parts of the globe, or else a renunciation of communist ideology and a shift to a path of reconciliation, recovery, love of one's country, and care for one's people.

As a Russian, I find little consolation in the thought that Soviet communism might after all suffer defeat in the pursuit of the first alternative and that a certain number of today's bosses (those who fail to make a getaway) will face a military tribunal on the Nuremburg model. There is no comfort in this thought because the human cost of achieving this outcome would fall most heavily on the deceived and afflicted Russian people.

But how to make the second alternative attainable? It is extraordinarily difficult to achieve such an outcome with indigenous strength alone in the conditions of a communist dictatorship, especially because the rest of the world, in its blindness, shows little sympathy for our attempts to free ourselves from communism and at best washes its hands of us.

When I came to understand this problem, I decided seven years ago to undertake an action which it was within my limited powers to accomplish: I wrote my *Letter to the Soviet Leaders,* where I call on them to shake off the communist delirium and to minister to their own devastated country. The chances of success were naturally almost nil, but my aim was at least to pose the question loudly and publicly. If not the current leaders, then perhaps one of their successors might take note of my proposals. In the *Letter*, I attempted to formulate the minimum national policy which could be implemented without wresting power from the incumbent communist rulers. (It would surely have been entirely unrealistic to expect them to relinquish their personal power.) I proposed that they should discard communist ideology, at least for the time being. (But how painful it would be to renounce this weapon, insofar as it is precisely to communist ideas that the West yields most readily! . . .)

In the sphere of foreign policy, my proposal foresaw the following consequences: We were not to "concern ourselves with the fortunes of other hemispheres," we were to "renounce unattainable and irrelevant missions of world domination," to "give up our Mediterranean aspirations," and to "abandon the financing of South American revolutionaries." Africa should be left in peace; Soviet troops should be withdrawn from Eastern Europe (so that these puppet regimes would be left to face their own people without the support of Soviet divisions); no peripheral nation should be forcibly kept within the bounds of our country; the youth of Russia should be liberated from universal, compulsory military service. As I wrote: "The demands of internal growth are incomparably more important to us, as a people, than the need for an external expansion of our power."

The reaction of the addressees to my proposal was hardly surprising: they didn't bat an eye. But the reaction of the Western and in particular the American press simply astonished me. My program was construed as conservative, retrograde, isolationist, and as a tremendous threat to the world! It would seem that the consciousness of the West has been so debilitated by decades of capitulation that when the Soviet Union, after seizing half of Europe, ventures into Asia and Africa, this evokes respect: we must not anger them, we must try to find a common language with these progressive forces (no doubt a confusion with "aggressive" here). Yet when I called for an immediate halt to all aggression, and to any thought of aggression, when I proposed that all those peoples who so wished should be free to secede and that the Soviet Union should look to its domestic problems, this was interpreted as and even noisily proclaimed to be reactionary and dangerous isolationism.

But at the very least one should be able to draw a distinction between the isolationism of the world's chief defender (the United States) and the isolationism of the world's major assailant (the Soviet Union). The former withdrawal is certainly a grave danger to the world and to peace in general, while the latter would be highly beneficial. If Soviet (and today also Cuban and Vietnamese, tomorrow Chinese) troops would cease taking over the world and would go home, whom would this endanger? Could someone explain this to me? I cannot understand to this day.

Furthermore, I never proposed any kind of total isolationism (involving cultural and economic withdrawal, for instance), nor did I call for Russia to sequester herself as if there were no one else on the globe. To my nation—an organism gravely ill after 60 years of communism and after 60 million human victims (not counting war casualties)—I offered the only advice that can be offered to someone so seriously afflicted: stop wasting your valuable strength on fighting and pushing around healthy people; concentrate on your own recovery, conserving to this end every grain of the nation's strength. "Let us find strength, sense, and courage to put our own house in order before we busy ourselves with the cares of the entire planet"; "the physical and spiritual health of the people must be the goal." I envisaged an ascent from the material and moral abyss in which the people find themselves today. Children were to be preserved from having their heads stuffed with ideology, women were to be shielded from backbreaking physical labor, men saved from alcohol, and nature protected from poison; the shattered family upbringing was to be restored; schools were to be improved and the Russian language itself saved before it could be destroyed by the communist system. To achieve all this would require some 150 to 200 years of external peace and patient concentration on internal problems. Whom could this possibly endanger?

But this letter was a genuine address to very real rulers possessed of immeasurable power, and it was plain that the very most one could hope for would be concessions on their side, certainly not capitulation: neither free general elections nor a complete (or even partial) change of leadership could be expected. The most I called for was a renunciation of communist ideology and of its most cruel consequences, so as to allow at least a little more breathing space for the national spirit, for throughout history only national-minded individuals have been able to make constructive contributions to society. And the only path down from the icy cliff of totalitarianism that I could propose was the slow and smooth descent via an authoritarian system. (If an unprepared people were to jump off that cliff directly into democracy, it would be crushed to an anarchical pulp.) This "authoritarianism" of mine also drew immediate fire in the Western press.

But in the *Letter* I qualified this concept then and there: "an authoritarian order founded on love of one's fellow man"; "an authoritarianism with a firm basis in laws that reflect the will of the people"; "a calm and stable system" which does not "degenerate into arbitrariness and tyranny"; the toleration of all religions; a renunciation "once and for all, of psychiatric violence and secret trials, and of that brutal, immoral trap which the camps represent"; "free art and literature, the untrammeled publication of books." I doubt that anyone can offer any temporary measures more beneficial than these to take effect after we emerge from our prison.

As concerns the theoretical question whether Russia should choose or reject authoritarianism in the future, I have no final opinion and have not offered any. My criticism of certain aspects of democracy is well known. I do not think that the will of the English people was implemented when England was for years sapped of its strength by a Labor government—elected by only 40 percent of the voters. Nor was the will of the German people served when the left bloc had a majority of one seat in the Bundestag. Nor is any nation served when half the electorate is so disillusioned that it stays away from the polling booths. I cannot count among the virtues of democracy its impotence vis-à-vis small groups of terrorists and its inability to prevent the growth of organized crime or to check unrestrained profiteering at the expense of public morality. And I would note that the terrifying phenomenon of totalitarianism, which has been born into our world perhaps four times, did not issue from authoritarian systems, but in each case from a weak democracy: the ones created by the February Revolution in Russia, the Weimar and the Italian Republics, and Chiang Kai-shek's China. The majority of governments in human history have been authoritarian, but they have yet to give birth to a totalitarian regime.

I have never attempted to analyze this whole question in theoretical terms, nor do I intend to do so now, for I am neither a political scientist nor a politician. I am simply an artist who is distressed by the painfully clear events and crises of today. And in any case the problem cannot, I think, be settled by any journalistic debate or any hasty advice, even if it were buttressed by scholarship. The answer can only emerge through an organic development of accumulated national experience, and it must be free of any external coercion.

Here I would like to point once more to the respectful consideration which scholarship has always accorded the various unique features in the cultural development of even the smallest nations of Africa or Asia. And I would simply ask that the Russian people not be denied the same kind of treatment and that we not be dictated to, just as Africa is not. The Russian people have a 1,100-year-long history—longer than that of many of Russia's impatient teachers. Over this long period, the Russians have created a large store of their own traditional social concepts, which outside observers should not dismiss with a sneer. Here are a few examples. The traditional medieval Russian concept of justice (*pravda*) was understood as justice in the ultimate sense.[1] It was an ontological rather than a juridical concept, something granted by God. The social ideal was to live justly (*pravedno*), that is, live on a higher moral plane than any possible legal requirement. (This of course does not mean that everyone lived up to such precepts, but the ideal was accepted by all.) A number of Russian proverbs reflect this concern:

> The world itself weighs less than one just word (*odno slovo pravdy*).
> The Lord resides in justice (*v pravde*), not in strength.
> If all men lived justly (*po pravde*), no laws would be needed.

According to another traditional Russian concept, the truth cannot be determined by voting, since the majority does not necessarily have any deeper insight into the truth. (And what we know of mass psychology would suggest that the reverse is often true.) When representatives of the entire country gathered for important decisions (the so-called Assemblies of the Land), there was no voting. Truth was sought by a lengthy process of mutual persuasion, and it was determined when final accord was reached. While the decision of the Assembly was not legally binding on the tsar, it was morally incontestable. From this perspective, the creation of *parties,* that is of segments or parts which fight for their *partial interests* at the expense of the other segments of the people, seems an absurdity. (Indeed, this is less than worthy of mankind, at least of mankind in its potential.)

It is no accident that the powerful regime before which the free world trembles (including the free Western leaders, legislators, and journalists) has made no effort more concentrated and ferocious in 60 years than its attempt to eradicate Christianity—the worldview of its subjugated country. And yet they have proved incapable of destroying it!

And at this time the latest informants hasten to persuade the West that this ever-vital Christianity is in fact the greatest danger.

IX

ANY PUBLIC statement with social or political overtones always elicits a great deal of comment, much of it sober and scrupulous, but the distorted reactions are invariably the loudest; they acquire hysterical headlines and attempt to imprint themselves on the memory, not without occasional success.

---

[1] *Translator's note.* In modern Russian, this word means "truth." In medieval Russia, this term signified "justice," "right," "righteousness," as well as "law" in the broad sense. The first Russian code of laws (eleventh century) was called *Pravda Russkaya.*

My way of life, my work habits and principles of behavior, usually preclude any response on my part to all this cacophony. But now that I have touched upon some issues of consequence, I would like very briefly to comment on a number of distortions.

Apropos of my *Letter to the Soviet Leaders* and on other occasions since then, I have been repeatedly charged with being an advocate of a theocratic state, a system where the government would be under the direct control of religious leaders. This is a flagrant misrepresentation; I have never said or written anything of the sort. The day-to-day activity of governing in no sense belongs to the sphere of religion. What I do believe is that the state should not persecute religion and that, furthermore, religion should make an appropriate contribution to the spiritual life of the nation. Such a situation obtains in Israel, and no one condemns it; I cannot understand why the same thing should be forbidden to Russia—a land that has carried its faith through ten centuries and earned the right to it by 60 years of suffering and the blood of millions of laymen and tens of thousands of clergy. . . .

The path that I do propose is set forth in the conclusion of my Harvard speech and I can repeat it here: there is no other way left but—*upward*. I believe that the luxury-laden, materialistic twentieth century has all too long kept us in a subhuman state, be it of hunger or of excessive satiety.

The Harvard speech rewarded me with an outpouring of favorable responses from the American public at large (some of these found their way into newspapers). For that reason I was not perturbed by the outburst of reproaches which an angry press rained down upon me. I had not expected it to be so unreceptive to criticism: I was called a fanatic, a man possessed, a mind split apart, a cynic, a vindictive warmonger; I was even simply told to "get out of the country" (a fine way of applying the principle of free speech, but hardly distinguishable from Soviet practice). There were indignant questions about how I dare use the phrase "our country" in reference to the one that banished me. (The point of course is that the communist government, not Russia, had deported me.) Richard Pipes brought up the "freedom of speech which so annoys Solzhenitsyn." In fact it was stated plainly enough for all who can read that I had in mind not freedom of speech, but only the irresponsible and amoral abuse of this freedom.

But the most widespread allegation was that I "call upon the West" to liberate our people from the communists. This could not have been said by anyone who had made a conscientious effort to read and comprehend the text. I have never made any such appeal either in my Harvard address or at any time before that, indeed never once in all my public statements over the years have I appealed for help to a single Western government or parliament. I have always maintained that we shall liberate *ourselves*, that it is *our own* task, difficult as it may be. To the West I have made but one request and offered but one word of advice. First the request: Please do not force us into the grip of dictatorship, do not betray millions of our countrymen as you did in 1945, and do not use your technological resources to further strengthen our oppressors. And the advice: Take care lest your headlong retreat lead you into a pit from which there is no climbing out.

After the Harvard speech some members of the press asked with feigned surprise how I could defend the "right not to know" (as a rule they cut the quotation short, omitting: "not to have their divine souls stuffed with gossip, nonsense, vain talk"). My answer is already expressed in that omitted passage. They pointed out reproachfully that this is the same Solzhenitsyn who when in the U.S.S.R. struggled for the right *to know*. Yes, I did struggle for the right of the whole world to know—about the Gulag Archipelago, about the popular resistance to communism, about the millions of dead, about the famine of 1933, and the treachery of 1945. But we who have lived through these grim years are pained when the press offers us gratuitous details about a former British prime minister who has undergone surgery on one testicle, about the kind of blanket Jacqueline Kennedy uses, or about the favorite drink of some female pop star.

A more serious misunderstanding arose from the passage where I said that the deadly crush of life in the East has developed greater depth of character than the well-ordered life of the West. Some bewildered commentators interpreted this as praise for the virtues of communism and an assertion of the spiritual superiority of the Soviet system. Of course I meant no such thing. This is no more than the ancient truth that strength of character comes from suffering and adversity. Oppressed and driven as they are by constant poverty, it is inevitable that many of our people are crushed, debased, warped, or dehumanized. But evil which bears down openly upon men corrupts less insidiously than does the furtive, seductive variety of evil. Direct oppression can give birth to a contrary process too—a process of spiritual ascent, even of soaring flight. Russian faces seldom if ever wear a token smile, but we are more generous in our support of one another. This is all done voluntarily and informally, and such sacrifices are in no sense tax-deductible, indeed no such system even exists in our country. Taking risks for the sake of others is part of the moral climate in which we live, and I have more than once had occasion to witness the transformation which people from the West have undergone after living and working for a long period in Soviet conditions. It was reported that one American reader had offered his daughters one hundred dollars each to read the second volume of *The Gulag Archipelago*—but that the girls had refused. In our country, on the other hand, people read it even under threat of imprisonment. Or compare two young people—one a cowardly terrorist in Western Europe turning his bombs against peaceful citizens and a democratic government, the other a dissident in Eastern Europe stepping forth with bare hands against the dragon of communism. Compare, too, young Americans anxious to avoid the draft with the young Soviet soldiers who refused to fire upon insurgents—in Berlin, in Budapest, or in Afghanistan—and who were summarily executed (as they knew they would be!). . .

X

TODAY Afghanistan, yesterday Czechoslovakia and Angola, tomorrow some other Soviet takeover—yet even after all this, how good it would be to go on believing in détente! Could it really be over? "But the Soviet leaders haven't repudiated it at all! Brezhnev was quite clear about that: it was in *Pravda!*" (Thus Marshall Shulman and other like-minded experts.)

Yes indeed, the Soviet leaders are quite prepared to carry on détente, why shouldn't they be? This is the same détente that the West basked in so contentedly while millions were being exterminated in the jungles of Cambodia. The same détente that so gladdened Western hearts at a time when a thousand men, including 12-year-old boys, were being executed in one Afghan village. (And this was surely not a unique case!) We Russians immediately recognize an episode like this. That's the Soviet way of doing things! That's the way they slaughtered us too from 1918 on! Détente will continue to stand Soviet communism in very good stead: for the purpose of stifling the last flicker of dissidence in the Soviet Union and buying up whatever electronic equipment is necessary.

The West simply does not want to believe that the time for sacrifices has arrived; it is simply unprepared for sacrifices. Men who go on trading right until the first salvo is fired are incapable of sacrificing so much as their commercial profits: they have not the wit to realize that their children will never enjoy these gains, that today's illusory profits will return as tomorrow's devastation. The Western allies are maneuvering to see who can sacrifice the least. Behind all this lies that sleek god of affluence which is now proclaimed as the goal of life, replacing the high-minded view of the world which the West has lost.

Communism will never be halted by negotiations or through the machinations of détente. It can be halted only by force from without or by disintegration from within. The smooth and effortless course of the West's long retreat could not go on forever, and it is now coming to an end: the brink may not have been reached, but it is already the merest step away. Since the outlying borders were never defended, the nearer ones will have to be held. Today the Western world faces a greater danger than that which threatened it in 1939.

It would be disastrous for the world if America were to look upon the Beijing leadership as an ally while regarding the Russian people as no less a foe than communism: by so doing she would drive both these great nations into the maw of communism and plunge in after them. She would deprive both great peoples of their last hope of liberation. The indefatigable denigrators of Russia and all things Russian are forgetting to check their watches: all of America's mistakes and misconceptions about Russia might have been purely academic in the past, but not in the swift-moving world of today. On the eve of the global battle between world communism and world humanity, would that the West at least distinguished the enemies of humanity from its friends and that it sought an alliance not of foes but of friends. So much has been ceded, surrendered, and traded away that today even a fully united Western world can no longer prevail except by allying itself with the captive peoples of the communist world.

Can the Soviet Union Reform?

Richard Pipes

FALL 1984

AMERICAN-SOVIET RELATIONS can be approached in two ways. One approach avails itself of the techniques of meteorology, in that it concentrates on taking regular readings of the East-West climate as manifested in the level of rhetoric emanating from Washington and Moscow, the prevalence or absence of dialogues and negotiations, and the intensity of their competition in regions outside their immediate control. This approach is favored by journalists because it focuses on concrete events which they can report as news and subject to instant analysis. It also prevails in liberal circles whose adherents believe that there exist no genuine differences of either values or interests among nations and that such conflicts as do occur derive from mutual misunderstanding or lack of conciliatory spirit, mainly on the part of U.S. administrations.

The alternative approach has more in common with the science of geology. It perceives the East-West conflict as rooted in fundamental differences dividing the two societies, differences which are imbedded, as it were, in their respective ideological substances and political structures. Firm diplomacy and military preparedness may prevent these disagreements from erupting into overt hostility, but they cannot alter the reality of an inherent antagonism. This second approach, dominant among Western conservatives, happens also to be shared by the Soviet leadership.

Neither of these approaches is entirely satisfactory. Surely, relations among sovereign states involve more than atmospherics; there unquestionably exist significant differences in the nature and operations of democratic and communist societies that neither enhanced human contacts, nor good will, nor proper negotiating techniques can eliminate. These differences affect relations of the two societies because of the close and direct relationship

[453]

that exists between a country's internal condition and its external conduct: foreign policy, after all, is driven mainly by domestic interests and shaped by a society's political culture. If this is the case, then the decisive factors influencing the course of East-West relations must be sought elsewhere than in the day-to-day decisions of the leaders of the respective blocs, and an understanding of the drift in their relations requires a greater effort than that involved in readings of the political barometer with its fluctuations between the extremes of sunny détente and bleak Cold War. These factors reside in the political, social, and economic systems and cultures prevailing in Eastern and Western societies.

This point conceded, it must be said in criticism of the conservative view that nothing in nature is permanent and immutable: after all, even geological formations undergo evolution, slow and imperceptible as it may appear to the human eye. If continents shift, so do man-made institutions. If one postulates, therefore, that foreign policy is a function of domestic politics, then one has some assurance that as internal conditions in the blocs change, so too will their external conduct. The leadership of the Soviet Union is extremely anxious to create the impression that all changes occurring within its realm are the result of its own conscious and deliberate decisions; it is quite obvious, however, that it, too, must respond to the pressure of changing conditions brought about by such independent factors as the emergence of a large, well-educated technical intelligentsia, demographic developments, and the change in mood of the young generation.

II

WESTERN COMMENTATORS on East-West relations, however, persistently ignore the relationship between internal conditions in the U.S.S.R. and Soviet foreign policy. The level of analysis in the existing literature on the subject, including many academic monographs, rarely rises above that of journalism in that it concentrates attention on actions and events rather than on structures and processes, treating foreign conduct as if it were an entirely discretionary activity. This practice disregards the insights of the most outstanding dissidents from the U.S.S.R. and Eastern Europe—e.g., Andrei Sakharov, Aleksandr Solzhenitsyn, Milovan Djilas, and Adam Michnik—who see the root of Soviet aggressiveness and the threat to international peace that it represents in the internal conditions prevailing in the communist bloc. These writers argue that the manner in which the self-appointed and self-perpetuating elites of these countries treat their own citizens has critical bearing on the way they behave toward other states. From this premise they deduce that the West ought to concern itself with political and economic conditions inside communist societies, not only from philanthropic and idealistic motives but also from those of the most narrow self-interest. In an appeal issued recently to Western "peace" movements, which act on the premise that peace is endangered by the existence of weapons, a group of Polish Solidarity intellectuals sought to make this connection explicit:

> States with totalitarian political systems are a threat to world peace; the necessity for aggressive expansion arises wherever authority is based on force and lies, wherever societies are deprived of the possibility of influencing government policy, wherever governments fear those over whom they rule and against whom they conduct wars. . . . The sole ideology of the adherents of totalitarianism is the maintenance of power by any means. In the present crisis, even war can be considered an acceptable price for this aim.

In response it can be argued that even if this thesis is correct, it is irrelevant since totalitarian regimes are by definition incapable of evolution from within and impervious to change from without; hence Western attempts to attenuate Soviet aggressiveness must limit themselves to modest efforts at removing points of friction through treaties and "dialogues." This rejoinder is unconvincing. A deeper insight into internal conditions of communist societies, the Soviet Union included, indicates that they are in the throes of a serious systemic crisis which sooner or later will require action of a decisive kind—action which, in turn, will exert the most profound influence on Soviet external policy. It is much less clear whether this change of course at home will lead to heightened or to lessened truculence abroad, whether it will express itself in a turning inward toward peaceful reform or seek outlets abroad in enhanced military aggression as a surrogate for reform.

III

THE CURRENT crisis of the Soviet system has two aspects, a political one and an economic one. Speaking in the broadest terms, both arise from a growing discrepancy between the responsibilities assumed by the communist elites at home and abroad and the human and material resources with which to carry them out. The political crisis is, first and foremost, the crisis of the Communist Party establishment. The party was originally designed as an infinitely pliable instrument in the hands of its leadership with which to force a reluctant population toward the vision of a utopian society conceived by a band of radical intellectuals. Over the years, however, it has evolved into a self-serving, privileged class that in its highest echelons, the so-called nomenklatura, has turned into a completely parasitic stratum. Corrupted by privilege and peculation, it has lost, since Stalin's death, any sense of service or obligation, whether to the ideal of communism or to the nation: it so dreads any change in the Stalinist system, from which its power and privilege largely derive, that it chooses ever weaker general secretaries as party leaders. A party thus self-serving and estranged from the population, and weakened by lack of decisive leadership, is in grave danger of losing control. This was demonstrated in Poland in 1980–81, where the communist establishment found itself pushed aside by a discontented populace and forced to hand power over to the military. The political crisis also afflicts the Soviet empire, which is overexpanded and whose inhabitants make political and other demands that Moscow is ever less capable of either satisfying or beating back.

The economic crisis is due to inadequate productivity; this, in turn, is caused by two factors: excessive centralization of economic decision making in the hands of party organs and inadequate incentives offered to workers and farmers, who are essentially paid not in proportion to output but according to the time spent working. Declining rates of economic growth adversely affect the ability of Moscow to engage in its ambitious military and imperial ventures. For more than a decade now, Soviet planners have been forced to transfer resources from the capital investments sector into the military sector, which ensures in the long run further declines in industrial growth. The country's productive resources are stifled by an economic system that is designed primarily to ensure the security and power of the nomenklatura. The government theoretically could, but in reality does not dare to, decrease further the impoverished consumer sector for fear of strikes and riots in industrial centers, preferring instead to risk undermining the country's industrial future. One of the by-products of the economic crisis is declining birthrates, caused in good part by fantastic abortion rates (estimated at ten per Russian female): for the first time in recorded history, the Russian population, once with the highest reproduction rate in Europe, is not replacing itself, as each year more Russians die than are born.

IV

A CRISIS of such dimensions, camouflaged by massive disinformation and saber rattling, fits very well the concept of a "revolutionary situation" as defined by Lenin. The term meant to him a condition of stalemate between the ruling elite of a country and its population: the former could no longer rule, and the latter would no longer let themselves be ruled in the old way. Once a society reached this stage, it was objectively ready for revolution. But for revolution to break out, another element, subjective in nature, was required as well, and that was the ability and the will of the people to act—"it being a rule," in Lenin's words, that "the old government . . . never, not even in a period of crisis, 'falls,' if it is not toppled over." When this subjective element is missing, as, according to Lenin, it was at certain critical moments in nine-teenth-century Germany and Russia, then the "revolutionary situation" dissipates without issue.

Were Lenin alive today, he would very likely conclude that conditions in his country and its empire meet the criteria which he had established for "revolutionary situations." Certainly, the Soviet bloc is currently in the throes of a much graver economic and political crisis than either Russia or Germany had experienced a century ago. What is lacking today, as it was then, however, is the subjective element, the ability and the will of social groups and political parties to transform the "revolutionary situation" into a revolution. The ability to revolt is frustrated by the apparatus of repression which communist regimes have developed to a degree never before known; having come to power by revolution, they are determined to prevent being overthrown in the same way.

But a way could be found around even this obstacle, as events in Hungary, Czechoslovakia, and Poland have shown, if the revolutionary will were there. In Russia, at least, it is missing. Historical experience since 1917 has caused Russians of every political orientation to fear the collapse of authority even more than despotism and to reject violence as an instrument of change. Before 1917, the Russian intelligentsia had unbounded faith in the innate goodness and democratic spirit of its people. It was convinced that as soon as tsarism fell, democracy would emerge and triumph all along the line. These Rousseauean illusions were shattered by the experiences of the revolution. The present generation of the educated in the Soviet Union has been cured of all revolutionary romanticism. It believes that if the Soviet government were to collapse, the result would be a political vacuum that would only give license to the quarter of a billion inhabitants to settle old scores: village would move against city, nationalist against communist, Russian against Jew, Muslim against Russian, Armenian against Muslim, in a murderous Hobbesian war of all against all. But even the few who might be prepared to pay this price if it would rid the country of communist tyranny no longer believe that it will purchase anything worthwhile. Having experienced revolution in all its fury, Russians have learned not only its terrible costs but also its futility: no matter how many eggs it breaks, it somehow never produces an omelette.

Thus, there is universal disillusionment with political violence in the So-viet Union—at any rate, no prominent dissident of either the democratic or the nationalist opposition is known to advocate it. The two camps are in agreement that if Russia is to emerge from its crisis it must do so by means of gradual and peaceful changes; if this requires the Politburo and the rest of the nomenklatura to stay in power, so be it—at any rate, for the time being. . . .

Widespread conservatism of this kind among the educated classes provides no assurance, of course, that a revolution will not break out on its own, uncalled for and unwanted, from a collapse of authority. Lenin's insistence that if governments are to fall they must be toppled is too rigid, considering that the tsarist regime did fall under its own weight when it proved unable to cope with the strains of war. Nevertheless, the likelihood of a revolutionary explosion in the Soviet Union is certainly much reduced by virtue of the fact that the nomenklatura has public opinion on its side on this issue. Essentially, its opponents do not want to overthrow it and take power, but prefer to circumscribe its authority by expanding the private sphere; this desire may be dangerous to a totalitarian regime, but it does not threaten it with uncontrollable violence.

V

IF REVOLUTION is excluded, the Soviet regime faces three alternatives: reversion to Stalinism, intensified external aggression leading to a world war, and internal reform.

Among the nomenklatura and the less educated public there is much nostalgia for the days of Stalin—not, of course, for his genocidal savagery, but for an idealized regime of order and discipline, when everyone did his duty and corruption was pitilessly punished. Such glorified Stalinism seems to offer a way out of the difficulties that Soviet society faces, without resort to dangerous reforms. But this is an idle fantasy.

Stalinism cannot be restored for any number of reasons, the most weighty of which is the impossibility of running the country's present-day sophisticated industrial plant and military establishment by brute force and in isolation from the rest of the world. Nor can the nomenklatura have forgotten how insecure and hard its life under Stalin was and how many of its people perished in his wholesale massacres. In any event, after 30 years of gradual dismantling and decay of Stalinism, it is senseless to speak of its restoration; it would have to be recreated and reimposed anew. One suspects that those who recall it so wistfully realize this, and Stalinism is the last thing they want or would put up with if it really returned. The current nostalgia for Stalinism is very reminiscent of the longing of Russian bureaucratic and conservative circles during the "revolutionary situation" of the 1870s and 1880s for the "good old days" of Nicholas I (1825–55), when the peasants had been kept in their place by serfdom and the government suppressed all dissent. Then, as now, this habit of looking backward was symptomatic of the unwillingness of the ruling apparatus to face up to changed realities and to venture on painful but unavoidable reforms.

In some ways the easiest, if most dangerous, way out of a crisis is to keep raising the level of international tension. War scares, one of the major products of the Soviet propaganda industry since the 1920s, divert the masses' attention from their own condition and make it possible to demand extraordinary sacrifices from labor as well as to silence the opposition in the name of patriotism. The constant harping on memories of World War II in the Soviet Union and the linking of "fascism" with American "imperialism" serve this purpose. But war scares are risky, because they have a way of getting out of hand: the logical outcome of war scares is war. The possibility of the nomenklatura taking a chance on war as a way of avoiding internal reforms cannot be precluded; in the opinion of some East European observers, it is a risk that the nomenklatura would take if it felt sufficiently endangered internally. The greater the likelihood of quick and cheap victory, the greater the temptation to use this avenue of escape from an intolerable internal predicament. Clearly, the more the West forecloses this option with its own military counterpreparations, the less attractive will it appear.

VI

IF REVOLUTION is set aside because it lacks social support, a return to Stalinism because it is unrealistic, and recourse to war because of its uncertain outcome, reform looms as the only viable way of the "revolutionary situation" which the Soviet Union faces. The vital question for Russia, its subjugated nations, and the rest of the world is whether the nomenklatura will come to see its predicament in this light, whether a dispassionate analysis of the facts will prevail over bluster and the "after us the deluge" mentality. The nomenklatura is not the first ruling elite to face the choice between holding on to all its power and privilege at the risk of losing it all, or surrendering some of both in the hope of holding on to the rest. History knows both outcomes. England has avoided revolution for three centuries because its monarchy, aristocracy, and middle classes have always seen in time the inevitability of change and made the necessary concessions. In Imperial Russia, die-hard sentiment was much stronger, and so it is today in Latin America. . . .

Russia is an extremely conservative country, so much so that even its socialism has acquired a thoroughly reactionary character. It is so vast and complex and so loosely held together that its leaders have always feared and rarely volunteered changes. They have consented to make changes only under duress caused either by humiliations abroad or upheavals at home. Tsarism finally screwed up its courage to abolish serfdom and introduce both an independent judiciary and local self-government when the defeat in the Crimean War demonstrated Russia's backwardness. Nicholas II was determined to preserve the autocratic system that endowed him with a monopoly on legislative authority until Russia's drubbing at the hands of Japan, and the internal disorders which followed, compelled him to grant the country a constitution and a parliament. Even Lenin had to veer sharply toward more liberal economic practices in 1921, when social unrest and the near collapse of the economy placed his regime in jeopardy.

Russian history thus strongly suggests, and informed Russian opinion corroborates, that such *changes for the better that one can expect in the nature of the Soviet government and in its conduct of foreign relations will come about only from failures, instabilities, and fears of collapse and not from growing confidence and sense of security.* This assessment is antithetical to the one that underpinned détente and that continues to dominate thinking in the foreign services and liberal circles in Europe and the United States—that the more confident and secure the Soviet elite feels, the more restrained its conduct will be. The latter thesis cannot be supported by any evidence from the past and can only derive from ignorance of the mentality of the Soviet elite and the record of Russia's past.

VII

CLEARLY, it makes a profound difference for U.S. foreign policy which of these two interpretations is correct. Assuming that the crisis-reform thesis is correct and the "revolutionary situation" will ripen to the point where something must be done, what kind of reform can one reasonably expect from the Soviet leadership?

Speaking very generally, the trouble with the Soviet system as presently constituted is that it has the worst of both worlds: it suffers from all the drawbacks of a regime based on the command principle, but it no longer enjoys many of the benefits that this principle has to offer. Man can be motivated either by fear or by hope, either by threats or by inducements. Communists have always preferred to rely on the first of these methods. This practice has not given them the stability and productivity of democratic and free-market societies, but it has enabled them to concentrate the limited resources at their disposal on whatever goals to which they chose to assign high priority. What they lacked in quantity, quality, and diversity of resources, they made up for with the ability to mobilize resources for crash programs.

This ability has been eroding for some time. In a sense, the current crisis of communism is due to its vegetating in a kind of limbo between compulsion and freedom, unable to profit from either. The all-pervasive fear that Stalin's regime had instilled in the people is gone beyond recall, and one can no longer rely on the faint memory it evokes to exact hard work and unthinking obedience: for communist bloc citizens under 40—that is, the majority of them—Stalinism is ancient history. But fear has not been replaced with hope and inducements. As a result, the creative energies of the people living under regimes of the Soviet type are directed into private and opposition channels that not only bring those regimes no benefit but in many ways do them positive harm. The normal and healthy spirit of economic entrepreneurship, deprived of legitimate channels, seeks outlets in semilegal or illegal activity connected with the "second economy," bribery and the black market. Citizens concerned with public affairs take to overt or concealed dissent, which the regime is unable to wipe out and can only try to keep within safe bounds. In other words, everything dynamic and creative, whether in economic or intellectual activity, is driven by the system into criminal channels; forces which should strengthen the regime are made to undermine it.

This, in a nutshell, is the problem that post-Stalinist regimes have had to face and with which sooner or later they must come to terms. A way has to be found of reconciling the interests of the state and its ruling elite with the creative energies of its citizens. This cannot be accomplished unless the elite is prepared to sacrifice some of its authority and bring society into partnership, if only of a limited kind.

There is no need to spell out possible reform programs for the Soviet Union and its colonies in any detail. It is more useful to indicate the principles on which reforms must rest if they are to be of any benefit. The basic task is to harness the creative forces of the country in public service, to bridge the gap between the pursuit of private goals—presently the sole objective of the vast majority of citizens in communist countries, their leaders included— and the interests of the whole. To this end, three reforms appear essential.

One is legality. The citizen of communist society need not necessarily participate in the making of laws—this is a right which the nomenklatura would certainly not concede of its own will—but he must be assured that those laws that are on the books are binding on all, representatives of state authority included. For the citizen to know what he can and cannot do is a sine qua non of any properly functioning society. This requirement entails, among other things, strict judiciary control over the party bureaucracy—that is, an end to the tradition inherited from tsarism that servants of the government are above the law. Since legality is compatible with authoritarian methods of government, this innovation should not prove unacceptable, once reforms are decided upon.

The other is wider scope for private enterprise. The economy directly controlled by the regime must link up with the second, private sector, and draw on its dynamism. This calls for the decentralization of industrial decision making, the dismantling of collective farms, the adoption in industry and agriculture of the contractual principle as the rule rather than the exception, and the turning over of a good part of the consumer and service sectors to private enterprise. The consequence of such reforms would be a mixed economy, in which the state and the party establishment would continue to wield immense power but no longer stifle productive forces. That which the nomenklatura would give up in managerial authority it would gain many times over in increased productivity.

The third is administrative decentralization of the U.S.S.R. The nomenklatura will have to acknowledge that the days of colonialism are over, that it will never succeed in creating a synthetic "Soviet" nation by having the ethnic minorities dissolve tracelessly among the Russians. There is no likelihood that the Soviet government will voluntarily dissolve the Soviet Union into its constituent republics, but genuine federalism of some sort, with broad self-rule for the minorities, is not inconceivable; it calls only for making constitutional fiction constitutional reality. Such a step would go a long way toward reducing the ethnic tensions that now exist.

Viewed superficially, the fate of reforms in communist societies may appear to hold merely academic interest for citizens of other societies. After all, it is not for them to tell Russians how to manage their affairs; all that matters to them is that the Soviet Union respect international standards of conduct and cease its aggression. But because of the intimate relationship between a country's internal system and its conduct abroad, the issue is exceedingly relevant. Soviet militarism and aggressiveness are not, as widely believed, the product of a mythical paranoia brought about by centuries of foreign aggression: it requires only a slightly deeper acquaintance with the history of Russia to realize that that country has engaged in aggression against its neighbors far more often and more persistently than its neighbors have ever acted against it. Imperialism is endemic to the Soviet system in part because its ruling elite has no other justification for maintaining its power and privilege than to create the phantom of an ever-present external threat to the country's survival, and in part because it seeks to compensate its citizens for deprivations at home by manifestations of its might abroad. The root of the problem—and the principal threat to world peace today—is the political and economic system of Stalinism which the successors of Stalin have retained even as they turned its originator into a virtual non-person. As long as the nomenklatura remains what it is, as long as the Soviet Union lives in a state of lawlessness, as long as the energies of its peoples are not allowed to express themselves creatively, so long there can be no security for anyone else in the world.

VIII

THE KEY to peace, therefore, lies in an internal transformation of the Soviet system in the direction of legality, economic decentralization, greater scope for contractual work and free enterprise, and national self-determination. The obstacles to such reforms are formidable. The nomenklatura will resist changes of this nature as long as it can, and that means, in effect, as long as it is able to compensate for internal failures with triumphs abroad. It will always find the pursuit of an aggressive foreign policy preferable to coping with internal problems, because in the former case it can buy time with tactical maneuvers of all sorts, whereas internal problems call for structural changes which are far more difficult to undo.

The point is that the majority of inhabitants of any country, the U.S.S.R. included, are not deeply concerned with foreign policy. They may be disgusted with their country's humiliations and elated by its triumphs, but they experience the effects of such events only indirectly. What happens at home, however, is to them of immediate and direct relevance; here, every citizen is an expert. Competing against democracies, which only want to be left in peace to pursue their commercial interests, a government like the Soviet one can always stay on the offensive. At home, by contrast, it is forever waging a defensive campaign against its own people, who are ready to exploit every opportunity, every sign of weakness, to arrogate for themselves more economic and political power. Once they have seized a position, they are difficult to dislodge.

These difficulties conceded, it is nevertheless true that the Stalinist system now prevailing in the Soviet Union has outlived its usefulness and that the forces making for change are becoming well-nigh irresistible.

A Soviet Union that will turn its energies inward will of necessity become less militaristic and expansionist. It is a precondition of all Soviet reforms that the nomenklatura surrender some of its authority to the people over whom it rules, that it restrain the arbitrary powers of its members, that it allow law and contractual relations to replace bureaucratic whim. Anything that occurs in this direction has to act as a brake on the regime's hitherto unbridled appetite for conquests because, much as they may be flattered by the might of Russia, its citizens have other concerns closer to home. The immense task of internal reconstruction that confronts the country cannot be undertaken as long as military expenditures remain at their present levels Cutbacks in military budgets, however, demand a more pacific foreign policy. In other words, the greater the pressures on the Soviet regime to deal with genuine crises at home instead of artificially created crises abroad, the greater its dependence on its citizens, and the greater, in consequence, the ability of these citizens to deflect their governments from foreign adventures. This point was already made by Friedrich Engels a century ago:

> This entire danger of a world war will vanish on the day when a change of affairs in Russia will permit the Russian people to put an end to its tsars' traditional policy of conquest and attend to its own vital domestic interests—interests which are endangered in the extreme—instead of fantasies of world conquest.

Anyone who doubts this prospect has only to consider the evolution of China since Mao's death. As long as Mao ruled China, that country conducted an exceedingly truculent foreign policy, threatening to set the Third World afire with campaigns of "national liberation" and even making light of nuclear war. Washington took these threats so much to heart that it sent hundreds of thousands of men halfway around the world to prove its ability to cope with them. Mao's successors, however, decided that their first priority had to be economic modernization; once this decision had fallen, aggressive actions and words miraculously ceased. Economic modernization entailed a series of reforms, including decentralization of decision making, the gradual dismantling of the collective farm system, and greater latitude for the private sector. Concurrently, attempts have been made to introduce greater legality into relations between state and citizenry. The entrenched bureaucracy has been sabotaging these measures in its own quiet way, but even so their effect on foreign policy has been startling. Realizing that better relations with the West were essential to the modernization program, China has cautiously moved to establish with it closer economic, political, and military relations.

Thus, it was not success but failure that caused Communist China to turn from a mortal enemy of the "capitalist" countries into their quasi-partner—not promises of assistance from the West, but the desperate need for such assistance. And even after due allowance is made for the fact that Russia is not China, it is difficult to see why the experience of the one Stalinist state is not of immediate relevance to the other.

The implications which these observations hold for Western policy should not be difficult to draw. The West would be well advised to do all in its power to assist the indigenous forces making for change in the U.S.S.R. and its client states, forces that are eating away at the Stalinist foundations of communist regimes. This end it can partly promote by staunch resistance to Soviet expansion and military blackmail: such resistance will have the effect of foreclosing for the nomenklatura the opportunity of compensating for internal failures with triumphs abroad. Secondly, by denying to the Soviet bloc various forms of economic aid, it can help intensify the formidable pressures which are being exerted on their creaky economies. This will push them in the direction of general liberalization as well as accommodation with the West, since this is the only way of reducing military expenditures and gaining access to Western help in modernization.

Experience has repeatedly shown that attempts to restrain Soviet aggressiveness by a mixture of punishments and rewards fail in their purpose because they address the symptoms of the problem, namely aggression, rather than the cause, which is a political and economic system that induces aggressive behavior. The West, therefore, should in its own interest encourage anti-Stalinist forces and processes active inside the Soviet bloc. Such a policy calls not for subverting communism but for letting communism subvert itself.

Communism in Russian History

George F. Kennan

WINTER 1990/91

RUSSIA WAS FOR many centuries separated, geographically and politically, from the development of Western civilization and culture, and thus came late into what, for most of Europe, would be called the modern age. But the eighteenth and nineteenth centuries, witnessing as they did an extensive overcoming of these earlier barriers, permitted a very considerable progress in the modernization of Russian society. By the time the country was overtaken by the First World War, its situation was not entirely discouraging. Industrialization was proceeding at a level only two or three decades behind that of the United States. There was under implementation a program of education reform which, if allowed to continue unimpeded, would have assured total literacy within another two decades. And the first really promising program for the modernization of Russian agriculture (the so-called Stolypin reforms), while by no means yet completed, was proceeding steadily and with good chances for ultimate success.

These achievements, of course, had not been reached without conflicts and setbacks. Nor were they, alone, all that was needed. Still to be overcome as the war interceded were many archaic features in the system of government, among them the absolutism of the crown, the absence of any proper parliamentary institutions, and the inordinate powers of the secret police. Still to be overcome, too, was the problem of the non-Russian nationalities within the Russian Empire. This empire, like other multinational and multilingual political constellations, was rapidly becoming an anachronism; the maintenance of it was beginning to come under considerable pressure.

But none of these problems required a bloody revolution for their solution. The removal of the autocracy was, after all, destined to be achieved relatively bloodlessly, and the foundations of a proper parliamentary system laid, in the first months of 1917. And there was no reason to despair of the possibility that Russia, if allowed to develop without war or violent revolution, might still encompass a successful and reasonably peaceful advance into the modern age. It was, however, just this situation, and just these expectations, that were to be shattered by the events of the final months in that fateful year of 1917.

II

THE RUSSIAN oppositional movement of the last half of the nineteenth century and the first years of the twentieth had always included extreme radical factions that did not want reform to proceed gradually, peacefully, and successfully. They wanted nothing less than the immediate and total destruction of tsarist power and of the social order in which it operated. The fact that their own ideas of what might follow upon that destruction were vague, unformed, and largely utopian was not allowed to moderate the violence of their intentions. Participating, though in quite different ways, in both of the major revolutionary parties, the Socialist Revolutionaries and the Social Democrats (out of whom the Communists emerged), these factions found themselves, in their bitter opposition to gradual reform, in a state of limited and involuntary alliance with the most radical reactionary circles at the conservative end of the political spectrum. After all, these latter also did not want to see change proceed gradually and peacefully, for they did not want it to occur at all. So it was not by accident that the ideas and aims of both extremist elements were to find a common expression, as Robert C. Tucker has so persuasively pointed out in his recent work, in the Stalin of the future.

Up to the outbreak of war, to 1917 in fact, the leftist extremists had met with very limited success. In the final prewar years they had actually been losing political position and support. What changed all this, and gave them opportunities few of them had ever expected, was Russia's involvement in the war, and particularly the ill-considered attempt by the provisional government to continue the war effort into the summer of 1917, in the face of the epochal internal political crisis already brought about by the recent fall of the monarchy.

It had been a folly, of course, for Russia to involve itself a decade earlier in 1904–05 in the war against Japan. This alone had brought the country to the very brink of revolution. It was a greater folly (and this might have been clear, one would think, to Russian statesmen at the time) to involve Russia in the far larger strains of participation in a great European war. The war was, of course, not the only cause of the breakdown of the tsarist system in 1917; it may be fairly said, however, that without Russia's involvement in the war, that breakdown would not have come when it did or taken the forms that it did, and that anything like a seizure of power by the Bolshevist faction would have been improbable in the extreme. Seen in this way, the establishment of communist power in Russia in November 1917 has to be regarded as only one part of the immense tragedy that World War I spelled for most of European civilization. But the consequences of the Russian Revolution were destined long to outlive the other immediate effects of the war and to complicate the world situation over most of the remainder of the century.

By mid-1917 in any case, the die was cast for Russia. The stresses of the first two and a half years of war, together with those of the earlier months of that year—the exhaustion of army and society, the sudden collapse of the tsarist police force, and the program of land reform that lent itself so easily to demagogic exploitation—made possible the successful seizure of power, first in the major cities, then throughout the country, by Lenin and his associates. Thus the straitjacket of communist dictatorship—the restraint under which it was destined to writhe throughout the life span not only of the generation then alive but of its children and grandchildren as well—was fastened upon an unprepared and bewildered Russian society.

One hesitates to summarize what this development was to mean for Russia. No summary could be other than inadequate. But the effort must be made, for without it the communist epoch now coming to an end cannot be seen in historical perspective.

Let us start with what happened to most of the educated and culturally important elements of the Russian society of that time. The Leninist regime, in the initial years of Soviet power, succeeded in physically destroying or driving out of the country the greater part—most of an entire generation, in fact—of what would have been called, in the Marxist vocabulary of that day, the "bourgeois" intelligentsia. Stalin later completed the process by doing the same to most of the Marxist intelligentsia that remained. Thus Lenin and Stalin contrived, between the two of them, to eliminate a very large portion of the rather formidable cultural community that had come into being in the final decades of tsardom. And with this loss there went, more important still, the loss of much of the very cultural continuity of which this generation was an indispensable part. It would never thereafter be possible to reunite fully the two frayed ends of this great chain of national development, now so brutally severed.

Not content with these heavy blows to the country's intellectual and cultural substance, Stalin, as soon as his power was consolidated in 1928, turned to the peasantry and proceeded to inflict upon this great portion of the population (some 80 percent at that time) an even more terrible injury. In the Stolypin reforms, emphasis had wisely been placed on the support and encouragement of the most competent and successful segment of the farming population. Stalin, in his sweeping campaign of collectivization launched in 1929, did exactly the opposite. He set out to eliminate precisely this element (now referred to by the pejorative Russian term of "kulaks"), to eliminate it by ruthless confiscation of what little property most of its members possessed, by deportation of a high proportion of those and other peasant families, and by the punishment—in many cases the execution—of those who resisted.

The results were simply calamitous. They included a major famine in certain key agricultural regions of the country and the loss, within a short time, of some two-thirds of the country's livestock. Through these cruel and ill-considered measures, a blow was dealt to Russian agriculture that set it back by decades and from which it has not fully recovered to the present day.

The collectivization campaign roughly coincided in time with the First Five Year Plan, the announcement of which in 1928–29 made so deep and so favorable an impression upon many well-meaning people in the West. Actually, the plan as announced, and later the claimed statistics on its completion, masked a ruthless and reckless program of military industrialization. This program did indeed provide certain basic components of a great military industry, but did so in an extremely hasty and wasteful manner, at vast expense in human deprivation and suffering, and with reckless abuse of the natural environment. Despite limited improvements in later years, these same features were destined to mark much of Soviet industrialization down through the ensuing decades.

It was on the heels of these early Stalinist efforts at revolutionizing the Soviet economy that there was then unleashed upon Soviet society that terrible and almost incomprehensible series of events known historically as "the purges." Beginning with an obvious effort on Stalin's part to remove from office and destroy all those remnants from the Lenin leadership in whom he suspected even the slightest traces of resistance to his personal rule, these initial efforts, savage enough in themselves, soon grew into a massive wave of reprisals against a great portion of those who at that time were taking any part in the governing of the country or who enjoyed any prominence as members of the cultural intelligentsia. So terrible were these measures, so arbitrary, indiscriminate, and unpredictable was their application, that they culminated, in the years 1937 and 1938, in a deliberately induced mass frenzy of denunciation—a frenzy overcoming millions of innocent but frightened people who had been encouraged to see in the reckless denunciation of others, even others they knew to be as guiltless as themselves, the only possible assurance of their own immunity to arrest and punishment. In the course of this hysteria, friend was set against friend, neighbor against neighbor, colleague against colleague, brother against brother, and child against parent, until most of Soviet society was reduced to a quivering mass of terror and panic. In this way a very considerable proportion of the administrative and cultural elite of the Soviet Union—tens of thousands upon tens of thousands of them—were induced to destroy each other for the edification, perhaps even the enjoyment, of a single leader, and this, while lending themselves to the most extravagant demonstrations of admiration for and devotion to this same man. One searches the annals of modern civilization in vain for anything approaching, in cynicism if not in heartlessness, this appalling spectacle.

So preposterous, so bizarre, so monstrously destructive, and so lacking in any conceivable necessity or advantage to anyone at all were these measures that it is impossible to imagine any rational explanation for them, even from the standpoint of the most fearful, jealous, and suspicious of tyrants. What, in these circumstances, explained Stalin's motives in launching and directing them? And how was it possible that an entire society could submit passively to so dreadful an abuse of its social intactness and moral integrity? These are crucial questions.

Suffice it to say that when Stalin finally perceived that things had gone too far, when he realized that even his own interests were being endangered and finally began to take measures to dampen the terror and the slaughter, several million people were already either languishing or dying in the labor camps, and a further number, sometimes estimated in the neighborhood of a million, had been executed or had died of mistreatment. To which tragic count must be added those further millions who had themselves escaped persecution but who cared about the immediate victims—their parents, lovers, children, or friends, and for whom much of the meaning of life went out with the knowledge, or the suspicion, of the sufferings of the latter. Bereavement, in short, had taken its toll on enthusiasm for life. Fear and uncertainty had shattered nerves, hopes, and inner security.

III

IT WAS, THEN, on a shaken, badly depleted, socially and spiritually weakened Russian people that there fell, in the first years of the 1940s, the even greater strains of the Second World War. Russia, to be sure, did not become formally involved in that war as such until June 1941. But the interval had been in part taken up with the war with Finland, which alone had caused some hundreds of thousands of Russian casualties. And what was then to follow, after the German attack, was horror on a scale that put into shade all the sufferings of the previous decades: the sweeping destruction of physical installations—dwellings, other buildings, railways, everything—in great parts of European Russia, and a loss of life the exact amount of which is not easy to determine but which must have run to close to 30 million souls. It is virtually impossible to envisage, behind these bare words and figures, the enormity of the suffering involved.

It will of course be observed that, if the tragedies of the 1920s and 1930s were brought to Russia by its own communist regime, the same cannot be said of those of the 1940s. These were the doing of Hitler; Stalin had actually gone to great lengths to appease Hitler with a view to diverting the attack; it was not his fault that he did not succeed.

There is much truth in this statement. Nothing can diminish Hitler's responsibility for bringing on what the Soviets have subsequently referred to (ignoring most of the other theaters of operation in World War II) as the Great Patriotic War. But it was not the whole truth. Stalin himself heightened in many ways the horrors of the struggle: by the cynicism of his deal with Hitler in 1939; by the subsequent treatment of Russians who had become prisoners of war in Germany; by his similar treatment of those civilians who had found themselves on territory that fell under German control; by the brutal deportation of entire subordinate nationalities suspected of harboring sympathies for the German invader; by the excesses of his own police in the occupied areas, of which even the appalling Katyn massacre of Polish officers was only a small part; and by the liberties allowed to his own soldiery as they made their entry into Europe. More important still, one will never know what might have been the collaboration in the prewar years between Russia and the Western powers in the confrontation with Hitler had the regime with which those powers were faced on the Russian side been a normal, friendly, and open one. Instead, to many in Europe, the Soviet state looked little if any more reliable and reassuring as a partner than did the Nazi regime. Let us, however, leave such speculations aside and proceed with our recitation of the miseries that overtook the Russian people in these seven decades of communist power.

It was an even more weary, even more decimated and ravaged Russian people that survived the trials and sacrifices of the war. And their miseries, as it turned out, were not yet at an end.

War against a hated enemy had aroused elementary nationalistic feelings among the Russian people. So long as hostilities were in progress, Stalin had wisely (if presumably cynically) associated himself with those feelings. The people and regime had thus, as it seemed, been brought together in the common effort of resistance to the Nazi invasion. And this had produced new expectations. Not unnaturally, there was hope in all quarters, as the war neared its end, that victory would be followed by a change in the habits and methods of the regime—a change that would make possible something resembling a normal relationship between ruler and ruled, and would open up new possibilities for self-expression, cultural and political, on the part of a people long deprived of any at all.

But Stalin soon made it clear that this was not to be. Government would continue as it had before. There would be no concessions to the Soviet consumer; there would only be more of the same ruthless effort of military industrialization, the same suppression of living standards, the same familiar yoke of secret police control. Seldom, surely, has a more bitter disillusionment been brought to an entire people than this callous indifference on Stalin's part to the needs of a sorely tried population just emerging from the sufferings of a great and terrible war.

This, however, was the way things were to be. And the final years of Stalin's life, from 1945 to 1953, wore their way much as the final prewar years had done: the same tired litanies of the propaganda machine; the same secrecy and mystification about the doings of the Kremlin; the same material discomforts; and the same exactions of a police regime the ferocity of which seemed, if anything, to be heightened as an aging Stalin became increasingly aware of his dependence upon it for his personal security and for the preservation of his own power.

Even Stalin's death, in 1953, brought about no sudden or drastic change in the situation. Stalinism, as a governing system, was by now far too deeply planted in Russian life to be removed or basically changed in any short space of time. There was no organized alternative to it, and no organized opposition. It took four more years before Khrushchev and his associates succeeded in removing from power even those in the leadership who had been most closely associated with Stalin in the worst excesses of his rule and who would have preferred to carry on in much the same manner.

But Khrushchev himself did not last very long thereafter, and in the ensuing years, down to the mid-1980s, the country was ruled by a number of mediocre men (Yuri Andropov, Mikhail Gorbachev's patron, was an exception). While they had no taste for the pathological excesses of Stalinist rule (which, as they correctly saw, had endangered everyone, themselves included), these men were heirs to the system that had made these excesses possible, and they saw no reason to change it. It represented, in their eyes, the only conceivable legitimation of their power and the only apparent assurance of its continuation. It was all they had and all they knew. The sort of systemic changes Gorbachev would eventually endeavor to bring about would have surpassed the reaches of their imaginations. And after all, from their standpoint, the system appeared to work.

But it did not, of course, work very well. The Soviet system involved the continuing necessity of suppressing a restless younger intelligentsia, increasingly open to the influences of the outside world in an age of electronic communication and increasingly resentful of the remaining limitations on its ability to travel and to express itself. Beyond that, it rested upon an economy that, just at the time when the remainder of the industrialized world was recovering from the war and moving into the economic revolution of the computer age, was continuing to live in many respects in the conceptual and technological world of the nineteenth century and was consequently becoming, on the international scene, increasingly uncompetitive.

Finally, the ideology as inherited from Lenin was no longer really there to support this system. It remained as a lifeless orthodoxy, and Soviet leaders would continue on all ceremonial occasions to take recourse to its rituals and vocabulary. But it had been killed in the hearts of the people: killed by the great abuses of earlier decades, killed by the circumstances of the great war for which Marxist doctrine offered no explanations, killed by the great disillusionment that followed that war.

It began to become evident, in short, in those years of the 1970s and early 1980s, that time was running out on all that was left of the great structure of power Lenin and Stalin had created. Still able to command a feigned and reluctant obedience, it had lost all capacity to inspire and was no longer able to confront creatively the challenge of its own future. The first leader to perceive this, to read its implications, and to give a dying system the *coup de grace* it deserved, was Gorbachev.

One cannot end this review of the blows suffered by Russian society at the hands of its own rulers over the decades of communist power without being aware of the danger of a certain Manichaean extremism in the judging of those rulers and of those who tried faithfully to follow them. Not all that went by the name of communism in Russia was bad; nor were all of those who believed in it. And to recognize the tragic consequences of its exercise of power is not to question the intellectual seriousness or the legitimacy or the idealism of the world socialist movement out of which, initially, communism arose. One's heart can go out, in fact, to those many well-meaning people in Russia and elsewhere who placed their faith and their enthusiasm in what they viewed as socialism and who saw in it a way of bringing Russia into the modern age without incurring what they had been taught to see as the dark side of Western capitalism. It is important to recognize that Russian communism was a tragedy not just in its relations to others, but also a tragedy within itself, on its own terms.

But it is impossible, in the view of this writer, to review the history of communism-in-power in Russia without recognizing that the left-extremist wing of the Russian revolutionary movement, as it seized power in 1917 and exercised it for so many years, was the captive of certain profound and dangerous misconceptions of a political-philosophical nature, revolving around the relationships between means and ends, between personal and collective morality, between moderation and unrestrained extremism in the exercise of political power—misconceptions that were destined to have the most dire effects on the nature of the authority it was assuming to itself. It was the Russian people who had to pay the price for these misconceptions, in the form of some of the most terrible passages in their nation's long and tortured history. Seen in this way, the October Revolution of 1917 cannot be viewed otherwise than as a calamity of epochal dimensions for the peoples upon whom it was imposed.

IV

AND WHAT of the future?

It is not easy, in any discussion of Russia's future, to avoid preoccupation with the distressing and dangerous state of disarray that prevails in that country today and to distinguish the short-term aspects of this situation from those causal features that may be expected to have determining significance in the longer future.

The postcommunist Russia we now have before us finds itself not only confronted with, but heavily involved in, the Herculean effort to carry out three fundamental changes in the national life of the country.

The first of these changes is the shift of the vital center of political power from the Communist Party, which has had a monopoly on power for so many years, to an elected and basically democratic governmental structure. The second is the shift of the economy from the highly centralized and authoritarian administrative basis that has governed it since the 1920s to a decentralized free-enterprise system. The third is the decentralization of the structure of interrelationships among the various national components, originally of the tsarist empire and more recently of the Soviet Union, that has generally prevailed over the last three centuries.

These three changes, if successfully implemented, would represent in many respects an alteration of the life of the Russian state more fundamental than that which the communists endeavored to introduce into Russian life in 1917—more fundamental, because whereas the communists' changes purported, rather vaingloriously, to deny, ignore, and consign to oblivion the Russian past, the present efforts at change are linked, consciously or otherwise, to that past, and reflect an inclination not only to respect but in part to resume the struggles for modernization that marked the final decades of tsardom. If successfully carried through, these changes would constitute the greatest watershed in Russian life since the Petrine reforms of the early eighteenth century.

What are the chances for success in this momentous effort? Many factors would have to enter into any adequate answer to that question; they cannot all be treated here. But certain outstanding ones may well deserve attention in this context.

First, in estimating the chances for success of the first two of these efforts at change—the basic reforms of the political and economic systems—one has to take account of the enduring effects of seven decades of communist power. One is obliged to note that, when it comes to the bulk of the population, the state of preparedness to meet these challenges is smaller than it probably would have been in 1917. It is sad to reflect that among the many other disservices that the Soviet regime did to traditional Russia, not the least was the fact that it left, as it departed, a people so poorly qualified to displace it with anything better.

It would be easy to regard the communist decades as a tragic 70-year interruption in the normal progress of a great country and to assume that, the interruption now being over, the country could pick up where things left off in 1917 and proceed as though the interruption had never occurred. The temptation to view things that way is heightened by the evidence that many of the problems the country now faces, as the heavy communist hand withdraws, represent the unfinished business of 1917, existing much as it then did because so little of it was, in the interval, sensibly and effectively addressed.

But things are not quite like that. The people we now have before us in Russia are not those who experienced the events of 1917; they are the children and grandchildren of the people of that time—of those of them, at least, who survived enough of the horrors of the ensuing years to leave progeny at all. And these children and grandchildren are divided from their parents and grandparents by something more than just the normal generational change. The intervening events, primarily Stalinism and the carnage of the wartime battlefields, were decisive, each in its own way, in their legacy for future generations. Certain people were more likely than others to survive them; it is to these latter that the next generation was born. We have already noted the decimation of much of the prerevolutionary Russian intelligentsia in the early years of communist power. This has had its effects; of those who saw something of Russia before that decimation was completed, this writer surely is not alone in noting a certain comparative brutalization in the faces one now encounters on the Moscow streets—a result, no doubt, of long exposure to not only the exactions of a pitiless dictatorship but also the ferocious petty frictions of daily life in a shortage economy.

Nor may we ignore the social effects of all these upheavals. Political persecution and war left tragic gaps in the male parental population, particularly in the villages. Family structure was deeply destabilized, and with its stability there were forfeited those sources of inner personal security that only the family can provide. As so often before in the more violent passages of Russian history, it has been the broad and long-suffering back of the Russian woman, capable of bearing a great deal but also not without its limits, on which an inordinate share of the burdens of the maintenance of civilization has come to rest. The effects are painfully visible in a whole series of phenomena of that woman's life: the weariness, the cynicism, the multitudinous abortions, the fatherless families.

Particularly distressing is the fact that so many of the present younger generation have very little idea of what has happened to Russia in these past decades, of why it happened, or of its effects. With the lives of the tens of millions who perished in the earlier vicissitudes went also their memories and the lessons learned from the events of those times. This younger generation has been thrust with little parental guidance and almost no historical memory into a world whose origins it does not know or comprehend.

It was inevitable that this state of affairs should have had its effects on intellectual outlooks. It is true that a larger part of the population than was the case at the time of the revolution has now received at least a grade school education and some technological training. But on the philosophical, intellectual, and economic sides, the picture is a disturbing one.

The governmental structure to which the center of gravity of political power is now being transferred from what was formerly the party's political monopoly may adequately serve as the outward framework for a new and democratic form of political life, but only that. It will have to be filled in at many points with an entirely new body of methods, habits, and—eventually—traditions of self-rule. For this, the minds of the younger generation are poorly prepared. It is not too much to say that there was much more real understanding for the principles and necessities of democratic rule—for the compromises, the restraints, the patience, and the tolerance it demands—in the Russia of 1910 than is the case today.

And the same applies when it comes to an understanding of economic realities. Seven decades of relentless suppression of every form of private initiative or spontaneity have left a people trained to regard themselves as the helpless and passive wards of the state. Seven decades of economic hardship and low living standards have largely destroyed good-neighborly relations and have produced an atmosphere in which a great many people peer spitefully and jealously every day over the backyard fence to assure themselves that their neighbors have not contrived to get something they themselves do not possess, and if the neighbors have done so, to denounce them. All this has encouraged the prevalence of a sweeping and exaggerated egalitarianism, under the influence of which it is sometimes held to be better that all should continue to live in a state of semi-poverty and abject dependence upon centralized power than that any should be permitted to take the lead, by their own effort and initiative, in elevating themselves even temporarily over the living standards of others.

Faced with such attitudes, it will not be easy to make quick progress in the systemic changes Gorbachev and others are trying to bring about. These are not the only handicaps of this sort, but they will perhaps prove the most recalcitrant and long-lasting. For what will be required for their correction will be a long and persistent educational effort—an effort for which, in many instances, a new generation of teachers will have to be provided, and one that will presumably have to proceed in the face of much instability in Russian life.

If the full seriousness of the problem is recognized and taken into account, and if the requisite patience and persistence can be mustered, there is no reason to preclude the possibility of eventual success. But the effort cannot be other than a long one; until it is completed, the prejudices and the forms of ignorance just described will continue to lie heavily across the path of Gorbachev's efforts at reform.

We come now to the third of the great elements in the process of change in which Russia is now involved: the readjustment of the interrelationships among the various national and ethnic elements that have heretofore made up the tsarist/Soviet state.

This readjustment is inevitable. The complete maintenance in any of its former forms of the multinational and multilingual empire of past decades and centuries is incompatible with the powerful force of modern nationalism. Most of the other empires of this nature have already been compelled to yield to that force. Russia, too, had begun to yield to it in 1917; but here, too, the process was interrupted and long postponed by the establishment of communist power. Now the demand for it has reasserted itself with redoubled vigor, and not all of it, surely, is to be withstood. But this is a highly complex and even dangerous problem, which even the benevolently inclined outsider should approach only with greatest circumspection.

That the three Baltic states deserve their independence, and will eventually have it, seems beyond question. There are others that are demanding sovereign status but in whom the requisite experience and maturity of leadership, as well as other essential resources, have yet to be demonstrated. There are still other non-Russian entities where the demand for independence has not even been seriously raised and where the ability to bear the strains and responsibilities of an independent status is even more questionable. There is, in short, no uniformity in the needs and the qualifications that the respective Soviet peoples bring to any far-reaching alteration in their relationship to the Russian center. And no single model, not even one from the outside world, could possibly provide a useful response to all the problems such an alteration would present. . . .

Pregnant with problems of equal, if not greater, gravity are the demands for a virtual independence on the part of the Russian center that now embraces nearly half of the population, and an even larger proportion of the material resources, of the Soviet Union. These demands, too, are not lacking in serious foundation. Russian national feeling, while not without weaknesses and distortions (notably in the tendencies toward xenophobia and intolerance), is deeply rooted in the culture, the religion, and the traditions of the Russian people. No less than the similar feelings of the other national parts of the Soviet Union do they deserve recognition and consideration. To which must be added the fact that the recent discussion within Russia proper of the separate future of that part of the country has been marked, notwithstanding all the handicaps noted above in this article, by an encouraging level of seriousness and responsibility.

But here, very serious complications present themselves. For were the process of designing an independent future for the Russian people alone to go too far, this would place in question the very *raison d'être* for any supranational center such as the Soviet government now presents. Were the Russians, in other words, to establish a separate sovereignty, or even a far-reaching degree of national independence, this, coming together with the similar detachment of other nationalities of the present Soviet Union, would raise the question as to whether enough would be left of the traditional tsarist/Soviet empire to justify any great coordinating center at all.

The relationships that have existed between the many non-Russian parts of this traditional multinational structure and the Russian center have deep historical roots. Few would be prepared for the situation that would develop if all these ties were to be abruptly severed. The economic confusion would be enormous. Worse still is the growing evidence that certain of these non-Russian entities, if left suddenly to themselves, would either make war against each other or become subject to highly destructive civil conflicts within their own confines. Finally, there is the very serious problem that would be created by the fragmentation of responsibility for the nuclear weaponry now in Soviet hands.

Beyond this, there is the need of this entire region for a single voice—a mature and experienced voice—in world affairs. The importance of this problem is apparent in the commanding figure and present position of Gorbachev, a statesman of world stature and competence, without whose service as a spokesman for peoples of this entire area, all would be impoverished. It is hard to think of any of the aspirants for independence who, trying to "go it alone," could be as useful to world peace, or even to themselves, as this one common and enlightened voice in world affairs could be to all of them. The preservation of the Soviet government as a coordinating center will demand, most certainly, a far higher level of input on the part of these other entities into the development of a common foreign policy than they have enjoyed in the past, but to forfeit the advantages of this arrangement would be, for most if not all of them, to lose more than they would gain.

Of greatest importance in this connection would be the effect on international life of any complete breakup of the Russian/Soviet state. The abandonment of any general political center for the peoples of the region would mean the removal from the international scene of one of those great powers whose interrelationships, with all their ups and downs, have constituted a central feature of the structure of international life for most of this century. Experience has shown (not least in the sudden breakup of the Austro-Hungarian Empire in 1918–19) that any major change in the composition of the international community, although perhaps unavoidable or even desirable over the long term, is pregnant with possibilities for unpredictable complications and for grave dangers if it takes place too abruptly and without careful preparation.

It is clear, then, that no satisfactory solution to these problems will be found at either of the extremes of contemporary opinion in the Soviet Union—neither at that of total independence for everyone nor at that of a total preservation of the sort of subordination to a single central political authority that its component national entities have known in the past. Compromises will have to be found, restraint and patience will have to be observed on all sides.

All this would suggest the necessity for some sort of a federated interrelationship among those of the present components of the Soviet Union that are not to become entirely independent. This would have to be a highly flexible arrangement and probably a looser one than that which Gorbachev now envisages. But the total absence of such ties would present dangers of great gravity for Russia itself, for the other Soviet nationalities, and for the peace of surrounding regions.

V

LET THE FOLLOWING stand, then, as a summary of the considerations set forth above.

What is now emerging on the territory traditionally known as Russia will not be—cannot be—the Russia of the tsars. Nor can it be the Russia of the communists. It can only be something essentially new, the contours of which are still, for us and for the Russians themselves, obscure.

The tasks to be encompassed are immense. A workable system of humane representative government—something of which Russian history provides only the most rudimentary experience—will have to be devised and rendered acceptable to a people among whom the principle of reasonable compromise, essential to its success, is largely foreign. A new economic system, compatible with Russian traditions but not limited by them, will have to be devised; and an essential feature of this new system will have to be a wholly new organization of the agricultural process for which, in the main, there will be no precedent in Russian experience. And, finally, the immensely complex and dangerous process of political and institutional decentralization of the traditional Russian state will have to be in some way managed.

For the meeting of these demands the Russian people are today poorly prepared. The events of this century have, as we have seen, taken a terrible toll on their social and spiritual resources. Their own history has pathetically little to tell them. A great deal will have to be started from scratch. The road will be long, rough, and perilous.

How can we best relate to a people that finds itself in such straits, confronted with such tremendous and difficult tasks? The lingering tendencies in this country to see Russia as a great and dangerous enemy are simply silly and should have no place in our thinking. We have never been at war with Russia, should never need to be, and must not be. As Gorbachev has often pointed out, we live in an age when other people's problems are essentially our own. This is the way we must come to view Russia's.

The Russians will need help from wherever they can get it. Some of that help, in our case, may from time to time take the form of economic assistance; but this will be of minor importance. The greatest help we can give will be of two kinds: understanding and example.

The *example* will of course depend upon the quality of our own civilization. It is our responsibility to assure that this quality is such as to be useful in this respect. We must ask ourselves what sort of example is going to be set for Russia by a country that finds itself unable to solve such problems as drugs, crime, decay of the inner cities, declining educational levels, a crumbling material substructure, and a deteriorating environment.

The *understanding*, on the other hand, will have to include the recognition that this is in many ways a hard and low moment in the historical development of the Russian people. They are just in process of recovery from all the heartrending reverses that this brutal century has brought to them. They are not, seen in the historical dimension, entirely themselves. We should bear this in mind. We, too, may someday have our low moments. And while we should beware of our American tendency to idealize those foreign peoples whom we consider to be particularly unfortunate, there is no reason why an understanding American attitude toward Russia at this juncture in its history should not include a reasonable measure of compassion.

Beyond this, while we speak of understanding, we can try to bear in mind that along with all the dark aspects of their development, the Russians have shown themselves historically to be a great people—a people of many talents, capable of rendering significant contributions, spiritual, intellectual, and aesthetic, to the development of world civilization. They have made such contributions at times in the past. They have the potentiality for doing it again—in a better future.

The obligation to respect and cherish that potentiality is primarily their own. But in another sense it is ours as well. Let us accept that responsibility, and meet it thoughtfully, imaginatively, and creatively wherever we can.

The Cold War
and Its Aftermath

Zbigniew Brzezinski

FALL 1992

KARL VON CLAUSEWITZ defined war as the continuation of policy by other means. By extension the Cold War can be defined as warfare by other (non-lethal) means. Nonetheless, warfare it was. And the stakes were monumental. Geopolitically the struggle, in the first instance, was for control over the Eurasian landmass and, eventually, even for global preponderance. Each side understood that either the successful ejection of the one from the western and eastern fringes of Eurasia or the effective containment of the other would ultimately determine the geostrategic outcome of the contest.

Also fueling the conflict were sharply conflicting, ideologically motivated conceptions of social organization and even of the human being itself. Not only geopolitics but philosophy—in the deepest sense of the self-definition of mankind—were very much at issue.

After some 45 years of political combat, including some secondary military skirmishes, the Cold War did indeed come to a final end. And given its designation as a form of war, it is appropriate to begin with an assessment deliberately expressed in terminology derived from the usual outcomes of wars, that is, in terms of victory and defeat, capitulation and postwar settlement. The Cold War did end in the victory of one side and in the defeat of the other. This reality cannot be denied, despite the understandable sensitivities that such a conclusion provokes among the tenderhearted in the West and some of the former leaders of the defeated side.

A simple test reinforces the above assertion. Suppose at some stage of the Cold War—say, ten years ago or even earlier—one were to have asked: What might be a reasonable but also substantive definition of a Western or American victory? Or, alternatively, what might a communist or Soviet victory look like? The answers are revealing, for they indicate that the final outcome was even more one-sided than most dared to expect.

Until 1956 some in the West might have defined victory as the liberation of central Europe from Soviet domination. Western passivity during the Hungarian uprising, however, indicated that the Western, and especially the American, commitment to a policy of liberation was largely rhetorical. Thereafter most serious Westerners probably would have defined victory as involving primarily a combination of the following arrangements: German reunification by mutual agreement, with at least the former East Germany neutralized and with many in the West (and especially in Germany itself) even willing to accept German neutrality in exchange for unity; a mutual NATO–Warsaw Pact treaty, providing for significant troop reductions on both sides but also for the retention of some political-military links between Moscow and the central European states; genuine liberalization of the Soviet-imposed regimes, but with many liberal Westerners quite happy to settle for Kadar-type versions; a comprehensive strategic and conventional arms reduction agreement; and the termination of ideological hostility.

In brief, victory would have been defined largely as an accommodation in some respects consistent with the Western understanding of the Yalta agreement: de facto acceptance of a somewhat benign Soviet sphere of influence in central Europe, in return for Soviet acceptance of America's ties to Western Europe (and also to Japan and South Korea). To be sure, a more militant Western minority would have viewed the above as inadequate, while liberal progressives were in general inclined to accept the status quo as the basis for terminating the Cold War.

A Soviet definition of victory is somewhat more difficult to delineate, given the universalist aspirations of communist ideology and the more limited scope of actual Soviet power. Moreover one can also differentiate in the Soviet case between the radicals and the conservatives. The former favored the energetic pursuit of world revolution, exploiting what they perceived to be the general postwar crisis of capitalism. Others warned that caution dictated first consolidating the postwar Soviet gains. One can also deduce to some extent the basic geostrategic assumptions of the Soviet leadership from the top-level and confidential Soviet-Nazi exchanges in late 1940 regarding the postwar division of spoils in the event of the then anticipated Nazi victory. Both Hitler and Stalin agreed that America should be excluded from any role whatsoever in Eurasia, and that appears to have been the continuing Soviet goal during the Cold War.

Thus it seems reasonable to conclude that a working definition of a Soviet strategic victory in the Cold War would have entailed the submissive neutralization of both Western Europe (through the dismantling of NATO) and Japan and the withdrawal of U.S. political and military presence across the oceans. Moreover, following adoption of the 1962 program of the Communist Party of the Soviet Union (CPSU), victory was also defined as attaining the worldwide economic supremacy of communism over capitalism, said to be inevitable by 1980. In the meantime anti-Western "national liberation" struggles would isolate "the imperialist camp," with the rest being only a global mop-up operation.

It is a useful exercise to ponder these two alternative notions of victory. Not only did the Soviet victory not come to pass (whether it could have ever been attained is discussed later), but the most likely conventional Western scenario of victory has been exceeded to a degree that is truly staggering. Germany is reunited and already wholly in NATO, with Soviet forces to be withdrawn altogether by 1994; the Warsaw Pact has been abolished, and Soviet forces have been evicted from Hungary and Czechoslovakia and are in process of their final departure from Poland; the Soviet-imposed regimes in central Europe have not only been overthrown but Poland, Hungary, and Czechoslovakia are moving toward joining the European Community (EC) and even knocking at the doors of NATO.

Most important of all, the Soviet Union itself has crumbled, and central Eurasia is now a geopolitical vacuum. The former Soviet army is being demobilized and is already demoralized. The Baltic states are free, Ukraine is consolidating its independent statehood, and so are the Central Asian republics. Russia's own unity may soon also be at stake, with perhaps the Far Eastern provinces tempted before too long to set up a separate Siberian–Far Eastern republic of their own. Indeed the economic and even the political destiny of what was not long ago a threatening superpower is now increasingly passing to de facto Western receivership. Instead of the once acclaimed theory of "convergence" of the two competing systems, the reality is that of one-sided conversion.

This is an outcome historically no less decisive and no less one-sided than the defeat of Napoleonic France in 1815, or of Imperial Germany in 1918, or of Nazi Germany and Imperial Japan in 1945. Unlike the Peace of Westphalia, which ended the Thirty Years War in a grand religious compromise, *cuius regio, cuius religio* does not apply here. Rather, from a doctrinal point of view, the outcome is more similar to 1815 or 1945: the ideology of the losing side has itself been repudiated. Geopolitically the outcome is also suggestive of 1918: the defeated empire is in the process of dismantlement.

As in previous terminations of war, there was a discernible moment of capitulation, followed by postwar political upheavals in the losing state. That moment came most probably in Paris on November 19, 1990. At a conclave marked by ostentatious displays of amity designed to mask the underlying reality, the erstwhile Soviet leader, Mikhail Gorbachev, who had led the Soviet Union during the final stages of the Cold War, accepted the conditions of the victors by describing in veiled and elegant language the unification of Germany that had taken place entirely on Western terms as "a major event." This was the functional equivalent of the act of capitulation in the railroad car in Compiègne in 1918 or on the U.S.S. *Missouri* in August 1945, even though the key message was subtly couched in "friendship."

Defeats tend to be politically unsettling. Not only do war-losing regimes tend to be overthrown, but the leaders who accept the necessity of capitulation also tend to pay the political price. The kaiser's regime collapsed within days after November 11, 1918—Armistice Day. Within a year the Soviet leader who had accepted the thinly disguised defeat of the Soviet Union was himself overthrown. More than that: the doctrinal past was also formally condemned, the red flag was officially lowered, the ideology and systemic features of the victorious side were henceforth to be formally imitated. The Cold War was, indeed, over.

The critical question on history's agenda now is this: What kind of peace? To what end? On what models of previous postwar settlements? But before those issues are addressed, a second set of major, as well as some subordinate, questions still need to be examined:

—How was the Cold War actually played? More specifically, were there discernible phases to it? Which side was on the offensive and which on the defensive, and when?

—Was the outcome foreordained? Was an earlier Western victory possible? Could there have been a compromise outcome? And, finally, could the Soviet Union have won and, if so, when?

Both sets of questions are not only of historical interest. There are lessons to be learned for the kind of relations that should now be fostered in the new postwar settlement era, both from the mistakes as well as the accomplishments of the past, and from the very nature of the grand contest itself.

II

IT NOW SEEMS clear that in the Cold War's initial phase, which lasted until after Stalin's death in March 1953, both sides were motivated more by fear than by aggressive designs, but each also perceived the other as, indeed, intent on aggression. In fact *both* significantly demobilized their forces, though the traditional Stalinist secrecy that masked the Soviet demobilization fed

Western fears of a possible Soviet conventional sweep westward by a huge Soviet land army that actually no longer existed.

It is now evident that for Stalin the central concern then was to keep and to digest his principal war gain—control over central Europe—while avoiding a premature collision with the ascending Western power, America. He was no doubt motivated also by the hope that America would eventually disengage from Europe. He thus counseled caution and restraint to his more radical and impatient revolutionary allies, notably Yugoslavia's Marshal Tito and China's Mao Zedong.

Stalin was also convinced that the West would seek to contest his primacy in central Europe. He interpreted the Western demands for democratic elections as an effort to inject Trojan horses into his domain. He saw in the introduction of the new West German currency a deliberate effort to undermine his own occupation of East Germany. As the Cold War heated up, he became increasingly paranoid, prompting massive purges of his own satellite communist elites and witch-hunts against any and all manifestations of independent political thinking.

This does not mean that Stalin's intentions were altogether defensive. Rather one can argue that Stalin had a realistic appreciation of the correlation of forces, that he knew how to bide his time, and that he wanted first to consolidate his gains before moving forward. Eventually he did expect that with the hoped-for American disengagement from Europe, continental domination (and thus ideological victory) would be his. In a revealing exchange at Potsdam, Stalin responded to Churchill's congratulations on the Russian capture of Berlin by noting wistfully that in 1815 Alexander I had triumphantly marched into Paris.

During this first phase the West also maintained a defensive posture. The West condemned the Soviet subjugation of central Europe but did not contest it. Then the Berlin blockade in 1947 was perceived as the beginning of a Soviet westward push, meant to force the West not only out of Berlin itself but also out of Germany. The Korean War was viewed at a minimum as a diversionary offensive tactic, preliminary to the central showdown in Europe, but also as a part of the effort to complete the expulsion of America from the mainland of Asia and an effort to intimidate Japan.

The Western, and especially the American, response remained cautious throughout. Preventive war against the Soviet Union was not seriously contemplated, despite the U.S. nuclear monopoly. "Massive retaliation," based on U.S. strategic superiority, was in effect a defensive doctrine. The Berlin blockade was contested only indirectly. China was not attacked, despite its massive intervention in the Korean War. The West, instead, placed increased emphasis on the political integration of its slowly recovering former enemies,

Germany and Japan, and America undertook explicit commitments to remain militarily present both in the western and eastern extremities of Eurasia. The Korean War demonstrated the American resolve to remain in shattered Korea and Japan, while the creation of NATO in 1949 represented a binding security marriage between America and the still weak Western Europe. The lines were thus clearly drawn. They endured for some 40 years.

Stalin's death brought this first phase of the Cold War to an end. Not only were both sides ready for a respite, but the West seemed poised for an offensive. American self-restraint in the Korean War was becoming increasingly strained, and the new Republican administration was broadly hinting that nuclear weapons might be employed. More important, the new U.S. secretary of state, John Foster Dulles, had publicly committed the United States to a policy of "liberation" of central Europe from Soviet domination. With NATO in existence, with German rearmament under active consideration, and with the United States assertively proclaiming a forward strategy of its own, the proclamation of the policy of liberation appeared to foreshadow a comprehensive Western offensive on the central front, boldly directed at the enemy's weakest sector.

The offensive never materialized. The reasons were basically twofold. The first is that the American side never fully meant it. The policy of liberation was a strategic sham, designed to a significant degree for domestic political reasons. To the extent that it was taken seriously by U.S. policymakers, it prompted more intensified Radio Free Europe broadcasts to the satellite nations, more financial support for émigré political activities, and larger-scale efforts to support anti-Soviet undergrounds behind the Iron Curtain. The policy was basically rhetorical, at most tactical.

America's European allies, in any case, not only had never embraced the concept but in fact had been basically against it. The strategic hollowness of the liberation policy was fully exposed during the dramatic months of October and November 1956, when the communist regimes in Hungary and Poland were teetering and when the post-Stalin regime in Moscow was torn by fear and uncertainty. America did nothing to deter the eventual Soviet intervention in Hungary, while the Anglo-French invasion of Egypt signaled that America's principal allies had other priorities.

The other reason the offensive never emerged was that the post-Stalin Soviet leadership was so fearful that the West might actually attempt to exploit the consequences of the tyrant's death that it promptly moved in the direction of diffusing the more dangerous facets of the ongoing Cold War. One of the principal contenders for Stalin's mantle, the secret police boss Lavrenti Beria, even explored the notion of German reunification (in exchange for neutrality). If implemented, it would have meant an unprecedented pullback of Soviet power. The other Soviet leaders were not prepared to go quite that far, but they did strive to facilitate the end of the Korean War and, led by the comical duo of Nikita Khrushchev and Nikolai Bulganin, they eagerly embraced "the spirit of Geneva" that the British and French (fearful of the new American rhetoric) were promoting.

The interlude did not last long. The American-led Western offensive that the post-Stalin leadership so feared never materialized, while before long the spirit of Geneva fizzled out as well. In the meantime the new Soviet leadership, increasingly consolidated under Khrushchev, gradually regained self-confidence and began to craft a new and comprehensive strategy, designed to break out of the Eurasian containment that the West had fashioned. That strategy was to be based on three elements: growing Soviet strategic power, which was beginning to neutralize the U.S. deterrent; Soviet economic vitality, which Moscow hoped would before long match the industrial might of the United States and become an ideological magnet for the developing countries; and the promotion of "national liberation" struggles around the world, thereby forging a de facto alliance between the newly emancipated Third World and the Soviet-led bloc.

III

THE SOVIET UNION now moved to the offensive. Eurasia was still the central stake but no longer the central front. Containment was to be defeated by encirclement. Since it could not be pierced without a central war, it would be enveloped. Victory would come somewhere around 1980. This target date was postulated with extraordinary optimism—and supported by massive statistics—in the new CPSU platform proclaimed by Khrushchev in 1962. By that date not only was the Soviet Union to surpass the United States economically, but the communist world as a whole was to become economically stronger than the capitalist world. At that point the scales of history would tip.

This second major phase, with its various ups and downs, including some temporary Soviet setbacks, lasted almost 20 years, from the late 1950s to the late 1970s. Although there were brief periods of Western tactical assertiveness as well as occasional "cease-fires," the Cold War on the geostrategic level during this phase was characterized by an offensive Soviet posture. It was marked by boastful assertions of Soviet rocket superiority, by the expansion of Soviet political-military influence into the Middle East, and by the successful acquisition of the highly symbolic but potentially geostrategically important base in Cuba. It even involved two brief but dangerous U.S.-Soviet confrontations, one in Berlin and the other in Cuba, both precipitated by Soviet assertiveness.

Despite the prevailing view of the time that these two dangerous clashes ended as American victories, the U.S. successes were largely tactical while the Soviet gains were more strategic. The uncontested Soviet construction of the Berlin Wall consolidated Soviet control over East Germany—thereby terminating Soviet fears of Western subversion of its domination over central Europe—while the withdrawal of Soviet missiles from Cuba was purchased by the Kennedy administration through a blanket guarantee of the continued existence of a pro-Soviet regime. In effect, immunity was successfully extorted for a geopolitically important Soviet forward base in defiance of the line drawn by the once inviolable Monroe Doctrine.

Despite the fall of Khrushchev in 1964, the basic thrust of the Soviet strategy was sustained under the less colorful and more bureaucratic Brezhnev regime. The strategic buildup continued for the next two decades, imposing such enormous strains on the Soviet economy that, in the end, they vitiated the (in any case, unrealistic) goal of surpassing the United States in the economic domain. The efforts to expand the Soviet role in the Third World, thereby piercing Western containment within Eurasia, were likewise sustained, despite tactical accommodations with the Johnson and Nixon administrations, both of them burdened by the Vietnam War and eager for some respite in the Cold War.

The resulting U.S.-Soviet accommodations were, however, confined to only two areas: some modest progress in arms control negotiations and some relaxation of tensions in Europe. But though the Soviet expansion into the Third World and the Soviet strategic buildup continued, even that limited progress on several occasions led the West to proclaim the premature end of the Cold War. In the late 1960s and early 1970s, "détente" became a fashionable concept, "beyond the Cold War" a frequent title for op-ed pieces, and a U.S. president even announced in the early 1970s that "a generation of peace" had been attained.

During this phase of the contest, America's European allies, fully recovered and protected by containment based on American power, tended to act as if they were increasingly neutral in the global Cold War and ready to negotiate separate cease-fires in Europe itself. While this posture was not formally opposed by the United States, it did tend to create tensions in the alliance as well as openings for Soviet diplomacy. To many people the slogan "Europe to the Urals" or the term "Ostpolitik" were code words for a separate European posture on the critical East-West issues. The unpopularity of the Vietnam War tended to contribute to a sense of American isolation, and that in turn fed into U.S. slogans advocating "Come home, America."

The Soviet offensive thrust reached its apogee in the 1970s. Soviet momentum interacted with America's post-Vietnam fatigue and with the widespread Western eagerness for détente to a degree that America seemed ready to settle the Cold War even on the basis of accepting strategic inferiority. President Nixon's brilliant coup in opening the U.S.-Chinese relationship altered the geostrategic context, but it could not compensate for internal American dissension and demoralization. That condition prompted Secretary of State Henry Kissinger—himself inclined toward historical pessimism—to diligently seek an accommodation modeled on the Peace of Westphalia: each side was to retain its geopolitical and ideological realms. It would be stabilized by a new emphasis on arms control, thereby slowing down the massive Soviet buildup but at the price even of accepting (in SALT I) Soviet strategic superiority.

The Soviet global offensive continued unabated into the second half of the 1970s. No longer politically deterred by American strategic power, Soviet troops were deployed in Vietnam, Ethiopia, Yemen, Cuba, not to mention the geopolitically vital Middle East, while Soviet military surrogates were active in Mozambique, Angola, and elsewhere. The Soviet military buildup reached unprecedented and truly threatening proportions. The SS-20 deployments aimed at Western Europe and Japan were specifically designed for intimidation. For the first time during the entire Cold War, the Soviet Union seemed to be genuinely preparing to dictate the outcome, both by encirclement and perhaps even on the central front.

Yet self-delusion lingered in the Western capitals and in Washington. French and German leaders competed in courting Brezhnev and in extolling his virtues. . . . Détente came to be viewed as an end in itself.

The moment seemed ripe for a historical turning point, but it did not occur. Instead the dramatic reversal only gradually took shape, mushroomed, and eventually produced an outcome beyond the wildest expectations even of the few historical optimists who persisted in the conviction that the Soviet drive, if confronted, could be stopped; and once stopped, that it could be reversed. As often in history, this happened for a variety of reasons, ranging from human folly to fortune. Most important perhaps were the errors and miscalculations of the Soviets themselves. Misjudging the historical situation, they pushed their forward thrust beyond the limits of toleration of even the most accommodationist elements in the West, while at the same time they strained Soviet internal resources to a point that the inherent weaknesses and corruption of the Soviet system assumed dynamic dimensions. Their conduct, in brief, fitted well Paul Kennedy's concept of "imperial overstretch."

IV

THE RESULT was the final phase of the Cold War, roughly from 1979 until 1991. It was marked by the West's gradual recapture of the ideological initiative, by the eruption of a philosophical and political crisis in the adversary's camp, and by the final and decisive push by the United States in the arms race. This phase lasted slightly more than a decade. Its outcome was victory.

The historically dramatic turnabout was precipitated by three critical cases of Soviet overstretch. Geopolitically the Soviet invasion of Afghanistan in December 1979—apparently taken on the assumption that the United States would not react—propelled the United States to adopt, for the first time ever during the entire Cold War, a policy of directly supporting actions aimed at killing Soviet troops. The Carter administration not only undertook immediately to support the Mujahedeen, but it also quietly put together a coalition embracing Pakistan, China, Saudi Arabia, Egypt, and Britain on behalf of the Afghan resistance. Equally important was the American public guarantee of Pakistan's security against any major Soviet military attack, thereby creating a sanctuary for the guerrillas. The scale and quality of U.S. support steadily expanded during the 1980s under the subsequent Reagan administration. America—along with Pakistan, which played a courageous and decisive role in the effort—thus succeeded in bogging down the Soviet Union in its own equivalent of Vietnam.

Moreover, with the influence of the accommodationist school of thought undercut by Soviet assertiveness, the United States qualitatively expanded its relationship with China. As early as 1980 U.S.-Chinese cooperation assumed a more direct strategic dimension, with sensitive undertakings not only toward Afghanistan but also on other matters. Thus the Soviet Union faced the growing geopolitical menace of a counter encirclement. . . .

The massive U.S. defense buildup of the early 1980s—including the decision to proceed with the Strategic Defense Initiative—both shocked the Soviets and then strained their resources. Its scale, momentum, and technological daring had been totally unexpected in Moscow. By 1983 a genuine war scare began to develop in the Kremlin, with the United States seen as bent perhaps even on a military solution. And then by the middle of the decade it dawned on Soviet leaders that they could neither match nor even keep up with the American efforts.

This realization interacted dynamically with the third reversal, on the ideological and social planes. In the second half of the 1970s, President Carter launched his human rights campaign. Within Soviet-controlled Eastern Europe and then within the Soviet Union itself, it first encouraged a few individuals, then larger groups, to pick up the standard of human rights, counting on Western moral and even political support. The struggle for human rights mushroomed, especially in Poland, galvanized by the election of the first Polish pope in Rome. By the late 1970s Solidarity's mass movement was beginning to threaten the communist regime of the Soviet Union's most important European satellite.

The Soviets were poised to intervene militarily in Poland, once in December 1980 and then again in March 1981. In both cases two successive U.S. administrations made clear, through direct and indirect signals, that such intervention would produce grave consequences, a message in the meantime made more credible by U.S. support for the Afghan resistance. Under these circumstances the Kremlin leaders chose to rely on an only partially effective imposition of martial law by the Polish communists themselves. As a result the Polish crisis festered throughout the decade, progressively undermining not only the Polish communist regime but gradually infecting other East European states.

The human rights campaign and the arms buildup thus became the mutually reinforcing central prongs of a U.S. response that not only blunted the Soviet offensive but also intensified the crisis of the Soviet political and socioeconomic system itself. Power and principle combined to reverse the Soviet momentum. Neither one alone would have sufficed.

By the mid-1980s a new and younger Soviet leadership had come to power. Imbued with the realization that Soviet policies, both internal and external, were a failure, Moscow was determined to repair the communist system through energetic reforms and to place its satellite regimes on a more domestically acceptable basis. To do that it needed a period of respite. These Soviet leaders thus eagerly seized the olive branch extended by the Reagan administration in 1985—especially in connection with the December 1985 Geneva summit—in the hope of gaining relief from the arms race.

The recent past is still fresh in memory. The domestic reforms, conducted pell-mell, did not revitalize the Soviet system but merely brought to the surface its hypocrisies and weaknesses. The arms race had exhausted the Soviet economy while refuting its ideological expectations. Failure to crush the Solidarity underground in Poland gradually forced the Polish communist regime into a compromise that rapidly turned into a progressive concession of power, with contagious effects in the neighboring satellites. Gorbachev's willingness to tolerate what he thought would be limited change in east-central Europe—in order to gain a breathing spell for his own domestic reforms—precipitated not the emergence of more popularly endorsed and reformist communist leadership but eventually the collapse of the communist systems as a whole.

By 1989 the choice left to Moscow was either a last-gasp effort to reimpose its rule through massive bloodshed—which not only could have precipitated violent domestic or external explosions but in all probability an intensification of the arms race and hostility with America—or to acquiesce.

The reformist Gorbachev leadership—flattered, courted, even bribed by the West, and in the final phases skillfully manipulated personally by President Bush and German Chancellor Helmut Kohl—chose the second course. The result was chaos in east-central Europe and then capitulation.

V

COULD THE outcome have been different? And what of the future, given the past?

The West perhaps might have won sooner, but at a higher cost and with a greater risk of war. The key opportunity for the West came in the period 1953–56. Greater Western elasticity in 1953 might have facilitated a Soviet pullback from Germany. But the Kremlin almost certainly would have used the Soviet army to maintain its grip on Warsaw and Prague, while in the West the neutralization of Germany might have precluded the establishment of binding NATO links between America and Europe. In contrast greater Western toughness in 1956—still a time of decisive U.S. strategic superiority—might have resulted in forcing the Soviet Union out of Hungary and Poland. The communist regimes in these countries were crumbling, and the Soviet leadership itself was in a state of panic.

The Cold War, however, would not have ended. Communism was not ripe for a collapse within Russia itself, and on the global scale the ideological momentum of communism was far from spent. Communist movements were strong even in Western Europe, and the communist wave in the Far East was still cresting. Thus any respite in the Cold War would have been just temporary. Moreover one cannot exclude the possibility that in these circumstances at least a conventional war might have broken out in central Europe.

The only other opportunity for ending the Cold War may have existed in the early 1970s, on the basis of what might be called "the Peace of Westphalia formula." But both sides would have had then to accept the status quo in Europe as fixed. The West seemed ready to do so. However, by the mid-1970s, the Soviets saw themselves as being on a historical roll. Hence Moscow wanted the status quo in Europe as well as American acquiescence to continued Soviet global expansion and to a gradual shift in "the correlation of forces." In effect any acceptance of the European status quo would have been for the Soviets merely a temporary expedient.

This is why it is historically important to reiterate here the fact that the Kremlin was in no mood to be propitiated either through arms control or an acceptance by the West of the existing division of Europe. The Cold War eventually ended because the West succeeded in combining firm containment with an active offensive on human rights and a strategic buildup of its own, while aiding the resistance in Afghanistan and Poland. . . .

Throughout the Cold War, it was America that bore most of the burden and displayed the strongest will to persist. America's allies were generally steadfast in critical moments, but otherwise they were more tempted to settle for a compromise. It was America that sustained large-scale efforts—especially by means of radio—to pierce the Iron Curtain, and it was America that in the later phases of the Cold War most directly supported the resistance in Afghanistan and the underground in Poland while intimidating Moscow through its crash strategic buildup. And it was America that throughout the Cold War deterred Soviet power with a posture and a leadership that was on the whole remarkably consistent.

In that regard the historical credit for fashioning the winning strategy and for forging the victorious coalition must go to one man above all: Harry Truman. He committed America because he understood the stakes. Eisenhower then built on Truman regarding NATO; Carter built on Nixon regarding China; Bush built on Reagan regarding the arms race. American policy may not have been brilliant, and at times, it was overly defensive, but it was steady. It also remained tactically focused on the weakest link in the Soviet "front": east-central Europe. From the 1960s onward the United States consistently sought, overtly and covertly, to soften Soviet control over the region by a policy of peaceful engagement, with the payoff coming finally in the 1980s.

In contrast Soviet policy lacked consistency. With the exception of Stalin himself the Soviet leadership proved to be less steady and operationally inferior to America's. Stalin was the Great Calculator, carefully husbanding his resources, devouring his enemies, while cautiously bluffing in order to obscure his system's weaknesses. But even he made a basic and historically decisive error: his brutal policies in east-central Europe united the West, and that unity precluded America's disengagement from Europe. Once that became clear, a conclusive Soviet victory was no longer possible.

Stalin's successors were second rate. Khrushchev was the Master Bumbler, pressing and posturing, creating the illusion of historical momentum at a time of Western indecision. But he could not achieve a breakthrough, even though he brought both sides dangerously close to a military collision at a time of still relative Soviet strategic inferiority. Brezhnev, the Gray Plodder, posed more of a threat, with his steady buildup of Soviet strategic might, but he did not know when to exploit that might for political gain. Had Brezhnev proved more imaginative, he might have taken advantage of Nixon's realism to reach an advantageous Peace of Westphalia or the goodwill of the American president in the latter 1970s, and of the naivete of some of his advisers, to conclude an even more beneficial accommodation. Instead, Brezhnev pursued the policy of global encirclement, with some peripheral successes but no breakthrough on the central front.

The last Soviet leader, Gorbachev, can be considered operationally the Grand Miscalculator and historically a tragic figure. He thought he could revitalize the Soviet economy that Brezhnev, through his military spending, had ruined, but he did not know how. He thought he could reach a broad détente with the West, but he underestimated the corrosive effects of the war in Afghanistan and of the survival of the Solidarity movement in Poland. Attempts at East-West accommodation, instead of stabilizing Soviet rule in east-central Europe, exploded in his face, especially once the fear of Soviet intervention had been dissipated by Gorbachev's cultivation of the West and by the Soviet military's failures in Afghanistan.

Could the Soviets have won the Cold War? The final outcome was the product of objective and subjective factors, and on both scores the Soviet side turned out to have been at a disadvantage. The Western socioeconomic system proved much stronger and its underlying ideas ultimately much more appealing. In effect, despite some illusions propagated by Khrushchev and entertained by Brezhnev, the Soviet Union was forced to play "catch-up ball" throughout the Cold War.

The bottom line thus has to be that a full-blown Soviet victory was never in the cards, except very briefly right after World War II. Had America disengaged, the outcome would have been quite different. But that alternative was foreclosed early on. Thereafter the Kremlin could have sought and perhaps obtained favorable settlements that could have served as launchpads for later offensives, but its leaders failed to exploit the occasional opportunities. These knocked on history's doors early in the 1950s and even more so in the 1970s. Finally, the grand scale of the final defeat in the late 1980s could also have been minimized if the Gorbachev leadership had been more skillful in handling its domestic reforms and had moved more rapidly in the mid-1980s to resolve the Afghan and Polish problems.

VI

WHAT SHOULD now be the West's central strategic objective toward its former Cold War rival?

The point of departure for a meaningful answer is to recognize that, from a historical point of view, the collapse of the Soviet Union, which endured for some 70 years, is more than overshadowed by the disintegration of the great Russian empire, which lasted for more than 300 years. This is an event of truly historic magnitude, pregnant with geopolitical uncertainties. It will be many years before the dust finally settles, but it is already clear that the postcommunist transition in the former empire will be more difficult and much more prolonged than the democratic reconstruction of either Germany or Japan after 1945.

The West must support that transition with the same commitment and magnanimity with which America acted after the victory in 1945. That commitment, however, must be guided by a longer range geopolitical vision that goes beyond the West's currently one-sided concentration on facilitating Russia's socioeconomic recovery. While that recovery is desirable, its attainment should be seen as part of a broader effort designed to accomplish two interrelated objectives: the emergence of a truly postimperial Russia that can assume its proper place in the concert of the world's leading democratic nations; and the stable consolidation of the newly independent non-Russian states, some of which are only in the early stages of their own nation building, in order to create an enduring geopolitical context that by itself reinforces Russia's transformation into a post-imperial state. Each of the foregoing is dependent on the other, and hence both must be deliberately sought.

Any Western ambiguity on this matter could prove historically shortsighted. Just as it would have been a historic mistake to settle for less than the liberation of east-central Europe from Moscow's domination, so now a recovery program for the Russian economy that does not at the same time seek to transform Russia into a post-imperial state could prove to be ephemeral. Accordingly any Russian efforts to isolate and eventually again to subordinate Ukraine through the maintenance of a Moscow-controlled outpost in Crimea, for example, or to delay the evacuation of Russian troops from the Baltic republics should be unambiguously viewed as obstacles to effective financial and economic assistance.

However, it is also essential to provide the Russians with a meaningful alternative to their long-standing imperial status, and that has to be the offer of partnership with the West. The West is correct in stressing that it sees Russia's eventual destiny as a major player in the European concert of nations and as one of America's partners in dealing with the world's wider problems. But to become such a player, the transformation of Russia requires—as earlier in the cases of Germany and Japan—the shedding of its imperial aspirations.

Since as a practical matter any formal association of Russia with Europe is still a long way off, some thought should now be given to the creation of intermediary forms of involvement with Europe. . . . Russia should not be made to feel that a new *cordon sanitaire* separates it from the West.

The above must be matched by sustained Western efforts to promote nation building in the former Soviet empire. Above all it is geopolitically essential that Ukraine succeed in stabilizing itself as a secure and independent state. That will automatically increase the chances of Russia's evolution as a democratizing and increasingly European post-imperial state. Accordingly a critical component of Western strategy has to be the deliberate effort—not only economic but also political—to consolidate a stable and sovereign Ukraine. Elsewhere in the former empire, the process of nation building is likely to be even more complex than in Ukraine, and yet it too will have to be supported simultaneously with the postcommunist socioeconomic transformation itself.

That socioeconomic transformation will be long and painful. The West, in proffering aid and advice, must be careful not to replace old communist dogmas with new dogmas of its own regarding the application of capitalist practices. Any attempt to create simultaneously a free-market economy and a political democracy that does not carefully seek to minimize the social pains of the needed transition could precipitate a destructive collision between these two objectives. This collision could then discredit both goals in the eyes of the affected peoples and enhance the appeal of some new escapist doctrines.

The aftermath of the Cold War thus poses an agenda for the West that is truly daunting. Its essence is to make certain that the disintegration of the Soviet Union becomes the peaceful and enduring end of the Russian empire, and that the collapse of communism truly means the end of the utopian phase in modern political history. But these grand goals will come to pass only if the West again demonstrates strategic staying power, focused on clear-headed geopolitical—and not just on narrow socioeconomic or vaguely idealistic—aims.

An Uncertain New Order

THE NINETEEN NINETIES

ⓔSCHOLARS SEEKING perspective on the 1990s might lament a paradigm lost. Without the overarching bipolar dynamic of the Cold War, students of U.S. foreign relations have groped in vain for a new way to explain the nature of the world around them; thus far, the overall theme of the 1990s is that there is no overall theme to the 1990s. The trends seem to move in different directions. The Soviet Union's corpse was not yet cold when it seemed that the new post–Cold War world might look depressingly like the old one. On August 2, 1990, Iraqi troops stormed across the Kuwaiti frontier. In response, the Bush administration assembled an astonishing coalition, uniting the United States and the Soviet Union—not to mention most of the Arab world—against Iraqi President Saddam Hussein. President George Bush began touting "a new world order," stirring memories of the old Wilsonian dream of collective security.

For some the world has changed fundamentally—completely transforming the old politics into a genuinely new order whose hallmarks are the declining importance of the nation-state and a sweeping restructuring of international power due to technology, economics, and globalization. Walter B. Wriston, the longtime chairman of Citibank, argues in "Technology and Sovereignty" that scientific advances will undermine states as we have known them. In "Power Shift," Jessica T. Mathews, the president of the Carnegie Endowment for International Peace, sees the unprecedented rise of nongovernmental organizations as the building blocks of a global civil society. Increasingly, economics seems to be the dominant force in the world, though for some this only means that the global game will be played with different cards. Geoeconomics became a new catchphrase, and U.S. trade policy under Bush and his successor, Bill Clinton, seemed influenced by it. But Paul Krugman, the iconoclastic MIT economist, explains in "Competitiveness: A Dangerous Obsession" that the view that countries compete with each other just like businesses is simply wrong.

But even with the rise of new technologies to bind the planet closer together, old forces from the past remain. Nationalism has roared back to life, perhaps most dangerously in the Soviet Union's former sphere of influence. In 1972, when rationalist ideologies like communism, socialism, and capitalism were flourishing, the great Oxford philosopher Isaiah Berlin's "The Bent Twig: A Note on Nationalism" prophetically warned of the power and resilience of nationalism. Two decades later, looking at the rise of religious fundamentalism from India's Bharatiya Janata Party to the Sudan's Islamists to Israel's radical right, Samuel P. Huntington drew a broader conclusion. In "The Clash of Civilizations?" the eminent Harvard political scientist predicted that the "great divisions among humankind and the dominating source of conflict will be cultural." Huntington's essay sees a world of civilizations that compete and collaborate but are defined by cultural unity. The former Yugoslavia, where a multiethnic nation was torn into its religious parts, is often held up as the prime example of such a culture clash. But Warren Zimmermann, the final U.S. envoy to the former Yugoslavia, in his memoir "The Last Ambassador" saw not immutable cultural differences but the cynical lust for power of the demagogues in Pale, Zagreb, and Belgrade. Whether it is nations that create nationalisms or the other way around, these hatreds are here to stay.

At a century's ending, however, America's attention is turning increasingly not to Europe but to the Pacific Rim, where a funny thing has happened over the last three decades. The countries of Southeast Asia, especially Japan and the so-called four tigers (South Korea, Taiwan, Singapore, and Hong Kong), moved from centuries of poverty to prosperity in one generation. China has begun following suit, and given its size the growth of this giant could well reconfigure world politics. In Fareed Zakaria's "Culture Is Destiny," the managing editor of *Foreign Affairs* interviewed the most outspoken voice representing the rise of East Asia: Lee Kuan Yew, the architect of prosperous, clean, and authoritarian Singapore. Lee argues that Confucianism's values will make the coming century the era of Asia. Zakaria politely demurs. The West has left its mark—both material and moral—on the world so firmly that it may prove impossible to escape it. After all, the twentieth century has turned out the way it has because of the power and purpose of one Western country. And the twenty-first century may also prove to be shaped by the American encounter.

Technology and Sovereignty

Walter B. Wriston

WINTER 1988/89

ONE OF HISTORY'S recurring themes is man's inability to credit information which conflicts with his prejudgments. Examples abound. In her book *Practicing History,* the American historian Barbara Tuchman uses the Japanese attack on Pearl Harbor as one illustration of this. Despite the fact that Japan had opened the Russo-Japanese War in 1904 by a surprise attack against the Russian fleet, American authorities dismissed the possibility of a similar maneuver in 1941: "We had broken the Japanese code, we had warnings on radar, we had a constant flow of accurate intelligence . . . we had all the evidence and refused to interpret it correctly, just as the Germans in 1944 refused to believe the evidence of a landing in Normandy." Tuchman concludes: "Men will not believe what does not fit in with their plans or suit their prearrangements." This phenomenon, unfortunately, is not limited to discrete events.

When major tides of change wash over the world, power structures almost inevitably reject the notion that the world really is changing, and they cling to their old beliefs. In the past some changes came slowly and gave us the time we needed to adjust to a new reality. In the last years of this century, however, the velocity of change in the world has become so great that there are literally no precedents to guide us. Policymakers are discovering that many of the events that are altering the world come not in response to their actions, but are driven by technologies which they may only dimly understand.

II

ABOUT 85 PERCENT of all the scientists who have ever lived are alive today. With their advanced tools and increased creative opportunities, it is not surprising that the rate of change is now more rapid than at any time in human

[503]

history. "The entire Industrial Revolution," says Dr. Carver Mead of the California Institute of Technology, "enhanced productivity by a factor of about a hundred," but "the microelectronic revolution has already enhanced productivity in information-based technology by a factor of more than a million—and the end isn't in sight yet." The immense consequences of this technological revolution have not always been grasped by policymakers.

Politicians and diplomats are by nature attracted to those political historians who record the rise and fall of nation-states, but they generally display little interest in the history of science. This lack of interest compounds the difficulty of understanding what is happening. Indeed, many renowned history books barely mention the impact of science on the course of political events. Even in ancient Greece, as Plato records, engineers were not held in high regard by philosophers: "You despise him and his art," he wrote, "and sneeringly call him an engine-maker, and you will not allow your daughter to marry his son or marry your son to his daughter." Very little has changed, even though scientific achievements are altering the shape of national and international events in fundamental ways.

A good example is the launching of sputnik by the Soviet Union on October 4, 1957. At the time, world reaction was divided. Dr. Edward Teller opined that the United States "had lost a battle more important and greater than Pearl Harbor. President Eisenhower, however, took a more sanguine view:

> So far as the satellite itself is concerned, that does not raise my apprehensions, not one iota. I see nothing at this moment . . . that is significant in that development so far as security is concerned, except . . . it does definitely prove the possession by the Russian scientists of a very powerful thrust in their rocketry.

The chancellor of West Germany, Konrad Adenauer, related the event to European geography: "Five hundred and sixty miles is only the distance from Bonn to Vienna. It does not prove they can fire anything parallel to the earth over a distance of many thousand miles."

In the blinding clarity of hindsight, Dr. Teller was probably closer to the mark in some ways than the politicians. Despite the initial reactions to sputnik's launch, what should no longer be in dispute is that satellite technology changed the world forever. Even today the full consequences are not yet known. On the other hand, the fallout from the event did galvanize America to mount a program that would put a man on the moon.

The convergence of computers with telecommunications has created an information revolution. One observer, the journalist Mike O'Neil, has said that this revolution is "hurrying the collapse of old orders, accelerating the velocity of social and political change, creating informed and politically active publics, and inciting conflict by publicizing the differences between people and nations."

The impact of information technology, moreover, has a profound effect on the rate of advance of all science, since calculations that used to take years can now be made in minutes. Scientific knowledge is currently doubling about every 13 to 15 years. The old industrial age is being slowly replaced by a new era of the information society. This transition does not mean that manufacturing does not matter, or that it will disappear, any more than the advent of the industrial age meant that agriculture disappeared. What it does imply is that, like agriculture today, manufacturing will produce more goods for more people with less labor. It also means that the relative importance of intellectual capital invested in software and systems will increase in relation to the capital invested in physical plants and equipment. Traditional accounting systems designed for an earlier age no longer reflect what is really happening, either in business or national economics.

III

THE INFORMATION revolution is changing our global economy, transforming national political and business institutions, and altering national foreign policy objectives and the methods of achieving them.

Changes of this magnitude are profoundly disturbing to the power structure, and with good reason. The mismatch between the fruits of new technology and the operation of the political process, whether in government, business, or the family, has often produced unrest, changing value systems, and sometimes, indeed, revolution. Just as the spread of rudimentary medical knowledge took away the power of the tribal witch doctor, the spread of information about alternate lifestyles in other countries threatens the validity of some official doctrines and thus some governments' power bases.

Knowledge has always conferred power on those who have it and know how to use it, and the proliferation and dissemination of information to huge numbers of people can be, and more often than not is, a precursor to a shift in the power structure. But the effects of the information revolution go even deeper: the very nature and definition of national sovereignty is being altered.

The currently accepted tenets of national sovereignty, like most man-made concepts, did not emerge full-blown upon a waiting world, but evolved over time. Those with a vested interest in any given definition want to sustain their own power and naturally resist any change which might undermine their authority.

Perhaps one of the first organized presentations of a concept of sovereignty appeared toward the end of the sixteenth century from the French scholar Jean Bodin. He argued for the unlimited and autocratic power of the state unrestrained by law. This idea was embraced by kings but challenged by others, including Johannes Althusius, who argued that the state's power was limited by the laws of God and nature and by the social contract between the state and the governed.

It was left to the great Dutch jurist, Hugo Grotius, to give us the definition of sovereignty that exists more or less intact to this day. Grotius defined sovereignty in broad terms as "that power whose acts are not subject to the control of another, so that they may be made void by the act of any other human will." This definition obviously covers many different facets of the exercise of power.

One of the fundamental prerogatives assumed by all sovereign governments has been to pursue their national interest by waging war. This has been true since ancient times, but today it is an aspect of sovereignty that is being severely circumscribed by the effects of information technology. No one who lived through the Vietnam War can fail to understand the enormous impact that television had in frustrating the American government's objective in Southeast Asia. A general recognition that war produces violent death is one thing, but witnessing the carnage of a battle or the body bags being unloaded at Dover Air Force Base on the television set is quite another. While debate will rage for years about whether Vietnam was lost on the battlefield or on the home front, few observers would fail to give at least some significant weight to television's impact on the citizens at home.

When the British engaged in war over the Falkland Islands, they severely limited the press and television coverage of the hostilities. Whether that military operation could have been successfully conducted under the glare of full television coverage is an open question; in any case, British rules on press coverage differ from those in America. In the United States, we have seen the names of American agents overseas published and have read accounts in national newspapers detailing American naval and troop movements at a time of national emergency.

Such episodes puzzle both domestic and foreign observers. Aleksandr Solzhenitsyn, in his address at Harvard in 1978, put it this way: "We may see terrorists heroized, or secret matters, pertaining to one's national defense, publicly revealed, or we may witness shameless intrusion on the privacy of well-known people."

This process has repercussions on the effectiveness of leadership. We are all familiar with the old saying that no man is a hero to his valet, and it can be argued that television has become the valet of today's world leaders.

In the absence of a major threat to the integrity of one's own borders or to the independence of the nation, one can at least question whether a democratic government operating in the full glare of television cameras could, in fact, conduct any sustained military operation that produces heavy casualties. If the answer is no, one important aspect of national sovereignty has been substantially altered.

IV

IF WE look at national domestic politics, we observe a similar phenomenon.

The quality, speed, and nature of information spread by the mass media has altered the relationship between the people and their government. Representative government in America is changing. Information technology has made it both possible and politically profitable for politicians to bypass traditional political structures that supported the orderly process of government and instead move toward the TV cameras to push a particular issue. As more and more leaders do this, the traditional cement of party discipline and consensus government begins to crumble. Adversarial confrontations make good TV drama but may often lead to bad policy decisions.

The national and international agendas are increasingly being set by the media in the sense that policymakers have to spend a good share of their time and energy dealing with whatever crisis or pseudocrisis has been identified by the media that particular day. Real issues, deliberative thought, and long-range strategic plans are often casualties of whatever damage-control actions are required at the moment. In these circumstances, the old bipartisanship in American foreign affairs has fallen prey to a new divisiveness. The so-called TV docudramas, part fact, part fiction, have even attempted to change the record of past events. The merging of media and message has created a situation wherein, according to Daniel Boorstin, a "larger and larger proportion of our experience, of what we read and see and hear, has come to consist of pseudo-events."

This kind of information is rarely a solid foundation for good policy judgments. However, it characterizes the age in which we live. We live in a world where Yasir Arafat works with a media consultant; where Mohammed Abbas, who hijacked the *Achille Lauro* and murdered an old man in cold blood, appears on American network television, even though he was a fugitive from justice at the time; where the Iranians stage marches for the cameras; and where Soviet spokesmen appear regularly on American TV. The world today is very different from that of Citizen Edmond Genet—now, instead of being asked to leave the country, he would be on Ted Koppel's "Nightline" to protest President George Washington's outrageous policies.

Without passing a value judgment, the fact is that representative government, as envisaged by the Founding Fathers, is no longer operating in the manner originally intended. We may have to think anew about old relationships, but for the moment, the use of information technology has far outstripped the political process.

This problem is not limited to Western governments. If democratic societies face the problem of adapting to what amounts to a wholly new definition of sovereignty, closed societies like the Soviet Union will have a much more difficult time. Their problem is twofold: first, communist regimes have always relied to some extent on their ability to control what their citizens see and hear. This control is now beginning to slip, and from the Soviets' point of view, the situation will get much worse. In addition to borders becoming increasingly porous to TV and radio transmissions, studies at Harvard's Center for Information Policy Research reveal that citizens of the Eastern-bloc countries have little difficulty gaining access to VCRs; the number available in Moscow is growing daily. The KGB is concerned that videotapes will be used for *magnitizdat*—a word coined for "tape publishing"—by political opposition groups.

The Soviet government's second major problem is whether the U.S.S.R. can continue to be a leader in science. Modern scientific research increasingly requires the ability to have access to huge databases at remote locations. If access is limited to a very small number of scientists, progress will be slowed. On the other hand, opening up supercomputers and databases to large numbers of men and women obviously loosens the state's control of data. It is a very real Hobson's choice, and the dilemma will only get worse over time.

The phenomenon of eroding government control over the management of institutions and how citizens live and work is not limited to closed societies but is becoming increasingly evident in the West. National sovereignty and political saliency have traditionally entailed the government's power to regulate major sectors of society, ranging from health care to heavy industries. The increasing difficulty of exercising this power in the information age as opposed to the industrial age was summed up, in the March/April issue of *Chief Executive* magazine, by the economist George Gilder: "A steel mill, the exemplary industry of the material age," lends itself to control by governments. Gilder continued:

> [A steel mill's] massive output is easily measured and regulated at every point by government. By contrast, the typical means of production of the new epoch is a man at a computer workstation, with access to data bases

around the world, designing microchips comparable in complexity to the entire steel facility, to be manufactured from software programs comprising a coded sequence of electronic pulses that can elude every export control and run a production line anywhere on the globe.

The advent of the silicon compiler, which is analogous to desktop publishing for chip design, opens up, in Gilder's words, "a great economic cleavage between the interests of entrepreneurs and the authority of national governments." As technology continues to progress, the cleavage will deepen.

v

THE GROWING inability of sovereign governments to regulate their affairs in the information age will have profound foreign policy implications.

Recently a private company forced a superpower to change its policy. This occurred when the government's monopoly on photographs from space was broken by the launching in February 1986 of the privately owned French satellite SPOT. When the pictures of the Chernobyl nuclear disaster taken by SPOT appeared on the front pages of the world's newspapers, the Soviet Union was forced to change its story and admit that the event was much more serious than it had previously claimed. In this instance, the technology was not new, but the power to use the information shifted from the government to the private sector. However, the event posed a continuing dilemma: what SPOT revealed about Chernobyl, it can also reveal about American military sites. There is no American censorship of SPOT pictures, as there has been on a de facto basis of America's Landsat photos.

While the resolution of SPOT's picture is only ten meters, it will undoubtedly be improved. It is not beyond the realm of possibility that the next logical development might be for an international news agency to purchase its own high-resolution satellite. As a cost comparison, the purchase of a satellite would be a good deal less expensive for a television network than covering the Olympics. If this occurs, the guardians of national security will clash in space with the defenders of the First Amendment.

The policy dilemma posed by SPOT was further sharpened by the offer of the Soviet Union to sell high-quality imagery, which has a five-meter resolution, to anyone beyond their borders who could meet the price. National rules, including those of the Department of Defense and President Carter's secret directive in 1978 limiting the power of civilian satellites, are eroding to the point of ineffectuality. One can wonder about the course of events if SPOT had produced a picture of Pearl Harbor on December 8, 1941, when the world was being told our fleet was intact. What is certain is that it will become progressively harder for nations to assert what is not true if the "spy in the sky" is not controlled by the government.

Another traditional aspect of sovereignty has been the ability of nation-states to issue currency and mandate its value. In the past, what kings said their currency was worth was not always congruent with the facts. In the seventeenth century the Amsterdam bankers made themselves unpopular by weighing coins and announcing their true metallic values. However, those bankers spoke to a very small audience, and their voices were not heard far beyond the city limits. Technology now carries the market's judgments on the value of currencies to all parts of the planet within minutes.

Today we are witnessing a galloping new system of international finance. Our new international financial regime differs radically from its precursors in that it was not built by politicians, economists, central bankers, or finance ministers, nor did high-level international conferences produce a master plan. It was built by technology. It is doubtful if the men and women who interconnected the planet with telecommunications and computers realized that they were assembling a global financial marketplace that would replace the Bretton Woods agreements and, over time, alter political structures. Although only a few politicians recognized the possibilities of instant global communications, the money traders of the world immediately drove their trades over the new global electronic infrastructure, creating a new international monetary system governed by the Information Standard.

Today, information about all countries' diplomatic, fiscal, and monetary policies is instantly transmitted to more than two hundred thousand screens in hundreds of trading rooms in dozens of countries. As the screens light up with the latest statement of the president or the chairman of the Federal Reserve, traders judge the effect of the new policies on the relative values of the country's currency and buy or sell accordingly.

Although innumerable speeches are made giving lip service to the idea of a global marketplace, many people still fail to understand the reality. The entire globe is linked electronically, with no place to hide. Finance ministers who believe in sound monetary and fiscal policies are starting to perceive that the new technology is on their side. And politicians who wish to evade responsibility for the results of their imprudent actions on fiscal and monetary matters correctly perceive that the new Information Standard will punish them. The consequences are, in fact, more draconian than the gold exchange standard and a great deal faster in coming.

VI

LIKE ALL technological advances, the new Information Standard makes the world's power structures very nervous, and with good reason. The rapid dissemination of information has always changed societies and, thus, the way governments operate. In the United States, perhaps the most dramatic example of this dynamic was the civil rights movement. The plight of black people in many sections of the nation went almost unnoticed by many Americans for almost a hundred years. Suddenly the TV cameras brought into our living rooms the image of Bull Connor with his dogs and whips. Americans quickly decided together that this was wrong, and the civil rights movement made a quantum leap forward, drastically changing the country's political landscape.

Even though American politicians have come to accept universal suffrage and the ballot box as arbiter of who holds office and who does not, the similar new global vote on a nation's fiscal and monetary policies is profoundly disturbing to many.

The world's financial marketplace will never recede to its old national borders. Lines on the maps, traditionally the cause of wars, are now porous. Money and ideas move across borders in a manner and at a speed never before seen. Markets are no longer geographical locations but data on a screen transmitted from anywhere in the world. It is difficult to suddenly accept the judgment of thousands of traders who translate politicians' actions into new monetary values, because this situation has arisen so quickly. Nevertheless, it is about as useful to curse the thermometer for recording a heat wave as it is to rail against the values the global market puts on a nation's currency.

This state of affairs does not sit well with many governments, because they correctly perceive that the new Information Standard is an attack on their sovereign powers. Since global financial markets are a kind of free speech, many complain about what the markets reveal about their country's policies.

In the past, if a country did not like the way a particular financial standard was working, be it the gold standard or the Bretton Woods agreements, the leader of the country could call a press conference and simply opt out of the system. This has happened many times in history. What will eventually harness politicians' attention is that there is no longer any way for a nation to resign from the Information Standard. No matter how a country attempts to escape from the system, the world's trading room screens will continue to light up, and the market will continue to make judgments.

Since the underlying technology of the new financial system will not disappear, it is reasonable to assume that the Information Standard will be with us for a long time. The good news is that since it is here to stay, there will be increasing pressure on all governments to implement sound fiscal and monetary policies, which will in turn enhance the chances of international financial cooperation. While each nation will continue to pursue what it perceives to be its national interests, there will be increasing pressure to harmonize various economic policies. Progress is already visible in these areas.

VII

IN THE FIELD of foreign policy, new technology is rewriting old concepts of sovereignty and over time will also change national objectives. As early as 1945, British Foreign Secretary Anthony Eden noted that "every succeeding scientific discovery makes greater nonsense of old-time conceptions of sovereignty." Although Eden was among the first leaders to recognize the impact of science on national sovereignty, the current shift in the power structure is not unique in history. There have been many instances throughout history of technology's impact on international relations, altering the balance of power between sectors of society and between countries.

The early science of blue-water navigation is a case in point. Although mariners from many countries had for years crossed oceans and explored foreign climes, only the Europeans exploited the political potential presented by this new knowledge. The historian Fernand Braudel has pointed out that "the conquest of the high seas gave Europe a world supremacy that lasted for centuries." The historical mystery is why the technology of ocean navigation, once demonstrated, was not grasped by other maritime civilizations to expand their own political power.

In more recent times, even the most jaded diplomat might have to concede that the balance of power in the world shifted decisively on July 16, 1945, in the desert at Alamogordo, New Mexico, when the first atomic explosion took place. (For the modern Luddites who explain almost daily that the Strategic Defense Initiative will not work, it is useful to remember that almost half of the scientists at Los Alamos thought the atomic bomb would not fire.) When it did, relations between nations were instantly altered, and indeed, the very survival of our planet came into question. The process works both ways: scientists suddenly also discovered the desirability of a world framework of international law and order to protect society from their own discoveries.

Some will say that while new technologies may affect the balance of power on a temporary basis, they cannot change the basic geopolitical interests of a country. This argument rests, in part, on the fact that it is vital for a country to have assured access to certain critical raw materials. Countries having these desired natural resources within their borders are therefore of strategic importance to the United States. The oil-rich nations in the Middle East are the most obvious examples, but there are other countries whose soils contain important minerals ranging from copper to titanium.

Not that long ago, armies fought and men died for control of the iron and steel in the Ruhr Basin because ownership of these assets conferred economic and political power. Indeed, the idea of a nation-state was based on the concept of territoriality. Today, these once coveted assets may be a liability. To the extent that new technology replaces once essential commodities with plastics or other synthetic materials, the relative importance of these areas to the vital interest of nations is bound to change.

When World War II cut the United States off from a supply of natural rubber from the Far East, we turned to synthetic rubber, the basic research on which had been completed before World War I. The technology had not been exploited because it was too expensive. The war emergency caused us to set aside economics in order to produce tires, but as we went up the learning curve, production costs were driven down. When we reached the point where synthetic rubber became cost-effective, the significance of rubber-producing countries to our strategic interests tended to decline.

Today, as fiber-optic cable replaces the twisted copper pair, the relative strategic importance of copper-producing countries will also shift. Sand, the most common substance in the world, is the raw material for computer chips. Clay is the base for superconducting ceramics that will speed data by a factor of a hundred, generally enhance the power of magnets, and thus further shift the value of traditional natural resources. Over a period of years this same pattern, in various degrees, will continue to apply to other natural resources, even oil.

As scientific advances continue to unfold, diplomatic priorities are bound to change. Even the strategic importance of critical areas of the world is altered by technology. It was not so long ago that conventional wisdom held that lights would go out all over the world if the Suez Canal were ever to be closed. However, conventional wisdom did not take into account the technology that would allow the building of huge supertankers able to carry oil economically around the Cape of Good Hope. This feat was achieved by relatively simple technology, but it altered the importance of the physical control of a specific territory.

Today the velocity of change is so great in all aspects of science, technology, economics, and politics that the tectonic plates of national sovereignty and power have begun to shift. Political scientists and statesmen are fond of remarking that generals usually prepare to fight the previous war. Now the policymakers may be guilty of similar errors. If today's leaders in government and business fail to recognize that the world has changed because what they see, in Tuchman's words, "does not fit in with their plans or suit their pre-arrangements," they will follow into oblivion a long list of leaders who have made similar mistakes. Those who can understand and master change will be tomorrow's winners.

Power Shift

Jessica T. Mathews

JANUARY/FEBRUARY 1997

THE RISE OF GLOBAL CIVIL SOCIETY

THE END of the Cold War has brought no mere adjustment among states but a novel redistribution of power among states, markets, and civil society. National governments are not simply losing autonomy in a globalizing economy. They are sharing powers—including political, social, and security roles at the core of sovereignty—with businesses, with international organizations, and with a multitude of citizens groups, known as nongovernmental organizations (NGOs). The steady concentration of power in the hands of states that began in 1648 with the Peace of Westphalia is over, at least for a while.

The absolutes of the Westphalian system—territorially fixed states where everything of value lies within some state's borders; a single, secular authority governing each territory and representing it outside its borders; and no authority above states—are all dissolving. Increasingly, resources and threats that matter, including money, information, pollution, and popular culture, circulate and shape lives and economies with little regard for political boundaries. International standards of conduct are gradually beginning to override claims of national or regional singularity. Even the most powerful states find the marketplace and international public opinion compelling them more often to follow a particular course.

The state's central task of assuring security is the least affected, but still not exempt. War will not disappear, but with the shrinkage of U.S. and Russian nuclear arsenals, the transformation of the Nuclear Nonproliferation Treaty into a permanent covenant in 1995, agreement on the long-sought Comprehensive Test Ban treaty in 1996, and the likely entry into force of the Chemical Weapons Convention in 1997, the security threat to states from other states is on a downward course. Nontraditional threats, however, are

[515]

rising—terrorism, organized crime, drug trafficking, ethnic conflict, and the combination of rapid population growth, environmental decline, and poverty that breeds economic stagnation, political instability, and sometimes, state collapse. The nearly 100 armed conflicts since the end of the Cold War have virtually all been intrastate affairs. Many began with governments acting against their own citizens, through extreme corruption, violence, incompetence, or complete breakdown, as in Somalia.

These trends have fed a growing sense that individuals' security may not in fact reliably derive from their nation's security. A competing notion of "human security" is creeping around the edges of official thinking, suggesting that security be viewed as emerging from the conditions of daily life—food, shelter, employment, health, public safety—rather than flowing downward from a country's foreign relations and military strength.

The most powerful engine of change in the relative decline of states and the rise of nonstate actors is the computer and telecommunications revolution, whose deep political and social consequences have been almost completely ignored. Widely accessible and affordable technology has broken governments' monopoly on the collection and management of large amounts of information and deprived governments of the deference they enjoyed because of it. In every sphere of activity, instantaneous access to information and the ability to put it to use multiplies the number of players who matter and reduces the number who command great authority. The effect on the loudest voice—which has been government's—has been the greatest.

By drastically reducing the importance of proximity, the new technologies change people's perceptions of community. Fax machines, satellite hookups, and the Internet connect people across borders with exponentially growing ease while separating them from natural and historical associations within nations. In this sense a powerful globalizing force, they can also have the opposite effect, amplifying political and social fragmentation by enabling more and more identities and interests scattered around the globe to coalesce and thrive.

These technologies have the potential to divide society along new lines, separating ordinary people from elites with the wealth and education to command technology's power. Those elites are not only the rich but also citizens groups with transnational interests and identities that frequently have more in common with counterparts in other countries, whether industrialized or developing, than with countrymen.

Above all, the information technologies disrupt hierarchies, spreading power among more people and groups. In drastically lowering the costs of communication, consultation, and coordination, they favor decentralized networks over other modes of organization. In a network, individuals or groups link for joint action without building a physical or formal institutional presence. Networks have no person at the top and no center. Instead, they have multiple nodes where collections of individuals or groups interact for different purposes. Businesses, citizens organizations, ethnic groups, and crime cartels have all readily adopted the network model. Governments, on the other hand, are quintessential hierarchies, wedded to an organizational form incompatible with all that the new technologies make possible.

Today's powerful nonstate actors are not without precedent. The British East India Company ran a subcontinent, and a few influential NGOs go back more than a century. But these are exceptions. Both in numbers and in impact, nonstate actors have never before approached their current strength. And a still larger role likely lies ahead.

DIAL LOCALLY, ACT GLOBALLY

NO ONE knows how many NGOs there are or how fast the tally is growing. Published figures are badly misleading. One widely cited estimate claims there are 35,000 NGOs in the developing countries; another points to 12,000 irrigation cooperatives in South Asia alone. In fact, it is impossible to measure a swiftly growing universe that includes neighborhood, professional, service, and advocacy groups, both secular and church-based, promoting every conceivable cause and funded by donations, fees, foundations, governments, international organizations, or the sale of products and services. The true number is certainly in the millions, from the tiniest village association to influential but modestly funded international groups like Amnesty International to larger global activist organizations like Greenpeace and giant service providers like CARE, which has an annual budget of nearly $400 million.

Except in China, Japan, the Middle East, and a few other places where culture or authoritarian governments severely limit civil society, NGOs' role and influence have exploded in the last half-decade. Their financial resources and—often more important—their expertise approximate and sometimes exceed those of smaller governments and of international organizations. "We have less money and fewer resources than Amnesty International, and we are the arm of the U.N. for human rights," noted Ibrahima Fall, head of the U.N. Centre for Human Rights, in 1993. "This is clearly ridiculous." Today NGOs deliver more official development assistance than the entire U.N. system (excluding the World Bank and the International Monetary Fund). In many countries they are delivering the services—in urban and rural community development, education, and health care—that faltering governments can no longer manage.

The range of these groups' work is almost as broad as their interests. They breed new ideas; advocate, protest, and mobilize public support; do legal, scientific, technical, and policy analysis; provide services; shape, implement, monitor, and enforce national and international commitments; and change institutions and norms.

Increasingly, NGOs are able to push around even the largest governments. When the United States and Mexico set out to reach a trade agreement, the two governments planned on the usual narrowly defined negotiations behind closed doors. But NGOs had a very different vision. Groups from Canada, the United States, and Mexico wanted to see provisions in the North American Free Trade Agreement on health and safety, transboundary pollution, consumer protection, immigration, labor mobility, child labor, sustainable agriculture, social charters, and debt relief. Coalitions of NGOs formed in each country and across both borders. The opposition they generated in early 1991 endangered congressional approval of the crucial "fast track" negotiating authority for the U.S. government. After months of resistance, the Bush administration capitulated, opening the agreement to environmental and labor concerns. Although progress in other trade venues will be slow, the tightly closed world of trade negotiations has been changed forever.

Technology is fundamental to NGOs' new clout. The nonprofit Association for Progressive Communications provides 50,000 NGOs in 133 countries access to the tens of millions of Internet users for the price of a local call. The dramatically lower costs of international communication have altered NGOs' goals and changed international outcomes. Within hours of the first gunshots of the Chiapas rebellion in southern Mexico in January 1994, for example, the Internet swarmed with messages from human rights activists. The worldwide media attention they and their groups focused on Chiapas, along with the influx of rights activists to the area, sharply limited the Mexican government's response. What in other times would have been a bloody insurgency turned out to be a largely nonviolent conflict. "The shots lasted ten days," José Angel Gurría, Mexico's foreign minister, later remarked, "and ever since, the war has been . . . a war on the Internet."

NGOs' easy reach behind other states' borders forces governments to consider domestic public opinion in countries with which they are dealing, even on matters that governments have traditionally handled strictly between themselves. At the same time, cross-border NGO networks offer citizens groups unprecedented channels of influence. Women's and human rights groups in many developing countries have linked up with more experienced, better funded, and more powerful groups in Europe and the United States.

The latter work the global media and lobby their own governments to pressure leaders in developing countries, creating a circle of influence that is accelerating change in many parts of the world.

OUT OF THE HALLWAY, AROUND THE TABLE

IN INTERNATIONAL organizations, as with governments at home, NGOs were once largely relegated to the hallways. Even when they were able to shape governments' agendas, as the Helsinki Watch human rights groups did in the Conference on Security and Cooperation in Europe in the 1980s, their influence was largely determined by how receptive their own government's delegation happened to be. Their only option was to work through governments.

All that changed with the negotiation of the global climate treaty, culminating at the Earth Summit in Rio de Janeiro in 1992. With the broader independent base of public support that environmental groups command, NGOs set the original goal of negotiating an agreement to control greenhouse gases long before governments were ready to do so, proposed most of its structure and content, and lobbied and mobilized public pressure to force through a pact that virtually no one else thought possible when the talks began.

More members of NGOs served on government delegations than ever before, and they penetrated deeply into official decision making. They were allowed to attend the small working group meetings where the real decisions in international negotiations are made. The tiny nation of Vanuatu turned its delegation over to an NGO with expertise in international law (a group based in London and funded by an American foundation), thereby making itself and the other sea-level island states major players in the fight to control global warming. *ECO*, an NGO-published daily newspaper, was negotiators' best source of information on the progress of the official talks and became the forum where governments tested ideas for breaking deadlocks.

Whether from developing or developed countries, NGOs were tightly organized in a global and half a dozen regional Climate Action Networks, which were able to bridge North-South differences among governments that many had expected would prevent an agreement. United in their passionate pursuit of a treaty, NGOs would fight out contentious issues among themselves, then take an agreed position to their respective delegations. When they could not agree, NGOs served as invaluable back channels, letting both sides know where the other's problems lay or where a compromise might be found.

As a result, delegates completed the framework of a global climate accord in the blink of a diplomat's eye—16 months—over the opposition of the three energy superpowers, the United States, Russia, and Saudi Arabia. The treaty entered into force in record time just two years later. Although only a framework accord whose binding requirements are still to be negotiated, the treaty could force sweeping changes in energy use, with potentially enormous implications for every economy.

The influence of NGOs at the climate talks has not yet been matched in any other arena and indeed has provoked a backlash among some governments. A handful of authoritarian regimes, most notably China, led the charge, but many others share their unease about the role NGOs are assuming. Nevertheless, NGOs have worked their way into the heart of international negotiations and into the day-to-day operations of international organizations, bringing new priorities, demands for procedures that give a voice to groups outside government, and new standards of accountability.

ONE WORLD BUSINESS

THE MULTINATIONAL corporations of the 1960s were virtually all American and prided themselves on their insularity. Foreigners might run subsidiaries, but they were never partners. A foreign posting was a setback for a rising executive.

Today, a global marketplace is developing for retail sales as well as manufacturing. Law, advertising, business consulting, and financial and other services are also marketed internationally. Firms of all nationalities attempt to look and act like locals wherever they operate. Foreign language skills and lengthy experience abroad are an asset, and increasingly a requirement, for top management. Sometimes corporate headquarters are not even in a company's home country.

Amid shifting alliances and joint ventures, made possible by computers and advanced communications, nationalities blur. Offshore banking encourages widespread evasion of national taxes. Whereas the fear in the 1970s was that multinationals would become an arm of government, the concern now is that they are disconnecting from their home countries' national interests, moving jobs, evading taxes, and eroding economic sovereignty in the process.

The even more rapid globalization of financial markets has left governments far behind. Where governments once set foreign exchange rates, private currency traders, accountable only to their bottom line, now trade $1.3 trillion a day, 100 times the volume of world trade. The amount exceeds the total foreign exchange reserves of all governments and is more than even an alliance of strong states can buck.

Despite the enormous attention given to governments' conflicts over trade rules, private capital flows have been growing twice as fast as trade for years. International portfolio transactions by U.S. investors, 9 percent of U.S. GDP in 1980, had grown to 135 percent of GDP by 1993. Growth in Germany, Britain, and elsewhere has been even more rapid. Direct investment has surged as well. All in all, the global financial market will grow to a staggering $83 trillion by 2000, a 1994 McKinsey & Co. study estimated, triple the aggregate GDP of the affluent nations of the Organization for Economic Cooperation and Development.

Again, technology has been a driving force, shifting financial clout from states to the market with its offer of unprecedented speed in transactions—states cannot match market reaction times measured in seconds—and its dissemination of financial information to a broad range of players. States could choose whether they would belong to rule-based economic systems like the gold standard, but as former Citicorp Chairman Walter Wriston has pointed out, they cannot withdraw from the technology-based marketplace, unless they seek autarky and poverty.

More and more frequently today, governments have only the appearance of free choice when they set economic rules. Markets are setting de facto rules enforced by their own power. States can flout them, but the penalties are severe—loss of vital foreign capital, foreign technology, and domestic jobs. Even the most powerful economy must pay heed. The U.S. government could choose to rescue the Mexican peso in 1994, for example, but it had to do so on terms designed to satisfy the bond markets, not the countries doing the rescuing.

The forces shaping the legitimate global economy are also nourishing globally integrated crime—which U.N. officials peg at a staggering $750 billion a year, $400 billion to $500 billion of that in narcotics, according to U.S. Drug Enforcement Agency estimates. Huge increases in the volume of goods and people crossing borders and competitive pressures to speed the flow of trade by easing inspections and reducing paperwork make it easier to hide contraband. Deregulation and privatization of government-owned businesses, modern communications, rapidly shifting commercial alliances, and the emergence of global financial systems have all helped transform local drug operations into global enterprises. The largely unregulated multitrillion-dollar pool of money in supranational cyberspace, accessible by computer 24 hours a day, eases the drug trade's toughest problem: transforming huge sums of hot cash into investments in legitimate business.

Globalized crime is a security threat that neither police nor the military—the state's traditional responses—can meet. Controlling it will require states to pool their efforts and to establish unprecedented cooperation with the private sector, thereby compromising two cherished sovereign roles. If states fail, if criminal groups can continue to take advantage of porous bor-

ders and transnational financial spaces while governments are limited to acting within their own territory, crime will have the winning edge.

BORN-AGAIN INSTITUTIONS

UNTIL RECENTLY, international organizations were institutions of, by, and
for nation-states. Now they are building constituencies of their own and,
through NGOs, establishing direct connections to the peoples of the world.
The shift is infusing them with new life and influence, but it is also creating
tensions.

States feel they need more capable international organizations to deal
with a lengthening list of transnational challenges but at the same time fear
competitors. Thus they vote for new forms of international intervention
while reasserting sovereignty's first principle: no interference in the domestic
affairs of states. They hand international organizations sweeping new responsibilities and then rein them in with circumscribed mandates or inadequate
funding. With states ambivalent about intervention, a host of new problems
demanding attention, and NGOs bursting with energy, ideas, and calls for a
larger role, international organizations are lurching toward an unpredictable,
but certainly different, future.

International organizations are still coming to terms with unprecedented
growth in the volume of international problem-solving. Between 1972 and 1992
the number of environmental treaties rocketed from a few dozen to more than
900. While collaboration in other fields is not growing at quite that rate,
treaties, regimes, and intergovernmental institutions dealing with human
rights, trade, narcotics, corruption, crime, refugees, antiterrorism measures,
arms control, and democracy are multiplying. "Soft law" in the form of guidelines, recommended practices, nonbinding resolutions, and the like is also
rapidly expanding. Behind each new agreement are scientists and lawyers who
worked on it, diplomats who negotiated it, and NGOs that back it, most of
them committed for the long haul. The new constituency also includes a burgeoning, influential class of international civil servants responsible for imple-
menting, monitoring, and enforcing this enormous new body of law.

At the same time, governments, while ambivalent about the international community mixing in states' domestic affairs, have driven some gaping
holes in the wall that has separated the two. In the triumphant months after
the Berlin Wall came down, international accords, particularly ones agreed
on by what is now the Organization for Security and Cooperation in Europe
and by the Organization of American States (OAS), drew explicit links between democracy, human rights, and international security, establishing new
legal bases for international interventions. In 1991 the U.N. General Assem-

bly declared itself in favor of humanitarian intervention without the request or consent of the state involved. A year later the Security Council took the unprecedented step of authorizing the use of force "on behalf of civilian populations" in Somalia. Suddenly an interest in citizens began to compete with, and occasionally override, the formerly unquestioned primacy of state interests.

Since 1990 the Security Council has declared a formal threat to international peace and security 61 times, after having done so only six times in the preceding 45 years. It is not that security has been abruptly and terribly threatened; rather, the change reflects the broadened scope of what the international community now feels it should poke its nose into. As with Haiti in 1992, many of the so-called Chapter VII resolutions authorizing forceful intervention concerned domestic situations that involved awful human suffering or offended international norms but posed little if any danger to international peace.

Almost as intrusive as a Chapter VII intervention, though always invited, election monitoring has also become a growth industry. The United Nations monitored no election in a member state during the Cold War, only in colonies. But beginning in 1990 it responded to a deluge of requests from governments that felt compelled to prove their legitimacy by the new standards. In Latin America, where countries most jealously guard their sovereignty, the OAS monitored 11 national elections in four years.

And monitoring is no longer the passive observation it was in earlier decades. Carried out by a close-knit mix of international organizations and NGOs, it involves a large foreign presence dispensing advice and recommending standards for voter registration, campaign law, campaign practices, and the training of clerks and judiciaries. Observers even carry out parallel vote counts that can block fraud but at the same time second-guess the integrity of national counts.

International financial institutions, too, have inserted themselves more into states' domestic affairs. During the 1980s the World Bank attached conditions to loans concerning recipient governments' policies on poverty, the environment, and even, occasionally, military spending, a once sacrosanct domain of national prerogative. In 1991 a statement of bank policy holding that "efficient and accountable public sector management" is crucial to economic growth provided the rationale for subjecting to international oversight everything from official corruption to government competence.

Beyond involving them in an array of domestic economic and social decisions, the new policies force the World Bank, the International Monetary Fund, and other international financial institutions to forge alliances with business, NGOs, and civil society if they are to achieve broad changes in target countries. In the process, they have opened themselves to the same demands they are making of their clients: broader public participation and greater openness in decision making. As a result, yet another set of doors behind which only officials sat has been thrown open to the private sector and to civil society.

LEAPS OF IMAGINATION

AFTER three and a half centuries, it requires a mental leap to think of world politics in any terms other than occasionally cooperating but generally competing states, each defined by its territory and representing all the people therein. Nor is it easy to imagine political entities that could compete with the emotional attachment of a shared landscape, national history, language, flag, and currency.

Yet history proves that there are alternatives other than tribal anarchy. Empires, both tightly and loosely ruled, achieved success and won allegiance. In the Middle Ages, emperors, kings, dukes, knights, popes, archbishops, guilds, and cities exercised overlapping secular power over the same territory in a system that looks much more like a modern, three-dimensional network than the clean-lined, hierarchical state order that replaced it. The question now is whether there are new geographic or functional entities that might grow up alongside the state, taking over some of its powers and emotional resonance.

The kernels of several such entities already exist. The European Union is the most obvious example. Neither a union of states nor an international organization, the EU leaves experts groping for inadequate descriptions like "postsovereign system" or "unprecedented hybrid." It respects members' borders for some purposes, particularly in foreign and defense policy, but ignores them for others. The union's judiciary can override national law, and its Council of Ministers can overrule certain domestic executive decisions. In its thousands of councils, committees, and working groups, national ministers increasingly find themselves working with their counterparts from other countries to oppose colleagues in their own government; agriculture ministers, for example, ally against finance ministers. In this sense the union penetrates and to some extent weakens the internal bonds of its member states. Whether Frenchmen, Danes, and Greeks will ever think of themselves first as Europeans remains to be seen, but the EU has already come much further than most Americans realize.

Meanwhile, units below the national level are taking on formal international roles. Nearly all 50 American states have trade offices abroad, up from four in 1970, and all have official standing in the World Trade Organization (WTO). German *Länder* and British local governments have offices at EU headquarters in Brussels. France's Rhône-Alpes region, centered in Lyon, maintains what it calls "embassies" abroad on behalf of a regional economy that includes Geneva, Switzerland, and Turin, Italy.

Emerging political identities not linked to territory pose a more direct challenge to the geographically fixed state system. The WTO is struggling to find a method of handling environmental disputes in the global commons, outside all states' boundaries, that the General Agreement on Tariffs and Trade, drafted 50 years ago, simply never envisioned. Proposals have been floated for a Parliamentary Assembly in the United Nations, parallel to the General Assembly, to represent the people rather than the states of the world. Ideas are under discussion that would give ethnic nations political and legal status, so that the Kurds, for example, could be legally represented as a people in addition to being Turkish, Iranian, or Iraqi citizens.

Further in the future is a proposed Global Environmental Authority with independent regulatory powers. This is not as far-fetched as it sounds. The burden of participating in several hundred international environmental bodies is heavy for the richest governments and is becoming prohibitive for others. As the number of international agreements mounts, the pressure to streamline the system—in environmental protection as in other areas—will grow.

The realm of most rapid change is hybrid authorities that include state and nonstate bodies such as the International Telecommunications Union, the International Union for the Conservation of Nature, and hundreds more. In many of these, businesses or NGOs take on formerly public roles. The Geneva-based International Standards Organization, essentially a business NGO, sets widely observed standards on everything from products to internal corporate procedures. The International Securities Markets Association, another private regulator, oversees international trade in private securities markets—the world's second-largest capital market after domestic government bond markets. In another crossover, markets become government enforcers when they adopt treaty standards as the basis for market judgments. States and NGOs are collaborating ad hoc in large-scale humanitarian relief operations that involve both military and civilian forces. Other NGOs have taken on standing operational roles for international organizations in refugee work and development assistance. Almost unnoticed, hybrids like these, in which states are often the junior partners, are becoming a new international norm.

FOR BETTER OR WORSE?

A WORLD that is more adaptable and in which power is more diffused could mean more peace, justice, and capacity to manage the burgeoning list of humankind's interconnected problems. At a time of accelerating change, NGOs are quicker than governments to respond to new demands and opportunities. Internationally, in both the poorest and richest countries, NGOs, when adequately funded, can outperform government in the delivery of many public services. Their growth, along with that of the other elements of civil society, can strengthen the fabric of the many still-fragile democracies. And they are better than governments at dealing with problems that grow slowly and affect society through their cumulative effect on individuals—the "soft" threats of environmental degradation, denial of human rights, population growth, poverty, and lack of development that may already be causing more deaths in conflict than are traditional acts of aggression.

As the computer and telecommunications revolution continues, NGOs will become more capable of large-scale activity across national borders. Their loyalties and orientation, like those of international civil servants and citizens of non-national entities like the EU, are better matched than those of governments to problems that demand transnational solutions. International NGOs and cross-border networks of local groups have bridged North-South differences that in earlier years paralyzed cooperation among countries.

On the economic front, expanding private markets can avoid economically destructive but politically seductive policies, such as excessive borrowing or overly burdensome taxation, to which governments succumb. Unhindered by ideology, private capital flows to where it is best treated and thus can do the most good.

International organizations, given a longer rein by governments and connected to the grassroots by deepening ties with NGOs, could, with adequate funding, take on larger roles in global housekeeping (transportation, communications, environment, health), security (controlling weapons of mass destruction, preventive diplomacy, peacekeeping), human rights, and emergency relief. As various international panels have suggested, the funds could come from fees on international activities, such as currency transactions and air travel, independent of state appropriations. Finally, that new force on the global scene, international public opinion, informed by worldwide media coverage and mobilized by NGOs, can be extraordinarily potent in getting things done and done quickly.

There are at least as many reasons, however, to believe that the continuing diffusion of power away from nation-states will mean more conflict and less problem solving both within states and among them.

For all their strengths, NGOs are special interests, albeit not motivated by personal profit. The best of them, the ablest and most passionate, often suffer most from tunnel vision, judging every public act by how it affects their particular interest. Generally, they have limited capacity for large-scale endeavors, and as they grow, the need to sustain growing budgets can compromise the independence of mind and approach that is their greatest asset.

A society in which the piling up of special interests replaces a single strong voice for the common good is unlikely to fare well. Single-issue voters, as Americans know all too well, polarize and freeze public debate. In the longer run, a stronger civil society could also be more fragmented, producing a weakened sense of common identity and purpose and less willingness to invest in public goods, whether health and education or roads and ports. More and more groups promoting worthy but narrow causes could ultimately threaten democratic government.

Internationally, excessive pluralism could have similar consequences. Two hundred nation-states is a barely manageable number. Add hundreds of influential nonstate forces—businesses, NGOs, international organizations, ethnic and religious groups—and the international system may represent more voices but be unable to advance any of them.

Moreover, there are roles that only the state—at least among today's polities—can perform. States are the only nonvoluntary political unit, the one that can impose order and is invested with the power to tax. Severely weakened states will encourage conflict, as they have in Africa, Central America, and elsewhere. Moreover, it may be that only the nation-state can meet crucial social needs that markets do not value. Providing a modicum of job security, avoiding higher unemployment, preserving a livable environment and a stable climate, and protecting consumer health and safety are but a few of the tasks that could be left dangling in a world of expanding markets and retreating states.

More international decision-making will also exacerbate the so-called democratic deficit, as decisions that elected representatives once made shift to unelected international bodies; this is already a sore point for EU members. It also arises when legislatures are forced to make a single take-it-or-leave-it judgment on huge international agreements, like the several-thousand-page Uruguay Round trade accord. With citizens already feeling that their national governments do not hear individual voices, the trend could well provoke deeper and more dangerous alienation, which in turn could trigger new ethnic and even religious separatism. The end result could be a proliferation of states too weak for either individual economic success or effective international cooperation.

Finally, fearsome dislocations are bound to accompany the weakening of the central institution of modern society. The prophets of an internetted world, in which national identities gradually fade, proclaim its revolutionary nature and yet believe the changes will be wholly benign. They won't be. The shift from national to some other political allegiance, if it comes, will be an emotional, cultural, and political earthquake.

DISSOLVING AND EVOLVING

MIGHT THE decline in state power prove transitory? Present disenchantment with national governments could dissipate as quickly as it arose. Continuing globalization may well spark a vigorous reassertion of economic or cultural nationalism. By helping solve problems governments cannot handle, business, NGOs, and international organizations may actually be strengthening the nation-state system.

These are all possibilities, but the clash between the fixed geography of states and the nonterritorial nature of today's problems and solutions, which is only likely to escalate, strongly suggests that the relative power of states will continue to decline. Nation-states may simply no longer be the natural problem-solving unit. Local government addresses citizens' growing desire for a role in decision-making, while transnational, regional, and even global entities better fit the dimensions of trends in economics, resources, and security.

The evolution of information and communications technology, which has only just begun, will probably heavily favor nonstate entities, including those not yet envisaged, over states. The new technologies encourage noninstitutional, shifting networks over the fixed bureaucratic hierarchies that are the hallmark of the single-voiced sovereign state. They dissolve issues' and institutions' ties to a fixed place. And by greatly empowering individuals, they weaken the relative attachment to community, of which the preeminent one in modern society is the nation-state.

If current trends continue, the international system 50 years hence will be profoundly different. During the transition, the Westphalian system and an evolving one will exist side by side. States will set the rules by which all other actors operate, but outside forces will increasingly make decisions for them. In using business, NGOs, and international organizations to address problems they cannot or do not want to take on, states will, more often than not, inadvertently weaken themselves further. Thus governments' unwillingness to adequately fund international organizations helped NGOs move from a peripheral to a central role in shaping multilateral agreements, since the NGOs provided expertise the international organizations lacked. At least for a time, the transition is likely to weaken rather than bolster the world's capacity to solve its problems. If states, with the overwhelming share of power, wealth, and capacity, can do less, less will get done.

Whether the rise of nonstate actors ultimately turns out to be good news or bad will depend on whether humanity can launch itself on a course of rapid social innovation, as it did after World War II. Needed adaptations include a business sector that can shoulder a broader policy role, NGOs that are less parochial and better able to operate on a large scale, international institutions that can efficiently serve the dual masters of states and citizenry, and, above all, new institutions and political entities that match the transnational scope of today's challenges while meeting citizens' demands for accountable democratic governance.

The Bent Twig

A Note on Nationalism

Isaiah Berlin

OCTOBER 1972

THE RICH DEVELOPMENT of historical studies in the nineteenth century transformed men's views about their origins and the importance of growth, development, and time. The causes of the emergence of the new historical consciousness were many and diverse. Those most often given are the rapid and profound transformation of human lives and thought in the West by the unparalleled progress of the natural sciences since the Renaissance, by the impact on society of new technology, and in particular, the growth of large-scale industry; the disintegration of the unity of Christendom and the rise of new states, classes, social and political formations, and the search for origins, pedigrees, connections with, or return to, a real or imaginary past. All of this culminated in the most transforming event of all—the French Revolution, which exploded, or at the very least profoundly altered, some of the most deeply rooted presuppositions and concepts by which men lived. It made men acutely conscious of change and excited interest in the laws that governed it.

All these are truisms that need no restating; nor does the corollary, no less platitudinous, that the theories claiming to account for social change in the past could not be confined to it: if they were valid at all, they must work equally well for the future. Prophecy, which had hitherto been the province of religion and the preserve of mystics and astrologers, moved from preoccupation with the apocalyptic books of the Bible—the four Great Beasts of the Book of David or of the Gospel according to St. John—and other occult regions, and became the province of philosophers of history and the fathers of sociology. It seemed reasonable to assume that the realm of historical change could be dealt with by the same kind of powerful new weapons as those which had unlocked the secrets of the external world in so astonishing a fashion.

Nor did this prove to be an altogether idle hope. Some of the historical prophets of the late eighteenth and nineteenth centuries, even the visionary among them, proved to have a firmer grasp of reality than their theological predecessors. Some thinkers of the Enlightenment were optimistic, some less hopeful. Voltaire and Rousseau were equally clear about the very different worlds they wished to see, but wondered gloomily whether human folly and vice would ever permit their realization. Melchior Grimm thought it would take centuries to improve human nature. Turgot and Condorcet were the most sanguine: Condorcet was sure that the application of mathematical methods—in particular social statistics—to social policy would usher in the reign of virtue, knowledge, and happiness, "bound by an indissoluble chain," that would put an end forever to the reign of cruelty, misery, and oppression whereby kings and priests and their wretched tools had kept mankind in subjection for so long.

What these men believed was not absurd. The new scientific methods did put vast new power in the hands of those who knew how to organize and rationalize the new society. The bright new world that Condorcet conceived in the darkness of his prison cell was that very world of "sophisters [i.e., Condorcet's rational men], economists, and calculators" which Burke, who had perceived its coming no less clearly, had lamented only three years before. This great mutation did in due course come to pass, even though its consequences turned out very differently from Condorcet's dreams. So, too, Condorcet's disciple Saint-Simon, at the beginning of the century, correctly foretold the revolutionary role to be played by the union of applied science, finance, and industrial organization, and still more accurately, the replacement of religious by secular propaganda, into the service of which artists and poets would be drafted as they had once worked for the glory of the Church. And he wrote lyrical but acutely prophetic chapters about the vast increase of social human power, in particular over nature, that was in process of realization. His secretary and collaborator, Auguste Comte, saw that to achieve this a species of secular religion, organized by an authoritarian church dedicated to rational, but not liberal or democratic, ideals would be needed.

Events have proved him right. The transformation in our century of political and social movements into monolithic bodies, imposing a total discipline upon their followers, exercised by a secular priesthood claiming absolute authority, both spiritual and lay, in the name of unique scientific knowledge of the nature of men and things, has, in fact, occurred, and on a vaster scale than even that most fanatical systematizer seems to have imagined. This was duly echoed by the fathers of science fiction, Jules Verne and

H. G. Wells. Jules Verne confined himself to brilliant predictions of technological discoveries and inventions. Wells is the last preacher of the morality of the Enlightenment, of the faith that the great mass of prejudice and ignorance and superstition, and the absurd and repressive rules in which it is embodied, economic, political, racial, and sexual, would be destroyed by the new élite of scientific planners. It was this type of approach that seemed so vulgar and dehumanizing to Victorian romantics, Carlyle or Disraeli or Ruskin. It alarmed even so rational a thinker as John Stuart Mill, who wished to believe in scientific method, but perceived in Comte's authoritarian arrangements a menace to both individual liberty and democratic government, and so became involved in a conflict of values which he was never able to resolve.

"The government of persons will be succeeded by the administration of things": this Saint-Simonian formula was common to Comte and Marx. Marx became convinced that this would be brought about by the true motor of all social change—the productive forces of society, the relationships of which were the primary factors that determined, and were as a rule disguised by outer forms—"the superstructure"—of social relationships. These included legal and social institutions as well as ideas in men's heads, ideologies that consciously or unconsciously performed the task of defending the status quo, that is the power of the class in control against the historical forces embodied in the victims of the prevailing system, which in the end would prove victorious. Whatever his errors, no one can today deny that Marx displayed unique powers of prognosis in identifying the central trend at work—the concentration and centralization of capitalist enterprise—the inexorable trend toward ever-increasing size on the part of Big Business, then in its embryo, and the sharpening social and political conflicts that this involved. He also set himself to unmask the conservative and liberal, patriotic and humanitarian, religious and ethical disguises in which some of the most brutal manifestations of these conflicts, and their social and intellectual consequences, would be concealed.

These were genuinely prophetic thinkers. And there were others. The unsystematic and wayward Bakunin predicted more accurately than his great rival Marx the circumstances in which the revolutions by the dispossessed would occur. He saw that they were liable to develop not in the most industrialized societies on an ascending curve of economic progress, but on the contrary, where the majority of the population was near subsistence level and had least to lose by an upheaval, that is, in the most backward regions of the world, inhabited by primitive peasants in conditions of desperate poverty, where capitalism was weakest—Spain, Russia. This doctrine was reformulated later but never attributed to anarchist inspiration by later Marxists such as Parvus (Helphand) and Trotsky.

These were the optimists. But by the early 1830s the first pessimists begin. The poet Heine warned the French in 1832 that one fine day their German neighbors, fired by a terrible combination of absolutist metaphysics, historical memories and resentments, fanaticism, and savage strength and fury, would fall upon them, and would destroy the great monuments of Western civilization: "Implacable Kantians . . . with axe and sword, will root the soil of our European life in order to tear out the roots of the past. . . . armed Fichteans will appear," restrained neither by fear nor greed, like those "early Christians, whom neither physical torture nor physical pleasure could break." The most terrible of all will be Schelling's disciples, the Philosophers of Nature, who, isolated and unapproachable beyond the barriers of their own obsessive ideas, will identify themselves with the elemental forces of "the demonic powers of ancient German pantheism." When these metaphysically intoxicated barbarians get going, then let the French beware: the French Revolution will seem like a peaceful idyll.

Who can say that this, too, has not come to pass in a form more horrible than any conceived even in Wagner's most sinister moments? A few decades later Jakob Burckhardt foretold the inevitability of the military-industrial complex that would, or at any rate might, dominate the decadent countries of the West. There follow the fears of Max Weber, and all the black utopias of Zamyatin, Aldous Huxley, Orwell, and the long row of blood-chilling Cassandras, half satirists, half prophets, of our day. Some of these vaticinations were pure predictions; others, like those of Marxists and of the Francophobe neopagans who terrified Heine, can be regarded as to some extent self-fulfilling.

These are examples of genuinely successful diagnoses and prognoses of the direction in which Western society was moving. Besides these there have been all those justly forgotten utopias—from Plato or Fourier or Cabet or Bellamy or Hertzka—embalmed in the pages of the more voluminous histories of socialist doctrines. On the other side, there were the liberal and technocratic or neo-medieval fantasies, which rest either on a return to a precapitalist and pre-industrial type of *Gemeinschaft;* or, alternatively, the construction of one single, technocratically organized, managerial, Saint-Simonian world. But in all this great array of elaborate, statistically supported serious futurology mingled with free fantasy, there took place one movement which dominated much of the nineteenth century, for which no significant future was predicted, a movement so familiar to us now, so decisive both within, and in relationships between, nations, that it is only by some effort of the imagination that one can conceive of a world in which it played no part. Its existence and its power (especially outside the English-speaking world) seem to us so self-evident today that it appears strange to have to draw attention to it as a phenomenon the prophets before our day, and in our time too, virtually ignored; in the case of the latter, at times with fatal consequences to themselves and those who believed them. This movement is nationalism.

II

NO SOCIAL or political thinker in the nineteenth century was unaware of nationalism as a dominant movement of his age. Nevertheless, in the second half of the century, indeed up to the First World War, it was thought to be waning. Consciousness of national identity may well be as old as social consciousness itself. But nationalism, unlike tribal feeling or xenophobia, to which it is related but with which it is not identical, seems scarcely to have existed in ancient or classical times. There were other foci of collective loyalty. It seems to emerge at the end of the Middle Ages in the West, particularly in France, in the form of the defense of customs and privileges of localities, regions, corporations, and of course states, and then of the nation itself, against the encroachment of some external power—Roman law or papal authority, or against related forms of universalism—Natural law and other claims of supranational authority. Its emergence as a coherent doctrine may perhaps be placed and dated in the last third of the eighteenth century in Germany, more particularly in the conceptions of the *Volksgeist* and *Nationalgeist*, in the writings of the vastly influential poet and philosopher Johann Gottfried Herder.

The roots of this go back to the beginnings of the eighteenth century, and indeed before it, at any rate in East Prussia, where it grew and whence it spread. Herder's thought is dominated by his conviction that among the basic needs of men, as elemental as that for food or procreation or communication, is the need to belong to a group. More fervently and imaginatively than Burke, and with a wealth of historical and psychological examples, he argued that every human community had its own unique shape and pattern. Its members were born in a stream of tradition which shaped their emotional and physical development no less than their ideas. Indeed, distinctions between reason, imagination, emotion, sensation were for him largely artificial. There was a central historically developing pattern that characterized the life and activity of every identifiable community and, most deeply, that unit which, by his own time, had come to be the nation. The way in which a German lived at home and the way in which he conducted his public life, German song, and German legislation—the collective genius, not attributable to individual authors, that created the myths and legends, the ballads and historical chronicles, was the same as that which made the style of Luther's Bible, or the arts and crafts and images and categories of thought of the Germans of his own time. The way in which Germans spoke or dressed or moved had more in common with the way in which they built their cathedrals, or organized their civic lives—a central German essence, as it were, an identifiable pattern and quality—than it had with analogous activities among the inhabitants of China or Peru.

Human customs, activities, forms of life, art, ideas, were (and must be) of value to men not in terms of timeless criteria, applicable to all men and societies, irrespective of time and place, as the French *lumières* taught, but because they were their own, expressions of their local, regional, national life, and spoke to them as they could speak to no other human group. This is why men withered in exile, that is what nostalgia ("the noblest of pains") was a yearning for. To understand the Bible one must imaginatively enter into the life of the Judean shepherds of primitive times; to understand the Eddas, the savage struggle with the elements of a barbarous northern race. Everything valuable was unique.

Universalism, by reducing everything to the lowest common denominator which applies to all men at all times, drained both lives and ideals of that specific content which alone gave them point. Hence Herder's implacable crusade against French universalism, and his concept and glorification of individual cultures—Indian, Chinese, Norse, Hebrew—and his hatred of the great levellers, Caesar and Charlemagne, Romans, Christian knights, British empire-builders and missionaries, who eliminated native cultures and replaced them with their own, historically, and therefore spiritually, foreign and oppressive to their victims. Herder and his disciples believed in the peaceful coexistence of a rich multiplicity and variety of national forms of life, the more diverse the better. Under the impact of the French revolutionary and Napoleonic invasions, cultural or spiritual autonomy, for which Herder had originally pleaded, turned into embittered and aggressive nationalist self-assertion.

The origins of cultural change and national attitudes are difficult to establish. Nationalism is an inflamed condition of national consciousness which can be, and has on occasion been, tolerant and peaceful. It usually seems to be caused by wounds, some form of collective humiliation. It may be that this happened in German lands because they had remained on the edges of the great renaissance of Western Europe. In the late sixteenth century, during the great creative age, which was far from spent even in Italy, which had risen to an unparalleled height a hundred years before, and marked an immense upsurge of creative activity in France, in Elizabethan England, in Spain, in the Low Countries; German towns and principalities, both those dominated by the imperial power of Vienna and those outside it, were by comparison profoundly provincial. They excelled only in architecture and, perhaps, Protestant theology. The terrible devastation of the Thirty Years

War doubtless made this cultural gap even wider. To be the object of contempt or patronizing tolerance on the part of proud neighbors is one of the most traumatic experiences that individuals or societies can suffer. The response, as often as not, is pathological exaggeration of one's real or imaginary virtues, and resentment and hostility toward the proud, the happy, the successful. This, indeed, characterized much German feeling about the West, more especially about France, in the eighteenth century.

The French dominated the Western world, politically, culturally, militarily. The humiliated and defeated Germans, particularly the traditional, religious, economically backward East Prussians, bullied by French officials imported by Frederick the Great, responded, like the bent twig of the poet Schiller's theory, by lashing back and refusing to accept their alleged inferiority. They discovered in themselves qualities far superior to those of their tormentors. They contrasted their own deep, inner life of the spirit, their own profound humility, their selfless pursuit of true values—simple, noble, sublime—with the rich, worldly, successful, superficial, smooth, heartless, morally empty French. This mood rose to fever pitch during the national resistance to Napoleon and was indeed the original exemplar of the reaction of many a backward, exploited, or at any rate patronized society, which, resentful of the apparent inferiority of its status, reacted by turning to real or imaginary triumphs and glories in its past or enviable attributes of its own national or cultural character. Those who cannot boast of great political, military, or economic achievements, or a magnificent tradition of art or thought, seek comfort and strength in the notion of the free and creative life of the spirit within them, uncorrupted by the vices of power or sophistication.

There is much of this in the writings of the German Romantics, and, after them, of the Russian Slavophiles, and many an awakener of the national spirit in Central Europe, Poland, the Balkans, Asia, Africa. Hence, the value of a real or imaginary rich historical past to inferiority-ridden peoples, for it promises, perhaps, an even more glorious future. If no such past can be invoked, then its very absence will be ground for optimism. We may today be primitive, poor, even barbarian, but our very backwardness is a symptom of our youth, our unexhausted vital power; we are the inheritors of the future which the old, worn-out, corrupt, declining nations, for all their vaunted present-day superiority, can no longer hope for. This messianic theme is sounded strongly by Germans, then by Poles and Russians, and after that, in our time, by many states and nations which feel that they have not yet played their part (but soon will do so) in the great drama of history.

III

THIS ATTITUDE, almost universal among the developing nations, is plain to the most untutored eye today. But in the home of political prophecy, the nineteenth century, when the future was discerned through many historical, sociological, and philosophical telescopes, it was evidently not plain at all. The great masters did not foretell the huge proliferation of national pride, indeed, did not predict it at all. Hegel, in his emphasis on "historic," as opposed to "unhistoric," nations as the carriers of the ever forward-thrusting cosmic *Geist,* may have flattered the self-esteem of Western and Northern Europe or fed the ambitions of those who sought German or Nordic unity and power. But he was no less opposed than Metternich to the wild, violent, emotional nationalism of Francophobe and anti-Semitic students, with their chauvinism and book burnings, which seemed to him barbarous excesses, as they did to Goethe, who forbade his son to fight against the French. To trace to Hegel's writings the fierce nationalism of later German writers who derive from them is certainly unjust. Even the fanatical early chauvinists—the Jahns, the Arndts, the Goerreses, and indeed, Fichte, who is in part responsible for this mood, with his paeans to the uncontaminated German language as a vehicle for the uniquely liberating German mission in the world—even they did not consciously view nationalism as the dominant force in the future of Europe, still less of mankind. They were merely struggling to liberate their nations from disabling dynastic or foreign or skeptical influences. Jahn and Arndt and Körner are German chauvinists, but they are not theorists of nationalism as such, still less prophets of its universal sway; inferior nations, indeed, are not entitled to it.

The rationalists and liberals, and, of course, the early socialists virtually ignore nationalism. For them, it is a mere sign of immaturity, an irrational relic of, or retrogressive return to, a barbarous past: fanatics like De Maistre (who for all his ultramontanism was an early believer in natural "integralism") or Friis or Gobineau or Houston Stewart Chamberlain and Wagner or, later, Maurras, Barrès, Drumont, are not taken seriously until the Boulanger and Dreyfus affairs; these, in their turn, are regarded as temporary aberrations, due to the abnormal mood following on defeat in war, which will make way once again for the return of sanity, reason, and progress. These thinkers, who look to the past for strength, do not play the part of social seers: with varying degrees of pessimism, they seek to revive a national spirit that has been undermined, perhaps fatally, by the enemy—liberals, Freemasons, scientists, atheists, skeptics, Jews. With a great effort something may yet be saved. But they believe that it is the other, "destructive" tendencies which work against the national spirit, that are there in menacing strength and hold the field and must be resisted, if only to preserve islands of purity and strength and "integral" life. Gobineau is the most pessimistic of these, and in any case, he is concerned with race rather than nations, Treitschke the most hopeful, reflecting, no doubt, respective national moods.

As for Marx and Engels, for them, I need hardly repeat, it is the emergence of classes, economically determined by division of labor and accumulation of capital, and the war between these classes, that account for social change in human history. Nationalism, like religion, is a temporary phenomenon which, generated by the ascendancy of the bourgeoisie, is one of the self-sustaining spiritual weapons against the proletariat. If, too often, it penetrates the masses, it does so as a form of "false consciousness" which disguises their true condition from them and breeds illusions that provide them with deceptive comfort in their benighted state. After the end of the conditions that have given rise to it—the class war—nationalism, like religion, will evaporate together with other politically potent and historically conditioned illusions. It may acquire a certain independent influence of its own, as many such by-products of the evolution of productive forces do, but it cannot survive the destruction of its primary source, the capitalist system.

This tenet became a dogma for every school of Marxism. No matter how wide the disagreements on other issues, this was common ground, from the peaceful gradualism of Eduard Bernstein to the most left-wing members of the Bolshevik Party. The belief that nationalism was a reactionary bourgeois ideology was tantamount to the belief that it was doomed. At most, national risings on the part of colonial peoples against imperialist masters might be considered as historically determined, a tactical step on the road to the true socialist revolution, which could not be too far behind. Even so, a national rising was one thing, and nationalism another. It was this belief that caused such disappointment and indignation to the internationalist left, led by Lenin, Karl Liebknecht, and their friends, when the socialist parties in the belligerent countries, instead of claiming a general strike which should have stopped the war in 1914, joined the national colors and went to war against each other. It was this that caused Rosa Luxemburg to protest against the very formation of a national state by the Poles at the end of the war. The October Revolution, it is fair to say, was genuinely antinationalist in character.

The contrast, enunciated in some quarters, between Lenin, as the authentic voice of Russian feeling, as against the "rootless cosmopolitanism" of men like Trotsky or Zinoviev or Radek, has no foundation. Lenin looked on the Russian Revolution as the breaking of the weakest link in the capitalist chain, whose value consisted in precipitating the world revolution, since, as Marx and Engels were convinced, communism in one country could not survive. Events decreed otherwise, but the doctrine itself was altered only under Stalin. The initial mood among the early Bolsheviks was genuinely antinationalist: so much so that Bolshevik critics in Russia vied with each other in disparaging the glories of their own national literature—Pushkin, for example—in order to express their contempt for national tradition as a central bourgeois value.

There was a similar mood among the leaders of the abortive communist revolutions that followed in Hungary and Munich. "National-chauvinism," "social-chauvinism" became terms of abuse, battle cries used to crush autonomous movements in some of the non-Russian provinces of the old Russian Empire. But after this, the genuine internationalist phase was over. Every revolution and upheaval thereafter contained a nationalist component. The rise of fascism or national socialism was interpreted by Marxist theorists as the final and extreme, but desperate, resistance on the part of capitalism in these countries against the inevitable victory of international socialism. The systematic underestimate of the strength of totalitarian or authoritarian nationalist movements, and their triumph in central and northeastern Europe, the Iberian peninsula, and elsewhere, was due to ideologically caused miscalculation.

The economic autarky which followed the great crisis of 1931, plausibly enough interpreted as a culmination of the internal contradictions of the capitalist system, was, whatever else it might indicate, a form of acute economic nationalism, which outlived its putative economic causes and gravely obstructed the advance of the enlightenment, whether liberal or socialist. What followed in the newly liberated territories in Asia and Africa seems to support the view that after the 1920s neither socialism nor any other political movement in the postwar world could be successful unless it came arm in arm not only with anti-imperialism but with pronounced nationalism.

IV

THE RISE of nationalism is today a worldwide phenomenon, probably the strongest single factor in the newly established states, and in some cases among the minority populations of the older nations. Who, in the nineteenth century, would have predicted the rise of acute nationalism in Canada, in Pakistan (indeed, the very possibility of Pakistan itself would have met with considerable skepticism among Indian nationalist leaders a hundred years ago), or in Wales or Brittany or Scotland or the Basque country? It might be said that this is an automatic psychological accompaniment of liberation from foreign rule—a natural reaction, on Schiller's "bent twig" theory, against oppression or humiliation of a society that possesses national characteristics.

In most of these cases the desire for national independence is intertwined with social resistance to exploitation. This kind of nationalism is, perhaps, as much a form of social class resistance as of purely national self-assertion, creating a mood in which men prefer to be ordered about, even if this entails ill-treatment, by members of their own faith or nation class, to tutelage, however benevolent, on the part of ultimately patronizing superiors from a foreign land or alien class or milieu.

So, too, it may be that no minority that has preserved its own cultural tradition or religious or racial characteristics can indefinitely tolerate the prospect of remaining a minority forever, governed by a majority with a different outlook or habits. And this may indeed account for the reaction of wounded pride, the sense of collective injustice, which animates, for example, Zionism or its mirror-image, the movement of the Palestinian Arabs, or such "ethnic" minorities as Negroes in the United States or Irish Catholics in Ulster, the Nagas in India, and the like. Certainly contemporary nationalism seldom comes in its pure, romantic form as it did in Italy or Poland or Hungary in the early nineteenth century but is connected far more closely with social and religious and economic grievances. Yet it seems undeniable that the central feeling is deeply nationalistic. More ominous still (and even more rarely, if indeed ever, foreseen a century ago), racial hatreds seem to be at the core of the most hideous expressions of violent collective emotion of this kind: genocide and near-genocide in India, in the Sudan, in Nigeria and Burundi indicate that, no matter what other factors may be present in such explosive situations, they always possess a national or racialist core, which other factors may exacerbate, but which they do not generate, and without which they do not combine into the socially and politically critical mass. Passionate nationalism appears to be the sine qua non of contemporary revolutions.

Whatever may be the explanation of this phenomenon, which, in its own way, is just as menacing as the other dangers that loom over mankind—pollution or overpopulation or the nuclear holocaust—its rise is incompatible with nineteenth-century notions of the relative unimportance of race or nationality or even culture, as opposed to, say, class or economic competition, or of psychological and anthropological factors as against sociological or economic ones. Yet these were the assumptions upon which predictions of the emergence of a rational society, whether founded upon the principles of liberal individualism or on technocratic centralization, once rested. Unanticipated outbreaks of such dissimilar yet equally nationalist movements in the communist societies of our day—from the Hungarian resistance in 1956 to anti-Semitism and nationalism in Poland, and indeed in the Soviet Union itself—seem, to say the least, to weaken the orthodox Marxist thesis.[1] Yet they certainly cannot be described, as they sometimes are by those who are embarrassed by them, as mere relics and survivals of an earlier ideology. Neither Nagy in Hungary nor Moczar in Poland, despite the vast differences of their purposes, were in any sense bourgeois nationalists.

In the face of this, faith in countervailing forces—in multinational corporations which, whatever their relationship with class war and social conflict, at any rate do cross national borders or in the United Nations as a barrier to unbridled chauvinism—seems about as realistic (at least so far as lands outside Western Europe are concerned) as Cobden's belief that the development of free trade throughout the world would of itself ensure peace

---

[1] The attitude of the founders of Marxism to national or local patriotism, autonomist movements, self-determination of small states, and the like is not in doubt. Apart from the direct implications of their theory of social development, their attitude to Danish resistance to Prussia over Schleswig-Holstein, to the Italian fight for unity and independence (when Marx in his dispatches to *The New York Times* so sharply differed from the pro-Italian Lasalle), to the efforts by the Czechs to defend their culture from German hegemony, and even to the outcome of the Franco-Prussian War, is quite clear. The charge brought by the Swiss anarchist leader James Guillaume against Marx, of supporting Pan-Germanism, was only a piece of absurd propaganda during the 1914–18 war. Like other historicists who believe in a single progressive universal civilization, Marx regarded national or regional loyalties as irrational resistance by lower forms of development, which history would render obsolete. In this sense German civilization (and the developed workers' organization in it) represented a more advanced stage of (admittedly capitalist) development than, say, Danish or Bohemian or any other *Kleinstaaterei*. Similarly, it was more desirable from the point of view of the International Workingmen's Movement that the Germans—with their superior workers' organizations—should win rather than the French, riddled with Proudhonism, Bakuninism, etc.; there is no trace of nationalism in Marx's conception of the stages of world progress toward communism and beyond it. It is all the more significant, therefore, that the creation of states founded on Marxist doctrines should, nevertheless, display acute national feeling. The latest and sharpest expression of this is contained in the report presented to the National Conference of the Rumanian Communist Party by its leader Nicolae Ceauçescu on July 19, 1972:

> Some people think that the nation is a concept which is historically obsolete, and that the policy of national unity and the development of the nation, particularly in Socialist conditions, would even be a wrong

and harmonious cooperation between nations. One is also reminded of Norman Angell's apparently unanswered argument a short while before 1914 that the economic interests of modern capitalist states alone made large-scale wars impossible.

V

WHAT WE are seeing, it seems to me, is a world reaction against the central doctrines of nineteenth-century liberal rationalism itself, a confused effort to return to an older morality. The lines of battle in the eighteenth and nineteenth centuries were more or less clearly drawn. On one side stood the supporters of tradition, of political and social hierarchies, whether "natural" or hallowed by history, or belief in, and obedience to, divine, or at any rate transcendent, authority. These were men who believed that the operations of untrammeled reason must be kept within bounds and should, above all, be prevented from questioning the validity of the laws and customs and ancient ways of life—those impalpable and unanalyzable bonds that hold society together and alone preserve the moral health of states and individuals. This is the faith in the "integral" community which critical examination by skeptical intellectuals, using rationalist methods, can only discredit in theory and un-

---

policy, would represent the expression of narrow-minded nationalism. Sometimes it is said that this policy is opposed to Socialist internationalism. . . . With respect to the national problem in Socialist conditions, we have to say that the victory of the new society has opened up the way to achieving true national unity, to strengthening and developing the nation on a new basis. . . . The dialectical process of bringing together [different] nations presupposes their strong affirmation [of their national characteristics]. . . . Between national and international interests not only is there no contradiction, but on the contrary, there is a full dialectical unit (*Scinteia*, July 20, 1972, p. 8).

Ceauçescu is perhaps the most impeccably Leninist-Stalinist of all the leaders of communist states. The fact that he should have chosen to make a doctrinal issue of what has, in practice, for many years been the line of many communist governments and parties in the East and West is surely an event of some importance. The conflict between Marxist discipline and nationalist forces, which is a fairly constant factor in contemporary communism—indeed, the entire topic of Marxism and nationalism, both its theoretical aspects and in practice—deserves closer study than it has obtained.

dermine, and in the end, disintegrate in practice. On the other side stood the unswerving champions of reason, who rejected faith in tradition, intuition, transcendent sources of authority as mere smoke screens to justify irrationality, ignorance, bias, fear of the truth in matters of theory, and stupidity, injustice, oppression, and the corrupt power of Bentham's sinister interests in practice.

The party of progress, liberal or socialist, appealed to the methods of reason, especially the methods employed in the natural sciences, by which any rational being could verify the truth of a principle, or the effectiveness of a policy, or the reliability of the evidence on which these conclusions were founded. He could test such claims for himself by the use of techniques open to anyone, at any time, anywhere, without appeal to special faculties or mystical intuition with which only a chosen few were mysteriously endowed— magical ways of knowing for which infallibility was often claimed. Each side knew its enemies: on the right stood monarchists and conservatives, clericals and authoritarians, nationalists and imperialists, men whom their opponents called reactionaries and obscurantists; on the other side, rationalists, scientific materialists, skeptical intellectuals, egalitarians and positivists of many hues. Whatever the differences within each group, whether about ends or about means, the main lines of division between them were clearly discernible; and in spite of mixed and intermediate positions, each side was conscious of where it belonged and who its natural allies and opponents were.

There is a sense in which, in our time, Burke's "sophisters, economists and calculators," the rationalists, the Victorian progressives, have won. Condorcet had once observed that all real issues of the future could be decided on the basis of rational calculation of utilitarian consequences. *Calculemus* was to be the new watchword, the key to the solution both of social and of personal problems. This method, with its stress on systems analysis, cost-effectiveness, reduction to statistical and quantitative terms, reliance on the authority and power of organization and experts, is today the common property of both sides. The application of technological techniques in organizing the lives and productive activities of human beings is the policy of governments, of industrial enterprises, indeed of all large-scale economic (and cultural) activities in capitalist and communist states alike. Scientific knowledge and scientific organization, which alone have succeeded in revealing the secrets of nature, animate and inanimate, can surely be made to rationalize social life and so bring about the maximum satisfaction of discoverable human needs provided that the system is organized by disinterested experts.

Physicists and biologists, geographers and urban and rural planners, psychologists and anthropologists, mathematicians and engineers (including Stalin's "engineers of human souls"), specialists of every kind, can be, and to a larger degree have been, harnessed into the service of those who, sometimes with pure motives and a fanatical devotion to what they see as the cause of reason and human happiness, are determined to make the best use possible of available resources, natural and artificial, human and nonhuman. Marxists, or inhabitants of underdeveloped countries, may protest against the use of such methods in their own interest by the class enemy, internal or external, capitalists, "neo-colonialists," imperialists. But they do not protest against the technological approach itself, and indeed seek to adapt and perfect it for the promotion of their own interests. It is against this that a worldwide protest has begun.

The effectiveness of this revolt, for such it seems to be since it is still in its early beginnings, is hard to foretell. It springs from the feeling that human rights, rooted in the sense of human beings as specifically human, that is, as individuated, as possessing wills, sentiments, beliefs, ideals, ways of living of their own, have been lost sight of in the "global" calculations and vast extrapolations which guide the plans of policy planners and executives in the gigantic operations in which governments, corporations, and interlocking élites of various kinds are engaged. Quantitative computation cannot but ignore the specific wishes and hopes and fears and goals of individual human beings. This must always be so, whenever policies for large numbers must be devised, but it has today gone very far indeed.

There is a growing number among the young of our day who see their future as a process of being fitted into some scientifically well-constructed program, after the data of their life expectancy and capacities and utilizability have been classified, computerized, and analyzed for conduciveness to the purpose, at the very best, of producing the greatest happiness of the greatest number. This will determine the organization of life on a national or regional or world scale, and this without undue attention to, or interest in (since this is not needed for the completion of the task), their individual characters, ways of life, wishes, quirks, ideals. This moves them to gloom and fury or despair. They wish to be and do something, and not merely be acted upon, or for, or on behalf of. They demand recognition of their dignity as human beings. They do not wish to be reduced to human material, to being counters in a game played by others, even when it is played, at least in part, for the benefit of these counters themselves. A revolt breaks out at all levels.

The dissident young opt out or attack universities, intellectual activities, organized education, because they identify them with this huge and dehumanizing machinery. Whether they know it or not, what they are appealing to is some species of Natural law, or Kantian absolutism, which forbids the treatment of human beings as means to ends, no matter how benevolently this is conceived. Their protests sometimes take rational forms, at other times violently irrational ones, mostly exhibitionistic and often hysterical attempts to defy the ruling powers, to insult them into awareness of the totalitarian effect of such policies, whether intended or unintended (the authentic Marxist component of such protests, the denunciation of exploitation and class rule, is not, as a rule, the dominant note). They protest against the destructive effect to individuals of global planning, of the substitution of figures and curves for the direct perception of actual human beings for whose ostensible good all this is being done, especially of those remote from them whose lives the planners seek to determine, sometimes by exceedingly brutal means, hidden from their own sight by the opaque medium of impersonal statistics.

In industrial or post-industrial societies, the protest is that of individuals or groups whose members do not wish to be dragged along by the chariot wheels of scientific progress, interpreted as the accumulation of material goods and services and of utilitarian arrangements to dispose of them. In poor or ex-colonial territories, the desire of the majority to be treated as equals of their former masters—as full human beings—often takes the form of nationalist self-assertion. The cry for individual and national independence—the demand not to be interfered with or dictated to or organized by others—springs from the same sense of outraged human dignity. It is true that the movement for national independence at times itself leads to the creation of larger units, to centralization, and often to the suppression by the new elite of its own fellow-citizens, and it can lead to the crushing of various minorities, ethnic, political, religious. At other times it is inspired by the opposite ideal—escape from huge impersonal authority that ignores ethnic, regional, and religious differences, a craving for "natural" units of "human" size.

But the original impulse, the desire *fare da se,* appears to be the same in both cases; it is the *se* that varies. The self that seeks liberty of action, determination of its own life, can be large or small, regional or linguistic; today it is liable to be collective and national or ethnic-religious rather than individual; it is always resistant to dilution, assimilation, depersonalization. It is the very triumph of scientific rationalism everywhere, the great eighteenth-century movement for the liberation of men from superstition and ignorance, from the selfishness and greed of kings, priests, and oligarchies, above all, from the vagaries of natural forces, that, by a curious paradox, has imposed a yoke that, in its turn, evoked an all-too-human cry for independence from its rule. It is a cry for room in which men can seek to realize their natures, quirks and all, to live lives free from dictation or coercion from teachers, masters, bullies, and persuaders and dominators of various kinds. No doubt to do entirely as one likes could destroy not only one's neighbors but oneself. Freedom is only one value among others, and cannot be realized without rules and limits. But in the hour of revolt this is inevitably forgotten.

VI

ANTINOMIANISM is nothing new. Mutiny against the life of the barracks, the suffocation of "closed" societies against the laws and institutions that are felt to be unjust or oppressive or corrupt or indifferent to some of the deepest aspirations of human beings, occur in the history of every long-lived state and church and social order. Sometimes these institutions, whatever their official professions and ideologies, are felt to favor a particular class or group at the expense of others, whom they seek, consciously or unconsciously, to deceive or coerce into conformity. At other times the system is felt to be mechanically self-perpetuating and the reasons for its existence, even if once valid, have become obsolete. Its supporters delude men (and are themselves deluded) into supposing that human arrangements, which may have originally responded to real needs, are objective necessities, laws of nature (at least human nature) which it is idle and irrational to seek to alter. Diderot spoke of the war within each human being, of the natural man seeking to liberate himself from the artificial man, who is compounded of social conventions, irrational pressures, and the "interested error" of the ruling class which rational criticism would blow sky-high but upon which contemporary society rests.

Protest against this takes the form sometimes of a nostalgic longing for earlier times, when men were virtuous or happy or free, or dreams of a golden age in the future, or of a restoration of simplicity, spontaneity, natural humanity, the self-subsistent rural economy, in which man, no longer dependent on the whims of others, can recover moral (and physical) health. The result would presumably be the reign of those eternal values which all but the hopelessly corrupt can easily recognize simply by looking within themselves; this is what Rousseau and Tolstoy and a good many peaceful anarchists and their modern followers still believe. Populist movements in the nineteenth century which idealized peasants, or the poor, or the "true" nation, very different from its self-appointed bureaucratic rulers, represented attempts of this kind—a return to "the people" in order to escape from a world of false values, "inauthentic" lives, organization men, or Ibsen's or Chekhov's crushed or repressed beings, where human capacity for love and friendship, justice and creative work, enjoyment, curiosity, pursuit of the truth, have been aborted and frustrated. Some wish to improve contemporary society by reforms. Others feel, as the Anabaptists of the sixteenth century may have felt, that the corruption has gone too far, that the wicked must be destroyed root and branch, in the hope that a new and pure society will arise miraculously upon its ruins.

These are extreme cases, chosen to illustrate the predicament at its most characteristic. It is with this mood and this predicament that nationalism is connected. It, too, is a pathological form of a self-protective resistance. Rousseau, the most spellbinding voice of this general revolt, told the Poles to resist encroachment by the Russians by obstinately clinging to their national institutions, their clothes, their habits, their ways of life, not to conform, not to assimilate; the claims of universal humanity were incarnated, for the time being, in their resistance. There is something of the same attitude in the Russian populists of the last century. It is to be found among those hitherto suppressed peoples or minorities—those ethnic groups which feel humiliated or oppressed, to whom nationalism represents the straightening of bent backs, the recovery of a freedom that they may never have had (it is all a matter of ideas in men's heads), revenge for their insulted humanity.

This is less acutely felt in societies which have enjoyed political independence for long periods. The West has, by and large, satisfied that hunger for recognition, the desire for the *Anerkennung* which Hegel analyzed very memorably; it is lack of this that, more than any other cause, seems to lead to nationalist excesses. Nationalism to many liberals and socialists in the West appears to be mere chauvinism or imperialism, part and parcel of the ideology of that very establishment which has robbed the victims of their birthright. What could be more paradoxical or more pathetic than that they should seek to realize the very values of the monstrous system which has reduced them to poverty and degradation? Is this not one of the best illustrations of the Marxist thesis that one of the greatest wrongs the ruling class does to its subjects is to blind them to their true interest, to infect them with its ideology dictated by its own interests, as if they were identical with those of the oppressed?

In fact, nationalism does not necessarily and exclusively militate in favor of the ruling class. It animates revolts against it, too, for it expresses the inflamed desire of the insufficiently regarded to count for something among the cultures of the world. The brutal and destructive side of modern nationalism needs no stressing in a world torn by its excesses. Yet it must be recognized for what it is—a worldwide response to a profound and natural need on the part of newly liberated slaves—"the decolonized"—a phenomenon unpredicted in the Europe-centered society of the nineteenth century. How did the possibility of this development come to be ignored? To this question, I volunteer no answer.

The Clash of Civilizations?

Samuel P. Huntington

SUMMER 1993

THE NEXT PATTERN OF CONFLICT

WORLD POLITICS is entering a new phase, and intellectuals have not hesitated to proliferate visions of what it will be—the end of history, the return of traditional rivalries between nation states, and the decline of the nation state from the conflicting pulls of tribalism and globalism, among others. Each of these visions catches aspects of the emerging reality. Yet they all miss a crucial, indeed a central, aspect of what global politics is likely to be in the coming years.

It is my hypothesis that the fundamental source of conflict in this new world will not be primarily ideological or primarily economic. The great divisions among humankind and the dominating source of conflict will be cultural. Nation states will remain the most powerful actors in world affairs, but the principal conflicts of global politics will occur between nations and groups of different civilizations. The clash of civilizations will dominate global politics. The fault lines between civilizations will be the battle lines of the future.

Conflict between civilizations will be the latest phase in the evolution of conflict in the modern world. For a century and a half after the emergence of the modern international system with the Peace of Westphalia, the conflicts of the Western world were largely among princes—emperors, absolute monarchs, and constitutional monarchs attempting to expand their bureaucracies, their armies, their mercantilist economic strength, and most important, the territory they ruled. In the process they created nation-states, and beginning with the French Revolution, the principal lines of conflict were between nations rather than princes. In 1793, as R. R. Palmer put it, "The wars of kings were over; the wars of peoples had begun." This nineteenth-century pattern

[548]

lasted until the end of World War I. Then, as a result of the Russian Revolution and the reaction against it, the conflict of nations yielded to the conflict of ideologies, first among communism, fascism-Nazism and liberal democracy, and then between communism and liberal democracy. During the Cold War, this latter conflict became embodied in the struggle between the two superpowers, neither of which was a nation state in the classical European sense and each of which defined its identity in terms of its ideology.

These conflicts between princes, nation-states, and ideologies were primarily conflicts within Western civilization, "Western civil wars," as William Lind has labeled them. This was as true of the Cold War as it was of the world wars and the earlier wars of the seventeenth, eighteenth, and nineteenth centuries. With the end of the Cold War, international politics moves out of its Western phase, and its centerpiece becomes the interaction between the West and non-Western civilizations and among non-Western civilizations. In the politics of civilizations, the peoples and governments of non-Western civilizations no longer remain the objects of history as targets of Western colonialism but join the West as movers and shapers of history.

THE NATURE OF CIVILIZATIONS

DURING THE Cold War, the world was divided into the First, Second, and Third Worlds. Those divisions are no longer relevant. It is far more meaningful now to group countries not in terms of their political or economic systems or in terms of their level of economic development but rather in terms of their culture and civilization.

What do we mean when we talk of a civilization? A civilization is a cultural entity. Villages, regions, ethnic groups, nationalities, religious groups all have distinct cultures at different levels of cultural heterogeneity. The culture of a village in southern Italy may be different from that of a village in northern Italy, but both will share in a common Italian culture that distinguishes them from German villages. European communities, in turn, will share cultural features that distinguish them from Arab or Chinese communities. Arabs, Chinese, and Westerners, however, are not part of any broader cultural entity. They constitute civilizations. A civilization is thus the highest cultural grouping of people and the broadest level of cultural identity people have short of that which distinguishes humans from other species. It is defined both by common objective elements, such as language, history, religion, customs, institutions, and by the subjective self-identification of people. People have levels of identity: a resident of Rome may define himself with varying degrees of intensity as a Roman, an Italian, a Catholic, a Christian, a European, a Westerner. The civilization to which he belongs is the broadest level

of identification with which he intensely identifies. People can and do redefine their identities, and as a result, the composition and boundaries of civilizations change.

Civilizations may involve a large number of people, as with China ("a
civilization pretending to be a state," as Lucian Pye put it), or a very small
number of people, such as the Anglophone Caribbean. A civilization may include several nation states, as is the case with Western, Latin American, and
Arab civilizations, or only one, as is the case with Japanese civilization. Civilizations obviously blend and overlap and may include subcivilizations. Western civilization has two major variants, European and North American, and
Islam has its Arab, Turkic, and Malay subdivisions. Civilizations are
nonetheless meaningful entities, and while the lines between them are seldom sharp, they are real. Civilizations are dynamic; they rise and fall; they divide and merge. And, as any student of history knows, civilizations disappear
and are buried in the sands of time.

Westerners tend to think of nation states as the principal actors in global
affairs. They have been that, however, for only a few centuries. The broader
reaches of human history have been the history of civilizations. In *A Study of
History,* Arnold Toynbee identified 21 major civilizations; only 6 of them exist
in the contemporary world.

WHY CIVILIZATIONS WILL CLASH

CIVILIZATION identity will be increasingly important in the future, and the
world will be shaped in large measure by the interactions among seven or
eight major civilizations. These include Western, Confucian, Japanese, Islamic, Hindu, Slavic-Orthodox, Latin American, and possibly African civilization. The most important conflicts of the future will occur along the
cultural fault lines separating these civilizations from one another.

Why will this be the case?

First, differences among civilizations are not only real; they are basic.
Civilizations are differentiated from each other by history, language, culture,
tradition, and most important, religion. The people of different civilizations
have different views on the relations between God and man, the individual
and the group, the citizen and the state, parents and children, husband and
wife, as well as differing views of the relative importance of rights and responsibilities, liberty and authority, equality and hierarchy. These differences
are the product of centuries. They will not soon disappear. They are far more
fundamental than differences among political ideologies and political
regimes. Differences do not necessarily mean conflict, and conflict does not
necessarily mean violence. Over the centuries, however, differences among

civilizations have generated the most prolonged and the most violent conflicts.

Second, the world is becoming a smaller place. The interactions between peoples of different civilizations are increasing; these increasing interactions intensify civilization-consciousness and awareness of differences between civilizations and commonalities within civilizations. North African immigration to France generates hostility among Frenchmen and at the same time increased receptivity to immigration by "good" European Catholic Poles. Americans react far more negatively to Japanese investment than to larger investments from Canada and European countries. Similarly, as Donald Horowitz has pointed out, "An Ibo may be. . . an Owerri Ibo or an Onitsha Ibo in what was the Eastern region of Nigeria. In Lagos, he is simply an Ibo. In London, he is a Nigerian. In New York, he is an African." The interactions among peoples of different civilizations enhance the civilization-consciousness of people that, in turn, invigorates differences and animosities stretching or thought to stretch back deep into history.

Third, the processes of economic modernization and social change throughout the world are separating people from long-standing local identities. They also weaken the nation state as a source of identity. In much of the world, religion has moved in to fill this gap, often in the form of movements that are labeled "fundamentalist." Such movements are found in Western Christianity, Judaism, Buddhism, and Hinduism, as well as in Islam. In most countries and most religions, the people active in fundamentalist movements are young, college-educated, middle-class technicians, professionals, and businesspersons. The "unsecularization of the world," George Weigel has remarked, "is one of the dominant social facts of life in the late twentieth century." The revival of religion, "la revanche de Dieu," as Gilles Kepel labeled it, provides a basis for identity and commitment that transcends national boundaries and unites civilizations.

Fourth, the growth of civilization-consciousness is enhanced by the dual role of the West. On the one hand, the West is at a peak of power. At the same time, however, and perhaps as a result, a return to the roots phenomenon is occurring among non-Western civilizations. Increasingly one hears references to trends toward a turning inward and "Asianization" in Japan, the end of the Nehru legacy and the "Hinduization" of India, the failure of Western ideas of socialism and nationalism and hence "re-Islamization" of the Middle East, and now a debate over Westernization versus Russianization in Boris Yeltsin's country. A West at the peak of its power confronts non-Wests that increasingly have the desire, the will, and the resources to shape the world in non-Western ways.

In the past, the elites of non-Western societies were usually the people who were most involved with the West, had been educated at Oxford, the Sorbonne, or Sandhurst, and had absorbed Western attitudes and values. At the same time, the populace in non-Western countries often remained deeply imbued with the indigenous culture. Now, however, these relationships are being reversed. A de-Westernization and indigenization of elites is occurring in many non-Western countries at the same time that Western, usually American, cultures, styles, and habits become more popular among the mass of the people.

Fifth, cultural characteristics and differences are less mutable and hence less easily compromised and resolved than political and economic ones. In the former Soviet Union, communists can become democrats, the rich can become poor and the poor rich, but Russians cannot become Estonians and Azeris cannot become Armenians. In class and ideological conflicts, the key question was "Which side are you on?" and people could and did choose sides and change sides. In conflicts between civilizations, the question is "What are you?" That is a given that cannot be changed. And as we know, from Bosnia to the Caucasus to the Sudan, the wrong answer to that question can mean a bullet in the head. Even more than ethnicity, religion discriminates sharply and exclusively among people. A person can be half-French and half-Arab and simultaneously even a citizen of two countries. It is more difficult to be half-Catholic and half-Muslim.

Finally, economic regionalism is increasing. The proportions of total trade that were intraregional rose between 1980 and 1989 from 51 percent to 59 percent in Europe, 33 percent to 37 percent in East Asia, and 32 percent to 36 percent in North America. The importance of regional economic blocs is likely to continue to increase in the future. On the one hand, successful economic regionalism will reinforce civilization-consciousness. On the other hand, economic regionalism may succeed only when it is rooted in a common civilization. The European Community rests on the shared foundation of European culture and Western Christianity. The success of the North American Free Trade Area depends on the convergence now underway of Mexican, Canadian, and American cultures. Japan, in contrast, faces difficulties in creating a comparable economic entity in East Asia because Japan is a society and civilization unique to itself. However strong the trade and investment links Japan may develop with other East Asian countries, its cultural differences with those countries inhibit and perhaps preclude its promoting regional economic integration like that in Europe and North America.

Common culture, in contrast, is clearly facilitating the rapid expansion of the economic relations between the People's Republic of China and Hong Kong, Taiwan, Singapore, and the overseas Chinese communities in other Asian countries. With the Cold War over, cultural commonalities increasingly overcome ideological differences, and mainland China and Taiwan move closer together. If cultural commonality is a prerequisite for economic integration, the principal East Asian economic bloc of the future is likely to be centered on China. This bloc is, in fact, already coming into existence. As Murray Weidenbaum has observed,

> Despite the current Japanese dominance of the region, the Chinese-based economy of Asia is rapidly emerging as a new epicenter for industry, commerce and finance. This strategic area contains substantial amounts of technology and manufacturing capability (Taiwan), outstanding entrepreneurial, marketing and services acumen (Hong Kong), a fine communications network (Singapore), a tremendous pool of financial capital (all three), and very large endowments of land, resources and labor (mainland China). . . . From Guangzhou to Singapore, from Kuala Lumpur to Manila, this influential network—often based on extensions of the traditional clans—has been described as the backbone of the East Asian economy.[1]

Culture and religion also form the basis of the Economic Cooperation Organization, which brings together ten non-Arab Muslim countries: Iran, Pakistan, Turkey, Azerbaijan, Kazakhstan, Kyrgyzstan, Turkmenistan, Tadjikistan, Uzbekistan, and Afghanistan. One impetus to the revival and expansion of this organization, founded originally in the 1960s by Turkey, Pakistan, and Iran, is the realization by the leaders of several of these countries that they had no chance of admission to the European Community. Similarly, Caricom, the Central American Common Market, and Mercosur rest on common cultural foundations. Efforts to build a broader Caribbean–Central American economic entity bridging the Anglo-Latin divide, however, have to date failed.

As people define their identity in ethnic and religious terms, they are likely to see an "us" versus "them" relation existing between themselves and people of different ethnicity or religion. The end of ideologically defined states in Eastern Europe and the former Soviet Union permits traditional ethnic identities and animosities to come to the fore. Differences in culture and religion create differences over policy issues, ranging from human rights to immigration to trade and commerce to the environment. Geographical propinquity gives rise to conflicting territorial claims from Bosnia to Mindanao. Most important, the efforts of the West to promote its values of

---

[1] Murray Weidenbaum, *Greater China: The Next Superpower?*, St. Louis: Washington University Center for the Study of American Business, Contemporary Issues, Series 57, February 1993, pp. 2–3.

democracy and liberalism as universal values, to maintain its military predominance, and to advance its economic interests engender countering responses from other civilizations. Decreasingly able to mobilize support and form coalitions on the basis of ideology, governments and groups will increasingly attempt to mobilize support by appealing to common religion and civilization identity.

The clash of civilizations thus occurs at two levels. At the micro-level, adjacent groups along the fault lines between civilizations struggle, often violently, over the control of territory and each other. At the macro-level, states from different civilizations compete for relative military and economic power, struggle over the control of international institutions and third parties, and competitively promote their particular political and religious values.

THE FAULT LINES BETWEEN CIVILIZATIONS

THE FAULT LINES between civilizations are replacing the political and ideological boundaries of the Cold War as the flash points for crisis and bloodshed. The Cold War began when the Iron Curtain divided Europe politically and ideologically. The Cold War ended with the end of the Iron Curtain. As the ideological division of Europe has disappeared, the cultural division of Europe between Western Christianity, on the one hand, and Orthodox Christianity and Islam, on the other, has reemerged. The most significant dividing line in Europe, as William Wallace has suggested, may well be the eastern boundary of Western Christianity in the year 1500. This line runs along what are now the boundaries between Finland and Russia and between the Baltic states and Russia, cuts through Belarus and Ukraine separating the more Catholic western Ukraine from Orthodox eastern Ukraine, swings westward separating Transylvania from the rest of Rumania, and then goes through Yugoslavia almost exactly along the line now separating Croatia and Slovenia from the rest of Yugoslavia. In the Balkans this line, of course, coincides with the historic boundary between the Hapsburg and Ottoman empires. The peoples to the north and west of this line are Protestant or Catholic; they shared the common experiences of European history—feudalism, the Renaissance, the Reformation, the Enlightenment, the French Revolution, the Industrial Revolution; they are generally economically better off than the peoples to the east; and they may now look forward to increasing involvement in a common European economy and to the consolidation of democratic political systems. The peoples to the east and south of this line are Orthodox or Muslim; they historically belonged to the Ottoman or tsarist empires, and were only lightly touched by the shaping events in the rest of Europe; they are generally less advanced economically; they seem much less likely to develop stable democratic political systems. The Velvet Curtain of culture has replaced the Iron Curtain of ideology as the most significant dividing line in Europe. As the events in Yugoslavia show, it is not only a line of difference; it is also at times a line of bloody conflict.

Conflict along the fault line between Western and Islamic civilizations has been going on for 1,300 years. After the founding of Islam, the Arab and Moorish surge west and north only ended at Tours in 732. From the eleventh to the thirteenth century, the Crusaders attempted with temporary success to bring Christianity and Christian rule to the Holy Land. From the fourteenth to the seventeenth century, the Ottoman Turks reversed the balance, extended their sway over the Middle East and the Balkans, captured Constantinople, and twice laid siege to Vienna. In the nineteenth and early twentieth centuries, as Ottoman power declined, Britain, France, and Italy established Western control over most of North Africa and the Middle East.

After World War II, the West, in turn, began to retreat; the colonial empires disappeared; first Arab nationalism and then Islamic fundamentalism manifested themselves; the West became heavily dependent on the Persian Gulf countries for its energy; the oil-rich Muslim countries became money-rich and, when they wished to, weapons-rich. Several wars occurred between Arabs and Israel (created by the West). France fought a bloody and ruthless war in Algeria for most of the 1950s; British and French forces invaded Egypt in 1956; American forces went into Lebanon in 1958; subsequently American forces returned to Lebanon, attacked Libya, and engaged in various military encounters with Iran; Arab and Islamic terrorists, supported by at least three Middle Eastern governments, employed the weapon of the weak and bombed Western planes and installations and seized Western hostages. This warfare between Arabs and the West culminated in 1990, when the United States sent a massive army to the Persian Gulf to defend some Arab countries against aggression by another. In its aftermath, NATO planning is increasingly directed to potential threats and instability along its "southern tier."

This centuries-old military interaction between the West and Islam is unlikely to decline. It could become more virulent. The Gulf War left some Arabs feeling proud that Saddam Hussein had attacked Israel and stood up to the West. It also left many feeling humiliated and resentful of the West's military presence in the Persian Gulf, the West's overwhelming military dominance, and their apparent inability to shape their own destiny. Many Arab countries, in addition to the oil exporters, are reaching levels of economic and social development where autocratic forms of government become inappropriate and efforts to introduce democracy become stronger. Some openings in Arab political systems have already occurred. The principal beneficiaries of these openings have been Islamist movements. In the Arab world, in short, Western democracy strengthens anti-Western political forces. This may be a passing phenomenon, but it surely complicates relations between Islamic countries and the West.

Those relations are also complicated by demography. The spectacular population growth in Arab countries, particularly in North Africa, has led to increased migration to Western Europe. The movement within Western Europe toward minimizing internal boundaries has sharpened political sensitivities with respect to this development. In Italy, France, and Germany, racism is increasingly open, and political reactions and violence against Arab and Turkish migrants have become more intense and more widespread since 1990.

On both sides the interaction between Islam and the West is seen as a clash of civilizations. The West's "next confrontation," observes M. J. Akbar, an Indian Muslim author, "is definitely going to come from the Muslim world. It is in the sweep of the Islamic nations from the Maghreb to Pakistan that the struggle for a new world order will begin." Bernard Lewis comes to a similar conclusion:

> We are facing a mood and a movement far transcending the level of issues and policies and the governments that pursue them. This is no less than a clash of civilizations—the perhaps irrational but surely historic reaction of an ancient rival against our Judeo-Christian heritage, our secular present, and the worldwide expansion of both.[2]

Historically, the other great antagonistic interaction of Arab Islamic civilization has been with the pagan, animist, and now increasingly Christian black peoples to the south. In the past, this antagonism was epitomized in the image of Arab slave dealers and black slaves. It has been reflected in the ongoing civil war in the Sudan between Arabs and blacks, the fighting in Chad between Libyan-supported insurgents and the government, the tensions between Orthodox Christians and Muslims in the Horn of Africa, and the political conflicts, recurring riots, and communal violence between Muslims and Christians in Nigeria. The modernization of Africa and the spread of Christianity are likely to enhance the probability of violence along this fault line. Symptomatic of the intensification of this conflict was Pope John Paul II's speech in Khartoum in February 1993 attacking the actions of the Sudan's Islamist government against the Christian minority there.

On the northern border of Islam, conflict has increasingly erupted be-

---

[2] Bernard Lewis, "The Roots of Muslim Rage," *The Atlantic Monthly*, vol. 266, September 1990, p. 60; *Time*, June 15, 1992, pp. 24–28.

tween Orthodox and Muslim peoples, including the carnage of Bosnia and Sarajevo, the simmering violence between Serb and Albanian, the tenuous relations between Bulgarians and their Turkish minority, the violence between Ossetians and Ingush, the unremitting slaughter of each other by Armenians and Azeris, the tense relations between Russians and Muslims in Central Asia, and the deployment of Russian troops to protect Russian interests in the Caucasus and Central Asia. Religion reinforces the revival of ethnic identities and restimulates Russian fears about the security of their southern borders. This concern is well captured by Archie Roosevelt:

> Much of Russian history concerns the struggle between the Slavs and the Turkic peoples on their borders, which dates back to the foundation of the Russian state more than a thousand years ago. In the Slavs' millennium-long confrontation with their eastern neighbors lies the key to an understanding not only of Russian history, but Russian character. To understand Russian realities today one has to have a concept of the great Turkic ethnic group that has preoccupied Russians through the centuries.[3]

The conflict of civilizations is deeply rooted elsewhere in Asia. The historic clash between Muslim and Hindu in the subcontinent manifests itself now not only in the rivalry between Pakistan and India but also in intensifying religious strife within India between increasingly militant Hindu groups and India's substantial Muslim minority. The destruction of the Ayodhya mosque in December 1992 brought to the fore the issue of whether India will remain a secular democratic state or become a Hindu one. In East Asia, China has outstanding territorial disputes with most of its neighbors. It has pursued a ruthless policy toward the Buddhist people of Tibet, and it is pursuing an increasingly ruthless policy toward its Turkic-Muslim minority. With the Cold War over, the underlying differences between China and the United States have reasserted themselves in areas such as human rights, trade, and weapons proliferation. These differences are unlikely to moderate. A "new cold war," Deng Xiaoping reportedly asserted in 1991, is underway between China and America.

The same phrase has been applied to the increasingly difficult relations between Japan and the United States. Here cultural difference exacerbates economic conflict. People on each side allege racism on the other, but at least on the American side the antipathies are not racial but cultural. The basic values, attitudes, behavioral patterns of the two societies could hardly be

---

[3] Archie Roosevelt, *For Lust of Knowing*, Boston: Little, Brown, 1988, pp. 332–33.

more different. The economic issues between the United States and Europe are no less serious than those between the United States and Japan, but they do not have the same political salience and emotional intensity because the differences between American culture and European culture are so much less than those between American civilization and Japanese civilization.

The interactions between civilizations vary greatly in the extent to which they are likely to be characterized by violence. Economic competition clearly predominates between the American and European subcivilizations of the West and between both of them and Japan. On the Eurasian continent, however, the proliferation of ethnic conflict, epitomized at the extreme in "ethnic cleansing," has not been totally random. It has been most frequent and most violent between groups belonging to different civilizations. In Eurasia the great historic fault lines between civilizations are once more aflame. This is particularly true along the boundaries of the crescent-shaped Islamic bloc of nations from the bulge of Africa to central Asia. Violence also occurs between Muslims, on the one hand, and Orthodox Serbs in the Balkans, Jews in Israel, Hindus in India, Buddhists in Burma, and Catholics in the Philippines. Islam has bloody borders.

CIVILIZATION RALLYING: THE KIN-COUNTRY SYNDROME

GROUPS OR STATES belonging to one civilization that become involved in war with people from a different civilization naturally try to rally support from other members of their own civilization. As the post–Cold War world evolves, civilization commonality, what H.D.S. Greenway has termed the "kin-country" syndrome, is replacing political ideology and traditional balance of power considerations as the principal basis for cooperation and coalitions. It can be seen gradually emerging in the post–Cold War conflicts in the Persian Gulf, the Caucasus, and Bosnia. None of these was a full-scale war between civilizations, but each involved some elements of civilizational rallying which seemed to become more important as the conflict continued and which may provide a foretaste of the future.

First, in the Gulf War one Arab state invaded another and then fought a coalition of Arab, Western, and other states. While only a few Muslim governments overtly supported Saddam Hussein, many Arab elites privately cheered him on, and he was highly popular among large sections of the Arab publics. Islamic fundamentalist movements universally supported Iraq rather than the Western-backed governments of Kuwait and Saudi Arabia. Forswearing Arab nationalism, Saddam Hussein explicitly invoked an Islamic appeal. He and his supporters attempted to define the war as a war between civilizations. "It is not the world against Iraq," as Safar Al-Hawali, dean of

Islamic Studies at the Umm Al-Qura University in Mecca, put it in a widely circulated tape. "It is the West against Islam." Ignoring the rivalry between Iran and Iraq, the chief Iranian religious leader, Ayatollah Ali Khamenei, called for a holy war against the West: "The struggle against American aggression, greed, plans and policies will be counted as a jihad, and anybody who is killed on that path is a martyr." "This is a war," King Hussein of Jordan argued, "against all Arabs and all Muslims and not against Iraq alone."

The rallying of substantial sections of Arab elites and publics behind Saddam Hussein caused those Arab governments in the anti-Iraq coalition to moderate their activities and temper their public statements. Arab governments opposed or distanced themselves from subsequent Western efforts to apply pressure on Iraq, including enforcement of a no-fly zone in the summer of 1992 and the bombing of Iraq in January 1993. The Western-Soviet-Turkish-Arab anti-Iraq coalition of 1990 had by 1993 become a coalition of almost only the West and Kuwait against Iraq.

Muslims contrasted Western actions against Iraq with the West's failure to protect Bosnians against Serbs and to impose sanctions on Israel for violating U.N. resolutions. The West, they alleged, was using a double standard. A world of clashing civilizations, however, is inevitably a world of double standards: people apply one standard to their kin-countries and a different standard to others.

Second, the kin-country syndrome also appeared in conflicts in the former Soviet Union. Armenian military successes in 1992 and 1993 stimulated Turkey to become increasingly supportive of its religious, ethnic, and linguistic brethren in Azerbaijan. "We have a Turkish nation feeling the same sentiments as the Azerbaijanis," said one Turkish official in 1992. "We are under pressure. Our newspapers are full of the photos of atrocities and are asking us if we are still serious about pursuing our neutral policy. Maybe we should show Armenia that there's a big Turkey in the region." President Turgut Özal agreed, remarking that Turkey should at least "scare the Armenians a little bit." Turkey, Özal threatened again in 1993, would "show its fangs." Turkish Air Force jets flew reconnaissance flights along the Armenian border; Turkey suspended food shipments and air flights to Armenia; and Turkey and Iran announced they would not accept dismemberment of Azerbaijan. In the last years of its existence, the Soviet government supported Azerbaijan because its government was dominated by former communists. With the end of the Soviet Union, however, political considerations gave way to religious ones. Russian troops fought on the side of the Armenians, and Azerbaijan accused the "Russian government of turning 180 degrees" toward support for Christian Armenia.

Third, with respect to the fighting in the former Yugoslavia, Western publics manifested sympathy and support for the Bosnian Muslims and the horrors they suffered at the hands of the Serbs. Relatively little concern was expressed, however, over Croatian attacks on Muslims and participation in the dismemberment of Bosnia-Herzegovina. In the early stages of the Yugoslav breakup, Germany, in an unusual display of diplomatic initiative and muscle, induced the other 11 members of the European Community to follow its lead in recognizing Slovenia and Croatia. As a result of the pope's determination to provide strong backing to the two Catholic countries, the Vatican extended recognition even before the Community did. The United States followed the European lead. Thus the leading actors in Western civilization rallied behind their coreligionists. Subsequently Croatia was reported to be receiving substantial quantities of arms from Central European and other Western countries. Boris Yeltsin's government, on the other hand, attempted to pursue a middle course that would be sympathetic to the Orthodox Serbs but not alienate Russia from the West. Russian conservative and nationalist groups, however, including many legislators, attacked the government for not being more forthcoming in its support for the Serbs. By early 1993 several hundred Russians apparently were serving with the Serbian forces, and reports circulated of Russian arms being supplied to Serbia.

Islamic governments and groups, on the other hand, castigated the West for not coming to the defense of the Bosnians. Iranian leaders urged Muslims from all countries to provide help to Bosnia; in violation of the U.N. arms embargo, Iran supplied weapons and men for the Bosnians; Iranian-supported Lebanese groups sent guerrillas to train and organize the Bosnian forces. In 1993 up to 4,000 Muslims from over two dozen Islamic countries were reported to be fighting in Bosnia. The governments of Saudi Arabia and other countries felt under increasing pressure from fundamentalist groups in their own societies to provide more vigorous support for the Bosnians. By the end of 1992, Saudi Arabia had reportedly supplied substantial funding for weapons and supplies for the Bosnians, which significantly increased their military capabilities vis-à-vis the Serbs.

In the 1930s the Spanish Civil War provoked intervention from countries that politically were fascist, communist, and democratic. In the 1990s the Yugoslav conflict is provoking intervention from countries that are Muslim, Orthodox, and Western Christian. The parallel has not gone unnoticed. "The war in Bosnia-Herzegovina has become the emotional equivalent of the fight against fascism in the Spanish Civil War," one Saudi editor observed. "Those who died there are regarded as martyrs who tried to save their fellow Muslims."

Conflicts and violence will also occur between states and groups within the same civilization. Such conflicts, however, are likely to be less intense and less likely to expand than conflicts between civilizations. Common membership in a civilization reduces the probability of violence in situations where it might otherwise occur. In 1991 and 1992 many people were alarmed by the possibility of violent conflict between Russia and Ukraine over territory, particularly Crimea, the Black Sea fleet, nuclear weapons, and economic issues. If civilization is what counts, however, the likelihood of violence between Ukrainians and Russians should be low. They are two Slavic, primarily Orthodox peoples who have had close relationships with each other for centuries. As of early 1993, despite all the reasons for conflict, the leaders of the two countries were effectively negotiating and defusing the issues between the two countries. While there has been serious fighting between Muslims and Christians elsewhere in the former Soviet Union and much tension and some fighting between Western and Orthodox Christians in the Baltic states, there has been virtually no violence between Russians and Ukrainians.

Civilization rallying to date has been limited, but it has been growing, and it clearly has the potential to spread much further. As the conflicts in the Persian Gulf, the Caucasus, and Bosnia continued, the positions of nations and the cleavages between them increasingly were along civilizational lines. Populist politicians, religious leaders, and the media have found it a potent means of arousing mass support and of pressuring hesitant governments. In the coming years, the local conflicts most likely to escalate into major wars will be those, as in Bosnia and the Caucasus, along the fault lines between civilizations. The next world war, if there is one, will be a war between civilizations.

THE WEST VERSUS THE REST

THE WEST is now at an extraordinary peak of power in relation to other civilizations. Its superpower opponent has disappeared from the map. Military conflict among Western states is unthinkable, and Western military power is unrivaled. Apart from Japan, the West faces no economic challenge. It dominates international political and security institutions and, with Japan, international economic institutions. Global political and security issues are effectively settled by a directorate of the United States, Britain, and France; world economic issues by a directorate of the United States, Germany, and Japan, all of which maintain extraordinarily close relations with each other to the exclusion of lesser and largely non-Western countries. Decisions made at the U.N. Security Council or in the International Monetary Fund that reflect the interests of the West are presented to the world as reflecting the desires of the world community. The very phrase "the world community" has become the euphemistic collective noun (replacing "the Free World") to give global legitimacy to actions reflecting the interests of the United States and other Western powers.[4] Through the IMF and other international economic institutions, the West promotes its economic interests and imposes on other nations the economic policies it thinks appropriate. In any poll of non-Western peoples, the IMF undoubtedly would win the support of finance ministers and a few others but get an overwhelmingly unfavorable rating from just about everyone else, who would agree with Georgy Arbatov's characterization of IMF officials as "neo-Bolsheviks who love expropriating other people's money, imposing undemocratic and alien rules of economic and political conduct and stifling economic freedom."

Western domination of the U.N. Security Council and its decisions, tempered only by occasional abstention by China, produced U.N. legitimation of the West's use of force to drive Iraq out of Kuwait and its elimination of Iraq's sophisticated weapons and capacity to produce such weapons. It also produced the quite unprecedented action by the United States, Britain, and France in getting the Security Council to demand that Libya hand over the Pan Am 103 bombing suspects and then to impose sanctions when Libya refused. After defeating the largest Arab army, the West did not hesitate to throw its weight around in the Arab world. The West in effect is using international institutions, military power, and economic resources to run the world in ways that will maintain Western predominance, protect Western interests, and promote Western political and economic values.

That at least is the way in which non-Westerners see the new world, and there is a significant element of truth in their view. Differences in power and struggles for military, economic, and institutional power are thus one source of conflict between the West and other civilizations. Differences in culture, that is, basic values and beliefs, are a second source of conflict. V. S. Naipaul has argued that Western civilization is the "universal civilization" that "fits all men." At a superficial level, much of Western culture has indeed permeated the rest of the world. At a more basic level, however, Western concepts differ fundamentally from those prevalent in other civi-

---

[4]Almost invariably Western leaders claim they are acting on behalf of "the world community." One minor lapse occurred during the run-up to the Gulf War. In an interview on "Good Morning America," Dec. 21, 1990, British Prime Minister John Major referred to the actions "the West" was taking against Saddam Hussein. He quickly corrected himself and subsequently referred to "the world community." He was, however, right when he erred.

lizations. Western ideas of individualism, liberalism, constitutionalism, human rights, equality, liberty, the rule of law, democracy, free markets, the separation of church and state, often have little resonance in Islamic, Confucian, Japanese, Hindu, Buddhist, or Orthodox cultures. Western efforts to propagate such ideas produce instead a reaction against "human rights imperialism" and a reaffirmation of indigenous values, as can be seen in the support for religious fundamentalism by the younger generation in non-Western cultures. The very notion that there could be a "universal civilization" is a Western idea, directly at odds with the particularism of most Asian societies and their emphasis on what distinguishes one people from another. Indeed, the author of a review of 100 comparative studies of values in different societies concluded that "the values that are most important in the West are least important worldwide."[5] In the political realm, of course, these differences are most manifest in the efforts of the United States and other Western powers to induce other peoples to adopt Western ideas concerning democracy and human rights. Modern democratic government originated in the West. When it has developed in non-Western societies, it has usually been the product of Western colonialism or imposition.

The central axis of world politics in the future is likely to be, in Kishore Mahbubani's phrase, the conflict between "the West and the Rest" and the responses of non-Western civilizations to Western power and values.[6] Those responses generally take one or a combination of three forms. At one extreme, non-Western states can, like Burma and North Korea, attempt to pursue a course of isolation, to insulate their societies from penetration or "corruption" by the West, and in effect, to opt out of participation in the Western-dominated global community. The costs of this course, however, are high, and few states have pursued it exclusively. A second alternative, the equivalent of "band-wagoning" in international relations theory, is to attempt to join the West and accept its values and institutions. The third alternative is to attempt to "balance" the West by developing economic and military power and cooperating with other non-Western societies against the West, while preserving indigenous values and institutions; in short, to modernize but not to Westernize.

---

[5] Harry C. Triandis, *The New York Times*, Dec. 25, 1990, p. 41, and "Cross-Cultural Studies of Individualism and Collectivism," Nebraska Symposium on Motivation, vol. 37, 1989, pp. 41–133.

[6] Kishore Mahbubani, "The West and the Rest," *The National Interest*, Summer 1992, pp. 3–13.

THE TORN COUNTRIES

IN THE FUTURE, as people differentiate themselves by civilization, countries with large numbers of peoples of different civilizations, such as the Soviet Union and Yugoslavia, are candidates for dismemberment. Some other countries have a fair degree of cultural homogeneity but are divided over whether their society belongs to one civilization or another. These are torn countries. Their leaders typically wish to pursue a band-wagoning strategy and to make their countries members of the West, but the history, culture, and traditions of their countries are non-Western. The most obvious and prototypical torn country is Turkey. The late-twentieth-century leaders of Turkey have followed in the Atatürk tradition and defined Turkey as a modern, secular, Western nation-state. They allied Turkey with the West in NATO and in the Gulf War; they applied for membership in the European Community. At the same time, however, elements in Turkish society have supported an Islamic revival and have argued that Turkey is basically a Middle Eastern Muslim society. In addition, while the elite of Turkey has defined Turkey as a Western society, the elite of the West refuses to accept Turkey as such. Turkey will not become a member of the European Community, and the real reason, as President Özal said, "is that we are Muslim and they are Christian and they don't say that." Having rejected Mecca, and then being rejected by Brussels, where does Turkey look? Tashkent may be the answer. The end of the Soviet Union gives Turkey the opportunity to become the leader of a revived Turkic civilization involving seven countries from the borders of Greece to those of China. Encouraged by the West, Turkey is making strenuous efforts to carve out this new identity for itself.

During the past decade, Mexico has assumed a position somewhat similar to that of Turkey. Just as Turkey abandoned its historic opposition to Europe and attempted to join Europe, Mexico has stopped defining itself by its opposition to the United States and is instead attempting to imitate the United States and to join it in the North American Free Trade Area. Mexican leaders are engaged in the great task of redefining Mexican identity and have introduced fundamental economic reforms that eventually will lead to fundamental political change. In 1991 a top adviser to President Carlos Salinas de Gortari described at length to me all the changes the Salinas government was making. When he finished, I remarked: "That's most impressive. It seems to me that basically you want to change Mexico from a Latin American country into a North American country." He looked at me with surprise and exclaimed: "Exactly! That's precisely what we are trying to do, but of course we could never say so publicly." As his remark indicates, in Mexico as in Turkey, significant elements in society resist the redefinition of their country's identity. In Turkey, European-oriented leaders have to make gestures to Islam (Özal's pilgrimage to Mecca); so also Mexico's North American–oriented leaders have to make gestures to those who hold Mexico to be a Latin American country (Salinas's Ibero-American Guadalajara summit).

Historically Turkey has been the most profoundly torn country. For the United States, Mexico is the most immediate torn country. Globally the most important torn country is Russia. The question of whether Russia is part of the West or the leader of a distinct Slavic-Orthodox civilization has been a recurring one in Russian history. That issue was obscured by the communist victory in Russia, which imported a Western ideology, adapted it to Russian conditions, and then challenged the West in the name of that ideology. The dominance of communism shut off the historic debate over Westernization versus Russification. With communism discredited Russians once again face that question.

President Yeltsin is adopting Western principles and goals and seeking to make Russia a "normal" country and a part of the West. Yet both the Russian elite and the Russian public are divided on this issue. Among the more moderate dissenters, Sergei Stankevich argues that Russia should reject the "Atlanticist" course, which would lead it "to become European, to become a part of the world economy in rapid and organized fashion, to become the eighth member of the Seven, and to put particular emphasis on Germany and the United States as the two dominant members of the Atlantic alliance." While also rejecting an exclusively Eurasian policy, Stankevich nonetheless argues that Russia should give priority to the protection of Russians in other countries, emphasize its Turkic and Muslim connections, and promote "an appreciable redistribution of our resources, our options, our ties, and our interests in favor of Asia, of the eastern direction." People of this persuasion criticize Yeltsin for subordinating Russia's interests to those of the West, for reducing Russian military strength, for failing to support traditional friends such as Serbia, and for pushing economic and political reform in ways injurious to the Russian people. Indicative of this trend is the new popularity of the ideas of Petr Savitsky, who in the 1920s argued that Russia was a unique Eurasian civilization.[7] More extreme dissidents voice much more blatantly nationalist, anti-Western, and anti-Semitic views and urge Russia to redevelop its military strength and to establish closer ties with China and Muslim countries. The people of Russia are as divided as the elite. An opinion survey in Euro-

---

[7] Sergei Stankevich, "Russia in Search of Itself," *The National Interest,* Summer 1992, pp. 47–51; Daniel Schneider, "A Russian Movement Rejects Western Tilt," *Christian Science Monitor,* Feb. 5, 1993, pp. 5–7.

pean Russia in the spring of 1992 revealed that 40 percent of the public had positive attitudes toward the West and 36 percent had negative attitudes. As it has been for much of its history, Russia in the early 1990s is truly a torn country.

To redefine its civilization identity, a torn country must meet three requirements. First, its political and economic elite has to be generally supportive of and enthusiastic about this move. Second, its public has to be willing to acquiesce in the redefinition. Third, the dominant groups in the recipient civilization have to be willing to embrace the convert. All three requirements in large part exist with respect to Mexico. The first two in large part exist with respect to Turkey. It is not clear that any of them exist with respect to Russia's joining the West. The conflict between liberal democracy and Marxism-Leninism was between ideologies which, despite their major differences, ostensibly shared ultimate goals of freedom, equality, and prosperity. A traditional, authoritarian, nationalist Russia could have quite different goals. A Western democrat could carry on an intellectual debate with a Soviet Marxist. It would be virtually impossible for him to do that with a Russian traditionalist. If, as the Russians stop behaving like Marxists, they reject liberal democracy and begin behaving like Russians but not like Westerners, the relations between Russia and the West could again become distant and conflictual.[8]

THE CONFUCIAN-ISLAMIC CONNECTION

THE OBSTACLES to non-Western countries joining the West vary considerably. They are least for Latin American and East European countries. They are greater for the Orthodox countries of the former Soviet Union. They are still greater for Muslim, Confucian, Hindu, and Buddhist societies. Japan has established a unique position for itself as an associate member of the West: it

---

[8]Owen Harries has pointed out that Australia is trying (unwisely in his view) to become a torn country in reverse. Although it has been a full member not only of the West but also of the ABCA military and intelligence core of the West, its current leaders are in effect proposing that it defect from the West, redefine itself as an Asian country and cultivate close ties with its neighbors. Australia's future, they argue, is with the dynamic economies of East Asia. But, as I have suggested, close economic cooperation normally requires a common cultural base. In addition, none of the three conditions necessary for a torn country to join another civilization is likely to exist in Australia's case.

is in the West in some respects but clearly not of the West in important dimensions. Those countries that for reason of culture and power do not wish to, or cannot, join the West compete with the West by developing their own economic, military, and political power. They do this by promoting their internal development and by cooperating with other non-Western countries. The most prominent form of this cooperation is the Confucian-Islamic connection that has emerged to challenge Western interests, values, and power.

Almost without exception, Western countries are reducing their military power; under Yeltsin's leadership so also is Russia. China, North Korea, and several Middle Eastern states, however, are significantly expanding their military capabilities. They are doing this by the import of arms from Western and non-Western sources and by the development of indigenous arms industries. One result is the emergence of what Charles Krauthammer has called "Weapon States," and the Weapon States are not Western states. Another result is the redefinition of arms control, which is a Western concept and a Western goal. During the Cold War the primary purpose of arms control was to establish a stable military balance between the United States and its allies and the Soviet Union and its allies. In the post–Cold War world, the primary objective of arms control is to prevent the development by non-Western societies of military capabilities that could threaten Western interests. The West attempts to do this through international agreements, economic pressure, and controls on the transfer of arms and weapons technologies.

The conflict between the West and the Confucian-Islamic states focuses largely, although not exclusively, on nuclear, chemical, and biological weapons, ballistic missiles and other sophisticated means for delivering them, and the guidance, intelligence, and other electronic capabilities for achieving that goal. The West promotes nonproliferation as a universal norm and nonproliferation treaties and inspections as means of realizing that norm. It also threatens a variety of sanctions against those who promote the spread of sophisticated weapons and proposes some benefits for those who do not. The attention of the West focuses, naturally, on nations that are actually or potentially hostile to the West.

The non-Western nations, on the other hand, assert their right to acquire and to deploy whatever weapons they think necessary for their security. They also have absorbed, to the full, the truth of the response of the Indian defense minister when asked what lesson he learned from the Gulf War: "Don't fight the United States unless you have nuclear weapons." Nuclear weapons, chemical weapons, and missiles are viewed, probably erroneously, as the potential equalizer of superior Western conventional power. China, of course, already has nuclear weapons; Pakistan and India have the capability to deploy them. North Korea, Iran, Iraq, Libya, and Algeria appear to be attempting to acquire them. A top Iranian official has declared that all Muslim states should acquire nuclear weapons, and in 1988 the president of Iran reportedly issued a directive calling for development of "offensive and defensive chemical, biological, and radiological weapons."

Centrally important to the development of counter-West military capabilities is the sustained expansion of China's military power and its means to create military power. Buoyed by spectacular economic development, China is rapidly increasing its military spending and vigorously moving forward with the modernization of its armed forces. It is purchasing weapons from the former Soviet states; it is developing long-range missiles; in 1992 it tested a one-megaton nuclear device. It is developing power-projection capabilities, acquiring aerial refueling technology, and trying to purchase an aircraft carrier. Its military buildup and assertion of sovereignty over the South China Sea are provoking a multilateral regional arms race in East Asia. China is also a major exporter of arms and weapons technology. It has exported materials to Libya and Iraq that could be used to manufacture nuclear weapons and nerve gas. It has helped Algeria build a reactor suitable for nuclear weapons research and production. China has sold to Iran nuclear technology that American officials believe could only be used to create weapons and apparently has shipped components of 300-mile-range missiles to Pakistan. North Korea has had a nuclear weapons program under way for some while and has sold advanced missiles and missile technology to Syria and Iran. The flow of weapons and weapons technology is generally from East Asia to the Middle East. There is, however, some movement in the reverse direction; China has received Stinger missiles from Pakistan.

A Confucian-Islamic military connection has thus come into being, designed to promote acquisition by its members of the weapons and weapons technologies needed to counter the military power of the West. It may or may not last. At present, however, it is, as Dave McCurdy has said, "a renegades' mutual support pact, run by the proliferators and their backers." A new form of arms competition is thus occurring between Islamic-Confucian states and the West. In an old-fashioned arms race, each side developed its own arms to balance or to achieve superiority against the other side. In this new form of arms competition, one side is developing its arms and the other side is attempting not to balance but to limit and prevent that arms buildup while at the same time reducing its own military capabilities.

IMPLICATIONS FOR THE WEST

THIS ARTICLE does not argue that civilization identities will replace all other identities, that nation states will disappear, that each civilization will become a single coherent political entity, that groups within a civilization will not conflict with and even fight each other. This paper does set forth the hypotheses that differences between civilizations are real and important; civilization-consciousness is increasing; conflict between civilizations will supplant ideological and other forms of conflict as the dominant global form of conflict; international relations, historically a game played out within Western civilization, will increasingly be de-Westernized and become a game in which non-Western civilizations are actors and not simply objects; successful political, security, and economic international institutions are more likely to develop within civilizations than across civilizations; conflicts between groups in different civilizations will be more frequent, more sustained, and more violent than conflicts between groups in the same civilization; violent conflicts between groups in different civilizations are the most likely and most dangerous source of escalation that could lead to global wars; the paramount axis of world politics will be the relations between "the West and the Rest"; the elites in some torn non-Western countries will try to make their countries part of the West but in most cases face major obstacles to accomplishing this; a central focus of conflict for the immediate future will be between the West and several Islamic-Confucian states.

This is not to advocate the desirability of conflicts between civilizations. It is to set forth descriptive hypotheses as to what the future may be like. If these are plausible hypotheses, however, it is necessary to consider their implications for Western policy. These implications should be divided between short-term advantage and long-term accommodation. In the short term it is clearly in the interest of the West to promote greater cooperation and unity within its own civilization, particularly between its European and North American components; to incorporate into the West societies in Eastern Europe and Latin America whose cultures are close to those of the West; to promote and maintain cooperative relations with Russia and Japan; to prevent escalation of local intercivilization conflicts into major intercivilization wars; to limit the expansion of the military strength of Confucian and Islamic states; to moderate the reduction of Western military capabilities and maintain military superiority in East and Southwest Asia; to exploit differences and conflicts among Confucian and Islamic states; to support in other civilizations groups sympathetic to Western values and interests; to strengthen international institutions that reflect and legitimate Western interests and values and to promote the involvement of non-Western states in those institutions.

In the longer term other measures would be called for. Western civilization is both Western and modern. Non-Western civilizations have attempted to become modern without becoming Western. To date only Japan has fully succeeded in this quest. Non-Western civilizations will continue to attempt to acquire the wealth, technology, skills, machines, and weapons that are part of being modern. They will also attempt to reconcile this modernity with their traditional culture and values. Their economic and military strength relative to the West will increase. Hence the West will increasingly have to accommodate these non-Western modern civilizations whose power approaches that of the West but whose values and interests differ significantly from those of the West. This will require the West to maintain the economic and military power necessary to protect its interests in relation to these civilizations. It will also, however, require the West to develop a more profound understanding of the basic religious and philosophical assumptions underlying other civilizations and the ways in which people in those civilizations see their interests. It will require an effort to identify elements of commonality between Western and other civilizations. For the relevant future, there will be no universal civilization, but instead a world of different civilizations, each of which will have to learn to coexist with the others.

The Last Ambassador

A Memoir of the Collapse of Yugoslavia

Warren Zimmermann

MARCH/APRIL 1995

IN EARLY 1989, shortly after I was confirmed as the new—and as it turned out the last—U.S. ambassador to Yugoslavia, I sought out Lawrence Eagleburger. Eagleburger had been named deputy secretary of state for the incoming Bush administration but had not yet been approved by the Senate. His temporary office was in the small back room adjoining the opulent deputy secretary's office, and there he could be found inhaling a cigarette, which, as an asthma sufferer, he was not supposed to have.

Larry Eagleburger remains one of the foremost American experts on the Balkans. Like an unusually large number of Foreign Service officers—myself included—he served twice in Yugoslavia. He and I shared a love of the country and its people. As we talked, we discovered a mutual view that the traditional American approach to Yugoslavia no longer made sense, given the revolutionary changes sweeping Europe.

By 1989 the world had changed dramatically. The Cold War was over and the Soviet Union was breaking up. The East European countries had already slipped Moscow's leash, and Poland and Hungary had achieved quasi-Western political systems, with Czechoslovakia soon to follow. In such circumstances, Eagleburger and I agreed that in my introductory calls in Belgrade and the republican capitals, I would deliver a new message: Yugoslavia no longer enjoyed the geopolitical importance that the United States had given it during the Cold War. Then, Marshal Josip Tito had made Yugoslavia a model for independence from the Soviet Union as well as for a brand of communism that was more open politically and less centralized economically.

Now Yugoslavia had been surpassed by both Poland and Hungary in economic and political openness. In addition, human rights had become a

[571]

major element of U.S. policy, and Yugoslavia's record on that issue was not good—particularly in the province of Kosovo, where an authoritarian Serbian regime was systematically depriving the Albanian majority of its basic civil liberties. Finally, I was to reassert the traditional mantra of U.S. support for Yugoslavia's unity, independence, and territorial integrity. But I would add that the United States could only support unity in the context of democracy; it would strongly oppose unity imposed or preserved by force.

Thus equipped, my wife and I arrived in Belgrade on March 9, 1989, after an absence of 21 years. The city had not changed much from the dusty half-Slav, half-Turkish town we remembered. Everybody still talked politics in the outdoor cafés, shaded by splendid chestnut trees. Belgrade was an acquired taste, and I had acquired it. What had changed was the character of the Serbian politics that people were busy discussing. Slobodan Milošević, an ambitious and ruthless Communist Party official, had clawed his way to power several years before. In early 1989, his efforts were focused on Kosovo.

Kosovo is to Serbs what Jerusalem is to Jews—a sacred ancestral homeland. In the postwar period, the Albanians in Kosovo—about 90 percent of the population—had carved out a dominant position in the province. Milošević was intent on wresting back that control, and he had no qualms about doing it unconstitutionally. Working through the intimidating powers of the communist apparatus, he took over or suspended Kosovo's governing bodies. He replaced bureaucratic and party incumbents with Serbs or pliant Albanians, one of whom, party chief Rahman Morina, sweated through his shirt during each of my meetings with him. Morina was later carried off prematurely by a heart attack brought on, no doubt, by stress.

On Kosovo, the message that Eagleburger and I had worked out was simple: if Yugoslavia wanted to continue its close relations with the United States, it would have to curb human rights abuses in the province. The point was naturally welcomed by the Albanians in Kosovo and also by Slovenia, an already democratic republic, which was proclaiming that Kosovo was the most egregious example of Milošević's dictatorial rule. Milošević, on the other hand, took my criticism personally; he later cited it as the reason he waited nearly a year before agreeing to meet me.

AN OBSESSION WITH HISTORY

MILOŠEVIĆ'S SERBIA was at the heart of the complex of issues that destroyed Yugoslavia. Serbs are a naturally talented and ebullient people with an instinctive liking for Americans that is based partly on a shared garrulity and partly on a military alliance spanning both world wars. Their tragic defect is an obsession with their own history; their hearts are in the past, not the future. In the Balkans, intellectuals tend to be the standard-bearers of nationalism; in Serbia, this is carried to fetishistic lengths.

A lugubrious, paranoid, and Serbocentric view of the past enables the Serbs to blame everyone but themselves for whatever goes wrong. They had a real grievance against Tito, in some measure justified, for creating a postwar Yugoslavia that denied them a role that they believed their large population (40 percent of the nation—similar to Russians in the old Soviet Union) and historical mission entitled them. When Tito died, leaving a Yugoslavia too decentralized for any ethnic group to dominate, it became inevitable that a Serbian nationalist would rise up to redress the perceived wrongs dealt his people. It was a tragedy for Serbia, its neighbors, and Europe as a whole that the nationalist turned out to be Slobodan Milošević.

After the year from the spring of 1989 to 1990 in which Milošević left me cooling my heels, I grew to know him well. We had many long conversations, all of them contentious but none of them shouting matches. "You see, Mr. Zimmermann," he would say, "only we Serbs really believe in Yugoslavia. We're not trying to secede like the Croats and Slovenes and we're not trying to create an Islamic state like the Muslims in Bosnia. They all fought against you in World War II. We were your allies." On Kosovo, Milošević painted a picture without shadings: "Kosovo has always been Serbian, except for a brief period during World War II. Yet we have given the Albanians their own government, their own parliament, their own national library, and their own schools [none of these assertions was true at the time he made them to me]. We have even given them their own academy of sciences. Have you Americans given your blacks their own academy of sciences?"

Milošević makes a stunning first impression on those who do not have the information to refute his often erroneous assertions. Many is the U.S. senator or congressman who has reeled out of his office exclaiming, "Why, he's not nearly as bad as I expected!" One congressman even invited him to a White House prayer breakfast. Milošević knows how to act with Americans. He dresses in the Western style (he spent considerable time in New York in his banking days), drinks Scotch on the rocks, and smokes Italian cigarillos. His cherubic cheeks do not fit the strongman image; in fact, he has to work hard at looking tough for his public posters. His manner is affable and displays his light side. Unfortunately, the man is almost totally dominated by his dark side.

Milošević began his career as a communist apparatchik of extremely authoritarian mien, even for Serbia. He rose to the leadership of the Serbian party by betraying the man who gave him his chance in politics, Ivan Stambolić, whose purge Milošević organized. Milošević is an opportunist, not an ideologue, a man driven by power rather than nationalism. He has made a Faustian pact with nationalism as a way to gain and hold power.

He is a man of extraordinary coldness. I never saw him moved by an individual case of human suffering; for him, people are groups (Serbs, Muslims) or simply abstractions. Nor did I ever hear him say a charitable or generous word about any human being, not even a Serb. This chilling personality trait made it possible for Milošević to condone, encourage, and even organize the unspeakable atrocities committed by Serbian citizens in the Bosnian war. It also accounts for his habitual mendacity, as in his outrageous distortion of Serbian behavior in Kosovo. For Milošević, truth has only a relative value. If it serves his objectives, it is employed; if not, it can be discarded.

When the unity of Yugoslavia was threatened in the late 1980s by Slovenia—Yugoslavia's only Serbless republic—Milošević cast himself as the apostle of unity. Not interested in unity per se, he wanted a unity that Serbia could dominate, working through the Yugoslav People's Army, whose officer corps was over 50 percent Serbian. Milošević's concept of unity did not extend to democracy or power sharing with other national groups.

In fact, in his verbal attacks on Slovenia and Croatia and his subsequent trade sanctions against them, he became the major wrecker of Yugoslavia. When the Slovenian and Croatian independence movements, together with Milošević's own disruptive actions in the name of unity, made the preservation of Yugoslavia impossible, he fell back on an even more aggressive approach. If Yugoslavia could not encompass all Serbs, then Serbia would. The Serbian populations of Croatia, Bosnia, Montenegro, and possibly Macedonia would be incorporated—along with generous pieces of territory—into a Milošević-dominated "Yugoslavia." His rallying cry was that all Serbs have the right to live in a single state—a doctrine that, if applied globally, would cause the disintegration of dozens of multinational states.

WORST-CASE SCENARIOS

FROM THE beginning of my ambassadorship in Yugoslavia, I pressed the talented and highly professional group of political and economic officers in the U.S. embassy in Belgrade and the consulate general in Zagreb, Croatia, to consider worst-case scenarios for Yugoslavia. The worst case we could think of was the breakup of the country. We reported to Washington that no breakup of Yugoslavia could happen peacefully. The ethnic hatred sown by Milošević and his ilk and the mixture of ethnic groups in every republic except Slovenia meant that Yugoslavia's shattering would lead to extreme violence, perhaps even war. . . .

In January 1990, the Communist Party created by Tito breathed its last; a party congress split by quarreling was adjourned, never to meet again. Yugoslavia lurched into its first democratic elections. The two most anti-Yugoslav republics, Slovenia and Croatia, were the first to vote. By the end of the year, the four southern republics had voted as well. Even the Serbian government held elections, despite Milošević's occasional assertions to me that Serbia's needs were much better met by a one-party system.

The republican elections turned out to be a disaster for those who hoped to keep Yugoslavia together in a democratic framework. People had no opportunity to vote on a Yugoslavia-wide level once Prime Minister Marković failed to win approval for federal elections. They vented their pent-up frustrations by voting for nationalists who hammered on ethnic themes. The elections became a test of ethnic loyalty. Ethnic parties won power in five of the six republics, all but Macedonia.

NATIONALISM UNLEASHED

BY BRINGING nationalism to power almost everywhere, the elections helped snuff out the very flame of democracy that they had kindled. Nationalism is by nature uncivil, antidemocratic, and separatist because it empowers one ethnic group over all others. If the elections weakened the democratic element so necessary for Yugoslavia, they also weakened the necessary unifying element. I visited all six republics to evaluate the new leaders. I found that not only was the country breaking up into different power centers, but each local region was developing a nationalist ideology, each different from the other. The age of naked nationalism had begun.

Slovenian nationalists, now in power, quickly broke almost all Slovenia's remaining political and economic ties with the Yugoslav government. The Slovenes' separatist nationalism was unique in Yugoslavia—it had no victims and no enemies; while the Slovenes hated Milošević, they built no ideology against him. They practiced a "Garbo nationalism"—they just wanted to be left alone. Their virtue was democracy and their vice was selfishness. In their drive to separate from Yugoslavia, they simply ignored the 22 million Yugoslavs who were not Slovenes. They bear considerable responsibility for the bloodbath that followed their secession.

No Yugoslav republic was more transformed by the elections of 1990 than Croatia. The decisive victory of the Croatian Democratic Union in May brought to the presidency an implacable nationalist, Franjo Tudjman. I first met Tudjman in Zagreb on the morning of his victory; before then I had avoided him because of the extreme nature of some of his campaign statements. If Milošević recalls a slick con man, Tudjman resembles an inflexible schoolteacher. He is a former general and communist, expelled from the party under Tito and twice jailed for nationalism. Prim steel eyeglasses hang on a square face whose natural expression is a scowl. His mouth occasionally creases into a nervous chuckle or mirthless laugh. In our first meeting, he treated the colleagues who accompanied him with extreme disdain. Then, on the spot, he appointed two of them to high-ranking positions—to their surprise, since the venue for this solemn act was the breakfast table of the American consul general.

Tudjman's temper flared when I asked him about his remark during the campaign that he was glad his wife was neither a Serb nor a Jew. He launched into a ten-minute defense of his ethnic humanity, claiming, among other things, that some of his best friends were Serbs. While he didn't profess similar affinities with Jews (and his earlier writings had denigrated the Holocaust), he did promise to make restitution to the Zagreb Jewish community for the destruction of its synagogue by Croatian fascists during World War II. He kept that promise.

Unlike Milošević, who is driven by power, Tudjman is obsessed by nationalism. His devotion to Croatia is of the most narrow-minded sort, and he has never shown much understanding of or interest in democratic values. He presided over serious violations of the rights of Serbs, who made up 12 percent of the population of Croatia. They were dismissed from work, required to take loyalty oaths, and subjected to attacks on their homes and property. I have sat at Tudjman's lunch table and listened to several of his ministers revile Serbs in the most racist terms. He didn't join in, but he didn't stop them either. He has also stifled the independence of the press as much as Milošević, and maybe even more.

Tudjman's saving grace, which distinguishes him from Milošević, is that he really wants to be a Western statesman. He therefore listens to Western expressions of concern and criticism and often does something about them. For better or worse, Croatian nationalism is defined by Tudjman—intolerant, anti-Serb, and authoritarian. These attributes—together with an aura of wartime fascism, which Tudjman has done nothing to dispel—help explain why many Serbs in Croatia reject Croatian rule and why the core hostility in the former Yugoslavia is still between Serbs and Croats.

During 1990, Serbian nationalism under Milošević became even more aggressive. No longer was it enough for Serbs living outside Serbia to have their rights protected. They also had to own and control the territory they inhabited, regardless of prior sovereignty. These Serbian claims had no consistent principles behind them. Where Serbs were a minority, as in Kosovo, they asserted a historical, rather than a numerical, right to rule. Where no such historical right was plausible, as in the Krajina area of Croatia, they claimed self-determination on the majority principle. Revealingly, Milošević was unwilling to give the Albanians in Kosovo the same right of self-determination that he demanded for Serbs in Croatia and Bosnia. . . .

ELEVENTH-HOUR MANEUVERS

THE LAST YEAR of Yugoslavia's existence—1991—saw the unfolding of unilateral and conflicting nationalist strategies. Slovenia, where a December 1990 referendum showed overwhelming popular support for independence, announced its decision to secede in June 1991 if a loose confederal solution was not found. Wittingly making his republic a hostage to Slovenian policy, Tudjman said Croatia would do what Slovenia did. Milošević countered that the breakup of Yugoslavia would lead to Serbia's incorporating all Serbs into a single state. Bosnian leader Alija Izetbegović argued that the survival of Yugoslavia in some form was essential to Bosnia's survival as well.

Izetbegović was mild-mannered, deferential, and perpetually anxious; he wore the mantle of leadership with great discomfort. A devout Muslim but no extremist, he consistently advocated the preservation of a multinational Bosnia. Ironically, it was Milošević and Tudjman, in their professed desire for Bosnian Serbs and Bosnian Croats to live apart from Muslims, who laid the philosophical groundwork for a separate Muslim entity. Bosnia had a strong multiethnic character and the highest percentage of ethnically mixed marriages of any republic. While its history since the fifteenth-century Turkish occupation was no more bloody than the history of England or France, Bosnia was the major Balkan killing ground during World War II. Izetbegović was succinct with me: "If Croatia goes independent, Bosnia will be destroyed."

In early 1991, the supporters of a unified and democratic Yugoslavia were becoming marginalized. The leaders of the two republics with the most to lose from the breakup of Yugoslavia—Alija Izetbegović of Bosnia and Kiro Gligorov of Macedonia—proposed to hold it together in an even weaker configuration. Milošević gave their plan lip service; the Croats and Slovenes rejected it flatly for leaving too many powers with the central government.

During this period the Yugoslav People's Army (JNA in its Serbo-Croatian acronym) emerged as a major political player, an unusual role for a communist army. I met regularly with the defense minister, General Veljko Kadijević, a brooding, humorless officer who spoke with antipathy about Slovenes and Croats and with paranoia about Germans, whom he saw as bent on incorporating the Balkans into a Fourth Reich. The JNA enjoyed a proud tradition, with roots in Tito's Partisan fighters, who stood up to the

Germans in World War II. The fifth-largest army in Europe, well supplied by the Soviet Union and an enormous domestic arms industry, it was seen by many as the most important unifying institution in Yugoslavia. Its officer corps, however, had a Serbian majority who, when events forced them to choose, followed Milošević.

The JNA was soon on a collision course with the breakaway republics. Both Croatia and Slovenia were trying to create their own military forces by calling on their young men to desert the JNA and by weakening the JNA's control over the republican Territorial Defense Forces, a sort of national guard. The JNA went berserk over this proliferation of armies. "How many armies does the United States have?" Kadijević stormed at me. In early 1991, the JNA tried to force the Yugoslav presidency—a comically weak, collective, eight-person chief of state—to declare a national emergency and authorize the army to disarm the Slovenian and Croatian militaries. This bid, which amounted to a military coup, was frustrated politically by the democratically inclined presidency members from Macedonia and Slovenia, Vasil Tupurkovski and Janez Drnovšek. The defeat led Milošević to use the four votes he controlled in the eight-member presidency to subvert the scheduled rotation of its "president" from a Serb to a Croat. I asked Milošević several days before the May 15 election by the presidency if he would block the accession of the Croat Stipe Mesić, even though it was called for by constitutional precedent. "Serbia will always act in the spirit of the highest democratic principles," replied Milošević, who was always at his most mellifluous when expatiating on his devotion to democracy. "There will be a democratic vote in the presidency."

"But are you going to accept a fair transition from a Serb to a Croat president?" I pursued. "Mr. Zimmermann," he said, "you can tell your government that it has absolutely nothing to worry about." I cabled Washington that Mesić was not a sure thing. Two days later Milošević's allies on the presidency blocked Mesić's ascension, throwing Yugoslavia into a constitutional crisis. When I accused Milošević later of lying to me, he asserted that he had not actually promised that Mesić would be named. The incident illustrated three important traits of Milošević's character: his cynicism about Yugoslavia's unity and institutions, his natural mendacity, and the pains he always took to avoid direct responsibility for aggressive actions. The third trait was to become particularly relevant to Milošević's hidden hand in the Bosnia crisis.

ENTER BAKER

IT WAS IN the context of Milošević's move against the Yugoslav presidency and its Croatian president-designate, Croatian actions against the jobs and property of Serbs in Croatia, growing violence between Serbs and Croats, and the threat by both Slovenia and Croatia to withdraw from Yugoslavia at midyear that Secretary of State James Baker arrived in Belgrade on June 21, 1991. . . .

To Milošević and (indirectly) the army, Baker made clear that the United States strongly opposed any use of force, intimidation, or incitement to violence that would block democratic change. Yugoslavia could not be held together at gunpoint. In his encounter with Milošević—the most contentious of the nine meetings—Baker hammered the Serb leader on his human rights violations in Kosovo, urged his acquiescence to a looser constitutional arrangement for Yugoslavia, and pressed him to stop destabilizing the Yugoslav presidency.

Never was a green light given or implied to Milošević or the army to invade the seceding republics, as has since been alleged in some press accounts. But was there a red light? Not as such, because the United States had given no consideration to using force to stop a Serbian/JNA attack on Slovenia or Croatia. Nor, at that point, had a single member of Congress, as far as I know, advocated the introduction of American military power. Baker did, however, leave a strong political message. He said to Prime Minister Marković, a conduit to the army, "If you force the United States to choose between unity and democracy, we will always choose democracy."

Baker's message was the right one, but it came too late. If a mistake was made, it was that the secretary of state had not come six months earlier, a time that unfortunately coincided with the massive American preparations for the Persian Gulf War. By June 1991, Baker was making a last-ditch effort. Even so, it is not clear that an earlier visit by Baker would have made a difference. The aggressive nationalism emanating like noxious fumes from the leaders of Serbia and Croatia and their even more extreme advisers, officials, media manipulators, and allies had cast the die for disintegration and violence.

The breakup of Yugoslavia is a classic example of nationalism from the top down—a manipulated nationalism in a region where peace has historically prevailed more than war and in which a quarter of the population were in mixed marriages. The manipulators condoned and even provoked local ethnic violence in order to engender animosities that could then be magnified by the press, leading to further violence. Milošević gave prime television time to fanatic nationalists like Vojislav Šešelj, who once said that the way to deal with the Kosovo Albanians was to kill them all. Tudjman also used his control of the media to sow hate. Nationalist "intellectuals," wrapped in the mantle of august academies of sciences, expounded their pseudohistory of the victimization of Serbs (or Croats) through the ages. One of them seriously asserted to me that Serbs had committed no crimes or moral transgressions at any point in their long history. Worst of all, the media, under the thumb of most republican regimes, spewed an endless daily torrent of violence and enmity. As a reporter for *Vreme*, one of the few independent magazines left in the former Yugoslavia, said, "You Americans would become nationalists and racists too if your media were totally in the hands of the Ku Klux Klan."

SECESSION AND WAR

IN LATE JUNE 1991, just a few days after Baker's departure from Belgrade and almost exactly according to their timetable, Croatia and Slovenia declared independence. Fighting began in Slovenia almost immediately. Contrary to the general view, it was the Slovenes who started the war. Their independence declaration, which had not been preceded by even the most token effort to negotiate, effectively put under their control all the border and customs posts between Slovenia and its two neighbors, Italy and Austria. This meant that Slovenia, the only international gateway between the West and Yugoslavia, had unilaterally appropriated the right to goods destined for other republics, as well as customs revenues estimated at some 75 percent of the Yugoslav federal budget. Even an army less primitive than the JNA would have reacted. Worst of all, the Slovenes' understandable desire to be independent condemned the rest of Yugoslavia to war.

The Yugoslav generals, thinking they could intimidate the Slovenes, roared their tanks through peaceful Slovenian streets, slapping aside compact cars as they lumbered through. The Slovenes, trained by the JNA itself in territorial defense, fought back. After ten days, at Milošević's direction or with his acquiescence, the JNA withdrew from Slovenia, leaving the republic effectively independent. Compared to the Croatian and Bosnian wars that followed, the casualty figures in Slovenia seem ludicrously small: 37 JNA and 12 Slovenes killed. They do not bear out the generally held assumption that the Yugoslav army waged an extermination campaign in Slovenia. In provoking war, the Slovenes won the support of the world's television viewers and consolidated their entire population behind independence. Unlike the JNA, they welcomed foreign journalists, to whom they retailed the epic struggle of their tiny republic against the Yugoslav colossus. It was the most brilliant public relations coup in the history of Yugoslavia.

It was no surprise to me that Milošević was willing to let Slovenia go. His policy since 1989 provoked the Slovenes to secede by making it clear that he would not tolerate their liberal, independent ways. With Slovenia out of the game, he and the JNA were now free to take on a Croatia no longer able to count on Slovenia's support.

The fighting in Croatia began with the illusion of evenhandedness. The Yugoslav army would step in to separate the Serbian and Croatian combatants. During the summer of 1991, however, it soon became clear that the JNA, while claiming neutrality, was in fact turning territory over to Serbs. The war in Croatia had become a war of aggression. . . .

The pretty Croatian city of Vukovar, with a mixed population, of which over a third was Serb, first came under JNA shelling in August, apparently because of its location on the Danube River between Serbia and Croatia. For three months the army, shrinking from an attack that might have cost it casualties, sat outside the city and shelled it to pieces. The civilian population of the city—Serbs and Croats alike—huddled in cellars. Over 2,000 civilians were killed before the JNA finally "liberated" the city.

One of the employees in our embassy residence, a young Croatian woman named Danijela Hajnal, was from Vukovar; her mother was trapped in a cellar during the siege. During her stay with my wife and me after Vukovar fell, Danijela's mother described the relations between Serbs and Croats during the attack: "There were a hundred people in that cellar," she said, "half of us Croats and half Serbs. We were friends when we went into the cellar, and three months later when we came out, we were still friends." About the same time I asked Danijela how many Serbs and Croats were in her high school class in Vukovar. She replied that she didn't have the faintest idea. These vignettes, which could be multiplied thousands of times over, show how natural it was for Yugoslavs to get along with each other, despite the ranting of their leaders.

Notwithstanding solemn guarantees by General Kadijević, the JNA in October 1991 also shelled Dubrovnik from the hills and the sea. This medieval town, which glowed in the Adriatic like a piece of pink marble, had withstood the depredations of Turks, Venetians, and many other would-be conquerors. Now it was falling under the guns of an army whose constitutional duty was to defend it. Dubrovnik was not destroyed, but the damage inflicted by the Yugoslav army exceeded the best efforts of any previous marauder. Only Milošević pretended that there was any military objective in Dubrovnik. Denying, as usual, any personal responsibility for what the army did, he told me with a straight face that there were foreign mercenaries hiding in the city. Kadijević didn't even pretend that Dubrovnik was a military target. "I give you my word," he told me, "that the shelling of Dubrovnik was unauthorized. Those who did it will be punished." My repeated requests for the details of their punishment went unanswered.

Shelling civilian populations is a war crime. Vukovar and Dubrovnik led directly to the merciless attacks on Sarajevo and other Bosnian cities. Yet no Western government at the time called on NATO's military force to get the

JNA to stop shelling Dubrovnik, although NATO's supreme commander, General John Galvin, had prepared contingency plans for doing so. The use of force was simply too big a step to consider in late 1991. I did not recommend it myself—a major mistake. The JNA's artillery on the hills surrounding Dubrovnik and its small craft on the water would have been easy targets. Not only would damage to the city have been averted, but the Serbs would have been taught a lesson about Western resolve that might have deterred at least some of their aggression against Bosnia. As it was, the Serbs learned another lesson—that there was no Western resolve, and that they could push about as far as their power could take them.

A TAR BABY IN WASHINGTON

SECRETARY OF STATE BAKER'S failure to head off the Slovenian and Croatian declarations of independence cooled whatever ardor he may have had for projecting the United States into the Yugoslav imbroglio. During the summer of 1991, it had been fair enough to give the EC a chance to deal with what it called a "European problem." But by autumn, the Serbian/JNA plan for taking over parts of Croatia had crystallized in the attacks on Vukovar and Dubrovnik. Threats to the integrity of Bosnia were growing, and the EC, under German cajoling, was stumbling toward recognition of the breakaway republics. Even without threatening force, the United States could have thrown more weight behind the effort to prevent greater violence. However, between July 1991 and March 1992, the United States was not a major factor in the Yugoslav crisis. In the fall of 1991, at a U.S. ambassadors' meeting in Berlin, a friend from the State Department's European Bureau told me that Yugoslavia had become a tar baby in Washington. Nobody wanted to touch it. With the American presidential election just a year away, it was seen as a loser.

Unfortunately, American immobility coincided with growing pressure on Bosnia. Neither Milošević nor Tudjman made any effort to conceal their designs on Bosnia from me. As a place where Serbs, Croats, and Muslims had coexisted more or less peacefully for centuries, Bosnia was an affront and a challenge to these two ethnic supremacists.

At the end of a long meeting with me, Tudjman erupted into a diatribe against Izetbegović and the Muslims of Bosnia. "They're dangerous fundamentalists," he charged, "and they're using Bosnia as a beachhead to spread their ideology throughout Europe and even to the United States. The civilized nations should join together to repel this threat. Bosnia has never had any real existence. It should be divided between Serbia and Croatia.". . .

Milošević's strategy for Bosnia, unlike Tudjman's, was calculating rather than emotional. When Slovenia and Croatia declared independence and stopped participating in the Yugoslav government, Milošević, notwithstanding all he had done to destroy Yugoslavia, now claimed to be its heir. He contended that all those who wanted to "remain" in Yugoslavia should have the right to do so. This included, of course, the Serbs of Croatia and the Serbs of Bosnia. As Milošević explained this to me, he added that while the Muslims in Bosnia tended to live in cities, the Serbs were a rural people living on 70 percent of the land, to which they therefore had a right. Thus, at least six months before the Bosnian Serb army and the irregulars from Serbia shattered the peace in Bosnia, Milošević was laying the groundwork for a Serbian claim. . . .

FATAL RECOGNITION

WHEN CROATIA opted for independence in mid–1991, Bosnian President Izetbegović saw the writing on the wall for his republic. He scurried throughout Europe and the United States looking for ways to head off disaster. He pushed, without success, the dying Izetbegović-Gligorov plan for a loosely connected Yugoslavia. He asked for and got EC observers in Bosnia. He asked for, but did not get, U.N. peacekeepers there. Vance and the U.N. leadership in New York took the traditional if puzzling line that peacekeepers are used after a conflict, not before. The U.S. government did not support Izetbegović on the request for peacekeepers either. In a cable to Washington, I urged this innovative step, but did not press for it as hard as I should have. As an unsatisfactory compromise, when the U.N. peacekeepers arrived in Croatia in March 1992, they set up their headquarters in Sarajevo.

In the fall of 1991, German Foreign Minister Hans-Dietrich Genscher pressed his EC colleagues to recognize Slovenia and Croatia and to offer recognition to Bosnia and Macedonia. Izetbegović, briefed by the German ambassador to Yugoslavia on how to make his point with Genscher that EC recognition would bring violence to Bosnia, unaccountably failed to do so in his November meeting with the German foreign minister. The omission can only have led Genscher to assume that he had a green light from Izetbegović for recognition.

I was urging Washington to defer recognition, as the EC ambassadors in Belgrade were urging their governments. Although Washington was opposed to premature recognition, U.S. appeals to EC governments were perfunctory. On December 17, 1991, an EC summit decided to grant recognition. Carrington and Vance both complained loudly and publicly. The State Department's statement, to avoid ruffling the EC, was nuanced. War in Bosnia, which had until then been probable, now became virtually inevitable.

A few days after the EC's decision, I had lunch in Belgrade with Izetbegović's deputy, Ejup Ganić, a Muslim hard-liner who had trained at MIT. I asked him, "Is Bosnia really going to ask for recognition in the face of all the dangers Izetbegović has repeatedly warned about? Wouldn't it be better to tell the European Community that you need more time to work out the political issues involved?" Ganić looked at me as if I had just dropped out of the sky. He said, "Of course we're going to move ahead on recognition. With Croatia and Slovenia now gone, we can't consign Bosnia to a truncated Yugoslavia controlled by Serbia."

I concluded from the abrupt change of tack by Ganić that Izetbegović was now playing a double game. With the European Community heading toward recognition, he thought he could get away with it under the guns of the Serbs. Perhaps he counted on Western military support, though nobody had promised him that. Whatever his motives, it was a disastrous political mistake. Serbia, Bosnia's vastly more powerful neighbor, now had the pretext it needed to strike—the claim that 1.3 million Serbs were being taken out of "Yugoslavia" against their will. I believe that Milošević and Bosnian Serb leader Radovan Karadžić had already decided to annex the majority of Bosnia by military force (Milošević had spoken to me of 70 percent). The EC's irresponsibility, the United States' passivity, and Izetbegović's miscalculation made their job easier. . . .

PARTNERS IN CRIME

DURING THE first few months of 1992, events in Bosnia careened down two parallel tracks. On one, the Izetbegović government, following the EC lead, prepared for independence. Its referendum on February 29 and March 1 produced predictable results. Practically all the Muslims and Croats voted for independence, yielding a 64 percent majority, while practically all the Serbs boycotted the election. On the other track, the leaders of the Serbian minority prepared for secession and war. Since the 1990 Bosnian election, I had paid periodic visits to Karadžić. The Bosnian Serb leader is a large man with flamboyant hair, an outwardly friendly manner, and the unlikely profession of psychiatry. In the great tradition of nationalists who do not come from their nation (Hitler, Napoleon, Stalin), Karadžić is from Montenegro, not Bosnia. I learned from experience that his outstanding characteristics were his stubbornness and deep-seated hostility to Muslims, Croats, and any other non-Serb ethnic group in his neighborhood.

I was startled to hear the extravagance of Karadžić's claims on behalf of the Serbs. He told me that "Serbs have a right to territory not only where they're now living but also where they're buried, since the earth they lie in was taken unjustly from them." When I asked whether he would accept parallel claims on behalf of Croats or Muslims, he answered, "No, because Croats are fascists and Muslims are Islamic fanatics." His disdain for the truth was absolute; he insisted that "Sarajevo is a Serbian city," which it has never been. His apartheid philosophy was as extreme as anything concocted in South Africa. He was the architect of massacres in the Muslim villages, ethnic cleansing, and artillery attacks on civilian populations. In his fanaticism, ruthlessness, and contempt for human values, he invites comparison with a monster from another generation, Heinrich Himmler.

Karadžić and Milošević both made an elaborate pretense to me of not knowing each other very well and having no operational contacts. Milošević always reacted with cherubic innocence when I accosted him over Bosnia. "But why do you come to me, Mr. Zimmermann? Serbia has nothing to do with Bosnia. It's not our problem." This fiction suited each leader—Milošević to escape responsibility for aggression, Karadžić to avoid the charge that he was a henchman of Milošević's rather than a Serbian folk hero in his own right.

There is no doubt, however, that the two were partners in war crimes. Copying Milošević's strategy in Croatia, Karadžić's followers—beginning a year before the Bosnian war broke out—declared three "Serb Autonomous Regions" in Bosnia, began an arms supply relationship with the JNA, and accepted JNA intervention in September to define their borders. They established artillery positions around Sarajevo and other towns, created a "Bosnian Serb" army (effectively a branch of the JNA, commanded by a JNA general and using JNA-supplied heavy artillery, tanks, and air power), established their own parliament, and attempted a putsch in Sarajevo on March 2, 1992. In March 1992—before any country had recognized the independence of Bosnia—they declared a "Serbian Republic." These steps, particularly those involving the JNA, would not have been possible without Milošević's direct involvement.

In response to the evidence of Serbian collusion and the results of the Bosnian referendum, and in hopes that recognition might deter a Serbian attack, the United States and other NATO countries recognized Bosnia in early April 1992. However, a few days before, Serbs had launched an attack from Serbia across the Drina River, which forms the border between Serbia and Bosnia. Milošević, Karadžić, and their spokesmen have asserted that the Western recognition of Bosnia had forced the Serbs to move. I doubt this. The two Serbian leaders already had a joint strategy for dividing Bosnia and they were going to carry it out, regardless of what the rest of the world did.

The attack on Bosnia showed that Milošević and Karadžić are apostles of the most aggressive form of nationalism. Milošević-style nationalism has proven singularly resistant to economic inducements, penalties, or any other pressures short of force. Unfortunately, neither the Bush nor the Clinton administration was willing to step up to the challenge of using force in Bosnia, despite significant American interests in the Balkans. Moreover, the two Serbian strongmen, behind their propaganda, espouse the doctrine of the single nation-state, a deeply uncivilized concept. Nation-states have nothing to unify them but their nationalism, and power within them will naturally gravitate to the most strident nationalists. Multinational states, a majority in the world, can be deeply conflicted, as Yugoslavia proves. But they can also be schools of tolerance, since the need to take account of minority interests moderates behavior. Yugoslavia had its democrats as well as its demagogues. The attackers across the Drina, however, were barbarians, pure and simple.

The Serbian attack was directed at towns with large Muslim majorities. Gangsters from Serbia proper, including the notorious Arkan, who had left a trail of murder and pillage during the Croatian war, were displayed on Belgrade television swaggering on the debris of Bijeljina and other Muslim towns. Those Serbia-based marauders accounted for the high volume of atrocities committed in the early days of the war—the gang rapes, ethnic cleansing, and wanton murder of Muslim villagers. The presence in Bosnia of irregulars from Serbia drained all credibility from Milošević's assertion that Serbia had nothing to do with what was going on there.

During one of the meetings in which, on Washington's instructions, I accused Milošević of aggression in Bosnia, he asserted, "There isn't a single Serb from Serbia involved in the fighting in Bosnia."

"But," I said, "I saw Arkan on your own Belgrade television boasting about his capture of Bosnian villages."

"Our television is free to broadcast whatever it wants," said Milošević. "You shouldn't take it so seriously. Besides, you needn't worry about trouble in Bosnia. Serbs have no serious grievances in Bosnia; they're not being abused there. This is a big difference with Serbs in Croatia." Via this backhanded compliment to the Izetbegović government, Milošević reduced the Serbian argument for naked aggression to the assumption that Serbs had a right to murder, torture, and expel simply because they did not want to live under an independent multiethnic government that was not abusing them.

LAST WORDS

JUST A FEW weeks before I was recalled in protest against the Serbian aggression in Bosnia, I had my last talk with Karadžić in Belgrade, where he was pretending not to see Milošević. He came to the U.S. embassy, bringing with him as usual his deputy and pilot fish, Nikola Koljević, a Bosnian Serb who had taught in the United States and was an expert on Shakespeare. Koljević's specialty was sidling up to me after my meetings with Karadžić and portraying himself as the humane influence on Bosnian Serb policy. Several months after my departure from Belgrade, I saw a photograph of Koljević directing artillery fire on the civilian population of Sarajevo from a hill above the city.

Perhaps it was fitting that I should have one of my last meetings in doomed Yugoslavia with this macabre pair, the professor of English literature and the psychiatrist. At least Shakespeare and Freud would have understood the power of the irrational that provoked these and other madmen to destroy the human fabric of Yugoslavia.

Karadžić began the conversation by running down his usual litany of criticisms of the Europeans, attacks on Izetbegović's character and ideology, and laments that the United States should be so blind as to abandon its traditional Serbian allies. He then launched into a stream-of-consciousness justification for everything he was doing. "You have to understand Serbs, Mr. Zimmermann. They have been betrayed for centuries. Today they cannot live with other nations. They must have their own separate existence. They are a warrior race and they can trust only themselves to take by force what is their due. But this doesn't mean that Serbs can hate. Serbs are incapable of hatred."

I sought to pin him down. "What sort of Bosnian Serb republic do you have in mind?" I asked. "Will it be a part of Serbia?"

"That will be for the Bosnian Serb people to decide," he said. "But our first goal is independence, so we can live separately from others."

"Where will your capital be?" I asked.

"Why, Sarajevo, of course."

"But how can a city which is nearly 50 percent Muslim and only 30 percent Serb be the capital for the Serbs alone?"

Karadžić had a ready answer. "The city will be divided into Muslim, Serbian, and Croatian sections, so that no ethnic groups will have to live or work together."

"Just how will it be divided?"

"By walls," he said matter-of-factly. "Of course people will be able to pass from one part of the city to another, as long as they have permission and go through the checkpoints."

I thought of Sarajevo, which for centuries had been a moving symbol of the civility that comes from people of different ethnicities living in harmony. Then I thought of Berlin, where the wall, which had symbolized all the hatreds and divisions of the Cold War, had been torn down just over a year before.

"Do you mean," I asked, "that Sarajevo will be like Berlin before the wall was destroyed?"

"Yes," he answered, "our vision of Sarajevo is like Berlin when the wall was still standing."

Competitiveness:
A Dangerous Obsession

Paul Krugman

MARCH/APRIL 1994

THE HYPOTHESIS IS WRONG

IN JUNE 1993, Jacques Delors made a special presentation to the leaders of the nations of the European Community, meeting in Copenhagen, on the growing problem of European unemployment. Economists who study the European situation were curious to see what Delors, president of the EC Commission, would say. Most of them share more or less the same diagnosis of the European problem: the taxes and regulations imposed by Europe's elaborate welfare states have made employers reluctant to create new jobs, while the relatively generous level of unemployment benefits has made workers unwilling to accept the kinds of low-wage jobs that help keep unemployment comparatively low in the United States. The monetary difficulties associated with preserving the European Monetary System in the face of the costs of German reunification have reinforced this structural problem.

It is a persuasive diagnosis, but a politically explosive one, and everyone wanted to see how Delors would handle it. Would he dare tell European leaders that their efforts to pursue economic justice have produced unemployment as an unintended by-product? Would he admit that the EMS could be sustained only at the cost of a recession and face the implications of that admission for European monetary union?

Guess what? Delors didn't confront the problems of either the welfare state or the EMS. He explained that the root cause of European unemployment was a lack of competitiveness with the United States and Japan and that the solution was a program of investment in infrastructure and high technology.

It was a disappointing evasion, but not a surprising one. After all, the rhetoric of competitiveness—the view that, in the words of President Clinton, each nation is "like a big corporation competing in the global marketplace"—has become pervasive among opinion leaders throughout the world. People who believe themselves to be sophisticated about the subject take it for granted that the economic problem facing any modern nation is essentially one of competing on world markets—that the United States and Japan are competitors in the same sense that Coca-Cola competes with Pepsi—and are unaware that anyone might seriously question that proposition. Every few months a new best-seller warns the American public of the dire consequences of losing the "race" for the twenty-first century.[1] A whole industry of councils on competitiveness, "geo-economists," and managed trade theorists has sprung up in Washington. Many of these people, having diagnosed America's economic problems in much the same terms as Delors did Europe's, are now in the highest reaches of the Clinton administration formulating economic and trade policy for the United States. So Delors was using a language that was not only convenient but comfortable for him and a wide audience on both sides of the Atlantic.

---

[1] See, for just a few examples, Laura D'Andrea Tyson, *Who's Bashing Whom: Trade Conflict in High-Technology Industries*, Washington: Institute for International Economics, 1992; Lester C. Thurow, *Head to Head: The Coming Economic Battle among Japan, Europe, and America*, New York: Morrow, 1992; Ira C. Magaziner and Robert B. Reich, *Minding America's Business: The Decline and Rise of the American Economy*, New York: Vintage Books, 1983; Ira C. Magaziner and Mark Patinkin, *The Silent War: Inside the Global Business Battles Shaping America's Future*, New York: Vintage Books, 1990; Edward N. Luttwak, *The Endangered American Dream: How to Stop the United States from Becoming a Third World Country and How to Win the Geo-economic Struggle for Industrial Supremacy*, New York: Simon & Schuster, 1993; Kevin P. Phillips, *Staying on Top: The Business Case for a National Industrial Strategy*, New York: Random House, 1984; Clyde V. Prestowitz, Jr., *Trading Places: How We Allowed Japan to Tale the Lead*, New York: Basic Books, 1988; William S. Dietrich, *In the Shadow of the Rising Sun: The Political Roots of American Economic Decline*, University Park: Pennsylvania State University Press, 1992; Jeffrey E. Garten, *A Cold Peace: America, Japan, Germany, and the Struggle for Supremacy*, New York: Times Books, 1992; and Wayne Sandholtz et al., *The Highest Stakes: The Economic Foundations of the Next Security System*, Berkeley Roundtable on the International Economy (BRIE), Oxford University Press, 1992.

Unfortunately, his diagnosis was deeply misleading as a guide to what ails Europe, and similar diagnoses in the United States are equally misleading. The idea that a country's economic fortunes are largely determined by its success on world markets is a hypothesis, not a necessary truth; and as a practical, empirical matter, that hypothesis is flatly wrong. That is, it is simply not the case that the world's leading nations are to any important degree in economic competition with each other or that any of their major economic problems can be attributed to failures to compete on world markets. The growing obsession in most advanced nations with international competitiveness should be seen, not as a well-founded concern, but as a view held in the face of overwhelming contrary evidence. And yet it is clearly a view that people very much want to hold—a desire to believe that is reflected in a remarkable tendency of those who preach the doctrine of competitiveness to support their case with careless, flawed arithmetic.

This article makes three points. First, it argues that concerns about competitiveness are, as an empirical matter, almost completely unfounded. Second, it tries to explain why defining the economic problem as one of international competition is nonetheless so attractive to so many people. Finally, it argues that the obsession with competitiveness is not only wrong but dangerous, skewing domestic policies and threatening the international economic system. This last issue is, of course, the most consequential from the standpoint of public policy. Thinking in terms of competitiveness leads, directly and indirectly, to bad economic policies on a wide range of issues, domestic and foreign, whether it be in health care or trade.

MINDLESS COMPETITION

MOST PEOPLE who use the term "competitiveness" do so without a second thought. It seems obvious to them that the analogy between a country and a corporation is reasonable and that to ask whether the United States is competitive in the world market is no different in principle from asking whether General Motors is competitive in the North American minivan market.

In fact, however, trying to define the competitiveness of a nation is much more problematic than defining that of a corporation. The bottom line for a corporation is literally its bottom line: if a corporation cannot afford to pay its workers, suppliers, and bondholders, it will go out of business. So when we say that a corporation is uncompetitive, we mean that its market position is unsustainable—that unless it improves its performance, it will cease to exist. Countries, on the other hand, do not go out of business. They may be happy or unhappy with their economic performance, but they have no well-defined bottom line. As a result, the concept of national competitiveness is elusive.

One might suppose, naively, that the bottom line of a national economy is simply its trade balance, that competitiveness can be measured by the ability of a country to sell more abroad than it buys. But in both theory and practice a trade surplus may be a sign of national weakness, a deficit a sign of strength. For example, Mexico was forced to run huge trade surpluses in the 1980s in order to pay the interest on its foreign debt since international investors refused to lend it any more money; it began to run large trade deficits after 1990 as foreign investors recovered confidence and began to pour in new funds. Would anyone want to describe Mexico as a highly competitive nation during the debt crisis era or describe what has happened since 1990 as a loss in competitiveness?

Most writers who worry about the issue at all have therefore tried to define competitiveness as the combination of favorable trade performance and something else. In particular, the most popular definition of competitiveness nowadays runs along the lines of the one given in Council of Economic Advisors Chairman Laura D'Andrea Tyson's *Who's Bashing Whom?:* competitiveness is "our ability to produce goods and services that meet the test of international competition while our citizens enjoy a standard of living that is both rising and sustainable." This sounds reasonable. If you think about it, however, and test your thoughts against the facts, you will find out that there is much less to this definition than meets the eye.

Consider, for a moment, what the definition would mean for an economy that conducted very little international trade, like the United States in the 1950s. For such an economy, the ability to balance its trade is mostly a matter of getting the exchange rate right. But because trade is such a small factor in the economy, the level of the exchange rate is a minor influence on the standard of living. So in an economy with very little international trade, the growth in living standards—and thus "competitiveness" according to Tyson's definition—would be determined almost entirely by domestic factors, primarily the rate of productivity growth. That's domestic productivity growth, period—not productivity growth relative to other countries. In other words, for an economy with very little international trade, "competitiveness" would turn out to be a funny way of saying "productivity" and would have nothing to do with international competition.

But surely this changes when trade becomes more important, as indeed it has for all major economies? It certainly could change. Suppose that a country finds that although its productivity is steadily rising, it can succeed in exporting only if it repeatedly devalues its currency, selling its exports ever more cheaply on world markets. Then its standard of living, which depends on its purchasing power over imports as well as domestically produced goods, might actually decline. In the jargon of economists, domestic growth might be outweighed by deteriorating terms of trade.[2] So "competitiveness" could turn out really to be about international competition after all.

There is no reason, however, to leave this as a pure speculation; it can easily be checked against the data. Have deteriorating terms of trade in fact been a major drag on the U.S. standard of living? Or has the rate of growth of U.S. real income continued essentially to equal the rate of domestic productivity growth, even though trade is a larger share of income than it used to be?

To answer this question, one need only look at the national income accounts data the Commerce Department publishes regularly in the Survey of Current Business. The standard measure of economic growth in the United States is, of course, real GNP—a measure that divides the value of goods and services produced in the United States by appropriate price indexes to come up with an estimate of real national output. The Commerce Department also, however, publishes something called "command GNP." This is similar to real GNP except that it divides U.S. exports not by the export price index, but by the price index for U.S. imports. That is, exports are valued by what Americans can buy with the money exports bring. Command GNP therefore measures the volume of goods and services the U.S. economy can "command"—the nation's purchasing power—rather than the volume it produces.[3] And as we have just

---

[2]An example may be helpful here. Suppose that a country spends 20 percent of its income on imports, and that the prices of its imports are set not in domestic but in foreign currency. Then if the country is forced to devalue its currency—reduce its value in foreign currency—by 10 percent, this will raise the price of 20 percent of the country's spending basket by 10 percent, thus raising the overall price index by 2 percent. Even if domestic *output* has not changed, the country's real *income* will therefore have fallen by 2 percent. If the country must repeatedly devalue in the face of competitive pressure, growth in real income will persistently lag behind growth in real output

It's important to notice, however, that the size of this lag depends not only on the amount of devaluation but on the share of imports in spending. A 10 percent devaluation of the dollar against the yen does not reduce U.S. real income by 10 percent—in fact, it reduces U.S. real income by only about 0.2 percent because only about 2 percent of U.S. income is spent on goods produced in Japan.

[3]In the example in the previous footnote, the devaluation would have no effect on real GNP, but command GNP would have fallen by 2 percent. The finding that in practice command GNP has grown almost as fast as real GNP therefore amounts to saying that events like the hypothetical case in footnote one are unimportant in practice.

seen, "competitiveness" means something different from "productivity" if and only if purchasing power grows significantly more slowly than output.

Well, here are the numbers. Over the period 1959–73, a period of vigorous growth in U.S. living standards and few concerns about international competition, real GNP per worker-hour grew 1.85 percent annually, while command GNP per hour grew a bit faster, 1.87 percent. From 1973 to 1990, a period of stagnating living standards, command GNP growth per hour slowed to 0.65 percent. Almost all (91 percent) of that slowdown, however, was explained by a decline in domestic productivity growth: real GNP per hour grew only 0.73 percent.

Similar calculations for the European Community and Japan yield similar results. In each case, the growth rate of living standards essentially equals the growth rate of domestic productivity—not productivity relative to competitors, but simply domestic productivity. Even though world trade is larger than ever before, national living standards are overwhelmingly determined by domestic factors rather than by some competition for world markets.

How can this be in our interdependent world? Part of the answer is that the world is not as interdependent as you might think: countries are nothing at all like corporations. Even today, U.S. exports are only 10 percent of the value-added in the economy (which is equal to GNP). That is, the United States is still almost 90 percent an economy that produces goods and services for its own use. By contrast, even the largest corporation sells hardly any of its output to its own workers; the "exports" of General Motors—its sales to people who do not work there—are virtually all of its sales, which are more than 2.5 times the corporation's value-added.

Moreover, countries do not compete with each other the way corporations do. Coke and Pepsi are almost purely rivals: only a negligible fraction of Coca-Cola's sales go to Pepsi workers, only a negligible fraction of the goods Coca-Cola workers buy are Pepsi products. So if Pepsi is successful, it tends to be at Coke's expense. But the major industrial countries, while they sell products that compete with each other, are also each other's main export markets and each other's main suppliers of useful imports. If the European economy does well, it need not be at U.S. expense; indeed, if anything, a successful European economy is likely to help the U.S. economy by providing it with larger markets and selling it goods of superior quality at lower prices.

International trade, then, is not a zero-sum game. When productivity rises in Japan, the main result is a rise in Japanese real wages; American or European wages are in principle at least as likely to rise as to fall and in practice seem to be virtually unaffected.

It would be possible to belabor the point, but the moral is clear: while competitive problems could arise in principle, as a practical, empirical matter the major nations of the world are not to any significant degree in economic competition with each other. Of course, there is always a rivalry for status and power—countries that grow faster will see their political rank rise. So it is always interesting to compare countries. But asserting that Japanese growth diminishes U.S. status is very different from saying that it reduces the U.S. standard of living—and it is the latter that the rhetoric of competitiveness asserts.

One can, of course, take the position that words mean what we want them to mean, that all are free, if they wish, to use the term "competitiveness" as a poetic way of saying productivity, without actually implying that international competition has anything to do with it. But few writers on competitiveness would accept this view. They believe that the facts tell a very different story, that we live, as Lester Thurow put it in his best-selling book *Head to Head,* in a world of "win-lose" competition between the leading economies. How is this belief possible?

CARELESS ARITHMETIC

ONE OF THE remarkable, startling features of the vast literature on competitiveness is the repeated tendency of highly intelligent authors to engage in what may perhaps most tactfully be described as "careless arithmetic." Assertions are made that sound like quantifiable pronouncements about measurable magnitudes, but the writers do not actually present any data on these magnitudes and thus fail to notice that the actual numbers contradict their assertions. Or data are presented that are supposed to support an assertion, but the writer fails to notice that his own numbers imply that what he is saying cannot be true. Over and over again one finds books and articles on competitiveness that seem to the unwary reader to be full of convincing evidence but that strike anyone familiar with the data as strangely, almost eerily inept in their handling of the numbers. Some examples can best illustrate this point. Here are three cases of careless arithmetic, each of some interest in its own right.

Trade Deficits and the Loss of Good Jobs. In a recent article published in Japan, Lester Thurow explained to his audience the importance of reducing the Japanese trade surplus with the United States. U.S. real wages, he pointed out, had fallen 6 percent during the Reagan and Bush years, and the reason was that trade deficits in manufactured goods had forced workers out of high-paying manufacturing jobs into much lower-paying service jobs.

This is not an original view; it is very widely held. But Thurow was more concrete than most people, giving actual numbers for the job and wage loss. A million manufacturing jobs have been lost because of the deficit, he asserted, and manufacturing jobs pay 30 percent more than service jobs.

Both numbers are dubious. The million-job number is too high, and the 30 percent wage differential between manufacturing and services is primarily due to a difference in the length of the workweek, not a difference in the hourly wage rate. But let's grant Thurow his numbers. Do they tell the story he suggests?

The key point is that total U.S. employment is well over 100 million workers. Suppose that a million workers were forced from manufacturing into services and as a result lost the 30 percent manufacturing wage premium. Since these workers are less than 1 percent of the U.S. labor force, this would reduce the average U.S. wage rate by less than 1/100 of 30 percent—that is, by less than 0.3 percent.

This is too small to explain the 6 percent real wage decline by a factor of 20. Or to look at it another way, the annual wage loss from deficit-induced deindustrialization, which Thurow clearly implies is at the heart of U.S. economic difficulties, is on the basis of his own numbers roughly equal to what the U.S. spends on health care every week.

Something puzzling is going on here. How could someone as intelligent as Thurow, in writing an article that purports to offer hard quantitative evidence of the importance of international competition to the U.S. economy, fail to realize that the evidence he offers clearly shows that the channel of harm that he identifies was not the culprit?

High Value-added Sectors. Ira Magaziner and Robert Reich, both now influential figures in the Clinton administration, first reached a broad audience with their 1982 book, *Minding America's Business.* The book advocated a U.S. industrial policy, and in the introduction the authors offered a seemingly concrete quantitative basis for such a policy: "Our standard of living can only rise if (i) capital and labor increasingly flow to industries with high value-added per worker and (ii) we maintain a position in those industries that is superior to that of our competitors."

Economists were skeptical of this idea on principle. If targeting the right industries was simply a matter of moving into sectors with high value-added, why weren't private markets already doing the job?[4] But one might dismiss this as simply the usual boundless faith of economists in the market;

---

[4]"Value-added" has a precise, standard meaning in national income accounting: the value added of a firm is the dollar value of its sales, minus the dollar value of the inputs it purchases from other firms, and as such it is easily measured. Some people who use the term, however, may be unaware of this definition and simply use "high value-added" as a synonym for "desirable."

didn't Magaziner and Reich back their case with a great deal of real-world evidence?

Well, *Minding America's Business* contains a lot of facts. One thing it never does, however, is actually justify the criteria set out in the introduction. The choice of industries to cover clearly implied a belief among the authors that high value-added is more or less synonymous with high technology, but nowhere in the book do any numbers compare actual value-added per worker in different industries.

VALUE ADDED PER WORKER, 1988
(in thousands of dollars)

CIGARETTES	488
PETROLEUM REFINING	283
AUTOS	99
STEEL	97
AIRCRAFT	68
ELECTRONICS	64
ALL MANUFACTURING	66

Such numbers are not hard to find. Indeed, every public library in America has a copy of the *Statistical Abstract of the United States,* which each year contains a table presenting value-added and employment by industry in U.S. manufacturing. All one needs to do, then, is spend a few minutes in the library with a calculator to come up with a table that ranks U.S. industries by value-added per worker.

The table on this page shows selected entries from pages 740–44 of the 1991 *Statistical Abstract.* It turns out that the U.S. industries with really high value-added per worker are in sectors with very high ratios of capital to labor, like cigarettes and petroleum refining. (This was predictable: because capital-intensive industries must earn a normal return on large investments, they must charge prices that are a larger markup over labor costs than labor-intensive industries, which means that they have high value-added per worker.) Among large industries, value-added per worker tends to be high in traditional heavy manufacturing sectors like steel and autos. High-technology sectors like aerospace and electronics turn out to be only roughly average.

This result does not surprise conventional economists. High value-added per worker occurs in sectors that are highly capital-intensive, that is, sectors in which an additional dollar of capital buys little extra value-added. In other words, there is no free lunch.

But let's leave on one side what the table says about the way the economy works and simply note the strangeness of the lapse by Magaziner and Reich. Surely they were not calling for an industrial policy that would funnel capital and labor into the steel and auto industries in preference to high-tech. How, then, could they write a whole book dedicated to the proposition that we should target high value-added industries without ever checking to see which industries they meant?

Labor Costs. In his own presentation at the Copenhagen summit, British Prime Minister John Major showed a chart indicating that European unit labor costs have risen more rapidly than those in the United States and Japan. Thus he argued that European workers have been pricing themselves out of world markets.

But a few weeks later, Sam Brittan of the *Financial Times* pointed out a strange thing about Major's calculations: the labor costs were not adjusted for exchange rates. In international competition, of course, what matters for a U.S. firm are the costs of its overseas rivals measured in dollars, not marks or yen. So international comparisons of labor costs, like the tables the Bank of England routinely publishes, always convert them into a common currency. The numbers presented by Major, however, did not make this standard adjustment. And it was a good thing for his presentation that they didn't. As Brittan pointed out, European labor costs have not risen in relative terms when the exchange rate adjustment is made.

If anything, this lapse is even odder than those of Thurow or Magaziner and Reich. How could John Major, with the sophisticated statistical resources of the U.K. Treasury behind him, present an analysis that failed to make the most standard of adjustments?

These examples of strangely careless arithmetic, chosen from among dozens of similar cases, by people who surely had both the cleverness and the resources to get it right, cry out for an explanation. The best working hypothesis is that in each case the author or speaker wanted to believe in the competitive hypothesis so much that he felt no urge to question it; if data were used at all, it was only to lend credibility to a predetermined belief, not to test it. But why are people apparently so anxious to define economic problems as issues of international competition?

THE THRILL OF COMPETITION

THE COMPETITIVE metaphor—the image of countries competing with each other in world markets in the same way that corporations do—derives much of its attractiveness from its seeming comprehensibility. Tell a group of businessmen that a country is like a corporation writ large, and you give them the comfort of feeling that they already understand the basics. Try to tell them about economic concepts like comparative advantage, and you are asking them to learn something new. It should not be surprising if many prefer a doctrine that offers the gain of apparent sophistication without the pain of hard thinking. The rhetoric of competitiveness has become so widespread, however, for three deeper reasons.

First, competitive images are exciting, and thrills sell tickets. The subtitle of Lester Thurow's huge best-seller, *Head to Head,* is "The Coming Economic Battle Among Japan, Europe, and America"; the jacket proclaims that "the decisive war of the century has begun . . . and America may already have decided to lose." Suppose that the subtitle had described the real situation: "The coming struggle in which each big economy will succeed or fail based on its own efforts, pretty much independently of how well the others do." Would Thurow have sold a tenth as many books?

Second, the idea that U.S. economic difficulties hinge crucially on our failures in international competition somewhat paradoxically makes those difficulties seem easier to solve. The productivity of the average American worker is determined by a complex array of factors, most of them unreachable by any likely government policy. So if you accept the reality that our "competitive" problem is really a domestic productivity problem, pure and simple, you are unlikely to be optimistic about any dramatic turnaround. But if you can convince yourself that the problem is really one of failures in international competition—that imports are pushing workers out of high-wage jobs, or subsidized foreign competition is driving the United States out of the high value-added sectors—then the answers to economic malaise may seem to you to involve simple things like subsidizing high technology and being tough on Japan.

Finally, many of the world's leaders have found the competitive metaphor extremely useful as a political device. The rhetoric of competitiveness turns out to provide a good way either to justify hard choices or to avoid them. The example of Delors in Copenhagen shows the usefulness of competitive metaphors as an evasion. Delors had to say something at the EC summit; yet to say anything that addressed the real roots of European unemployment would have involved huge political risks. By turning the discussion to essentially irrelevant but plausible-sounding questions of competitiveness, he bought himself some time to come up with a better answer (which to some extent he provided in December's white paper on the European economy—a paper that still, however, retained "competitiveness" in its title).

By contrast, the well-received presentation of Bill Clinton's initial economic program in February 1993 showed the usefulness of competitive rhetoric as a motivation for tough policies. Clinton proposed a set of painful spending cuts and tax increases to reduce the Federal deficit. Why? The real reasons for cutting the deficit are disappointingly undramatic: the deficit siphons off funds that might otherwise have been productively invested and thereby exerts a steady if small drag on U.S. economic growth. But Clinton was able instead to offer a stirring patriotic appeal, calling on the nation to act now in order to make the economy competitive in the global market—with the implication that dire economic consequences would follow if the United States does not.

Many people who know that "competitiveness" is a largely meaningless concept have been willing to indulge competitive rhetoric precisely because they believe they can harness it in the service of good policies. An overblown fear of the Soviet Union was used in the 1950s to justify the building of the interstate highway system and the expansion of math and science education. Cannot the unjustified fears about foreign competition similarly be turned to good, used to justify serious efforts to reduce the budget deficit, rebuild infrastructure, and so on?

A few years ago this was a reasonable hope. At this point, however, the obsession with competitiveness has reached the point where it has already begun dangerously to distort economic policies.

THE DANGERS OF OBSESSION

THINKING AND speaking in terms of competitiveness poses three real dangers. First, it could result in the wasteful spending of government money supposedly to enhance U.S. competitiveness. Second, it could lead to protectionism and trade wars. Finally, and most important, it could result in bad public policy on a spectrum of important issues.

During the 1950s, fear of the Soviet Union induced the U.S. government to spend money on useful things like highways and science education. It also, however, led to considerable spending on more doubtful items like bomb shelters. The most obvious if least worrisome danger of the growing obsession with competitiveness is that it might lead to a similar misallocation of resources. To take an example, recent guidelines for government research funding have stressed the importance of supporting research that can improve U.S. international competitiveness. This exerts at least some bias toward inventions that can help manufacturing firms, which generally compete on international markets, rather than service producers, which generally do not. Yet most of our employment and value-added is now in services, and lagging productivity in services rather than manufactures has been the single most important factor in the stagnation of U.S. living standards.

A much more serious risk is that the obsession with competitiveness will lead to trade conflict, perhaps even to a world trade war. Most of those who have preached the doctrine of competitiveness have not been old-fashioned protectionists. They want their countries to win the global trade game, not drop out. But what if, despite its best efforts, a country does not seem to be winning, or lacks confidence that it can? Then the competitive diagnosis inevitably suggests that to close the borders is better than to risk having foreigners take away high-wage jobs and high-value sectors. At the very least, the focus on the supposedly competitive nature of international economic relations greases the rails for those who want confrontational if not frankly protectionist policies.

We can already see this process at work, in both the United States and Europe. In the United States, it was remarkable how quickly the sophisticated interventionist arguments advanced by Laura Tyson in her published work gave way to the simple-minded claim by U.S. Trade Representative Mickey Kantor that Japan's bilateral trade surplus was costing the United States millions of jobs. And the trade rhetoric of President Clinton, who stresses the supposed creation of high-wage jobs rather than the gains from specialization, left his administration in a weak position when it tried to argue with the claims of NAFTA foes that competition from cheap Mexican labor will destroy the U.S. manufacturing base.

Perhaps the most serious risk from the obsession with competitiveness, however, is its subtle indirect effect on the quality of economic discussion and policymaking. If top government officials are strongly committed to a particular economic doctrine, their commitment inevitably sets the tone for policymaking on all issues, even those which may seem to have nothing to do with that doctrine. And if an economic doctrine is flatly, completely, and demonstrably wrong, the insistence that discussion adhere to that doctrine inevitably blurs the focus and diminishes the quality of policy discussion across a broad range of issues, including some that are very far from trade policy per se.

Consider, for example, the issue of health care reform, undoubtedly the most important economic initiative of the Clinton administration, almost surely an order of magnitude more important to U.S. living standards than anything that might be done about trade policy (unless the United States provokes a full-blown trade war). Since health care is an issue with few direct international linkages, one might have expected it to be largely insulated from any distortions of policy resulting from misguided concerns about competitiveness.

But the administration placed the development of the health care plan in the hands of Ira Magaziner, the same Magaziner who so conspicuously failed to do his homework in arguing for government promotion of high value-added industries. Magaziner's prior writings and consulting on economic policy focused almost entirely on the issue of international competition, his views on which may be summarized by the title of his 1990 book, *The Silent War*. His appointment reflected many factors, of course, not least his long personal friendship with the first couple. Still, it was not irrelevant that in an administration committed to the ideology of competitiveness, Magaziner, who has consistently recommended that national industrial policies be based on the corporate strategy concepts he learned during his years at the Boston Consulting Group, was regarded as an economic policy expert.

We might also note the unusual process by which the health care reform was developed. In spite of the huge size of the task force, recognized experts in the health care field were almost completely absent, notably though not exclusively economists specializing in health care, including economists with impeccable liberal credentials like Henry Aaron of the Brookings Institution. Again, this may have reflected a number of factors, but it is probably not ir-relevant that anyone who, like Magaziner, is strongly committed to the ideol-ogy of competitiveness is bound to have found professional economists notably unsympathetic in the past—and to be unwilling to deal with them on any other issue.

To make a harsh but not entirely unjustified analogy, a government wedded to the ideology of competitiveness is as unlikely to make good eco-nomic policy as a government committed to creationism is to make good science policy, even in areas that have no direct relationship to the theory of evolution.

ADVISERS WITH NO CLOTHES

IF THE obsession with competitiveness is as misguided and damaging as this article claims, why aren't more voices saying so? The answer is, a mixture of hope and fear.

On the side of hope, many sensible people have imagined that they can appropriate the rhetoric of competitiveness on behalf of desirable economic policies. Suppose that you believe that the United States needs to raise its savings rate and improve its educational system in order to raise its produc-tivity. Even if you know that the benefits of higher productivity have nothing to do with international competition, why not describe this as a policy to en-hance competitiveness if you think that it can widen your audience? It's tempting to pander to popular prejudices on behalf of a good cause, and I have myself succumbed to that temptation.

As for fear, it takes either a very courageous or very reckless economist to say publicly that a doctrine that many, perhaps most, of the world's opinion leaders have embraced is flatly wrong. The insult is all the greater when many of those men and women think that by using the rhetoric of competitiveness they are demonstrating their sophistication about economics. This article may influence people, but it will not make many friends.

Unfortunately, those economists who have hoped to appropriate the rhetoric of competitiveness for good economic policies have instead had their own credibility appropriated on behalf of bad ideas. And somebody has to point out when the emperor's intellectual wardrobe isn't all he thinks it is.

So let's start telling the truth: competitiveness is a meaningless word when applied to national economies. And the obsession with competitiveness is both wrong and dangerous.

Culture Is Destiny

A Conversation with Lee Kuan Yew

Fareed Zakaria

MARCH/APRIL 1994

MEETING THE MINISTER

"ONE OF THE ASYMMETRIES of history," wrote Henry Kissinger of Singapore's patriarch Lee Kuan Yew, "is the lack of correspondence between the abilities of some leaders and the power of their countries." Kissinger's one time boss, Richard Nixon, was even more flattering. He speculated that, had Lee lived in another time and another place, he might have "attained the world stature of a Churchill, a Disraeli, or a Gladstone." This tag line of a big man on a small stage has been attached to Lee since the 1970s. Today, however, his stage does not look quite so small. Singapore's per capita GNP is now higher than that of its erstwhile colonizer, Great Britain. It has the world's busiest port, is the third-largest oil refiner and a major center of global manufacturing and service industries. And this move from poverty to plenty has taken place within one generation. In 1965 Singapore ranked economically with Chile, Argentina, and Mexico; today its per capita GNP is four or five times theirs.

Lee managed this miraculous transformation in Singapore's economy while maintaining tight political control over the country; Singapore's government can best be described as a "soft" authoritarian regime, and at times it has not been so soft. He was prime minister of Singapore from its independence in 1959 (it became part of a federation with Malaysia in 1963 but was expelled in 1965) until 1990, when he allowed his deputy to succeed him. He is now "Senior Minister" and still commands enormous influence and power in the country. Since his retirement, Lee has embarked on another career of sorts as a world-class pundit, speaking his mind with impolitic frankness. And what is often on his mind is American-style democracy and its perils. He travels often to East Asian capitals from Beijing to Hanoi to Manila dispensing advice on how to achieve economic growth while retaining political stability and control. It is a formula that the governing elites of these countries are anxious to learn.

The rulers of former British colonies have been spared the embarrassment of building grandiose monuments to house their offices; they simply occupy the ones that the British built. So it is with Singapore. The president, prime minister, and senior minister work out of *Istana* (palace), the old colonial governor's house, a gleaming white bungalow surrounded by luxuriant lawns. The interior is modern—light wood paneling and leather sofas. The atmosphere is hushed. I waited in a large anteroom for the "SM," which is how everybody refers to Lee. I did not wait long. The SM was standing in the middle of a large, sparsely furnished office. He is of medium build. His once-compact physique is now slightly shrunken. Still, he does not look 70.

Lee Kuan Yew is unlike any politician I have met. There were no smiles, no jokes, no bonhomie. He looked straight at me—he has an inexpressive face but an intense gaze—shook hands, and motioned toward one of the room's pale blue leather sofas (I had already been told by his press secretary on which one to sit). After 30 awkward seconds, I realized that there would be no small talk.

FZ: With the end of the Cold War, many Americans were surprised to hear growing criticism of their political and economic and social system from elites in East Asia, who were considered staunchly pro-American. What, in your view, is wrong with the American system?

LKY: It is not my business to tell people what's wrong with their system. It is my business to tell people not to foist their system indiscriminately on societies in which it will not work.

FZ: But you do not view the United States as a model for other countries?

LKY: As an East Asian looking at America, I find attractive and unattractive features. I like, for example, the free, easy, and open relations between people regardless of social status, ethnicity, or religion. And the things that I have always admired about America, as against the communist system, I still do: a certain openness in argument about what is good or bad for society; the accountability of public officials; none of the secrecy and terror that's part and parcel of communist government.

But as a total system, I find parts of it totally unacceptable: guns, drugs, violent crime, vagrancy, unbecoming behavior in public—in sum, the breakdown of civil society. The expansion of the right of the individual to behave or misbehave as he pleases has come at the expense of orderly society. In the East the main object is to have a well-ordered society so that everybody can have maximum enjoyment of his freedoms. This freedom can only exist in an ordered state and not in a natural state of contention and anarchy.

Let me give you an example that encapsulates the whole difference between America and Singapore. America has a vicious drug problem. How does it solve it? It goes around the world helping other anti-narcotic agencies to try and stop the suppliers. It pays for helicopters, defoliating agents, and so on. And when it is provoked, it captures the president of Panama and brings him to trial in Florida. Singapore does not have that option. We can't go to Burma and capture warlords there. What we can do is to pass a law which says that any customs officer or policeman who sees anybody in Singapore behaving suspiciously, leading him to suspect the person is under the influence of drugs, can require that man to have his urine tested. If the sample is found to contain drugs, the man immediately goes for treatment. In America if you did that it would be an invasion of the individual's rights and you would be sued.

I was interested to read Colin Powell, when he was chairman of the Joint Chiefs of Staff, saying that the military followed our approach because when a recruit signs up he agrees that he can be tested. Now, I would have thought this kind of approach would be quite an effective way to deal with the terrible drug problem you have. But the idea of the inviolability of the individual has been turned into dogma. And yet nobody minds when the army goes and captures the president of another state and brings him to Florida and puts him in jail. I find that incomprehensible. And in any case this approach will not solve America's drug problem. Whereas Singapore's way, we may not solve it, but we will lessen it considerably, as we have done.

FZ: Would it be fair to say that you admired America more 25 years ago? What, in your view, went wrong?

LKY: Yes, things have changed. I would hazard a guess that it has a lot to do with the erosion of the moral underpinnings of a society and the diminution of personal responsibility. The liberal, intellectual tradition that developed after World War II claimed that human beings had arrived at this perfect state where everybody would be better off if they were allowed to do their own thing and flourish. It has not worked out, and I doubt if it will. Certain basics about human nature do not change. Man needs a certain moral sense of right and wrong. There is such a thing called evil, and it is not the result of being a victim of society. You are just an evil man, prone to do evil things, and you have to be stopped from doing them. Westerners have abandoned an ethical basis for society, believing that all problems are solvable by a good government, which we in the East never believed possible.

FZ: Is such a fundamental shift in culture irreversible?

LKY: No, it is a swing of the pendulum. I think it will swing back. I don't know how long it will take, but there's already a backlash in America against failed social policies that have resulted in people urinating in public, in aggressive begging in the streets, in social breakdown.

THE ASIAN MODEL

FZ: You say that your real concern is that this system not be foisted on other societies because it will not work there. Is there another viable model for political and economic development? Is there an "Asian model"?

LKY: I don't think there is an Asian model as such. But Asian societies are unlike Western ones. The fundamental difference between Western concepts of society and government and East Asian concepts—when I say East Asians, I mean Korea, Japan, China, Vietnam, as distinct from Southeast Asia, which is a mix between the Sinic and the Indian, though Indian culture also emphasizes similar values—is that Eastern societies believe that the individual exists in the context of his family. He is not pristine and separate. The family is part of the extended family, and then friends and the wider society. The ruler or the government does not try to provide for a person what the family best provides.

In the West, especially after World War II, the government came to be seen as so successful that it could fulfill all the obligations that in less modern societies are fulfilled by the family. This approach encouraged alternative families, single mothers for instance, believing that government could provide the support to make up for the absent father. This is a bold, Huxleyan view of life, but one from which I as an East Asian shy away. I would be afraid to experiment with it. I'm not sure what the consequences are, and I don't like the consequences that I see in the West. You will find this view widely shared in East Asia. It's not that we don't have single mothers here. We are also caught in the same social problems of change when we educate our women and they become independent financially and no longer need to put up with unhappy marriages. But there is grave disquiet when we break away from tested norms, and the tested norm is the family unit. It is the building brick of society.

There is a little Chinese aphorism which encapsulates this idea: *Xiushen qijia zhiguo pingtianxia. Xiushen* means look after yourself, cultivate yourself, do everything to make yourself useful; *Qijia*, look after the family; *Zhiguo,* look after your country; *Pingtianxia*, all is peaceful under heaven. We have a whole people immersed in these beliefs. My granddaughter has the name *Xiu-qi*. My son picked out the first two words, instructing his daughter to cultivate herself and look after her family. It is the basic concept of our civilization. Governments will come, governments will go, but this endures. We start with self-reliance. In the West today it is the opposite. The government says give me a popular mandate and I will solve all society's problems.

FZ: What would you do instead to address America's problems?

LKY: What would I do if I were an American? First, you must have order in society. Guns, drugs, and violent crime all go together, threatening social order. Then the schools; when you have violence in schools, you are not going to have education, so you've got to put that right. Then you have to educate rigorously and train a whole generation of skilled, intelligent, knowledgeable people who can be productive. I would start off with basics, working on the individual, looking at him within the context of his family, his friends, his society. But the Westerner says I'll fix things at the top. One magic formula, one grand plan. I will wave a wand and everything will work out. It's an interesting theory but not a proven method.

BACK TO BASICS

FZ: You are very skeptical of government's ability to solve deeper social issues. But you're more confident, certainly than many Americans are, in the government's ability to promote economic growth and technological advancement. Isn't this a contradiction?

LKY: No. We have focused on basics in Singapore. We used the family to push economic growth, factoring the ambitions of a person and his family into our planning. We have tried, for example, to improve the lot of children through education. The government can create a setting in which people can live happily and succeed and express themselves, but finally it is what people do with their lives that determines economic success or failure. Again, we were fortunate we had this cultural backdrop, the belief in thrift, hard work, filial piety, and loyalty in the extended family, and most of all, the respect for scholarship and learning.

There is, of course, another reason for our success. We have been able to create economic growth because we facilitated certain changes while we moved from an agricultural society to an industrial society. We had the advantage of knowing what the end result should be by looking at the West and later Japan. We knew where we were, and we knew where we had to go. We said to ourselves, "Let's hasten, let's see if we can get there faster." But soon we will face a different situation. In the near future, all of us will get to the stage of Japan. Where do we go next? How do we hasten getting there when we don't know where we're going? That will be a new situation.

FZ: Some people say that the Asian model is too rigid to adapt well to change. The sociologist Mancur Olson argues that national decline is caused most fundamentally by sclerosis—the rigidity of interest groups, firms, labor, capital, and the state. An American-type system that is very flexible, laissez-faire, and constantly adapting is better suited to the emerging era of rapid change than a government-directed economic policy and a Confucian value system.

LKY: That is an optimistic and attractive philosophy of life, and I hope it will come true. But if you look at societies over the millennia, you find certain basic patterns. American civilization from the Pilgrim fathers on is one of optimism and the growth of orderly government. History in China is of dynasties which have risen and fallen, of the waxing and waning of societies. And through all that turbulence, the family, the extended family, the clan, has provided a kind of survival raft for the individual. Civilizations have collapsed, dynasties have been swept away by conquering hordes, but this life raft enables the civilization to carry on and get to its next phase.

Nobody here really believes that the government can provide in all circumstances. The government itself does not believe it. In the ultimate crisis, even in earthquakes and typhoons, it is your human relationships that will see you through. So the thesis you quote, that the government is always capable of reinventing itself in new shapes and forms, has not been proven in history. But the family and the way human relationships are structured do increase the survival chances of its members. That has been tested over thousands of years in many different situations.

THE CULTURE OF SUCCESS

FZ: A key ingredient of national economic success in the past has been a culture of innovation and experimentation. During their rise to great wealth and power, the centers of growth—Venice, Holland, Britain, the United States—all had an atmosphere of intellectual freedom in which new ideas, technologies, methods, and products could emerge. In East Asian countries, however, the government frowns upon an open and free-wheeling intellectual climate. Leaving aside any kind of human rights questions this raises, does it create a productivity problem?

LKY: Intellectually that sounds like a reasonable conclusion, but I'm not sure things will work out this way. The Japanese, for instance, have not been all that disadvantaged in creating new products. I think that if governments are aware of your thesis and of the need to test out new areas, to break out of existing formats, they can counter the trend. East Asians, who all share a tradition of strict discipline, respect for the teacher, no talking back to the teacher, and rote learning, must make sure that there is this random intellectual search for new technologies and products. In any case, in a world where electronic communications are instantaneous, I do not see anyone lagging behind. Anything new that happens spreads quickly, whether it's superconductivity or some new lifestyle.

FZ: Would you agree with the World Bank report on East Asian economic success, which I interpret to have concluded that all the governments that succeeded got fundamentals right—encouraging savings and investment, keeping inflation low, providing high-quality education. The tinkering of industrial policies here and targeting sectors there was not as crucial an element in explaining these countries' extraordinary economic growth as were these basic factors.

LKY: I think the World Bank had a very difficult job. It had to write up these very, very complex series of situations. But there are cultural factors which have been lightly touched over, which deserved more weightage. This would have made it a more complex study and of less universal application, but it would have been more accurate, explaining the differences, for example, between the Philippines and Taiwan.

FZ: If culture is so important, then countries with very different cultures may not, in fact, succeed in the way that East Asia did by getting economic fundamentals right. Are you not hopeful for the countries around the world that are liberalizing their economies?

LKY: Getting the fundamentals right would help, but these societies will not succeed in the same way as East Asia did because certain driving forces will be absent. If you have a culture that doesn't place much value in learning and scholarship and hard work and thrift and deferment of present enjoyment for future gain, the going will be much slower.

But, you know, the World Bank report's conclusions are part of the culture of America and, by extension, of international institutions. It had to present its findings in a bland and universalizable way, which I find unsatisfying because it doesn't grapple with the real problems. It makes the hopeful assumption that all men are equal, that people all over the world are the same. They are not. Groups of people develop different characteristics when they have evolved for thousands of years separately. Genetics and history interact. The Native American Indian is genetically of the same stock as the Mongoloids of East Asia—the Chinese, the Koreans, and the Japanese. But one group got cut off after the Bering Straits melted away. Without that land bridge, they were totally isolated in America for thousands of years. The other, in East Asia, met successive invading forces from Central Asia and interacted with waves of people moving back and forth. The two groups may share certain characteristics, for instance if you measure the shape of their skulls and so on, but if you start testing them you find that they are different, most particularly in their neurological development and their cultural values.

Now if you gloss over these kinds of issues because it is politically incorrect to study them, then you have laid a land mine for yourself. This is what leads to the disappointments with social policies, embarked upon in America with great enthusiasm and expectations, but which yield such meager results. There isn't a willingness to see things in their stark reality. But then I am not being politically correct.

FZ: Culture may be important, but it does change. The Asian "model" may prove to be a transitional phenomenon. After all, Western countries also went through a period in the eighteenth and nineteenth centuries when they were capitalist and had limited participatory democracy. Elites then worried—as you do today—that "too much" democracy and "too many" individual rights would destabilize social order. But as these societies modernized and as economic growth spread to all sections of society, things changed. Isn't East Asia changing because of a growing middle class that demands a say in its own future?

LKY: There is acute change in East Asia. We are agricultural societies that have industrialized within one or two generations. What happened in the West over 200 years or more is happening here in about 50 years or less. It is all crammed and crushed into a very tight time frame, so there are bound to be dislocations and malfunctions. If you look at the fast-growing countries—Korea, Thailand, Hong Kong, and Singapore—there's been one remarkable phenomenon: the rise of religion. Koreans have taken to Christianity in large numbers, I think some 25 percent. This is a country that was never colonized by a Christian nation. The old customs and religions—ancestor worship, shamanism—no longer completely satisfy. There is a quest for some higher explanations about man's purpose, about why we are here. This is associated with periods of great stress in society. You will find in Japan that every time it goes through a period of stress, new sects crop up and new religions proliferate. In Taiwan—and also in Hong Kong and Singapore—you see a rise in the number of new temples; Confucianist temples, Taoist temples, and many Christian sects.

We are all in the midst of very rapid change and at the same time we are all groping towards a destination which we hope will be identifiable with our past. We have left the past behind, and there is an underlying unease that there will be nothing left of us which is part of the old. The Japanese have solved this problem to some extent. Japan has become an industrial society, while remaining essentially Japanese in its human relations. They have industrialized and shed some of their feudal values. The Taiwanese and the Koreans are trying to do the same. But whether these societies can preserve their core values and make this transition is a problem which they alone can solve. It is not something Americans can solve for them. Therefore, you will find people unreceptive to the idea that they be Westernized. Modernized, yes, in the sense that they have accepted the inevitability of science and technology and the change in the lifestyles they bring.

FZ: But won't these economic and technological changes produce changes in the mind-sets of people?

LKY: It is not just mind-sets that would have to change but value systems. Let me give anecdotal evidence of this. Many Chinese families in Malaysia migrated in periods of stress, when there were race riots in Malaysia in the 1960s, and they settled in Australia and Canada. They did this for the sake of their children so that they would get a better education in the English language because then Malaysia was switching to Malay as its primary language. The children grew up, reached their late teens, and left home. And suddenly the parents discovered the emptiness of the whole exercise. They had given their children a modern education in the English language and in the process lost their children altogether. That was a very sobering experience. Something less dramatic is happening in Singapore now because we are not bringing up our children in the same circumstances in which we grew up.

FZ: But these children are absorbing influences different from your generation. You say that knowledge, lifestyles, culture all spread rapidly in this world. Will not the idea of democracy and individual rights also spread?

LKY: Let's not get into a debate on semantics. The system of government in China will change. It will change in Korea, Taiwan, Vietnam. It is changing in Singapore. But it will not end up like the American or British or French or German systems. What are we all seeking? A form of government that will be comfortable, because it meets our needs, is not oppressive, and maximizes our opportunities. And whether you have one-man, one-vote or some-men, one vote or other men, two votes, those are forms which should be worked out. I'm not intellectually convinced that one-man, one-vote is the best. We practice it because that's what the British bequeathed us and we haven't really found a need to challenge that. But I'm convinced, personally, that we would have a better system if we gave every man over the age of 40 who has a family two votes because he's likely to be more careful, voting also for his children. He is more likely to vote in a serious way than a capricious young man under 30. But we haven't found it necessary yet. If it became necessary, we should do it. At the same time, once a person gets beyond 65, then it is a problem. Between the ages of 40 and 60 is ideal, and at 60 they should go back to one vote, but that will be difficult to arrange.

Culture Is Destiny

MULTICULTURAL SCHISMS

FZ: Change is often most threatening when it occurs in multiethnic societies. You have been part of both a multiethnic state that failed and one that has succeeded. Malaysia was unwilling to allow what it saw as a Chinese city-state to be part of it and expelled Singapore from its federation in 1965. Singapore itself, however, exists peacefully as a multiethnic state. Is there a solution for those states that have ethnic and religious groups mixed within them?

LKY: Each state faces a different set of problems and I would be most reluctant to dish out general solutions. From my own experience, I would say, *make haste slowly.* Nobody likes to lose his ethnic, cultural, religious, even linguistic identity. To exist as one state you need to share certain attributes, have things in common. If you pressure-cook you are in for problems. If you go gently, but steadily, the logic of events will bring about not assimilation, but integration. If I had tried to foist the English language on the people of Singapore, I would have faced rebellion all around. If I had tried to foist the Chinese language, I'd have had immediate revolt and disaster. But I offered every parent a choice of English and their mother tongue, in whatever order they chose. By their free choice, plus the rewards of the marketplace over a period of 30 years, we have ended up with English first and the mother tongue second. We have switched one university already established in the Chinese language from Chinese into English. Had this change been forced in five or ten years instead of being done over 30 years—and by free choice—it would have been a disaster.

FZ: This sounds like a live-and-let-live kind of approach. Many Western countries, particularly the United States and France, respectively, have traditionally attempted to assimilate people toward a national mainstream—with English and French as the national language, respectively. Today this approach is being questioned, as you know, with some minority groups in the United States and France arguing for "multiculturalism," which would allow distinct and unassimilated minority groups to coexist within the nation. How does this debate strike you as you read about it in Singapore?

LKY: You cannot have too many distinct components and be one nation. It makes interchangeability difficult. If you want complete separateness, then you should not come to live in the host country. But there are circumstances where it is wise to leave things be. For instance, all races in Singapore are eligible for jobs and for many other things. But we put the Muslims in a slightly different category because they are extremely sensitive about their customs, especially diet. In such matters one has to find a middle path between uniformity and a certain freedom to be somewhat different. I think it is wise to leave alone questions of fundamental beliefs and give time to sort matters out.

FZ: So you would look at the French handling of their Muslim minorities and say "Go slow, don't push these people so hard."

LKY: I would not want to say that because the French, having ruled Algeria for many years, know the kind of problems that they are faced with. My approach would be, if some Muslim girl insists on coming to school with her headdress on and is prepared to put up with that discomfort, we should be prepared to put up with the strangeness. But if she joined the customs or immigration department where it would be confusing to the millions of people who stream through to have some customs officer looking different, she must wear the uniform. That approach has worked in Singapore so far.

IS EUROPE'S PAST ASIA'S FUTURE?

FZ: Let me shift gears somewhat and ask you some questions about the international climate in East Asia. The part of the world you live in is experiencing the kind of growth that the West has experienced for the last 400 years. The West has not only been the world's great producer of wealth for four centuries, it has also been the world's great producer of war. Today East Asia is the locus of great and unsettling growth, with several newly rising powers close to each other, many with different political systems, historical animosities, border disputes, and all with ever-increasing quantities of arms. Should one look at this and ask whether Europe's past will be East Asia's future?

LKY: No, it's too simplistic. One reason why growth is likely to last for many years in East Asia—and this is just a guess—is that the peoples and the governments of East Asia have learned some powerful lessons about the viciousness and destructiveness of wars. Not only full-scale wars like in Korea, but guerrilla wars as in Vietnam, in Cambodia, and in the jungles of Malaysia, Thailand, Indonesia, and the Philippines. We all know that the more you engage in conflict, the poorer and the more desperate you become. Visit Cambodia and Vietnam; *the world just passed them by.* That lesson will live for a very long time, at least as long as this generation is alive.

FZ: The most unsettling change in an international system is the rise of a new great power. Can the rise of China be accommodated into the East Asian order? Isn't that kind of growth inevitably destabilizing?

LKY: I don't think we can speak in terms of just the East Asian order. The question is: Can the world develop a system in which a country the size of China becomes part of the management of international peace and stability? Sometime in the next 20 or 30 years, the world, by which I mean the major powers, will have to agree among themselves how to manage peace and stability, how to create a system that is both viable and fair. Wars between small countries won't destroy the whole world but will only destroy themselves. But big conflicts between big powers will destroy the world many times over. That's just too disastrous to contemplate.

At the end of the last war, what they could foresee was the United Nations. The hope was that the permanent five would maintain the rule of law or gradually spread the rule of law in international relations. It did not come off because of Stalin and the Cold War. This is now a new phase. The great powers—by which I mean America, Western Europe as a group if they become a union, Japan, China, and in 20 to 30 years time, the Russian republic—have got to find a balance between themselves. I think the best way forward is through the United Nations. It already has 48 years of experience. It is imperfect, but what is the alternative? You cannot have a consortium of five big powers lording it over the rest of mankind. They will not have the moral authority or legitimacy to do it. Are they going to divide the world into five spheres of influence? So they have to fall back on some multilateral framework and work out a set of rules that makes it viable. There may be conflicts of a minor nature, for instance between two Latin American countries or two small Southeast Asian countries; that doesn't really matter. Now if you have two big countries in South Asia like India and Pakistan and both with nuclear capabilities, then something has to be done. It is in that context that we have to find a place for China when it becomes a major economic and military power.

FZ: Is the Chinese regime stable? Is the growth that's going on there sustainable? Is the balancing act between economic reform and political control that Deng Xiaoping is trying to keep going sustainable after his death?

LKY: The regime in Beijing is more stable than any alternative government that can be formed in China. Let us assume that the students had carried the day at Tiananmen and they had formed a government. The same students who were at Tiananmen went to France and America. They've been quarreling with each other ever since. What kind of China would they have today? Something worse than the Soviet Union. China is a vast, disparate country; there is no alternative to strong central power.

FZ: Do you worry that the kind of rapid and unequal growth taking place in China might cause the country to break up?

LKY: First, the economy is growing everywhere, even in Sichuan, in the heart of the interior. Disparate growth rates are inevitable. It is the difference between, say, California before the recession and the Rust Belt. There will be enormous stresses because of the size of the country and the intractable nature of the problems—the poor infrastructure, the weak institutions, the wrong systems that they have installed, modeling themselves upon the Soviet system in Stalin's time. Given all those handicaps, I am amazed that they have got so far.

FZ: What about the other great East Asian power? If Japan continues on the current trajectory, should the world encourage the expansion of its political and military responsibilities and power?

LKY: No. I know that the present generation of Japanese leaders do not want to project power. I'm not sure what follows when leaders born after the war take charge. I doubt if there will be a sudden change. If Japan can carry on with its current policy, leaving security to the Americans and concentrating on the economic and the political, the world will be better off. And the Japanese are quite happy to do this. It is when America feels that it's too burdensome and not worth the candle to be present in East Asia to protect Japan that it will have to look after its own security. When Japan becomes a separate player, it is an extra joker in the pack of cards.

FZ: You've said recently that allowing Japan to send its forces abroad is like giving liquor to an alcoholic.

LKY: The Japanese have always had this cultural trait, that whatever they do they carry it to the nth degree. I think they know this. I have Japanese friends who have told me this. They admit that this is a problem with them.

FZ: What if Japan did follow the trajectory that most great powers have; that it was not content simply to be an economic superpower, "a bank with a flag" in a writer's phrase? What if they decided they wanted to have the ultimate mark of a great power—nuclear weapons? What should the world do?

LKY: If they decided on that, the world will not be able to stop them. You are unable to stop North Korea. Nobody believes that an American government that could not sustain its mission in Somalia because of an ambush and one television snippet of a dead American pulled through the streets in Mogadishu could contemplate a strike on North Korean nuclear facilities like the Israeli strike on Iraq. Therefore it can only be sanctions in the U.N. Security Council. That requires that there be no vetoes. Similarly, if the Japanese decide to go nuclear, I don't believe you will be able to stop them. But they know that they face a nuclear power in China and in Russia, and so they would have to posture themselves in such a way as not to invite a preemptive strike. If they can avoid a preemptive strike then a balance will be established. Each will deter the others.

FZ: So it's the transition period that you are worried about.

LKY: I would prefer that the matter never arises and I believe so does the world. Whether the Japanese go down the military path will depend largely on America's strength and its willingness to be engaged.

Culture Is Destiny

VIVE LA DIFFERENCE

FZ: Is there some contradiction here between your role as a politician and your new role as an intellectual, speaking out on all matters? As a politician you want America as a strong balancer in the region, a country that is feared and respected all over the world. As an intellectual, however, you choose to speak out forcefully against the American model in a way that has to undermine America's credibility abroad.

LKY: That's preposterous. The last thing I would want to do is to undermine her credibility. America has been unusual in the history of the world, being the sole possessor of power—the nuclear weapon—and the one and only government in the world unaffected by war damage whilst the others were in ruins. Any old and established nation would have ensured its supremacy for as long as it could. But America set out to put her defeated enemies on their feet, to ward off an evil force, the Soviet Union, brought about technological change by transferring technology generously and freely to Europeans and to Japanese, and enabled them to become her challengers within 30 years. By 1975 they were at her heels. That's unprecedented in history. There was a certain greatness of spirit born out of the fear of communism plus American idealism that brought that about. But that does not mean that we all admire everything about America.

Let me be frank; if we did not have the good points of the West to guide us, we wouldn't have got out of our backwardness. We would have been a backward economy with a backward society. But we do not want all of the West.

A CODA ON CULTURE

THE DOMINANT theme throughout our conversation was culture. Lee returned again and again to his views on the importance of culture and the differences between Confucianism and Western values. In this respect, Lee is very much part of a trend. Culture is in. From business consultants to military strategists, people talk about culture as the deepest and most determinative aspect of human life.

I remain skeptical. If culture is destiny, what explains a culture's failure in one era and success in another? If Confucianism explains the economic boom in East Asia today, does it not also explain that region's stagnation for four centuries? In fact, when East Asia seemed immutably poor, many scholars—most famously Max Weber—made precisely that case, arguing that Confucian-based cultures discouraged all the attributes necessary for success in capitalism. Today scholars explain how Confucianism emphasizes the essen-

tial traits for economic dynamism. Were Latin American countries to succeed in the next few decades, we shall surely read encomiums to Latin culture. I suspect that since we cannot find one simple answer to why certain
societies succeed at certain times, we examine successful societies and search
within their cultures for the seeds of success. Cultures being complex, one
finds in them what one wants.

What explains Lee Kuan Yew's fascination with culture? It is not something he was born with. Until his 30s he was called "Harry" Lee (and still is
by family and friends). In the 1960s the British foreign secretary could say to
him, "Harry, you're the best bloody Englishman east of the Suez." This is not
a man untouched by the West. Part of his interest in cultural differences is
surely that they provide a coherent defense against what he sees as Western
democratic imperialism. But a deeper reason is revealed in something he said
in our conversation: "We have left the past behind, and there is an underlying
unease that there will be nothing left of us which is part of the old."

Cultures change. Under the impact of economic growth, technological
change, and social transformation, no culture has remained the same. Most
of the attributes that Lee sees in Eastern cultures were once part of the West.
Four hundred years of economic growth changed things. From the very beginning of England's economic boom, many Englishmen worried that as
their country became rich it was losing its moral and ethical base. "Wealth
accumulates and men decay," wrote Oliver Goldsmith in 1770. It is this "decay" that Lee is trying to stave off. He speaks of the anxious search for religion in East Asia today, and while he never says this, his own quest for a
Confucian alternative to the West is part of this search.

But to be modern without becoming more Western is difficult; the two
are not wholly separable. The West has left a mark on "the rest," and it is not
simply a legacy of technology and material products. It is, perhaps most profoundly, in the realm of ideas. At the close of the interview, Lee handed me
three pages. This was, he explained, to emphasize how alien Confucian culture is to the West. The pages were from the book *East Asia: Tradition and
Transformation*, by John Fairbank, an American scholar.

Contributors

FOUAD AJAMI (1945–) is a professor of Middle Eastern studies at the Paul H. Nitze School of Advanced International Studies of The Johns Hopkins University. He is the author of *The Arab Predicament* and *The Vanished Imam*.

HAMILTON FISH ARMSTRONG (1893–1973) was editor of *Foreign Affairs* from 1928 to 1972. He worked at the *New York Evening Post* before becoming managing editor to Archibald Cary Coolidge, *Foreign Affairs'* first editor. Armstrong was the author of dozens of articles and several books including *Peace and Counterpeace*.

JULIEN BENDA (1867–1956) was a French writer and critic. A humanist philosopher, Benda became famous for his attack on romanticism in *The Treason of the Intellectuals*.

ISAIAH BERLIN (1909–) is a historian of ideas and philosopher. Born in Latvia, he was the first president of Wolfson College, Oxford, and is a Fellow of All Souls. A former president of the British Academy, Berlin is the author of *Russian Thinkers*, *Against the Current*, *Four Essays on Liberty*, and *The Crooked Timber of Humanity*, among other works.

ZBIGNIEW BRZEZINSKI (1928–) was President Jimmy Carter's national security adviser. A former political science professor at Columbia University, Brzezinski is the author of numerous books, including *Power and Principle*, *The Soviet Bloc: Unity and Conflict*, and *The Grand Chessboard*.. He is currently a counselor at the Center for Strategic and International Studies and a professor at the Paul H. Nitze School of Advanced International Studies of The Johns Hopkins University.

WILLIAM F. BUCKLEY, JR. (1925–), is the founder and longtime editor of *National Review*. He is now its editor at large. His 38 books include *God and Man at Yale* as well as several novels.

NIKOLAI BUKHARIN (1888–1938) was a Marxist theoretician and revolutionary. Called "the darling of the party" by Lenin, Bukharin was a leader of the October Revolution, a member of the Politburo, and head of the editorial board of *Izvestia*. He was arrested in 1937 during Stalin's purges and shot dead. Bukharin was posthumously rehabilitated during the Gorbachev era.

VICTOR CHERNOV (1876–1952) was the leader of Russia's Socialist Revolutionary Party and served as agriculture minister in the 1917 provisional government. After Lenin's henchmen forcibly dispersed the Constituent Assembly, in which Chernov's party held a substantial majority, Chernov worked underground against Bolshevik control of the Kremlin for several years until fleeing to the West in 1920.

CLARK M. CLIFFORD (1906–) is a Washington lawyer and political aide. He was White House counsel to President Harry S Truman, was President John F. Kennedy's personal lawyer, and served as President Lyndon B. Johnson's defense secretary during the Vietnam War.

RICHARD N. COOPER (1934–) is a professor of international economics at Harvard University. He was undersecretary of state for economic affairs during the Carter administration and is a former provost of Yale University. His books include *The Economics of Interdependence* and *The International Monetary System*.

BENEDETTO CROCE (1866–1952) was an Italian philosopher, historian, and politician. He served as minister of education, was editor of *La Critica*, and was appointed senator for life in 1910. His books include *History as the Story of Liberty*.

W. E. B. DU BOIS (1868–1963) was a sociologist, historian, and prominent black protest leader. An ardent proponent of equal rights, he was one of the founders of the National Association for the Advancement of Colored People and the editor of its magazine, *Crisis*. Du Bois was the author of numerous works including *The Souls of Black Folk*, *Black Reconstruction*, and *Dusk of Dawn*.

DAVID FROMKIN (1932–) is chairman of the international relations department and a professor of law, international relations, and history at Boston University. He is an international attorney and the author of *In the Time of the Americans* and *A Peace to End All Peace*.

EDWIN F. GAY (1867–1946) was a professor of economic history at Harvard University. He was the first dean of its Graduate School of Business Administration.

A. WHITNEY GRISWOLD (1906–1963) was president of Yale University. Before becoming president, he was a professor of history, international relations, and political science. Griswold's books include *In the University Tradition*, *Liberal Education and the Democratic Ideal*, and *The Far Eastern Policy of the United States*.

JAMES F. HOGE, JR. (1935–), is editor of *Foreign Affairs*. His three decades in newspaper journalism included serving as editor-in-chief and publisher of *The Chicago Sun-Times* and publisher of *The New York Daily News;* under his leadership, the newspapers won seven Pulitzer Prizes. Hoge is a former fellow at Harvard University's John F. Kennedy School of Government.

SAMUEL P. HUNTINGTON (1927–) is a university professor at Harvard University. He served as director of security planning for the Carter administration's National Security Council and was president of the American Political Science Association. His books include *Political Order in Changing Societies*, *The Third Wave*, and *The Clash of Civilizations and the Remaking of World Order*.

KARL KAUTSKY (1854–1938) was a leading German socialist and, as a key figure pushing Germany's Social Democratic Party toward orthodox Marxism, one of the most prominent members of the Second International. His books include *Ethics and the Materialist Conception of History* and *Bolshevism at a Deadlock*.

GEORGE F. KENNAN (1904–) is professor emeritus in the School of Historical Studies at the Institute for Advanced Study in Princeton, New Jersey. While on staff at the U.S. embassy in Moscow, he drafted the famous "Long Telegram" on Soviet intentions. As director of the State Department's policy planning staff, he pseudonymously wrote "The Sources of Soviet Conduct" in *Foreign Affairs* in 1947 under the byline "X." The author of numerous works of diplomatic history and two volumes of memoirs, Kennan served as U.S. ambassador to the Soviet Union and Yugoslavia.

HENRY A. KISSINGER (1923–) was secretary of state in the Nixon and Ford administrations and national security adviser to President Richard M. Nixon. He shared the 1973 Nobel Peace Prize with Le Duc Tho for their negotiations to end the Vietnam War. A refugee from Nazi Germany and a former professor of government at Harvard University, Kissinger is the author of *A World Restored, Nuclear Weapons and Foreign Policy, Diplomacy,* and two volumes of memoirs.

IRVING KRISTOL (1920–) was one of the founders of *Encounter* and is co-editor of *The Public Interest.* A former professor of social thought at New York University, he is the author of *Reflections of a Neoconservative, On the Democratic Idea in America,* and *Two Cheers for Capitalism.*

PAUL KRUGMAN (1953–) is a professor of economics at MIT. His books include *The Age of Diminished Expectations, Peddling Prosperity,* and *Pop Internationalism.*

WALTER LIPPMANN (1889–1974) was a columnist for *The New York Herald Tribune.* The leading commentator of his day and one of the founders of *The New Republic,* he won the Pulitzer Prize for international reporting in 1962. His books include *Public Opinion, The Cold War,* and *U.S. Foreign Policy: Shield of the Republic.*

HEINRICH MANN (1871–1950) was a German novelist. The brother of Thomas Mann, his writings include *The Little Town* and *Professor Unrat,* which later became the basis for the film *The Blue Angel.*

JESSICA T. MATHEWS (1946–) is president of the Carnegie Endowment for International Peace. She was director of the National Security Council's Office of Global Issues and deputy to the undersecretary of state for global affairs.

MARGARET MEAD (1901–1978) was an anthropologist and commentator. Educated at Columbia University, she did groundbreaking field research in the Pacific. Her numerous books include *Coming of Age in Samoa, Growing Up in New Guinea,* and *Culture and Commitment.*

HANS J. MORGENTHAU (1904–1980) was one of the first theorists of the realist school of international relations. He taught history and political science at the University of Chicago and the New School of Social Research. Morgenthau's books include *Politics Among Nations* and *In Defense of the National Interest.*

RICHARD PIPES (1923–) is a professor of history emeritus at Harvard University. He was an adviser on Soviet and East European affairs to President Ronald Reagan. His books include *The Russian Revolution* and *Russia Under the Old Regime.*

ELIHU ROOT (1845–1937) was secretary of state under President Theodore Roosevelt; he was before that secretary of war and a U.S. senator. He helped found both the League of Nations and the Council on Foreign Relations. Root was awarded the Nobel Peace Prize in 1912.

JAMES B. RESTON (1909–1995) joined the London bureau of *The New York Times* on the first day of World War II. He subsequently served as the *Times'* Washington bureau chief, diplomatic correspondent, columnist, and executive editor. Reston won the Pulitzer Prize in 1944 for diplomatic reporting and again in 1956 for national political reporting.

ARTHUR SCHLESINGER, JR. (1917–), is professor emeritus in the humanities at the Graduate School and University Center, City University of New York. Formerly a professor of history at Harvard University, he was a special assistant to President John F. Kennedy. Twice a winner of the Pulitzer Prize, he is the author of numerous books, including *The Age of Jackson, A Thousand Days: John F. Kennedy in the White House,* and *The Cycles of American History.*

ALEKSANDR SOLZHENITSYN (1918–) is a Russian author and critic of Soviet rule. His books include *One Day in the Life of Ivan Denisovich, Cancer Ward,* and *The Gulag Archipelago.* He was awarded the Nobel Prize for Literature in 1970. After the Soviet authorities expelled Solzhenitsyn in 1974 for his indictment of Stalinism, he lived in Vermont until returning recently to post-Soviet Russia.

HENRY L. STIMSON (1867–1950) was President Franklin Delano Roosevelt's secretary of war throughout World War II. He held the same portfolio under President William Howard Taft and was secretary of state during the Hoover administration.

ARNOLD J. TOYNBEE (1889–1975) was a British historian, best-known for his ten-volume *A Study of History.* He served as director of the Royal Institute of International Affairs.

H. G. WELLS (1866–1946) was a British author. His science fiction novels include *The Time Machine* and *War of the Worlds.* A member of the Fabian Society, he wrote several influential nonfiction works including *The Outline of History.*

ALBERT WOHLSTETTER (1913–1997) was a leading nuclear theorist and national security strategist. He worked at the University of Chicago and the Rand Corporation and was a frequent consultant to the Pentagon. An advocate of flexibility in nuclear strategy, Wohlstetter's studies helped pioneer "second strike" doctrines to let the United States retain a nuclear response after a Soviet first strike.

WALTER B. WRISTON (1919–) is a former chairman of Citicorp/Citibank. He is the author of *The Twilight of Sovereignty.*

FAREED ZAKARIA (1964–) is managing editor of *Foreign Affairs.* He writes an occasional column in *Newsweek* on international affairs, and is the author of a forthcoming book on the rise of America to world power.

WARREN ZIMMERMANN (1934–) is a professor of diplomacy at Columbia University. He spent 33 years in the U.S. Foreign Service and was U.S. ambassador to Yugoslavia from 1989 to 1992. Zimmermann is the author of *Origins of a Catastrophe: Yugoslavia and Its Destroyers.*

ALFRED ZIMMERN (1879–1957) was a British scholar. He helped found the Geneva School of International Studies and was a professor of international relations at Oxford. Zimmern was knighted in 1936. His books include *The Prospects of Democracy* and *Spiritual Values and World Affairs.*

Photo Acknowledgments

1920s—Versailles	Archive Photos
1930s—Nazi troops	UPI/Corbis-Bettmann
1940s—D-Day	Corbis-Bettmann
1950s—Red Square parade	UPI/Corbis-Bettmann
1960s—Vietnam quagmire	UPI/Bettmann
1970s—U.S. flag burning	UPI/Corbis-Bettmann
1980s—Lenin statue in noose	Reuters/Corbis-Bettmann
1990s I—Seoul Olympic bridge	Archive Photos
1990s II—Mostar bridge	Magnum/Gilles Peress

Index

Printed in the United States
110998LV00003B/4-6/A

9 780465 001712